Alabama in Africa

AMERICA IN THE WORLD

SVEN BECKERT AND JEREMI SURI, *Series Editors*

Alabama in Africa

BOOKER T. WASHINGTON,

THE GERMAN EMPIRE, AND

THE GLOBALIZATION OF THE NEW SOUTH

Andrew Zimmerman

PRINCETON UNIVERSITY PRESS

PRINCETON AND OXFORD

Copyright © 2010 by Princeton University Press
Published by Princeton University Press, 41 William Street,
Princeton, New Jersey 08540
In the United Kingdom: Princeton University Press, 6 Oxford Street,
Woodstock, Oxfordshire OX20 1TW

press.princeton.edu

Second printing, and first paperback printing, 2012
Paperback ISBN 978-0-691-15586-9

The Library of Congress has cataloged the cloth edition of
this book as follows

Zimmerman, Andrew.
Alabama in Africa : Booker T. Washington, the German empire,
and the globalization of the new South / Andrew Zimmerman.
p.   cm. — (America in the world)
Includes bibliographical references and index.
ISBN 978-0-691-12362-2 (cloth : alk. paper)
1. Cotton trade—Togo—History. 2. Agricultural laborers—
Togo—History. 3. Germany—Colonies—Africa. 4. Tuskegee Institute.
5. Washington, Booker T., 1856–1915. I. Title.
HD9087.T62Z56 2010
338.1′35109668109041—dc22   2009044502

British Library Cataloging-in-Publication Data is available

This book has been composed in Sabon

Printed on acid-free paper. ∞

Printed in the United States of America

7   9   10   8   6

CONTENTS

ILLUSTRATIONS

PREFACE

IN JANUARY 1901 four African American men from Tuskegee Institute, the Alabama teacher-training school founded by Booker T. Washington, arrived in the German colony of Togo, West Africa, to help transform the territory into a source of cotton for the European spinning industry. *Alabama in Africa* reconstructs this expedition and its global consequences from the perspectives of its American, African, and German participants. It explores the transnational economic, political, and ideological networks that connected Booker T. Washington's American South, the kaiser's Germany, and colonial West Africa. The global collapse of unfree labor—both Atlantic slavery and European serfdom—profoundly affected each of these regions in the nineteenth century. The Atlantic transition to free labor unleashed new political and economic energies among former bondspeople, energies that employers and states endeavored to redirect for their own profit and power.

Alabama in Africa reveals how early, tentative efforts by Booker T. Washington to transform the place of blacks in the American South gave way to his better-known "accommodationism" as a result of his work with German imperialism in Africa. The pioneering interest of German colonial personnel in Tuskegee Institute, in turn, helped make the American South of segregation and sharecropping a model for the supposedly humanitarian internationalism of the League of Nations. The model of the American South and individual African Americans, including Washington and W.E.B. Du Bois, also influenced the history of free labor inside the borders of Germany, shaping the development of the social sciences and the state social policies for which Germany has been so admired, as well as the treatment of Poles for which it has been so reviled. *Alabama in Africa* rejects empire-centered approaches to colonialism that regard Africans as raw clay for colonial sculpting, demonstrating rather that the history of Togolese self-fashioning in the aftermath of Atlantic slavery structured and resisted the various attempts by missionaries, colonial states, and Tuskegee Institute to create an Africa after their own desires. *Alabama in Africa* offers a transnational historical narrative, grounded in archival research and recent methods in the history of culture, gender, and sexuality as an answer to a now venerable topic of comparative social science about the rise of capitalism around the world. It suggests, finally, that racism and imperialism, as well as struggles of class, culture, gender, and sexuality are as relevant as ever to understanding the essentially modern human drama, the struggle for political and economic freedom in a divided world.

Part of the pleasure of writing a transnational history encompassing the United States, Africa, and Germany has been the intellectual debts I have accumulated and the generosity I have enjoyed from scholars in so many fields and from friends and acquaintances in so many places. Those who made time to read earlier versions of this text have offered such important guidance that I believe many of them would not recognize the book I have finally produced. I alone am responsible for the many shortcomings that no doubt remain, but there are far fewer of them, thanks especially to those whom I would like to mention here, as well as to many others whom limitations of space prevent me from naming individually.

I am a newcomer to American history. John David Smith has, from the beginning of this project, shared his tremendous expertise in the history of the American South and African American history, as well as his own current research on German and American racial ideology. His meticulous and insightful reading of the entire manuscript crowned years of conversations and advice about my project. My colleague Adele Alexander also read the entire manuscript, and she has been equally generous with her knowledge of African American history and especially the world of Tuskegee Institute. I have also been fortunate for the advice of Sven Beckert, one of the editors of the series in which this book appears and an expert on, among other things, the global cotton economy of the nineteenth century and the Tuskegee expedition to Togo. Michael Bieze kindly shared his research on Booker T. Washington and the family of James Nathan Calloway, the head of the expedition. Very early in this project, James Campbell got me started on the transnational study of African Americans and Africa and, at the end of this project, Jay Mandle gave me an insider's insight into the historiography of the "Prussian path" and the American South. Tyler Anbinder, Ed Berkowitz, and Adam Rothman have also been unstinting sources of advice and encouragement in my study of American history.

I am equally new to African history, and my gratitude is no less great to my friends and colleagues in this field. I was fortunate to have the chance to discuss my work with colleagues at the University of Lomé, Togo, where Professors N'buéké Adovi Goeh-Akue and Pierre Ali Napo generously shared their time and expertise and supported my research. I am also grateful to four other Togo specialists—Dennis Laumann, Birgit Meyer, Paul Nugent, and Michel Verdon—who each read earlier versions of chapter 3 and provided invaluable guidance. Nemata Blyden, Jan-Bart

Gewald, Paul Landau, and Peter Pels also each taught me much about the study of African history.

I have needed as much guidance in German history, the field most familiar to me, as I have in American and African history, and here I have been equally lucky in having generous colleagues and friends. Geoff Eley has been a wellspring of insight and inspiration, and kindly commented on the entire manuscript. Guenther Roth has shared his expertise on Max Weber and the *Verein für Sozialpolitik* with unmatched generosity. His critical and constructive comments substantially improved this manuscript. I have worked out many of my arguments during the intellectually intense meetings of the German Modernity Group organized by Edward Ross Dickenson, Geoff Eley, Jennifer Jenkins, and Tracie Matysik. My research on Germany has also benefited greatly from the comments and suggestions of Sebastian Conrad, Sara Lennox, Bradley Naranch, George Steinmetz, and Keith Tribe, as well as from more friends and colleagues than I can name here.

I would also like to thank a number of individuals related to John Winfrey Robinson and James Nathan Calloway, the leaders of the Tuskegee expedition to Togo, who offered family memories and reflections. Monica Eklou of Togo sought me out after researching her American great-great-grandfather, John Robinson, on the Internet. She kindly shared family memories of Robinson and sent me a copy of his Togolese family tree. Nathan Calloway similarly found me while researching his own great-grandfather James Calloway and also discussed his family history with me. Two other members of the Calloway family, Constance Calloway Margerum and Sondra Crusor, met with me in their homes and shared family photographs, one of which is figure I.2 of this book. My discussions with these four descendants of two of the main figures in this book not only furthered my research but were also enjoyable and inspiring. If parts of my interpretation of John Robinson and James Calloway strike their descendants as excessively critical, I hope they will also recognize in their ancestors complex and ultimately sympathetic individuals pursuing projects in good faith in an era, I hope like our own, bound to appear wanting in equality and humanity to future generations.

I have been more fortunate than I could ever have hoped in being a part of the History Department at George Washington University. I have received helpful advice from nearly every colleague and many graduate students in the department. I single out here a number of colleagues with whom I have enjoyed wide-ranging conversations on transnational history and on the history of empires: Muriel Atkin, Nemata Blyden, Dane Kennedy, Dina Rizk Khoury, Shawn F. McHale, and Marcy Norton, as well as Melani McAlister of the American Studies Department.

My research has received external support from the American Council of Learned Societies, the American Philosophical Society, and the National Endowment for the Humanities (FT-46516-02). The George Washington University, including the Columbian College of Arts and Sciences, the Department of History, and the Institute for European, Russian and Eurasian Studies, has been generous in its support of my research and travel. I am also grateful for the research assistance of Elizabeth Fine, Steven Bulthuis, and Brett Morrison.

I have conducted research in numerous archives, listed individually in the bibliography of this book, and I am grateful to the staffs of each of them. I am also indebted to the staffs of the Library of Congress, the New York Public Library, the Burke Library at Union Theological Seminary, and the Staatsbibliothek in Berlin. I am especially thankful to the staff members of the interlibrary loan department of the George Washington University and to the librarians of the European Reading Room at the Library of Congress, who went well beyond reasonable expectations in tracking down texts that were essential to this project.

I have benefited enormously from the editorial guidance and support of Brigitta van Rheinberg and Clara Platter of Princeton University Press. I am also grateful to an anonymous reader for the press, whose extensive commentary on an earlier draft made this a better book than it otherwise would have been.

My family not only encouraged and supported me, but also read and discussed this project at every stage. My mother, Muriel Zimmerman, commented on the entire manuscript, and both she and my brother, Daniel Zimmerman, have been partners in the ongoing discussions that inform this book.

Johanna K. Bockman is my most important intellectual partner, and this book results from years of discussion with her on many topics, above all economic experimentation and human freedom. Her commentary has contributed to every aspect of this book, and I have also been educated and inspired by her research and writings, published and not-yet-published, on dissident socialisms and variant capitalisms around the world in the twentieth century. These I list in the bibliography.

My father, Everett Zimmerman, who was born on a farm in Lancaster County, Pennsylvania, and became a professor of English literature at the University of California, Santa Barbara, taught me something about nearly everything in what follows, from plowing with mules to political theory. Each of the many individuals in this book who abandoned the countryside to "live by their wits," as Booker T. Washington liked to put it, reminded me of him. As far as I know, there was not a day in his life when he did not appreciate the good fortune of having been able to do so. I am sorry that he died before I could show him what I made of it all.

Alabama in Africa

INTRODUCTION

GERMAN COLONIAL AUTHORITIES turned to Booker T. Washington because they hoped that the prominent African American educator would bring to Africa the industrial education that he often suggested trained blacks in the New South to become diligent and compliant laborers contributing to a modern, postslavery economy. Germany, like other European powers, desired similarly subordinate and productive black labor in its own African colonies. The Tuskegee personnel who worked in Togo succeeded in transforming African cotton growing because they brought with them techniques and assumptions about agriculture, labor, race, and education from the American South. They found such ready partners in the German government because Germany, unlike any other colonial power in Africa, but like the United States, undertook the long transition from bound to free agricultural labor only in the nineteenth century, beginning with the abolition of serfdom in 1807.[1]

The Tuskegee cotton expedition to Togo brought together German and American models and ideologies of race and free agricultural labor. It brought together the long American history of slavery and emancipation, Jim Crow, sharecropping, and the promises of a "New South," with the long German history of the colonization of Eastern Europe, the partition of Poland, the end of serfdom, the migrations of Germans and Poles, and the promise of an expert state that used social science to control and develop its territory and population. These two histories converged in, and on, an even longer West African history of coastal trade with Europe, succeeding from gold, to slaves, to palm oil, of the promise of abolition wrecked by European colonial conquests in the nineteenth century, of the transformation of a once relatively independent participant in Atlantic trade networks into a subordinate agricultural producer in a capitalist world economy. The Tuskegee expedition to Togo helped transform the political economy of race and agricultural labor characteristic of the New South into a colonial political economy of the global South, separated from core capitalist countries by what W.E.B. Du Bois called the "color line" and the African American novelist Richard Wright later called the "color curtain," at least as important as the better known "iron curtain" that once separated East and West.[2]

The expedition is a mere curiosity, its narrative little more than a colonial adventure story, unless it is understood in its connection to the three regional histories it brought together—African, German, and American.

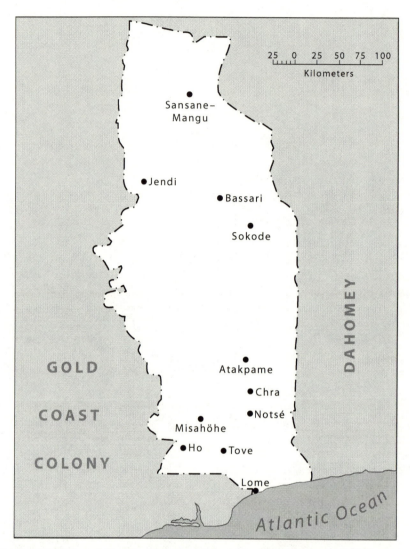

FIGURE I.1. Map of German Togo. The Republic of Togo today is slightly smaller than the German colony, part of which was annexed to the English colony of Gold Coast, today Ghana, after the First World War. Only the locations discussed in this book are indicated on the map. The two principal areas of operation of the Tuskegee expedition were Tove and Notsé. Map drawn by Meghan Kanabay, based on a map in Albert F. Calvert, *Togoland* (London: T. Werner Laurie, 1918).

Understanding the expedition, in turn, illuminates these three regional histories as elements of a transnational history of free labor, global agriculture, and the conscious and unconscious struggles waged by cultural, social, and economic producers against the rule of capital and the state. This transnational approach is all the more important because the histories of Africa, Germany, and the United States have, until recently, been cut off from global history by tendentious exceptionalisms. Exceptionalism has been central to American self-conceptions from the earliest Puritan settlers to the most recent American neoconservatives.[3] While German exceptionalism, the so-called German *Sonderweg*, or special historical path, has been widely and usefully criticized, the study of German imperialism has, until recently, been hobbled by the view that overseas expansion had more to do with the domestic politics and culture of Germany than with the societies it ruled or with its contributions to a political and economic hegemony far greater and longer-lived than its own brief colonial history.[4] The exceptional treatment of sub-Saharan African history has long consisted in excepting the region and its inhabitants from history altogether.[5] The Tuskegee expedition to Togo stands at a point where both historical exceptionalism and comparative history meet transnational history. Transnational history demands and allows historians to apply the microhistorical cultural methods that we have developed over the past decades to the macrohistorical political-economic questions that these newer methods once seemed—incorrectly, I believe—to have eclipsed.

Booker T. Washington came to the attention of German colonial authorities fortuitously, as a result of growing European interest in the American cotton industry.[6] In 1860, on the eve of the Civil War, the United States accounted for two-thirds of world cotton production. During the American Civil War, a "cotton famine," caused by declining southern production and the Union blockade of the South, made Europeans acutely aware of their economic dependence on American cotton. After the Civil War, while the United States produced ever more cotton each year, it also consumed an increasingly large portion of that cotton in its own domestic textile industry.[7] In the period 1902–14, America produced more than half the world's cotton crop, followed by India, which produced about a sixth. Industrial textile mills could use the short-stapled Indian crop only in limited quantities, however, and only by mixing it with American cotton. Cotton textile production grew in many other nations as well, heightening the pressure on the limited American supply of cotton. In the period 1904–14, the United States exported more than 60 percent of its total crop. Great Britain consumed about 40 percent of these exports, and Germany consumed between 25 and 30 percent, with France a distant third at around 10 percent.[8]

German interest in American cotton, as well as in the cheap Midwestern grain that threatened the Junker estates of eastern Germany, led the German embassy in Washington, D.C., to create the position of agricultural attaché. In 1895 Baron Beno von Herman auf Wain, from Württemberg in southwestern Germany, became the first to take this position. Upon arriving in Washington, D.C., he immediately turned his attention to cotton growing.[9] Baron von Herman traveled to Atlanta for the 1895 Cotton States and International Exposition, and he may even have been part of the audience that heard Booker T. Washington make his famous "Atlanta Compromise" address.[10] Two years later, in 1897, Baron von Herman toured the cotton-growing regions of the South and concluded that American preeminence in the global cotton market resulted from its large population of black growers, both in slavery and in freedom. The residents of regions of the South that did not produce cotton explained to the baron, he reported, that there was no cotton because there were no mules, there were no mules because there were no Negroes, and there were no Negroes because there was no cotton.[11]

Though clearly mocking the circular logic of southern wiseacres, Herman, like many experts, believed that cotton had to be grown by blacks, both because of their supposed unique ability to withstand labor in hot weather and also because of a vague sense of a natural connection between blacks and cotton. This connection, Herman concluded, presented an opportunity for Germany in its African colonies, since, he related to the German *Reichskanzler*, the "Negro" (*Neger*) in Africa required less than a fifth of the wages paid in the United States, which would more than compensate for any comparative inefficiencies in production.[12] For the entire period of his service in the Washington embassy, Herman worked assiduously to transfer American cotton expertise to German Africa, reporting on American cotton growing, encouraging German agricultural experts to inspect cotton farming in the American South, and even traveling to study cotton growing in the German East Africa (present-day Tanzania) toward the end of his tenure in Washington, in 1901.[13]

While Germans did not, by any means, invent the idea that there existed a fundamental connection between industrial-grade cotton and American blacks, those involved in Germany's colonial cotton projects made more of this idea than any before them had. Baron von Herman worked closely with the Colonial Economic Committee (Kolonialwirtschaftliches Komitee, hereafter KWK), a private organization that supported research in colonial agriculture, to reproduce the American economy of black cotton growing in Africa. The corporate members of the KWK represented many types of business, including large banks and heavy industry, but textile manufacturers set the agenda of the organization, which focused its efforts on improving cotton growing in the German colonies.[14] The KWK agreed with Baron von Herman that, since black labor was the most important factor in American cotton production, Germany might develop its African colonies along American lines to compete with the United States.[15] At least one official in the Colonial Department of the German Foreign Office agreed with the KWK and Baron von Herman that it would be "very practical" to use "colored young" men from America to teach cotton growing to Africans.[16] In the summer of 1900 Herman traveled to Boston to meet with Booker T. Washington, who was there to address the National Negro Business League. The Baron persuaded Washington to recruit "two negro-cottonplanters and one negro-mechanic . . . who would be willing to come over to . . . the colony of Togo in West-Africa to teach the negroes there how to plant and harvest cotton in a rational and scientific way."[17] The expedition would be financed by the KWK and supported by the German government in Togo.

A Tuskegee faculty member, James Nathan Calloway, led the expedition, helping the other members, as Herman put it, "in finding the necessary authority towards the native population and in having at the same time the necessary respect towards the German government official."[18] Born in Tennessee in 1865, Calloway began working for Tuskegee Institute immediately after graduating from Fisk University in 1890. He joined the agriculture department in 1897, the year after George Washington Carver established it, and managed the institute's 800-acre Marshall Farm.[19] Calloway's younger brother, Thomas Junius, was a lifelong friend of W.E.B. Du Bois, with whom he had roomed at Fisk.[20] The summer before his older brother traveled to Togo, Thomas J. Calloway and W.E.B. Du Bois mounted an exhibit on African Americans at the Paris Exposition of 1900.[21] While James N. Calloway worked in Togo, his youngest brother, Clinton Joseph, joined the agriculture department at Tuskegee, and later became director of agricultural extension programs at the institute.[22] Coming from a family close to Tuskegee, James Nathan Calloway evidently won the trust of Booker T. Washington to represent the institute in Africa.

Less is known about the three younger Tuskegee men who accompanied Calloway. Allen Lynn Burks had graduated from Tuskegee in agriculture the year before the expedition. Shepherd Lincoln Harris had come to Tuskegee from Union, Georgia, in 1886 to study mechanics, but had never completed a degree. John Winfrey Robinson graduated from Tuskegee in 1897, spending a year teaching school in Alabama before returning to Tuskegee for postgraduate training in agriculture.[23] Robinson would have undertaken his agricultural studies under James N. Calloway, the expedition leader, and George Washington Carver, the famous director of Tuskegee's agriculture department. The twenty-seven-year-old Robinson would soon become the most important member of the expedition.

Figure I.2. James Nathan Calloway, the leader of the Tuskegee expedition, travels by hammock, as was customary for dignitaries in German Togo. German officials used hammocks made of African cloth because it was sturdier than the European cloth sold in West Africa. The man grasping Calloway's hand is likely John Winfrey Robinson, who would soon become the head of Tuskegee efforts in Togo. Source: Personal collection of Constance Calloway Margerum, granddaughter of James Nathan Calloway. Reprinted with permission.

The group first landed in Lome, the capital of the German colony on the West African coast between French Dahomey (present-day Benin) to the east and British Gold Coast (present-day Ghana) to the west. Calloway and Robinson, assisted by Burks, established and supervised an experimental cotton farm in Tove, a group of six villages about sixty miles inland from Lome. On the experimental farm, Robinson bred a strain of cotton whose staple resembled American Upland cotton closely enough to be used as a raw material in industrial textile mills, and the Tove plantation produced these seeds for the entire German colony. Local government stations compelled Togolese growers to cultivate this new cotton varietal and to sell their produce to European firms. Shepherd L. Harris, the fourth member of the expedition, established his own cotton farm, which was to set an example of cotton growing and domestic economy that Africans might imitate.

FIGURE I.3. John Winfrey Robinson at the twenty-fifth-anniversary celebration of Tuskegee Institute, 1906. Robinson returned from his work in Togo to participate in the celebrations. He poses here in a robe he brought back from Togo, along with a collection of Ewe and Hausa objects. He resumed his work in Togo after the celebrations until his death in 1909. Source: The Frances Benjamin Johnston Collection, Prints and Photographs Division, Library of Congress.

After a year in Togo, Calloway traveled briefly to the United States, returning in May 1902 with five Tuskegee students who planned to join Harris in setting up model cotton farms. These new settlers met with disaster when their landing boat capsized in the notoriously rough surf off the coast of Togo. Two of these settlers, Hiram Dozier Simpson and William Drake, drowned. The remaining three—Hiram Simpson's wife, Walter Bryant, and Horace Greeley Griffin—made it to shore. Simpson's widow soon married Griffin, and the new couple set up a model farm, as did the bachelor Bryant.[24] Later that summer, Harris, the first model farmer from Tuskegee, died of a fever. Burks, another of the original four expedition members, returned to the United States at the end of that year, in December 1902. Calloway himself returned to his position at Tuskegee several months later, at the beginning of 1903, leaving Robinson in charge of Tuskegee's work in Togo.[25] Calloway's experience in Africa imparted in him a lifelong interest in international education, even after he left

Tuskegee for Langston University in Oklahoma, before finally settling in Chicago.[26] The last Tuskegee settlers, Walter Bryant and Mr. and Mrs. Griffin, stuck it out in Togo through the end of 1904. The deaths of Simpson, Drake, and Harris dissuaded the remaining Tuskegee students scheduled to go to Togo, and George Washington Carver, whom Booker T. Washington had charged with recruiting students for Africa, failed to enlist any others for work in the German colony.[27]

John W. Robinson remained in Togo to set up a cotton school in Notsé (Nuatjä in German and Notsie in English), near the town of Atakpame, that would train Togolese themselves, rather than African Americans, to serve as model cotton farmers. Robinson had by then made himself at home in Togo. He learned to speak Ewe, the main language of southern Togo, and married two Togolese women, one at Tove, the location of the experimental plantation, and another at Notsé, the location of the new school. (Togolese women commonly shared a single husband, and there was nothing illicit about these multiple marriages.) Robinson's family ties to Togo did not prevent him from participating in the coercive programs of the German colonial state. German officials forced a number of young men from each of the seven districts in Togo to attend the three-year program at Robinson's school. The government then forced the cotton-school graduates, about fifty each year, to settle as model cotton growers under the supervision of district officials. The government took over the school from the Colonial Economic Committee in 1908 so that Robinson could travel to the North of Togo, where he planned to found a similar cotton school. Before he could do so, however, he drowned in the Mono River, when his boat capsized.[28]

The cotton projects that Robinson and the other Tuskegee expedition members carried out at Tove and Notsé were remarkably successful, breeding and propogating a cotton varietal that flourished in Togo and produced a staple suitable for European industry. The agricultural institutions that Tuskegee founded at Tove and Notsé remained in nearly continuous operation under the French government after 1914 and under the independent Togolese Republic since 1960, although their approaches and goals have changed considerably. The Tuskegee cotton program taught all the European colonial powers in Africa that it was possible to replace indigenous cotton with varietals suitable for mechanized spinning and weaving, to train Africans to grow cotton extensively, and to persuade growers to export this cotton as a raw material, rather than spinning and weaving it locally. Colonial cotton programs, including the efforts of Tuskegee in Togo, though carried out in the name of, and sometimes even with a sincere belief in, economic progress, have been a political and economic disaster for Africans because of the coercion they involved, the economic opportunities Africans had to forgo to grow cotton, and, today, the terms of trade that force West African growers to compete with lavishly subsidized American and European growers.[29]

Readers may be surprised by the colonial undertakings of Tuskegee Institute, a normal school established and run by African Americans. European and American interventions in Africa were oppressive and exploitative, to be sure, and the Tuskegee expedition to Togo was no exception. Yet, these interventions were part of a colonial "civilizing mission" in which many Europeans and Americans, including Booker T. Washington and the participants in the expedition, believed as earnestly as their present-day counterparts believe in economic development, democracy, and human rights.[30] Writing at the end of his life, as a citizen of independent Ghana, W.E.B. Du Bois reflected on his own youthful enthusiasm for the colonial civilizing mission: "French, English and Germans pushed on in Africa, but I did not question the interpretation which pictures this as the advance of civilization and the benevolent tutelage of barbarians."[31] Du Bois rejected his youthful view only after years of practical political experience, including his gradual rejection of Tuskegee ideas in the early twentieth century, his study of Marxism in the middle of the century, and his later experience with anticolonial revolutionaries, including Kwame Nkrumah, president of Ghana.

The histories of empire and of the global South provide a transnational perspective that helps answer the question of whether Washington opposed or cooperated with southern racism, a question that remains central to many areas of scholarship, political thought, and activism to this day. Historian Robert J. Norrell has recently come to the defense of Washington, arguing that the struggle against the racist terror raging in the United States in the 1890s and after was more important to Washington's life than were his more banal political machinations or his well-known conflicts with W.E.B. Du Bois.[32] Earlier scholars of Washington and African American thought at this time, including Louis R. Harlan and August Meier, similarly showed how Washington worked behind the scenes against segregation and disfranchisement, even while publicly seeming to accept or even to endorse the ever-worsening disfranchisement and segregation in the New South.[33] In a glowing review of August Meier's book, the sociologist St. Clair Drake, a graduate of Hampton Institute and the University of Chicago, wished that the author had "explored the quite considerable influence of Washington's confidante, Robert Ezra Park, and had he made some mention of Washington's attempts to apply his ideas in Africa."[34] *Alabama in Africa* explores these strands connecting Tuskegee Institute to European colonialism in Africa and to the distinct school of sociology that the German-trained social scientist Robert E. Park founded at the University of Chicago. Placing Tuskegee in transnational political, economic, and intellectual histories not only fills gaps in the literature on Booker T. Washington, but also clarifies his apparently inscrutable politics by indicating how they functioned in multiple contexts in Germany and Africa, as well as in the United States.

Considering Booker T. Washington from the perspective of empire reveals not only the ambivalent politics of Tuskegee Institute, but also how these politics changed over time. Tuskegee Institute contained an emancipatory, even revolutionary—and finally unrealized—potential. Both Washington and Du Bois participated in the African American struggles against racism in the United States, in the international and imperial politics of the United States, in the transnational politics of European colonialism and of Pan-African anti-imperialism, and even in the rise of Germany as a world power. What in retrospect appears as a clear distinction between Du Bois and Washington in fact emerged only gradually. In the 1890s, Washington sought to employ Du Bois at Tuskegee to add a sociological component to the agricultural research with which George Washington Carver hoped to transform the political and economic position of rural blacks in the American South. Washington's work with the German empire in the first decade of the twentieth century ended these plans, and led Washington to the conservative positions for which he is remembered today. In their engagement with American, African, German, and transnational histories, Du Bois and Washington each elaborated views about race and emancipation, about imperialism, civilization, and uplift, and about the role of African Americans in the United States and in the world. Their fraught encounters with empire in the crucial decades around the turn of the twentieth century, we shall see, finally shaped both the radical politics of Du Bois and the conservative politics of Washington.

When European powers met in Berlin in 1884–85 to work out the terms under which they would divide nearly all of Africa among themselves, they claimed sovereignty not by right of conquest but rather as a common humanitarian effort to end slavery in Africa and to replace the slave trade with "legitimate" trade, for example in agricultural commodities grown with free labor.[35] These colonial powers took up the abolitionist claim that Christianity, commerce, and civilization would help bring an end to the slave trade in Africa.[36] Sierra Leone, a colony founded in 1787 by British abolitionists, became, after Britain outlawed the slave trade in 1807, a settlement for Africans freed from illegal slavers. In 1816 Americans opposed to the presence of free blacks in the United States founded the American Colonization Society, an organization that established Liberia in 1822 as a settlement of manumitted American slaves. While many supported colonization as a means of gradually ending slavery, leading abolitionists detected covert support for slavery and racism in the plan to remove free blacks from the United States.[37] President Abraham Lincoln espoused colonization almost his entire life, and historians continue to debate whether he did so out of genuine conviction or only to win wider support for abolition.[38] Slavery, in fact, continued to exist within many European colonies in Africa, and Europeans ruled their colonies, for all the rhetoric of international humanitarianism, with brutal force. The colonization of Africa, nonetheless, formed a central part of the abolition of the slave trade. This paradoxical juxtaposition of liberty and domination was in fact a—perhaps the—fundamental feature of the global economy that emerged in the period between the American Civil War and the First World War.

Germany was neither as recent nor as insignificant an imperial power as is often suggested.[39] Germany stood behind Britain and France in the size of its overseas colonial empire, but emerged as the premier European land power after 1871 and, by the 1890s, had surpassed Britain as an industrial economy and challenged the island nation as a global naval power. Merchants from Bremen and Hamburg played a major role in the European trade with West Africa from the middle of the nineteenth century. Already in 1847, the North German Mission Society of Bremen worked closely with the Vietor trading firm, also based in Bremen, to evangelize the region of West Africa that would become southern Togo and Gold Coast. Germany also played a leading diplomatic role in establishing European sovereignty over Africa, beginning with the West Africa Conference held in Otto von Bismarck's Berlin residence in the late fall and winter of 1884–85, presided over by the German *Reichskanzler*. By the time of this conference, Germany had already established protectorates in Southwest Africa (present-day Namibia), Togo, and Cameroon. On February 27, 1885, the day after the Berlin conference closed, the German East Africa Company, headed by the infamously brutal Carl Peters, received imperial status, making present-day mainland Tanzania, Rwanda, and Burundi the fourth German protectorate in Africa. Germany also claimed Pacific island colonies in the 1880s and after, building, as in Africa, on decades of involvement by German merchants. These included northeast New Guinea, the Solomon Islands, the Marshall Islands, Western Samoa, the Caroline Islands, and the Mariana Islands. The German navy also controlled the Shandong Peninsula of China as a base for operations in the Pacific Ocean. Germany further pursued an informal empire in the Middle East by cultivating commercial ties with, and offering military training to, the Ottoman Empire, and undertaking a Berlin-Baghdad railroad project. It is often pointed out the German state lost more money than it earned in most of its colonial enterprises. Such accounting, however, reveals little, for colonial states, then as now, do not serve themselves or, patriotic rhetoric aside, a nation, but rather provide infrastructure, administration, and military and police support, typically at taxpayers' expense, to private firms working overseas.[40]

Cotton occupied a special place in attempts to replace the Atlantic slave trade with legitimate commerce. People in every corner of the earth have grown cotton since antiquity, but the spinning and weaving machines of the industrial revolution required American cotton, which had long been grown by slave labor. The voracious appetite of European industry for American cotton had made slavery more profitable than ever in the United States in the decades before abolition. Cotton nearly won the Confederacy English and French support during the Civil War.[41] Even after abolition, European consumption of American cotton made the gross oppression and exploitation of blacks in the South economically viable, even profitable. For some abolitionists and antiracists, cotton grown with free labor in Africa would be more than just one item of legitimate trade among others; it would challenge the economic power that southern landlords had built up with the labor of blacks, both in slavery and in the partial freedom that replaced it in the Jim Crow South.

Booker T. Washington was not the first African American to intervene in African cotton growing. In 1859 and 1860 the African American abolitionist and physician Martin R. Delany explored the Niger Valley to determine whether cotton growing in Africa might simultaneously support a black exodus from American slavery and racism and also challenge the economic power of the slave South.[42] While Africans in many parts of the continent grew cotton for their own textile industries, African cotton, like cotton from most parts of the world outside the United States, was unsuitable for mechanized spinning and weaving. Delany chose the Niger Valley because, as in much of West Africa, its residents had long produced high-quality cloth from locally grown cotton.[43] Delany shared the assumption, common at the time, that, as he put it, "cotton cannot be produced without negro labor and skill in raising it," and he hoped that cotton grown by free labor in Africa would allow Africans and African Americans to "enrich themselves, and regenerate their race" rather than "enrich the white men who oppress them."[44] Delany also hoped that African Americans would bring "the habits of civilized life" to Africans, for he, like many white and black visitors to the continent, regarded Africa as a primitive region whose people needed outside assistance to become "civilized." Like many Europeans and Americans, Delany hoped to liberate blacks in Africa from their supposed backwardness and at the same time liberate blacks in America from slavery and racial oppression.[45] Settling African Americans in Africa as cotton growers might, Delany ventured, achieve both of these ends, but nothing, ultimately, came of his scheme.

Many European textile experts believed, like Delany, that black people had a special affinity for growing cotton, and so, while they also tried to get American cotton to grow in many parts of the world, Africa figured prominently in their cotton efforts. French colonists began promoting cotton growing in Senegal as early as 1817.[46] When, in the 1840s, the British East India Company sought to grow American cotton in India, the land that had taught the world how to grow, spin, and weave the fiber, it recruited cotton experts from Mississippi.[47] In the nineteenth century, Egypt developed a fine, long-stapled cotton that has been used ever since to produce particularly soft fabrics, but in quantities too limited to cover the massive needs of the European textile industry.[48] Whereas Delany hoped that growing cotton in Africa would challenge the oppressive and exploitative conditions under which blacks grew cotton in the United States, many European colonial powers hoped to grow cotton in Africa by reproducing the oppressive and exploitative conditions of the United States. The collaboration of Tuskegee Institute with the German government of Togo brought together two dimensions of African cotton growing, which reflected two dimensions of the colonization of Africa: on the one hand, an emancipatory, if misguided and ethnocentric, effort to improve the conditions of blacks on both sides of the Atlantic; and, on the other, an anti-emancipatory effort to establish black cotton farming in Africa that would enrich white economic elites in Europe as much as it did their counterparts in the United States.

The events of the Tuskegee expedition to Togo emerged from, and also helped create, a structure of capitalism in the period between the Civil War and the First World War that prefigures our own era of globalization.[49] In the nineteenth century the European economy cast an ever-widening net over the globe, so that, for example, German workers might operate English machines lubricated with West African palm oil to spin American cotton. As the scale and technology of production increased, manufacturing moved from the privacy of producers' households to the supervision and discipline of the factory. The agricultural labor that supplied the raw materials for such industrial production, however, took place far from centers of capital and involved relatively little mechanization. As steamships, railroads, and canals facilitated the transportation of agricultural raw materials to industrial areas, manufacturers became exposed to the climate, the labor, and the agricultural markets of far-flung regions about which they had only minimal information. Commodity bourses in Chicago, New York, Liverpool, Bremen, and elsewhere, in the course of the nineteenth century, established reliable standards for various global raw materials, including cotton. Standardizing agricultural products for these bourses required exercising ever-greater discipline over producers from Alabama to East-Elbian Germany to West Africa and beyond.

Political and economic domination based on racist hierarchies in the southern United States and elsewhere established regimes of labor discipline that were, in their own way, as necessary in the fields that produced agricultural raw materials as were the very different regimes in the factories that processed them.[50] Race, to be sure, was not dreamed up in the nineteenth century, but racial types did come to serve new economic functions as old categories like "slave" and "serf" ceased to organize agricultural production. Racism functions, as sociologist Robert Miles has suggested, as part of the labor process—not merely as an ideology—because it shapes the way work is organized and exploited.[51] Specifically, describing a group as a race suggests that it is an exceptional instance of the generic category "human," requiring special treatment. Singling out a group as a race often involved social-scientific study, excessive political and managerial control, and especially poor pay. The production of cotton for the world market after slavery depended on placing African Americans in such a racist state of exception. The production of German sugarbeets relied on placing Polish migrant workers in an analogous position of racial subordination. The transition in Africa from precolonial coastal trade to European capitalist control of African agricultural labor also brought with it a new racial classification. Africans, with the help of Tuskegee Institute, would become "Negroes" only in the early twentieth century.

Race is, at one level, totally imaginary, a hallucination that organized populations transnationally, much as national identity organized the inhabitants of a territory ruled by a single state.[52] A racial image grouped blacks in Africa, the United States, and elsewhere, giving rise to the idea that Tuskegee Institute might reproduce the American South in Africa, but also inspiring various Pan-African forms of anticolonial solidarity. Whiteness similarly produced transnational solidarities that furthered the project of colonial domination. Even as European states competed for overseas territories, they usually assumed certain allegiances based on their common "race." When disagreements among white people did lead to shooting, the warring parties even used less harmful bullets against each other than they did against nonwhites, on whom they fired the gruesome expanding bullets that the British produced in their arsenal at Dum Dum, near Calcutta.[53] Individuals defined themselves as white in relation, primarily, to blacks, but also to a whole gradation of people of color and of white people perceived as not fully white, groups such as Poles that we would today call ethnicities, as well as whites who, because of their poverty, did not exhibit all the traits that white elites liked to attribute to their own "race."[54]

In addition to its imaginary function, race is also a kinship system, neither more nor less real than those studied by Lewis Henry Morgan, Claude Lévi-Strauss, Gayle Rubin, or Monique Wittig.[55] Race assigns identities to individuals based on various conventional laws of biological descent, such as matrilinearity or the "one drop" rule. Like all kinship systems, race assigns age and gender roles and regulates sexual behavior, compelling reproductive, often patriarchal heterosexuality, and prohibiting not only incest but also certain forms of exogamy that violate various, and variously enforced, racial taboos. The complex of race, patriarchal heterosexuality, and political and economic power continues to shape much of the world today. This complex appears clearly, for example, in the 1965 Moynihan report, an official study that has had a great influence on United States policy toward African Americans. "Ours is a society," concluded that U.S. Labor Department report, "which presumes male leadership in private and public affairs. The arrangements of society facilitate such leadership and reward it. A subculture, such as that of the Negro American, in which this is not the pattern, is placed at a distinct disadvantage."[56] This book studies the emergence of this complex of oppression and exploitation undergirded by race and sexuality in the transnational world of imperialism.

In postemancipation plantation agriculture around the world, sexuality, gender, kinship, and race became central to many regimes of political and economic control in the apparently "natural" form of the heterosexual, monogamous family. German smallhold farmers, African peasants, and American sharecroppers all appeared in domestic spheres that seemed at least partly independent of the global economies for which they worked. In fact, the paternal control of fathers over wives and children in such households, and the monogamous heterosexuality that this presupposed, became essential aspects of the over supervised and underpaid labor basic to the production of agricultural goods as cheap raw materials for industry elsewhere. German and American social scientists agreed that family farming presented an ideal model of controlling emancipated workers. Such domestic economies committed families, these social scientists believed, to an existing social order as much as they did to specific houses on specific plots of land. Smallholding checked the mobility and slowed the urbanization of workers that seemed to many social scientists to threaten the social order. Smallholding also, many social scientists held, kept farmers in paternal relations of domination with large landowners, often former masters of slaves or serfs, who might rent them land or employ their occasional labor. Smallholding furthermore tied individuals to monogamous, heterosexual patriarchies that brought paternal relations of domination inside the household, controlled sexuality, and thereby maintained racial lines of descent.

Sharecropping in the American New South became an important transatlantic paradigm of labor control. The labor-repressive function of the agricultural tenant household in the New South was especially tragic for African American freedpeople, who had struggled, in the aftermath of slavery, to establish family farms as means of defending their liberty and autonomy against would-be white masters. Faced with widespread black resistance to reintroducing the gang-labor system characteristic of the slave plantation, planters subverted African American demands for autonomous family farms through a particular sharecropping system that provided a brutally effective form of labor coercion. While the resulting sharecropping arrangements did foil the most authoritarian ambitions of planters, they also defeated, to much more devastating effect, the self-emancipatory efforts of freedpeople.

Social scientists on both sides of the Atlantic helped states make the family farm a general model for social control, pointing to the advantages of the patriarchal household and the smallhold farm. The smallhold farm, the peasant household, was hardly an autochthonous social unit, preceding and resisting the intrusions of the state and capital.[57] Small agricultural producers in the global South have long had complex and dynamic relations to larger structures of colonial and neocolonial exploitation and oppression, relations that the static label "peasant" tends to mask.[58] Creating peasantries became an important strategy of political and economic control in the reconfigured plantation belt that emerged in the wake of emancipation.[59]

Sociology became a transatlantic science in the last decades of the nineteenth century in part because the family farm became a transatlantic structure of political and economic control, promoted by state and business elites in the American South, the German East, and Colonial Africa. German social scientists regarded sharecropping, the smallhold of the American New South, as a model for the control of free agricultural labor, one that became particularly important as they began advising their own government on policies of "internal colonization" to check the "Polonization" of the Prussian East. The social policy and the political economy of the American South thus already informed the German social scientists who, as historian Daniel T. Rodgers and others have shown, deeply influenced the many American sociologists and economists who studied with them.[60] German social scientists not only trained W.E.B. Du Bois in the most advanced methods of sociology, but also learned from him about the "Negro question" in the United States, often drawing lessons from the African American sociologist at odds with his own antiracist writings. The German decision to request help from Booker T. Washington in transforming the political economy of Togo resulted from decades of mutual influence between German and American social science and social policy.

The Tuskegee expedition to Togo, in turn, made these transatlantic networks even broader and denser, as it brought smallholding to West Africa for purposes of agricultural production, social control, and racial ordering similar to those in the American South and the German East.

The school of sociology that emerged at the University of Chicago after the First World War became the most important American variant of this transatlantic social science. It was founded by Robert E. Park, the Tuskegee Institute sociologist and close adviser to Booker T. Washington, who combined his own scholarship on black labor in Africa and the United States with the expertise of William I. Thomas, the colleague who had recruited him to the sociology department, on Polish labor in Europe and the United States. The Chicago school of sociology emerged from the study of the two groups, blacks and Poles, that had inspired the study of free agricultural labor in the United States and Germany in the first place, and that had provided models for colonial synthesis in Togo. Park and Thomas hoped that their sociology would help states and economic elites devise pedagogies that could accommodate workers of various racial and ethnic backgrounds to the global capitalist division of labor. They would expand to the workers of the world the projects advocated by the Verein für Sozialpolitik for eastern Germany, by Tuskegee Institute for the New South, and by the German colonial state for Togo. In Chicago, however, Park and Thomas encountered blacks and Poles who were urban rather than rural and thus challenged their normative and analytic models of smallhold farming. During the First World War, Chicago became a major destination for African Americans leaving the South, and for decades the city had also been a major destination for Poles seeking better opportunities in the United States than those offered by seasonal labor in German agriculture. Chicago school sociology became urban sociology because the rural people who served it as models for the racial division of labor fled the countryside.

The regionally differentiated and globally interdependent capitalist economy of the nineteenth century emerged through the proliferation of a network of stable identities, both human and nonhuman. The globally traded raw materials of the nineteenth century were the products of biological and social control, much like the people who grew them. Agriculture had always involved modification through selection, and the global commodities markets of the nineteenth century expanded this ancient element of agriculture into a means of labor coercion. American cotton and European sugarbeets acquired traits useful to industry because managers and overseers controlled their biological reproduction and the processes by which they were planted, cultivated, and harvested. West African palm oil had much greater flexibility, both as a biological organism and as a good used by humans, and thus became an inextricable part of the political and economic autonomy that many West Africans enjoyed between the end of the slave trade and the beginning of colonial domination. Introducing cotton into West Africa did not simply mean scattering American seeds on African soil, but rather introducing to Africa a simultaneously biological, economic, and political regime of control. Industrial-grade cotton and confining racial categories of blackness were both causes and effects of this regime of control. Agricultural workers in the global South found themselves incorporated as members of specific races into a social-biological regime of control that also included the engineered crops they grew and the farms on which they grew these crops.

Charging race and kinship with stabilizing capitalist orders in the global South gave extraordinary importance to sexual desire, perhaps the only force more mobile and fungible than capital itself. In every case studied in this book, sexuality provided an avenue of rebellion against the capitalist household. Anxieties about sex between black men and white women plagued white elites around the world, and assuaging these fears may have been foremost in Washington's mind when he spoke of the races remaining socially "separate as the fingers" in his Atlanta address. Washington's interest in domesticity, both in Alabama and in Africa, also reflected his recognition of both the fragility and the importance of particular forms of monogamous heterosexuality. Polish migrant laborers, at least half of whom were young women, enjoyed a sexual autonomy unavailable to their brothers and sisters in the households of their fatherland. They engaged in extramarital sex in farm workers' barracks and even chose their own partners for marriage. Polish and German authorities alike decried this sexual autonomy, especially among young women. German colonial attacks on African economic autonomy concentrated on the independence of women's households in polygamous marriages and on women's physical, sexual, and economic mobility. Colonial authorities sought to replace the individual autonomy of the Togolese extended household with the personal and sexual constraint of a patriarchal family farm.

Capitalism produced not only the stability of biosocial identities, the fixity of fields and households that ensured the predictable flow of cotton and other crops to the commodity markets of the global North. It also simultaneously undermined the constraints on which the political economy of empire depended. The routines of capitalist production often allowed, often impelled, individuals to leave family and home, as seasonal or permanent migrants. Indeed, the imperatives of kinship also, through the functioning of the incest taboo, expelled individuals from the very households to which they also bound them. Many individuals chose to disregard Booker T. Washington's famous advice to "cast down your buckets where you are," and capitalism made many kinds of exodus possible. Political and economic authorities used racial identities to integrate individuals into specific places in an order of capitalist production, based, in the era after slavery, on cash and contracts, but individuals could also use the mechanisms of cash and contracts to challenge not only the meaning of racial identity but even political and economic authorities themselves. The kinship systems of "race" stabilized capitalism in many regions of the world, but capitalism also destabilized these kinship systems, sometimes even producing that dreadful and hopeful flash of bare capitalism, of bourgeoisie and proletariat, a moment when, as Marx wrote, "all that is solid melts into air."[61] Capitalism has created a thousand ways to trap workers but also a thousand ways for workers to revolt and, ultimately, again to borrow Marx's words, to expropriate the expropriators.[62]

The October Revolution challenged the global political and economic conditions that had fostered conservative academic sociology, Tuskegee Institute, German internal colonization, and the European "civilizing mission" in Africa. Before the First World War, Social Democrats, including Karl Kautsky and Rosa Luxemburg, subjected the work of the Verein für Sozialpolitik to careful criticism, rejecting the authoritarian statism of German social scientists, their valorization of the patriarchal household, their calls to keep workers in the countryside as small farmers, and their support for overseas colonization. The workers' movements inspired by the Russian Revolution, which soon came to call themselves "communist," took an even more aggressive stance against colonialism and racism. The failings of the Soviet Union to live up to its early promises are well documented. Most important for this study are the international support and the less quantifiable inspiration that the communist movements gave to many African and African American radicals. Many of the first generation of University of Chicago students, the intellectual grandchildren, in a sense, of Booker T. Washington and Gustav Schmoller, incorporated the radical environment of Chicago, as well as communist ideas about racism, imperialism, and capitalism, to create a sociology that criticized and sought to transform the conditions of oppression and exploitation, conditions to which sociology had also contributed. This book ends at that hopeful period between the two world wars, when workers and colonized societies around the world struggled against exploitation and oppression, inspiring new political alliances and new sciences and pointing toward new forms of democracy and prosperity.

Chapter 1

COTTON, THE "NEGRO QUESTION,"

AND INDUSTRIAL EDUCATION

IN THE NEW SOUTH

THE NEW SOUTH that Tuskegee Institute would help reproduce in West Africa was a temporary outcome of a long-standing conflict between workers and employers over the meaning of the freedom of labor. Workers, black and white, enslaved and emancipated, sought a kind of economic freedom given one of its now-classic formulations by Garrison Frazier, an African American Baptist minister interviewed in Savannah, Georgia, by General William T. Sherman and Secretary of War Edwin M. Stanton in January 1865. "Slavery," explained Frazier, "is receiving by irresistible power the work of another man, and not by his consent. The freedom, as I understand it, promised by the [1863 Emancipation] proclamation, is taking us from under the yoke of bondage and placing us where we can reap the fruit of our own labor, and take care of ourselves and assist the Government in maintaining our freedom."[1] Frazier not only contrasted economic freedom with slavery but also implied that economic freedom stood in tension with wage labor, in which employers also took the "work of another," compensating employees for their labor time only. Workers around the Atlantic, sometimes implicitly, sometimes explicitly, demanded, like Frazier, economic autonomy as a foundation of political and personal self-reliance, seeking to attain a freedom suggested by, but also antithetical to, emerging capitalist relations of production. Employers sought to direct the autonomous and self-emancipatory activity of workers into myriad channels, including the routines of factory, plantation, and tenant farm. The resulting economic forms were hybrids of emancipation and exploitation, rarely satisfactory to workers or to employers. The New South, both in the United States and as European authorities reproduced it across the Atlantic, represented one such hybrid.[2]

The American South interested European and American elites, and finally made the region a model for European colonial rule, because of the interdependent social constructions of industrial-grade cotton and submissive, hardworking, and poorly paid "Negroes."[3] Both of these constructions were vigorously resisted by the entities that they were meant to describe. The particular quality of American cotton came from constant control of varietals and, more importantly, strict supervision of African American cotton growers. As one British cotton expert warned: "Where the negro is his own master, custom, not the condition of the crop, dictates when he shall begin the harvest. Should the crop mature early, while the full heat of August is still felt, nothing will persuade the negro to face the arduous task of a day's work in the fields, with the result that his fields may be seen white with cotton for a week or a fortnight before work is started."[4] American cotton emerged from the racist division of labor in the South as much as it did from processes of natural selection and artificial breeding. Growing American cotton in Africa or anywhere else outside the United States would involve significantly more than transplanting American cotton seeds. It would involve reproducing an approximation of the entire biological-social complex of American cotton growing, as it had developed in slavery and in freedom.

The permanent coercion needed to maintain American cotton also maintained the status of millions of southerners as "Negroes." African Americans themselves contradicted the image of the "Negro" presupposed by ideologies of slavery and of the New South through their self-conscious political action, their everyday forms of resistance, and the simple fact of their complex humanity.[5] An alleged affinity for cotton growing has long been central to racist images of African Americans, suggesting that blacks need and even enjoy the hard work, low pay, and coercive treatment of the southern cotton plantation. Even after the turn of the century, when the number of white cotton growers approached, and finally exceeded, the number of black cotton growers, many experts continued to assert that cotton could only be grown profitably with black labor.[6] Industrial-quality cotton and the "Negro" of New South ideology were indeed codependent images whose failures to correspond to reality—natural, social, economic, and political—authorized coercive interventions that gave these images, in the end, a superficial plausibility. The Negro-cotton pair, interdependent in ways inconceivable to most white elites, founded a New South that would prove as attractive to the colonial rulers of Africa as it did to their counterparts in the northern and southern United States.[7]

The connection between blacks and cotton hardly merited discussion before emancipation, for slavery had ensured that blacks alone worked America's cotton fields. With the end of slavery, the meaning of black freedom for political and economic elites in America and around the world came to be formulated around a so-called Negro question, which concerned the nature and the proper treatment of African Americans. The "Negro question" was largely reactive, seeking to reinterpret and thus deflect African American self-emancipation onto paths that maintained white political and economic domination. Thus, the peculiar forms of sharecropping that emerged in the southern United States travestied prior African American demands for independent family farming. Sharecropping remained the main force responsible for continuing the coercion of African American cotton growers after emancipation, even as it stymied the most coercive designs of planters.

The type of industrial education promoted by Hampton and Tuskegee Institutes similarly represented an attempt to redirect African American efforts at self-education into channels supportive of the political and economic status quo. Industrial education did not mean vocational schooling but rather imparting an aptitude and enthusiasm for physical labor and personal virtues, such as cleanliness, sobriety, and thrift, that many African Americans were supposed to lack. Proponents of "industrial education" defined it against a literary or academic education, which, they claimed, had little relevance for poor, rural blacks in the South. Critics argued that industrial education accommodated and even encouraged segregation, disfranchisement, and the economic exploitation of blacks. Most scholars today side with the critics of Hampton and Tuskegee Institutes, and one historian has even described industrial education as "schooling for the new slavery."[8]

Industrial education, however, contained black self-emancipation in a double sense: it sought to control black struggles for freedom, but it also preserved these efforts. Indeed, the founder and president of Tuskegee Institute, the African American Booker T. Washington, became, at the end of the nineteenth century, the best known and most widely admired global representative of the New South, ironically by encouraging blacks to limit their economic and political aspirations and to remain in the South. His national and international fame gave him the authority to begin working with the agricultural scientist George Washington Carver and the sociologist W.E.B. Du Bois on a program to transform, rather than reinforce, the dismal political and economic conditions of blacks in the South. Carver conducted agricultural research to make black farmers economically independent, producing their own means of subsistence and ending their dependence on the cotton industry. Du Bois, had he come to Tuskegee, would have worked in tandem with Carver to challenge the racist political and economic structures that prevented blacks from gaining the independence that Garrison Frazier had understood by freedom. This global renown, however, also brought Booker T. Washington to the attention of European colonial authorities, who persuaded him to help them reproduce the New South of cotton and coercion in Africa rather than revolutionize the New South in America.

Cotton and Coercion

The biological diversity of cotton made it an unlikely candidate for a major industrial commodity of the nineteenth and twentieth centuries. The mechanical spinning and weaving of the industrial revolution required precisely standardized fibers, yet the term *cotton* could refer to any number of varieties of any of the four species of the genus *Gossypium* that had been cultivated from Asia to the Americas since antiquity. These four cultivated species were themselves artificial entities, the product of perhaps millennia of selective breeding that turned the single-cell filaments that once assisted, like dandelion fluff, in seed distribution into freakishly long and extraordinarily durable fibers, separable from the seeds they had once carried on the wind and suitable for spinning and weaving. The four species of *Gossypium* are themselves hardly stable, for cotton plants cross-pollinate easily and vary widely.[9] The unpredictable characteristics of cotton fibers had posed few obstacles to hand spinning and weaving, since human fingers could make constant adjustments to irregularities in cotton staple. The transition from hand to factory spinning and weaving required not only the discipline of workers but also the standardization of cotton fibers. The discipline of workers and the standardization of cotton were, in fact, two aspects of a single agricultural, economic, and political process.

Long before British rule, India dominated the cotton textile industry in the Old World, a prominence it maintained until the eighteenth century, exporting textiles to markets from China to West Africa. Egyptians also cultivated cotton, beginning as early as the fifth century B.C.E. New World cottons, woven throughout Central and South America, had little role in the world market before the eighteenth century. In the eighteenth and nineteenth centuries, Europe and the United States came to exercise a near global monopoly over cotton textile manufacture because British manufacturers and American planters gradually subjected every stage of cotton production—from the selection of seeds to the cultivation of fields, to the grading of the product, to the labor of spinning and weaving—to the institutionalized coercion of the factory and the plantation.

Both mechanical- and hand-processing of textiles require similar steps. Cotton fibers have first to be separated from the seeds. The seeds can be used as fertilizer or animal feed. Oil extracted from the seeds served as a lubricant, as food, and in soap- and candle-making. Carding and combing removed dirt, pieces of stalk, and other extraneous material from the fibers and untangled and straightened them into parallel lines. Spinners then twisted the fiber into yarn, one thread at a time with spinning wheels and distaffs for most of human history. The yarn itself could be dyed before weaving, or it could be left undyed to produce "gray" cloth that could then be bleached, dyed, printed, and finished in other ways.

Cotton textiles became widely available in Europe in the twelfth century, thanks to the expansion of trade routes and to the greater contact between Europe and the Middle East resulting from the Crusades. By the thirteenth century, cotton cloth and cotton-linen blends, or fustians, became popular fabrics throughout Europe. Europeans already produced textiles from the indigenous fibers of wool and linen, and they were soon able to incorporate some cotton, exported from Arab markets to Italian cities, into their own spinning and weaving. By the fourteenth century, weavers began importing raw cotton fiber from Italy into southern Germany, turning the region into a major center of cotton weaving, a role it would resume in the nineteenth century. The terminology of cotton and cotton cloth in European languages reflects this early international economy. The term *cotton*, used with various spellings in Italian, French, and English, is taken directly from the Arabic *al Kotn*, as is the Spanish term *algodón*. The term *calico*, for printed cotton, derives from the name of the Indian city Calcutta; muslin, a fine cotton fabric, from the name of the city Mosul; and fustian, the cotton-linen mix, from Al-Fustat, a former capital of Egypt that has since been incorporated into Cairo. The German term, *Baumwolle*, literally "tree wool," reflects how Europeans incorporated cotton into already existing spinning technologies.[10]

In the early seventeenth century, the East India Company began importing Indian calicos and muslins to Britain, where, by the middle of the century, they became popular consumer items, threatening the indigenous silk, wool, and linen textile industry. These trades persuaded the government to ban the sale of imported cottons in Britain. The East India Company continued to re-export Indian cotton textiles, including to markets in West Africa as part of the infamous triangle trade that brought enslaved Africans to the Americas. In a classic case of industrialization through import substitution, as historian Joseph E. Inikori has shown, weavers and spinners in England and Scotland, protected from Indian competition in domestic markets, gradually introduced a number of labor-saving devices in cotton spinning and weaving that soon made British labor costs cheaper per unit of output than Indian labor costs. English textile manufacturers soon competed in global markets, imitating the check fabrics popular in West African and New World markets to compete with Indian textiles sold by English and European merchants.[11]

Textile manufacturing in this period typically occurred in households, with a wife spinning and a husband weaving.[12] At first, the low output of spinners using the distaff or wheel limited the amount of yarn available to weavers in the household organization of the textile industry. In 1764 the weaver James Hargreaves increased the amount of yarn available to him by inventing a machine that essentially simulated the fingers of several female spinners. Hargreaves called the machine a "spinning jenny," giving a generic woman's name to the machine that replicated this characteristically female work (see figure 1.1). The number of threads spun by a single spinner gradually increased from the single strand of the spinning wheel or distaff to the 120 spindles of the biggest spinning jennies. The spinning jenny, however, could only produce the relatively weak threads used for weft, and were thus more suitable for making fustian, with a cotton weft and linen warp. Richard Arkwright invented a water-driven spinning machine, the water frame, that employed a series of rollers to stretch and spin a stronger cotton yarn, suitable for warp. This invention allowed him to produce the first all-cotton English fabric in 1773 at his Nottingham mill. Samuel Crompton, a weaver, combined the inventions of Hargreaves and Arkwright into a "mule" (that is, a combination of the two) that could spin a much finer thread than the water frame and a much stronger thread than the jenny. This was sometimes called the "muslin wheel," since it could spin threads fine enough for that delicate fabric. The further automation of the jenny drove spinning out of the household and into factories. These innovations in spinning at first improved the earning power of handloom weavers, who now had more raw material for their own looms. This privileged position did not last long. Engineers first automated the loom in 1785 and powered it by steam later that year. This power loom slowly displaced handloom weavers, much as the mule had displaced hand spinners.[13]

Whereas Britain produced large quantities of relatively inexpensive textiles for markets in China, India, West Africa, and the Americas, German manufacturers produced smaller quantities of more luxurious textiles, including velvet and velour, for European markets. Southern Germany regained its prominent position in the cotton textile industry in the late eighteenth century, after recovering from the devastation of the Thirty Years' War. The cotton textile industry soon spread to Saxony, and, in the early nineteenth century, to Alsace in the West, which became part of Germany in 1871.[14] German mill workers were less efficient than their English counterparts, but their high-quality products were well suited to European markets. By 1913, even though its textiles could not compete successfully on the world market, Germany had become the second largest textile exporter globally thanks to its sales within Europe and other relatively wealthy regions, including Latin America and South Africa.[15]

The mechanization of the textile industry brought with it a dislocation of textile production from households, where workers controlled the labor process and owned spinning wheels, looms, and other equipment, to factories, where workers received wages to operate machines owned by employers. The chemist and political economist Andrew Ure celebrated

Figure 1.1. Spinning jenny. This spinning machine, invented by a weaver, increased the output of yarn by mimicking and multiplying the actions of a spinner's fingers. At first giving more economic power to household producers, the jenny initiated a process of mechanization that soon subjected workers to employers inside centralized factories, increased the global demand for industrialized cotton, and pushed European states to mimic the American cotton South in the colonial global South. Source: Alwin Oppel, *Die Baumwolle nach Geschichte, Anbau, Verarbeitung und Handel, sowie nach ihrer Stellung im Volksleben und in der Staatswirtschaft* (Leipzig: Duncker and Humblot, 1902).

mechanization as a weapon allowing employers to defeat workers in the class struggles that raged in Britain in the first half of the nineteenth century. Ure, writing in 1835, described industrialization as a "progression . . . according to which every process peculiarly nice, and therefore liable to injury from the ignorance and waywardness of workmen, is withdrawn from handicraft control, and placed under the guidance of self-acting machinery." An improved spinning mule was, according to Ure, so obviously "destined to restore order among the industrious classes" that it "strangled the Hydra of misrule" even before employers introduced it into factories.[16] The industrial revolution, which emerged from efforts to protect the English textile industry from superior Indian cottons, soon led to European preeminence in the global textile market and to a greater authority of factory owners and managers over textile producers.

The mechanization of European spinning depended upon the cotton grown in the United States.[17] British planters had initially grown Indian cotton plants in the American colonies, but soon learned that New World varieties produced stronger and longer fibers that withstood the high speeds and tensions of mechanized spinning and weaving better than the short-staple cotton of India did. In coastal areas of the American South, planters grew Sea Island cotton, which produced bolls with a long-stapled, fine fiber and with easily removed black seeds. A second variety of American cotton produced a staple shorter and coarser than that of Sea Island, though still superior to Indian cotton, but with the advantage of growing over a much wider range than its longer-stapled cousin. The green seeds that easily distinguished this so-called Upland cotton from Sea Island could not, however, be removed by the roller gin, an ancient invention of India that pushed seeds out of bolls by rolling a cylinder over cotton resting on a flat, hard surface. Upland cotton seeds could only be removed by hand until 1793, when Eli Whitney invented a gin that could remove these green seeds. This saw gin made it possible to supply a global market with textiles woven from American Upland cotton.[18]

The American Civil War of 1861–65 emphatically reminded the global textile industry of its dependence on cotton from the United States, even as it temporarily cut off supplies of southern cotton to European markets and inspired a short boom in markets outside the United States.[19] Cotton prices skyrocketed as the so-called cotton famine made British and continental mills desperate for raw materials. (Large stores of cotton in European warehouses meant that few suffered from a real shortage of cotton for the first years of the conflict, but the blockade of the South worried European manufacturers from the beginning.) British India sought to meet this demand by increasing the output and trying to improve the notoriously poor quality of its cotton. Indian peasant cultivators sometimes mixed extraneous matter in with their cotton or even wetted bales to make them heavier, since they sold them by weight. This practice only increased with global demand and prices. Government steps to control this practice could not succeed, since authorities had little control over the production process and market pressures dictated that peasants concern themselves more with the weight than the quality of cotton bales. Nonetheless, during the American Civil war, India provided 55 percent of Britain's cotton supply, and some growers became wealthy. Initially cotton planters in the United States feared, and cotton growers in India hoped, that the end of slavery would mean the end of the near monopoly of the United States over cotton production. The consumption of Indian cotton was limited, however, even during the Civil War, by the inability of spinning machines to process short-staple cotton and the unwillingness of European firms to introduce new machinery for the duration of what they hoped would be only a short interruption in American cotton supplies.[20] As cotton prices came down after the war, many Indian growers were ruined. Smaller cotton booms took place in other cotton-producing regions, including Togo, during the war. In India and in much of the world, the short boom followed by crashing cotton prices and demand as America reentered the market after the war chastened peasant producers and established more firmly the global importance of American cotton.

The dominance of Upland cotton came to sustain itself, for, as the textile industry developed specialized machines to handle its medium fiber, mills became less and less able to process other types of cotton. As one British observer noted, "It is probably more true to say that cotton spinning has been elaborated so as to handle in the best possible way the cotton from America, than to claim that America has evolved cotton specially suitable for spinners."[21] In the course of the nineteenth century, China and Japan became major markets for Indian cotton. Japanese spinners spun a relatively fine yarn from raw Indian cotton, while Chinese weavers produced so-called nankeen fabrics from rough Indian yarn. European textile mills also used limited quantities of Indian cotton by mixing it with American Upland. Indians themselves wore fabrics made primarily from American cotton, whether woven in Britain or in local mills. In the early twentieth century, when the Swadeshi movement encouraged Indians to boycott the economy of the British Empire by weaving fabrics from local cotton, Indian mill proprietors turned to their Japanese colleagues to learn how to make fine yarn from their own cotton.[22] Today American Upland cotton—*Gossypium hirsutum*—accounts for 90 percent of the cotton cultivated around the world.[23] Before the Tuskegee efforts in German Togo, however, only growers in the United States cultivated significant quantities of cotton that could be used as an industrial raw material.

The global commodities bourses that emerged in the nineteenth century guaranteed that American cotton had predictable qualities, so that spinning, weaving, and other processing machines did not have to be recalibrated for each new bale.[24] Markets in Liverpool and New York were the first to introduce techniques for grading cotton, techniques gradually adopted by other markets, including in the city of Bremen in 1872.[25] Commodities markets forced growers to standardize the cotton they grew, ensuring not only that they delivered American Upland but also that it was of a predictable grade, length, and character. The amount of trash—leaves, dirt, and other extraneous matter—that a bale of cotton contained affected its price more than any other variation. "Classers" deemed cotton with a certain amount of trash middling, which became the basis for all futures contracts.[26] Cotton with much trash descended through a series of classes down to ordinary. Classers categorized cotton with little trash in ranks ascending to fair. Trained classers learned to determine the

FIGURE 1.2. Bales of American cotton in a warehouse of the Bremen Cotton Exchange. Cotton exchanges demanded a consistency in cotton, necessary both for commodifying and industrially processing the fiber, that required severe labor discipline in the cotton fields of the Southern United States and, later, Africa. Source: Oppel, *Die Baumwolle.*

amount of trash in a bale of cotton by scrutinizing a sample in carefully controlled conditions.

Measuring the length of cotton staple was by no means easy or mechanical, for every fiber of an individual cotton boll is not, obviously, of an identical length. A cotton classing manual of 1938 described how classers measured staple length by pulling a sample of cotton repeatedly, without looking or measuring, to determine the length of the cotton through "kinaesthetic impression . . . the drag of the cotton between fingers and thumb." "Cotton stapling," this manual continued, "is an art based on a fine delicacy of the senses and on skills built up by experience; the cotton classer has hands as well educated and trained as the hands of an expert violinist" (see figure 1.3).[27] While intuiting the length of cotton fiber, classers also judged the "character" of the cotton. Even as late as 1938, the U.S. Department of Agriculture admitted that "there are no character standards, nor is there entire agreement as to all the quality elements that should be included in character" even though cottons of a given staple length and grade produced varying quality yarns based upon this indefin-

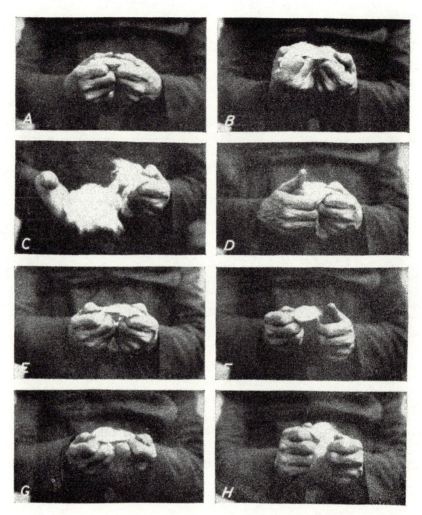

Figure 1.3. The "kinaesthetic" process by which classers determined the staple length and "character" of cotton. Although the images make it appear as if the stapler separated and then measured the fiber, in fact both the staple length and the cotton character were determined by the feel of the cotton as the classer pulled it between his hands. As another manual explained, "the cotton classer has hands as well educated and trained as the hands of an expert violinist." The minute precision with which markets classed cotton translated into the strict control of the labor of cotton growers. Source: *The Classification of Cotton* (Washington, DC: U.S. Department of Agriculture, 1938), 40–41.

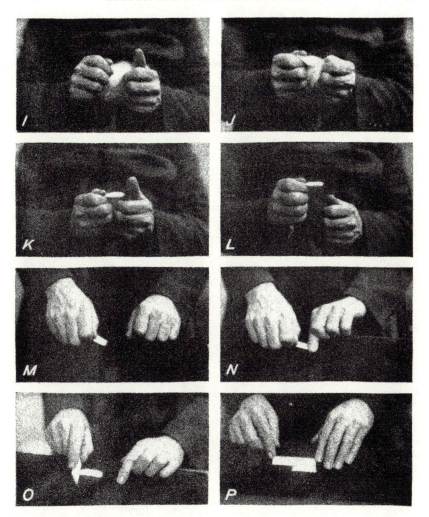

FIGURE 1.3. *continued.*

able trait.[28] No matter how precisely markets specified the standards for cotton, all agreed that classers had to possess special aesthetic abilities to determine the grade of a bale of cotton by inspecting just a small sample. As an American guide for cotton farmers put it: "[T]he classing of cotton is not a mechanical art; it is the work of artists essentially. Classing cotton is a great deal more than matching samples. It is a matter of the eye and the judgment, a certain feeling that only a man with an artistic temperament can have. All good classers are in a way artists."[29] Perhaps this supposed artistic element of cotton classing inspired Edgar Degas to illustrate each of the processes of classing cotton in his well-known 1873 painting, *New Orleans Cotton Exchange.*

Every factor judged in the cotton exchanges of New Orleans, New York, Liverpool, Bremen, and elsewhere had a counterpart in the exacting control of labor in the cotton fields of the American South. To ensure high prices for their cotton in ever more vigilant markets, growers had to destroy cotton plants at the end of a growing season, although the plants are perennials able to produce bolls for several seasons, in order to ensure maximum productivity. Growers had to be prevented from replanting seeds obtained from their own crops, purchasing instead seeds produced under controlled circumstances.[30] There were dozens of varieties of American Upland, and if growers reused seeds from their own plants they might produce hybrids of different varieties and of unknown character. Commodities markets also demanded cotton of a pure white color, which resulted largely from the work of pickers. Dirt stained any cotton that pickers allowed to rest on the ground instead of putting directly into their sacks. If pickers did not harvest cotton immediately after the bolls opened, rain or sun could alter its color and frost or mildew could give it a bluish hue. If pickers harvested bolls too early, however, gins could not process the cotton properly. Since the bolls on any given plant do not open simultaneously, pickers had to go through the fields several, typically three, times each season. Because the grade of cotton depended on its trash content, pickers had to pluck the bolls nimbly by hand from the surrounding leaves. Cotton picking was not mechanized until after the Second World War.[31] Before this, hand labor in the United States had to achieve levels of precision and productivity commensurate with the exact standardization of mechanized mills. Commodities markets, of course, did not talk directly to growers, nor did they have an invisible hand that directed growers with cash incentives; the demands of the market came through the quite visible hands of plantation owners and managers. The meticulous control of labor remained essential to the production of cotton in both slavery and freedom.

GROWING COTTON IN THE OLD SOUTH AND THE NEW

Even as it reminded most manufacturers of their dependence on American cotton, the Civil War also emancipated the enslaved workers who had made it possible for the United States to produce such superior industrial-grade cotton in the first place. Often fleeing plantations at the first sign of approaching Union soldiers, slaves forced Union commanders to address the issue of black freedom even while President Abraham Lincoln

FIGURE 1.4. Cotton harvest. Much of the value of a given bale of cotton derived from the care and speed with which it was picked, a process done entirely by hand before the middle of the twentieth century. This was one of the principal reasons that cotton growing required such intense levels of coercion. In Togo, colonial authorities would seek to reproduce not only the coercive supervision characteristic of American cotton growing, but also many specific techniques, including the use of sacks seen in this image. Source: Oppel, *Die Baumwolle*.

continued to insist that emancipation was not a war aim. These African Americans did not concern themselves with the political delicacies of legal emancipation occupying Lincoln as he negotiated a fragile wartime alliance that included both abolitionists and slaveholders in border states still loyal to the Union. During the Civil War, fleeing slaves, writes historian Eric Foner, "propelled a reluctant white America down the road to abolition."[32]

While some Radical Republicans welcomed abolition without reservations, most officers in the Union army sought to maintain white control over African American labor. During the war, General Nathaniel P. Banks, Union commander at New Orleans, pioneered a system that required blacks, although ostensibly free, to sign yearly labor contracts, often on the plantations of their former masters. Many who did not sign such contracts were forced to work for the Union army. Vagrancy laws made it difficult for workers to avoid signing contracts, and the contracts themselves gave former slaveholders great authority over former slaves. Banks's narrow interpretation of freedom, although criticized by radicals as too close to the slave system it had replaced, shaped the labor policy of the Union army and later that of the Bureau of Refugees, Freedmen, and Abandoned Lands (more commonly known as the Freedmen's Bureau). It was of a piece with bourgeois notions of free labor on both sides of the Atlantic, which sought to ensure that workers remained free only until they were hired, after which they became subject to the will of owners and managers. Racism added a further element of brutality to this bourgeois conception of free labor in the South.[33]

In contrast to many white elites, African Americans in the rural South understood free labor to mean, above all else, the autonomy afforded by land ownership. When slaves demanded freedom they did not envision the system of master-servant codes, contracts, and vagrancy laws that characterized free labor in most parts of the world.[34] A parcel of land, when planted with both subsistence and cash crops, would allow freedpeople to manage their own labor and to keep much of the value they created for themselves. Free labor would be freedom from laboring under the authority, and for the profit, of another. The chaos of the war did provide opportunities for thousands of African Americans to appropriate the lands of former masters, in many cases with the approval of Union authorities. Following his 1865 discussion with the African American minister Garrison Frazier, discussed at the beginning of this chapter, General Sherman issued his famous Special Field Order No. 15, which divided a strip of coastal land from South Carolina to Florida into forty-acre parcels for the families of freedpeople. This project distributed approximately 400,000 acres in six months.[35] The first case of mass land redistribution occurred earlier in the war, in Hampton Roads, the area around Fort Monroe on the Virginia coast where Samuel Chapman Armstrong would later found Hampton Institute.[36] The Union army had retained control of Fort Monroe after Virginia had seceded, and, during the war, the Federal stronghold attracted thousands of blacks fleeing slavery, who occupied and farmed land abandoned by fleeing Confederates. The commander of Fort Monroe, General Benjamin Butler, was the first to classify escaped slaves as "contraband of war" who could be held by the Union during hostilities, even though slavery remained legal in the United States. Escaping to Union lines was one of the many steps taken by enslaved African Americans that eventually forced legal abolition.

The American Civil War brought with it not only legal emancipation but also an attempt at social change far more profound and democratic than anything that occurred during Reconstruction. Neither northern nor southern authorities supported such a social revolution, or even reforms that would have afforded blacks the limited liberty enjoyed by white workers.[37] President Andrew Johnson's Amnesty Proclamation of 1865 required the Freedmen's Bureau to remove freedpeople from the land they had settled during the war. The federal government replaced Bureau officers who sympathized with new black landowners, such as C. B. Wilder of Hampton, Virginia, with others, such as the one who took Wilder's place, General Samuel Chapman Armstrong, willing to restore lands to former slaveholders. Once the Freedmen's Bureau had removed freedpeople from the lands they had cultivated, its officers, following the model established by General Banks in Louisiana, set about pressuring African Americans to sign year-long labor contracts, often with former slaveholders.[38] Former slaveholders were joined by planters from the North, who were at least as eager as their Southern counterparts to take advantage of the political and economic subordination of African American laborers and perhaps more enthusiastic about employing new mechanisms of formal economic freedom to do so.[39] The Freedmen's Bureau helped northern and southern elites transform the economic emancipation briefly achieved by many freedpeople into, at best, the merely formal freedom of the contract. In many cases the Freedmen's Bureau was no agent of emancipation, but rather limited or even undermined the personal freedom and economic autonomy achieved by African Americans during the war.

One of the many ways that African Americans resisted efforts to limit their freedom after emancipation was to continue a struggle, waged also in slavery, for the autonomy of nuclear families. Slaveholders had sought to define African American gender and kinship roles to suit their interlinked aims of exploitation and control, and often to serve their sadistic caprice as well. Slaveholders forced most slaves, male and female, to work plantation fields, refusing to recognize a gendered division of labor in blacks that they thought important for whites. The ubiquitous rape of enslaved African American women by white men attacked both individual women and also assaulted monogamous marriage and the role of the husband as protector of the family and father of his wife's children. The children of enslaved women became slaves themselves, "property" of a slaveholder, who could forever separate them from their families. Even in slavery, African American men and women managed to create gender and kinship roles apart from those that slaveholders sought to impose.[40] After 1865 many African Americans sought to preserve some of the individual and family autonomy that they had gained through their wartime self-emancipation. After the war, many women and children refused to work in plantation labor gangs, and few men wished to work under conditions reminiscent of the slave plantation either. A family farm promised many African Americans security and autonomy in their property and in their gender and household roles, as well as some safety from the violence and sexual assaults of white authorities.[41] The patriarchal, monogamous household has long been one of the most effective forms of social control, but for many freedpeople it also represented a rebellion against the even more oppressive family arrangements of slavery, as well as a means of defending themselves against further white exploitation and oppression.

Complaining of labor shortages, many landlords compromised with African American aspirations for land ownership and family autonomy, but in such a way that they might continue the coercive labor discipline essential to the global cotton market and thus to their own incomes. To induce African Americans to continue producing staple crops, planters adopted a sharecropping, coercive form of tenancy that gave agricultural laborers some of the autonomy of land ownership and family independence, while preserving the property relations and much of the coercion of the plantation. Although sharecropping may initially have seemed to provide a means for landless farmers to gain some independence, it soon created a widespread system of dependent labor.[42] A family in a share contract rented a plot on a plantation in exchange for providing the owner with a share—often half—of the cash crops they grew. The landlord or another creditor would also advance the family cash, supplies, and equipment necessary for the season. At the end of the year, the landlord sold the crop to a mercantile agent, or factor, retaining his share of the profits, the cost of the goods, and the cash advanced to the tenant, plus interest, before giving anything that remained to the cropper. The law classified croppers as employees rather than renters, thus allowing landlords to intervene in the labor process in ways that would have otherwise been difficult with tenant farmers. Since the landlord earned money from a share of the cash crop only, share contracts required tenants to devote the majority of their land to staples, and to cotton above all. Landlords could require whole families and even neighboring croppers to work extra hours on a plot if they determined that it was inadequately cultivated. The transition from the plantation gang-labor system to smallhold tenant farming represented a victory of African American workers over white planters; the sharecropping that emerged in the South represented a counterattack by planters seeking to maintain some of the economic and political authority they had lost with the end of slavery.

The credit mechanisms of sharecropping further subjected tenants to landlords, although they also encumbered landlords. Tenants had to live on borrowed money until the cotton was harvested and sold and they received their share from the landlord. Because of low cotton prices, exorbitant interest rates, and frequent dishonesty by landlords, it was common for families to remain in debt to their landlords or to other lien holders even after the crop was sold. Tenant indebtedness gave more direct eco-

nomic advantage to banks and merchants than to landlords, but, indirectly, it gave landlords the extraordinary authority, once provided by
slavery, necessary to grow cotton. Sharecroppers seeking to leave their
landlords while in debt could be imprisoned for fraud or charged a fine
that was added to their debt. An 1867 law had outlawed debt peonage in
the United States, but courts could imprison debtors for fraud and then
force them to work. The Thirteenth Amendment that abolished slavery
in 1865 still allowed "involuntary servitude" "as a punishment for
crime," and millions of individuals found themselves forced into virtual
slavery through this constitutional loophole.[43] Croppers trying to escape
debts could easily end up, as convicts, in "involuntary servitude" on the
plantation they had sought to flee in the first place. Indebted sharecroppers could move only by finding a landlord willing to assume responsibility for their debts, but the sharecropper would then be legally bound to
this new landlord. One British cotton expert explained that, after emancipation, planters introduced sharecropping as a financial constraint "to
secure a hold on the negro, whose nomadic peculiarities are not in the
interest of successful cotton cultivation."[44] Southern sharecropping uti-
lized the mechanisms of the free market and the appearance of family
farming to create a new form of unfree labor.

After the Civil War, whites also found themselves caught up in the economic trap of tenant cotton farming. The common assumption that tenant farmers were black was incorrect; in fact, tenant farmers of all races
were subjected to the harsh exploitation of share tenancy and crop liens.
As figure 1.5 illustrates, by 1910 the number of white tenant farmers in
the cotton states approached, and by 1930 exceeded, the number of black
tenant farmers in the region. According to historian Gavin Wright, increasing numbers of white tenant farmers accounted for the expansion of
cotton acreage after the Civil War, allowing the South to produce more
cotton after emancipation than it had before.[45] Despite these facts, cotton
remained principally associated with black growers working under white
supervision. Speaking in 1907 to an international cotton congress in Vienna, Austria, the president of the Southern Cotton Planters' Association
of Atlanta, Georgia, explained that growing cotton required so much
labor that, when undertaken by white growers, it "is carried on at the
expense of the education of the children of the growers and of the man-
hood and independence of that type of the Anglo-Saxon race of which
every American is so proud."[46] When whites grew cotton they became,
this speaker suggested, not fully white. A 1935 study led by the African
American sociologist Charles S. Johnson found that white sharecroppers
resisted cooperating with African Americans to fight against the abuses
both suffered. "Because," Johnson remarked, "of their insistence upon
the degrading of three million Negro tenants, five and a half million white

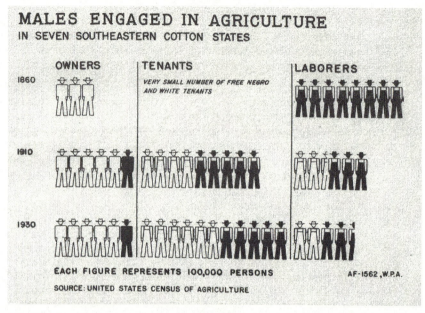

FIGURE 1.5. Males Engaged in Agriculture in Seven Southeastern States. The number of white tenant farmers grew until, by 1930, there were more white than black tenant farmers. In 1930 black farm laborers still outnumbered white farm laborers, and white owners far outnumbered black owners. Source: T. J. Woofter Jr., *Landlord and Tenant on the Cotton Plantation* (Washington, DC: Works Progress Administration, 1936), 13.

workers continue to keep themselves in virtual peonage."[47] The common belief that cotton corresponded to a race was an absurd, but effective, fiction. Imagining cotton as a "black man's crop," as one British expert described it, resulted from, underwrote, and obscured the high levels of coercion and poor pay that really were necessary to produce the type of cotton demanded by mechanized textile mills—mills that themselves depended on other forms of labor coercion.[48]

The "Negro Question" and the New South

For New South boosters and international manufacturers, African Americans were not an unwelcome remnant of a defunct slave system—as they were for some abolitionists—but rather a regional resource. Blacks, these boosters claimed, worked harder, obeyed authority more willingly, and engaged in strikes less readily than white workers did. In the decade before Booker T. Washington's Atlanta Compromise address, Henry Grady, editor of the *Atlanta Constitution*, was the best known promoter of the New South. In a speech at an 1886 banquet of the New England Club in New York City, Grady depicted the "Negro," not as an awkward reminder of the "feudal" Old South of slavery, but rather as a superior laborer in a modern capitalist economy: "No section," Grady informed his audience, "shows a more prosperous laboring population than the negroes of the South, none in fuller sympathy with the employing and land-owning class."[49] The Virginia businessman Lewis H. Blair, though opposed to segregation because he thought it made the Negro "an extremely defective tool," reminded his readers that "the Negro . . . being our principal source of labor, is our principal dependence for prosperity."[50] Booker T. Washington would expand upon these New South representations of African Americans, often remarking that blacks were brought to America because of their superior abilities as laborers, touting black indifference to labor unions and strikes, and promising ever increasing national prosperity as black labor improved with the industrial education promoted by Tuskegee Institute.[51]

Authorities in the New South, in their optimism about the economic value of African American workers, avidly discussed what they called "the Negro question," the question of how best to realize the benefits of free black labor. The authorities discussed the labor of freedpeople as a question about racial identity rather than, for example, about capital investment, land reform, or even—despite their talk of "industrial" education—acquisition of technical skills. The question about black labor in the South revolved around the nature of "Negroes" and what those defined as "Negroes" might become. Under slavery there had been no "Negro question," although there had, of course, been racist views of African Americans among whites both opposed to, and in favor of, slavery.[52] Elites never succeeded in arriving at a stable definition of the "Negro" or at a stable political and economic regime for those defined as "Negroes." Rather, they formulated a "Negro question." The failed and contradictory answers that these elites offered to their own "Negro question," the always insufficient solutions to their own "Negro problem," produced a diverse array of political and economic traps that subjected millions to a process of capital accumulation akin to extortion and robbery, bolstered by a murderous system of coercion.

Those elites concerned with the "Negro" defined this racial identity around a contradiction: the "Negro" was a servile, hard-working, and inexpensive laborer; at the same time, the "Negro" was a rebellious, lazy, and excessively demanding threat to the political and economic order. Those who posed the "Negro question" asked how to make "Negroes" servile rather than rebellious, hardworking rather than lazy, and willing to settle for poverty wages. There could be no final solution to this "Negro question" for two reasons. First, any solution acceptable to white elites would require those defined as "Negroes" to abandon their every aspiration for economic autonomy, even while incentives supposed to motivate free laborers depended on precisely those aspirations. Second, those who would resolve the "Negro question" were stymied by a contradiction: admitting that "Negroes" were essentially rebellious and lazy meant that there could be no solution to the question; yet denying that "Negroes" were rebellious and lazy took away the justification for subjecting them to coercion in the name of eventual freedom. "How does it feel to be a problem?" According to W.E.B. Du Bois, this inquiry lay at the basis of any specific question asked of him about African Americans.[53] Those identified as "Negroes" were always defined as a problem, and thus subject to extraordinary coercion that was misrepresented as a solution to this "problem" but in fact functioned as a political and economic end in itself. At the root of the "Negro question" was the problem for all free labor in hierarchical societies: for workers, free labor meant economic autonomy, including the freedom not to work; for employers, free labor meant economic dependency and the need to work for others in order to survive.[54]

Fundamental to any understanding of racial ideology and industrial education in the New South is the brutal violence to which African Americans were subjected in the decades after emancipation. Racism and racist violence in the New South were not simply survivals from slavery and the Old South, but innovations of whites in the New South seeking to prevent blacks from enjoying the freedom won in the Civil War. White mobs, often with the consent of police and other local authorities, lynched two or three black southerners every *week* in the period 1890–1917. While even today the noose remains the icon of lynching, lynching was even worse than extrajudicial execution; lynch mobs publicly tortured their victims to death, typically by burning and mutilation, after which their dead or dying bodies were hanged for public display. Lynchings terrorized every African American, reinforcing the conditions of their exploitation and oppression and making resistance to racism exceedingly dangerous— and thus all the more heroic.[55] Racist ideas and the racialized political economy of the New South depended upon a constant threat of horrific violence looming over every African American.

HAMPTON INSTITUTE: FROM COLONIAL EDUCATION TO INDUSTRIAL EDUCATION

Education, like free labor and land ownership, became a central element of the "Negro question," and of white attempts to control black labor, not only because it fit with ideological concepts of the "Negro," but also because African Americans in slavery and in freedom had made education a fundamental part of their own self-emancipation.[56] In the early nineteenth century, most Southern states criminalized black education, and African Americans made heroic efforts to educate themselves, most importantly to read and write. Literacy conferred a range of benefits on African Americans, including social mobility; political and cultural emancipation; religious salvation through Bible study; the ability to forge travel passes; and, after slavery, the ability to read the tenancy and other employment contracts that they were forced to sign.

After emancipation, freedpeople organized schools to obtain the education denied them under slavery. They cautiously welcomed the assistance of educators from both the American Missionary Assocation and the Freedmen's Bureau, but sought to retain control of their own education and, insofar as possible, to ensure that black schools employed black teachers. African Americans seem to have perceived, correctly, that many whites, even in the Freedmen's Bureau, lacked enthusiasm for, or even outright opposed, black education. Schools in the South remained segregated by race before the 1954 Supreme Court decision in *Brown vs. Board of Education*, but in the nineteenth century the majority of public school teachers were whites, some committed abolitionists, others former Confederates driven into teaching by postwar poverty rather than by any commitment to black education.[57] The vast majority of black students had access only to primary schooling. In rural areas this consisted, typically, of four months of instruction in a one-room schoolhouse. The labor demands placed on children, especially in farming families, meant that they could attend only irregularly even for these months. Still, this school system, created in response to the demands of freedpeople, provided the first public education to members of any race in many southern states.

The American Missionary Association (hereafter AMA) pursued educational goals for African Americans more academic and literary than those of the Freedmen's Bureau, which, as a federal agency, followed the Johnson administration in restoring much of the political and economic power of the planters.[58] The AMA had been founded in 1846 by abolitionist missionaries dissatisfied with the weak opposition of their own organizations to slavery. Members of the AMA, which had worked at Fort Monroe throughout the war, protested the Union policy of treating slaves as "contraband of war" rather than as free people; they sought to protect blacks in the region from violence by Union troops and opposed the restoration of the lands occupied by freedpeople to large landowners. The Freedmen's Bureau and the AMA would continue clashing over the process of emancipation and Reconstruction, including over the education of freedpeople at Hampton Institute and elsewhere.

In the years immediately after the war, the AMA dominated primary schooling for blacks in the South, and its primers, while hardly radical, did stand unequivocally against slavery and the Confederacy and supported civil rights for blacks. The monthly newspaper of the AMA, the *Freedman*, also opposed President Johnson's conservative approach to Reconstruction. Between 1866 and 1869 the AMA founded seven colleges and assisted in founding Howard University in Washington, D.C. The faculty and administration of these schools were white, and the students, apart from some faculty children, were mostly black. Atlanta University and Fisk University soon stood out as the AMA's two premier universities. Along with Talladega, Atlanta and Fisk upheld standards similar to those of northern white universities. The rigorous college curriculum at Fisk University, in Nashville, Tennessee, for example, included a range of social and natural sciences and the study of classical Latin and Greek, as well as modern German and French.[59] It was the German taught at Fisk that made it possible for W.E.B. Du Bois to do graduate work in Berlin and for James Nathan Calloway to communicate in German with officials in Togo. Even though Washington and others contrasted industrial education to this kind of academic education, Tuskegee Institute hired many Fisk graduates as academic instructors.[60]

While the AMA had founded and continued to support Hampton Institute, General Samuel Chapman Armstrong of the Freedmen's Bureau gradually established personal control over the school. Thanks to Armstrong and, later, to his student Booker T. Washington, the "industrial" education promoted by Hampton, marked by the more conservative policies of the Freedmen's Bureau, gradually displaced AMA pedagogy in black schools throughout the South.[61] The AMA had already come into conflict with Armstrong, the Union army, and the Freedmen's Bureau over the treatment of black "contrabands" and the expulsion of black farmers from seized Confederate land. The AMA tried, unsuccessfully, to keep Armstrong from becoming director of Hampton Institute. With government funding made available by the 1862 Morrill Land-Grant Colleges Act, Armstrong made Hampton virtually independent of the American Missionary Association and the academic standards they promoted. Hampton Institute trained African American primary school teachers to promote "industrial education"—rather than the more conventional academic pedagogy of the AMA—in the black primary schools where most would teach. Armstrong used Hampton to divert freedpeople's educational aspirations in ways that not only did not challenge, but actually supported, the racial and economic hierarchies of the South in the age of free labor.

Armstrong refashioned a progressive American pedagogical tradition of manual education by incorporating a colonial pedagogy designed for white rule over perceived racial inferiors. In the first half of the nineteenth century, a number of schools, including Oberlin College, embraced industrial education to democratize higher education. Combining work and study allowed less wealthy students to earn their tuition and taught more wealthy students the dignity of labor. A growing progressive consensus in the United States espoused the educational value of manual and industrial education for all children, a view given its greatest formulation by John Dewey.[62] American abolitionists also cited industrial education as proof, as historian Paul Goodman has shown, that free blacks could be integrated as workers into American society.[63] However, as W.E.B. Du Bois pointed out, "manual training" made up only a small portion of the education at white schools, while students at Hampton and Tuskegee Institutes spent as much time in the workshops or fields as in the classroom.[64]

Samuel Armstrong had learned a colonial tradition of manual education from his father, Richard, a Presbyterian missionary in charge of education in Hawaii.[65] Armstrong senior had adapted his style of industrial education from British missionaries in Africa who, since the middle of the nineteenth century, had advocated an education emphasizing the "domestic and social duties of the coloured races."[66] In 1848 Richard Armstrong wrote of his Hawaiian flock: "This is a lazy people and if they are ever to be made industrious the work must begin with the young. So I am making strenuous efforts to have some sort of manual labour connected with the school."[67] Armstrong junior thought his father's conception of colonial education appropriate for African Americans because, as he put it in his 1884 "Lessons from the Hawaiian Islands," "The negro and the Polynesian have many striking similarities. . . . Especially in weak tropical races idleness, like ignorance, breeds vice . . . [I]f man is to work out his own salvation, he must learn how to work."[68] Whereas missionary educators like Armstrong's father had supplemented traditional academic studies with manual education, Samuel sought to replace academic education for colonized people with industrial education. The academic education offered at missionary schools, Samuel thought, undermined the virtues instilled by industrial education. "The sharp brain of the savage," the younger Armstrong remarked, "easily outstrips his sluggish moral nature. . . . The mental food which is given him creates a sense of power, over which his blunt sense of obligation has little control."[69] Armstrong also took northern reformatories as a model, historian James D. Anderson has argued, and students at Hampton thus devoted up to half of their days to unskilled manual labor.[70] Hampton students had an extremely regimented schedule, including military drill for male students, that consumed nearly every waking hour. Instructors enforced strict discipline and expelled many students for minor infractions. In adapting industrial education from its colonial context, Armstrong emphasized those elements that reinforced the subordination of African Americans to a white political and economic elite. Armstrong continued to run Hampton until his death in 1893, when he was succeeded by Hollis Burke Frissell, the school chaplain.

Two conferences on the "Negro question," held in 1890 and 1891 at a hotel on Lake Mohonk, New York, made Armstrong's evaluation of the "Negro question" canonical for many white elites.[71] Ex-President Rutherford B. Hayes, who had run conferences of Indian Affairs Commissioners at Mohonk since 1883, presided over these conferences of white delegates from the North and the South. Organizers excluded blacks from the conference, and Booker T. Washington privately complained that the organizers planned "to consult *about* the Negro instead of *with*."[72] At these conferences, as well as in other work directing northern philanthropy to black education, Hayes continued to abet southern racism as he had when, as president of the United States, he withdrew federal troops from the former Confederate states, ending Reconstruction in 1877.

In a lecture opening the first Mohonk conference, Armstrong affirmed the New South characterization of the "Negro" as simultaneously docile and rebellious, productive and lazy. These contradictions meant, according to Armstrong, that the "Negro" required the special, coercive pedagogy that Hampton Institute disseminated: "The Negroes are a laboring people," Armstrong declared. "They do not like work, however, because they have had it forced on them. . . . They work under pressure. The great thing is to give them an idea of the dignity of labor; that is, to change their standpoint. Nothing is more important than that they should see that."[73] To untangle the logical mess of Armstrong's pronouncement would be to misunderstand how, like countless similar responses to the "Negro question," it supported oppression through its illogic. As Armstrong explained it, "Negroes" were, as New South boosters never tired of proclaiming, essentially hard working. However, the propensity of blacks to work hard had been tainted by their having been forced to work under slavery. Therefore, they currently only worked when forced to ("under pressure"). Armstrong advocated education not to liberate African Americans from labor that they detested, but rather to "change their standpoint," to have them undertake freely the labor that slavery and postemancipation "pressure" had, till that point, forced them to carry out.

Black freedom, as rendered by Armstrong and others, required constraints—ostensibly temporary—to make those defined as "Negroes" freely labor for others. To become freely what they were essentially, Armstrong suggested, Negroes would have, in the short term, to continue to be forced to work, while education would eventually help "their standpoint" to correspond to their nature as a "laboring people." Education promised a future solution to the "Negro question" by relating the desirable (docile and productive) and undesirable (rebellious and lazy) characteristics supposed to inhere in "Negroes" as chronological stages of development. Prior to education, Negroes, both as individuals and as a "race," displayed only their undesirable characteristics. Education would train "Negroes" to realize their supposed unique potential as docile and productive workers. Education further identified those characteristics deemed threatening to political and economic elites with the folly of childhood, and justified suppressing those supposedly childish characteristics by placing authority in loco parentis.

TUSKEGEE INSTITUTE: AN AMBIVALENT CHALLENGE TO THE NEW SOUTH

Hampton's most famous graduate, Booker T. Washington, became one of the most important national and international spokespeople for industrial education and for the New South. Washington thus, paradoxically, rose to power by disseminating an educational philosophy that had been designed to keep him and other African Americans in subordinate roles. He also transformed industrial education as Armstrong had conceived it at Hampton, first tentatively moving it toward an emancipatory challenge to the New South before decisively returning it to its colonial origins in an era of renewed imperial expansion.

Born in Franklin County, Virginia, in 1856, Washington spent the first years of his life in slavery.[74] According to his celebrated 1901 autobiography, *Up from Slavery*, his earliest childhood memory was his "intense longing to read."[75] After emancipation, African Americans in Franklin County, as in other areas, organized and funded their own schools, even before educators from the Freedmen's Bureau or the American Missionary Association arrived. Washington's education was limited by his stepfather, who sent for his wife and stepchildren to join him in the salt-processing town of Malden, West Virginia. In Malden, Washington could attend the local school only rarely, when he could get away from work in the salt furnace or the coal mine that supported it. Washington found better employment as a domestic servant in the household of the mine owner. Under the strict discipline of the lady of the house, a Vermonter, Washington learned housekeeping and the exacting sanitary standards for which he was later so well known. After a year in this strict environment, in 1872, Washington set out for Hampton to seek entrance to Armstrong's institute.

As Washington tells it in *Up from Slavery*, his domestic service and the severe standards of his mistress in Malden proved more useful for his further education than did the schooling that he had been forced to abandon. His entrance examination to Hampton apparently consisted of cleaning a classroom, a task for which his domestic service had prepared him superbly. Washington enthusiastically embraced Hampton and Samuel Armstrong, finding "the General," as he liked to be called, "a perfect man" with "something about him that was superhuman." Washington speculated that, even if all the educational staff and facilities had been taken from Hampton, "daily contact with General Armstrong . . . alone would have been a liberal education." "The General," in fact, designed Hampton to promote a model of education that avoided the supposed political and economic dangers of giving a liberal education to blacks. Washington, however, would even speak of the "school of American slavery" that had, in the long run, benefited African Americans.[76]

After graduating from Hampton in 1875, Washington returned to Malden, West Virginia, where he taught school for three years. In his first year of teaching, he emphasized, he later recalled, "the proper use of the toothbrush and the bath" and opposed "the two ideas constantly agitating the minds of the coloured people. . . . One of these was the craze for Greek and Latin learning, and the other was a desire to hold office."[77] In Malden, Washington also established a reading room for blacks and founded a debating society, although he did not record this fact in his autobiography.[78] In 1878 Washington, considering a career as a Baptist minister, traveled to Washington, D.C., where he attended Wayland Seminary for a year. His observations of middle-class African Americans in the District of Columbia only confirmed his commitment to industrial education against literary education. In *Up from Slavery*, he complained that "six or eight years of book education had weaned" female high school students in the District of Columbia "away from the occupation of their mothers," laundering.[79]

Up from Slavery perhaps reveals less about Washington himself than it does about the extraordinary elitism and racism of even those northern whites who *supported* black education. It also hints at the far worse racism of those southern whites who opposed black education. Washington crafted *Up from Slavery*, like all of his published writings, to appeal to the northern philanthropists who did so much to support industrial education. Washington's pronouncements against learning Latin and Greek and other supposedly useless topics reflected common sentiments of Gilded Age elites. Andrew Carnegie, for example, a major donor to both Hampton and Tuskegee, expressed similar feelings about ancient languages for students of any race when he inveighed against the waste of "obtaining a knowledge of such languages as Greek and Latin, which are of no more practical use to them than Choctaw."[80] In Germany, no less an authority than Kaiser Wilhelm II denounced an "excess of mental work," and especially the focus on classical languages, in education.[81] In his published writings, Washington exaggerated the anti-intellectual aspects of his own life and of his pedagogical program, stressing the extent to which he helped his students accommodate themselves and their own pupils to subordinate political and economic roles.

Hampton and Tuskegee gained an overwhelming influence over black schooling in the South because northern philanthropists supported pedagogies that placed blacks in subordinate positions in the division of labor.[82] Neither Tuskegee nor Hampton persuaded African American educators of the superiority of industrial education. Rutherford B. Hayes, the spirit behind the Mohonk conferences, had presided over the John F. Slater Fund, the first fund devoted entirely to the education of African Americans, since its inception in 1882, and he sat on the boards of all the major funds for black education in the South, including the Southern Education Board, founded in 1897 and merged with John D. Rockefeller's General Education Board in 1902.[83] These philanthropists remained as committed as most American and European elites to the place of African Americans in the cotton economy of the South. William H. Baldwin, the first president of the General Education Board, commented that "The Negro and the mule is the only combination so far to grow cotton" and that, if "properly educated" the Negro "will willingly fill the more menial positions, and do the heavy work, at less wages, than the American white man or any foreign race which has yet come to our shores."[84] After philanthropic support ensured that Tuskegee and Hampton dominated the training of black teachers, these patrons of education turned their attention to transforming individual public schools. In 1907 the Anna T. Jeanes Fund, in close cooperation with Booker T. Washington, hired visiting teachers to introduce Tuskegee ideals to rural schools that had not yet adopted them.[85]

Washington began pursuing a pedagogical agenda distinct from Armstrong's after he returned to Hampton in 1879, eventually to work as "house father" to captured Native American students at the institute. The year before, Armstrong had persuaded the United States government to enroll a group of Native Americans taken prisoner in the wars of westward expansion.[86] Armstrong did not place the Native American captives in the teacher-training program at Hampton but rather, as Washington tells it in *Up from Slavery*, sought only to "teach them to speak English and to acquire civilized habits."[87] For Armstrong, Hampton education suited all "weak tropical races," and it would work as well for Native Americans as it did for African Americans. For Washington, however,

African Americans, trained in the "school of slavery," had a superior "civilization" to Native Americans. As Washington would later explain: "The Indian refused to submit to bondage and to learn the white man's ways. The result is that the greater portion of American Indians have disappeared, and the greater portion of those who remain are not civilized. The Negro, wiser and more enduring than the Indian, patiently endured slavery; and the contact with the white man has given the Negro in America a civilization vastly superior to that of the Indian."[88] Washington did not only hold that Native Americans, like African Americans, might benefit from the discipline of industrial education; he also suggested that African Americans might bring the "civilization" they had learned in the United States to nonwhites around the globe. While Armstrong treated African Americans as just one of many "weak tropical races," Washington saw African Americans as an elite who might play a special role in the global development of race relations.

In 1881 Booker T. Washington, with General Armstrong's support, traveled to Tuskegee, the county seat of Macon County, Alabama, to found a normal school modeled on Hampton Institute. Tuskegee Institute required even more manual labor from its students than its parent institution did. The purpose of all the toil, Tuskegee's catalogue clarified, was "to teach the dignity of labor," "to teach the student how to work" (although students were taught a trade only "when thought best"), and to allow students to work off some of the expenses of their education. The institute forbade its students "to take part in political mass meetings or conventions."[89] At least in Washington's own representation, Tuskegee institute remained true to the Armstrong's Hampton pedagogy. Students had to be at least fifteen years old to enroll in Tuskegee Institute; their average age was a little over eighteen. In 1889 four hundred students attended Tuskegee. The number grew to around fifteen hundred after the turn of the century. Close to two-thirds of the students were male. Close to a third of the students came from Alabama, with most of the remainder coming from other southern states.[90]

With a speech at the opening ceremonies of the 1895 Cotton States and International Exposition in Atlanta, Georgia, Booker T. Washington attained, as he put it, "the place of 'leader of the Negro people' left vacant by Fredrick Douglass's death" earlier that year.[91] The Atlanta Exposition communicated to national and international audiences a New South ideology that emphasized the value of emancipated, though subordinate, black labor. The 1893 Columbian Exposition in Chicago had excluded African Americans; the Atlanta Exposition demonstrated that the New South valued blacks.[92] The Atlanta Exposition, its organizers declared, was "the largest, and first announcement in comprehensive form, of the results of a gigantic experiment involving millions of human beings and forecasting the future, not only of these, but of many more millions of the same race on other continents."[93] Orators on the opening day made clear that the incorporation of blacks in the New South, as advocated by the exposition, would not erode the political power of white authorities.[94]

Central to the self-promotion of the New South at the Atlanta Exposition was a "Negro building," presenting African American arts, manufacturing, and agriculture from every state of the Union (see figure 1.6). Booker T. Washington and two bishops of the African Methodist Episcopal Church, Wesley J. Gaines and Abraham Grant, organized the exhibits.[95] Bishop Grant explained to the U.S. Congress, in testimony designed to secure funding for this exhibit, that the importance of the "Negro" lay in his conservatism and his role in cotton cultivation: "The negro was more interested in the culture and manufacture of cotton than in all other products put together. . . . The negro makes that crop, and he is the finest laborer on earth. He is the conservative element in this country, seldom in any riot or organized disturbance, and never in a strike." The exhibits in the Negro building, promoters hoped, would demonstrate to the world the "good will of the white people" and "stimulate the [black] race by an exhibition of its progress." The Negro building had exhibits of arts and manufactures, put together by individual state commissions. Visitors to the exposition could also catch a glimpse of the Old South at an "Old Plantation . . . with real negroes as the actors on the midway at the fair" alongside ethnographic performances by Native Americans, Africans, and Asians. The "Old Plantation," according to the official guide to the exposition, was "as much superior to negro minstrelsy by white men as real life is to acting" and was "one of the popular features of the Midway," the only one visited by President Grover Cleveland (see figure 1.7).[96]

Many African Americans resisted the message of black subordination presented at the exposition. Some artists refused to send their work to be displayed in the Negro section, fearing it would be used by the white organizers to mock the accomplishments of their race. Still others emphasized achievements that drew blacks away from agricultural labor. A Hampton faculty member found that many of the exhibits showed "too great a preponderance of school exhibits and of fancy work" and not enough on "the industrial contribution of the colored people" and their agricultural work.[97] Hampton Institute had its own exhibit that appears, in a surviving stereoscopic photograph, to have featured the uniforms that male Hampton students wore, an exhibit that, like the school itself, was not particularly industrial or agricultural.

Booker T. Washington delivered a speech at the exposition still remembered as the "Atlanta Compromise," the scornful title W.E.B. Du Bois gave it in 1903.[98] The speech appeared to many at the time and ever since

FIGURE 1.6. Interior of the "Negro building" at the Atlanta Exposition. The Negro building contained exhibits of arts and crafts, organized by state. The District of Columbia exhibition, pictured here, was at the entrance to the building. The Atlanta Exposition announced a New South that did not exclude blacks, but rather incorporated them, albeit in subordinate political and economic roles. Source, Walter G. Cooper, *The Cotton States and International Exposition and South, Illustrated* (Atlanta: The Illustrator Company, 1896), 57.

to accept segregation and disfranchisement and to relegate blacks to a subordinate place in the southern economy. Many heard this message in the famous simile that has since come to stand for the entire speech: "In all things that are purely social, we can be as separate as the fingers, yet one as the hand in all things essential to mutual progress."[99] Yet, the "Atlanta Compromise" speech did not unambiguously accept segregation or black subordination. At the time, even W.E.B Du Bois, who would later become one of Washington's most important critics, saw nothing hostile to the interests of African Americans in the address and congratulated the principal of Tuskegee for "a word fitly spoken."[100] Washington himself rejected the segregationist understanding of the speech that emerged soon after he delivered it. As he revealed in a private letter written less than a month after the speech: "If anybody understands me as meaning that riding in the same railroad car or sitting in the same room at a railroad station is social intercourse they certainly got a wrong idea of my posi-

FIGURE 1.7. The "Old Plantation" on the midway of the Atlanta Exposition. The sign on the right of the building advertises performances of a "cake walk," a mainstay of minstrel shows. The midway had numerous ethnographic spectacles, with African, Asian, and Native American performers. Source: Cooper, *The Cotton States and International Exposition*, 91.

tion."[101] The "separate as the fingers" message, the "wrong idea of [his] position," however, appealed to many whites and this wrong idea, at least in part, would be responsible for Washington's international renown.

Washington rejected racism but accepted a hierarchical class society in which most blacks, as well as many whites, belonged to a poor and oppressed rural working class.[102] The most important advice he offered blacks in his Atlanta address was to "cast down your bucket where you are" and cultivate good relations with southern whites, rather than leaving for Africa or northern cities. Indeed, in 1908, when Washington shortened this speech to fit on a 78 rpm recording for Columbia Records, he focused on the "cast down your bucket where you are" portion and did not even include the "separate as the fingers" line.[103] The place of blacks (where they should cast down their buckets) included not just the South, but also their social and economic status in the South: "No race," Washington admonished his audience, "can prosper till it learns that there is as much dignity in tilling a field as in writing a poem. It is at the bottom of life we must begin, and not the top." In his Atlanta address, Washington promised that blacks would be better workers than the new European immigrants, reminding his audience of the loyalty that slaves were said to have displayed to their masters and promising "we shall stand by you with a devotion that no foreigner can approach." Washington's elitism, conservatism, and apparent reconciliation to segregation won him many friends and enemies. In the two decades between his 1895 speech and his death in 1915, Booker T. Washington enjoyed national and international recognition as the most important African American leader.

With the power he won with his "Atlanta compromise," Washington developed a pedagogical and political agenda that, for a brief time, promised to improve the economic conditions of blacks in ways that might have challenged the social order of the New South. This agenda has been mostly unnoticed, in large part because he abandoned these plans after the turn of the century, when he began working with the German colonial state in Togo to reproduce the New South cotton economy in Africa, rather than transforming it at home. Thus no trace of this potentially transformative Tuskegee appears in his 1901 autobiography, written after he began the colonial phase of his work. However, an examination of Tuskegee education, as well as of Washington's own writings in the period between 1895 and 1900, suggests both what Tuskegee might have become and the extent to which its colonial entanglements after 1900 altered Tuskegee itself.

Both Hampton and Tuskegee won the support of northern philanthropists, as well as the toleration of virulently racist southern white leaders, by highlighting the academic knowledge that they denied their students, rather than that which they imparted to them. Booker T. Washington's *Up from Slavery* reads as a kind of inverted *Bildungsroman*, where the narrator's progress results from the education he does not get. Tuskegee and Hampton both promised to prevent black students from succumbing, in Washington's memorable phrase, "to the temptation of trying to live by their wits," even though their "chief ambition . . . was to get an education so that they would not have to work any longer with their hands."[104] Yet Hampton and Tuskegee were teacher-training schools, whose pupils would, in fact, "live by their wits" as primary school instructors, even if the low pay offered most black teachers meant they would be forced to supplement their income with manual labor. The ideals of industrial education that Hampton and Tuskegee claimed their own students would impart in primary schools have obscured the academic education that did go on at each.

Both Hampton and Tuskegee devoted a significant portion of their curriculum to academic subjects, stressing sociology, political economy, and pedagogy. The texts assigned for these courses suggest that both institutes aimed to inculcate students with a conservative ideology that accepted much of the status quo in the South and encouraged the same in their pupils. This conservatism, however, also pervaded much of the education available to white students, even at elite universities. Carter G. Woodson famously argued that what he called "the mis-education of the Negro" resulted from giving blacks the same dismal education given to whites, an education that "justified slavery, peonage, segregation, and lynching."[105] Tuskegee and Hampton academic education was conservative because it adhered to the standards of education for whites. The schools would have had to go off the white "standard" if they were to embrace a pedagogy that challenged, rather than endorsed, hierarchies of race and class. While the academic education at Tuskegee and Hampton did adhere to the white standard, however, it was necessarily limited by the sheer amount of manual labor required of students at both institutes. Still, much of the well-justified criticism of Tuskegee and Hampton could be better directed toward American education more generally. It is inaccurate to attribute inequalities created by racist elites in the United States, inequalities of a type that may even be structural features of American capitalism, to moral or political failings of the principal of Tuskegee Institute.

Hampton Institute, unlike Tuskegee, designed special texts for its students. Hampton texts, like texts at nearly every white and black college, justified black subordination within capitalism. One of the main teaching texts at Hampton was the school's monthly magazine, the *Southern Workman*, published also to spread the ideals of the institute beyond its campus. The main political economy text at Hampton, compiled in 1879 from *Southern Workman* articles, taught that all who participated in the economy, employers and employees, were workers, and that there were, therefore, "no class feelings to irritate, no color line to fight over."[106] Unions, this text explained, were equivalent to slavery, since when unions called for strikes they sought, like slaveholders, to control how individuals disposed of their own labor.

Before the turn of the century, at least, Tuskegee went further than Hampton in providing its students an academic education comparable to that offered in white schools. Tuskegee used standard college texts for its academic instruction. Washington himself taught "mental and moral sciences," the core of Tuskegee academic education. The Tuskegee catalogue directed students to a series of mainstream texts connecting pedagogy and psychology with a conformist notion of the role of the individual in society. Thus Daniel Putnam's *Manual of Pedagogics*, one of the texts most commonly recommended in the Tuskegee catalogue, criticized Johann Heinrich Pestalozzi—a Swiss educational reformer often cited as an influence on American industrial education—for his Rousseauian individualism and his dangerous neglect of "the interests and legitimate demands of society and the state." Putnam also criticized those who saw industrial education as a panacea, which suggests that Tuskegee's principal and students had a more complicated sense of the relation between academic and industrial education than they let on to those outside the institute.[107] The Kentucky pedagogue Ruric Nevel Roark, a second favorite author at Tuskegee, similarly advocated training students to fit into their "individual, national, and race environment." Roark favored manual training to a greater extent than Putnam did, praising the "splendid discipline" of "drudgery."[108] The political economy taught at Tuskegee followed a standard textbook by J. Laurence Laughlin of Harvard, and later the University of Chicago.[109] Laughlin explained, among other things, that low wages resulted from the tendency of less skilled laborers to have more children than skilled laborers and thus to drive their own wages down. No Malthusian pessimist, however, Laughlin concluded his text with the promise that, if poor workers developed "Christian character" and learned "to do what is disagreeable and repugnant to one's inclinations, provided it is right and honorable," they would experience social advancement.[110] Tuskegee students also studied other academic topics, including history and ethics, and read Shakespeare in a literature course.[111] In 1902 Washington would hire a new academic director, the Harvard-educated Roscoe Conkling Bruce, to reduce the academic education at Tuskegee. This, however, resulted from a reorientation of Tuskegee that took place after the expedition to Togo had persuaded Washington to work closely with colonial elites, and it met much protest from Tuskegee faculty and students alike.[112]

Tuskegee students also educated themselves outside the classroom, even after the institute began reducing classroom instruction. Milton's *Paradise Lost*, for example, was one of the most popular books in the Tuskegee library. Novels by Sir Walter Scott and Charles Dickens were also in high demand. So popular was a biography of Abraham Lincoln that, even with four copies, the library had trouble keeping it on its shelves.[113] Tuskegee reading habits suggest that students had more interest in political questions than Washington's publicity would have led one to believe, and the institute's library even requested copies of Edward Bellamy's socialist classic, *Looking Backward*.[114] Nor did Tuskegee students neglect entirely their own classical education, despite Washington's recurrent fulminations against Latin and Greek, for Homer's *Iliad* and *Odyssey*, though probably in English translation, were also among the most popular library texts.[115] Tuskegee academic faculty, many of whom had graduated from Fisk University with educational backgrounds that included both modern and classical languages, may have discreetly educated students in topics excluded from the published Tuskegee curriculum. For the most part, only black colleges would hire black faculty, so the decision of an African American scholar to teach at Tuskegee did not necessarily reflect a commitment to industrial education. The African American sociologist Richard R. Wright Jr., for example, remembered that instructors at his own college, Georgia State Industrial School, continued to teach Latin and Greek, as well as advanced mathematics, privately in their own homes after white school commissioners forbade them to teach these topics. By the time Wright entered the University of Chicago he had studied three years of Greek and seven years of Latin.[116] Although Washington presented Tuskegee education as unambitious and even anti-intellectual, many Tuskegee students were likely anything but. Tuskegee offered an education far beyond what most black Southerners could otherwise have obtained, and many students may have submitted to its manual drudgery and strict discipline and paid lip service to Tuskegee ideals for the chance to "live by their wits," for at least part of each day.

In the last decade of the nineteenth century, Booker T. Washington supplemented the training of students enrolled in Tuskegee Institute with annual "Negro Conferences" for a broader African American public. These conferences addressed political and economic problems of black southerners, mostly in a manner consistent with the most conservative aspects of Tuskegee ideology. About five hundred attended the first conference in 1892, a number that almost doubled by the 1894 conference.[117] Lectures at the Tuskegee Negro conferences encouraged attendees to purchase land, stay out of debt and avoid mortgages, improve and diversify farming, extend the length of the school year, and replace their one-room cabins with dwellings that did not render "privacy an impossibility." They were told that "the negro of the South is very wasteful, both of time and money" and should be induced to work on Saturdays instead of congregating on "the street corner." To save money, Washington informed conferees, African Americans should be discouraged from purchasing "cheap jewelry" or pistols, and refrain from "excursions," which were "a useless way to spend money."[118]

The conferences illustrate the limits of Washington's willingness to openly challenge the political and economic order of the New South. Washington recognized many of the problems facing black southerners, but tended, at least in public, to blame these problems on black southerners themselves. His moral bromides sometimes even contradicted themselves, for example his advice simultaneously to avoid mortgages and other kinds of debt and also to purchase land and build better houses. Sometimes he simply refused to acknowledge barriers that would have required confronting white southerners. Diversifying agriculture by planting subsistence crops in addition to cotton, for example, certainly would have helped black farmers, but the restrictive terms of share leases required that most rented farmland be devoted to cotton or other cash crops. Sometimes this advice may even have exacerbated the problems it was meant to solve. Discouraging African Americans from purchasing pistols in an era when the legal authorities did not protect blacks from lynch mobs meant allowing white terror to reign freely. Du Bois later recalled that fellow Fisk students carried pistols for protection when looking for summer-school teaching jobs in the South.[119] Demanding that blacks work more and consume less amounted to endorsing poverty as a way of life, rather than seeking to overcome it. Avoiding "the street corner" on Saturdays meant limiting black civil society, a possible basis for political organization against the structures that produced the deprivation that Washington himself decried.

Yet evidence also exists suggesting that Washington himself sensed that black southerners needed more than moralistic exhortations to improve their situation and that southern society and especially southern agriculture presented structural obstacles to black advancement. The conservative aspect of Tuskegee was also its most conventional, repeating borrowed formulas from elite white universities, and even using textbooks written by faculty at those universities. As Washington's fame and power increased after his Atlanta speech, however, Tuskegee Institute supplemented—though it did not supplant—this reactionary pedagogy with knowledge produced by African American scholars and scientists for the purposes of improving the lives of ordinary African Americans in the South. In 1896 Booker T. Washington brought George Washington Carver to Tuskegee to devise new approaches to agriculture that might transform black farming. That year he also began efforts to recruit W.E.B. Du Bois to conduct social-scientific research that would similarly assist in transforming the lives of African Americans, much as he hoped Carver's agricultural science would. While philosophical differences between Du Bois and Washington may have doomed any common project from the start, they both earnestly sought to develop an emancipatory social science at Tuskegee.

The efforts of George Washington Carver to help black farmers achieve a greater degree of prosperity and economic independence represented a real, material challenge to the cotton economy that both reproduced, and also depended upon, the subordination of African Americans. Carver hoped to use his agricultural experimental station and extension service to turn the rural economy of the South from labor-intensive, low-skilled farming to more productive scientific agriculture through "a mighty campaign of education, which will lead the masses to be students of nature."

Carver hoped that improved agriculture would, in addition to making farmers independent and prosperous, help combat the racism that plagued the South for, Carver wrote, "the markets have become more fastidious; and he who puts such a product upon the market as it demands, controls that market, regardless of color. It is simply a survival of the fittest."[120] Had workers and farmers been able to carry out, against all odds, a social democratic revolution in the American South, Carver might have been one of the leaders in building a new, more free and prosperous society.

Born into slavery during the Civil War, George Washington Carver came to Tuskegee in 1896, after graduating as a star student with a master's degree from Iowa State Agricultural College.[121] Carver did conduct some experiments on cotton almost from the beginning of his tenure at Tuskegee, but, before the turn of the century, he devoted most of his attention to subsistence crops, like sweet potatoes, cowpeas, and peanuts, that would shield black farmers from the fluctuations and depredations of the southern cotton economy. These crops would also restore soil depleted of nitrogen by decades of cotton cultivation. Carver also devised recipes to help farmers prepare appealing dishes from peanuts and other crops. Some of these recipes, like peanut milk, never came into wide use, while others, like peanut butter cookies, have become great and original elements of American cuisine. Significantly, Carver's station received none of the federal funding for agricultural stations that the Alabama state government distributed under the Hatch Act of 1887.

Agriculture was not, apparently, a popular subject among Tuskegee students, many of whom attended the institute to become teachers and thereby escape a life of farming. Indeed, Tuskegee Institute sometimes punished students with work in the agricultural department.[122] Those Tuskegee students who did study agriculture, however, made important contributions. John W. Robinson and Allen L. Burks, two of the first members of the expedition to Togo, had graduated in agriculture from Tuskegee. James N. Calloway, the Tuskegee faculty member in charge of the expedition, was a colleague of Carver's in the agriculture department. Tuskegee agricultural education would face obstacles in Togo similar to those it faced in Alabama, where students generally attended school in order to leave the land rather than to learn improved farming techniques. Carver's audience, however, did not consist only of Tuskegee students. The agricultural department ran short courses for local farmers, and the Tuskegee Institute press printed pamphlets by Carver that provided advice on growing and preparing new crops like peanuts and sweet potatoes. In 1906 the Tuskegee agriculture department began sending around the Jesup Wagon—named after the New York philanthropist who financed it—to offer on-the-spot agricultural instruction to farmers of any race.[123]

The agricultural transformations that Carver encouraged were limited by the unwillingness of Booker T. Washington to advocate political measures that would allow, for example, sharecroppers to grow more crops for their own consumption. As historian Mark Hersey has argued, Carver's emancipatory agricultural ideals foundered on the political economy of the cotton South.[124] Landlords benefited from the dependency of their tenants on cotton, and sharecropping contracts generally specified that farmers devote their land to that crop. Improving black agriculture required ending the political and economic subordination of tenant farmers to landlords. To help transform these southern social conditions, Booker T. Washington sought to recruit W.E.B. Du Bois for Tuskegee Institute. Had he succeeded, Du Bois might have helped Tuskegee attack the political and economic, as well as the agricultural, foundations of black poverty in the South. The split between W.E.B. Du Bois and Booker T. Washington, which has become a canonical feature of narratives of American intellectual history, emerged only in the twentieth century as a result of the new political engagements of each thinker with European imperialism.

W.E.B. Du Bois was born in 1868 in Great Barrington in western Massachusetts.[125] After graduating from Fisk in 1888, where he roomed with James Nathan Calloway's younger brother, Thomas Junius, Du Bois attended Harvard University, graduating with a B.A. in philosophy in 1890 and an M.A. two years later. Like many of the leading American social scientists of the day, Du Bois went on to graduate work at the University of Berlin. The unwillingness of the Slater Fund to support a final semester in Berlin forced Du Bois to return to the United States in 1894, before finishing his degree. He took a position teaching classical languages at Wilberforce University in Ohio while completing a Ph.D. in history at Harvard, which he earned in 1895 with a dissertation on the abolition of the slave trade.[126] After two years at Wilberforce, in 1896, Du Bois moved to Philadelphia, to take a temporary position at the University of Pennsylvania studying African Americans in that city. He would published this research as *The Philadelphia Negro* in 1899.[127] In 1897, while still completing that work, Du Bois took a position at Atlanta University, where he taught, with lengthy interruptions for his work for the National Association for the Advancement of Colored People, from 1898 until, hounded by the U.S. Department of Justice for his communist sympathies, he fled the United States for Ghana in 1961, where he died in 1963.

In the nineteenth century, Du Bois, like Washington, pursued an elitist strategy that accepted class and other social hierarchies while fighting racism. Du Bois's own views of social science and the problems facing African Americans did not become significantly more radical than those of Washington until the early twentieth century. This intellectual elitism led Du Bois to the American Negro Academy, founded in 1897 by Alexander Crummell.[128] Crummell, an American-born, British-educated minister who had spent much of his life working in Liberia, proclaimed the purpose of the Academy to be "the civilization of the Negro race in the United States, by the scientific processes of literature, art, and philosophy, through the agency of the cultured men of this same Negro race." Crummell criticized Tuskegee and Hampton Institutes, as well as every other pedagogy that encouraged blacks to "begin at the bottom": "thoughtless toilers," Crummell maintained, "are destined to be forever a race of senseless *boys*; for only beings who think are men."[129] Crummell's view, however, resembled Washington's more closely than he recognized. Washington never objected to the existence of a black elite (to which he, after all, belonged), but focused instead on training those Crummell called "the masses." In an 1897 address to the academy, Du Bois demonstrated his sympathies with Crummell's project of building a unique black "civilization" but also expressed the view, which would become more pronounced over the course of his life, that this elite knowledge should be used to transform the lives of all African Americans and, indeed, all victims of racism and imperialism. Du Bois suggested in his address that the academy work toward "the settlement of the present friction between the races—commonly called the Negro Problem" through "the correction of the immorality, crime, and laziness among the Negroes themselves, which still remains as a heritage from slavery."[130]

In the 1890s, Du Bois encouraged black sociologists to assist an African American struggle for political rights and economic advancement congruent with, if more radical than, the sort of racial uplift that Washington sought in his own less conservative period, between his 1895 "Atlanta compromise" and his work with the German Empire after the turn of the century. In *The Philadelphia Negro*, for example, Du Bois exhorted African Americans to "impress upon Negro children" that "work, although it be menial and poorly rewarded," is "the road to salvation." He also admonished whites to look past the highly unlikely possibility that black men and white women would marry and to cease discriminating against blacks in matters of employment, as well as in everyday social interactions.[131] Booker T. Washington may have hoped, similarly, that his "separate as the fingers, yet one as the hand" image would calm white anxieties about intermarriage and thus reduce other forms of white racism. Aspects of the least radical phase in Du Bois's political life overlapped with the most radical phase in Washington's.

At Atlanta University, Du Bois established sociology as a rigorous discipline that would "throw as much light as possible upon the intricate social problems affecting [the] masses."[132] Addressing fellow sociologists shortly after he arrived at Atlanta in 1897, Du Bois defined the "Negro Problem" as a social rather than a racial concern, challenging racist explanations of black poverty in America even as he endorsed elitist solutions to those problems. "Among the masses," he explained, "we have problems but not Negro problems—there are problems of crime, of poverty, of sexual lewdness, of ill-health, of heredity. The Negro problem is the question whether those who have raised themselves above this dead level of degradation can do as other nations have done—cooperate, investigate, sacrifice and lift as they climb." [133] Du Bois established a seven-semester introduction to social science at Atlanta and transformed the university into a center for research about African Americans. As a university associated with the American Missionary Association, Atlanta confronted the southern status quo more directly than did Hampton or Tuskegee Institutes, and it lost support from some of its funders because it refused to segregate campus facilities.[134] Du Bois introduced greater sociological rigor to the annual conferences initiated by the president of Atlanta University, Horace Bumstead, on the political and economic problems facing African Americans. He followed the survey methods that his German teachers employed to answer questions of broad social-policy interest, distributing questionnaires throughout the South to be filled out by knowledgeable local observers on such topics as businesses, churches, families, and criminality.[135] For him, the "Negro problem" was not a racial problem about black people, but rather a political and economic problem of the United States to which African American sociologists should devote themselves.

Booker T. Washington worked closely with Du Bois to bring this more emancipatory social science to Tuskegee.[136] In 1896, while teaching at Wilberforce, Du Bois proposed to Washington that they set up at Tuskegee "a school of Negro History and social investigation which might serve to help place, more and more, the Negro problem on a basis of sober fact."[137] At this time, Du Bois may simply have wanted to leave unpleasant conditions at Wilberforce, but had this been the only motivation for his interest in Tuskegee he would not have continued to pursue the project after moving to Atlanta University in 1897.[138] Two years later, Booker T. Washington offered Du Bois a position at Tuskegee Institute to "conduct sociological studies that will prove useful to our people, especially in the Gulf States, including both the country districts, smaller towns and cities." Du Bois would have access to the Tuskegee printing press, so that he, like Carver, could disseminate his research in pamphlet form, addressing African Americans directly, as well as through the schoolteachers he would have instructed. Du Bois would also have taught an annual course at Tuskegee about the results of his own research.[139] Fearing that his department would "be regarded by the public as a sort of superfluous addition not quite in consonance with the fundamental Tuskegee idea," however, Du Bois ultimately rejected Washington's offer in 1900. He nonetheless expressed hope that Atlanta would work even more closely with Hampton and Tuskegee than it had in the past.[140] Du Bois had congratulated Washington on his 1895 Atlanta address and continued to praise Washington as late as 1901, even after he had begun mildly criticizing industrial education.[141] The influential Tuskegee board member William Baldwin arranged two final meetings in New York between Washington and Du Bois in 1902 to bring the social scientist to Tuskegee, but, once again, without success.[142]

Perhaps the split between the two men became irrevocable in 1903, with Du Bois's claim in *Souls of Black Folk* that the industrial education promoted by Booker T. Washington did not merely accommodate the measures that kept blacks economically and politically subordinate in the United States, but also "helped their speedier accomplishment."[143] In his work with the Niagara Movement, founded in 1905, and in its better-known successor organization, the National Association for the Advancement of Colored People, founded in 1909, Du Bois challenged racism more directly than Washington did. He also confronted European imperialism and what he dubbed the global "color line" in his international work with the Pan-African Conference. Washington, meanwhile, began working with the German colonial government, helping globalize, rather than transform, the conditions of agriculture in the New South that he had perhaps briefly, through George Washington Carver and W.E.B. Du Bois, hoped to transform.

BOOKER T. WASHINGTON'S PAN-AFRICANISM AND THE TURN TO EMPIRE

At the turn of the century, Washington began to rethink the relationship of Tuskegee Institute to blacks in Africa and in the diaspora, even becoming, for a brief time, a critic of European imperialism. In his 1895 address in Atlanta he had urged blacks to "cast down your bucket where you are" in the New South. Soon, however, he began to consider the international position of African Americans and Tuskegee Institute. In the summer of 1899, northern philanthropists sent Washington, who had become visibly exhausted from his relentless fund-raising and other activities, on a vacation with his wife to Europe, where the two visited Belgium, the Netherlands, Paris, and London.[144] In Paris that June, Washington spoke with a number of Haitians, "well educated and cultured" individuals who, Washington thought, would do better to focus attention on "physical science, agriculture, mechanics and domestic science" to help their country. He took great interest in the progress of Haiti, and planned a visit to the grave of Toussaint L'Ouverture, a leader of the revolution that had overthrown French slavery on the island. To read Booker T. Washington praise as a "great hero" the man who led an armed uprising against slavery suggests that he had perhaps begun to question his own well-known political quietism. In London later that summer Washington met with the planning committee for what would be, the following year, the first Pan-African Conference, held to take advantage of the visitors who would already be present in Europe for an international exposition in Paris. Washington endorsed the call for a conference to expose the mistreatment of blacks in "South Africa, West Africa, the West Indies and the United States." The conference would expose, its organizers promised, "the cruelty of civilized paganism, of which our race is the victim," and demand "Europe's atonement for her blood-guiltiness to Africa." "Organized plunder versus human progress," the organizers proclaimed, "has made our race its battlefield." In his published letters from Europe, Washington wrote: "I beg and advise as many of our people as can possibly do so, to attend this conference. In my opinion it is going to be one of the most effective and far-reaching gatherings that has ever been held in connection with the development of our race."[145] Washington had, it seemed, temporarily taken a more confrontational approach to racist abuse in colonial Africa and in the United States.

Pan-Africanists have long had an ambivalent attitude toward Tuskegee Institute. Generally critical of Booker T. Washington for seeming to acquiesce to the subordination of American blacks, many nonetheless saw Tuskegee, and indeed Washington's own life, as great instances of black self-help.[146] Marcus Garvey, for example, admired Washington.[147] Many Pan-Africanists shared Booker T. Washington's view of African Americans as a black elite who could raise up—economically and culturally— blacks in Africa and the Caribbean. Just two months after Booker T. Washington's 1895 address, Atlanta's Gammon Theological Seminary, a Methodist Episcopal institution for African Americans, sponsored a Congress on Africa at the Atlanta Exposition. African and African American speakers at this conference stressed the responsibility of African Americans to christianize Africans. Bishop Henry M. Turner of the African Methodist Episcopal Church was surely thinking of Booker T. Washington and his recent Atlanta address when he excoriated those "would-be colored leaders" who accepted the exclusion of African Americans from politics. "For the Negro to stay out of politics is to level himself with a horse or a cow." Yet Turner also regarded the United States as a "heaven-permitted if not a divine-sanctioned manual laboring school" that had also brought Christianity to African Americans. He advised African Americans to emigrate to Africa to bring these valuable traits to their "fatherland."[148] Alexander Crummell, who would later found the American Negro Academy, delivered a speech much closer to Tuskegee ideals. Crummell explained that Christianizing Africa meant bringing "civilization" to the "naked pagan" so that this "crude, undeveloped and benighted child," this "shadow of a man" could be a better "head of a family" and "member of the community in which he lives."[149] For Turner, Crummell, and others at the conference, American blacks constituted a global elite that could raise up Africans, rather than a politically and economically subordinate caste confined to the United States.

As Washington began to think more internationally, perhaps in part as a result of the international fame his address at the Atlanta Exposition brought him, he began to move closer to the positions held by these Pan-Africanists. At least since his duties as "house father" to Native American students at Hampton Institute, Washington conceived of African Americans as an elite group that could bring "civilization" and an aptitude for hard work to nonwhites anywhere. African Americans serving in the Spanish-American War of 1898 gave Booker T. Washington and others an image of what they called a "New Negro" outside the confines of the New South, taking part in American westward expansion and overseas conquest, from the Indian wars to the occupation of the Philippines.[150] By the turn of the century, Booker T. Washington also began presenting African Americans as a colonial labor force superior to all indigenous peoples: "Within the last two months," he wrote in 1900, "I have had letters from the Sandwich Islands, Cuba, and South America, all asking that the American Negro be induced to go to these places as laborers. In each case there would seem to be abundant labor already in the places named. It is there, but it seems not to be of the quality and value of that of the Negro in America."[151] African Americans were no longer only superior laborers in the American South; they might now become, Washington suggested, an elite labor force in the colonial regions of the world.

The U.S. government also supported the type of colonial Pan-Africanism advocated by Booker T. Washington, and it promoted the New South as a model for European imperialism in its official representation at the Paris Exposition of 1900. The Paris Exposition commission appointed, almost certainly on Booker T. Washington's recommendation, Thomas J. Calloway, the brother of Togo expedition leader James N. Calloway, to mount an "exhibition on the present condition and progress of the Afro-American" for the "Social Economy Building" of the U.S. representation at the Exposition.[152] Thomas Calloway had his former Fisk roommate, W.E.B. Du Bois, assemble photographs of African American life for the exhibition.[153] Calloway and Du Bois presented evidence of growing prosperity among African Americans and portrayed the New South as a model of "racial adjustment," "since most of the countries of Europe are now engaged in colonizing Africa." "To the statecraft of Europe," Thomas Calloway predicted "the 'Negro Problem' is destined to become a burning reality in their African colonies, and it is our privilege to furnish them the best evidence at hand to prove that the only solution that will ever succeed is that of an equal chance in the race of life without regard to 'color, race or previous condition.' "[154] W.E.B. Du Bois compared this exhibit on African Americans to other presentations at the Paris Exposition of social reform, such as Belgian working man's circles, the Red Cross Society, or the German state insurance programs. African Americans of the New South, Du Bois explained, functioned as part of an international discussion about applied sociology and "the larger aspects of human benevolence."[155] The exhibit Calloway and Du Bois mounted in Paris was a great success, winning numerous awards, including a gold medal for the section devoted to Tuskegee Institute.[156] The following year, Calloway would take the Negro exhibit to the South Carolina Interstate and West Indian Exposition.[157] Calloway and Du Bois shared Washington's ambivalent Pan-Africanism, helping disseminate, even if not endorsing, a colonial variety that would reproduce the New South in Africa, even while simultaneously committed to more radical variants of Pan-Africanism.

That July, Thomas Calloway and W.E.B. Du Bois left Paris to attend the first Pan-African Conference in London.[158] Du Bois coined the iconic phrase of the conference when he announced: "The problem of the twentieth century is the problem of the color line."[159] Du Bois's observation is in its own way as ambiguous as Washington's "separate as the fingers, yet one as the hand" image. Both statements represent a moment when individuals on both sides of the Atlantic had just begun to draw practical conclusions from a growing sense that Africans and African Americans, because they belonged to the same "race," were susceptible to similar political and economic policies, both oppressive and emancipatory. While Washington had already abandoned his 1895 opinion that African Americans should "cast down their buckets" in the southern states alone, he retained a conservatism that would soon put him at odds with Du Bois and other Pan-Africanists at the London conference. The representations of European colonialism and of the "Negro question" differed fundamentally in Paris and London in the summer of 1900. They also shared and disseminated a common view that the American South in the age of Jim Crow would shape, for better or for worse, a global color line.

When delegates met in London that summer of 1900 to criticize European imperialism and American racism, Booker T. Washington had already begun negotiations with Baron von Herman, the agricultural attaché to the German embassy in Washington, D.C. Herman persuaded Washington to send Tuskegee students to the German colony of Togo in West Africa to teach the "Negroes" there American methods of cotton growing. While Washington was just one of the many African American intellectuals who interested themselves in Africa, the expedition to Togo would give his Pan-Africanism a palpable practicality. With the expedition to Togo, Washington would raise the mutually sustaining constructs of "cotton" and "Negroes" to an international level. Africans would experience a version of the New South that emerged from the efforts of political and economic elites to divert and subvert the African American drive toward free, autonomous labor, land reform, and education. By the end of the nineteenth century, many African Americans had also taken their struggles for emancipation to a global level, working with blacks in both northern and southern hemispheres, on both sides of the Atlantic, against imperialism and its global racist division of labor. These new international self-emancipatory efforts, like the early self-emancipation struggles of African Americans in the South, presented a radical challenge to the political and economic status quo. Like the elites who had helped turn African American emancipation into the racialized labor exploitation of the New South, international elites also sought to hijack Pan-Africanism, attempting to turn an emancipated black Atlantic into a global New South.

Chapter 2

SOZIALPOLITIK AND THE
NEW SOUTH IN GERMANY

GERMAN WRITERS across the political spectrum recognized the global political significance of the American Civil War, of the abolition of slavery in the United States, and of the New South. Like the American South, the German East produced agricultural staples—grain and, later, sugar-beets—on large estates employing unfree labor, serfs, until the nineteenth century, when these agricultural enterprises were forced to deal with the legal emancipation of their workers. Like their American counterparts, German landowners, policy makers, and workers struggled over contradictory meanings of free labor. At the root of these conflicts was the question of whether free labor meant the autonomy of workers or new regimes of labor control. Academic and political elites, both in Germany and in the United States, rallied to the cause of landowners, helping to keep formerly bound laborers, as well as their children and grandchildren, on the land of their erstwhile masters, carrying out the oversupervised and underpaid work of staple cultivation.

Workers and employers the world over engaged in practical struggles over the meaning of free labor. In Germany, social scientists involved themselves self-consciously in this partisan struggle. Karl Marx, even during the American Civil War, began to contextualize that sectional conflict as a global war over the freedom of labor. The German Social Democratic Party, the strongest Marxist party in the world before the October Revolution, continued this struggle over the meaning of free labor both in their theoretical writings and in their political work. German academic social scientists provided an antirevolutionary counterpart to this social democratic perspective, looking to postwar America for models of the constraint of free labor, particularly in agriculture. These social scientists advocated family farming carried out under landlord or state supervision as a means of controlling free labor, a program adopted by the Prussian state under the name of "internal colonization." The Prussian state also pursued internal colonization as a national or even a racial struggle, settling German farmers in predominantly Polish areas in the eastern provinces of the kingdom. While today most would regard Poles as an ethnicity rather than a race, it was not uncommon in the years before the First

World War to conceive of Poles and other "ethnic" groups as biological "races."[1] By the turn of the twentieth century, German social scientists and policy makers followed their American counterparts in synthesizing race and class anxieties, creating a model of economically and sexually controlled household farming based on comparative studies of free labor in Germany and the United States. German colonial authorities would then cooperate with Tuskegee educators to employ this German-American synthesis as a component of colonial rule in Togo.

German Social Thought and the American Civil War

No foreign observer welcomed the Union victory with greater enthusiasm than did Karl Marx. Just two years after the Civil War, Marx explained in a preface to the first volume of *Capital* that the defeat of slavery had "sounded the tocsin . . . for the European working class," just as "the American War of Independence sounded the tocsin for the European middle class."[2] Specifically, as Marx had earlier written to President Abraham Lincoln, the conflict that defeated slavery also opened "the virgin soil of immense tracts" for "the labor of the emigrant" rather than placing it under the "tramp of the slave driver."[3] Paying, it must be noted, no heed to prior Native American territorial rights, Marx embraced America as an open frontier where individuals could freely work for themselves rather than for the profit of employers or slaveholders. He thus embraced free labor and free soil ideology in an endlessly expansive sense, outside the capitalist limits within which mainstream American politicians circumscribed these views.[4] "The phase of the Civil War over," wrote Marx in an 1866 letter to Friedrich Engels, "only now have the United States really entered the revolutionary phase, and the European wiseacres who believe in the omnipotence of Mr. Johnson"—presumably in the ability of the new American president to limit the social change inaugurated by the Civil War—"will soon be disappointed."[5]

Marx commented less on the liberation of African Americans from slavery than on the victory of free labor in general in the United States. In contrast to many communists of the twentieth century, Marx did not consider racism an especially important phenomenon, because, like nationalism, or "the motley feudal ties that bound man to his 'natural superiors,' " it would disappear on its own with the proletarianization of the work force under capitalism.[6] Political economic conditions, rather than any supposed racial characteristics, interested Marx, for race was a patently false category, merely an artifact of the political economic systems in which it functioned. Marx's critique of capitalism rested not on skepticism about free labor ideology, but rather on a belief in free labor greater than that of any other economist. Marx applauded a truly free labor that would triumph over those elites, from factory owners to plantation managers, who sought to subvert the freedom of workers even while speaking the language of the free market. For Marx, free labor would outlast capitalism, as workers eventually liberated themselves from the constraints required to make their labor contribute to the expansion of capital and to generate profits for private appropriation. Marx overestimated, at least in the short run, the revolutionary consequences of free labor in the United States, but in doing so conceptualized a proletarian counterpart of bourgeois free labor ideology that emphasized the freedom of workers against all economic authorities.

The German economist Gustav Schmoller saw the Union victory in the American Civil War and the end of slavery in the United States in quite different terms than did Marx. In contrast to Marx, Schmoller, at the time a professor at the University of Halle, anticipated the role that race and racism would play in channeling free labor into new regimes of exploitation in the American South. Writing in 1866, immediately after the Civil War, Schmoller predicted that, with the end of slavery, racism alone would function to keep African Americans subordinate, impoverished, and bound to cotton plantations. Because of the high price of cotton in the years after the war, he noted, white elites preferred to keep black freedpeople bound to the land rather than seeing them move into more skilled and better-paid occupations. White racism, which Schmoller deplored, as well as, to a lesser extent, what Schmoller called the "original and natural abilities of the black race," had thus far succeeded in suppressing African American freedom even after emancipation. Despite these failures of emancipation, the Union victory over slavery and the Confederacy represented a triumph of "ethical life" (*sittliche Leben*) over concerns about "economic loss." Prussia, wrote Schmoller in 1866, faced a similar opportunity to embrace "ethical life" over more mundane concerns. Under Bismarck's leadership, the powerful kingdom had just defeated Austria, its only potential rival among the German states, in what really was a war of northern aggression. Schmoller admonished "the best" in Germany to rally around Prussia, helping the government to unify the nation, creating "with blood and iron" a "higher law" that transcended "all economic concerns" and "all formal law."[7] Schmoller would soon lead German economists in doing just that, advising the newly founded German state on preserving political and economic hierarchies in an era of free labor. From the beginning, the New South served Schmoller and his colleagues as a model of social order, and its importance would only expand in the two decades before the First World War.

The divergent ways in which Marx and Schmoller characterized free agricultural labor in the United States after the Civil War represented two sides of a dialectic that would shape the history of capitalism in Europe, the United States, and Africa. On the one hand, as Marx maintained, the emergence of free labor within capitalism foreshadowed a free labor that exceeded the boundaries of capitalism. Bourgeois economists did not recognize the revolutionary potential of their own doctrines of economic freedom, Marx held, misapplying the concept of personal private property to social goods like factories, fields, and other means of production to imagine that economic freedom would automatically allow the "owners" of these goods to live from the labor of "their" employees. In fact, as Schmoller correctly surmised, economic elites did not embrace economic freedom and the absolute reign of private property, for they, like Marx, recognized the subversive potential of these doctrines of political economy. Rather than laissez-faire economics, political and economic authorities around the world introduced various regimes designed to undermine economic freedom, including master-servant codes, vagrancy laws, sharecropping, racial segregation, lynching, and prison labor. Schmoller and his colleagues called for a benevolent and paternalist treatment of workers to prevent both the extremes of exploitation and oppression and also the chaos they thought would result from the unconstrained freedom of workers.

Economic elites were in a particularly sticky position, for capitalism depended for its mobility, flexibility, and freedom on the mobility, flexibility, and freedom of workers themselves, the very traits that also threatened the dominant position of economic and political elites. Marx was more committed to free labor than to maintaining the political economic status quo; Schmoller by contrast, would throw himself on the side of political and economic elites, even when doing so meant advocating policies that limited not only the freedom of labor but also the profitability of business enterprises. Both Marx and Schmoller, as well as elites around the world, recognized a fatal dynamic in capitalism such that, if left unchecked, what passed for economic freedom in capitalism might eventually become real economic freedom, overthrowing established political and economic hierarchies. Capitalist elites thus, in a sense, sometimes opposed capitalism to a greater extent than the most militant workers. This dynamic played itself out in Germany in the struggle between members of the Social Democratic Party who followed Marx and the economists and social scientists who followed Schmoller. The American New South played an important role in this struggle, serving as a model for colonial and capitalist elites to emulate and, after the October Revolution, as a model for revolutionary struggles of national liberation.

Emancipation and Free Labor in Germany

The Civil War and the American South became significant components of German discussions of free labor because German social scientists perceived similarities between the situation in the American South and that in the Prussian East. Large capitalist agricultural concerns employing unfree labor to produce cash crops for international markets spanned much of the globe, from the Americas to Russia, in the nineteenth century. On the eve of emancipation, Prussia supplied half of Britain's grain and, even after the abolition of serfdom, remained a major exporter of grain for much of the nineteenth century. In Prussia east of the River Elbe, as in Austria and Russia, lords had succeeded in imposing serfdom on the tenants living on their estates, a condition of involuntary, hereditary servitude akin to slavery. In Prussia at the end of the eighteenth century, about half of the rural lower classes, or about 35 percent of the total population of the kingdom, were serfs.[8] All members of a dependent family worked on a lord's demesne or in his household for a specified number of days each week, outside of which they worked a private plot of land on the lord's estate. The conditions of serfdom varied, and, like slaves in the United States, serfs could, even under the most brutally oppressive conditions, exercise a certain amount of control over their lives.[9]

In October 1807 King Friedrich Wilhelm III of Prussia, advised by his chief minister, Baron Karl vom Stein, ended unfree labor in his kingdom by decreeing that, after St. Martin's Day, 1810, "there will only be free people" in Prussia.[10] The liberation of serfs was part of the Prussian reform movement, a program of administrative and economic modernization designed to restore the territory, status, and power that the kingdom had possessed before its defeat by Napoleon's army in 1806. The Prussian reformers who orchestrated the abolition of serfdom had been influenced by the free labor ideology of Adam Smith, whose doctrines influenced the teaching of political and economic, or cameral, sciences in Göttingen, Königsberg, and Halle in the late eighteenth and early nineteenth centuries.[11] Baron vom Stein described liberating the serfs as a measure "removing everything that has up till now prevented the individual from reaching the level of affluence that his powers enable him to achieve."[12] Stein did not imagine serfs freed from work, but rather freed to work more than ever before.

As in the American South half a century later, declaring agricultural labor free without redistributing land not only left the gross inequalities of unfree labor in place, but also in many ways increased the economic power of former lords. After emancipation, large estates ruled by lords and worked by dependent laborers (a system called *Gutsherrschaft*) remained predominant in German agriculture east of the River Elbe. This contrasted with the region west of the Elbe, where independent peasants farmed land rented from lords (a system called *Grundherrschaft*). In western Germany, as in much of western Europe, feudal dues in labor or in kind had gradually been commuted to cash rent. The lord in the West was, in essence, a landlord. In the East, by contrast, German and Polish nobles had for centuries controlled large tracts of land, their demesnes, worked by estate-bound laborers. The reforms that ended serfdom also opened land ownership to all social classes, so that, by the last decades of the nineteenth century, more than half of all estate owners in eastern Germany were of bourgeois origin.[13] As in the American South, however, as emancipation transformed the class structure of estates, new relations of production maintained much of the old unfreedom of agricultural labor.[14]

The liberation of serfs led, in fact, to an expansion of estate agriculture in the East under conditions of de facto unfreedom. The legal and political-economic framework in which the Prussian government introduced free labor kept many German freedpeople, like their American counterparts, on the land, subject to the authority of former masters and new landowners. In Prussia, freedpeople retained the plots to which they had been entitled as serfs, although they had typically to part with some of this land to compensate former lords for the loss of their services. Through such additions to their demesnes, landlords soon possessed more land after emancipation than they had before. Landlords continued to employ agricultural day laborers, many of whom had been serfs, now unable to support themselves with their reduced plots. In the first half of the nineteenth century, landlords also began employing cottagers (*Insten*), families who bound themselves with yearly contracts to labor for the landlord in exchange for the use of less than two acres of land. While the de jure political authority of landlords over local farmers and laborers diminished, it did not disappear. Until the November Revolution of 1918, German law defined agricultural laborers as subject members of their employer's household, regulated by servants' law (*Gesindeordnung*) rather than employment law (*Gewerbeordnung*). In his patriarchal role, a landlord could, for example, administer corporal punishment to his employees.[15] Landlords might also require the children of cottagers, as they had required the children of serfs, to perform several years of domestic service.[16] German freedpeople did not suffer anything resembling the horrors of lynching and convict labor that their American counterparts endured, but they did find themselves in economic conditions of agrarian dependency comparable to those in the United States.

The relations of agricultural production east of the River Elbe were more radically transformed by the mobilization of agricultural workers

at the end of the nineteenth century than they had been by the decrees of
Baron vom Stein and other Prussian reformers decades earlier. German
agricultural laborers sought the freedom and prosperity only promised by
their formal emancipation in a mass exodus from the land of their former
masters, as American freedpeople would during their great migration to
northern cities half a century later. In the century between the defeat
of Napoleon and the beginning of the First World War, approximately
5.5 million Germans moved to the United States. In the period before
German unification in 1871, most German emigrants originated from the
South and the West. In the final wave of German emigration, from 1880
to 1893, most left from northeastern Germany, the area dominated by
the *Gutsherrschaft*. The almost 1.8 million Germans who made up
this wave constituted the largest single immigrant group to the United
States during this period.[17] Added to this overseas emigration from eastern
Germany was an even larger internal migration of the descendants of
dependent farmers to industrial employment in western Germany. Between 1880 and 1910, 2 million individuals left eastern Germany for
other regions within Germany.[18]

The improved rail and ship transportation on which German workers
escaped eastern estates also forced these estates to compete with foreign
agriculture. The export of grain to Great Britain and elsewhere had long
been the backbone of the agrarian capitalism of eastern Prussia. Indeed,
the outlook for grain exports had been rosy enough that Germany had
eliminated its grain tariffs in 1853. In the second half of the nineteenth
century, however, improvements in railroad and ocean transportation
made grain from all over the world, and especially from Russia and the
United States, increasingly competitive on the Liverpool grain exchange,
the center of the European market. As falling prices made Prussian grain
less profitable, landlords shifted in part to livestock herding for wool and
meat production, and, in some locations, to chemical- and labor-intensive
sugarbeet farming.[19] Sugarbeet cultivation increased the demand for
workers on many estates, even as internal and overseas migration reduced
the labor force available in these regions. Polish seasonal migrants covered many of these labor shortages.

The agricultural transformations of the East made up only one half of
the picture of free labor in nineteenth-century Germany. The West saw a
dramatic growth of urban and industrial employment, and the state
worked to preserve the legal authority of employers in these new, less
hierarchical areas of the economy. An 1845 law allowing freedom of profession in Prussia also specified fines and prison sentences for employees
"who leave work without permission and without legal justification, or
are guilty of shirking, gross disobedience or insistent obstinacy."[20] The
German Employment Law (Gewerbeordnung) of 1869 limited—although

did not eliminate—the use of penal sanctions against most artisans and industrial workers. The law continued the practice of treating apprentices as members of their master's household, rather than as employees, and thus bolstered the authority of their masters with legal sanctions. Apprentices who left work without permission or who performed unsatisfactory work could be arrested, fined, imprisoned, and returned by the police to their masters. The 1869 law even allowed factories to define some of their workers as apprentices, thus continuing to back the authority of employers and managers with the police power of the state.[21] The 1869 law did not extend even its limited protection to agricultural workers, who remained subject to the Servants' Law (Gesindeordnung), defining them as dependent members of their employers' households. While industrial workers remained subject to a whole host of legal constraints, they enjoyed significantly more freedom than agricultural workers in the period before the revolution of 1918. As in the United States, the emancipation of agricultural workers inaugurated a new struggle between workers and landlords as each group fought for fundamentally incompatible versions of free labor.

GERMANY'S NEW SOUTH: SOCIAL SCIENCE, SOCIAL POLICY, AND THE FREEDOM OF FREE LABOR

Gustav Schmoller and other German economists, out of anxiety about the social and political consequences of the growing freedom of labor, founded the Verein für Sozialpolitik (Social Policy Association) in 1872.[22] The Verein, whose members also included Adolph Wagner, Georg Friedrich Knapp, Lujo Brentano, and, later, Max Weber, provided important advice to the Prussian and the German state, continuing a longer tradition of conservative social-welfare thought and policy in Prussia.[23] The Verein für Sozialpolitik founded the discipline of sociology in Germany and, through its American students, arguably also in the United States. Though authoritarian, nationalist, and defensive of a hierarchical and exploitative status quo, the Verein also inspired many American progressives because of its regard for the welfare of the weak and the defense of society.

The economists of the Verein für Sozialpolitik developed an empiricist, historical economics as an alternative to laissez-faire doctrines associated with Adam Smith and subsequent classical political economy. The economics of Adam Smith inspired the Prussian reformers who emancipated the serfs in 1807, and, though the members of the Verein never called for the reestablishment of serfdom or other forms of dependent labor, they did seek new means of controlling free labor. Georg Friedrich Knapp, a Verein member specializing in the history of serfdom and unfree labor, characteristically lamented that the social science of the eighteenth century had condemned serfdom without finding "a replacement" (*Ersatz*) for it.[24] Like the architects of the New South and experts on the "Negro question" in the United States, the members of the Verein für Sozialpolitik sought to devise new forms of constraint to maintain what they regarded as a proper social order in an era of legal freedom. Few of these individuals on either side of the Atlantic perceived themselves as malicious oppressors, and most had genuinely humanitarian, though deeply paternalist, attitudes toward freedpeople. They exemplify the limits of a humanitarianism committed to preserving the social order whose ills it seeks to redress.

At the first meeting of the Verein für Sozialpolitik, Gustav Schmoller warned that economic conflicts threatened a "social revolution" in Germany, and thus cast doubt on the enthusiasm of certain economic "hotheads" for "the introduction of freedom of trade and profession [*Gewerbefreiheit*]" and for "the abolition of the whole archaic medieval economic legislation." Schmoller and his audience rejected limiting the state's role in economic life according to principles of free trade and free labor. Schmoller admitted that workers did enjoy freedom and prosperity in the economic boom of the so-called *Gründerzeit* following the founding of the German Empire in 1871. However, this freedom and prosperity had led to a split between workers and the "owning and educated classes," particularly in "ethics, education, views, and ideals," a split similar to that which had brought down all previous "higher civilizations," including the ancient Greeks and Romans. Opposing the "leveling" tendencies he attributed to social democracy, Schmoller spoke for most Verein für Sozialpolitik members when he called on the state to foster a gradated society, with a large middle class bridging the gap between rich and poor.[25]

The Verein für Sozialpolitik defined its economic theories against classical, free-trade economics and in favor of what many came to call state socialism. Members of the Verein für Sozialpolitik dubbed those economists who supported free trade and classical economics the "Manchester School," suggesting a loyalty to industry rather, presumably, than the state, and dismissed their writing as "abstract and unhistorical" in contrast to their own "realistic" approach.[26] While laissez-faire economics had shaped the views of the Prussian reformers of the first decade of the nineteenth century, by the 1870s the historical economics of the Verein für Sozialpolitik represented a venerable academic orthodoxy in Germany. Friedrich List set the tone for much subsequent German economic thought in his 1841 *National System of Political Economy*, in which he criticized followers of Adam Smith for ignoring the distinct needs of individual nations in their pell-mell endorsement of free trade.[27] Free traders once again obtained a voice in Germany with the founding of the Economic Congress (Volkswirtschaftliche Kongress) in 1858, the year the future Kaiser Wilhelm I became regent in Prussia, proclaiming a "New Era" of liberalism in the kingdom.[28] Led by the English-born Prussian Cobdenite John Prince-Smith and by Hermann Schulze-Delitzsch, a liberal founder of credit, producer, and other cooperatives for workers and artisans, the Economic Congress hoped to provide liberal alternatives to social democracy. German free traders sought to discredit the economists in the Verein für Sozialpolitik, with its academic leadership, as *Kathedersozialisten*, or socialists of the lectern, suggesting a connection to a social democracy reviled by both groups of economists.[29] Both the Verein für Sozialpolitik and the Economic Congress agreed on the importance of combating social democracy more than they disagreed with each other. In their opposition to worker militancy, the "Manchesterist" Economic Congress and the "*Kathedersozialist*" Verein für Sozialpolitik had much to agree on, and, indeed, in 1885 the two organizations fused. While the dispute between historical economics and non-Marxist abstract economics emerged again in Gustav Schmoller's disputes with Carl Menger and other members of the Austrian school of economics, the principal theoretical and political target of Schmoller and his colleagues in the Verein remained social democracy and Marxism, not liberal economics.[30]

The members of the Verein für Sozialpolitik vehemently and repeatedly rejected social democracy and any revolutionary movement of workers. Writing in 1871, Verein member Lujo Brentano decried the Paris Commune, in the year the French Third Republic crushed it under the eyes of the German occupation, to distance his own organization from social democracy. The Verein für Sozialpolitik, Brentano wrote, had no sympathy for the Commune, for "the abolition of property and marriage," or for the "*pétroleuses*."[31] The *pétroleuses*, female communards armed with petrol bombs, became an icon of antirevolutionary propaganda, for they highlighted the threat that worker militancy posed not only to political and economic hierarchies, but also to bourgeois notions of masculinity and femininity.[32] Focusing on those aspects of social democracy most threatening to patriarchal domesticity, Brentano signaled the commitment of his organization to a complex of public and private hierarchies that made up the status quo. Even Werner Sombart, who stood out as the only member of the Verein für Sozialpolitik who wrote seriously about Marxist theory and who even flirted with the idea of joining the Social Democrats, remained committed to an antirevolutionary politics that ultimately kept him out of the party. Sombart even wrote an explanation of the labor theory of value that Friedrich Engels declared "the first time that a German university professor has managed to see by and large in Marx's writings what Marx actually said."[33] Yet Sombart turned to the

Social Democrats primarily to enlist their support for the state socialist politics of the Verein, and the party ultimately rejected his views as those of an opponent.[34]

In 1875 Reichskanzler Otto von Bismarck, certainly the most powerful enemy of social democracy in Germany, informed Schmoller that he himself was a Kathedersozialist, a claim born out at least in part by the famous health and disability insurance and pension legislation that he sponsored in the following decade.[35] Thanks to the high opinion that Bismarck and other Prussian officials held of the Verein für Sozialpolitik, the new Imperial University in Strassburg, Alsace-Lorraine, offered Knapp, Schmoller, and Brentano academic appointments. Germany had annexed Alsace-Lorraine in the 1870–71 Franco-Prussian War, and the founders of the Imperial University hoped to demonstrate the scientific and cultural achievements of the empire that had emerged from that conflict.

In criticizing classical economics, the members of the Verein not only rejected the laissez-faire doctrines behind the abolition of serfdom in Prussia, but also the Marxist economics of social democracy. The Social Democrat Rosa Luxemburg, for one, noted the antisocial-democratic aspect of the opposition of the Verein to "Manchesterism" and perceived the critique of classical economics by Schmoller and other German economists as an attempt to muddle with empirical trivia the conclusions of Adam Smith and David Ricardo, which remained, after all, essential parts of Marx's own economic analysis.[36] Luxemburg suggested that Schmoller, like many German professors, "believes . . . he puts science in the service of social progress in that he serves the ruling reactionaries."[37]

The term *Kathedersozialist* had a longer career as a term of abuse among Social Democrats and, later, communists, than it did among advocates of free trade. Writers on the left employed the term not only against members of the Verein für Sozialpolitik but also, later, against other proponents of conservative or state socialism. Engels mocked those "German economists of the Katheder-Socialist school" who had once been consoled by the English worker's "respectful regard for the position of his master." With the growth of social democracy in England, Engels chided, Professor Brentano and "his brother *Katheder-Socialists*" would see that England also displayed "the incurable communistic and revolutionary tendencies of their own working-men at home."[38] In 1895 the Italian Marxist philosopher Antonio Labriola criticized "Katheder- and State socialism" as a "bureaucratic and fiscal utopia, that is, the utopia of cretins."[39] Communists of the Third International, including Lenin, Bukharin, and Trotsky, would similarly scorn the state socialism of the Verein für Sozialpolitik as an authoritarian defense of class society.[40]

The German Social Democratic Party, like Karl Marx himself, rejected paternalistic socialism, opting for a classical political economy made revolutionary by a radicalized concept of free labor. This commitment to political economy and free labor set Marxism at odds with a whole range of socialisms, including the authoritarian state socialism developed by Saint-Simon and embraced by Napoleon III or that advocated by the Verein für Sozialpolitik and embraced by Otto von Bismarck. While the history of Soviet-style state socialism has obscured the libertarian impulse of Marxian socialism, it is impossible to understand the politics and ideology of the Verein für Sozialpolitik, the German state, or the German labor movement without grasping the connection of laissez-faire political economy, Marxism, and the self-emancipatory efforts of workers, both in their concerted actions through the Social Democratic Party and their everyday assertions of personal autonomy. While the party itself pursued fairly conventional, nonrevolutionary strategies, it nonetheless demanded an end to the exploitation of labor by capitalists, not the state handouts and paternalistic control that the Verein demanded.[41]

To avoid confusion, I follow the terminology of the period, using *state socialism* to refer to paternalist schemes defending the status quo and *social democracy* to refer to the democratic socialism and worker autonomy demanded by Marxists. For the sake of simplicity, I will refer to the party representing this position in Germany as the Social Democratic Party of Germany (Sozialdemokratische Partei Deutschlands, or SPD), although the party only took this name in 1890 and only adopted Marxism as its official ideology a year later. To a greater extent than the communist parties that emerged after the October Revolution, the parties of the Second (Socialist) International included diverse and contradictory political and theoretical positions, from Fabianism and reformism to revolutionary Marxism. Here I focus only on revolutionary Marxism, since, before the First World War, Marxism, represented by such figures as August Bebel, Karl Kautsky, and Clara Zetkin, dominated the SPD.

Although it would soon be better known for its work on rural labor, in its first years, the Verein für Sozialpolitik concerned itself with the control of workers in manufacturing. In 1874, at its second annual meeting, the organization considered whether the state could maintain the economic and social order sufficiently after the Employment Code of 1869 abolished criminal sanctions against workers who broke contracts with employers in most nonagricultural sectors. Members of the Verein agreed that the state did not need to expand its powers to punish contract-breaking workers, but encouraged authorities to enforce more thoroughly existing laws against a practice that "produces and encourages the moral

barbarization [*Verwilderung*] of the working class." The Verein für Sozialpolitik explained its interest in contract breaking as part of its struggle
against social democracy. "We are," one member announced in his lecture
on contract breaking, "above all unconditional enemies of social democracy. . . . We regard social democracy as a materialistic enemy of the
Reich, destructive of all ideals, a party to be combated with all means."[42]

In the 1880s, politicians identifying themselves as "social conservatives" or "Christian socialists" sought to chip away at the electoral base
of the Social Democrats by providing paternalist protection for workers
in lieu of democracy and economic autonomy. The Verein für Sozialpolitik not only offered social-scientific advice for such policies; some of its
members, above all Adolph Wagner, became noisy political agitators,
speaking to mass audiences.[43] Many of these conservative socialists, including Adolph Wagner, adopted anti-Semitic rhetoric, presenting themselves as defenders of the poor and downtrodden against ills of modern
society that they characterized as un-Christian and Jewish. The phrase
"anti-Semitism is the socialism of fools," commonly attributed to the Social Democrat August Bebel, emerged in response to these new political
movements. In the late 1880s and early 1890s, voters elected to the Reichstag more than a dozen members of parties identifying themselves as anti-
Semitic. In 1892, seeking to co-opt these movements, and certainly not
averse to the doctrine themselves, the Conservatives incorporated anti-
Semitism into their party platform.[44]

The Verein für Sozialpolitik first turned to agricultural topics in 1878,
the year the German state passed laws forbidding the Social Democratic
Party from campaigning, organizing, or publishing party literature, although still permitting the party to stand for election to the Reichstag.
With the party of urban workers hamstrung, the Verein could safely turn
its attention to agricultural workers. For members of the Verein für Sozialpolitik, the end of serfdom and the subsequent decline of manorial control
demanded new forms of labor coercion suited to an era of free labor.
Georg Friedrich Knapp, perhaps the greatest historian of German agriculture, and one of the founders of the Verein für Sozialpolitik, framed this
problem as one of finding a capitalist replacement for feudal labor relations.[45] Knapp's interest in modern agriculture may have come from his
uncle, the famous organic chemist Justus von Liebig. Liebig's work on
chemical fertilizer allowed eastern landlords to abandon the three-field
system, expanding the area under cultivation at any given time by a third,
and thus increasing the labor demanded by these agriculturalists. Knapp's
principal work on emancipation, his 1887 *Liberation of the Serfs* (*Bauernbefreiung*), criticized those liberals who assumed that, with the abolition
of serfdom in Prussia, the free market would work out labor relations as
a matter of course.[46] "Every age has its task," Gustav Schmoller wrote

in a review of *Liberation of the Serfs*: "the century 1750–1850 had the obligation to save and liberate the peasants. The century 1850–1950 stands before the even greater task of elevating the working class and reconciling it to our economic order." Schmoller elaborated the political implications of Knapp's historical research, noting that a kind of repeasantization of the working class could prevent the spread of social democracy after the decline of "patriarchal relations" and calling for mass settlement of workers on smallholds in the Prussian East.[47] Knapp similarly called on the state to pursue a "scientific social policy" that would allow it "gradually to lift up the rural proletarians of the eastern provinces, so that we might recognize them as equal compatriots."[48]

Many members of the Verein für Sozialpolitik regarded the United States as a model for the control of free agricultural labor. One agricultural economist, Max Sering, looked to homesteading in the American Midwest as a model of independent small farming and the settlement and colonization of territory.[49] Marx also idealized the independent farmers of the Midwest, probably following the ideology of American Free-Soilers, but Sering cited these small proprietors as evidence against social democracy.[50] For many members of the Verein für Sozialpolitik, however, the American South presented a better example of the control of free labor. While agricultural laborers fled the estates of eastern Germany in the three decades before the First World War, in the southern United States, at this time, white elites continued to keep the counterparts of the former serfs, African American freedpeople, bound to the land through sharecropping and a host of legal measures and informal racist violence. African American freedpeople would begin their own Great Migration to northern cities during the First World War, but, in the decades before that conflict, the American South, with its "Negro question," still offered a model of constrained agricultural labor that German social scientists and policy makers would observe with interest, first as a model for the Prussian East and later as a model for German Africa.

Racial hierarchies at first appeared to Verein as means of controlling free agricultural labor peculiar to the American South and other colonial plantation societies. As early as 1866, in his discussion of the United States immediately after the Civil War, Gustav Schmoller identified the role that racism would play in coercing rural labor in America with the decline of slavery.[51] In the late 1880s, Georg Friedrich Knapp began studying black labor in Africa and the New World as comparative cases for his study of the transition from bound to free labor in Germany. In Africa and the New World, as in Germany, Knapp argued, the psychological motivations promised by free labor ideology could never sufficiently guarantee labor discipline, and thus emancipation required new forms of control. Around the time he published *Liberation of the Serfs*, Knapp began studying contemporary literature on European overseas colonies, often taking extensive notes, as well as histories of slavery and emancipation in the United States.[52] The following year, Knapp wrote on the "Negro question" in the New World, mostly in the Spanish and Portuguese colonies, arguing that "Negro slavery" was a solution to "the worker question on the large-scale agricultural-industrial business of the plantation" that took advantage of the fact that, at the time, blacks, as a race, "stood outside the law of nations [*Völkerrecht*]."[53] Knapp further maintained that, despite the proclaimed opposition to slavery by European rulers of Africa, the institution of the plantation maintained structural continuities between slavery and colonization.

For Knapp, antiblack racism functioned as a labor-coercive regime that could replace slavery as a means of maintaining and controlling a plantation labor force. Knapp already detected a tendency toward forced labor or even slavery in the common white complaint that the "Negro" was lazy and did not like to work. In fact, Knapp noted, it was only the case that Negroes did not wish to work for European plantations. Knapp expressed the hope that German rulers of Africa would find methods of extracting labor from their colonial subjects at least more humane than slavery.[54] In a 1900 lecture, Knapp elaborated the role of racism in New World plantation economies, noting that the United States had abandoned slavery but still used racism to control black labor: "The Negro cannot lose the marks of his race; he remains subordinated, even when he becomes a Christian and a free man, and is restricted to lower jobs. . . . Under these circumstances, it is economically possible to free slaves without ruining the plantation. . . . There remains just one final question: that of the racially alien proletariat."[55] Knapp, like Schmoller, regarded race and racism as just one of the myriad ways that labor could be controlled in specific economic and social conjunctures. In the 1880s, neither man concerned himself with "race" inside Germany.

GERMAN SETTLERS AND POLISH MIGRANTS: INTERNAL COLONIZATION AND THE STRUGGLE OVER LABOR, SEXUALITY, AND RACE

With its turn to agricultural topics, the Verein called for "the preservation and economic strengthening of the rural middle class" as a means of preserving the social order against the growth of a mobile, free, and presumably social democratic proletariat.[56] Participants in an 1884 conference devoted to rural conditions in Germany demanded that the state support small farming, at least in part as a bulwark against social democracy.[57] Farming attached workers to the land, keeping them available for nearby large agricultural enterprises and discouraging both physical movement and political mobilization. Authorities regarded farmers as a conservative force in German politics, and counted on them to reject Social Democrats at the polls and to provide obedient soldiers who, in times of social upheaval, would be willing to fire on revolutionaries if ordered to do so.[58] The smallhold farm also grouped workers into households imagined as bastions of paternalist hierarchy that might confine the threatening, if limited, economic autonomy conventional for working-class women and preserve the social order from the revolutionary female pétroleuses cited by Brentano.

In 1886 the Verein published a volume advocating "internal colonization," the state-sponsored settlement of small farmers, and the topic was discussed at its annual meeting.[59] Schmoller, by then an influential professor at the University of Berlin, applauded the "building, settling, agricultural activity" that distinguished "internal colonization" from the territorial conquest of "external colonization." Internal colonization amounted, in Schmoller's words, to the "definitive settling [*Sesshaftwerdung*] of a people" and "the transition to agriculture." Agriculture, for Schmoller, involved the advance of "higher moral, intellectual, and technical civilization" and therefore represented an "earnest struggle with the opposing natural forces, with the traditional morals and customs of one's own people and with hostile or recalcitrant elements of foreign peoples."[60] The volume also included practical recommendations based on an experiment of the early 1870s, in which the state divided some unrented crown land among a number of small farmers. These recommendations covered topics from irrigation, to the organization of villages, to the valuation of the farms; all encouraged the state to take a greater role in managing such settlements.[61] Smallhold farming soon became the centerpiece of nearly every policy recommendation by members of the Verein.

The Prussian state embraced the proposals put forward by the Verein for internal colonization, but, in the first instance, as measures to increase the number of ethnic Germans living in Posen and West Prussia. These eastern provinces of Prussia had been parts of Poland and contained large, and in many areas majority, Polish populations. Prussia, Russia, and Austria had annexed all of Poland in a sequence of three partitions in 1772, 1793, and 1795, and thus each had sizeable Polish populations. Polish and German workers alike became more mobile in the nineteenth century, and German nationalists began to speak of a growing threat of "Polonization" in the East. Prussia had already turned on its Polish citizens in the series of anti-Catholic measures enacted in 1871–78, commonly described as a *Kulturkampf*, or "struggle for civilization."[62] Bismarck later described his interest in the Kulturkampf as related "overwhelmingly" to "its Polish aspect."[63] Between 1883 and 1885 Bismarck had further ordered the expulsion of around 32,000 Poles who did not possess Prussian citizenship.[64] Concerns about free labor in eastern agriculture thus included fears that Polish residents threatened the ethnic and even racial purity of Prussia.

Despite official concerns about the number of Poles living in Prussia, German agriculture continued to attract Polish migration from across the Austrian and Russian borders. Most Russian and Austrian Poles who worked in German agriculture did so as seasonal laborers rather than as permanent residents. For Poles interested in permanent relocation, the United States, Canada, and Brazil all proved more attractive than eastern Germany. However, eastern Germany became a major destination for Polish seasonal labor migration. Even as hundreds of thousands of Germans emigrated abroad, more foreign workers traveled to Germany than to any country other than the United States.[65] In the last decade of the nineteenth century, an average of 30,000 seasonal migrants left Russian Poland for Germany each year, and, in the first decade of the twentieth century, this annual average rose to 160,000. Figures from Austrian Poland are similarly significant: in 1900, 70,000 left for seasonal employment in Germany, and the annual average from 1910 to 1913 was a massive 240,000 per year.[66]

The demand for Polish workers in eastern agriculture arose not only from the need to replace Germans who left for the West, but also from the new labor demands brought about by the introduction of sugarbeet cultivation. Between 1880 and 1910, the peak of German emigration from the rural northeast, German sugarbeet production nearly quadrupled.[67] The conditions of sugarbeet production shaped both the image and the lives of Polish migrant laborers, much as conditions of cotton production did for African American farmers.

The sugarbeet was a triumph of German agrarian science. In 1747 Andreas Siegmund Marggraf of the Prussian Royal Academy of Sciences discovered that sucrose, previously thought to derive only from sugarcane, could be obtained from beets and other crops grown in Europe.[68] In 1799 Margraf's student Franz Carl Achard produced the first sugarbeet, the Silesian white beet, by crossbreeding varieties grown to feed cattle. German agronomists introduced the imperial beet in the 1840s, a hardier plant with a higher sugar content than its predecessors, and selective breeding continued to improve beets dramatically, even into the twentieth century.[69] Sugarbeets required relatively little acreage, so even when German production accounted for more than an eighth of sugar from all sources on the world market, German agriculturalists devoted a relatively small area to the crop. Furthermore, although sugarbeets required nearly constant cultivation, they did not interfere with other crops because grains and potatoes were sown before sugarbeets and harvested after

FIGURE 2.1. Sugarbeet. Source: George H. Coons, "The Sugar Beet: Product of Science," *Scientific Monthly* 68 (1949): 149–64. Reprinted with permission from AAAS.

them.[70] In 1896 Prussia boasted four hundred sugar refineries, which produced almost 1.5 million tons of sugar from 12 million tons of sugarbeets.[71]

The sugarbeet, like cotton, combined capital-intensive and technically sophisticated breeding and processing with labor-intensive planting, cultivating, and harvesting. Perhaps to an even greater extent than cotton, sugarbeets required constant hoeing, from the time they were planted until the time they were harvested. Hoeing had to begin immediately if the ground crusted over, if weeds sprouted, or to kill larvae in the soil if insects appeared.[72] "The German peasants," noted the American geographer Edith Muriel Poggi in 1930, "have the idea that they hoe sugar into the beets, and this is not far from the truth, since on the same quality soil the sugar content varies from 10 to 18 percent depending on the method of cultivation."[73] Preparing and sowing the beet fields, as well as harvest-

FIGURE 2.2. Weeding sugarbeet fields with hoes. The original caption explains: "Gangs of women frequently do this work, supervised by one man." Cotton similarly had to be weeded with hoes, a process known as "chopping cotton." Source: E. Muriel Poggi, "The German Sugar Beet Industry," *Economic Geography* 6 (1930): 81–93, 85.

ing the beets, required a similarly large amount of work. When it came time to harvest the beets, for example, one worker loosened each beet with a spade, a second worker pulled out two beets at a time, knocked them together to remove excess soil clinging to the beets, and placed them on a wagon, where a third worker cut the leaves off the top.

Both cotton and sugarbeets were the products of careful selective breeding, and the value of crops thus depended on purchasing seeds chosen by technical experts. Sugarbeet cultivation also required extensive application of chemical fertilizer to maintain profitable levels of sugar in the crop. Sugarbeet farms required skilled technical supervision, usually carried out

FIGURE 2.3. The original caption reads: "Thinning out the young beets. This work is done almost entirely by hand." Source: Poggi, 83.

by a manager rather than a landlord. Most experts applauded, as one put it, "that sugarbeet farming stimulates the intelligence of the farmer" by forcing him to abandon "the rules handed down from antiquity" in favor of "rational, contemporary farm management."[74] After harvest, the value of both cotton and sugarbeets could be realized only by industrial processing. The factories that extracted sucrose from sugarbeets tended to be located close to areas of cultivation in order to save transportation costs, something that distinguished beets from American cotton, which industrial centers distant from the southern cotton belt processed.[75]

The labor-intensive cultivation and harvesting of sugarbeets was carried out in large part by Polish migrants, who, like African American cotton growers, were regarded as ideally suited for such arduous and poorly paid labor because of their supposed racial inferiority. Polish seasonal agricultural workers were known in Germany as *Sachsengänger*, those who go to Saxony. The first Sachsengänger left homes in Prussian Poland to work in sugarbeet growing areas farther west, first in Saxony and later in other parts of the Reich. In 1886, the Prussian government began providing a railway discount to these Prussian citizens—typically of Polish ancestry—traveling west for seasonal agricultural labor. This seasonal migration displeased landlords in the Prussian East, who were already losing agricultural workers to western German industry and to overseas migration. After 1890, Prussian authorities permitted these eastern landlords to employ Polish migrant laborers from across the Russian or Austrian borders. These migrant laborers who came to replace the original Sachsengänger soon came themselves to be called Sachsengänger.[76] The term later came to describe seasonal migrant workers in any part of Germany, and, by the turn of the century, Germans even used the term to refer to migrant African laborers in their colonies.[77]

During the winter months, Poles in their late teens and early twenties signed on for work beginning in the spring with labor recruiters who were often former Sachsengänger themselves.[78] At the beginning of April, recruiters would escort groups of migrant laborers by train, via Berlin, to their contracted place of employment, where the recruiters often became overseers. In 1907 the state set up thirty-nine border stations with barracks that could together process up to ten thousand foreign workers daily. Seasonal migrants could not enter Germany without a labor contract, but those who had not been recruited for a specific employer could usually sign contracts at the border. After undergoing medical examination, authorities provided migrants with a "legitimation card," colored according to their nationality (red for Poles). Without this card, migrants could be deported from Prussia at their own expense.[79]

At least half of the Sachsengänger were female. It was often said that employers desired Polish workers because they were "*willig und billig*"— willing and cheap—and Polish women were considered even *williger und billiger* than Polish men.[80] Booker T. Washington, traveling through Europe in 1910, noted that, in the area around Berlin, women, "coarsely clad, barefoot," sometimes outnumbered the men in the fields.[81] The young male and female Sachsengänger generally came to Prussia unmarried, and, to prevent them from marrying Germans, the state forced them to leave Germany in the winter. This forced absence from Germany also spared landlords the cost of feeding and housing these migrants when estates no longer required the extra hands. The Prussian government thus assured that male and female Polish migrants remained outside the patriarchal and normative heterosexual family while they were in Germany.

This non-normative sexuality of Sachsengänger, facilitated by the state to control race and reproductive sexuality, also raised moral concerns. The youth, mobility, and sexual freedom of the Sachsengänger, precisely those characteristics that made them so economically attractive and reproductively harmless to landlords and state authorities, summoned a specter of sexual debauchery. In the barracks that housed Polish migrants, we should not be surprised to learn, young Poles apparently enjoyed sex with each other outside of wedlock and, in such close living quarters, outside the privacy of the household, in full view of the other residents.[82] At first, male and female Sachsengänger had been housed together in barracks, or even in outbuildings with straw scattered on the floor. By 1890 the law put a stop to this, requiring that Sachsengänger be housed in separate men's and women's barracks, in iron beds with straw mattresses and woolen blankets. Typically, according to the social scientist Karl Kaerger, the overseer had a private apartment between the men's and women's barracks to maintain the separation of the sexes. He could even levy fines for "nighttime mischief."[83] Migrant labor gave young workers a range of personal freedoms that the patriarchal household denied. Their sexual freedom was part of a larger political and economic challenge that capitalism posed to itself and to the interlinked authority of nation, state, and household.

As state authorities began to decry what they referred to as the "Polonization" of parts of Germany, German efforts to regulate, even to combat, Polish sexuality extended beyond the simple pleasures of young Polish workers to a broad campaign to control sexuality, reproduction, kinship, and nationality. The president of Bromberg in the Prussian province of Posen and a close associate of Bismarck, Christoph von Tiedemann, asserted in an official memorandum of 1886 that Poles sought to educate "German children into Poles." Polish reproduction, Tiedemann implied, could operate through education, primarily by forcing the children of German parents to learn the Polish language in school. A central organization, ultimately controlled by the Catholic Church, directed Polish educational efforts, Tiedemann warned, and dedicated itself to "just one purpose: the Polonization of the province" of Posen. The idea that children could become Polish through education points to an understanding of race that is at once sociological and biological and, ultimately, sexual. The Catholic Church could direct Polish activities, according to Tiedemann, because of a "Polish custom" according to which women dominate men and priests dominate women.[84] The power of Polish women and the emasculation of Polish men threatened, indirectly, to make German children, produced through heterosexual unions, Polish. Poles also, according to concerned Prussians, outdid the Germans in the more conventional reproduction of national subjects in heterosexual, monogamous households, displaying an enviable "fertility, tenacity . . . and a willingness to make sacrifices for the nation."[85] German state building and racial politics in the East necessarily addressed the sexuality of Poles, including Sachsengänger, as well as the sexuality of Germans.

Some Prussian officials worried that the earnings that Sachsengänger brought back to their home territories helped Poles in what they imagined to be a "struggle of nationalities." The so-called Sachsengänger theory held that returning migrants deposited their savings in Polish-run banks that used the money to help Poles buy land from Germans and used the high profits on their low-interest accounts to fund the national struggle.[86] Kaiser Wilhelm II himself held this theory, explaining that "the significant sums earned from *Sachsengängerei*, which are deposited in Polish Banks under the control of their clergy" financed "Polish propaganda" and Polish land acquisition in Germany.[87] Polish banks did indeed support nationalist land acquisition in eastern Germany. In his 1886 memorandum, Tiedemann had warned that when Poles bought German estates, they immediately replaced all Germans with Poles, "from the top farm inspector to the last house boy." German farmers, however, also preferred to hire Polish laborers, for they were more obedient, less demanding, and accepted living quarters that no German would.[88] The economic incentives of capitalism undermined the racial purity and domestic stability of Germans, suggesting a further reason for Verein members to reject laissez-faire economic policies.[89] The politics of nationalism in Prussia involved a struggle about proper households, a struggle of what Germans imagined as a dissolute, sexually irregular, and reproductively uncontrollable Polish horde with monogamous, heterosexual, and patriarchal German families.

In its effort to promote stable German households, the Prussian state followed the recommendations of the Verein für Sozialpolitik to sponsor rural smallholding.[90] In 1886 the Prussian House of Deputies authorized the Ministry of Agriculture to establish a Settlement Commission (*Ansiedlungskomission*) "to strengthen the German element in the provinces of West Prussia and Posen against Polonizing efforts."[91] Funded with an initial 100 million marks, followed by further similar appropriations, the Settlement Commission purchased large estates to divide into small plots for German settlers.[92]

These anti-Polish policies violated royal Prussian tradition and precedent, which had once welcomed all productive workers, whether Huguenots, Poles, or any other religious or national group. Indeed, in an 1841 letter copied for the files of Prussian Settlement Commission, King Friedrich Wilhelm IV explicitly rejected any consideration of nationality when selling crown land to private individuals.[93] The *Ober-Präsident* of Posen, Baron von Wilamowitz, reasoned in 1895: "of course His Majesty's subjects are to be treated equally, whether they are of German or foreign origin and mother tongue; the question is simply to determine in which cases and to what extent exceptions to this rule are necessary. . . ." Such exceptional decisions were indeed necessary, the Baron continued, because Germans could no longer compete economically or demographically with Poles, and "a significant influx of Polish or Jewish immigrants from Russia and Galicia . . . can and must always be prevented."[94] The politics of race and free labor fit uneasily with older, aristocratic norms, and in the nineteenth century traditional authorities in Prussia, as in the American South, had to refashion themselves politically and economically and cooperate with new bourgeois allies and ideological and scientific experts.

The Settlement Commission placed each newly acquired estate under a manager who divided it into parcels suitable for a family of German settlers, with fields, access to water, a house, and outbuildings.[95] To recruit settlers, the commission employed traveling agents, set up permanent offices throughout Prussia, and published a newsletter. Commission agents arranged visits of potential settlers to estates, during which estate managers staged discussions with current settlers highlighting the benefits of the settlement.[96] The administrator was to select settlers carefully, collecting police reports from their previous places of residence and making a personal judgment if he had an opportunity to meet them before they moved permanently to the estate. He was advised to reject land speculators (although one strains to imagine a speculator interested in these settlements), or anybody with disabilities that might hinder farm work. Managers were also to turn away settlers wishing to move from other areas of eastern Prussia that were themselves threatened with "Polonization." The Settlement Commission instructed administrators to attend to the "diversity of the German tribes," taking into account, for example, that those from Saxony, southern Germany, and elsewhere preferred "heavy soil and good access to roads," whereas Brandenburgers, Pomeranians, Hanoverians, and others demanded less. Administrators grouped settlers in villages according to their confession so that they could all attend a single church. Nonetheless, the thirty to fifty inhabitants of a typical settler village, according to one account, shared little in common and were generally "dull and mistrustful."[97] In areas with opportunities for wage labor, either for other settlers, on larger estates, or in distilleries, brick-making, or other industries, the administrator might create smaller plots that could be farmed by a male worker's wife and children while he worked outside the household.

The Settlement Commission also recruited Russians of German descent, whom it termed "returnees." The commission singled out these Russian-Germans for special treatment because, although they were ethnically German, they still came from the East and were therefore considered inferior to German citizens. Upon arrival they had to be examined by the district physician, who also ensured that they had been immunized against small pox.[98] Large "troops" of related families often migrated together, hoping to settle on the same estate, but administrators were instructed to disperse them among western Germans in order to bring the individual families up to German standards. The Prussian government made efforts to help relieve the returnees of the duties of Russian citizenship—primarily military service—but discouraged them from returning to Russia, lest they be punished for leaving without permission.[99]

The Settlement Commission did not merely hope to replace Polish seasonal agricultural workers in the East with ethnic Germans, but also to settle ethnic Germans on supervised smallhold farms. To do so, the commission employed tenancy contracts, an economic form that had, by the last decades of the nineteenth century, become a well-established means of maintaining coercion over formally free labor. Prussian landlords themselves had responded to the end of serfdom by placing entire families under their household authority as contract-bound cottagers (*Insten*). Similarly, the sharecropping and crop lien system used contracts to keep American cotton growers in conditions of bondage even with the end of slavery. The Settlement Commission conceived of the farmers on its estates as owners, rather than renters, but sought to refashion mortgage agreements to mimic the labor coercion of the rental contract.

The mortgage agreement employed by the commission sought, like rental contracts elsewhere, to regulate the lives of the settlers and bolster the authority of estate supervisors. The mortgages of the settlers could not be amortized, that is, paid off, so the mortgage contract remained in effect as long as the settlers occupied the land. These mortgages did not seem designed to exploit settlers, who could collect 90 percent of their total payments if they left the estate, but rather to keep them under permanent contractual obligation.[100] This distinguished the German settlers from most contract-bound renters, including American sharecroppers, who were brutally exploited and abused. A settler family received, typically, about thirty-five acres, already furnished with a house and all necessary outbuildings.[101] Settlers had to supply a certain amount of capital to purchase cattle and farm implements and to maintain, at their own expense, trees, drainage, and meadows on their land. Every contract form had additional space for "personal obligations" particular to each settler.[102] A senior officer of the commission supervised the settlers in an area in all matters, not just agriculture but also "political, general economic, social, and communal things."[103] These were odd mortgage agreements indeed that stipulated work and family arrangements, political and economic life, but they were typical of the rental agreements that emerged on both sides of the Atlantic to control free agricultural workers.

Many of Russian-German "returnees" signed contracts as worker-settlers, which required less initial capital, but also subjected them to even stricter regulation than that to which settlers from within Germany had to submit. Rental contracts required these "returnees" to work six days of "customary" length each week. They could also, in exceptional cases, be forced to work overtime and on Sundays. Fines up to the equivalent of four days wages could be levied for missing work, drunkenness, disobedience, and other infractions. Workers could be evicted for repeated offences and also for "inciting other workers" (to what is not specified).[104] The commission guaranteed such high pay to these worker-settlers that, at first, they made local workers unwilling to accept employment at the prevailing wage. Responding to employer complaints, the Settlement Commission reduced settler wages but paid bonuses into an account that worker-settlers could use to acquire leaseholds when they left the land.[105] These Russian-German "returnees" performed, in common estimations, work that was not only more expensive, but also of an inferior quality to that of their Polish competitors.[106] Not only their high wages, but also the high costs of schooling children, caring for the poor, and other social obligations tempered the enthusiasm of local landlords for employing these settled workers.[107] Settlement Commission estate managers were thus directed to employ these German "returnees" where possible and assured that a "just, calm, and fatherly treatment" would improve their performance. Russian-Germans were not, in any case, to be insulted by unfavorable comparisons with Poles or by being made to work under Polish overseers or among Polish workers.

A 1908 census revealed that the commission had settled eighty-five thousand German farmers and agricultural laborers in West Prussia and Posen. The average settler family had between five and six members, including, typically, one or two school-aged children. There were about seven times as many settler families as worker families.[108] One survey found that most of the settlers were not the sons of farmers, but rather, for the most part, former agricultural day laborers, as well, occasionally, as craftsmen. The author of this study found that these settlers were motivated primarily by a desire for independence and personal private property, and that they worked diligently. The commission did not attract many western Germans, and most of the settlers were Germans who already lived in the East.[109] The settlements served neither the interests of labor nor capital: Prussian state elites framed these contracts to serve nationalist desires by combating Polonization and, at least in the view of members of the Verein für Sozialpolitik, to combat proletarianization and social democracy. Agents of the Settlement Commission exercised the combination of paternal authority and care over worker-settlers advocated by state socialists in the Verein.

The Verein applauded the work of the Settlement Commission at an 1886 meeting on internal colonization, "even if it only applied to the formerly Polish parts of the state." Schmoller commended the Settlement Commission for fostering small farms, which, in his estimation, influenced "the entire social structure," "the entire well-being of the nation" and "the political constitution and more," "the constitution of communities," and "the entire economic [*gewerblichen*] conditions, the livelihood of all classes." Other participants at the meeting endorsed the work of the Settlement Commission with equal enthusiasm, and the Verein resolved that the program should be expanded to all of Prussia.[110] In the 1880s, Schmoller and his colleagues commended smallhold farming as a bulwark against proletarianization and social democracy rather than against "Polonization."

Ever close to the Prussian state, the Verein für Sozialpolitik itself began conducting research in the 1890s to further internal colonization.[111] Verein members regularly discussed tenancy contracts as a means of preserving within the legal and economic framework of capitalism the social stability that had characterized feudalism and that might impede social democracy in the countryside. They explored how workers throughout Germany, even outside the Settlement Commission estates, might be subjected in ways similar to those on the estates.[112] The Verein für Sozialpolitik recognized that workers suspected—correctly—that detailed rental contracts functioned as means of constraining their freedom. Workers thus resisted such contracts in the same measure that landlords and their allies welcomed them. The formal freedom of the market demanded a certain degree of consent from workers, even when poverty was the only alternative to signing a contract.

Karl Kaerger, a student of Georg Friedrich Knapp, lecturer (*Privatdozent*) at the Royal Agricultural Academy in Berlin, and expert on Sachsengänger, led discussions in the Verein für Sozialpolitik about refining labor contracts as instruments of coercion. Kaerger recognized that the mobility of rural workers gave them more money, freedom, and access to "*Kultur*," but worried that, unless these workers settled in one place, they would lack "inner satisfaction." He had similarly worried that the technical character of sugarbeet cultivation made the farm manager a mere technical expert, "no longer the father of his workers."[113] Settling workers in the countryside would, Kaerger noted, secure a supply of workers for large landowners while ensuring "the material and ideal interests of workers," that is, keeping them under the paternal care of state and landlord. Workers would only sign binding rental agreements if, Kaerger reckoned, they could be made to "feel at home" on a smallhold and develop a desire to remain "in the service" of a large land owner. Such rental contracts should, therefore, avoid any "medieval flavor" by dispensing with terms (accurate though they might be) such as "estate-bound [*gutshörigen*] renter." Preferable would be terms imported from western Germany, which might "arouse the fantasies" of the renters. Kaerger rejected the

term *Insten,* the contract-bound cottager, for it still connoted the subservi-
ence of the serf in eastern Germany. Kaerger, like others in the Verein für
Sozialpolitik, preferred the term *Heuerling,* from the western province of
Westphalia, which described (as did all the other terms), a tenant whose
rental agreement required that he and his family work for his landlord.
Kaerger appended sample *Heuerling* contracts to his book, presumably
as models for landlords who chose to introduce this system.[114]

Kaerger was more optimistic than any other leading Verein member
about the possibility of preserving capitalist hierarchies through a kind
of refeudalization of the land. Knapp did agree with his former student
Kaerger on the desirability of bringing the legal form of the Westphalian
Heuerling to the East, but lamented that this would be more difficult than
simply borrowing new models for rental agreements. The problem,
Knapp explained, was more psychological than material: "in the East the
body [of the *Heuerling*] would not go hungry, but the thirst of his soul
would not be quenched."[115] As Max Weber elaborated, the "thoroughly
honest hatred of millions of German proletarians and broad sections of
the bourgeoisie" for "patriarchal large landowners" meant that, for reasons of "folk psychology," the patriarchal system of the East could not
be preserved or restored.[116] For Knapp, the Prussian program of "inner
colonization"—though done for "national political purposes that do
not interest us here"—would gradually make the Prussian East more
like Westphalia, with household farms that would weaken the appeal of
social democracy.[117]

With carefully constructed rental and mortgage agreements, small
farms in Germany, like tenant farms in the United States, offered means
of controlling workers of any ethnicity. While many imagined sharecropping in the United States as a tactic of controlling blacks, it also entrapped
millions of whites, and the anti-Polish rhetoric of the Settlement Commission similarly did not prevent estate managers from constraining Germans. The blacks in the American South suffered violence and racism
incomparably more brutal than any inhabitant of the German East in this
period. Both regions did, however, adopt contracts and other trappings
of economic freedom as means of constraining workers.

Polish nationalists fought against the Settlement Commission and other
Prussian anti-Polish policies, often appealing to a defensive nationalism
and class politics that mirrored the activities of their German opponents.
Both the Settlement Commission and Polish nationalists sought to outdo
each other in the political economy of the household, with its authoritarian defense of the status quo, its appeal to pure biological descent, and
its attempt to control sexuality. Polish parceling banks competed with the
Settlement Commission, sometimes outbidding the Prussian organization
and dividing German estates for settlement by Polish smallholders.[118]

Polish nationalists protested the German Settlement Commission as an assault by "Germans and Jews." At a 1912 demonstration against the commission, Polish nationalists distributed leaflets warning: "Any Pole who buys from Jews or Germans undermines the existence of the Catholic Church and the Fatherland."[119] Local Polish papers published the names or initials of local residents who purchased goods from local German or Jewish merchants, seeking to direct public opprobrium to these supposed traitors to their nation: "The Misses B.," wrote one paper, "are patronizing the Jews. Is this a proper way to show respect for their recently deceased mother?" Another Polish newspaper claimed to keep a "black book" in which it recorded "the names of those who for a Judas penny have sold their land into the hands of the colonization commission . . . in order that our posterity may know of the infamous deeds of these betrayers of their country."[120] Neither German nor Polish landowners wholly embraced the parcelization of estates, which replaced local landlords and their dependent laborers with smallholders dependent on the state Settlement Commission. One Polish agitator sought to turn German landowners against the Settlement Commission with a pamphlet quoting a German song "already current in the provinces" in which a peasant proclaims: "To the devil with the Barons, whether they're German or Polish, the devil should take all of them."[121] The Prussian anti-Polish campaigns, as well as some of the Polish responses to this campaign, fought to maintain class and national hierarchies on the land.

Polish nationalist authorities condemned the sexual freedom won by young Polish migrant laborers at least as fiercely as did their German counterparts. When Sachsengänger returned to their homes in the winter, as required by law, most had amassed considerable savings. Seasonal labor gave Polish youth unprecedented levels of economic and personal freedom, even as it subjected them to twelve-hour work days, often with additional mandatory overtime. These migrants were typically unmarried and still living with their parents. Both their experience abroad and the money that they brought home at the end of the season allowed them an autonomy that threatened paternal control of the household. Polish youth working in Germany, complained the *Gazeta Świąteczna*, a Russian-Polish newspaper, "do as they please; consequently the girls return home ruined and corrupted and the boys addicted to drinking." Their parents, the paper went on, "are aware of the corruption but they do not mind it as long as their children give them their earnings."[122] These young people marked their independence with new clothing styles, using some of their earnings to purchase German fashions that earned them the colloquial Polish name Westfaloki (Westphalian, after the region that employed the Polish industrial workers who had first brought these fashions to the East).[123] A decade later, the same newspaper complained that young people returning from Germany did not turn their earnings over to their parents at all, but instead "spend their days and evenings in the shops and waste all their earnings," living off the wages of their fathers.[124] With the economic independence these young workers earned in Germany, they also escaped, apparently, the control of the Church, leaving priests to "plead and beg from the pulpit" in vain.[125]

Like German authorities, Polish authorities deplored the sexual autonomy these migrants enjoyed, and, not surprisingly, expressed special hostility toward female autonomy. In 1907 the *Gazeta Świąteczna*, complained that Polish women working abroad now chose their own husbands, often men from other parts of Poland whom they met during the season in Prussia. Women no longer needed permission from their parents for these matches, since they now had enough money to pay for their own weddings.[126] Most descriptions of this sexual freedom suggested that it brought misery and ruin to women, but it seems just as likely that these tales of ruined women reflected an ideological defense of the authority of the patriarchal household rather than an accurate assessment of the consequences of sexual freedom.[127] "German women laugh," the *Gazeta Świąteczna* chided—positing a kind of emasculating alliance between women on both sides of the ethnic divide—"that a Polish girl earns more in Prussia than a Polish man" who remains at home.[128] Both the Prussian program of internal colonization and the nationalist Polish resistance to this program responded to the mobility and freedom of young workers through attempts at biological and social control, centered on the sexuality of Germans and Poles. Sexual freedom threatened political, racial-national, and economic hierarchies. Sexuality, in fact, so close to the individual sense of personality, desire, and even self-worth, often loomed much larger in personal and public perceptions than the other mutually sustaining elements in this political economic complex.

Social Democracy versus Internal Colonization and State Socialism

The leading theorists of the Social Democratic Party grasped the fundamental role that particular configurations of gender, sexuality, and the household played in regimes designed to control free labor. It is thus hardly surprising that some of the most important Social Democratic writings of the period before the First World War focused on questions of individual freedom in the household, drawing special attention to the unique oppression of women. In *Woman and Socialism*, the work perhaps most widely read by members of the Social Democratic Party, party leader August Bebel proclaimed that, with the end of capitalism, women would be economically, politically, socially, and sexually independent of, and equal to, men. He pointed to the exploitation of women's and children's labor in the household, including on small farms, which was in many cases more severe than that faced by individual workers outside the home.[129] Just as sexuality, kinship, and the household were fundamental to policies of racial and national domination, of opposition to social democracy, and of the control of free labor developed by the Prussian state and the Verein für Sozialpolitik, so too were they central to the critique of these policies by the Social Democrats.

The dual call of the German Social Democratic Party for the liberation of workers and the liberation of women was no marriage of convenience between partisans of class equality and partisans of gender equality but rather a necessary consequence of the Marxist theory to which the party committed itself after 1891, and which many party leaders embraced much earlier.[130] Marxist theory virtually compelled Social Democrats to reject ahistorical concepts of a "natural" role for women or inherent feminine characteristics. Many party members became, in the words of historian Jean Quataert, "reluctant feminists," and their political practice and personal lives did not always meet their own standards of gender equality.[131] The writings of Social Democrat Clara Zetkin sometimes give an impression of posing gender and class equality as alternatives in tension with each other, but, in fact, like the other major Social Democratic theorists, Zetkin saw total equality of men and women as necessary to social democracy. For Zetkin, industrialization had begun to liberate women from the household and from the domination of men, and only social democratic workers, not bourgeois feminists, could take these initial steps toward equality beyond the constraints imposed on all workers by capitalism. She acknowledged the validity of many of the individual goals of women's rights activists, but argued that the separation of gender and class by non-Marxist feminists undermined the struggle for gender equality.[132] The struggle by political and economic elites against the freedom of labor included imposing authoritarian households, and the struggle for the freedom of labor thus necessarily included an attack on such households. Feminism was not a happy adjunct of social democracy, resulting from benevolent democratic sentiments of the party, but rather was a basic part of the Marxist critique of capitalism and of the struggle of Social Democrats against the authority of employers and the state.

In a certain sense, opposition to patriarchal authority drove Social Democrats to Marxism as much as Marxism drove them to feminism. As historian Vernon Lidtke has shown, leading Social Democratic theorists like Karl Kautsky and Eduard Bernstein first engaged seriously with Marxist theory to respond to the paternalist state socialist policies that Bismarck, as well as various conservative and anti-Semitic, self-styled "social" politicians, began proposing in the 1880s.[133] State socialism not only aimed to control the workers on whose freedom social democracy, as well as capitalism, depended, but also, more immediately, threatened to peel away social democratic voters more concerned with issues of social welfare than with longer term social democratic goals. A state committed to preserving the social order, the "class state" in social democratic shorthand, could not, argued the party's official newspaper, "solve the social question" without destroying the class hierarchy on which its own existence depended.[134] In the course of their critique of state socialism, Social Democrats rejected even the concept of "the people" or "the nation" (*das Volk*) because it obscured social differences, and they thus repudiated the goal of a "free state of all the people" (*freie Volksstaat*) in favor of a "free socialist society" (*freie sozialistische Gesellschaft*).[135] Karl Kautsky, the leading theorist of the Social Democratic Party, rejected state authority as firmly as he rejected the domination of capital. Kautsky attacked even those proposals for state control of some parts of the economy offered in Marx and Engels's 1848 Communist Manifesto, noting that the previous half-century had revealed the state as an instrument of class oppression that could not, in any case, manage firms as efficiently as private capitalists could.[136] The Social Democrats refused the false unity of nation and state because these false unities depended on, obscured, and preserved differences of power, wealth, and freedom. Essential to state and nation, and also to the social democratic critique of these false unities, was the complex of gender, sexuality, and kinship in the household.

After the antisocialist law lapsed in 1890, the newly legalized Social Democratic Party took its struggle directly to the countryside. In Reichstag elections in February of that year, a fifth of all voters supported the Social Democrats, almost doubling the party's representation in the national parliament. German electoral districting, however, gave disproportional weight to votes cast in rural districts, so the party did not gain representation in the Reichstag even closely corresponding to the number of votes it received. In 1891 the party began a program of "rural agitation," sending party members out to the countryside to distribute leaflets, sing party songs, and organize rural workers.[137] Organizers met violent opposition from churches, police, and wealthy landowners, who also distributed counterpropaganda. The party had little success with small farmers who, like prosperous craftsmen, often employed labor and thus opposed the eight-hour day and other basic socialist demands. "Their servants and day laborers [*Knechte, Mägde und Taglöhner*]," wrote Engels, "of course interest us more than they do."[138] The Social Democratic Party did succeed in recruiting rural workers, and, in 1903, it received more than 17 percent of the rural vote (and 32 percent of the national vote), surging ahead of conservatives to become the second largest party in the countryside, after the Catholic Center Party. While urban workers remained the strongest support for the party, Social Democratic organizers did also recruit many among rural workers.

With its turn to rural issues, the Social Democratic Party became the proletarian and democratic counterpart of the state-socialist Verein für Sozialpolitik. In his 1899 *Agrarian Question*, Karl Kautsky provided the social democratic response to questions about rural labor and smallhold farming asked earlier by the Verein. Kautsky's book, hailed by Lenin in the year of its publication as "the most important event in present-day economic literature since the third volume of *Capital*," addressed the question of rural workers, social democracy, state socialism, and internal colonization.[139] Kautsky reinterpreted data gathered by the Verein für Sozialpolitik for its studies of rural life to provide a Marxist account of the transition on the land from feudalism to capitalism and beyond. Kautsky, like Bebel before him, refused to idealize the small farm, and subjected the household form of production to a thorough critique that ultimately, like Bebel's work, highlighted the importance of gender inequality to this particular capitalist organization of labor.

The small farm, Kautsky argued, did not afford economic independence to the family that lived on it, but rather forced the family to work for nearby large landholders in order to earn money to cover the expanding needs of modern farming and the increasing burdens of state and parish taxes. In the East, therefore, the small farm did not compete with large estates, but rather served as a reliable source of labor for those estates. The small farm, according to Kautsky, survived only because every member of a family worked on it for almost no compensation, living in miserable conditions and practicing a "farmer's hunger art." Rural women, Kautsky noted, suffered under the double burden of housework and farm work. He claimed that German social scientists exaggerated the economic viability of smallhold farming and, in any case, endorsed it primarily for nationalistic reasons, to give dependent renters (*Instleute*) a false sense of upward mobility and to ameliorate rural class conflict. Small farms served large farms, both ideologically and by providing laborers, which clarified, for Kautsky, why a state as subservient as the Prussian to the interests of large landholders would promote small farming through the Settlement Commission. The Social Democratic Party rejected a policy of *Bauernschutz*, the protection of farmers, Kautsky explained, because it amounted to "not the protection of farmers but rather the protection of farmers' property." Farmer's property, however, the smallhold farm, was "the main cause of the immiseration of the farmer."[140]

Kautsky also addressed migrant labor, relying primarily on Karl Kaerger's work on the Sachsengänger. He noted that employers hired these migrants because they could be paid less, having lower economic expectations, and also were less able to resist domination because they lived as foreigners among a hostile population, sometimes without a common language. Nonetheless, the experience of Polish seasonal workers in Germany gave them new demands that put them in a revolutionary position when they returned home: "The same elements that appear here as menials, gladly submitting to exploitation and oppression, become agitators stirring up dissatisfaction and class hatred" in their home regions. Kautsky bemoaned, like many of his conservative opponents, the employment of teenage female migrant workers, and criticized Kaerger for endorsing underage female labor as necessary for the cultivation of sugarbeets, or sugarbeet *Kultur*, as Germans termed it. "We social democratic vandals," he chided, "have no appreciation for the culture of beets through the unculture of humans."[141] It would have been more consistent with the social democratic spirit of his work had Kautsky, like Kaerger, endorsed teenage female migrant labor, for, as we have seen, these new proletarian subjects, defying the expectations of patriarchal households, created, in effect, a revolutionary culture that challenged class and gender hierarchies in their home villages and in Germany.

For Kautsky, the question of agriculture was less a question of the countryside than a question about the role of the patriarchal household in capitalism and in a future socialist society. He advocated ending the household as a site of capitalist labor in agriculture or anywhere else, and also ending the Gesindeordnung, the Servants' Code, which exempted agricultural workers from German employment law and made them instead dependent members of their employer's household. The historically changing sexual division of labor in agriculture, as well as industry, refuted, according to Kautsky, those who presented boundaries between men's work and women's work "as natural, that is, as 'eternal' in relation to social institutions." Kautsky promised that socialism would bring to an end the economic form of household labor, with the exploitation of women and children and the disproportionate authority of the father. Rather than as workers, or as guardians of an "inheritance" (*Erbe*), women and children would be part of a free association based on individual love, without an economic basis.[142] Kautsky meant "inheritance" here to refer to the property, whether rural smallhold, bourgeois fortune, or aristocratic manor, whose preservation the family guaranteed. In fact, the family guaranteed also a racial "inheritance," a biological "*Erbe*" whose preservation similarly required the control of women and children. Kautsky did not discuss race, regarding it, like most Marxists at that time, as an invalid category of social thought not worthy of serious discussion. This racial inheritance, however, was what the Prussian Settlement Commission meant to protect with the family farm, and it was for this reason that it sought to bolster the household as fervently as Kautsky looked forward to its demise.[143]

RACE AND THE "DARK URGE FOR PERSONAL FREEDOM": MAX WEBER AND W.E.B. DU BOIS

Members of the Verein für Sozialpolitik did not share the racial and national concerns of the Prussian Settlement Commission at first, remarking that smallholding should be encouraged all over Germany, and not only in those areas with large Polish populations. Schmoller and Knapp emphasized race and racism in their accounts of free labor in the United States and, thus, indirectly, in their studies of free labor in Germany. Before the 1890s they did not, however, apply the American "Negro question" directly to German conditions, seeing race as a means to control American free labor, much as rental contracts served as a means to control German free agricultural labor.

Max Weber finally made race a central concern of German sociology, bringing the racism of the Settlement Commission to the center of discussions in the Verein für Sozialpolitik about the control of free labor in Germany. Even before joining the Verein für Sozialpolitik in 1890, Max Weber had a special connection to the activities of the Settlement Commission. His father, Max Sr., a National Liberal member of the Prussian House of Deputies, had helped write the law establishing the Settlement Commission in 1886.[144] Two years later, in 1888, Max Weber Jr. moved with his Army reserve unit from Alsace to Posen, one of the areas of activity of the Prussian Settlement Commission. Bismarck had proposed, as one of a number of anti-Polish measures to supplement internal colonization, transferring predominantly German military units to Polish areas, and perhaps this explains the relocation of Weber's own unit.[145] At the end of his first year of service in that eastern province, Weber toured some of the estates set up by the Settlement Commission. Weber also participated in military exercises in Posen in 1888, 1891, and 1894, and much of what he saw in the East repelled him. "From that time on," his wife and biographer, Marianne Weber, would later recall, "he felt one of the most important political problems was the winning of the East by a policy of settlement."[146]

In the 1890s, race became an increasingly important political and economic category in Germany and the United States and, indeed, in much of the world. In that decade, much of the German right, as we have seen, including Verein für Sozialpolitik member Adolph Wagner, embraced anti-Semitism. To the East, anti-Semites in the Russian Empire had been carrying out pogroms since the 1880s, encouraged by the anti-

Semitism of the czarist government. To the West, a virulent political anti-Semitism emerged in France during the Dreyfus affair, beginning in 1894 and dragging on into the early twentieth century. Racism also increased its already considerable importance in the United States in the 1890s. The "Jim Crow" laws that spread segregation from schools and public transportation to everything from drinking fountains to the Bibles used to swear oaths in court were also created in the 1890s and after, no legacy of the Old South, but an innovation of the New South, as C. Van Woodward famously demonstrated in 1951.[147] A series of Supreme Court decisions, culminating in the 1896 *Plessy vs. Ferguson* case, gave laws enforcing racial segregation the blessing of the American Constitution. The lynching of blacks by white mobs, already all too common, became in the 1890s increasingly frequent, brutal, and public, with body parts taken as "trophies" from victims and openly celebratory newspaper coverage. As a result of its victories in the Spanish-American War, the United States joined European colonial powers in shouldering the "white man's burden" overseas. The 1890s also saw an increase in anti-immigrant agitation in the United States, culminating in such racist landmarks as Madison Grant's 1916 *Passing of the Great Race*, and the emergence of nativist and reactionary "100 per cent Americanism."[148] While racism certainly played a central role in European and American politics before the 1890s, the 1890s saw an intensification of racist politics on both sides of the Atlantic.

Anti-Polish racism distinguished Weber's political engagements and his intellectual development.[149] Weber joined the Eastern Marches Society, dedicated to "Germanizing" the Polish provinces of Prussia, and the Pan-German League, an ultranationalist pressure group. He also belonged to the National Social Union, one of the many new "social" parties offering a patriotic and religious alternative to the Social Democrats. In 1896, at the founding meeting of the National Social Union, Weber attacked the leader of the party, his friend Friedrich Naumann, for his lack of hostility toward Poles. Naumann should not protest, offered Weber, against "reducing the Poles to second-class citizens of Germany" because "the opposite is true: we were the first to make the Poles into humans."[150] In 1899 Weber resigned from the Pan-German League, explaining that, while he supported the aims and leaders of the organization, he believed it did not work with sufficient diligence against Poles in Germany, yielding to the interests of agrarian capitalists in cheap migrant labor.[151] In 1918 Weber would make an exception to his own strictures against professors acting as political leaders, calling on students to follow him "to see to it that the first Polish official who dares to enter Danzig is hit by a bullet." (No students volunteered, and Marianne Weber recalled that many listeners walked out on him.)[152] Weber stood at the racist extreme of a number of organizations, including the Verein für Sozialpolitik, pushing them to focus more attention on racial questions and advocating the exclusion of Poles from Germany. Weber made racism, moreover, a prominent element of his politics and scholarship, including the cultural studies of economic life for which he is widely admired today.

Weber concurred with the concerns of his colleagues in the Verein about the social instability brought about by free labor in capitalist agriculture. The rise of free labor in the Prussian East had, Weber and his colleagues in the Verein agreed, circumscribed the paternal authority of landlords, increasing the freedom of those workers who remained on the land and allowing many to leave the countryside for the greater prosperity of industrial employment. For Max Weber, Polish workers migrated to the West not so much for wages as to break with their subordination in "the entire ensemble of family and familiar environment." In fact, when Weber accounted for the miserable living conditions and long working hours of Sachsengänger, he found net wages no higher for Polish migrants than for Poles who remained in the East. The migrant was pushed, rather, by what Weber called a "dark urge for personal freedom."[153] Few members of the Verein, and certainly not Weber, had any nostalgia for, or desire to resuscitate, the feudal economy of the Junker estate. Rather than applauding the new freedom and prosperity gained by workers, however, Weber, like other members of the Verein, worried that it would lead to rural proletarianization, class conflict, and the growth of social democracy.

To these well established social and political anxieties, Weber added his own cultural and racial concerns. A "rapidly growing mass of foreign laborers with lower standards of living," Weber warned, was replacing the German farmers who left the land for urban employment or who migrated overseas. Weber worried that the "swarm of eastern nomads" would bring German workers down to the cultural level of the "Polish proletariat" in those eastern regions where Germans did not, as they did in Saxony, "look down with contempt on the low standard of living of the Sachsengänger."[154] Landlords, Weber recognized, benefited not only from the lower wages of these migrant workers but also from the ease of controlling such "precariously employed foreigners." The Prussian East had, through what Weber identified as its typical patriarchal forms of authority, preserved the "military virtue" of the rural population and "created the political might of the nation."[155] Polish migrants now threatened these German virtues. Weber also worried that the low economic and cultural standards of the Polish workers would degrade those of the German workers who had to compete with them. "It is not possible," Weber declared "to allow two nations with different bodily constitutions—differently constructed stomachs . . . —to compete freely as workers in the same area." German workers could only compete with Poles, Weber explained, by descending a "cultural step [*Kulturstufe*]." Weber thus called for the "absolute exclusion of the Russian-Polish workers from the German East."[156] Weber did not look back to feudalism with nostalgia, but rather called for a new racial politics for an era of free labor.

Max Sering, a professor of agricultural economics at the University of Berlin, agreed with Weber that Sachsengänger and others who wandered out of the East were motivated less by the prospect of higher wages than by a desire for "increased independence" and "personal respect." It was, Sering observed, "the ideal of freedom and human dignity" spread— "often in a crude form"—to the "lowest social levels." Sering hoped his research would help the Prussian state satisfy the new "feelings of independence of the worker" by encouraging smallhold farming. The state could thereby encourage a "social order that lessens the current differences of property and the opposition of classes and removes the causes of the depopulation of the East." By depopulation, Sering clearly meant the emigration of ethnic Germans from the East, for there was no shortage of Poles willing to work in Prussia. Settlement would make Polish migrant labor unnecessary, keep Germans workers in the East, and make a "protective barrier for the state against the external and internal enemy."[157]

Max Weber brought questions about race directly into discussions about German free labor, adding racial purity and racial contamination to the long-standing concerns in the Verein about free agricultural labor in the East. George Friedrich Knapp proclaimed in 1893 that Weber's research on agricultural labor in the East had showed members of the Verein that "our expertise has come to an end, and we must start to learn all over again."[158] Thanks to the wide admiration he won for his writings on eastern agriculture, Weber was appointed professor of economics at the University of Freiburg in 1895. That May, like all new professors in Germany, Weber delivered a public address on his current research. Weber's inaugural lecture treated agricultural labor in the German East as, he explained, "an *example* illustrating the role . . . that physical and mental race differences [*Rassendifferenzen*] between nationalities play in the economic struggle for existence." Weber elucidated for his audience how the Pole succeeded as a farmer in the East, "not *in spite*, but rather *because*, of his low physical and mental habits," which allowed him to flourish in conditions too difficult for Germans. Weber praised the "systematic colonization of German farmers" being carried out by the Prussian state in its eastern provinces, and reminded his audience that "our descendants will make us responsible before history . . . for the amount of elbowroom we wrest for ourselves in the world." Speaking just months before Booker T. Washington delivered his "Atlanta Compromise," Weber described to his audience the dangers emerging from "the German farmer" being driven from the land in the East by a "lower race" (*tiefer-stehenden Rasse*), the Poles.[159] Max Weber and Booker T. Washington held quite different political views, but they shared a sense that struggles for economic and political freedom involved, in a fundamental sense, struggles for and against racial equality.

Another young social scientist, W.E.B. Du Bois, brought expertise about African Americans to the Verein für Sozialpolitik when he joined the organization as a doctoral student in Berlin. After completing a master's degree at Harvard, Du Bois traveled to Berlin to complete perhaps the most prestigious social science degree in the world, a Ph.D. in economics at the University of Berlin. Many of the leading American economists and social scientists of the late nineteenth and early twentieth centuries pursued similar courses of study. Du Bois spent the entire 1892–93 academic year and the first semester of the 1893–94 year in Berlin. Historians have shown how much German social science contributed to W.E.B. Du Bois's education.[160] Du Bois's own contributions to German social science are less well known, at least in part because historians have paid little attention to the importance of race and racism, including the situation of African Americans, in the work of the Verein für Sozialpolitik.

Gustav Schmoller and other members of the Verein für Sozialpolitik must have welcomed the twenty-four-year-old W.E.B. Du Bois as an expert on African Americans when he arrived at the University of Berlin in the fall of 1892. Max Weber had just published his first major essay on free labor as a racial problem in eastern Prussia, bringing to the German context some of the questions Schmoller had been asking about black free labor in the United States since 1866. In addition to a number of lecture courses, including from Verein members Adolph Wagner and Max Sering, Du Bois enrolled in the political economy seminar run by Gustav Schmoller and his student Karl Rathgen. Such seminars, focusing on student research, formed the core of advanced university study in Germany. Schmoller set Du Bois to work on "the labor question in the southern United States."[161] Du Bois used, he reported, "material already in my possession, from the United States census reports, Agriculture and labor reports, etc." to produce a long paper titled: "Der Gross- und Klein Betrieb des Ackerbaus, in der Südstaaten der Vereinigten Staaten, 1840–90" ("Small- and large farming in the southern states of the United States, 1840–90"). Schmoller evidently appreciated the work, for he encouraged Du Bois to develop it into a doctoral thesis or publish it as an article in the *Jahrbuch für Gesetzgebung*, Schmoller's famous journal.[162] Du Bois chose to continue this research as a dissertation topic.

Du Bois encountered the racial politics of Weber and others in the Verein für Sozialpolitik during his second semester in Germany, at the March 1893 meeting of the organization in Berlin. Du Bois had joined the Verein earlier that month, presumably in order to attend that meeting, which the organization dedicated to the "rural labor question," questions about land ownership, and the preservation of small farming.[163] Du Bois was then writing a dissertation on small farming, and the meeting would have been of obvious interest to him. Perhaps in recognition of the centrality of internal colonization to rural labor, the Verein had originally planned to hold the meeting in the Prussian province of Posen, one of the areas of activity of the Settlement Commission. It relocated the meeting to Berlin, however, because a cholera outbreak in Posen threatened to diminish conference attendance.[164] Du Bois remembered having heard Weber speak while a student in Germany, and it may well have been at this meeting, where Weber instructed his colleagues about the danger of Polish racial inferiority in Germany.[165]

In his lecture at the 1893 meeting, Weber maintained that, "from a cultural standpoint," it would be preferable to bring Chinese contract laborers, or "coolies," to Germany than to allow Polish migrants, "since our German workers will not assimilate with coolies."[166] With the abolition of slavery during the nineteenth century, contract laborers from China and India came to do much of the plantation work around the world, and German discussions of employing "coolies" in Prussian agriculture were hardly unusual.[167] The year before, the government of German East Africa, after much debate, brought at least seven hundred Chinese "coolies" to work on plantations in the colony.[168] Karl Kaerger, the Verein expert on Sachsengänger, argued that it would be better to bring "Negroes" from the German colonies than to bring Chinese contract laborers or to admit Polish migrants. Since his study of the Sachsengänger in 1890, Kaerger had conducted research in German East Africa, primarily on means of compelling Africans to work for European enterprises, and he had been in the colony during the debates about Chinese contract laborers there.[169] Based on his observations in Africa, Kaerger testified to the meeting, "The Negroes work very well, just not for a long time." In Germany, he ventured, "it would be very easy to make them work consistently."[170] The published proceedings do not reveal whether Du Bois attended this discussion or whether Kaerger recognized the black doctoral student when making his remarks.

The audience at the Verein meeting, the proceedings record, burst out in laughter at Kaerger's suggestion of bringing African plantation workers to Germany. Anton Sombart, the father of the sociologist Werner Sombart and one of the founding members of the Verein für Sozialpolitik, objected to "the mulattoes and creoles that would result," proclaiming "we want to remain Teutonic [*Germanen*]."[171] The elder Sombart, like Max Weber's father a National Liberal member of the Prussian House of Deputies and an advocate of internal colonization, owned a sugarbeet estate in Saxony and thus possessed a more direct interest in the question of rural labor than any of his colleagues in the Verein.[172] Adolph Wagner, to vigorous applause, warned against discussing the "Chinese question" and the "Negro question," worrying that the press would report that the Verein had declared: "if there is no other means to keep the workers under control [in Ordnung], and if it furthers the interests of the . . . landlords, then we can call upon such foreign workers."[173] Max Weber cautioned against taking Kaerger's remark too seriously. Kaerger, Weber explained, was excessively enthusiastic about "the idea of patriarchal domination, on the model of an energetic rural patriarch over his workers," and thus understood the Negro here, as he had in his writings on German East Africa, "neither as a human nor as cattle, but rather as a dependent laborer [Kerl]." Weber, as we have seen, like Knapp and other Verein members, disagreed with Kaerger about the value and feasibility of restoring feudal, patriarchal relations on the land. He argued instead that Poles (as well, presumably, as blacks and Chinese) should be kept out of the East in the interest of the preserving the livelihood of German workers and the integrity of the German nation. Weber's interest in black workers as models of subordinated labor surviving the demise of feudalism would grow after his visit, a decade later, to Tuskegee Institute and his personal observations of African Americans in the South.

Du Bois presented his completed Ph.D. thesis, "Der landwirtschaftliche Gross- und Kleinbetrieb in den Vereinigten Staaten" ("Large- and Small Agricultural Enterprises in the United States"), later that year, in December 1893, to Schmoller's seminar.[174] The question of the relative advantages of small and large farms was an important and contested topic in Germany at the time. The Verein für Sozialpolitik and the Prussian Settlement Commission, as we have seen, hoped that state-sponsored small farms would both prevent the spread of social democracy and also further an internal colonial project of Germanizing the Polish provinces of Prussia. The thesis that Du Bois wrote does not survive. Coming from the United States, Du Bois would have seen the small farm from a different perspective than that of his German teachers. For African American freedpeople, small farms had initially served as a means to expropriate and divide the lands of their former masters, securing economic independence for families that had once been treated as chattel, who could be separated and sold for the profit of the landlord. Yet the sharecropping system of the United States produced a system analogous to, although even more exploitative and oppressive than, the small farming of the Prussian East. The hopes for small farming had been much greater for African American freedpeople and the reality much worse than that of their Prussian counterparts. In the judgment of Adolph Wagner, the second reader, Du Bois "succeeded in bringing much material together to prove that American experience offers no ground for the assumption that agriculture tends to develop toward the large-farming system, as the most advantageous."[175] Du Bois, Wagner related, defended the small farm with the example of farms in the American South. Du Bois's German dissertation may have been the source of Wagner's observation, in an 1894 textbook, that since emancipation African Americans had achieved some economic success in small farming on rented land, in a situation resembling colonial settlement.[176] All that stood between Du Bois and his German Ph.D. in the spring of 1894 was a fourth semester at the university and an examination. The Slater Fund, however, which had supported Du Bois's studies in Germany, refused to fund this final semester and thus forced Du Bois to return to the United States without a degree, despite having written a well-received dissertation for his advisors in Berlin.

Du Bois was an ambivalent student of Schmoller's and of other German social scientists. He provided his German teachers unique expertise on African American freedpeople, but he never accepted the anti-Polish racism that Weber introduced into the Verein für Sozialpolitik, or the ambivalence about free labor that had long been central to the organization. While he shared the commitment of his mentors to use social science for the public good, he had a quite different view of the public good, especially of the supposed social value of racial hierarchies. During his first winter in Berlin, before the 1893 meeting of the Verein, Du Bois visited Krakow, in Austrian Poland, at the invitation of an aristocratic Polish classmate who advised Du Bois to observe German-Polish "race antagonism" and compare it with that in the United States.[177] The dissertation that Du Bois wrote for his Harvard history Ph.D., *The Suppression of the African Slave-Trade to the United States of America, 1638–1870*, followed, he explained, "the general principles laid down in German universities" to produce "a chapter of history which is of peculiar interest to the sociologist." Du Bois did not equivocate about racism and free labor in his dissertation, however. He praised Toussaint Louverture for initiating the processes that would ultimately end slavery through "bloody terror, which contrived a Negro 'problem' for the Western Hemisphere." He condemned slavery in the United States as a result of "the cupidity and carelessness of our ancestors," not accepting it, as Knapp and others in fact did, as a once valid means of securing labor for plantation agriculture.[178] Yet, while some of the statements that Weber and his colleagues made about Poles and blacks, many in Du Bois's hearing, were quite racist by most twenty-first-century standards, they were mild by nineteenth-century American standards. Du Bois himself, coming from the United States of the 1890s, was, in fact, surprised by how little antiblack racism he experienced in Germany and elsewhere in Europe.[179]

Du Bois understood the political universe of the Verein für Sozialpolitik, even if he did not endorse its combination of paternalist state policy, nationalism, and even racism. In notes on "the Present Condition of German Politics," Du Bois described "socialism" as a "middle course" between the "militarism" necessary for German survival and the democracy desired by much of its population: "As the army cares for the national fortresses, so the wonderfully trained bureaucracy is to care for the people: to protect, guide, and educate them." Clearly, Du Bois understood socialism to mean the state socialism of his teachers rather than social democracy, for he categorized socialism as a right-wing doctrine. He reasoned that, while Social Democrats fit on the political right because they supported socialism, they should really be classified as leftist because they stood for "democracy far more than socialism." In another essay, probably written a few years later, Du Bois surmised that the state socialism supported by the Verein was too anti-democratic to find adherents among Social Democrats.[180] Du Bois noted the growing importance of anti-Semitism in German politics, describing it as the use of "racial hatred" as a motive force for "socialism," since "German industry is largely in the hands of the Jews" who also "practically control the stock-market, own the press, fill the bar and bench, are crowding the professions." Adolph Wagner, the second reader of Du Bois's dissertation, campaigned unsuccessfully as an anti-Semite in the Reichstag elections that year and Du Bois's assertions perhaps reflect Wagner's political lectures and the anti-Semitic fliers that his sympathizers distributed outside his classroom.[181] There is no evidence that Du Bois was anything but repelled by anti-Semitism, as well as by anti-Polish racism.

Yet Du Bois did not reject all that he had learned about race from his German teachers. From the Verein für Sozialpolitik Du Bois learned to see race as a transnational issue, as Schmoller, Weber, and other German social scientists did. Questions about race and racism no longer appeared to him confined to the American South. "Under these teachers and in this social setting," he later recalled of his studies in Germany, "I began to see the race problem in America, the problem of the peoples of Africa and Asia, and the political development of Europe as one."[182] In an 1897 address to Crummell's American Negro Academy, Du Bois maintained that every race had "to develop for civilization its particular message, its particular ideal, which shall help to guide the world nearer and nearer that perfection of human life for which we all long." He characterized the messages of the "English nation," "the German nation," and the "Romance nations," and called on the academy to formulate "the full, complete Negro message of the whole Negro race." Like his German teachers, Du Bois doubted the biological significance of race but insisted on race as an important social and historical category.[183] Less than a decade after his Berlin studies, he would formulate his famous statement about the transnational character of race at the Pan-African Conference in London: "The problem of the twentieth century is the problem of the color line, the question as to how far differences of race—which show themselves chiefly in the color of the skin and the texture of the hair—will hereafter be made the basis of denying to over half the world the right of sharing to their utmost ability the opportunities and privileges of modern civilization."[184] Du Bois came to share with his German teachers the sense that race and racism supported many types of political and economic domination around the world. He concentrated his attention on white oppression of blacks but, as his Polish classmate had taught him in Krakow, racial oppression existed also in Europe.

Members of the Verein combined the knowledge about blacks that Du Bois brought to the organization with Max Weber's racial sociology of the German East to make their empirical variety of economics as universal as the abstract political economy of both neoclassical economists and Marxists. Unlike individual nations, races are inherently transnational, as mobile as their individual members. In his 1900 textbook, *Outline of General Economics (Grundriß der allgemeinen Volkswirtschaftslehre)*, Schmoller outlined such a transnational racial political economy. Humanity, for Schmoller, was no abstract concept, and he faulted the political and economic sciences of the eighteenth century, as well as their nineteenth-century followers, for ignoring "the laws of national character." While suggesting that Arthur de Gobineau had exaggerated the importance of Aryans to human progress, Schmoller agreed with the well-known French theorist that race helped determine national character. "Economics makes sound judgments when it proceeds not merely from abstract humans or even from just their economic activity, but rather when it attends to the varieties of racial types." (Neither Schmoller nor any of his colleagues understood race in a narrowly biological sense. Not only racial "inherited properties" shaped individuals, Schmoller explained, but also "the influence of the great spiritual fluid . . . that surrounds them, that affects them through imitation, education, and social interaction.")[185] The attention to the transnational category of race allowed German social scientists to develop what they called national economics into a global, but nonetheless empirically grounded, economic theory.

Schmoller, like other German social scientists, pointed to blacks as a decisive case establishing the foundational importance of race to economic analysis. To correct earlier economists' inattention to racial characteristics, Schmoller surveyed the "lowest races," beginning with the "Negro" of Africa and America. Schmoller, like New South ideologues, defined the "Negro" around a contradiction between an aptitude for menial work and an inability to do this work without the intervention of external authority. Negroes, according to Schmoller, were all hand and no head: they had no sense for "ideals" or "truth" but they did have "strong muscles" and "naively sensual, strong sentiments." Schmoller suggested that blacks possessed a contradictory nature that could run amok without external control: They were, he ventured, "good natured and naturally gentle" but also subject to "unbridled fantasies and brutality"; they were "vain, exuberant like children in their joy" but "they eat human flesh and kill from passion without a sting of conscience; they die from homesickness, but every tune makes them dance." Blacks could be, Schmoller suggested, better laborers than Europeans, but only, again, with outside direction. "Their physical strength and skill exceeds Europeans," but adults suffer from "complete mental stagnation." They only work when they must, "never freely, out of pleasure in their work." The economy of Africa, Schmoller contended, was hindered by constraining customs and a lack of good transportation, as well as the political division of the continent into many "small tribes." Africa lacked, that is, precisely those interventions that European colonial rule promised.[186] After the turn of the twentieth century, Schmoller would thus lead a number of members of the Verein für Sozialpolitik to work closely with the German Colonial Office.

The racial thought of Max Weber, combined with the knowledge about African Americans that Du Bois and others brought to the Verein für Sozialpolitik, allowed German social scientists to begin to synthesize the internal and external forms of colonialism that Schmoller had originally distinguished. External colonization meant conquering foreign territory, while internal colonization involved, as Schmoller had put it in 1886, the "definitive settling" of Germans on previously conquered territory. Internal colonization involved settling populations on small farms, with their attendant social, sexual, economic, political, racial, and national constraints and hierarchies. As race became, for members of the Verein, including Du Bois, a transnational phenomenon, not localized in the southern United States or in eastern Prussia, but rather a global "color line," the difference between internal and external colonization began to fade. Internal colonization became ever more like racial conquest in the 1890s, as the struggle against mobile Polish migrants became an increasingly important component of the program to settle German farmers. External colonization, as we shall see in the next chapter, became ever more like internal colonization, as colonial authorities sought to control African populations by settling Africans, like Germans, on small family farms. In the half century before the First World War, an increasingly interconnected, transnational, and self-referential complex of ideologies and practices of race, sexuality, and labor emerged on both sides of the Atlantic. The first application of this complex outside Germany or the United States occurred in Togo, under the auspices of the German colonial state with assistance from Booker T. Washington and students and faculty from Tuskegee Institute.

Chapter 3

ALABAMA IN AFRICA:

TUSKEGEE AND THE COLONIAL

DECIVILIZING MISSION IN TOGO

IN THE MIDDLE DECADES of the nineteenth century, the region of West Africa that became the German colony of Togo enjoyed new economic opportunities as the Atlantic slave trade declined. Many West Africans established diverse household economies incorporating manufacturing and agriculture and carried on a profitable trade with European and Hausa merchants. The colonial states founded at the end of the century redirected these new African economies into channels that aggrandized state power and colonial capital. One of the principal means of subordinating Africans, both politically and economically, to European elites, involved forcing them to produce raw materials, like industrial-grade cotton, onerous and unprofitable for producers but essential for metropolitan industry. Central to African self-emancipation, as well as to colonial efforts to subvert this emancipation, was a series of struggles over African identity. Africans were not blank slates on which colonial elites could inscribe identities according to their desires. Indeed, colonial elites had changing and often contradictory desires, and Africans, like all human beings, had changing and often contradictory identities, often suited to changing political and economic opportunities. New identities that Africans or Europeans desired had to be superimposed on, and created and legitimized in terms borrowed from, previous identities.

Before the onset of colonial rule, Germans interacted on terms of relative equality with Africans in Togo who participated in the booming mercantile economy of the coast, based largely on African palm oil exports. Many West Africans attended missionary schools, present in Togo from the middle of the nineteenth century, to learn to read and write English so that they could obtain white-collar jobs as merchants or as clerks for European businesses and, later, for government offices. While colonial states and businesses depended on white-collar blacks, widespread African aspirations for upward mobility also threatened the colonial political economies that emerged at the end of the nineteenth century. In seeking to transform African identities, colonial states turned to mission schools because Africans themselves already employed these institutions as part of their own political and economic self-fashioning. The state persuaded missionary schools in Togo to promote an African ethnic identity, Ewe (pronounced EH-vey or EH-wey), among the population of southern Togo. This was a common technique of colonial rule, in which Europeans imposed constructed, homogenous ethnicities on indigenous populations to divide them from each other and from cosmopolitan African elites.[1]

In turning to Tuskegee Institute after the turn of the century, however, the German state inaugurated a new colonial strategy, proposing an identity constructed outside of Africa, the ideal of the "Negro" taken from the ideology of the New South and Tuskegee Institute. The German state had trouble persuading missionary teachers to promote this New South racial identity in their schools, for it meant, in the exaggerated terms in which the colonial state understood it, renouncing catechism, literacy, and academic study in favor of menial labor. Africans would have stayed away from schools offering such a curriculum, even if missionaries had been willing to found them. The Tuskegee expedition to Togo, in the mistaken belief that the conditions of the New South represented progress for Africans, assisted the colonial state in bringing to many Africans what counted, by African, American, and European standards, as downward mobility. The German state enlisted Tuskegee Institute and New South ideology in what could be called, borrowing from contemporary terminology, a colonial decivilizing mission in Africa. The Tuskegee expedition to Togo participated in a program of forced cotton cultivation and compulsory training designed not only to transform African agriculture, but also African gender, sexuality, and families, seeking to impose monogamous, patriarchal domesticity on extended households that had previously afforded husbands, wives, and children a great deal of personal autonomy. The "Negro" identity that emerged in Togo was shaped as much by the prior African identifications that it both built on and sought to undermine as it was by the New South ideology from which it originated.

TOGO BETWEEN ATLANTIC SLAVERY AND GERMAN COLONIAL RULE

The Atlantic slave trade devastated the small polities of southern Togo, stuck between the two major slave-trading states of Asante and Dahomey, feeding the practically inexhaustible appetite of European and American slave traders. Togo is located on the western end of the Bight of Benin, a section of the West African coast between the Volta River and the Niger Delta once known, for obvious reasons, as the Slave Coast. Germany gave its territorial claim on the Bight of Benin the name Togo to suggest that the "treaty of protection" that the German Gustav Nachtigal had concluded on July 5, 1884, with King Mlapa of Togoville, a village on the

northern shore of Lake Togo, applied to the entire region between French
Dahomey to the east and British Gold Coast to the west.[2] Between 1640
and 1870, slavers took more than 1.8 million Africans from the Bight of
Benin. This accounted for some 15–20 percent of the almost 12 million
taken in the Atlantic slave trade.[3] In the eighteenth century, slave traders
took almost half of those captured from the Bight of Benin to the French
sugar colony of St. Domingue, where they made up about a quarter of the
enslaved population.[4] The religious practices that slaves from the Bight
of Benin brought to St. Domingue contributed significantly to Vodou, a
religion important in organizing the first successful uprising against slavery in the New World, in 1791, when St. Domingue won independence
and its present name, Haiti.[5] In the nineteenth century, with Haiti free,
slaveholders in Brazil took the largest portion of the captives from the
Bight of Benin, about a third. Some free Afro-Brazilians even returned to
the Bight of Benin in the late eighteenth century to participate in the slave
trade, and Afro-Brazilians remain a powerful elite in Togo and elsewhere
in West Africa even to this day.[6]

   The Bight of Benin as a whole, in the estimate of historian Patrick Manning, suffered the most pronounced and long-term population decline of
any region in Africa affected by the slave trade. The disproportionate
export of male slaves meant that the male-to-female sex ratio in the region
recovered from its late-eighteenth-century low of approximately sixty
men for every hundred women only in the second half of the nineteenth
century.[7] The unusual economic and personal autonomy of women in
southern Togo, even in the early twentieth century, a common complaint
of European authorities and some African men, may even have resulted
in part from this demographic effect of the slave trade.

   The people of southern Togo enjoyed a brief period of relative freedom
and prosperity in the second half of the nineteenth century, as they recovered from the demographic, economic, and political catastrophe of the
slave trade, and before the new catastrophe of German colonial rule.[8] The
Ewe had had no unified state to protect them from the depredations of
the slave trade so, between the decline of the Atlantic slave trade and the
imposition of German rule, no state to oppress them either. In southern
Togo in this period, production occurred in extended households that
allowed every member personal autonomy. Several wives shared a single
husband, typically rotating four-day housekeeping shifts and thus retaining sufficient free time to pursue independent economic activities.
Husbands and wives lived separately, with their own houses, fields, property, cattle, and, if they could afford them, slaves. Men lived with their
older sons, and wives with their youngest children and their daughters.[9]
Children also possessed cattle independently of their parents. Men and
women carried out different economic tasks, so boys learned to work by

assisting their fathers, and girls by helping their mothers. Girls learned to farm, cook, keep house, and spin homegrown cotton into yarn. Boys learned to cultivate cassava, yams, and other produce, to make palm wine, and sometimes to weave. Boys could also work as porters, turning over the money they earned to their fathers, but receiving rewards for the cash.

Market exchanges and gifts linked separate household economies in southern Togo. Boys presented their mothers with produce, woven cloth, or game. These gifts gave a son a good reputation, which would later attract his own wives. "He who takes good care of his mother," ran one Ewe saying current at the turn of the century, "also honors his wife."[10] Husbands also paid bridewealth to the fathers of their wives.[11] Wives expected regular gifts from their husbands, including yearly allotments of clothing.[12] A woman could shame a stingy husband by wearing torn clothes, making his alleged neglect public.[13] The missionary teacher Anna Knüsli remembered that, when a missionary asked a group of African men to say something nice about women, the best they could offer was that "if you give a really nice gift to a woman, she can sometimes be friendly."[14] Women, in fact, had greater economic power than the language of gifts suggests, for they did not depend economically on men.

Men did indeed single out women for oppression and exploitation in the practice of debt peonage. Creditors did not earn interest from debtors but rather gained the use of collateral put up for the period of the loan. Thus, if land served as collateral, the creditor could cultivate it; if the borrower's clothes served as collateral, the creditor could wear them. A male debtor could also offer himself or one of his wives or an unmarried child as collateral. As with other forms of collateral, the creditor could use this human collateral by requiring a fixed number of days of work per week. If collateral humans died as a result of work they performed for the creditor, then the debt was discharged, but, if collateral humans died of other causes, then their bodies were exposed, unburied, until the debt was paid off and the family could reclaim the body. It is not surprising that such relationships could lead both to implacable enmity and to lasting friendships among debtor and creditor families.[15] This system remained in place throughout the entire period of German rule.[16]

With the decline of the slave trade, palm oil became the most important item of international commerce between West Africa and Europe.[17] Unlike cotton in the United States or sugarbeets in Germany, palm oil had been traded and consumed in West Africa long before it became a global commodity. Oil palms grow freely along the West African coast, and thus remained independent of the private land ownership, industrial cultivation, and biological engineering characteristic of cotton and sugarbeets. Small producers could profitably harvest palm oil for their own consumption or for sale in local or international markets. The international palm oil market thus neither required nor brought about the subordination of agricultural workers to large landowners, merchants, and industrial processors, as cotton and sugarbeets did. On the contrary, palm oil afforded its producers a certain economic autonomy.

Harvesters extracted palm oil by boiling the fruit of the oil palm, mashing it into a pulp, mixing the pulp with water, and skimming the reddish oil from the surface. Mixed with peppers and other ingredients, this oil became a basis for the sauce for fufu, dumplings of mashed cassava and African yams, whose importance to West African cuisine can hardly be overstated. Palm oil could also be used as an ointment and for other medicinal purposes. By fermenting the sap of the oil palm, individuals could make palm wine, an important intoxicant often used to conclude certain business transactions, including loans, in West Africa. Palm oil also had further household, industrial, and medicinal uses.[18]

Europeans found as many uses for palm oil as West Africans had. Like petroleum, palm oil can be refined into separate components, including a solid fat, liquid oleic acid, and glycerin. Palm oil grease lubricated the machines of the industrial revolution that accounted for the expanding demand for American cotton. The solid fat formed a base for candles and soaps, both objects, like sugar and cotton textiles, of increasingly popular consumption in nineteenth-century Europe and the United States. Palm oil served as flux in the tinplate industry, preventing sheets of steel from oxidizing before they were dipped in molten tin. A range of industries, including food canning and roofing, used tinplate because of its strength and imperviousness to rust. The liquid oil was used as a fuel for lamps, as a substitute for whale oil. Glycerin was a component of smokeless gunpowder, as well as a range of medicines and cosmetics.

The international palm oil trade that replaced the trade in slaves on the West African coast in the nineteenth century expanded the political, economic, and cultural contact zone between Africans and European merchants. Afro-Brazilians remained an important group in the palm oil trade in Togo, but competed with other groups to a greater extent than they had in the slave trade.[19] A few large British firms dominated the European side of the palm oil trade in the first two-thirds of the nineteenth century. Later in the century, however, new regular commercial shipping lines between Europe and West Africa allowed traders, working at a scale too small to support their own freighting, to compete with the established oligopoly of British oilmen. This competition among palm oil merchants, as well as competition from new oils, most importantly petroleum, lowered the price of palm oil by as much as half between 1850 and 1885. Increasing European demand, however, allowed the palm oil industry to remain profitable by increasing output as prices declined. The last third

FIGURE 3.1. Oil palms along the road to Tove. The political independence of Tove prior to the German conquest in 1894–95 rested on its abundant supply of oil palms, as well as its pottery industry. The area around Tove still has abundant oil palms. Photograph by author, January 2005.

of the nineteenth century thus saw ever more Africans and Europeans trading ever greater quantities of palm oil.[20]

A new palm kernel oil industry foreshadowed the colonial transformation of the West African economy. Extracting the clear, liquid oil of palm seeds required more labor and capital than rendering the thick red oil of the palm fruit, and palm kernel oil itself had more uses in Europe than in Africa. Palm kernel oil could be made into an inexpensive butter substitute more appealing than the mixture of suet and other fats that had previously gone under the name margarine. Palm kernels could also be made into a fattening cattle cake that increased milk yields, improved butterfat, and gave butter a more appealing color.[21] African processors dried and cracked seeds one by one before selling them to merchants, who shipped them to Hamburg for further processing. Before the First World War, German mills enjoyed a near monopoly over the palm kernel industry.[22] Like the later West African cotton economy, the trade in palm kernel oil made African workers dependent on European industrial capital, since African producers could not render their own palm kernel oil, and this oil did not possess the numerous local uses that the oil of the palm fruit did. The palm kernel industry indicated a larger transition in West Africa from the mercantile economy that emerged after emancipation to a colonial economy based on the exploitation of African labor by European industrial capital.

Germany gained prominence in the newer, more competitive palm oil markets of the later nineteenth century. Many of the new commercial shipping lines and oil-trading firms operated out of Hamburg and, to a lesser extent, Bremen. By 1880, Hamburg alone handled nearly a third of all overseas trade with West Africa.[23] A single German firm virtually monopolized the shipment of palm oil from Lagos, perhaps the most import oil exporting port in Africa.[24] Hamburg also dominated the marketing and processing of palm kernel oil. German merchant houses with West African interests sent men in their early twenties, typically for three-year periods, to run coastal warehouses, or "factories," with the help of African "clerks."[25] These factories sold European goods, including liquor, tobacco, perfumes, and other wares demanded by Africans and purchased palm oil and seeds. Merchants stored palm oil in these factories between arrivals of commercial liners. Clerks worked the factory stores, managed the factory stock, and weighed the palm kernels and oil that Africans came to sell. To increase their business, factories also advanced goods on credit to African intermediaries, who sold them at inland markets to which Europeans did not have easy access before the establishment of colonial hegemony. Local leaders sponsored markets of various sizes, collecting a small fee from those who entered. These markets met at set intervals, when work

FIGURE 3.2. Market day in Togo. Togo had a lively market economy before German conquest. Local leaders sponsored periodic markets, where Togolese met to trade and to socialize. Only with the expansion of the colonial state could European merchants operate in these inland markets. Source: Photography Collection of Anton Codelli (taken between 1911 and 1914), Slovenski etnografski muzej, Ljubljana, Slovenia (hereafter SEM), F 34420.

stopped and local inhabitants went to buy and sell, but also to socialize.[26] They sold all manner of local, European, and Hausa goods.[27]

There was a lively competition among the European factories for the business of Africans with palm oil to sell. Women dominated commerce in southern Togo, both at hinterland markets and in the trade with European merchants and their male African clerks. In urban households, women's economic role might even consist exclusively of marketing.[28] To this day, the most prestigious merchants in Lomé are women, the famous "Nana Benz" (as in Mercedes Benz).[29] European merchants evidently found the commercial role of women in Africa unsettling, and one German worried that French merchants charmed female African traders away with a "friendly smile and a glass of gin."[30]

Unlike palm kernels and oil, cotton, although an important local commodity, had virtually no role in the Togolese export economy before the German state, with the help of Tuskegee Institute, forced African workers to meet the needs of the European spinning industry. Earlier attempts to profit from the cotton famine during the American Civil War taught cotton growers in Togo, as in much of the world, that they could not compete on the world market. While European manufacturers demanded cotton from any part of the world when the American Civil War sharply reduced their supplies, they found most cotton from outside the United States difficult to process and ceased purchasing from Africa, India, and elsewhere as soon as they could obtain American cotton again. During the Civil War, some Togolese near the coast borrowed money to set up plantations and purchase slaves to produce cotton for French and English merchants. One established a plantation with more than forty slaves and a cotton gin and press that exported twenty to forty bales a month to Liverpool. When, however, by the early 1870s, cotton prices in Togo declined to a tenth of their wartime high, these cotton planters lost everything. Those who had neglected subsistence crops for cotton now found they could not earn enough to buy food. Some of these slaveholders had to sell their own children into slavery just to survive.[31] Togolese learned that local cotton, an important resource within Africa, had little value on the world market.

Togolese grew cotton, like all crops, in a complex system of intercropping that, in the memorable words of historian Paul Richards, "is one of the great glories of African science. It is to African agriculture as polyrhythmic drumming is to African music and carving to African art."[32] Because draft animals could not survive sleeping sickness in much of Africa, farmers cultivated with hand tools, which did not require neat rows of single crops. Interplanting meant that fields yielded a variety of crops and never lay fallow or became overgrown with weeds. For example, farmers would plant cassava among corn stalks that had been growing for two months. After an additional two months, they would harvest the corn, planting beans in the holes left after they pulled out the corn stalks. Farmers could also rotate in other crops, such as peanuts. After two or three years, rather than leaving the land fallow, farmers would abandon the field for years, allowing bush to take it over, and clear new fields to repeat the process.[33] Intercropped fields were thus intensively farmed and constantly productive.

Togolese patterns of interplanting also improved the productivity of individual crops. Togolese farmers planted cotton seeds among young corn, so that the cotton remained in the shade of the corn stalks until around mid-August. In the shade, the cotton would grow directly toward the sun, becoming a tall, straight stalk. Furthermore, the corn prevented weeds from growing among the cotton, which meant that African farmers avoided the hard work of "chopping" cotton that occupied growers in the United States. Only after farmers harvested the corn did the cotton plants, now exposed to direct sunlight, become bushy. Cotton grown this

FIGURE 3.3. Mixed cultivation in Togo, including cotton plants and yams. German colonial agriculture initially sought to replace this mixed cultivation, which carefully balanced multiple crops, with monocultures, including of cotton. Later they accepted the interplanting of corn and cotton. Source: Albert F. Calvert, *Togoland*.

way was said to survive the ensuing dry season better than cotton grown without the initial shade of the corn.[34]

Before the interventions of the Tuskegee expedition, only women cultivated cotton in Togo. Women could sell the raw cotton at a market or spin it into yarn themselves.[35] The seeds could be removed either by hand or with a roller gin, in which the bolls were placed on a hard surface and a cylinder rolled over them to squeeze out the seeds. The cotton might be bleached in the sun, after which women and girls spun it by hand, often displaying remarkable dexterity with fast-moving, weighted spindles (see figure 3.4). The yarn could then be dyed. While women could make blacks and grays from soot, reds from iron and yellows and greens from fruits and barks, indigo blue was the most widely produced dye. Dying yarn blue required much work, including burning a tree trunk to ashes to make lye, mixing it with locally grown indigo, and soaking yarn in the mixture for almost two weeks.[36] Spinners could sell this yarn to weavers, all of whom were male, or exchange the yarn with a weaver for a share of the cloth that he produced from it. This gendered division of labor, combined with the separation of male and female households, ensured that growing

FIGURE 3.4. Spinning cotton, Togo. Using a weighted spindle to produce yarn
was an important women's industry in Togo. A skilled hand spinner could produce yarn from cotton staple of varying length and character, thus obviating the
exacting standardization required for mechanical spinning. Hand spinning is,
however, labor intensive so, while European-made cloth never displaced superior
African fabrics, European yarn did hurt the market for handspun yarn in Togo.
Source: SEM, 063.

and spinning cotton and weaving cloth would be conducted by separate,
but interdependent, economic actors.[37]

Weavers in Togo, as in much of West Africa, used looms, operated with
their hands and feet, that produced long thin strips of sturdy cloth (see
figure 3.5). Tailors then sewed these strips together with such small
stitches that they appeared to form a single large piece of cloth. (In northern Togo women operated a special loom that produced a broad cloth,
unlike the characteristic strip weaving of much of West Africa.)[38] Local
Germans obviously appreciated the virtues of West African cloth, for they
insisted that only local cloth be used to construct the hammocks in which
they were carried about on longer trips; apparently hammocks from
cheap English fabrics could not be relied upon to support their girth.[39]
Imperial Commissioner Eugen von Zimmerer, the highest German official
in Togo at that time, reported, "the farther one goes from the coast to the

FIGURE 3.5. Weaving cotton, Togo. Operating a loom with their hands and feet, weavers in Togo, like elsewhere in West Africa, produced long strips of cloth that they later sewed together to make a strong material of higher quality than the cheap fabrics sold by European merchants. In most of Togo, only men wove cotton, except in the north, where a special woman's loom produced wide pieces of fabric. Source: SEM, 064.

interior . . . hideously printed cotton fabrics" from England and Europe yielded to better "fabrics produced by the natives."[40] The advantages of industrial textiles from Europe lay in their low cost and colorful dyes rather than in the quality of the material.

MISSION SCHOOLS, WHITE-COLLAR WORK, AND POLITICAL RESISTANCE

Togolese men, like men all along the West African coast, found an avenue toward social advancement through positions as clerks in European trading firms or, with the onset of colonial rule, in government offices. These office jobs promised high pay and prestige for men in Togo, as in much of West Africa and, indeed, in much of the world. Africans needed to learn to read and write English to become clerks, for English was the language of commerce along the West African Coast. Merchant houses, even those run by Germans, required their employees to speak English, not German. German merchants apparently spoke the German language among themselves as a kind of secret cant, and, in any case, most of their customers spoke English, not German.[41] European mission schools provided the English literacy necessary for Africans to become clerks both because these schools genuinely endorsed the kind of economic and cultural life led by white-collar employees and also because the mission societies active in Togo competed for students who would go to whichever school best met their own needs.[42] "The natives here," one German official observed in 1907, "want, after [attending school], to become either a merchant or to assume a higher position than their countrymen, specifically an office worker [*Angestellte*] with a regular salary."[43]

Catholic and North German Protestant missionaries dominated formal education in southern Togo. These two missions, as well as the smaller Wesleyan and Basel missions, offered four years of primary instruction at schools throughout the region.[44] The German government forbade Christian missionaries from working in the area north of Atakpame before 1913, for it did not control the region effectively enough to ensure their safety.[45] Fewer opportunities existed for girls to attend school in colonial Togo, and the education that missions did give girls aimed, as one missionary explained, "to educate African girls into Christian housewives and mothers."[46] Such bourgeois European ideals of domesticity afforded less economic autonomy to women in Togo than the economic roles they already typically occupied.

Throughout Togo, Hausa communities provided Muslim education and Arabic instruction to their own children, and their well-known openness to treat non-Hausa as Hausa meant that this education would have also been available to local Muslims in Togo.[47] Hausa traders, originally from Nigeria, worked throughout West Africa, establishing Hausa settlements and building important trade routes. As German merchants sent African middlemen from the South to ply their wares, Hausa merchants arrived from the North with their own goods, including weapons, leather articles, textiles, and clothing. As many coastal Africans adopted European fashions, many in the North began wearing Hausa fashions. Hausa clothing sold well enough in Togolese markets that European merchants even began selling cheap imitations of Hausa turbans and other garments.[48] Even after the colonial state pushed into the Togolese hinterland, the region north of Atakpame remained oriented toward the Hausa mercantile economy, as well as Hausa religion, education, and clothing.

The most popular missionary schools in southern Togo were those that taught the most English, the essential skill for upward mobility in the coastal economy of West Africa. African students seem to have been less concerned with the theological differences among the various denominations than with the amount of English education each offered. Before the Catholics arrived in 1892, the Wesleyans were the best-known teachers of English, and thus were the favorite of coastal elites.[49] Catholic missionaries came to Togo from French Dahomey in 1892 and, like the Wesleyans, conducted their lessons almost entirely in English. By the turn of the century, the Catholics ran the most popular schools in Togo, with approximately twice as many students as the North German Mission, and about four times as many as the much smaller Wesleyan or Basel missions.[50] While the North German and Basel missions taught students primarily in an African language, they too taught most of their students English as a second language. Only a tiny minority learned German.[51] If none of the missionary schools in Togo appealed to students or their families, individuals could flee to the Gold Coast, where, by the turn of the century, 138 schools taught English reading and writing, and arithmetic. Girls could also attend these schools.[52] If a mission school in Togo had refused to teach English it would likely have lost most of its students.

While many Africans chose the English academic education available at mission schools because white-collar positions furnished greater pay and social status than manual or agricultural labor, academic education also gave broader political advantages to Africans.[53] This was especially pronounced in Gold Coast, where more extensive English education provided not just vocational education for clerks but also allowed for a lively intellectual and political culture.[54] Ewe lived on both sides of the English-German border, and many Togolese traveled to the Gold Coast for work or for an English education, or to flee the brutality of German colonial officials. German and English colonial authorities agreed that literate Africans represented a threat to colonial rule, even while they also performed necessary functions in political and business administration.[55] West Africans who could write English could communicate with each other over long distances, across colonial and linguistic boundaries, and thus challenge the monopoly colonial states sought to exercise over information within their territories and that reaching the world outside their boundaries.

Independent African newspapers published in the Gold Coast also represented the concerns of Africans under the more repressive German regime in neighboring Togo, where a free press was out of the question. Togolese read, and sometimes published articles in, Gold Coast newspapers.[56] In this sense, the Gold Coast press played a role in Togo analogous to that of the *Chicago Defender* for African Americans in the South. The British had worked with African elites in administering the Gold Coast south of the Asante Empire informally since the mid-nineteenth century and formally since 1874, asking Africans to take a greater role in political institutions in their own colony than they did in neighboring Togo. As in many colonies, the elites that the Europeans had hoped would support their political and economic hegemony often became the most effective critics of, and later revolutionaries against, colonial domination.

No figure was more important in this Gold Coast political and intellectual milieu than J. E. Casely Hayford. Born in 1866 to a prominent Gold Coast family, he studied in Fourah Bay College in Sierra Leone and read law at Cambridge University and in London. As a barrister in Gold Coast, he involved himself in the Aborigines Rights Protection Society, an organization founded by Africans in 1898 to oppose the British confiscation of unoccupied land. A supporter of the Liberian Pan-Africanist E. W. Blyden, Casely Hayford edited a number of Gold Coast papers, including the *Gold Coast Echo*, the *Gold Coast Leader*, and the *Gold Coast Chronicle*. All of these newspapers challenged British rule, "depicting," as a British writer complained, "in novel and picturesque language how the long-suffering native population is ground under the iron heel of a British administration."[57]

Gold Coast newspapers also reported critically on German administration in Togo, which permitted no African press at all. These reports were often based on firsthand accounts by Togolese who had fled the German colony. An article by an anonymous inhabitant of Togo in the *African Times and Orient Review*, a paper distributed in Gold Coast, the United States, and elsewhere, explained that, since reporting abuses by German officials resulted in further mistreatment, if a Togolese wished to air grievances, "the best thing . . . is to escape to the Gold Coast Colony or Dahomey."[58] English literacy allowed Togolese to communicate with Africans in Gold Coast and elsewhere and to expose colonial abuses to the world.

West Africans could indicate their education and cosmopolitan status by wearing European fashions (see figure 3.6). A Togolese man born in 1913 remembered that dressing in the latest fashions from Europe indicated both wealth and learning. Of unschooled wealthy men, who did not, according to this observer, wear European clothing, he recalled: "How stupid these people seemed to us. You have to have gone to school to know what is nice and fashionable."[59] Like Polish Sachsengänger who returned from their seasonal labor as Westfaloki, wearing fashionable clothing purchased in Germany, African clerks did not sport European clothing to suggest their subordination to their employers but rather their status among their own people. In fact, African "dandies" as they were called in German, as well as English, tended to dress more formally than Europeans would have for similar occasions, and perhaps also to wear slightly different fashions. The explorer Heinrich Klose described the "black dandy with . . . yellow Nanking trousers, high collars, and black tailcoat." He described an inland chief who, after a stay on the coast, exchanged his loincloth for a "white dandy suit," yellow "dandy shoes," a large hat, and blue spectacles (the latter to appear like the "literate blacks on the coast") to become a "black gentleman."[60]

FIGURE 3.6. African dandies in Togo. Many men in Togo, as in much of Africa, expressed their social status by wearing European fashions. Such clothing suggested education, English literacy, and white collar employment. European states and business depended upon such educated Africans, but many Europeans found their claims to elite status threatening to colonial white supremacy. Education not only allowed Africans to work for European authorities, but also to challenge them. Source: Photography Collection of Anton Codelli (taken between 1911 and 1914), Map and Pictorial Collection of National and University Library, Ljubljana, Slovenia, 147.

The great West African trading families and the countless white-collar Africans upon whom the international mercantile economy of the West African coast depended also posed obstacles to the colonial capitalism that emerged at the turn of the twentieth century. New colonial authorities regarded black dandies, even while they remained essential to European government and commerce, as threats to European hegemony. Dandies challenged the singularity and superiority of European culture and the uniquely European face of political and economic authority in Africa. Many educated Africans did indeed challenge European domination, not least in order to defend their own elite status. Germans applied various disparaging terms to well-dressed African clerks, often combining references to their clothing or to the fact that they lived on the coast with the German word for "Negro" or with the common English and American epithet for black people.[61]

The vitriol against blacks wearing clothing considered too European or too fancy, common among whites on both sides of the Atlantic, reflects the real challenge that educated Africans and African Americans posed to the racist underpinnings of colonial economics and politics. Europeans could both praise their own higher "civilization" and disparage those Africans who seemed to come closest to this civilization by claiming that Africans merely imitated superficial aspects of European civilization, such as the clothing, while remaining alien to the supposedly deeper and superior aspects of European civilization.[62] Writing in 1909, the German governor of Togo complained that young Africans "want to appropriate a higher culture for themselves" to obtain less physically demanding jobs and higher wages.[63] Such desires were as much a part of upward mobility in Africa as they were in Europe and the United States. European concerns with elite Africans were not really about clothing: deriding African clothing provided a way to ignore and belittle as mere costumes African writing, political power, and demands for equality.

Ewe Education and German Colonial Rule

Around the turn of the century, the German colonial state sought to limit the freedom and independence many Africans gained through small-scale palm oil production, petty commerce, and independent household production, as well as high-status, white-collar employment. Such economic freedom, in Togo as in Germany or the United States, threatened capitalist profits, for it freed workers from laboring under the control, and for the profit, of owners of capital. In 1901 the *Gold Coast Chronicle* warned its readers: "the average white man of to-day is not the white man with whom our fathers had to do—the noble guest of theirs whose word was sacred and who would not have the native think aught of him but what is honourable, and warn them to be careful, or they would surely burn their fingers."[64] Whites, according to this writer, who had once traded on relatively equal terms with Africans, now invaded Africa as would-be masters and exploiters. Gustav Schmoller, writing at the turn of the century, expressed similar views, presenting the African merchant as an adversary, rather than a trading partner, of European merchants: "In commerce he is pushy, tireless, sometimes flattering, sometimes complaining. He visits markets almost more for entertainment than for profit, but often outwits the Europeans there anyway."[65] Neither Schmoller nor the African author in the *Gold Coast Chronicle* regarded Europeans and Africans as participating on equal terms in a common market. Each had become an illegitimate and untrustworthy economic rival for the other. This was but one reflection of the counterattack conducted by states and businesses on the economic, political, and personal freedom that individuals had recently won in Togo and elsewhere around the world.

In part to work against the political threat that the colonial state perceived in African literacy in English, the North German Mission, the oldest

Christian mission in Togo and the one closest to the German government, began promoting a unified Ewe identity in their educational and missionary work.[66] Africans became dandies in part by attending mission schools, and the colonial state thus turned to these schools in its efforts to cultivate an African identity less threatening to colonial rule. Based in Bremen, with a regional headquarters in Keta, in the English territory, the North German Mission began working in 1847 in the southern portions of the area that became Togo. By 1897 the North German Mission ran 15 elementary schools in the German protectorate; by 1911 the society taught pupils at 141 schools.[67] Early in the colonial period, in deference to demands of the state, the mission taught as little English as it could without driving too many students away.[68] Even the reduced English lessons offered at North German mission schools aroused government complaints of "Un-German behavior."[69] While the German government in Togo would have liked to ban the teaching of English from mission schools—and claimed to the Foreign Office that all the missions in Togo had agreed to help "eliminate" English[70]—the missions in fact persuaded the government that they could not cease offering English without drastically reducing student attendance.[71] Ewe education, as a writer in the *Deutsche Kolonialzeitung* explained, provided an alternative to a European education, which, he wrote, "ran the danger of spoiling our Negro youth, who in any case tend easily to dandyism and to superficial ostentation."[72] The Catholic Mission and the North German Mission even published Ewe newspapers, which the North Germans, at least, hoped would compete with the African press from Gold Coast and elsewhere.[73]

The North German Mission standardized a written Ewe language based on the version spoken in the Anlo region, just across the border with Gold Coast. The various languages defined as Ewe differed so greatly that Ewe speakers from different regions often could not understand one another.[74] The inhabitants of the Anlo region, however, had enough contact with other Ewe-speaking groups that most at least understood their dialect.[75] The standardized Ewe allowed German missionaries to communicate with Christians all over the South of the colony and to publish schoolbooks, catechisms, hymnals, and, eventually, a Bible in a language defined as native.[76] The missionaries also posited a unified and proto-Christian Ewe religion, reimagining as a single pantheon regionally diverse practices and beliefs around spiritually effective beings, known in English as fetishes and in Ewe languages as trɔ̄wo (sing.: trɔ̄). Missionaries promoted a particularly powerful trɔ̄, Mawu, as a supreme being who ruled over, or even created, this pantheon.[77] In addition to its efforts at stabilizing and standardizing the languages and religions of southern Togo, the North German Mission also codified an Ewe history. Central to this history, as historian Sandra Greene has shown, were narratives tracing the scattered Ewe polities to the city of Notsé (pronounced

NO-chey; spelled Nuatjä in German and Notsie in English), the original center of Mawu worship.[78] The North German Mission did not invent any element of this unified Ewe language, religion, and history, but rather systematized existing elements to present the Ewe as a unified, proto-Christian, *Volk*.

The missionary project of grouping the people of southern Togo under a single Ewe identity, however, proved insufficient to the needs of the colonial state for a number of reasons. An Ewe identity did not preclude English literacy or white-collar employment. Any mission school that taught only Ewe would have lost many, if not most, of its pupils. Furthermore, missionary education that involved only noncompulsory primary school for some Togolese children had little prospect of transforming the linguistic, religious, or historical identities of more than a small portion of the Togolese population. Moreover, as the German state sought to expand its reach beyond the southern third of the area it claimed as Togo, it dealt with populations that had no connection at all to Ewe languages, religion, or history.

More importantly, there is nothing inherently subordinate about adopting an Ewe identity, even if it did seem less threatening to many Germans than the cosmopolitan "dandy" identity of literate Africans. Indeed, Benjamin N. Lawrance has shown how the Ewe instruction that Germans provided for purposes of colonial control set the stage for a powerful Ewe nationalist movement after the Second World War.[79] The Ewe trɔwo, even when imagined as part of a proto-Christian pantheon, still provided ideological resources for Ewe to resist European control, for example by claiming that specific trɔwo forbade the presence of Europeans in some areas. At the turn of the century, Africans in Togo and Gold Coast even employed fetishism as an organized form of resistance to European rule in the Yewe secret society or cult. The members of this Yewe society spoke a secret language, took on new names, and established restricted compounds or courts that could be entered only by cult members.[80] The extended household and mixed economy that missionaries themselves recognized as a basic feature of Ewe life represented a further obstacle to German political and economic control. German efforts to use missionary education to promote a unified Ewe identity proved at best only partially successful in imposing ideological state control on southern Togo.[81]

COTTON, CONQUEST, AND THE SOUTHERN TURN OF COLONIAL RULE

The German state established political and economic control in Togo less with the construction of Ewe ethnic identities than with direct military force accompanied by economic transformations that robbed many Afri-

cans of their previous independence. Establishing African cotton cultivation for export to European industry played a central role in this process.
The three decades of German rule in Togo consisted, in large part, of a
series of battles that pushed German control gradually into the North of
the colony and continuous police actions to maintain German power. The
Tuskegee expedition followed German conquests, establishing cotton
farming to consolidate colonial rule in the aftermath of military conflicts.

One of the early, decisive battles that allowed Germans to establish
political and economic hegemony in Togo occurred in the spring of 1895
at Tove, the group of six villages about sixty miles inland from Lome
where the members of the Tuskegee expedition would first work.[82] The
population of Tove had long enjoyed political and economic independence. Indeed, in 1888 the inhabitants of Tove drove off a visiting German
official by brandishing their weapons and firing shots in his direction.[83]
Tove could afford this political defiance because of the economic independence it enjoyed as a regional center for the manufacture of pottery, a
product relatively immune from competition from European or Hausa
manufactures because its weight and unwieldiness made it unprofitable
to transport long distances.[84] In Tove, women alone produced pottery,
making them unusually independent, even by Ewe standards. Tove did
not possess a textile industry, which might have given men greater economic power as weavers. The Toveers rejected, for the most part, the
Christian proselytizing of an Ewe catechist who arrived in 1893, and they
remained hostile to German officials. The location of Tove on a major
north-south caravan route made its political, economic, and cultural autonomy especially threatening to German commerce and political rule.

Germans crushed resistance in Tove in an 1895 war. The Germans Hans
Gruner and Ernst von Carnap had established German state power in the
Misahöhe district, the area around Tove, the previous year with a series
of military assaults.[85] Gruner had been head of the Misahöhe district since
1892, a position he held, with several interruptions, for the entire German
colonial period, including the time that Tuskegee worked in the area.[86]
The 1895 Tove war began when a botanist, Ernst Baumann, from the
nearby Misahöhe station had a number of Tove residents arrested for
mocking him.[87] Residents of one of the Tove villages, Tove-Dzigbe, managed to free the prisoners in a conflict that escalated into a full-scale uprising, during which the Toveers controlled the main road for several weeks,
cutting off a German station to the North, at Kete-Kratschi. The German
government sent out more troops from the South, who killed many Toveers, wounded many others still, destroyed five of the six villages of Tove,
and laid waste to farms and houses.[88] The *Gold Coast Chronicle* reported
that the soldiers decapitated the fallen Toveers and shipped the heads to
Germany. German officers commonly took heads and other body parts

as battlefield trophies, which they sent to anthropologists in Germany.[89] Reports of these atrocities spread fear of the Germans throughout the colony and into the Gold Coast.[90] The Germans meted out punishments to all the men in Tove, probably floggings and forced labor, and took whatever property they had not already destroyed as tribute. Germans also made a point of destroying the local pottery industry.[91] For years after the uprising, observers still reported collapsing, empty houses in Tove and shattered pottery along the road.[92] The Germans established a garrison in the area with a German officer and a hundred African soldiers.[93] Through such punitive expeditions, as the Germans called the village raids designed to instill terror in Africans and destroy the sources of their economic independence, Germans gradually established control over much of Togo.

The attack on Tove and other military actions in the Misahöhe district allowed German merchants to set up warehouses in the hinterland, outside of the coastal strip to which they had formerly been confined. By 1902 one could purchase in the town of Palime, north of Tove—according to Tuskegee expedition head James Nathan Calloway—"flour from Minnesota, ham from Chicago, butter from Denmark, and canned fruits from California."[94] Hausa merchants continued to sell their wares in Palime, too, and Togolese women even continued to sell some pottery, despite the earlier destruction of the industry in Tove.[95] Lieutenant von Carnap, who had accompanied Gruner on his first expeditions in 1894–95, founded stations at Kpandu, north of Misahöhe, and Sasane-Mangu, in the far north of the protectorate. A series of raids in 1897 and a final conquest in 1898 allowed the Germans to set up a station at Atakpame, east of Tove, where the Tuskegee expedition would expand in 1904.[96]

German colonial rule depended as much on forced labor as it did on military conquest. Germans compelled prisoners of war to work, so that each conquest not only gave the German state new territory but also further subjected African labor to German control.[97] German authorities, like many European colonial governments, also used taxation to force populations to work. Most asserted that taxation induced Africans to labor because the more cash they needed, including to pay taxes, the more commercial crops they would grow.[98] Governor Zech thus described tax work as "pedagogically very good."[99] In fact, taxation, like so many other laws, worked through the failure of its stated purpose: those who did not have the cash to pay taxes had to perform twelve days of labor for the government, and those accused of dodging their taxes could be imprisoned and forced to work on a chain gang until somebody else paid their taxes.[100] The German government also forced those imprisoned for other offenses to work without pay and could even require prisoners to work beyond their sentences to pay for the meals they had been provided during their incarceration.[101] Corporal punishment, often meted out by African police, formed an important component of forced labor.[102] As in the southern United States, arbitrary and racist justice elevated prison labor to an important political and economic factor in colonial Togo.

For many colonial officials in Togo, cotton farming represented an especially effective means of undermining African political and economic autonomy, driving Africans into the state of abject dependency in which they believed African Americans lived and that they hoped to introduce in Togo. The Colonial Economic Committee, the organization sponsoring the Tuskegee expedition, maintained that introducing cotton cultivation for the world market would bolster the power of the German state in Togo, making the Togolese "economically dependent upon us," and thus making the Germans "finally the real masters" of Togo.[103] Apart from the value of cotton itself, German officials, including Gruner, saw in smallhold farming a possibility of stabilizing the African population, creating a patriarchal domesticity that promised to control everything from sexual reproduction, to the behavior of men and women, to the availability of labor, to the spatial location of inhabitants. In this, German hopes for smallhold farming were identical in Africa and in Germany.

The turn to cotton as a means of consolidating German political control and economic domination brought with it, perhaps at first as an unintended consequence, a new project of colonial identity formation, as innovative as the previous efforts to ethnicize or tribalize were conventional. Colonial cotton, because of the long-standing associations of cotton with American blacks, as well as the work with Tuskegee Institute that these associations led to, imposed a "Negro" identity from New South ideology, first on the Ewe and later on Africans throughout Togo. New South ideology provided the German government in Togo with a set of practices based on the racial identity "Negro" (the German word is *Neger*). Conceiving of the Togolese in starkly racial terms suggested that they, and, indeed, any population defined as black, might easily adopt the agriculture, and assume the subordinate political and economic positions, ascribed to African Americans in the New South. German colonial experts began referring to many colonized populations with the American term "Negro," but nowhere did they take this more literally than in Togo.[104] Since many Europeans and Americans regarded blacks as natural cotton growers, approaching the Togolese as black rather than as members of particular African societies opened the prospect of increasing cotton output through the voluntary participation of African growers. In reality, the cotton programs in Togo forced farmers to grow cotton against their will, but, as in the United States, the ideology of the "Negro" implied that blacks required this outside force to make them what they supposedly already were. A wide-ranging discussion about "educating of the Negro to work" (*Erziehung des Negers zur Arbeit*) emerged in German colonial circles, often referring to the New South and praising Booker T. Washington.[105]

Colonial officials superimposed policies addressing the Togolese as "Negroes" on earlier colonial constructions of the populations of southern Togo as members of a single Ewe ethnicity. Governing Togolese as "Negroes" or as "Ewe" seemed to penetrate history to an authentic culture or even to a biological nature. Both the cultural identification of individuals as "Ewe" and the racial identification of those individuals as "Negro" were aspects of a state policy of control, highlighting and standardizing aspects of culture and physical appearance as a means of constraining and directing African social and political mobility. The two appellations, Ewe and Negro, though having similar purposes, also contradicted each other, implying different political and economic roles for the individuals thus identified. The newer construction of the Togolese as "Negroes" also made use of elements of the slightly older construction of these societies, as diverse and polyglot as any, as a unified Ewe Volk.

In the first week of January 1901, Tuskegee expedition members James Nathan Calloway, John Winfrey Robinson, Shepherd Lincoln Harris, and Allen Lynn Burks arrived in Tove, to begin their work on cotton.[106] Accompanying the Tuskegee men were twenty-seven African employees and Hans Gruner, the German official in charge of the Misahöhe district who had led troops in the battle of Tove and in the subsequent destruction of the region a little more than five years earlier. Gruner acquired, for a "modest gift," land for the Tuskegee cotton experiments in Tove-Dzigbe, the still devastated village where the 1895 war had first broken out. The low price for the land may have reflected that Tove-Dzigbe remained in ruins from the 1895 war.[107] The expedition also leased fifty acres from the king of Tove, as well as twenty-five from the local North German Mission station.[108] The Tuskegee men occupied several of the huts in Tove-Dzigbe that had remained empty since the German attacks. Later, more permanent buildings were erected at Tove for the cotton expedition, some of which still stand (see figure 3.7). Gruner had local chiefs assemble about two hundred of their subjects to clear the fields and build additional housing. On the land that the expedition had cleared in Tove, Calloway and Robinson set up a cotton-seed plantation, worked by Africans whose once flourishing pottery industry had been destroyed by the German military. The majority of the African workers, not surprisingly, had no familiarity with the agricultural implements that the expedition had brought from the United States, and Robinson complained that

FIGURE 3.7. One of the Tuskegee plantation buildings still standing in Tove. Tove continued to serve as a cotton station under French rule and is now an agricultural school in independent Togo. Photograph by author, January 2005.

"it was more difficult to train the boys than it was to train the horses." Before Robinson learned Ewe, the expedition had no common language with the Africans at Tove, and, he admitted, both he and Calloway allowed "blue flames of English . . . occasionally [to] escape our lips."[109] African laborers sang work songs that reminded Calloway of "the plantation melodies of the colored people in the South."[110] The expedition members, like the expedition's organizers, proceeded from such superficial resemblances between Africans and African Americans to simulate a New South in Togo that was in some ways even more oppressive than the original.

John W. Robinson of Tuskegee Institute did not share the German government's enthusiasm for using cotton to control and subordinate Africans. "I stand," Robinson notified the governor of Togo, Count Julius Zech, "for more than cotton." Growing cotton for export should be taught, Robinson maintained, only where it would make people wealthy; if yams or maize yielded greater benefits to their growers in particular areas, these regions should not be induced to grow cotton. He imagined that people on the coast would remain traders, and "we"—Robinson and the German government—"wish to make them better traders," rather than turning them into cotton farmers.[111] Robinson's sentiments were ignored by Zech and other white elites eager to enrich themselves with cotton and to generate white political authority through the routines of subordination essential for industrial cotton growing.

In the first years of the expedition, the Tuskegee personnel sought to introduce Africans to this "Negro" *Volkskultur* by making African cotton farmers resemble African American cotton farmers, as well as by breeding cotton varietals whose fibers would mimic those of American Upland cotton. The cotton experiments conducted by Calloway and Robinson at Tove would support cotton farms cultivated by African American settlers who would, by force of their example, persuade Africans to set up the kind of small farms that produced cotton in the American South. Initially, the Tuskegee expedition members imagined these households in highly idealized terms, free of the coercion of sharecropping, although this soon would change.

German colonial authorities, working with Tuskegee instructors, sought to replace the extended Ewe households with the smallhold farming that had already proven effective in controlling agricultural labor in both eastern Germany and the southern United States. They defined this smallhold farming as *Volkskultur*, or "peoples' culture," suggesting that African "Negroes" customarily practiced this type of farming. The Tuskegee expedition, as the KWK explained, would "introduce a cotton *Volkskultur*" in Togo.[112] Much like the New South term "Negro," the term *Volkskultur* operated through its multiple, contradictory meanings. *Kultur* meant, simultaneously, agriculture, a people's way of life, and higher civilization. *Volk* meant people, but it remained productively unclear whether a "Volkskultur" was a culture (in any of the three senses of the word) that the people already had or any culture taken up by, or forced upon, a people. Tuskegee personnel arrived in southern Togo just as the North German Mission sought to teach the people of the region to consider themselves an Ewe Volk, and Africans and Europeans contested what the culture of this "Volk" might become.[113] J. K. Vietor, the head of the Bremen trading firm associated with the North German Mission, promised that the Togolese economy would flourish with agricultural smallholding, as "the natives get used to work and consumer demands," and colonial businesses and the state continued "educating the Negro more and more to economic independence" through "peaceful, gradual development of free trade."[114] Identifying cotton as a Volkskultur invited corrective intervention, much as identifying an individual as a "Negro" did in the United States. Volkskultur, like other forms of peasant production in West Africa and in much of the world, was not an ancient economic arrangement set upon by modern, transnational capitalism, but rather a modern economic form forced upon colonized people as part of a regime of political oppression and economic exploitation.

German social scientists and policy makers had long held that smallhold farming, in the German East and in the American South, helped control workers by binding them to specific plots of land, to households, to families, and to national or racial kinship networks. Members of the Verein für Sozialpolitik regarded African American sharecroppers as a particularly important model of this type of controlled smallhold farming. African American conditions became even more relevant as Germans tried to realize an African Volkskultur modeled on the Negro smallholders of the American South. Gustav Schmoller made these connections explicitly at a 1902 German Colonial Congress in Berlin. At the conference, Baron von Herman, the agricultural attaché who had, two years earlier, recruited Booker T. Washington for Togo, reported extensively on the Tuskegee expedition to Togo.[115] At the same conference, the Bremen merchant, J. K. Vietor praised African smallholding as a bulwark against proletarianization and worker mobility and warned that colonial plantations would "add millions of proletarians [abroad] to the millions of wage laborers already at home." Instead, "with strength, energy, and understanding" we can "work to create a class of free farmers" in Africa. The free farmer, Vietor applauded, "stays on his own plot, farms his own land, and lives a life without care, in peace and satisfaction, glad for the protection of the powerful German Empire."[116] Gustav Schmoller noted that he and his colleagues in the Verein für Sozialpolitik had long discussed questions of smallhold farming in the German context and agreed that the state, missionaries, and "all farsighted friends of the colonies" should support African smallholding for the "entire mental and economic development of the natives," for the "future of the conquered lower races."[117] At the next Colonial Congress, in 1905, Vietor praised a cotton school the Tuskegee expedition established in Togo as "the best institute I have seen in all the colonies I have visited."[118] German social theorists had long regarded African American smallholding as one model of the control of emancipated agricultural labor. The Tuskegee expedition to Togo both resulted from, and further elaborated, this transnational identification.

The model farm program in Togo rested on an assumption shared by Tuskegee expedition members and their German employers that black people imitated others more readily than white people did. Perhaps the most eminent colonial agronomist in Germany, Otto Warburg, described agricultural education in Africa as a matter of training select individuals to serve as models for the rest of the population to imitate. He cited the Tuskegee project in Togo as one of the best examples of this method.[119] Germans enthusiastic about the Tuskegee expedition and other colonial education projects argued that, as one put it, an "ability to imitate" characteristic of Negroes made them particularly susceptible to education (*"Bildungsfähig"*).[120] Booker T. Washington himself praised what he identified as a tendency of Negroes not merely to imitate, but to imitate the best in white people, while rejecting poor models for imitation, such as the Chinese.[121] James N. Calloway, the leader of the expedition, describing a stop in Liberia on his journey to Togo, remarked upon the good influence that African American settlers had exercised on Africans there: "The Negro who comes here from America must work and thus he teaches the natives to work." Calloway contrasted this situation with the bad imitation that he observed in Gold Coast, where he found "the natives, especially the boys, quite improved in education but not inclined to manual labor. They seek to imitate their masters and become English gentlemen."[122] Calloway echoed colonial sentiments that disparaged educated Africans as mere superficial imitators, and he promised that the Tuskegee expedition would provide models for imitation more amenable to the political and economic interests of white elites. In this, they gave an African version of the message that Washington had delivered at the Atlanta Exposition five years earlier.

At the most basic level, smallhold farming would, German officials hoped, prevent Africans from leaving Togo, especially for the freer political conditions in Gold Coast. Togolese resented the widespread practice of flogging and chain-gang labor for even minor infringements in the German colony.[123] Apparently some Africans in Gold Coast referred to the Togolese as "children of the chain and flog."[124] There were greater opportunities for education, and perhaps also higher wages in Gold Coast than in Togo. In 1899 the German government endeavored to slow emigration from Togo with a pass system, enforced by subjecting the families of those who left illegally to large fines and lengthy prison sentences, which included forced labor.[125] Many Togolese continued to cross the border surreptitiously, often with the help of labor recruiters, to work in Gold Coast.[126] Togolese emigration continued to increase throughout the entire German colonial period, eventually becoming so significant that one governor reckoned it reduced the agricultural output of the protectorate.[127] Tuskegee efforts to persuade Africans to found household cotton farms supported German efforts to keep a laboring population from emigrating, much the same purpose as the parcels of land provided for German settlers in the East by the Prussian Settlement Commission.

From Colonial Africans to New South "Negroes"

Gruner, after overseeing the military devastation that established German power, came to recognize that "the value of a colony" depended upon a "numerous, hard-working population." He advised district officials to avoid armed conflicts that might kill off or drive away residents and to pursue a policy of "education to labor" that included placing the "work-shy, the vagabonds, the habitual thieves and the like" in "reform settlements."[128] The extended households common in Togo, however, did not constrain their members to an extent consistent with these plans for social engineering.

The economic opportunities of the day, and even the emerging colonial economy in Togo, tended to discourage the sedentary, monogamous, patriarchal domesticity that the colonial state and the Tuskegee expedition advocated. In the extended households of southern Togo, women and children lived apart from the authority of the husband and father. Spending time in the patriarchal household required that women temporarily abandon their own household farms for those of their husbands. The heterogeneous manufacturing and agricultural production of these households, linked through periodic regional markets, kept Africans economically autonomous and required their mobility. The mercantile economy also brought many Togolese to the coast, both as traders and as porters. The economy that emerged between slavery and colonialism required individual mobility and economic autonomy, precisely those qualities inimical to colonial control. The German state and German firms also depended upon the mobility of African porters, merchants, and workers, even as many, especially in the state, also recognized African mobility as a threat to their own power. The simultaneous demands of the German state for Togolese mobility and immobility provide yet another example of the paradox of the freedom of labor, simultaneously necessary and threatening to capitalist polities.

The economic and domestic autonomy of Togolese women, often remarked upon by European visitors, had, in fact, already begun to wane early in the colonial period. The relative economic independence of women may even have been an unintended consequence of the slave trade, which had so drastically reduced the proportion of men to women in the Bight of Benin. The competition with European industry hurt the economic independence of African women earlier than it did that of men. European spinning mills could produce yarn of various colors with chemical dyes more cheaply than Togolese women could with weighted spindles and indigo and other natural dyes. This limited, although it did not entirely eliminate, the market in Togo for yarn spun from locally grown cotton by Togolese women.[129] European competition, however, did less harm to male weavers. English calicoes were notoriously shoddy, with neither the strength nor the quality of Togolese hand weaving. The uneven effects of European competition on men and women in Togo echoed, to a certain extent, the mechanization of the textile industry in Great Britain, where the spinning jenny displaced female home spinners before the mechanical loom displaced male handloom weavers.

Furthermore, as German police power made it possible for European merchants and their male clerks to set up shop in the hinterland, they also displaced the women who had previously dominated marketing in much of Togo. In Tove, as we have seen, the German military also destroyed the pottery industry, which had sustained women's prosperity and independence. Women and children carried out the labor of cracking palm kernels, and this may have taken up some of the economic slack from the decline of spinning and other women's industries. Cracking kernels, however, may have represented new drudgery rather than new prosperity. Meanwhile, the growing state and mercantile economy employed increasing numbers of male clerks. Men with little property or education could earn as much in daily wages as porters as they could by selling the produce of one or even two weeks of farming.[130] Some African men also found work as what Togolese called "black-skinned Germans," soldiers for the German colonial state, who took part in battles and punitive expeditions against Togolese and oversaw chain-gang labor (see figure 3.8).[131] While the interventions by Germans and Tuskegee personnel ultimately proved disastrous for most men and women in Togo, women initially lost more economic power than men did.

Some Togolese men participated in the colonial discourse of domesticity, for it promised them new opportunities to control women and children. Colonial domesticity may have allowed, paradoxically, some men to recover the masculinity that they felt they had lost from colonial rule itself. Compelling Ewe men to grow cotton, for example, forced them to carry out what had formerly been exclusively a women's task. For the Kabiye, in the northern part of Togo, forced labor for the German state also overturned conventional gender relations by subordinating one man to another. One Togolese man, interviewed in the early 1980s, remarked that, after the introduction of tax work, "the white man and his men could mistreat our people like 'their women.' " After the Germans left Togo, this man recalled, some Togolese castrated one of the African soldiers who had served the Germans with what they regarded as particularly sadistic zeal. As another African recalled: "they castrated that former violator of their wives and daughters, so that he also became a 'woman' of a sort for the rest of his days."[132]

FIGURE 3.8. *Polizeisoldaten*. African soldiers formed the bulk of German military units in Togo, carrying out deadly raids throughout the colony. Known to some Togolese as "black-skinned Germans," they oversaw forced labor, often meting out corporal punishment. Source: Photography Collection of the Norddeutsche Missionsgesellschaft, Staatsarchiv, Bremen, 7, 1025 (hereafter NDM), 4329.

Thus, even as the new colonial political economy eroded women's economic autonomy in Togo, some men pressed for further patriarchal authority. One African missionary accused women and children of taking unfair advantage of the peace and prosperity brought about, he asserted, by German rule, in order to free themselves from the control of men.[133] Another Togolese missionary explained "why the blacks cannot raise their children," by pointing to the independence of Togolese women. Because wives lived independently and raised their own children, fathers could not strike or otherwise punish their own young sons and daughters. "In the end," he remarked, "the woman becomes the complete master and man [*Herr*] of the children." As this missionary phrased it, the independence of women and children threatened, in the end, the foundation of sexual difference: women became men, and men, by implication, became unsexed.[134] It is unclear if only Christians, or even just African catechists, desired patriarchal domesticity. It may be that a prior interest in Christianity led these Africans to attack female independence, or that Togolese anxieties about female independence found practical outlet in Christianity.

Other African men also saw European colonial rule, not as a means of subjecting women to their own patriarchal authority, but rather as a moral scourge that corrupted already weak women. One observer in the *African Times and Orient Review* related that a woman who married a German could, if she were ever abandoned by her husband, never get an African man to marry her "for reasons that cannot be said here." Since every woman needs a husband, this writer reasoned, these unmarriageable Africans became prostitutes, usually, he wrote, in Dahomey and Nigeria.[135] (He presumably imagined these fallen Togolese traveling east to spare residents of Gold Coast, where the paper was published, the accusation of patronizing these prostitutes, as well as the possibility of finding empirical evidence for his assertions.) Governor Doering of Togo similarly worried that women who traveled outside of Togo did so to "give themselves over to debauchery [*Unzucht*]."[136] Some African writers seemed to assume that Germans were sexually depraved—one even singled out Gruner for particular excoriation—but also blamed African women for consorting with them. A Togolese man declared of such interracial unions: "Earlier this could not happen, because every whore [*Hure*] was sold [into slavery]."[137] The writer for the *Gold Coast Leader* who singled out Gruner in his discussion of "Togo-Germans and Immoralism" declared: "In what part of Africa can you picture such an animal desire? Even in Kafirland down to Mississippi the black man knows how to be moral."[138] While this writer connected Gruner to the racist sexuality of white supremacists in South Africa and the United States, he clearly regarded this sexual depravity as a characteristic of all whites. He accused Togolese women, unlike their American and South African counterparts, of doing little to resist this European sexuality.

This African moralist might have actually found in Gruner an ally against the supposed "immoralism" of independent women. Gruner saw in cotton farming a means of establishing a patriarchal monogamy that would consolidate the military gains he had made in Tove. Gruner enlisted the Tuskegee expedition in his efforts to transform the family structure of Tove to make individuals less mobile, discouraging women from traveling as merchants and men from traveling as porters or for other work. Cotton farming, he told an audience of African notables and missionaries in Tove, allowed a man to live as a "free farmer on his own plot, at home with his family." Men would no longer have to travel long distances to earn money as day laborers or porters and "the women would cease to ramble around." "Orderly family relations," Gruner concluded, "could take hold."[139] For Gruner, "orderly family relations" would settle the population under the control of male heads of households and, ultimately, of his station. Gruner, as well as other officials in the German government of Togo, sought to control a colonial population by replacing the polyga-

mous households and the female autonomy of southern Togo with patriarchal, monogamous, agricultural households. While such wide-ranging
plans for social engineering were unlikely to succeed without much
greater state control than existed in Togo (or anywhere else, for that matter), they did motivate state interventions that significantly shaped the
lives of many Africans.

Tuskegee personnel and German authorities held that more efficient
agriculture, most importantly the use of the plow, would facilitate a new
colonial domesticity by making the labor of multiple wives unnecessary.
Eduard Hahn, a sociologist of agriculture at the University of Berlin, explored most thoroughly the cultural advantages of, and obstacles to, plow
agriculture. For Hahn, the hoe was a tool of primitive agriculture carried
out by women, surviving in modern times among non-European peoples
and in the household gardens of Europe. Adopting plow culture required
a switch to male-dominated agriculture. Indeed the plow, for Hahn, had
a "phallic meaning" suggested by its role in penetrating and inseminating
the earth.[140] The switch to the plow further required and brought with it
major cultural changes, according to Hahn, including the domestication
of animals, the invention of an annual calendar, the introduction of the
wagon, the consumption of milk, the cultivation of grain, and thus, eventually, the development of bread. African Americans, according to one
colonial agricultural expert, had adopted the plow under the beneficial
direction of slavery; Africans would do so under the guidance of colonial
authorities.[141] The Colonial Office agreed, adding that Africans held in
"correct political distance from whites" and directed on a course of "cultural development" with a "practical, economical direction" might actually become better cotton growers than "the more civilized Negro in the
United States."[142] Colonial authorities in Germany and elsewhere proposed that, with the introduction of the plow, the work of draft animals
would replace the labor of wives and children, facilitating the transformation from polygamous, female-headed households farming with hoes to
monogamous, patriarchal family farms.

Togolese agriculturalists did not, however, customarily make use of
draft animals. Indeed, a district official near Lome noted that Togolese
mocked those forced to use plows as "cattle drivers," according to him an
insult in the Ewe language.[143] European draft animals imported to Africa,
furthermore, quickly succumbed to sleeping sickness, transmitted by
tsetse flies, and thus hardly survived long enough to repay the efforts of
breaking them to the yoke. Shortly after the expedition settled in Tove, all
forty-four draft animals sent to the plantation died from the fly. Robinson
quickly calculated that the plows the expedition had brought from the
United States could be drawn by four men, and thus helped establish the
use of humans as draft animals in Togo. He also found that the gin could

Figure 3.9. Plowing in Tove, 1905. Although draft animals did not live long enough to make breaking them to the yoke worthwhile, introducing "plow culture" was one of the most desired reforms for many colonial powers all over Africa, including Germans in Togo. Source: NDM, 4294.

be operated by putting six men to each sweep of the wheel powering it.[144] The short lifespan of cattle in Africa, thanks to the tsetse fly, meant that, in practice, Africans themselves generally supplied the power for these advanced agricultural implements.[145] The German agricultural expert Albrecht Zimmermann, in his guide for colonial cotton growing, would later encourage the purchase of plows light enough to be pulled by humans when no animals were available.[146] The expedition also employed humans to pull wagons, putting them in the position of draft animals even while claiming to introduce improved agriculture (see figure 3.10).[147] The commitment to improving African agriculture with draft animals meant, in practice, that many Africans themselves were employed as draft animals.

Tuskegee Educators and African Households

Each member of the Tuskegee expedition ran a household purported to inspire Africans to adopt the patriarchal monogamous domesticity thought necessary for plow agriculture and also desirable for German political and economic control. This was an unlikely prospect, especially

FIGURE 3.10. Transporting cotton on the road from Ho to Palime. Introducing European and American animal-powered agricultural equipment, like the wagons pictured here, did not elevate the Togolese, as the Tuskegee expedition and its German sponsors imagined, but rather forced some of them, as in this image, into the roles of draft animals. The men pulling the wagon are likely tax workers. The bales of cotton are labeled "KWK," the initials of the Colonial-Economic Committee that financed the Tuskegee expedition. Source: NDM, 4309.

at first when the expedition consisted of four single men, living in houses abandoned after the 1895 Tove war. In May 1902, the beginning of the second summer of the expedition in Togo, Calloway returned from a short visit to Tuskegee with five more Tuskegee students, who planned to settle in Togo as model cotton farmers. The landing boat overturned in the rough surf of Togo, drowning two of these new settlers, Hiram D. Simpson and William Drake. Simpson's widow soon married another survivor, Horace Greeley Griffin. The new couple and the third survivor, Walter Bryant, set up model cotton farms. For a brief period, then, at least four African American households existed in Togo, meant to serve as models to reform African families. A fever killed the first settler, Harris, in the summer of 1902, soon after the new settlers had arrived. Burks returned to the United States at the end of 1902. The Griffins remained in Togo until the end of 1904. When they returned, they brought a collection of African arts and crafts donated to the Tuskegee Institute museum by Dr. Kersting, a German official. Kersting himself had visited Tuskegee that year and donated the objects as a token of his admiration for Washington's institute.[148]

The households and farms founded by Tuskegee personnel did not correspond to the image of patriarchal, monogamous domesticity that the expedition's boosters portrayed. When a missionary and his wife visited the Tove plantation during its first year of operation, the two found themselves pleased with the fields, but "horrified by the parlor and dinning room" of Calloway's house and even more repelled by the tea he served.[149] The Griffins planted their cotton seeds too late and complained that they had difficulty finding workers and getting locals to sell them food. Their fields had too many stumps and roots to use a plow. Locals also complained of abuses by the Griffins' cook.[150] Bryant's ten-acre farm initially won praise from one German official, but by 1905 Gruner reported Bryant to be "dumb and arch-lazy" and suspected him of embezzling the wages of his employees.[151] Bryant was not the only member of the expedition accused by the Germans of abusing the Africans he was supposed to inspire with his example. Some of the Togolese under Calloway's tutelage allegedly fled when he threatened them with a gun.[152]

Robinson seems to have been the only successful Tuskegee householder in Africa, and he achieved his success by adapting to Togolese customs, not by modeling the normative sexuality supposed to prevail in Europe and the United States. Robinson, who learned to speak Ewe, married a woman at Tove, and the couple had a daughter, although she did not survive into adulthood. In 1906 Robinson married an American woman, Danella Foote, an assistant in the academic department at Tuskegee Institute. Robinson brought her to Togo, and the two established a household in Notsé, where Robinson managed a cotton school. Probably after Danella returned to the United States, Robinson married another Togolese woman, Alozoukè, with whom he had another daughter, Francisca Adjoa Robinson. Foote may have known her African co-wives, for her own daughter, Dicy Elizabeth Robinson, remained in contact with her African half-sister, Francisca Adjoa. Francisca Adjoa grew up to be a merchant in Togo, and her descendants still remember John Robinson from Alabama as part of their family.[153]

Gruner and other German officials similarly followed Togolese marriage customs, finding them more congenial to their own lives than they did the patriarchal domesticity they sought to impose on others. In addition to his German wife, Hans Gruner, the most vocal advocate of monogamous patriarchal domesticity in Tove, had, by 1905, acknowledged an African wife with whom he had two children.[154] He and another official, Julius Schmend, had both married women in the village Tomeglee, a location favored by German officials for its pleasant climate and friendly inhabitants.[155] When Gruner left Togo in 1914 he established a fund to educate one of these sons, Hans Komla Gruner.[156] Indeed, enough African women married German men in Togo that their children formed a "Brotherhood of German Mulattos" in the 1920s to communicate with their fathers, who by then all lived in Germany.[157] Gruner, at least, recognized patriarchal, monogamous domesticity as a political and economic trap, and there is no reason why he should have wished to spring it on himself.

Booker T. Washington claimed that the Tuskegee settlers in Togo did indeed transform gender and family relations in the African households with which they had contact. Thus, even after those landing in Togo had drowned, he remained committed to sending Tuskegee students to Togo, "even at considerable cost," worrying "that the success of the movement will be crippled if we do not send these men."[158] Ms. Griffin, he asserted, instructed African wives in sewing, cooking, and housework. Men, he maintained, built houses with shutters, doors, and bathrooms, and furnished with beds. Men took over all marketing, he ventured, leaving their wives and children in these model households to attend to housekeeping and farm work. This new domesticity, Washington concluded, led to a Christian life, and these Africans observed the Sabbath, dressing in holiday attire on Sundays and attending services at the mission.[159] Calloway described the domestic successes of Tuskegee in Africa more modestly than Washington did, claiming only that Africans became "better consumers" by learning to desire the kinds of household goods, furniture, and clothing enjoyed by the American expedition members.[160] Washington's depiction of the expedition is a flight of fancy, at odds with family life in Togo and especially in Tove.

Far from encouraging stable domesticity in Tove, the Tuskegee expedition seems to have encouraged Africans living in the area to leave in greater numbers than they otherwise might have. A drought beginning in 1902 exacerbated what was likely already a strong pressure to emigrate stemming from the German devastation, as well as the obligation to accept poorly paid work on the Tuskegee cotton farm.[161] Poor harvests further impelled many to seek employment outside Tove. These poor harvests may have been as much a result of cotton growing as of the weather, since the labor requirements of cotton, as historian John Tosh has shown, often interfered with the prior claims of food crops.[162] While working abroad, according to one North German missionary, students became less religious, having managed to "escape the supervision of the [missionary] teacher."[163] Some of the Tove youth, sharing common West African aspirations, left Tove, with its North German Mission school, for Gold Coast in order to learn English.[164]

In neither Tove nor anywhere else in the German colony did the monogamous, patriarchal domesticity of cotton Volkskultur take hold in the form that colonial authorities and Tuskegee expedition members had planned. In Togo the monogamous male cotton farmer and his housewife were unconventional gender roles that would have represented a loss of wealth, autonomy, and status for both spouses. Nonetheless, unsuccessful interventions in African sexuality by German and American authorities formed an important component of the cotton economy of Togo. While Tuskegee Institute did not succeed in establishing new gender and family arrangements in Togo, the coercion behind these failed efforts remained essential to the success of the cotton program.

The Transformation of Togolese Cotton

While the Tuskegee expedition could have only limited effects on African kinship and sexuality, it exercised greater control over the reproduction of cotton itself. Because of the peculiar nature of the colonial state, the distribution of cotton seeds produced at Tove had more wide-ranging effects on the Togolese cotton industry than any other aspect of the expedition. The German state in Togo, like most colonial states in Africa, possessed the capacity to impose draconian regulation and exercise enormous violence, but only in scattered local points. Colonial states, with their minuscule European staffs assisted by African soldiers and other auxiliaries, were, in comparison to their counterparts in Europe and elsewhere, dwarfed by the populations they struggled to rule. The colonial state could not impose the relatively omnipresent control characteristic of states in Europe and elsewhere. German officials did control the immediate areas around district stations and they could also regulate the large, periodic markets characteristic of Togolese commerce. The process of making Togo like the New South had to work through existing Togolese institutions, and the new cotton seeds allowed the power of the German state and capital to flow into the well-established system of periodic African markets that would otherwise have been inaccessible to these foreign powers.

Growing industrial-grade cotton equivalent to American Upland was not simply a matter of planting American seeds in African soil, although many colonial agriculturalists had tried this approach.[165] The plantation at Tove did not represent the type of cultivation that the expedition hoped to encourage, but rather propagated varieties of cotton that would grow on smallhold farms in Togo and yield a staple suitable for the international market.[166] Robinson crossed varieties of American cotton with a variety of cotton common around Tove, known as Ho cotton, to produce fibers that cotton experts in Bremen and elsewhere deemed identical to American Upland. Ho was already the most common of the five or six varieties of cotton found in Togo and was available in markets throughout the colony.[167] This new variety was called Togo Sea-Island.[168] Togolese growers still cultivate this variety, renamed "Anie" in 1948.[169] The

Tuskegee expedition established its success when, in its first year, the Tove station began sending cotton to Europe that could be classified in the cotton markets as "middling."[170] The expedition could count as very successful when the Association of Saxon Mill Owners described Togo cotton as "corresponding in class and appearance to a fully good middling to middling fair Louisiana creamy."[171] Togo cotton was no longer a "questionable experiment" but rather a "secure capital investment" when, in 1908, graders at the local cotton exchange in Galveston, Texas, rated it very highly.[172]

Cotton farming, like all agricultural production, encompasses humans, nature, and labor processes in a single field, and even something as apparently natural as new cotton seeds transformed this entire biosocial field. To prevent Togo Sea-Island from hybridizing with other cotton varieties, the state and businesses working with the Tuskegee expedition sought to eliminate most other cottons grown in Togo and to prevent Gold Coast or Dahomey cotton from entering the German protectorate. German authorities also sought to prevent farmers from replanting seeds saved from their own harvests, even of Togo Sea-Island cotton, since this could lead to a decline in the quality of Sea-Island itself. The well-known propensity of cotton plants to cross-pollinate made it particularly difficult to control the varieties.[173] According to the official view, at least, foreign cotton accounted for unwelcome anomalies in the preferred Togo Sea-Island variety.[174] The Tuskegee cotton stations at Tove, as well as the later station at Notsé, produced Togo Sea-Island seeds for local growers, a role they continued to play well after the end of German colonial rule.[175] Privately owned German ginning stations also collected and distributed Togo Sea-Island seed.

Distributing these new cotton seeds throughout Togo also involved spreading the coercion and oversight of labor that were necessary to produce industrial-grade cotton. German government stations and the ginning stations of the KWK distributed Togo Sea-Island Seed free of charge but claimed, as the KWK put it in 1904, "a certain right . . . to exercise pressure on those natives who have taken on obligations by choosing to accept seeds or other assistance for cotton growing."[176] The government did its best to ensure that German businesses and government stations were the only source of cotton in the protectorate, so that every farmer who wished to grow cotton had to accept this "assistance." Not surprisingly, fewer farmers than the government had hoped chose to grow cotton. The government thus eventually employed district agronomists to go directly to local farmers, providing them with seeds, an act of supposed generosity that gave the Germans the right to instruct farmers in what they considered proper cotton cultivation and picking and that imposed on the farmers the duty to obey them.[177]

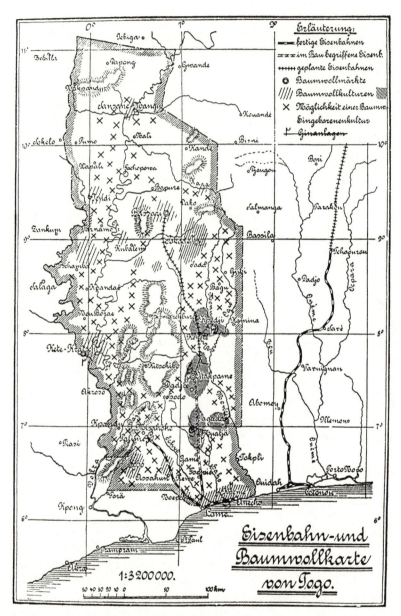

FIGURE 3.11. "Railroad and Cotton Map of Togo," c. 1909. The circles indicate cotton markets, the shaded areas existing cotton growing areas, and the crosses the "possibility of a native cotton culture." Source: *Arbeitsplan und Organization der Baumwoll-Kulturversuche 1910, 1911, 1912* (Berlin: Kolonial-Wirtschaftliches Komitee, n.d.), BArch R1001/8150, Bl. 123.

These district agronomists dealt in various ways with Togolese resistance. One abandoned his efforts to control the way women grew cotton for local spinning—the only type of cotton cultivation indigenous to Togo—to focus instead on compelling men to grow cotton for the world market in large fields that he could oversee.[178] Another of these district agronomists, finding that local growers did not wish to plant cotton, demanded that local chiefs send their subjects to the station to pick up an allotment of seed and to receive instruction "in connection also with a certain pressure from the district office" to plant and cultivate the cotton.[179] Another district agronomist required local farmers to grow cotton on every mound planted with cassava, the staple crop in much of Togo, and used government "pressure" to make them care for this cotton.[180] The state insinuated itself into African farming practices through these new seeds, distributing its own authority along with these new hybrids.

German state authority assured that cotton growers in Togo worked under supervision and coercion, as American cotton growers did. German business and state personnel pointed to cotton picking as an important area for control in Togo.[181] Those picking industrial-grade cotton in Africa, as in the United States, had to limit the amount of trash picked with each boll, prevent the bolls from being soiled, and work quickly to provide the vast quantities of the fiber demanded by the industry. The government officials who worked with the Tuskegee expedition directed their attention to the minutiae of African cotton picking, seeking, via an almost Taylorist analysis, to make every movement of African cotton pickers resemble that of their African American counterparts. African pickers, one government observer complained, placed cotton into a basket carried on their heads, gathering cotton in fields planted "without rule or order." American pickers, by contrast, walked along straight rows of cotton, using both hands to toss bolls into the mouths of large sacks held open with a strap under the arm. As they picked, Americans removed leaves and other trash with their teeth or lips, or by rubbing the cotton across their body, before tossing each boll in the sack.[182] Government cotton inspectors eventually introduced the American sack method into Togo and emphasized that using the sack required retraining of the precise movements of the picker's body. One wrote: "the art of picking lies in carrying out this maneuver precisely and rapidly: as long as the picker needs both hands to [pick] a boll and then both hands again to put the picked cotton in the sack, he will not achieve great output."[183] This meticulous control of the bodies of workers, in Africa as in the United States, could only occur under authorities who did not recognize the legitimate agency of workers, since workers would never freely choose such poorly paid drudgery. Following New South ideology in treating blacks as patho-

Figure 3.12. Packing cotton in Togo. SEM, 062.

logical provided one such type of domination in the cotton fields of the United States and German Africa.

The colonial state had to prevent free markets from emerging in Africa so that the commodities markets of Europe and the United States, conventionally defined as free, might flourish. Unlike their counterparts in the American South, Togolese had the option of spinning and weaving their own crop rather than selling it to industrial manufacturers. Such local spinning and weaving not only contributed nothing to European manufacturers, but it also afforded African producers and consumers an economic independence unwelcome to colonial authorities. In the first years of the expedition, Calloway, Robinson, and Burks purchased cotton grown throughout Togo, directing it away from local consumption to export for the world market. The KWK also had district stations in Togo acquire local cotton and transport it to Tove in carts pulled by tax workers.[184] The German state licensed cotton-purchasing agents to whom Togolese were required to sell their cotton or face punishments including fines, flogging, and forced labor.[185] Togolese growers actually preferred to sell their cotton to middlemen rather than directly to German government stations, even though this meant receiving less money for their cotton.[186] Many Africans sought to avoid contact with German officials, which might well result in forced labor, most commonly as a punishment for alleged tax evasion. Licensed purchasers were required to separate the cotton into two grades, a classification hardly as intricate as that employed in European and American cotton markets, but one that nonetheless had the same effect of increasing the discipline exercised over

FIGURE 3.13. Cotton purchasing agent, Noepe, Togo, 1906. The sale of cotton in German Togo was gradually restricted until only agents licensed by the government could purchase it, guaranteeing that the fiber would be sold on world markets rather than processed locally. The purchasing agent is the man in the white shirt facing the camera. Note that, despite Tuskegee efforts to make men grow cotton, most of the cotton here is being sold by women. Source: NDM, 4288.

cotton growers.[187] The biological control of commercial plants and animals, central to the global commodities markets of the nineteenth century, required confining the biological variability of cotton and many other organisms, but also preventing the economic freedom of those who produced many of these goods. Like the factory, the farm—and indeed much of the colony—was what Marx called a "hidden abode of production," defined by the absence of the very economic freedom that it sustained in the marketplace.[188]

UNDOING THE EXODUS: THE COLONIAL DECIVILIZING MISSION AT THE NOTSÉ COTTON SCHOOL

Expanding commercial cotton cultivation in Togo involved efforts to make the Togolese like American "Negroes." The nature of this African "Negro" identity, however, had necessarily to build upon the previous identities that it was designed to undermine. The "Negro" identity in German colonial ideology differed in important respects from its counter-

FIGURE 3.14. Purchasing cotton in a Togolese market. German authorities sought not only to force African growers to sell raw cotton to European exporters rather than processing it locally. They also sought to control the quality of cotton sold at markets by requiring licensed purchasers to separate it into two grades. Such an inspection appears to be taking place in this image. Source: SEM, 169.

part New South ideology. Indeed, some members of the German government in Togo, including the governor himself, Count Zech, began having second thoughts about welcoming African Americans to Togo. Zech obtained a different perspective on African Americans from Joseph Buvinghausen, a German American deputy sheriff from Harris County, Texas, whom the government had employed as a cotton inspector at least since 1902.[189] Buvinghausen explained to Zech that, while the Tuskegee personnel had rendered valuable service in Togo, "one cannot expect a beneficial influence from colored Americans on the natives here."[190] Other white experts echoed Buvinghausen's opposition to further African American settlement in Togo. An agronomist sent to Togo from the University of Berlin, though more sympathetic to Africans than Buvinghausen was, shared the Texan's hostility toward African Americans. He complained that Americans like Buvinghausen approached Negroes "with antipathy and coldness" whereas the "*African* Negro" requires "signs of good will" from his superiors, "exactly like a child." "The Togo Negro," he concluded—"with the exception of the . . . riff-raff on the coast"—"is not as far degraded as the American Negro."[191] Neither of these advisors encouraged African American settlement in Togo. A British observer for the Royal African Society had similarly worried that the African American might become a "noisy political agitator" in West Africa, but assured British colonial authorities, whom he hoped would also employ American blacks, that "where the autocratic Germans lead the way we surely need not fear to tread."[192] The interest of the government of Togo and the KWK in further African American settlement had been inspired by the New

South ideal of the "Negro," brought from Tuskegee, Alabama. This interest was muted by another dimension of the New South, racist anxieties like those brought to Togo from Texas.

The North German Mission also found reason to doubt the benefit of widespread African American influence in Africa after it encountered local competition from a mission in Gold Coast run by the African Methodist Episcopal (AME) Zion Church, an African American denomination. The head of that mission, Thomas B. Freeman, the son of an African American freedman and an English woman, had left the Wesleyans after a long and distinguished missionary career in Gold Coast. Freeman openly criticized North German Mission schools for their limited English instruction and attracted Togolese students to cross the border to his mission school.[193] Apparently many residents of Tove fled Togo to study with Freeman, who, they were reported to believe, could teach English reading and writing in a single day.[194] By 1904, the AME Zion mission in Gold Coast had begun holding what missionaries from the North German Mission described, using the English term, as "revival meetings" where "various people, especially women, comport themselves absurdly, shaking their heads and waving their arms about in the air, and shriek and scream like fetish women."[195] Such ecstatic African American religious observances, which Booker T. Washington also disdained, presented an aspect of black America that German authorities welcomed less than Tuskegee education.

Some Africans themselves may also have become skeptical of African American settlers. "As farmers and traders," explained a Gold Coast newspaper writer, African Americans "should be of great help to us," but they should not "come here with any high ideas about returning to a long-lost home, where brothers are ready with ever-open arms to receive and welcome them to a land flowing with milk and honey, and where they will have nothing to do but bask in the sun all day long . . . and eager, loving Africans will be running over one another's heads to fill the pockets of the American brothers with wealth untold."[196]

The German colonial version of "Negro" identity would thus involve rejecting real African Americans and transforming the New South ideology of blacks as born cotton growers so that it might serve as a weapon against the specific forms of African economic and political autonomy in Togo. Persuaded already in 1902 by the racism of his Texan advisor, Governor Zech decided it would be better to train "the more intelligent natives of Togo" in a local cotton school than to settle large numbers of "American colored cotton planters" in the colony.[197] In 1903 Calloway returned to his old position in the agriculture department at Tuskegee Institute, by which time all the African Americans but Robinson and the Griffins had returned to the United States or died. The Griffins would leave soon after that. While the KWK and Booker T. Washington continued to hope more African Americans would volunteer to settle in Togo as model cotton farmers, the misfortune of the first group of settlers had discouraged all subsequent Tuskegee volunteers.

John W. Robinson, the most enthusiastic and well respected member of the Tuskegee expedition, would found and direct this cotton school, so that specially trained Togolese, rather than African American settlers, would serve as examples of prosperous cotton growers to their countrymen.[198] The school, which opened in 1904, trained students from every district in Togo to grow cotton for the world market. Its graduates would, it was hoped, serve as examples to their countrymen when they returned to their home districts.

The government located this new cotton school in Notsé, a group of seven villages near Atakpame. The work that Tuskegee carried out at Notsé, like that at Tove, helped consolidate recent German military conquests by reshaping a local economy around cotton growing. The Germans founded Atakpame station, the main government outpost near Notsé, in 1898, after a year of combat to overcome local resistance. Atakpame station continued to direct these military expeditions, and German merchants soon established a foothold in the region.[199] Prior to the German conquest, the area had little contact with German missions or merchants, with an unusually wide use of cowries as currency, suggesting an orientation toward trade networks that did not include Europeans.[200] As in the Misahöhe district, German military force opened the Atakpame district to European merchant houses, which had formerly been confined to the coast.[201]

Germans had little contact with Notsé itself before Atakpame station founded a substation there in 1900, run by an African clerk.[202] Even after the German conquest, the inhabitants of the district, including in Notsé itself, continued to fight colonial rule. In early 1901 the Atakpame station chief, Geo Schmidt, reported that Notsé, and indeed the whole area, was "raging furiously."[203] Later that year, in August, the station chief at Atakpame learned that Notsé had once again "come to open insurrection." Accompanied by twenty soldiers, Schmidt marched to Notsé and had the chiefs assemble 450 of their subjects for punishment of forced labor. These workers cleared brush for the Tuskegee expedition's cotton school, which began teaching its first class less than a year later (see figure 3.16).[204] As at Tove, cotton and colonial conquest went hand in hand.

After conquering Atakpame, the German military turned its attention to the region of Togo north of Ewe territory. Fare Napo, an African veteran of the German military, remembered his service in the wars of "pacification" against the Konkomba in the Sokode-Bassari region in the North. On one occasion, Fare Napo and his comrades, commanded by a

FIGURE 3.15. Courtyard in Notsé, n.d. The German government established military control over Notsé less than a year before the Tuskegee expedition opened a cotton school there. Prisoners taken during the conquest of the region provided labor for clearing the school fields. Source: NDM, 4492.

German, entered a village deemed unfriendly to whites, where they "burned the huts, hunting down the villagers everywhere," and killing men, women, and children. They killed, in his estimate, "a good hundred," wounded more, and took dozens of prisoners. After this attack they extracted from the village chief an affirmation of submission to whites.[205] The battles to conquer the North delivered to the government great numbers of forced laborers, who built Togo's widely admired system of roads and railroads, lines of communication that themselves further extended German political and economic control into the hinterland.

During their conquest of the North, Germans sent many African captives to Chra, a penal colony located near Notsé.[206] Hans Georg Doering had founded the settlement when he took over Atakpame station from Geo Schmidt in 1902. German authorities had originally established Chra to hold Africans captured during the conquest of Atakpame itself, but when Doering moved to Sokode-Basari in the north of the colony, he continued to send prisoners to Chra. These prisoners included those who had fought against German control of the North, as well as, in the words of Gruner, "the work-shy, the vagrants, the habitual thieves, and others that make the roads unsafe."[207] Entire families were often forced to relo-

FIGURE 3.16. Cotton field in Notsé. According to the caption, the field was prepared by five hundred prison laborers in 1902–1903. District officer Geo A. Schmidt took the photograph. The white man in the field is identified as Director Schneider. The Africans in the field are from the first class of cotton school students. Source: BArch, R1001/ 8673, Bl. 179.

cate to Chra with the individual who had been sentenced. The population of Chra climbed to more than one hundred in 1905, and remained well above two hundred for the remainder of the German period.

Oral history interviews taken in 1980 and 1981 indicate that Togolese from the North understood the name *Chra* as a German misrendering of *Wahala*, the Hausa word for misery or trouble. In fact, the penal colony had been named for the river on which Germans located it, but the mistaken etymology is telling. Tiw, one of the interviewees, remembered that Germans drove him from his northern home in 1902, at the age of ten, along with his grandmother, her sister, and about a hundred other Kabiye. Germans had devastated the area, leaving what Tiw described as "a vast holocaust landscape," dotted with burning houses and corpses. Lorenz, another northerner, similarly left his home as a young child with his family, forced from their land to join a larger group of prisoners marching to Chra. Both interviewees remembered a long, exhausting march through the bush on which they were accompanied by African soldiers who offered few provisions but constant punishments. Both recounted numerous deaths from hunger, exhaustion, disease, and even, in Tiw's case, bites from venomous snakes. According to Tiw, of the hundred or more of his countrymen with whom he left, only a few dozen arrived in Chra.[208]

Because Germans imprisoned entire families in Chra, they could group individuals into the smallhold farms that were becoming an ever more prevalent method of political and economic control on both sides of the Atlantic. The prisoners were grouped in independent households, so that, according to one observer, people seemed to be "free farmers" rather than prisoners.[209] The particular conditions of Chra made the establishment of the monogamous patriarchy that Germans and the Tuskegee expedition advocated even less likely than in other parts of Togo. Unmarried men who came to Chra found it difficult to persuade women from outside the penal colony to relocate there, while women confined to the colony could sometimes be allowed to leave by marrying a man from the outside.[210] Chra provided forced labor for the south of the colony including, in all likelihood, the Tuskegee cotton school at Notsé.[211]

German authorities forced young men to leave their homes in every region of Togo to attend the Notsé cotton school. The first class of forty-six students arrived in Notsé during the first two weeks of April 1904. Earlier that year, in February, the government had commanded every district officer in Togo to send male students to the cotton school with "appropriate accompaniment," likely Togolese police.[212] Students were supposed to be between sixteen and nineteen years old, but a few were as young as twelve.[213] It seems that only two students ever volunteered for the school during the entire period of German colonial rule, and such voluntary attendance appeared so unlikely that it instigated an official inquiry.[214] Every other student entered the cotton school under some form of coercion. When the chiefs of Anecho protested to the government that "no one from their areas would register of their own free will as agricultural students," the government bluntly informed them that students would be registered from theirs and every other region of the country, whether or not of their own free will.[215] Apparently the district officer of the northernmost district in Togo, Sasane-Mangu, had misinformed residents about the length of the course at Notsé, and, after the first two classes of eleven students discovered that they were not permitted to leave the school for three years, the station found it could only recruit more students "through compulsory measures and punishments." "The native," remarked the officer, "would rather pay one hundred marks than send his son" to such a school.[216] The district office of Kete-Kratschi found that "the people fear training in Notsé and fear that . . . their freedom and status as non-bonded individuals [*Freiheit und Ungebundenheit*] would be too severely diminished."[217] The Notsé cotton school did indeed represent one of the many counterattacks on the freedom that workers on both side of the Atlantic won during the nineteenth century.

Locating the cotton school in Notsé had not only immediate strategic significance for the consolidation of German state power, but also symbolic consequences for the battle over Togolese identity.[218] North German missionaries had emphasized to Ewe students that their history had begun by fleeing Notsé, probably in the sixteenth century, to escape the despotic reign of King Agokoli. The Ewe, according to their own historical memory, had once lived together in Notsé until they decided to flee the despotic rule of Agokoli.[219] Seeking to aggrandize his own power, Agokoli ignored his royal counselors and killed all the elders who might have led popular resistance against his rule. Agokoli forced his subjects to perform excessive and difficult labors, most famously building an earthen wall around Notsé. Today portions of such a wall have been partially reconstructed, based on archaeological remains (see figure 3.17). King Agokoli III of Notsé, interviewed in 1976, explained that his predecessor had built the wall to protect Notsé from slave raiders.[220] Most accounts, however, present the construction of the wall as an arbitrary and onerous task or as a means of preventing Agokoli's subjects from fleeing his tyranny. Agokoli acquired the mud for this wall, according to some versions, by burying spikes that would lacerate the feet of passersby and soak the ground with blood. To escape Agokoli's tyranny, women agreed to empty washing and cooking basins on a specific place on the earthen wall around Notsé, softening it until it could be breached in the dark of the night. Many versions have the refugees walking through the gap backward, so their footprints appeared to be entering rather than leaving the city.

The historical origin of the Ewe in Notsé was not a capricious invention of missionaries cynically cooked up to achieve political or theological ends. The story was widely reported in Ewe oral histories collected by missionaries. By tracing their origin to an exodus from a walled city, from an absolute authority, and from submission to the labor demands of others, the Ewe understood themselves as a society marked by local, familial, and individual autonomy. This unity-in-dispersal also appeared in their relatively independent domestic lives. This Ewe historical memory ran counter to the despotism of state formation, capital accumulation, and patriarchal monogamous households. Promoting the Ewe origin story may well have appealed to Christian missionaries because of its apparent similarity to the Biblical exodus of the Israelites from Egyptian bondage.[221] The missionary Gottlob Härtter, however, claimed that the common origin in Notsé affirmed that the Ewe people were, as his North German Mission colleagues also insisted, a united Volk, but one left fragmented by historical accident, constantly fighting, he asserted, among themselves. German colonial rule, he argued, presented a means of bring-

FIGURE 3.17. Recent reconstruction of the mud wall built by King Agokoli's subjects. This was one of the cruel tasks that Agokoli was said to have forced upon the Ewe people. The wall also kept the Ewe trapped in the city. The Ewe polities, at least since the late nineteenth century, traced their history to an exodus from Notsé. It was thus an irony, and perhaps an intentional irony, that the Tuskegee cotton school, which the German government forced young men from all over Togo to attend, would be located in Notsé. Photograph by author, January 2005.

ing peace to the region and reuniting the Ewe.[222] Härtter thus put the German colonial state and his own mission, apparently without appreciating the irony, in the position of the despotic king Agokoli.

German authorities knew that Ewe historical narratives began with a flight from Notsé and, thus, by founding the cotton school in the city, reversed the exodus narrative that marked Ewe freedom. The cotton school at Notsé presented a concrete image of the regression brought about by the German state and the Tuskegee expedition, as they sought to transform parts of Togo's rich and complicated economy, comprised of diverse agriculture, manufacturing, and trade, into a cotton monoculture producing cheap raw materials for European industry. The location of the school assaulted the Ewe history that Germans sought to erase with the New South ideology of the "Negro." The return to Notsé emphasized to students that they were no longer Ewe, or part of any other African ethnic group, but rather "Negroes" defined by their race and their economic role as cotton farmers. Yet this New South ideological message, paradoxically, depended on narratives associated with the constructed Ewe identity that it was meant to overwrite.

While the school changed its name and adjusted its program several times, the purpose of the institution at Notsé remained constant: training students from all over Togo to grow cotton. Notsé students learned, in the words of an early report by the governor of Togo, "the handling of rational agricultural implements, the use of, and care for, work animals, the use of natural fertilizer, the proper use of crop rotation, the use of secondary crops, and the selection of good cotton seed."[223] "The boys," Robinson explained, "should learn first to select proper cotton soils and then to prepare the soil and how to plant the seeds perfectly and how to cultivate and harvest the cotton." Equally important was "How to use the plow and to manipulate common farm machinery."[224] "[O]n top of it all," complained Robinson, "we are expected to educate and to change the character of these boys within 1 to 2 years."[225] Students at Notsé were paid a sum ranging from twelve to fifteen marks a month, and the third-years were also allowed to retain the profits from a hectare (about two and a half acres) that they were allowed to farm themselves. From this money, students were expected to pay their own living expenses.[226]

Robinson worked tirelessly in Togo, putting in twelve-hour days, from sunup to sundown, all year round. He traveled, often in darkness, by bicycle and, as it was built, by railroad, shuttling between his seed-breeding work at Tove and his teaching at Notsé. Robinson also had a wife and a daughter in each location. Robinson's days at Notsé included teaching students in the fields and the classroom, supervising school employees, conducting correspondence, hosting visitors, and managing the buildings and facilities of the school, as well as overseeing the operation of a steam gin that turned out two hundred bales of cotton a year. He also had to train the draft animals for both the school and for the farms of its graduates, which, because of the short lives of these animals in Africa, was an ongoing enterprise. The school itself was a veritable business undertaking, and Robinson had to spend and account for thousands of marks each month.[227] Robinson evidently enjoyed good relations with King Komedja of Notsé, who became the godfather of his daughter Francisca and helped raise her after Robinson's death.[228]

Missionary Education and Industrial Education in Togo

The Notsé school allowed the German government to transform education in Togo much more directly than it had been able to through mission

FIGURE 3.18. Gin station, Notsé, 1906–1907. The bags of cotton on the ground, to the left, would have been purchased all over the Atakpame region and perhaps farther afield. Baskets of cotton in the front center are being weighed. An African worker or student shovels cotton seed to the right. On the raised platform is a bale of cotton, which has come out of the gin house to the right. Source: Detail from a photograph in NDM, 4298.

schools, which pursued their own agendas—economic, political, and theological—and also depended on the voluntary participation of African pupils. The school departed sharply from missionary pedagogy in Togo by teaching neither English reading and writing nor even the newer education in Ewe language and culture. Robinson, complying with the desire of the government to minimize English instruction, conducted the two hours of daily classroom instruction in Ewe.[229] Many students, however, recruited from all over Togo, had only limited understanding of Ewe, and, exhausted from their work, often slept in class.[230] That Robinson worked the students so hard that they gained little benefit from the classroom did not represent a failure of Notsé, but rather a logical result of the political and economic effort of which the school was a part: subverting Togolese aspirations for literacy and white-collar employment to make them a subject "Negro" peasant population.

Although the North German Mission worked closely with the German government in Togo, local missionaries rejected the idea that they should help impart labor discipline, as the state demanded. One missionary likened official concern about African labor discipline to Pharaoh's complaints that the Israelites in Egyptian bondage were lazy when they stopped work to worship God.[231] "Jesus did not come to the world," responded another to government demands, "to teach the people to be workers." Still, this missionary allowed, "it is never so good with the work and with the workers as where He has sent workers to do His [spiritual] work."[232] Against the KWK view that cotton was "the most valuable means for elevating the culture," the North German Mission retorted "the most valuable means of elevating real 'culture' of the Ewe is and remains the introduction of Christianity."[233] Missionaries, German officials, and Booker T. Washington all associated Christianity with hard labor. However, the mission saw hard work as the result of a spiritual conversion to Christianity whereas the others saw Christianity as the result of training to labor.

Washington had long reproached black Christianity for allegedly endorsing laziness and an aversion to work. At the 1890 commencement ceremonies at Fisk, when the first Tuskegee expedition leader, James Nathan Calloway, graduated, Washington delivered a speech that was, until his "Atlanta Compromise" address five years later, his most infamous. Black preachers, Washington asserted, too often took up their calling simply to avoid work. In his speech, he caricatured such preachers by parodying, as he often did, black English, and specified as cotton farming the valuable work that he accused some preachers of taking up their calling to shirk: "O Lord, de work is so hard, de cotton is so grassy, and de sun am *so* hot, I bleave dis darkey am called to preach." The result of such poorly qualified and lazy ministers, Washington concluded, was that "the seven million colored people in the South" might be "just as ignorant of true Christianity, as taught by Christ, as any people in Africa or Japan, and just as much in need of missionary efforts as those in foreign lands."[234] In Africa, Calloway endorsed Washington's skepticism about missionary Christianity, writing to Washington: "If Africa is ever reclaimed it will be through such missionary work as is done in school, shops and farms at Tuskegee."[235] Washington and Calloway both preferred proselytizing through the hard labor and patriarchal domesticity that they associated with Christian morality than through directly religious instruction.

Although missionaries working in Africa remained skeptical of the project of education to labor, the top leadership of the North German Mission in Bremen gradually came to admire the Tuskegee efforts at Notsé. J. K. Vietor, the head of the Togo trading firm closely allied with the mission, and a member of the mission's board, had singled out the Notsé school after its first year of operation as "the best establishment that I have seen in any colony I have ever visited."[236] Mission officials in Bremen soon echoed Vietor's view.[237] In 1907 the Bremen office sent the German translation of Washington's autobiography, *Up from Slavery*, to missionaries throughout Togo and encouraged them to familiarize themselves with the program at Notsé and to apply Tuskegee ideals to their own schools.[238] "What was possible for the Negroes in North America," promised one missionary, "will gradually happen for the Negroes of Africa."[239] Missionaries in Togo admitted to their superiors in Bremen that they admired Booker T. Washington's ideals but cautioned that industrial education had little place in their own pastoral efforts.[240] Two years later Bremen headquarters sent two representatives to Togo to impress upon local teachers the importance of manual labor in African education.[241] Missionaries in Togo, privately skeptical of mission officials with no classroom experience in Africa, remained distant from the ideals of Tuskegee.[242] Some rejected the idea of educating Africans for farm work or other menial tasks that did not require classroom preparation.[243] Most missionaries still emphasized *ora* (prayer) over *labora* (work) in their classrooms and congregations.[244] Even those missionaries who agreed that Africans had a particular need of instruction to overcome laziness hesitated, much to the annoyance of the head of the mission in Bremen, to devote more time to such education in their own schools.[245]

When missionary teachers in Togo did agree to incorporate industrial education in their curricula, student resistance ensured that they met with little success. "The natives here," Gruner wrote in 1907, "have no desire to attend school in order to become farmers."[246] Both the North German and Catholic Missions did send a number of African teachers to Notsé for a one-month summer course to learn agricultural methods that they might transmit to their students.[247] The special summer course for missionaries at Notsé did not emphasize cotton growing but rather sought to impart a more general appreciation for agricultural labor. Essays by teachers who participated in this course suggest that neither they nor their students found much value in agricultural education.[248] One teacher who did try to pass on what he learned at Notsé discovered the extent of student resistance to Tuskegee-style education. A student he asked to assist him in this rare lesson in agriculture refused to use his right hand to plant seeds, since he regarded the soil as unclean. The student also refused to fetch manure from the chicken coop for fertilizer, and, when the teacher went instead, the class erupted in laughter. The teacher finally threatened to punish his students to convey the importance of agricultural education.[249] Another North German Mission teacher, having asked his students to help construct new classrooms, complained that "many view their hands . . . as only there to use pencil and pen, like the 'book learned,' and also to eat, but not to swing a heavy hammer."[250] African missionary teachers resisted industrial education more stubbornly than their European supervisors did, perhaps detecting the racism behind this education for downward mobility. Like their white colleagues, these Africans had attained their own relatively comfortable positions through literary, not industrial, education. Mission officials recommended that Europeans alone teach industrial education since, when it was left to African teachers, "manual labor becomes a bitter obligation that has a highly undesirable effect on character building."[251]

GERMAN INTERNAL COLONIZATION
AND AMERICAN SHARECROPPING IN TOGO

To compel cotton-school graduates to become the natural cotton farmers
they supposedly already were, Tuskegee and German authorities relied
on well-established forms of coerced household farming from their own
countries: American sharecropping and the smallholds established by the
Prussian Settlement Commission for internal colonization. Nobody seems
to have believed that cotton-school graduates, who had been forced to
attend the school, would freely grow cotton after they graduated. [252] Before the first students graduated from Notsé, Robinson proposed an experiment in applying the sharecropping system in Togo. Identifying himself racially, as an African American, with the Togolese, Robinson
explained: "As a rule our people here are not rebellious but are docile,
submit readily to leadership and are easily encouraged. But are very im-
provident and full of childish simplicity. We are purely a pastorial [sic]
people and submit to the will of a good shepherd." Robinson thought
perhaps "the productive power of the people would be greatly effected
[sic] if their efforts are in a manner, under the control and supervision
of a more intelligent head." To test this hypothesis, Robinson proposed
selecting six families, some from among the laborers (not the students) at
his Notsé school, and treating them "halfway as a settler would be
treated, and halfway as a laborer or what we call a 'cropper' i.e. one who
makes a farm under the direction of another."[253] (The term *cropper* is
synonymous with *sharecropper.*) The German government approved of
Robinson's "cropper" plan, also because it would allow officials to measure how much cotton a "black farmer" could produce in Togo.[254] For
both Robinson and his supporters in the German government, this approach seemed plausible in Togo at least in part because the potential
African "croppers" seemed racially identical to African American croppers. Sharecropping in the United States involved different mechanisms
of supervision and coercion than those proposed by Robinson, but in
both regions authorities recognized the centrality of supervision and coercion to growing industrial-grade cotton.

   This cropper plan provided the basis for a settlement scheme to which
all graduates of the Notsé cotton school were subject. The German government used the German term *Ansiedler,* or settlers, for those whom
Robinson had called croppers. While this was surely, in part, simply to
avoid a foreign word, the term *Ansiedler* also invoked the techniques pioneered by the Prussian Ansiedlungskommission, the Settlement Commission, to create and control German smallholds in the program of internal
colonization. In Togo, as in Germany, *Ansiedlung,* settlement, meant

making workers less proletarian, less mobile, and more like the American Negroes whose supposed political docility and labor discipline they were to imitate. The regimes of economic control applied to African freedpeople had already become a model for the control of agricultural laborers in eastern Germany when these two models were combined for a second time in German Togo.

To maintain cotton-school graduates as supervised "settlers," the government concentrated them near one of the six districts offices in Togo, so that, even after students returned to their home district, they often had to live and work many miles from their homes. "Since the released students will continue to need oversight and control," the governor ruled, "they are not to be scattered across the district, but set up, if possible, in closed settlements."[255] Attending the cotton school meant exile and permanent subordination to the Germans. The district official of Kete-Kratschi found, after a few years, that people resented being separated from their "native land and tribe" to be permanently concentrated in a single settlement with various ethnic groups from every corner of the district.[256] The district official of Atakpame observed that the government, far from making cotton-school graduates into free farmers, simply continued the "oversight and forced labor that they had become accustomed to in the farming school."[257] The head of Kete-Kratschi station similarly found that, since few graduates wanted to be farmers, he had to subject them to "strict control . . . in order to use the day for diligent work."[258] A few years later, the Kete-Kratschi station head admitted that, unable to provide the "intensive oversight" necessary to prevent the settlers from "falling back into their customary defects of carelessness and laziness," and finding that "reminders and warnings" had no effect, he resorted to "hard punishments." He spoke, no doubt, of the whippings and forced labor that marked German rule in Togo.[259] During a 1912 tour of the entire colony, during which he spoke to many of the settlers, the governor of Togo "could not find a single one that did not long to leave the settlement." He also noted that the settlers enjoyed "diminished prestige" among other Togolese "because of the coercion under which they stand." He concluded that the settlement scheme offered little hope of inspiring imitation by other Togolese.[260]

G. H. Pape, a Texas A&M graduate who had come to Togo in 1904 as a government cotton inspector, took over the Notsé school from Robinson in 1908.[261] Pape brought some brutal Texas racism to the more rationalized Tuskegee model, and even had the government station a soldier at the school "for carrying out floggings."[262] After Pape left Notsé in 1911, his successor, a German, ended the "theoretical instruction" at the school, such as it was, and abandoned the settlement scheme. By that time, the

Atakpame district officer had drawn an obvious conclusion about the cotton school: the goal of "educating the settlers to become free, hard-working farmers, who serve as an example and an encouragement to the rest of the population" could not be reached, since the force required to make the settlers grow cotton meant that they were not, by definition, free farmers.[263] The Colonial Office explained that the Notsé School had overestimated students' "intelligence and independent motivation." The institute would thereafter focus on "the practical training in regular work of those natives to be used for work, correct farming, and better exploitation of their labor power [*Ausnutzung ihrer Arbeitskraft*]."[264] The KWK endorsed this new direction and urged the Togo government to get rid of "everything reminiscent of a school" at Notsé and to continue to refer to those trained at the institute as "students" (*Schüler*) only "in order to preserve certain ideals that exist here and there in the [institute's] relation to Germany."[265] Robinson had of course known that the students were forced to attend Notsé, and he himself had initiated the forced settlement scheme. The new Texan and German management, however, expressed the coercive nature of the cotton program more baldly.

The turn of the cotton school from "theoretical instruction" actually put the school more in line with its original impulse, combining the European colonial civilizing mission with American industrial education in the German program of *Erziehung des Negers zur Arbeit* ("educating the Negro to work"). Indeed, in 1905 Tuskegee Institute itself preceded Notsé in reducing academic instruction to make room for more industrial training, although Tuskegee offered immeasurably more academic instruction than Notsé did. Even as colonial authorities increased coercion to levels beyond those acknowledged by Robinson and the other Tuskegee expedition members, they remained committed to a notion of blacks as natural cotton growers who, because of an inherent laziness, needed outside force to realize this, their true nature. The Notsé school continued to offer summer agriculture courses for missionary teachers that these missionaries themselves regarded as Tuskegee-style education. Even the director of the school, whose missives acknowledged the coercive nature of the school in phrases plain enough to be censored by the German Colonial Office, remained committed to the Tuskegee-inspired Volkskultur model in Togo. For example, he described forcing farmers in a region to plant cotton as "free from unjustified severity, since it corresponds to the already existing custom of the Atakpame district, where cotton has already become a *Volkskultur*."[266] The school still pursued the often contradictory mixture of forced and free labor, racism and racial uplift, that remained at the heart of the New South ideology of the Negro.

Some students ran away from the Notsé school, often never to be found again. Graduates settled under government supervision escaped in greater numbers, and statistics from 1911 suggest that as many as half of all settlers ran away, likely to Gold Coast.[267] Since the cotton school lay on a major commercial route connecting Lome and Atakpame, many students from the hinterland found themselves for the first time with lucrative opportunities for porterage. Some students went truant, disappearing from the school, often for weeks, to work the roads as porters. As the Atakpame district official, despairing of preventing this economic autonomy, complained: "they go wild on the country roads" and learn "unpunctuality and indifference." The typical truant might have agreed with this official that porterage did not have "any utility for his future life as a farmer. A settled life is repugnant to him."[268] One example suggests a more subtle method that Notsé graduates may have employed to avoid cotton growing. Gbologa, a cotton-school graduate settled near Lome permitted by the German government to interplant cotton and corn, allowed his cotton to die off—giving the district official the impression that this was out of "laziness"—so that the corn he planted grew unimpeded, giving him a larger than normal harvest of a crop less labor intensive, more useful, and also with a greater market value than cotton.[269] These forms of resistance were, however, entirely individual, for the settlement program cut cotton growers off from family and regional networks that might otherwise have provided a way to turn individual resistance into collective action.

The Tuskegee cotton project seems to have done a better job of destroying the extended households of its students than in creating monogamous patriarchal households. The Notsé graduates forced to settle as cotton farmers under district office supervision were encouraged to marry and set up households. These young men, predictably, had difficulty convincing women to begin a life under such conditions, particularly given the independent households women were accustomed to maintaining in southern Togo. Observing settlements near the cotton school, one official remarked that many had a "dreary, joyless" appearance because the inhabitants, "completely separated from tribe and family," could not find wives.[270] The difficulties that graduates faced in establishing families not only made these young men unhappy and contradicted Tuskegee and German domestic ideals, they also interfered with cotton growing. Cotton growers, like other agriculturalists in Togo and throughout the world, depended upon the labor of their spouses and children. If cotton-school graduates could not marry, they would lack the necessary labor power to continue cotton farming.[271]

It was through its failures to create free, patriarchal, monogamous family cotton farms that the Tuskegee expedition succeeded in its stated aim of turning parts of Togo into an African version of the New South. Since the labor that the Tuskegee project and the farms of the Notsé graduates required could be provided neither by draft animals, as we have seen, nor by an extended family, growing industrial-grade cotton in Togo depended on the forced labor of prisoners and tax workers.[272] The district official of Atakpame complained that employing tax workers on the farms of Notsé graduates contradicted the goal of teaching students "to become independent farmers, who earn their own bread and gradually, through cotton growing, gain greater prosperity."[273] In Africa, as in the United States, industrial cotton depended on the economic unfreedom of farmers, for it became profitable only through the extreme exploitation and coercive supervision made possible by sharecropping and other forms of semi-free farming. Few, if any, free and economically rational actors in Togo would have grown cotton for the world market. The coastal oil trade continued to be the most profitable business in West Africa throughout the colonial period, and cotton growing did not always lead even to the meager economic rewards promised by the government. The official in charge of Kete Kratschi district explained that cotton growing paid so little that expansion of cotton in his region resulted only from the "gentle pressure" he exercised.[274] Even in Atakpame itself, the district containing the Notsé cotton school, graduates often did not earn enough from cotton growing to support themselves, and some were even forced to turn to local poor relief, such as it was.[275] The Tuskegee program isolated many of its graduates from family and community networks, separated from possibilities for collective resistance, and this isolation facilitated government control of these unfortunate young men. The Tuskegee efforts to create monogamous, patriarchal households that used plows and draft animals to grow cotton as a raw material for international markets worked through its many failures, leading to a forced cotton drive that seemed, in the end, to achieve the cotton output it had set out to achieve. Quintessentially American was the functioning of the ideological concept of the Negro through its self-contradictions and logical failures.

Between 1901 and 1909, cotton exports recorded by the Germans expanded almost sixty-fold before declining in 1911 to give a slightly less impressive figure of fifty-three-fold. This represented a quantitative increase of approximately ten thousand kilograms in 1901 to more than half a million kilograms per year in 1908–1909 and after.[276] This may understate the amount of cotton actually exported to the world market from German Togo, for, as historian Raymond E. Dumett has suggested, about half of the cotton exported from Gold Coast—more than twenty thousand kilograms in 1906—may have been grown in German Togo and smuggled into the English colony.[277] The importance of the Tuskegee cotton project in Togo, however, did not lie in the sheer amount of cotton exported from the colony, which was small both relative to the world market and to the export economy of Togo.[278] Rather, the Tuskegee project received wide international acclaim for three reasons: the apparent success in getting black farmers to grow cotton by introducing American agriculture and industrial education; the success in growing cotton equivalent to American Upland, essential for industrial spinning; and the marked increase in cotton output from the colony. Under the League of Nations mandate exercised by the French in Togo after the First World War, Notsé and Tove remained cotton stations. Notsé became a seed-production facility, while Tove became an agricultural school, still in operation today.[279]

Freed from his duties at Notsé, Robinson set out to follow the German state north of Atakpame, where the military continued to combat open Togolese resistance. Missionaries would not be allowed north for another four years, until 1913, only a year before French and British armies put an end to German rule in Togo. In addition to founding another cotton school, Robinson was to breed new cotton varietals better suited to the northern conditions than those he had introduced into southern Togo and also to "make propaganda for the introduction of the plow."[280] This northern cotton school would have followed the pattern already set by Tove and Notsé of introducing cotton growing to consolidate German military conquest. It would also have been the first non-Hausa educational facility in the northern region. Robinson, however, drowned crossing the Mono River in July 1909, before he could found this northern cotton school. He had insisted on ferrying workers to a cotton gin in a boat too small for the strong currents of the river. When the boat capsized just off the bank, the workers saved themselves by clinging to branches hanging over the river, but Robinson was swept away and his body never recovered.[281]

Members of the Tuskegee expedition, like their German sponsors and countless admirers ever since, believed they were bringing New South uplift to West Africans. Such views presuppose that African Americans were more culturally, technically, politically, or economically elevated than Africans.[282] In fact, the expedition succeeded in creating a cotton export market in Togo because it sent Africans backward along lines of progress commonly accepted by Germans, Africans, and Americans: from literate office work to agricultural labor, from domesticity to social disintegration, from prosperity to poverty, from skilled work to forced labor, and from freedom to domination. Such linear notions of progress are, of course, arbitrary constructions, but they were palpably real to those whose lives they structured.[283] Rather than bringing educational opportunities to Togo, Tuskegee normal-school graduates assisted the state in attacking the education offered by missions, which German authorities had decided was at odds with their own political and economic goals. Rather than bringing patriarchal domesticity to Togo, the cotton school in Notsé impeded family life for its students and graduates. Rather than bringing technological and economic uplift, cultivating raw cotton helped deindustrialize West Africa, limiting local spinning and weaving, working against the diverse economy of manufacturing, trade, and mixed agriculture, and even forcing some Africans into the position of draft animals. Rather than bringing freedom to Africa, the apostles of Tuskegee uplift brought unfreedom, following directly in the tracks of German military conquest. The failures of the expedition, paradoxically, made it successful, for if Tuskegee had succeeded in bringing uplift and freedom to Togo, West Africa may never have sent even a single bale of cotton to European markets. This paradoxical connection of freedom and force pervaded the forms of labor emerging in many capitalist economies, and it defined the position of "Negroes" in New South ideology and in the emerging global South.

Chapter 4

FROM A GERMAN ALABAMA IN AFRICA TO A

SEGREGATIONIST INTERNATIONAL:

THE LEAGUE OF NATIONS

AND THE GLOBAL SOUTH

THE COLONIAL EXTENSION of the New South that Tuskegee Institute and German colonial officials initiated in Togo quickly became a central element of a liberal imperialism that has shaped global politics ever since. German Togo gained a reputation as a model colony, or *Musterkolonie*, among colonial powers, a reputation that it continued to enjoy even after Germans ceded control to French and English colonial states.[1] In the decade before the First World War, liberal enthusiasts for progressive colonialism in Africa applauded both Tuskegee Institute and German colonial policy, not simply for their early successes in producing industrial-grade cotton in Africa, but also for the ostensibly humane and economically viable form of white rule in Africa that they established. Through an unpredictable cascade of events, many emerging directly from, or in imitation of, the Tuskegee expedition to Togo, the racial political and economic hierarchies of the New South became a model for a global South.

The Tuskegee expedition to Togo won wide international recognition because, in the first place, it succeeded in producing significant quantities of American-quality cotton in Africa. While German Togo was too small to have any effect by itself on the world cotton supply, international observers recognized the Tuskegee cotton work there as a milestone in the progress of the global cotton industry.[2] One American magazine even deemed the Tuskegee expedition, during its first month in Togo, "the most important step in the development of the cotton industry since Whitney invented the cotton gin."[3] Soon after their initial successes in Togo, German authorities attempted to reproduce the New South in German East Africa. The Colonial Economic Committee sent a German planter from German East Africa to tour the southern United States and to visit Tuskegee Institute and hired a German Texan to run a cotton school in East Africa.[4] In 1902, inspired by the KWK, the Manchester Chamber of Commerce founded the British Cotton Growing Association (BCGA).[5] British experts attributed much of the German success in growing cotton

FIGURE 4.1. Carrying cotton to a Société togolaise de coton (Sotoco) depot, near Atakpame. Photograph by the author, January 2005.

in Africa to their work with American experts and thus also approached Booker T. Washington to recruit Tuskegee students for British Africa.[6] The BCGA sent an official to Tuskegee Institute and to study cotton growing in the American South, and the Association hired Tuskegee students to run a cotton school in the Anglo-Egyptian Sudan.[7] The BCGA also sent American cotton experts—it is unclear whether white or black—to the other British territories in West Africa.[8] In France, the politically influential Parti Colonial, an umbrella organization bringing together numerous colonial groups, followed closely the progress of the Tuskegee work in Togo, emphasizing the importance of having African Americans run the program.[9] Following their German and British counterparts, French textile manufacturers founded the Association Cotonnière Coloniale (ACC) in 1904, an organization, like the KWK and BCGA, determined to expand production of industrial-quality cotton in overseas colonies, above all in West Africa.[10] Beginning in 1904 the KWK, the BCGA, and the ACC, as well as the smaller cotton associations of other colonial powers, organized an annual International Cotton Congress to foster collaboration in developing sources of industrial-grade cotton outside the United States. As late as 1925 a French colonial expert still cited the Tuskegee expedition to Togo as the premier West African cotton project and continued to hope that blacks from the American South would transform African cotton growing.[11] The work of Tuskegee personnel in German Togo began the colonial transformation of much of West Africa into the undercompensated exporter of raw cotton to international markets that it remains to this day.

Just as importantly, the Tuskegee expedition to Togo also transformed local questions of the American South into a global "Negro question" that shaped international colonial politics. In Germany itself, the Ameri-

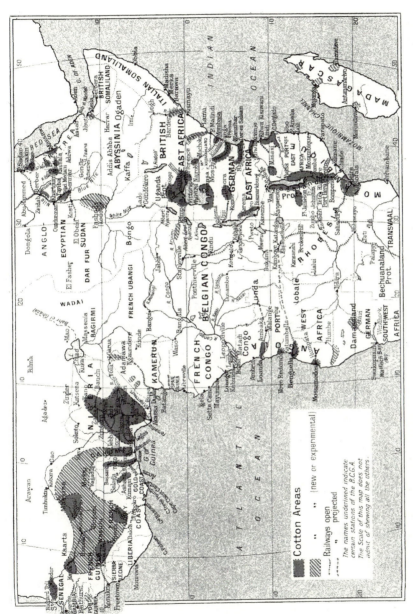

FIGURE 4.2. Colonial cotton cultivation in Africa, 1915. Source: John A. Todd, *The World's Cotton Crops* (London: A&C Black, 1915).

can "Negro question" became a colonial "*Negerfrage*" that drove debates around colonial policies and played a significant role in the most hotly contested elections of Imperial Germany, those of 1906–1907. These elections gave new influence to Bernhard Dernburg, secretary of state for the colonies, and his supporters in the Verein für Sozialpolitik, all of whom looked to the American South as a model for colonial Africa. Booker T. Washington began involving Tuskegee to an ever greater extent in international and colonial politics, taking advantage of his international influence to speak on African topics and to offer Tuskegee pedagogy as a panacea for the perceived ills of colonial Africa. Together, German colonialism and Tuskegee education gained international influence and credibility in the years before the First World War, an influence no less powerful for having been forgotten during that war when Washington died and Germany gained a reputation as a brutal "Hun" from its wartime enemies.

E. D. Morel, Congo Reform, and the German-Tuskegee Colonial Model

No figure was more responsible for the international prominence of Tuskegee and German colonialism than E. D. Morel, the tireless critic of colonial atrocities in the Belgian Congo (the Congo Free State before 1908). Morel, a Liverpool journalist, found that the Belgian concession companies in the Congo Free State employed whippings, executions, and mutilations to force indigenous populations to harvest rubber. In a series of pamphlets and books, including the famous *Red Rubber*, Morel documented these abuses and demanded international action against the Congo Free State.[12] King Leopold II of Belgium, the head of the African International Association, which ruled the Congo, paid great sums to counter Morel's charges, accusing the English humanitarian, for example, of fabricating evidence in order to support Liverpool merchants.

Morel is often misunderstood as an opponent of European imperialism.[13] In fact, the criticisms Morel leveled against the Congo Free State, as well as the solutions he proposed, showed him to be one of the most vocal and sincere believers in the principles of European colonial rule worked out at the Berlin Conference of 1884–85. Writing in 1905, Morel described the Berlin agreement that had laid the legal and diplomatic grounds for the European conquest of Africa as a rare case in which "humanitarian motives" drove international policy. The Congo Free State, for Morel, constituted a "great experiment which seemed to inaugurate an era of lofty effort and high moral purpose" that the conferees "entrusted" to King Leopold.[14] Morel's sincere belief in Europe's civilizing mission in Africa underlay his disappointed denunciations of Belgian atrocities in the Congo. Morel did not suggest freeing the Congo Basin from the imperial claims articulated at the Berlin Conference, but rather subjecting it more thoroughly to these international humanitarian principles. The solution, in short, to colonial atrocities, for Morel, was not less colonialism, but more.[15] For Morel, the collaborative work of Tuskegee Institute and the German government in Togo represented a humanitarian answer to the humanitarian catastrophe of Leopold's Congo.

Morel's colonial politics emerged from a group of Liverpool colonial reformers who, like the American philanthropists who supported Tuskegee, rejected both permanent subordination and also immediate political equality for blacks.[16] Taking its inspiration from the traveler and writer Mary Kingsley, who had recently died while serving as a nurse in the Boer War, the Liverpool group founded the African Society in 1901. (The organization took its present name, the Royal African Society, in 1935.) From the beginning, the African Society held German colonial methods up for admiration and imitation. The first substantial article in the journal of the African Society praised and studied "German Methods of Development in Africa," including the Tuskegee expedition to Togo. It concluded with a postscript on the latest achievements of Calloway and Robinson in the German colony, added just as the journal went to press.[17] The first issue of the journal also reprinted an article by a Frenchman on his country's efforts to cultivate cotton that began by praising the efforts undertaken by Germans in Togo "with the help of Negroes brought over from America" and noting British efforts in the same direction.[18] A lecture to the African Society by a German colonial expert, republished in the journal, touted German "education by labor." "In the first years," the German author allowed, "we ourselves followed too closely the steps of the Powers who had preceded us in Africa, and gave too much attention to literary education and too little to manual work, and like you we have now an excess of clerks, or of what is called in Germany 'Halbbildung' [half-education]."[19]

Morel regarded the German work with Tuskegee Institute in Togo as a model of the colonial rule he advocated and as an alternative to the abuses he decried in the Belgian Congo.[20] Morel, to be sure, also recognized the important role that the Tuskegee expedition to Togo played in the cotton industry. "It should never be forgotten," he wrote in 1909, "that in the modern revival of an export trade in cotton from West Africa, German enterprise led the way and Togo was the first field of experiment. Our cotton movement was to some extent the outcome of Germany's initiative."[21] But Morel applauded the African smallhold farming that Germans dubbed *Volkskultur* more than he applauded commercial cotton cultivation itself. Morel encouraged European colonial powers to foster an economy based on European commerce and the agricultural output of an independent African peasantry and to hinder the growth of both an African proletariat and an African bourgeoisie. The hybrid of the American New South and the German colonized East that emerged in Togo seemed to offer that amalgam of tutelage and commerce that Morel and his Liverpool comrades encouraged.[22] The *Gold Coast Nation* recognized such colonial support for African smallhold farming as an attempt to preserve European political and economic control from challenges by African elites. One writer for that West African newspaper remarked "that Morel on the Congo against the Belgian Government appears to be a totally different person from Morel on the Gold Coast against the English government." This author perceived correctly that, while Morel rushed to the defense of Congolese "steeped in ignorance and in darkness," he had no sympathy for the "'Educated Natives' and 'Cape Coast Barristers' " in Gold Coast.[23] Morel applauded collaboration in Togo between German colonialism and Tuskegee education as a model for peasantization that also, he remarked, bore an "indirect relation . . . to the Negro problem in the States."[24]

In 1912 Morel even endorsed transferring the Congo to Germany to safeguard the population and the freedom of trade in the region.[25] Before the First World War, British humanitarians paid little attention to Germany's genocidal campaign against the Herero of German Southwest Africa in 1904–1907, regarding the mass killing of African civilians as an unfortunate outcome of colonial warfare, rather than a sign of Germany's special brutality.[26] John H. Harris of the Aborigines Protection Society similarly proposed in 1912 that the Belgian Congo, along with portions of the French Congo, be transferred to Germany to improve colonial government of the region. Harris regarded Germany as "easily in the front rank" of colonial states in its encouragement of commerce. Were the German "treatment of the natives . . . equally farsighted," he speculated, "all students of African questions could view with equanimity her gradual absorption of the whole of Equatorial Africa." Even Harris's more limited proposal for a German Congo would have created a great central African Empire, "*Mittelafrika*," a territory crossing Africa from east to west, corresponding to the north-south "Cape to Cairo" ambitions of British imperialists and to the *Mitteleuropa* of German geopolitics.[27] Lord Cromer, since retired from his position as British consul general in Egypt, endorsed Harris's plan, provided it could be carried out without offending France.[28] While neither Morel, Harris, nor Cromer based their admiration for Germany on the Tuskegee expedition alone, for Morel, at least, the work of Germany with Tuskegee Institute exemplified its advanced colonial methods.

Perhaps the sincerest affirmations of the importance of the New South to Congo Reform were the attempts by King Leopold and, after 1908, the Belgian government, to improve their public image by associating themselves with Tuskegee and Hampton Institutes. Representatives of the Congo Free State approached Washington to secure African Americans to help develop the Congolese cotton industry in late 1903, and in 1905 the Congo Free State began employing an American cotton grower to encourage indigenous farmers to grow imported varieties of cotton for export.[29] In 1905, the year after the founding of the Congo Reform Association, King Leopold invited Washington to speak in Brussels, but Washington, advised that the Belgian king sought simply to enlist his good name for the Congo Free State, declined.[30] That same year, a representative of King Leopold offered the Hampton library a collection of books on Africa, which Hampton sociologist Thomas Jesse Jones suspected was a ploy to oblige the institute to the Congo Free State.[31] In 1912 the Belgian government announced that it would set up a "Tuskegee Institute" in the Congo, although it seems that nothing even representing itself as a Tuskegee Institute ever began work in the colony.[32] That was the year both E. D. Morel and John H. Harris made public their proposals to transfer Congo to Germany, and announcing a Tuskegee Institute for the colony may have been calculated to make Belgian rule appear as progressive to colonial liberals as German rule did at that time.

BOOKER T. WASHINGTON, CONGO REFORM, AND INDUSTRIAL EDUCATION IN AFRICA

In 1904, E. D. Morel recruited Booker T. Washington for the American branch of his Congo Reform Association, drawing Tuskegee Institute to an ever greater extent into the German overseas empire, Congo Reform, and other colonial projects. Just as northern white philanthropists had helped make Booker T. Washington the most widely recognized African American leader, now philanthropic colonial powers would seek to give him a corresponding global role as leader of colonized people everywhere. The Congo Reform Association also recruited other prominent Americans for its U.S. branch, including Mark Twain.[33] Morel may also have hoped Washington would have a special influence with President Theodore Roosevelt, who, in 1901, had famously (and, among many southern racists, infamously) hosted the principal of Tuskegee at a dinner with his family in the White House, the first time an African American had been granted that honor. More importantly, however, Morel sensed that Tuskegee Institute offered a model of colonial rule that did not depend upon the kind of atrocities committed in the Congo Free State. As early as 1902 Morel had claimed that the Tuskegee cotton expedition to German Togo had proven African farming to be a profitable alternative to forced plantation labor. Morel also considered the potential of Tuskegee Institute to facilitate the settlement of African Americans in Africa. He speculated that Americans might find African American emigration a threat to their own cotton industry, but also that this might help ameliorate "the Negro problem in the States" if white immigrant labor replaced black labor in the cotton South.[34]

With his increasing entanglements in colonial Africa, Washington began to transform Tuskegee Institute to bring it more in line with the image of an industrial school for blacks that had made him famous the world over, one that more thoroughly rejected academic education in favor of industrial training. Roscoe Conkling Bruce, son of the second African American elected to the United States Senate, Blanche K. Bruce of Mississippi, led this transformation when he became head of academic education at Tuskegee in 1902. From the beginning of his tenure at Tuskegee, Bruce, who had graduated from Harvard, urged Washington to extend Tuskegee internationally, suggesting that he "go to South Africa to attempt there the solution of the world-old race question." This, Bruce promised, "would mean service to the Negro, to South Africa, to England, to America, to civilization itself."[35] In 1905 Bruce began reducing the academic education at Tuskegee, eliminating courses in music and Bible study to make Tuskegee, he explained, "a first class industrial school rather than a second class academic." He demanded that every academic teacher "appreciably . . . diminish the amount of time required of his students for the preparation of his subjects" and threatened to eliminate "History or Literature or Education or some other" academic topic if they did not comply.[36] Students and teachers complained, but Bruce and Washington prevailed.[37] In 1906 Bruce would become assistant superintendent of schools in Washington, D.C. His partisanship for industrial education won him a friend in the white superintendent of schools, who saved his job when black residents organized to have Bruce removed from the position.[38] Tuskegee in Alabama gradually became more like the Tuskegee imagined by its colonial admirers, as it reduced its academic curriculum and began refashioning itself as an authority on black education in the United States and abroad. Booker T. Washington and W.E.B. Du Bois had broken with each other, and any chance of realizing the emancipatory challenge that Tuskegee Institute once might have posed to the New South had vanished.

After Tuskegee personnel began their work in Togo, Washington pressured George Washington Carver to devote more research to cotton.[39] Carver soon became known not only for his work on peanuts and other crops that might help black farmers gain economic independence, but also, internationally, for his work on cotton growing and colonial agriculture. Carver corresponded with John W. Robinson in Togo, who on one

FIGURE 4.3. Students hoeing cotton in experimental fields, Tuskegee Institute, 1902. While George Washington Carver, as this image shows, did some work on cotton from the beginning of his tenure at Tuskegee, his primary interest was in crops that would break the dependency of black farmers on cotton. After 1904, under pressure from Booker T. Washington, Carver devoted more time to cotton growing, the main interest of Europeans in Tuskegee Institute. The Frances Benjamin Johnston Collection, Prints and Photographs Division, Library of Congress.

occasion sent him insect specimens from Africa.[40] An Indian faculty member at the agricultural school at Benares, India, wrote to Carver not only about agricultural questions but also to get "popular and powerful organs conducted by your people on national lines," including the autobiography of Frederick Douglass, for the school library.[41] Carver also received inquiries from South Africa and from a Russian agricultural attaché in St. Louis.[42] He developed a reputation among personnel in agricultural experiment stations in Germany, as well as among Germans interested in cotton growing in East Africa, especially for his work on cotton fertilizer.[43]

Ten years after Washington had advised blacks in the South to "cast down your buckets where you are," he began to present Tuskegee Institute as an institution not only of the American New South but also of the colonial global South. In 1905 Washington began advertising his plans "to arouse interest and inform public opinion in regard to the importance of industrial education for the members of my own race as a means of solving the Negro problem or as it is called in South Africa, 'the native problem.' "[44] The twenty-fifth-anniversary celebrations of Tuskegee Institute in 1906 featured special exhibits of Tuskegee's international work in Africa and the Caribbean in a replica of the original church that had first housed the institute. John W. Robinson returned from Togo briefly to deliver a lecture at the anniversary celebrations.[45] After the turn of the century, increasing numbers of international students attended Tuskegee. Students came from Puerto Rico, Haiti, and elsewhere in the West Indies, as well as from Gold Coast, Southern Nigeria, and Liberia. One student, a nineteen-year-old named Edward Anthony, even came from Lome, Togo, to study at Tuskegee.[46] "[I]n the effort to solve the Negro problem by means of industrial education," Washington observed in 1909, "we have succeeded in working out in this country a practical and useful method of dealing with other primitive races."[47]

Not surprisingly, Booker T. Washington reserved special praise for the colonial state that had first offered him an international role, and he applauded the German "treatment of Negroes in Africa" as a model for other nations. The Germans, Washington claimed, "do not seek to oppress the African, but rather to help him to become more useful for himself and for the German people." Washington offered especially encouraging words to the German cotton textile industrialists who had been his greatest supporters: "The Negro is by nature a cotton grower," he declared in an article published in the *Tropenpflanzer*, a German journal devoted to colonial agriculture, "and if he is carefully led, encouraged, supported, and protected, he can just as easily become an important cotton grower as he now already is in the United States." In the United States, "the school of slavery" had taught the Negro to "use his hands as a good cotton farmer." After slavery, blacks had to "learn to work without the oversight of a master." Tuskegee trained blacks, according to Washington, to teach "their coracialists [*Rassengenossen*] the value of work and the shame of idleness."[48] Under German rule, he explained, "the Negro in Africa" learned "to plow by steam," while "the Sicilian farmer, clinging proudly to his ancient customs and methods, is still using the same plow that was used by the Greeks in the days of Homer, and he is threshing his grain as people did in the time of Abraham."[49]

White American elites came to concur with their European counterparts, as well as with Tuskegee boosters, that the New South's answers to the "Negro question" might serve as models for overseas colonial empires. Just after leaving his position as head of the Southern Education Board, in 1909, Edgar Gardner Murphy argued that the southern United States offered an exemplary solution to the contradiction between the two great principles of the modern world: democracy and empire. "The task which day by day engages us in our Southern States is but the characteristic problem of the modern world. . . . There is upon one hand the uncompromising reality of the negro, in his inexperience, his weakness, his racial contrasts; there is, upon the other hand, the uncompromising reality of the Constitution, both in the force of its written obligations and in that deeper force which our own instincts, interests, and preference have accorded it." Murphy maintained that the piecemeal adjustments achieved in the southern states through paternalistic policies of "the stronger race" toward "the weaker" offered every "imperial democracy" of the world an example to be followed.[50]

The American *Journal of Race Development,* the predecessor to *Foreign Affairs,* similarly placed race at the center of American international thought.[51] The journal was founded in 1910 by two Clark University professors, George H. Blakeslee, a historian of Asia who advised the U.S. Department of State, and the psychologist G. Stanley Hall, founding president of the university and president of the American branch of the Congo Reform Association. Blakeslee explained, in his opening introduction to the journal, that "races of a less developed civilization" were as important to the United States as they were to the colonial powers of Europe, for not only did the United States have a growing empire in the Pacific, but it had also faced, since before the Civil War, "the continuing struggle to find some solution for the negro problem."[52] Blakeslee sponsored annual historical conferences at Clark University that often dealt with themes of race and development, including a 1910 conference in which Booker T. Washington's personal secretary, Emmett Jay Scott, participated and that George Washington Carver had also hoped to attend.[53] Scott had been interested in Africa after having been appointed one of three commissioners to visit Liberia on behalf of the U.S. government to consider whether indebtedness to Great Britain or French and German expansionist ambitions endangered the republic's independence. (The other two commissioners, both white, insisted that each commissioner sail on a separate ship to avoid traveling on equal terms with a black man.)[54] African Americans, once representatives of America's "peculiar institution," now became part of a global black population. For many, like Edgar Gardner Murphy, the New South offered a model for other colonial powers to emulate. Booker T. Washington and the colonial authorities who enlisted the help of Tuskegee Institute further maintained that African Americans could educate the inhabitants of European colonial possessions so that these regions would come to resemble the American New South.

In 1912 Booker T. Washington presided over an "International Conference on the Negro" at Tuskegee, attended by black and white clergy, missionaries, and a few social scientists, representing twenty-one countries or colonies, thirty-six missionary organizations, and each of the black churches in the United States.[55] The conference, as Booker T. Washington announced in his opening address, brought together representatives of those European governments and missions "that have to do with the darker races of the world to come here and spend a few days, first of all in observing the methods that we are trying to employ at Tuskegee and then, in so far as it is possible, in informal discussion based upon their observations to see to what extent the methods employed here can be applied to the problems concerning the people in the countries that are peopled by the darker races."[56] The Tuskegee sociologist Monroe N. Work lectured to the conference on the Tuskegee expedition to German Togo.[57] The conference both reflected and furthered the process by which the efforts of John W. Robinson, James N. Calloway, and the other expedition members blossomed into a program for blacks around the world.

The 1912 Conference also gave African intellectuals, including some from Gold Coast familiar with German efforts in Togo, an opportunity to engage with Tuskegee and the New South. Gold Coast intellectuals, unlike many Europeans and Americans, did not regard the southern United States as a good model for Africa, and in fact used comparisons with the South to criticize colonial racism. A reader of the Gold Coast *African Times and Orient Review* suggested that "the idea that one drop of coloured blood makes a man socially unfit," which he found prevalent in German colonial law, "comes from the United States."[58] Another Gold Coast author, as we saw earlier, singled out Hans Gruner, the German official who worked closely with the Tuskegee expedition in Togo, as having an "animal desire" for African women worse than that found "in Kafirland down to Mississippi."[59] J. E. Casely Hayford, editor of the *Gold Coast Leader*, inveighed against the "new vile importation in terms of 'Negro' and 'nigger' " to Africa, reminding his readers, "We are Ethiopians—Africans."[60]

Many African intellectuals nonetheless praised Booker T. Washington, even while criticizing the American South and rejecting the industrial education that Tuskegee promoted in the United States and Africa.[61] The Liberian Pan-Africanist E. W. Blyden had hailed Booker T. Washington as a model of black success already in 1901 and, although he did not attend the 1912 conference, he did send formal greetings.[62] J. E. Casely Hayford, the Gold Coast newspaper editor, commenting on the 1912 conference, proclaimed "the great work that is being done at Tuskegee is a mighty uplifting force for the race." He hoped, however, that "the great national tendency which is the basis of our educational system here" in the Gold Coast might influence Washington and other African Americans to unite with Africans "in arriving at a national aim, purpose and aspiration."[63] J. E. Casely Hayford did not attend the conference, but his brother Mark did, traveling together with a Gold Coast clergyman, F. A. Pinanko. Even as J. E. Casely Hayford's newspaper, the *Gold Coast Nation*, hailed Booker T. Washington as a "Moses" who would lead his race out of the Egypt of white racist oppression, however, Casely Hayford rejected the education that Tuskegee promoted.[64] Writing the month after the 1912 conference, an author in the *Gold Coast Nation*, probably Casely Hayford, complained: "In name of Philanthropy Blacks are being kept down in Africa and the US." White philanthropists, the author continued, despite stellar examples of black success, including Booker T. Washington, still believed that the black's "proper place is that of a drawer of water and a hewer of wood—a being who must forever be kept under. Do even Philanthropists ever stop," this writer wondered, "to analyze their own sentiments, the motives which prompt them to action?"[65] Booker T. Washington himself had such power primarily because white philanthropists thought that the pedagogy promoted by Tuskegee would keep the black worker "a drawer of water and a hewer of wood." Washington's own position was, for this reason, self-contradictory, and these contradictions are reflected in the views of those Africans who admired Washington even while admonishing those who, like Washington, promoted programs of supposed racial uplift that in fact created obstacles to black freedom and prosperity.

Dusé Mohamed Ali, a black Londoner who founded and edited the *African Times and Orient Review*, a newspaper promoting anticolonial solidarity among the victims of imperialism, similarly welcomed the 1912 Tuskegee conference in terms suggesting a black nationalist understanding of Tuskegee.[66] "In West Africa," he reported, "the very announcement of the Conference seems to have given a new impetus to the sentiment in favour of an African nationality."[67] Dusé Mohamed Ali solicited an article on the conference and on Tuskegee Institute directly from Washington, who provided a portrait of Tuskegee unusual in its emphasis on the resistance of the institute to disfranchisement and other forms of white racism.[68] In 1920 Ali moved to New York to work with Marcus Garvey, a former associate from London, who had by then founded the Universal Negro Improvement Association (UNIA). Garvey, another nationalist admirer of Washington and Tuskegee Institute, would even name one of the ships of his Black Star shipping line the S.S. *Booker T. Washington*.[69]

The conference published no proceedings other than lectures by four prominent white men: Tuskegee sociologist Robert E. Park, University of Chicago professor of sociology William I. Thomas, the South African Maurice Evans, and E. D. Morel—even though Morel, in the end, did not attend the conference.[70] These lectures indicate how Tuskegee and the American South represented a model colonial society for white liberals.

They express none of the ambivalence about industrial education shown by the African attendees at the conference.

The lectures by E. D. Morel and Maurice S. Evans depicted racial separation as a prerequisite for black and white cooperation and progress. Morel and Evans were among the admirers of Tuskegee who understood Booker T. Washington's famous "separate as the fingers, yet one as the hand" image as an argument in favor of segregation. Morel recommended what he called, echoing German Colonial Secretary Bernhard Dernburg, "scientific" colonization. Such scientific colonization, according to Morel, required that the European colonial state preserve African smallholding, preventing Europeans or Africans from acquiring large tracts of land, and retaining government possession of "enough land for Africans so they can support future population growth." (This position had led the *Gold Coast Nation* to accuse Morel of playing "Mr. Jekyll and Mr. Hyde on this land question in the Congo and on the Gold Coast.")[71] Europeans would then rule this African smallholder in order to "build up by slow degrees a better *African* out of the raw material upon which [they] had to work."[72]

Like Morel, Maurice Evans advocated racial separation to maintain what he regarded as the true nature of Africans as smallholders, albeit a true nature to be improved by white rulers. Evans explained that Africans are "naturally a race of peasants living by and on the land, and to divorce them from it in their present unsettled and changing state would be to invite disintegration and chaos."[73] At the conference, Evans became an ardent admirer of Tuskegee Institute, which, he maintained, demonstrated that, "Whatever may be the failings of the negro race . . . they are very susceptible to wise guidance, they can be disciplined and led in the mass, as is perhaps not possible with a more individualistic race."[74] The year after the conference, Evans wrote an essay for a study by the Verein für Sozialpolitik on white settlement in the tropics in which he advocated racial separation for all of South Africa.[75] In 1915 he commended Tuskegee and Hampton Institutes for training American blacks to live in racially separated rural communities in the South, working in labor gangs or as "progressive peasant proprietor[s]" under white guidance. Citing Booker T. Washington as an authority, he sugested a similar policy of racial separation for South Africa, in which blacks would be placed under "white guidance." The southern United States served Evans as a model for the policy of segregation in South Africa that, after 1948, the white government would intensify and rename in Afrikaans, *apartheid*.[76]

Robert E. Park lectured on the role of Tuskegee pedagogy in colonial Africa, focusing on industrial education as an alternative to the type of colonial rule practiced in the Belgian Congo. "Africa must expect," Park warned, "to serve a long and hard apprenticeship to Europe, an appren-

ticeship not unlike that which Negroes in America underwent in slavery."
According to Park, "Tuskegee, Hampton, and some of the other industrial
schools in the South offer, perhaps, some suggestions as to the solution
of the Negro problem in Africa." The industrial education offered at
Tuskegee might serve, Park elaborated, "to abridge this apprenticeship of
the younger to the older races, or at least to make it less cruel and inhuman
than it now frequently is."[77] University of Chicago sociologist William I.
Thomas gave a lecture on Polish peasants in Europe and the United States,
the same population that had led Weber and others in the Verein für Sozialpolitik to connect race and free labor on both sides of the Atlantic.
Thomas found that "the peasant was and is mentally as backward as the
Negro is or as he was in slavery" but that industrial education could
civilize all races by making them accustomed to work.[78] Thomas and Park
would go on to found a school of sociology at the University of Chicago
that remains one of the most influential variants of the discipline to this
day. The 1912 conference brought together racial thought by white colonial elites like Morel and Evans with New South ideology represented by
Tuskegee Institute and with the sociology of the University of Chicago.
This new international synthesis would shape theories and practices of
racial divisions of labor for decades to come.

THE NEGERFRAGE IN GERMANY: COLONIAL POLICY,
COLONIAL SOCIAL SCIENCE, AND COLONIAL SCANDALS

Members of the German branch of the Congo Reform Association,
founded in 1910, included the colonial thinkers most enthusiastic about
bringing Tuskegee pedagogy to Africa. Indeed, Booker T. Washington's
German publisher, Ernst Vohsen, founded the German Kongo-Liga.[79]
Vohsen was the most important colonial publisher in Germany, one of
the most influential members of the Kolonialrat, an advisory board to the
German Colonial Office, and an early promoter of colonial cotton.[80] He
produced a translation of Washington's *Up from Slavery* soon after the
1901 English original. In his preface to the translation, Vohsen remarked
that Washington's famous words from his 1895 Atlanta address—"In all
things that are purely social, we can be as separate as the fingers, yet one
as the hand in all things essential to mutual progress"—"are also true for
us in Africa."[81] Vohsen's translation was the one that the leaders of the
North German Mission sent its mission teachers in Togo in 1907 to persuade them to follow the example of the Notsé cotton school by placing
more emphasis on agriculture than on English literacy. Vohsen also published German translations of other works by Washington with prefaces

that similarly praised Tuskegee Institute and African Americans as models for German colonies in Africa.[82]

As a result of both the success of the Tuskegee expedition in Togo and the wide international admiration it found, Germany began to develop its own colonial "Negro question," or Negerfrage. Like the American "Negro question," the German Negerfrage posited a contradictory identity for black people, holding that only with the outside authority of whites could their potentially valuable characteristics, like political docility and a contentment with poorly paid, menial labor, triumph over countervailing characteristics of political and economic restlessness and self-assertiveness. The white elites discussing the Negerfrage in Germany, like their counterparts in the United States, imagined this white authority as pedagogical and spoke of the colonial mission as "educating the Negro to work"—"*Erziehung des Negers zur Arbeit.*" Tuskegee, Booker T. Washington, and the New South remained reference points for these colonial thinkers, both because of the specific successes in Togo and because they found the New South ideology of the Negro congenial to the colonial capitalism they were introducing in Africa.

Colonial thinkers employed increasingly explicit comparisons of semi-free agricultural labor in the southern states, eastern Prussia, and colonial Africa. The presumed racial identity of Africans and African Americans laid the groundwork for a number of discussions of race and labor at a series of German Colonial Congresses held in 1902, 1905, and 1910. One German speaker at the 1902 Congress even offered the kind of scornful parody of black English employed by Booker T. Washington, as well as many white racists, in a comparative discussion of "white, yellow and back labor": "The Negro's, motto is," he explained, "'W'en de prophet sayed dat nothin' could be got widout hard work,' says Uncle Mose, 'he was plumb right, but dat don't of necessity mean dat you has to do de hard work yourself if you is smart enough to make some odder feller do it.' "[83] Each of the three Colonial Congresses emphasized the need to "educate the Negro to work," and many presentations relied on Tuskegee Institute as a model for colonial economic and political control.[84]

The German colonial Negerfrage incorporated not only the New South concept of the "Negro" but also the German concept of the Sachsengänger. The term *Sachsengänger* had originally referred only to Prussian Poles who went to Saxony for the sugarbeet season but soon came to refer to migrant labor in Africa and even to racially subordinated workers who did not migrate. In 1902 a German colonial publicist, addressing the African Society, the British group close to E. D. Morel, complained that reluctant plantation laborers in Cameroon "recall to memory the Russian Poles, the 'Sachsengänger,' who leave their homes in the summer for farm work in the eastern parts of Germany." The speaker invoked discussions from the New South when he offered that "education by labor" rather than "literary education" would improve these African Sachsengänger.[85] A writer in the liberal *Koloniale Rundschau* similarly worried that increasing "Sachsengängerei" in East Africa would spread syphilis among the men and infertility among the women.[86] German Colonial Secretary Bernhard Dernburg, as we shall see below, even compared African American sharecroppers to Sachsengänger. This generalization of the term "Sachsengängerei" reflected how knowledge about the Prussian East, produced decades earlier by the Verein für Sozialpolitik, had come to function globally. The "racial" struggle against Poles had always been part of the German version of the "Negro question."

Not only colonial reformers like Ernst Vohsen, whose plans depended upon the "improvability" of Africans, but also colonial racists who believed that German colonies should employ forced African labor, praised the work of Tuskegee Institute in Togo. Perhaps the most important of these colonial racists was Paul Rohrbach, a colonial writer who had headed a Settlement Commission (Ansiedlungskommission) in German Southwest Africa from 1903 to 1907, when the government carried out a genocidal campaign against the Herero.[87] Rohrbach recommended that the German government of Southwest Africa adopt the "Boer system" of racial segregation, forbidding "all instruction in writing and reading" for Africans.[88] He also advocated forced labor in Africa. "Natives," he declared, have no right "to live and die according to their own custom," if their custom created economic hardship for Europeans in the colony.[89] Yet Rohrbach invoked the New South and Tuskegee almost as often as Schmoller and others who favored African Volkskultur. Although he chastised those who believed that "blacks are human like us," Rohrbach, who had visited Togo in 1907, gave guarded praise for the Notsé cotton school. Noting that, in areas where the climate prevented white settlement on a large scale, colonial economies would have to depend upon African farmers, whose growing wealth might become "a means of political resistance [*Widersetzlichkeit*]," Rohrbach applauded the cotton projects in Togo and German East Africa for improving the agricultural output of African farmers without increasing their political or economic power. Even the "negrophilic English system in West Africa," Rohrbach noted, followed the example of these cotton projects.[90] Rohrbach would continue to discuss the Notsé cotton school in his writings on colonial topics during the Nazi period.[91]

The "Negro question" of the American New South gained increasing importance in German colonial and domestic politics during the so-called Hottentot elections of 1906–1907. A series of colonial scandals, including in German Togo, initially threatened to undermine parliamentary support for the German government. Catholic missionaries in Togo, including those in Atakpame, near Notsé, had, since 1905, sent numerous reports of colonial atrocities to members of the Catholic Center Party, which the young Reichstag member Matthias Erzberger and others publicized.[92] In the years following the foundation of the German Empire in 1871, the Catholic Center Party had found itself, along with the Social Democrats, classified as "enemies of the empire" (*Reichsfeinde*). With the end of anti-Catholic Kulturkampf laws in 1878, however, the Center Party gradually joined liberals and conservatives in supporting the government, primarily against Social Democrats. This alliance threatened to dissolve when the Center Party began excoriating the government of Chancellor Bernhard von Bülow on colonial issues in Togo and elsewhere. Major wars in German East Africa and in German Southwest Africa embarrassed the government especially, for they required large expenditures without promising correspondingly large profits. Although the Reichstag did not have the power to bring down a government, which the kaiser appointed, its assent was required for all legislation and it could thus make governing virtually impossible.

To address complaints about colonial scandals, Kaiser Wilhelm II sought to further Americanize German colonial policy. The Tuskegee expedition to Togo had, years before, brought Booker T. Washington and the value of the United States as a colonial model to the attention of the German emperor. In March 1902, during an official visit to the United States, Prince Henry, brother of Kaiser Wilhelm, met, at his own request, with Booker T. Washington at New York's Waldorf Astoria Hotel. The two men spoke cordially for ten or fifteen minutes, "chiefly," according to the *New York Times*, about the Tuskegee expedition to Togo.[93] Before their meeting, the prince had also asked Washington to arrange a performance of African American songs, "not the rag-time songs," he explained, "but the old negro melodies." The Hampton Singers, in New York with Washington to perform at Carnegie Hall at an event devoted to Hampton and Tuskegee, obliged him, likely in the "plantation dress" they wore for their other New York performances that March.[94] The prince asked Washington to send him a book of Negro melodies, and Washington obliged.[95] For Henry, as for many others on both sides of the Atlantic, Booker T. Washington simultaneously represented an admirable and authentic African American character—represented for Henry by "old negro melodies," not "rag-time songs"—and a colonial and industrial modernity represented by the cotton schemes in Togo.

Announcing "I need Americans," Kaiser Wilhelm appointed as top official in charge of the colonies the German banker Bernhard Dernburg.[96] The son of a prominent National Liberal Reichstag deputy, Dernburg had worked in his youth in a New York bank, and, when he eventually became head of the Darmstaedter bank in Germany, continued to cultivate American business contacts and business methods. The press in both the United States and Germany noted with surprise that the kaiser had appointed an official with a background in business rather than in the state bureaucracy or the military and also one who happened to be Jewish. The press attributed Dernburg's supposedly American style in part to these novel characteristics.[97] The liberal *Nationalzeitung*, formerly edited by Dernburg's father, called the kaiser's decision to appoint Dernburg a "triumph of Americanism." The *Vossische Zeitung* attributed to Dernburg "the characteristics of Mr. Rockefeller and Mr. Morgan, for whom no task is too great."[98] Dernburg's business expertise promised to bring a new style to the administration of individual colonies and to the Colonial Section of the Foreign Office, widely regarded as an "Augean stable" of corruption for the new colonial director to clean out.[99] The Tuskegee expedition had convinced the kaiser, like many Europeans, of the benefits of American methods and models for colonial rule.

The "American" Dernburg would serve Wilhelm II much as Bismarck had served his grandfather Wilhelm I in subduing, and finally winning over, parliamentary opposition. Dernburg, using the "jargon of the stock-jobber," responded so forcefully to Matthias Erzberger and other Catholic Center Party critics of German colonial policy that, the *New York Times* concluded, he made a break between the Center Party and the government virtually inevitable.[100] Dernburg even countered accusations against Gruner, district chief of Misahöhe, by pointing to the "cultural" development of the district, although he did not remark on the role that Tuskegee Institute played in this process.[101] After one particularly effective attack on the Center Party, Kaiser Wilhelm embraced and kissed Dernburg "with much warmth" at a reception at the Italian embassy. This gesture of affection was usually reserved for royalty, and the "warmth" of the kiss corresponded to the degree of honor and importance the kaiser attributed to its recipient.[102]

The Catholic Center Party finally broke, as predicted, with the government, and the kaiser dissolved the Reichstag on December 13, 1906, calling new elections to deliver a national parliament that would support the government he had appointed. Dernburg became the principal spokesperson for the government during these Reichstag elections.[103] Chancellor Bülow succeeded in reviving the Reichstag alliance that his predecessor, Otto von Bismarck, had forged between liberals and conservatives against Catholics and, as always, Social Democrats. Just as most liberals and conservatives had found common ground in support of the anti-Catholic Kulturkampf until 1878, they now found common ground in support for German colonialism, which many also regarded as a Kulturkampf, a struggle for civilization. Indeed, support for the colonial Kulturkampf also included opposition to political Catholicism. The largest liberal party, the National Liberals, viewed the struggle over colonies in the 1906–1907 campaign as in part a struggle against an ultramontane "second government, working through the Center Party and its leaders."[104] Catholic critics of colonialism nonetheless accepted the overseas "cultural mission" of Germany as much as the colonial politicians whom they criticized.[105]

To support Dernburg and the Bülow government in the 1906–1907 Reichstag elections, leading German social scientists, including Georg Friedrich Knapp, Max Sering, and Adolph Wagner, formed, under the leadership of Gustav Schmoller, a "Colonial-Political Action Committee" (CPAC).[106] This committee organized scientists, artists, writers, and other professionals to support the German "Volk" against the "petty and antinationalistic [*unnational denkende*] majority in the Reichstag."[107] The CPAC supported a view of colonialism that emerged from the smallholder model worked out in the Tuskegee expedition to Togo and advanced in the meetings of Colonial Congresses and elsewhere. The CPAC promised a reformed and reinvigorated colonialism to a German public dismayed by expensive colonial wars and individual colonial scandals. The older colonialism that grew out of the coastal trade, explained a 1907 CPAC pamphlet, gave Europeans insufficient control over indigenous labor to permit "the regulation and improvement of production." With the "education of the Negro to work" and increasing control over colonial production, Germany would, the pamphlet promised, soon produce enough cotton to cover all its needs, making its textile industry independent from American growers.[108] The CPAC worked closely with Dernburg in the campaign leading up to the January 1907 Reichstag elections.

At a widely publicized forum sponsored by the CPAC for an audience of scientists and artists at the Berlin Academy of Music in January 1907, Dernburg called on Germany, as the "nation of thinkers and poets," to employ science and technology as "the modern means of developing foreign parts of the world, raising up lower cultures, and improving the conditions of life for blacks and whites."[109] As newspapers in the United States were quick to note, Dernburg's speech presented the American South as a model for Germany's colonies, both for its organization of black labor and for its success in cotton growing.[110] Dernburg touted German efforts to turn colonial subjects into agricultural laborers after "slavery—thank God—has been abolished." He reminded his readers that the United States had similar problems with "the black population taken from the west coast of Africa, that is, from the same region where our Cameroon and Togo lie." Germany could congratulate itself on its "treatment of the black race" when it looked to the United States with "those nine million quarter- and half-educated Negroes, who do not lose their inherited characteristics, who have adopted only those aspects of civilization that increase their rights, and whose self-confidence stands in inverse proportion to their intelligence and ability."[111] Dernburg would later change his views of the racial division of labor in the United States, and would come to see African Americans as an example of what Africans in Germany's colonies might become, rather than an image of a politically active black population that Germany should prevent from emerging in its own colonies.[112] Max Sering and other members of the Verein für Sozialpolitik also spoke at the symposium, similarly praising the supposedly progressive colonialism of Bernhard Dernburg.[113] The 1907 election saved the Bülow government and gave new prestige to the German-American colonialism promoted by Bernhard Dernburg.

Dernburg institutionalized the close relationship between the Verein für Sozialpolitik and German colonial policy in the Hamburg Colonial Institute, founded in 1908.[114] In contrast to previous institutions of colonial education in Germany, the Hamburg Institute focused on all aspects of colonization, rather than just language instruction or agriculture, and undertook research that its advocates regarded as "scientific" rather than merely practical. This "colonial science," as historian Erik Grimmer-Solem has shown, emerged as a branch of the social science of the Verein für Sozialpolitik, especially in the work of the Gustav Schmoller student and Colonial Institute economist Karl Rathgen.[115] For Rathgen, conceiving of colonial policy (*Kolonialpolitik*) as a subspecialty of social policy (*Sozialpolitik*) meant focusing on improving the "Negro" rather than simply ensuring white domination over an abject population. As an example of this improvement, he cited German colonies where "polygamy is declining, the position of women is improving, and in agriculture modern implements are used, and small tribal conflicts disappear."[116] While a visiting professor at Columbia University in 1913, Rathgen traveled to Tuskegee Institute, where Booker T. Washington received him as an "important man" associated with the Colonial Economic Committee that had sponsored the Tuskegee expedition to Togo.[117]

In 1910 the Verein für Sozialpolitik again came to the defense of Germany's "New South" colonial policy, this time against Paul Rohrbach and others who called on the colonial state to cease its efforts to "improve" blacks and instead to force them to serve white settlers as unfree laborers. Supported by the Colonial Office, the Verein produced a series of regional studies on white settlement in the tropics, similar in format to those the organization had produced two decades earlier on agricultural labor in Germany. The studies did not reject white settlement outright, but they also reaffirmed the Colonial Office position that not every colonial economy could benefit from, or be profitable for, white settlers.[118] In 1914 G. K. Anton, a professor at the University of Jena and a member of the Verein für Sozialpolitik, met with one of Dernburg's successors in the Colonial Office, Wilhelm H. Solf, to discuss free labor in Africa. Anton warned that occasional "Sachsengängerei" might make Africans into "propertyless proletarians." Slavery had given way to "free labor" but without, he cautioned, leading to "satisfactory labor relations everywhere." As a solution, Anton advised compulsory "education to labor" modeled on "Negro education in the southern states of the North American Union."[119]

With the rise of the "American" Dernburg in the Colonial Office, the New South and Tuskegee Institute became ever more important to German colonial policy and colonial rhetoric. Shortly after the elections of 1907, Moritz Schanz of the Colonial Economic Committee traveled to the South to study cotton growing and African Americans. A German overseas merchant who had returned to run a spinning mill in his native Chemnitz, the center of the cotton textile industry in Saxony, Schanz became perhaps the most important colonial expert on African Americans.[120] During his visit to the United States, Schanz met with Booker T. Washington at Tuskegee, where Washington reaffirmed his willingness to send more of his graduates to Africa.[121] Despite Washington's warning to Schanz about Du Bois—"he's only a teacher, you know"—the German colonial expert also sought out the African American sociologist at Atlanta University. At Schanz's request, Du Bois prepared a report on "The Probability of Educated Negroes Going to Africa as Economic Leaders of the People." Apparently Du Bois had made a similar report for the Congo Free State a decade earlier. Du Bois warned that the "better class" of the American black population was already fighting for "full civil rights" and therefore would not want to travel to "a land with, on average, a lower civilization." "American blacks," concluded Schanz from Du Bois's report, "hold dark misgivings that European colonial powers might treat them with even more prejudice than Americans do." However, Du Bois offered, if Germany would guarantee that African Americans in Africa would "be treated as men," "have some share in their own government" and "have a chance for full and free development," "it will be possible to attract a small number and in time a considerable number of Negro Americans."[122] It was not overly far-fetched to hope that colonial governments might indeed establish political conditions for blacks more democratic and free than those in the American South, and Schanz and other Germans continued to hope that the brutal excesses of American racism might push African Americans to colonial Africa.[123] Schanz welcomed a 1909 book by William P. Pickett, a New York lawyer, advocating, as "Abraham Lincoln's Solution" to the "Negro Problem," the gradual expulsion of all blacks from the United States.[124] The antiblack riots of the summer of 1910, sparked by the victory of the African American heavyweight champion boxer Jack Johnson over a white challenger, renewed Schanz's hope that African Americans might choose to emigrate to Africa.[125]

In 1909 German Colonial Secretary Bernhard Dernburg visited Tuskegee and the southern United States to draw lessons for German colonialism. Although John W. Robinson, the last Tuskegee expedition member in Togo, had perished in Africa three months earlier, Tuskegee Institute continued to work closely with German colonial experts and officials. Booker T. Washington met Dernburg shortly after the German's arrival in New York, and the two dined together at a luncheon sponsored by the New York Cotton Exchange at Delmonico's restaurant.[126] After a consultation in Washington, D.C., at the U.S. Department of Agriculture, Dernburg traveled through Alabama, Mississippi, Louisiana, Texas, and Oklahoma, before meeting with Washington a second time in Tuskegee. Dernburg interested himself more in the tenant farming system than in Tuskegee, in part, he explained, because Schanz had already reported so extensively on Washington's institute.[127]

Dernburg, Schanz, and other colonial admirers of the United States applauded the control exercised over ostensibly free labor in the American South. Like many Germans, Schanz concurred with the dominant New South view that, as he put it, "the African negro requires some *outside* impetus in order to get him to take up the cultivation of some new produce for export."[128] Schanz described the advantages of debt peonage in the United States to the members of the International Cotton Congress, an organization of European industrialists interested primarily in promoting West African cotton: "The only way to force the *negro* to do regular work, according to the opinion expressed by many persons, is to keep him in debt. Among 600,000 coloured cotton farmers, 500,000 are in an intermediary state between free men and slaves."[129] Dernburg similarly found sharecropping in the United States an effective, and even admirable, means of controlling black labor, one "comparable in a certain degree with the Sachsengängerei of our fatherland." Dernburg could only have meant that both Sachsengänger and sharecroppers were particularly vulnerable to control by employers and labor contracts because of their racial subordination. The Sachsengänger were seasonal migrant laborers whose contracts stipulated that they leave Germany at the end of the season, whereas sharecroppers were hindered by their contracts, if not prevented entirely, from leaving the land that they worked. A better comparison might have been sharecroppers and the ethnic German smallholders settled by the Prussian Settlement Commission, although this would have ignored presumptions about racial inferiority and superiority. Dernburg translated in full for his German readers examples of two common types of tenancy contracts, each of which featured numerous obligations to the landlord.

Like Schanz, Dernburg noted how the obligation of tenants to buy from a furnishing merchant on credit kept them in "financial dependence."[130]

Dernburg, Schanz, and other proponents of New South colonialism, though sometimes criticized by the German right as excessively "Negro friendly," were in fact quite racist. The *Brooklyn Times* dubbed Bernhard Dernburg a "German Bourbon," using the term then common for Democrats nostalgic for the Old South. Dernburg, they reported, had announced in a speech in London "that his experience in the United States convinced him that cotton growing was essentially a Negro's job, and in his opinion an ideal system would be one in which the White man would act as director of Negro labor, subjecting his workers to discipline, so that they could be relied upon to work regularly." These views, the editors concluded, would make Dernburg "eagerly welcomed as a neighbor by Senator Tillman and ex-Gov. Vardaman."[131] Senator "Pitchfork" Ben Tillman, a populist Democrat from South Carolina, and James K. Vardaman, a one-term governor of Mississippi, were two of the most notoriously and vocally racist politicians in the South. Vardaman directed some of his most notorious racist invective against Booker T. Washington, and the comparison of Dernburg with the former Mississippi governor suggests that German colonial authorities distorted Tuskegee education, even as they claimed to admire it. The German application of the New South to Africa refashioned Tuskegee as an institute reproducing the racism of the New South, rather than challenging it, even in its own, limited fashion.

This racism lay at the heart of all the reforming colonialism that emerged out of the Tuskegee expedition to Togo, including much of the long tradition of international humanitarianism strengthened, if not inaugurated, by E. D. Morel and the Congo Reform Association. While African Americans did not share the antiblack racism common in Congo Reform Association or among those Catholic Center Party politicians critical of German colonial abuses, some did, as historian Tunde Adeleke has shown, support a colonial "civilizing mission" in the period before the First World War.[132] Supporters of humanitarian colonialism could criticize colonial abuses but remain certain that these abuses were contrary to, rather than inherent in, the colonial civilizing mission. The civilizing mission could thus live off its own failures, which, far from shaking the confidence of its proponents, caused them to redouble their efforts. The civilizing mission thus not only employed the New South concept of the "Negro," but also resembled this ideological concept structurally. The failure of the concept of "Negro" in New South ideology to correspond to the reality of black life in the New South authorized violent, supposedly corrective, interventions, which themselves constituted the reality of black life in the South. Similarly, the brutality of the colonial civilizing mission, its failure to correspond to its own ideological self-justifications, authorized new colonial efforts.

SOCIAL DEMOCRACY VERSUS THE CIVILIZING MISSION

European socialist parties of the Second International, apart from "revisionists" like Eduard Bernstein, were among the few organizations in Europe to maintain a principled opposition to imperialism, not simply decrying the abuses, but rejecting the premise, of a civilizing mission.[133] The principled critique and practical rejection of authoritarian state socialism and patriarchal domesticity by the German Social Democratic Party included a rejection of overseas, as well as internal, colonization. The colonial fervor surrounding the 1907 elections caused the Socialist International to revisit its earlier rejection of colonialism. The elections cost the German Social Democratic Party almost half of its seats in the Reichstag (although the percentage of votes cast for the party dropped by less than 3 percent and the number of SPD voters increased slightly). At the 1907 International Socialist Congress in Stuttgart, a Dutch socialist, Henri van Kol, attempted to reverse the organization's absolute rejection of colonialism, arguing that under a "socialist regime" colonialism "could have a civilizing effect."[134] A commission headed by Van Kol concluded that socialists should try to influence colonial policy rather than rejecting it out of hand, since, as Eduard Bernstein put it, to both applause and hissing from the audience, "civilized people" (*Kulturvölker*) had a responsibility to "uncivilized people" (*Nichtkulturvölker*). The majority at the conference opposed such socialist imperialism, and one member joked about "Comrade Dernburg," suggesting that the idea of a socialist colonialism was little better than the supposedly humane colonialism proposed by Dernburg and endorsed by the Verein für Sozialpolitik. Julian Baltazar Marchlewski, a Polish delegate who had written widely on Prussian internal colonization, the Settlement Commission, and Sachsengängerei, rejected this endorsement of a civilizing mission: "We Poles know the meaning of such tutelage, which we have received from the Russian Czars and the Prussian government."[135] Karl Kautsky, the leading theorist of the German Social Democratic Party, declared socialist colonial policy a "logical contradiction," and received a loud and lengthy ovation for comparing Bernstein's view that "there exist childish peoples unable to rule themselves" to the oldest justifications for despotism, common also to slaveholders in the American South. The Congress, over the objections of revisionists, including members of the German delegation, blocked van Kol's attempt to promote a social democratic colonial "civilizing mission."[136]

Karl Kautsky elaborated his position in a book published later that year, *Socialism and Colonial Policy*, in which he mounted a critique of the paternal colonial civilizing mission similar to the one he directed against agricultural smallholding and the patriarchal household in his 1899 *Agrarian Question*. Targeting Bernstein and other revisionists in his own party, and rejecting liberal and conservative variants of colonialism, Kautsky insisted that social democrats should never endorse "the right of peoples of higher culture to 'exercise tutelage' over peoples of lower culture" since that was precisely the "right" that the bourgeoisie claimed justified its own political and economic power over workers in Europe. Ironically, Kautsky explained, the poverty that capitalism brought to Europe and the rest of the world gave the domination of those few who profited from this system, the bourgeoisie, "the appearance of the rule of culture over barbarism [*Unkultur*], of select intelligence over . . . 'the great unwashed,' as the English say." The bourgeoisie thus could claim that "they do not exploit the proletariat for their personal advantage, nor for the sake of profit: they exercise tutelage over it in the general social interest." The proletariat could not, Kautsky wrote, endorse the colonial civilizing mission "without sanctioning its own exploitation and disavowing its own struggle for emancipation." Cultural and economic progress of subordinate groups, Kautsky reminded his readers, "has always occurred against and not through the upper classes."[137] Kautsky's Social Democratic Party, the largest party in Germany, rejected the colonial civilizing mission as part of its larger refusal of the paternalist state socialism advocated by the Verein für Sozialpolitik, including the interlinked, transnational complex of patriarchal households, racism, and the constraint of free labor that underwrote the power of the state and of capital.

The Versailles Treaty
and the Segregationist International

The years of the First World War erased historical memory of the German role in bringing the New South "Negro question" to the colonial civilizing mission. By the end of the First World War, most British observers, with the exception of E. D. Morel, came to view Germany as a peculiarly unfit colonizer in order to lend rhetorical support to their own nation's cause in the war and in the postwar settlement that expanded Britain's African territories under the aegis of the League of Nations. "The doctrine of Germany's guilt as a uniquely brutal and cruel colonial power," remarked historian William Roger Louis, "originated during the First World War, not before." The exigencies of war changed the views of John H. Harris, who had, as late as 1912, proposed transferring sovereignty over the Congo, if not all of tropical Africa, to Germany. During the conflict, Harris played a leading role in publicizing German colonial atrocities, and the British government nearly sent him to the United States on a lecturing campaign to drum up American enthusiasm for joining the war against Germany.[138] By this time, as William Roger Louis has shown, descriptions of German colonial atrocities served to bolster Britain's claim to a civilizing mission against those, like E. D. Morel, who had come to support internationalizing the colonies. The mainstream British press and politicians marginalized Morel, however, as pro-German. Belgium now functioned in the ideology of liberal internationalism primarily as a victim of German aggression needing protection rather than the brutal oppressor of the Congolese, who themselves needed international protection. Either way, liberal internationalism gained ideologically from the example of Belgium, and, even if E. D. Morel refused to accept the anti-German terms of the new liberal international, he nonetheless could claim partial responsibility for a politics that leveraged colonial atrocities to expand colonial rule.

The liberal international political order that emerged after the First World War both endorsed the type of colonialism that Germany had once exemplified and also justified itself in part by castigating German colonialism as barbaric. Many liberal internationalists posited German colonialism as a negative example justifying their own renewed civilizing mission while continuing to employ German colonialism, tacitly, as a model for this civilizing mission.[139] The administration of the former German colonies after the First World War first gave international liberalism territorial sovereignty and a historical role in the League of Nations. Through the League of Nations, Britain, France, and South Africa took Germany's African colonies not as the legitimate spoils of a war (which had long precedent in international law), but rather, as Article 22 of the Covenant of the League of Nations specified, as wards of "a sacred trust of civilization" under the "tutelage . . . exercised by Mandatories on behalf of the League." Soon the idea of a mandate of civilization, as well as Germany's unfitness to carry out that mandate, came to justify much European colonialism. Frederick Lugard's 1922 *Dual Mandate in British Tropical Africa* offered the greatest expression of this post-Versailles theory of imperial sovereignty.[140]

Africa, from the Berlin West Africa Conference of 1884–85 to the mandates of the League of Nations and beyond, played a central role in forging an international community, not despite, but precisely because, Europeans and Americans recognized Africans only as objects of policy and not as political actors in their own right. George Louis Beer, an American historian of the British Empire who served as chief advisor on colonial matters to Woodrow Wilson at the Paris Peace Conference, asserted that Africa could only function as an object of, not an actor in, international politics because of the nature of "the negro race." This race, he argued, "has hitherto shown no capacity for progressive development except under the tutelage of other peoples." Beer suggested that this inherent need for outside control, a long-standing feature of the New South conception of the Negro, resulted from the "established physiological fact that the cranial sutures of the negro close at an early age, which condition, it has been contended, prevents organic intellectual progress thereafter." Successively improved international orders, beginning with the Berlin West African Conference, had, according to Beer, emerged to address this inherent need of blacks for outside authority. For Beer, the League of Nations mandates would help to "eliminate the subordination of native interests to those of some of the colonizing Powers, and to emphasize the fact that the administration of tropical Africa is essentially an international trust, primarily for the benefit of the aboriginal peoples and only secondarily for the welfare of the outside world."[141] The American "Negro question" became a foundational feature, blacks themselves a constituent exclusion, of the international order that emerged between the Berlin West Africa Conference and the Paris Peace Conference. Excluding blacks not only from what was called civilization, but also from the possibility of achieving this civilization without outside intervention, helped Europeans and Americans found a League of Nations to enforce what was supposed to be universal.

Some Germans attributed their own exclusion from the civilizing mission to a colonial *Schuldluge*, or "guilt lie," that is, to a mischaracterization of their colonial policy as markedly brutal, even criminal. German officials responded to the *Schuldluge* in two ways. Defenders of German colonialism generally accepted the characterizations of their administrative style, but justified their actions as sound colonial practice. For example, in 1919 the German Colonial Office responded to the charge that Germans used whipping in their protectorates with the explanation that incarceration did not sufficiently deter Africans from committing crimes, so that Europeans had to resort to whipping, as even Lugard, it claimed, agreed.[142] Secondly, German opponents of the colonial "guilt lie" indicated, correctly, that German colonial methods had long been admired and imitated by other colonial powers, who now conveniently forgot the source of all they had learned in order to justify seizing new colonies. Lugard, for example, in his 1893 *Rise of Our East African Empire*, urged

Britain to imitate Germans in "the thorough and practical way in which they set about to develop their territories [in Africa]" (although, he allowed, "as regards tact with the natives, the advantage, perhaps, lies with us").[143] Germany won perhaps more admiration for its work with Booker T. Washington and Tuskegee Institute than for any of its other colonial achievements. Before the First World War, German colonial officials and experts stood at the vanguard, alongside Booker T. Washington and E. D. Morel, of an international collaboration about how best to educate and manage the "Negro"—whether in Alabama or West Africa. The final service of German colonial policy to international liberalism, after providing it with policy models, was to serve, paradoxically, as an other in contrast to which it could identify and justify itself. Had Booker T. Washington still been alive after the First World War he might have reminded the champions of the "sacred trust of civilization" that they had imitated German practices before they condemned them. Washington, however, died on November 15, 1915.

The "Negro Question" of the New South, important in its own right to progressive colonialism, and fundamental to the erstwhile status of Germany as a model colonizer, remained part of the colonial policies carried out by the mandatory powers after the First World War. The seeming paradox of President Woodrow Wilson, a southerner whose administration introduced segregation into the much of the federal government, championing the League of Nations is, in fact, no paradox at all. Nor should we be surprised by the leading role played in the founding of the League by Jan Smuts, a South African segregationist who saw to it that German Southwest Africa came under the "tutelage" of South Africa, which imposed segregation on the former German colony until Africans themselves expelled the armies of the apartheid state in 1988. It was consistent with the spirit of the interstate internationalism that had emerged since the Berlin Conference of 1884–85 that the majority of the delegates to the Paris Peace Conference of 1919 rejected an amendment to the Covenant of the League of Nations proposed by the Japanese delegation that mandated racial equality.[144] The segregated New South had become an important model for the liberal internationalism institutionalized in the League of Nations by, among others, two of the world's most influential segregationists, Woodrow Wilson and Jan Smuts.[145]

The apparent Americanization of the world has included not just northern efficiency and standardization, what the Italian Marxist Antonio Gramsci celebrated in the early twentieth century as "Fordism," and the American sociologist George Ritzer has more recently deplored as "McDonaldization," but also the capitalism underwritten by racism and gross inequality that characterized the American South in the decades after the end of slavery.[146] The transnational "Negro question," the attempts by white elites to impose interlinked regimes of political and economic control over African Americans and Africans, became fundamental to the renewed colonial civilizing mission of the League of Nations.

After the First World War, despite the death of Booker T. Washington, the New South became, if anything, even more important for European colonial rule in Africa. After the war Thomas Jesse Jones, a white sociologist from Hampton University, took over Washington's role in promoting industrial education in Africa. In 1902 Hollis Burke Frissell, president of Hampton Institute since the death of Samuel Chapman Armstrong in 1893, had hired Jones as an instructor and school chaplain, following Booker T. Washington in incorporating sociology into New South industrial education. Jones, an immigrant from Wales who had grown up in Ohio, had just completed a Ph.D. in sociology at Columbia University under the direction of Franklin Henry Giddings. Giddings employed sociology to teach high school and college students to assimilate to a society ruled by what he described, invoking both Aristotle and the eugenicist Francis Galton, as a "true elite" superior to all others in health, intelligence and creativity, and marked by a concern for their inferiors.[147] Giddings addressed Columbia students, of course, as individuals who would exercise this paternal authority, not as the docile objects of paternal control.[148] Giddings later claimed that permitting African Americans to vote was a mistake that would lead to revolution, as blacks demanded the equality that had been promised by emancipation.[149] At Hampton, Giddings's student Jones introduced a course in what he called "social studies" that preserved the goals and assumptions of his mentor's sociology, but adjusted his approach for students he perceived to be anything but the "true elite."[150] As Jones described it, the course taught Hampton students that political and economic inequalities between blacks and whites resulted from "vital differences in the dispositions, in the mental characteristics, and in the social organizations of races."[151] Blacks, Jones offered, might gradually ameliorate their situation by improving themselves individually, for example, through industrial education, but he discouraged political action against inequality. Thomas Jesse Jones proposed an industrial pedagogy more conservative than any that Booker T. Washington ever did.

Before turning his attention to Africa after the First World War, Jones employed sociology to strengthen the monopoly that Hampton and Tuskegee Institutes exercised over black education in the United States. In 1913 the Phelps Stokes Fund, founded in 1911 to support black education in the United States and Africa, hired Jones to direct a two-year survey of black schools in the American South.[152] Jones directed a cadre of researchers who collected data from all private schools and all public secondary schools for African Americans. The study recommended "simple manual training" for African Americans, not only to improve their economic situation by inducing pupils to work harder, but also because "the Negro's highly emotional nature requires for balance as much as possible of the concrete and definite." Jones advised northern philanthropy to support black schools subscribing to Tuskegee and Hampton ideals and to refuse funding to "[o]thers—and these comprise a majority of the institutions . . . following the traditional school curriculum with too exclusive emphasis upon bookish studies."[153] Du Bois detected in the Phelps-Stokes survey a "sinister danger" of denying black children academic education and the upward mobility it brought.[154] Jones gradually became known for using his control over northern philanthropy to manipulate black educational leaders, in a way reminiscent of the late Booker T. Washington. The African American historian Carter G. Woodson, in an obituary in the *Journal of Negro History*, remarked that the political agenda pursued by Jones, as well as his clandestine methods, led most African Americans to regard him as "an evil in the life of the Negro."[155]

After the First World War, Jones, again with the support of the Phelps Stokes Fund, carried out studies of black education throughout Africa similar to those he had carried out in the American South, also promoting industrial education to the exclusion of other pedagogies.[156] Education, in Africa as in the United States, should be adapted, Jones argued, to the specific needs of blacks in their subordinate positions in the economy and in "civilization." For Jones, industrial education for blacks had saved American democracy and served as a model for "what to do and what to avoid in race relations and in the education of peoples handicapped by causes within or without the group." Bringing Hampton and Tuskegee education to Africa would provide, through the League of Nations mandatory powers, "America's share in human betterment and in world peace."[157] In his African work, Jones combined a grim assessment of black laziness and dissolution, characteristic of American proponents of industrial education, with an equally characteristic optimism for the potential of blacks becoming, under the influence of industrial education, docile and productive workers.[158] For Jones, industrial education in Africa, as in the United States, offered a means of preserving an increasingly precarious political economic status quo, using "modern science and an enlightened public opinion" against a range of international "epidemics, whether of disease or of Bolshevism, or of warfare between groups."[159] South African educators, who had their own traditions of segregation and manual education, began describing their projects in terms borrowed from American industrial education, perhaps in part to appeal to the Phelps Stokes Fund and other American philanthropic organizations.[160] In 1929 the Phelps

Stokes Fund realized one of its original aims, when, in cooperation with
the American Colonization Society and other philanthropic organizations, it financed a Booker Washington Institute in Kakata, Liberia.[161]
Tuskegee had first gained a toehold in Africa with the expedition to German Togo in the decade before the First World War. After the war, New
South industrial education became a veritable orthodoxy of colonial administration and international humanitarianism.

The Tuskegee expedition to Togo laid the groundwork for a colonial New
South, a global South, that influenced the colonial policy and rhetoric not
only of Germany, but also of other European powers. European interest
in Tuskegee Institute grew beyond an initial enthusiasm for breaking the
American cotton monopoly. Soon, the New South, industrial education,
and the American ideology of the "Negro" also became important for
liberals attempting to work out a colonial civilizing mission in light of the
patent failure of that mission in the Congo Free State. Pointing to German
successes in Togo and elsewhere, to the potential of Booker T. Washington's industrial education for all of Africa, and to the example of the New
South itself, Morel and others renewed a colonial civilizing mission in
which a white elite exercised supposedly beneficial tutelage over a black
peasantry. When German colonial policy came under attack in the Reichstag, Tuskegee and the New South became reference points for the "scientific" and advanced colonial policy that gave German colonialism more
national and international authority than ever before. Thanks to this un-
expected influence of Tuskegee Institute, Washington became increasingly
interested in the colonial potential of the normal school he directed, first
in the Congo, and later throughout Africa. These colonial entanglements
also led Washington to reshape Tuskegee Institute itself: he directed
George Washington Carver, whom he had initially hired to help free black
farming from cotton dependency, to emphasize cotton; he abandoned any
transformative ideals he may have developed in his discussions with Du
Bois; and he reduced the academic component of Tuskegee education.
After the First World War, liberal internationalism, resting in part on the
globalized New South, gained new influence and territorial control in Africa, through the League of Nations and through expanded involvement
of American advocates of industrial education in Africa.

Chapter 5

FROM INDUSTRIAL EDUCATION FOR
THE NEW SOUTH TO A SOCIOLOGY
OF THE GLOBAL SOUTH

Booker T. Washington and the colonial authorities who brought Tuskegee to Togo relied on German and American social scientists to advise and to justify their political and economic projects. These political and economic projects, just as importantly, generated new social scientific knowledge. Tuskegee Institute did not only draw support from American sociology, but also played an important role in the development of sociology on both sides of the Atlantic. German social thought exercised a great influence on the United States through the large number of prominent American sociologists who studied in Germany and the great international prestige of German social science.[1] This intellectual history, however, depends on a deeper and broader political and economic history. The lines connecting German and American university scholars did not cross the Atlantic by the shortest route, but rather proceeded through the global South, through the racialized political economy of colonial Africa and the southern United States. Two figures loom largest in this broader Atlantic sociology: Max Weber, whose visit to Tuskegee Institute in 1904 profoundly shaped his work on the "Protestant Ethic and the 'Spirit' of Capitalism"; and Robert E. Park, who, after studying with the Verein für Sozialpolitik and working with Tuskegee Institute and the Congo Reform Association, founded a school of sociology at the University of Chicago that continues to influence American social science and racial thought to this day.

One of the most conspicuous features of the sociology of race and labor that emerged as part of the global South was its insistence on a sociological rather than a biological conception of race. This sociological gesture has led many observers into mistaking some of the most significant racial thought in the twentieth century for antiracism. In fact, this new sociology of the global South inaugurated what the philosopher Etienne Balibar called "neoracism," a racism that minimizes biological distinctions while working out a system of cultural differences that function as effectively as race to underwrite political and economic inequalities. Balibar writes:

"*culture can also function like a nature*, and it can in particular function as a way of locking individuals and groups a priori into a genealogy, into a determination that is immutable and intangible in origin."[2] Indeed, the opposition between biological and sociological conceptions of race is untenable, since race is always held to be passed from parent to child according to varying understandings of inheritance, from the one-drop rule to the continuity of a social, economic, or cultural milieu. The household from which race emerges includes the equally social and biological functions of kinship, from sexual reproduction to family nomenclature. Many sociological theorists of race, including Max Weber and Robert E. Park, believed that the racial differences they studied did rest, at least in part, on biology, although they acknowledged that their expertise did not extend to these supposedly natural differences. Both sociological and biological conceptions of race included a notion of the superiority of whites and the racial inferiority of blacks and perhaps other races. Unlike biological conceptions of race, sociological conceptions left room for reformist corrections to the perceived failings of supposedly inferior races, and in this sense emerged from and supported the "Negro question" of the New South and the global South.

This nonbiological, sociological racism emerged as colonial states and capital came to exercise hegemony over most of the globe, coming close to eliminating all territorial and racial exteriors in a massive, multinational empire in which imperial ambitions were coordinated and imperial conflicts minimized by the League of Nations. The sharp borders between self and other, inside and outside, characteristic of initial colonial conquest, gave way to a flexible field of others whom political and economic elites might assimilate, exploit, exclude, or deport as they saw fit.[3] The Polish seasonal migrant in Germany and the black sharecropper in the United States, not the "savage" untouched by civilization, were especially relevant cases for this new imperial situation, in which all populations were, at least in principle, internal minorities, "separate as the fingers, yet one as the hand in all things essential to mutual progress." This sociological racism was a racism of exploitation and subordination rather than a racism of conquest and annihilation. Weber worked out this new, imperial racism in a sociology of religion that divided the world into a patchwork of civilizations, each with a unique standard of labor. Park worked out a similar imperial racism, initially on a smaller scale, in the patchwork of ethnic neighborhoods in Chicago. Capital and colonial states move only against a background of fixed differences, and their mobility thus depends on the immobility of populations, races, cultures, and identities.[4] Weber and Park, each in their own way, theorized this world of cultural, economic, and political differences.

Max Weber, Booker T. Washington, and W.E.B. Du Bois

Max Weber had risen to prominence in the 1890s by bringing the anti-Polish racism of the Prussian Settlement Commission to bear on the questions about free labor that German social scientists had been asking for decades. After almost a decade of work placing racial and national conflict at the center of political and sociological questions about agrarian labor in Prussia, Weber sank, in 1898, into a profound and debilitating depression, into what his Heidelberg colleague Emil Kraeplin diagnosed as "neurasthenia."[5] His depression lifted enough in 1904 for Weber to publish the first half of "The Protestant Ethic and the 'Spirit' of Capitalism" and to undertake a trip to the United States with his wife, Marianne, a feminist and social reformer better known, at that time, than her husband.[6] The Webers' trip to the United States would bring the "Negro question" of the New South to the center of his thought and make possible his intellectual development from an anti-Polish sociologist of agricultural labor into a general theorist of culture and economics.

The Webers' trip through the United States was occasioned by Max's lecture at the International Congress of Arts and Science, part of the Universal Exposition at St. Louis. The psychologist Hugo Münsterberg, who had been a colleague of Weber's at Freiburg before moving to Harvard, organized the International Congress to foster further intellectual exchange between German and American scholars. In addition to Weber, Münsterberg invited such German luminaries as the scholars of religion Adolf Harnack and Ernst Troeltsch, the cultural historian Karl Lamprecht, the sociologists Werner Sombart and Ferdinand Tönnies, and the philosopher Wilhelm Windelband. The American contingent was no less impressive. It included the urban reformer Jane Addams, the anthropologist Franz Boas, the psychologist G. Stanley Hall, and the University of Chicago sociologists Albion W. Small and William I. Thomas. Also presenting was Columbia sociologist Franklin Henry Giddings, whose student, Thomas Jesse Jones, had recently joined the faculty at Hampton Institute. The American historians lecturing at the congress included Du Bois's Harvard mentor, Albert Bushnell Hart, as well as Frederick Jackson Turner and future U.S. president Woodrow Wilson, then president of Princeton University.[7] W.E.B. Du Bois also attended, but did not deliver a lecture at the conference.

A number of speakers at the Congress endeavored to relate their contributions to the politics of race and empire. Race had long been a concern of American politics, and empire had pushed its way into the foreground of American politics since the 1898 acquisition of Guam, Puerto Rico, and the Philippines from Spain, the occupation of Cuba, and the annex-

ation of Hawaii. The year of the conference, 1904, also saw the promulga-
tion of the Roosevelt Corollary to the Monroe Doctrine, which marked
the advent of a bloody century of U.S. military interventions in Latin
America. With a selection of ethnographic and anthropological performances larger than that of any previous world's fair, the St. Louis exposition placed questions of race and empire front and center, including in its
massive "Philippine reservation."[8] At the St. Louis Congress, the University of Chicago sociologist William I. Thomas called on social scientists
to "worked out from the mental standpoint" the problem of "the contact
of black and white in America," as well as the issues facing the American
occupation of the Philippines.[9] When, less than a decade later, Thomas
attended the International Conference on the Negro at Tuskegee, he became convinced that industrial education represented the best solution to
this racial problem, and would, with Booker T. Washington's associate
Robert E. Park, synthesize the imperial face of Tuskegee with German
sociology to lay the basis for a new global sociology of race and social
control. The principal speakers at the section on "Colonial Administration" were both German-trained American academics who praised liberal
American imperialism, contrasting it favorably with Dutch rule in Java
and tracing its origins to "that humanitarian optimism which animated
the period of the French Revolution."[10] The Yale sociologist Albert G.
Keller, an enthusiastic admiring expert on German "scientific" methods
of colonization, made a shorter contribution.[11]

At the St. Louis Congress, Weber offered his own expertise on, and
political engagement with, agricultural labor and German-Polish relations in Prussia as an example, and even a warning, to Americans dealing
with rural labor and racial conflict. According to Marianne Weber, the
lecture contained "many political points that interested the Americans."[12]
For Weber, rural society could not exist in a "developed capitalistic culture," which necessarily treated agriculture like any other business undertaking, with the landlord functioning as "a capitalist like others" and
laborers "of exactly the same class as other proletarians." As aristocrats
became capitalists, European civilization lost what Weber imagined as
economic independent bearers of traditional culture. As peasants became
proletarians, they turned increasingly to social democracy, weakening the
political power of the state and destabilizing the social order. While the
abundance of land in the United States meant that the nation would not
face a crisis of agricultural labor for years to come, the ethnic issues in
German agriculture did, Weber noted, parallel those in the United States.

Under conditions of capitalist competition, Weber remarked, "the peasant's struggle for existence" often led to "economic selection in favor of
the most frugal, i.e., those most lacking culture." Thus the success of
Polish farmers in parts of eastern Germany accorded with economic logic

but was "completely contrary" to "the advance of culture toward the East, during the Middle Ages, founded upon the superiority of the older and higher culture." Weber saw analogous tendencies in the United States, with the growing numbers of African American-owned farms and increasing African American migration into cities. The "present difficult social problems of the South" arose, for Weber, more from ethnicity—presumably he meant black-white relations—than from economics. Furthermore, the "enormous immigration of uncivilized elements from eastern Europe," according to Weber, similarly threatened "the expansive power of the Anglo-Saxon-German settlement of the rural districts." There might eventually arise, Weber warned, "a rural population" that "could not be assimilated by the historically transmitted culture of this country," a culture he described as "the great creation of the Anglo-Saxon spirit." Americans should look to German policy toward ethnic Poles, for "the greater part of the problems for whose solution we [Germans] are now working will approach America within but a few generations; the way in which they will be solved will determine the character of the future culture of this continent."[13]

Weber soon complemented his German lessons for America with American lessons for Germany. After the St. Louis Congress, Max and Marianne made a tour of the southern states, where both studied the situation of African Americans to draw lessons for Germany and for their own scholarly work. Max and Marianne visited Tuskegee in fall 1904. What the couple observed there, Marianne later recalled, "probably moved them more than anything else on their trip."[14] For Marianne, the "Negro school was truly worth the day's travel," vividly presenting "a piece of the life struggle and idealistic efforts that we had [only] read about in books." As Max Weber described the Tuskegee program in a letter to his mother, "no one is permitted to do only intellectual work. The purpose is the training of farmers; 'conquest of the soil' is a definite ideal."[15] Perhaps Weber had learned to regard farming as "conquest of the soil" from the Prussian Settlement Commission, which did indeed see smallholding by Germans as a means of pushing Polish populations from the East. The Tuskegee expedition to Togo offered a similar lesson to Booker T. Washington. In Togo, in an even more literal sense than in eastern Prussia, small farming amounted to "conquest of the soil" as the cotton expedition followed the path of destruction laid by the German military.

The Webers had great sympathy for African American leaders, including Booker T. Washington and W.E.B. Du Bois, both of whom they regarded as mixed-race individuals, unjustly defined as "Negroes" by the Manichaean racism of the United States. While these individuals, as Marianne Weber put it, "by virtue of their descent and talents belonged to the master race [Herrenrasse]," their destinies were bound to those whom

Max called the "semi-apes one encounters on the plantations and in the Negro huts of the '*Cotton Belt.*' " Marianne had similar views about the majority of African Americans. She described African American women whose faces, in contrast to those of "Frau Booker Washington and the female teachers at Tuskegee" reminded her "more of ape than of human countenances." These Negro leaders fought white racism by attempting, as Marianne put it, "nothing less than teaching 'culture' to a race which in an unmixed state actually seemed to have been relegated to the outer reaches of the human realm." From their visit to Tuskegee the Webers concluded that, in Marianne's words: "The tremendous, irremediable discord of America made the national life of Germany seem on a very small scale."[16] An interest in Tuskegee complemented, rather than overshadowed, Max Weber's own national political concerns.

Before returning to Germany, the Webers visited distant relatives of Max's, the Fallensteins, in Mount Airy, North Carolina, in the Appalachian Mountains.[17] Max, according to Marianne, was a hit with these American relatives, and "quickly won their heart with his beautiful '*Nigger-English*' and his stories."[18] Weber's private minstrel show, far from expressing glib scorn toward his recent host at Tuskegee, echoed Washington's own attitude toward poor blacks. In his speeches, Washington regularly caricatured black English to depict lazy, dissolute African Americans whom he thought would benefit from industrial education. Washington himself, by contrast, spoke with what the British Africa expert Harry Johnston described as close to a proper English accent. George Washington Carver, according to Johnston, "spoke English as though he had been brought up at Oxford."[19] The American trip marked the end of Weber's depression and the beginning of a new period of intellectual activity. The case of southern blacks would allow Weber to develop a broad economic sociology on the basis of concepts of race and labor that he had employed in his earlier work on German settlement and Polish Sachsengänger.

After returning to Germany, Max Weber contacted W.E.B. Du Bois to enlist his expertise on African Americans for the Verein für Sozialpolitik, asking the Atlanta University professor to resume a role that he had played during his student days in Berlin. Weber met Du Bois at the St. Louis Congress and planned to travel to Atlanta to continue his discussions with the African American sociologist, but Marianne could no longer tolerate the climate of the Deep South.[20] Weber solicited an article on "the Negro Question in the United States" from Du Bois for the *Archiv für Sozialwissenschaft und Sozialpolitik.*[21] As Weber explained, the article should treat "the relation between the (so-called) 'race-problem' and the (so-called) 'class-problem' in your country, although it is impossible to have any conversation with white people of the South without feeling the connection." Weber hoped Du Bois would produce an article concentrating on "the influence of socio-economic conditions upon the relations of races to each-other" as a correction to the purely biological theories of Houston Stewart Chamberlain and others in Germany.[22] Weber did not hope to demolish race as a category of social analysis, but to develop a sociological rather than a biological theory of race. "I am absolutely convinced," Weber wrote to Du Bois, echoing the phrase the latter had coined for the 1900 Pan-African Congress in London, "that the 'color-line' problem will be the permanent problem of the time to come, here and everywhere in the world."[23]

Du Bois's German article on the "Negro Question," which appeared in 1906, analyzed the sharecropping system that controlled black agricultural labor, much as his professors in Berlin had treated other regimes of labor control in Germany. Du Bois discussed frankly how debt peonage and the system of hiring out convict labor, as well as segregation, capitalist exploitation, and exclusion from labor unions, trapped African Americans in "a system of corvée labor, bound to their farms, under paternalistic domination." Du Bois cited increasing African American landownership, education, and professional advancement, even in the face of racial discrimination, to dispel the myth that black poverty resulted from inherent racial inferiority. Racism, Du Bois argued, facilitated capitalist exploitation of all workers, for "the fact that there is an ostracized race makes it easier to despise classes." Du Bois concluded with the warning that, no matter how intractable "racial antipathy" might be, it should not be allowed to continue poisoning American democracy.[24] In his article, Du Bois elaborated connections already made by Georg Friedrich Knapp between agricultural labor in Prussia and the "Negro question" in the United States. Like his German teachers and colleagues, Du Bois concerned himself with the ways in which forms of tenancy and ethnic relations shaped agricultural labor and class conflict, although, in contrast to his former teachers, Du Bois resolutely opposed the exploitation and oppression fostered by racism.

Weber responded so enthusiastically to Du Bois's manuscript that he worked—in the end unsuccessfully—to have Du Bois's 1903 *Souls of Black Folk* translated into German.[25] He also began work on a review of recent literature on African Americans, which would have included discussions of Du Bois and Washington.[26] Weber, like most German social scientists, probably disagreed with the political and ethical conclusions drawn by Du Bois. Nonetheless, the connection Du Bois made between racism and the exploitation of labor, his concern about capitalist agriculture, the stress he laid on forms of agricultural tenancy as means of controlling workers, and even, in a certain sense, the anxieties about the effect of these political economic processes on national cohesion had emerged during his study in the 1890s with the German sociologists for whom he wrote his 1906 article. Weber, like Moritz Schanz from the Colonial Economic Committee, as well as other German colonial experts, employed Du Bois's expertise on African Americans for purposes contrary to those that the Atlanta sociologist intended.

From "Teaching the Negro to Work" to the "Protestant Ethic"

The example of black labor allowed Weber, like Gustav Schmoller and other German economists, to develop the politics of internal colonization into a global sociology of race and labor. Weber adapted the German colonial policy of "educating the Negro to work" (*Erziehung des Negers zur Arbeit*) not only for politically and economically subordinate groups, such as Polish migrant laborers, but also for European Protestants. He showed, in his "Protestant Ethic and the 'Spirit' of Capitalism," how Protestants compelled themselves to work and suggested, especially in his later *Sociology of Religion*, that other racial or civilizational groups work in fundamentally different and, at least when left to their own devices, necessarily inferior, ways. The inner compulsion of European Protestants, in Weber's model, suggests the necessity of—although Weber did not state this explicitly—an external compulsion for all others. The "Protestant Ethic," originally published in two parts on either side of his 1904 visit to the United States, treats a problem similar to that addressed by Tuskegee Institute, namely, what makes people work?

Like Schmoller, Weber rejected the abstract models of classical economics and sought instead cultural explanations of economic behavior. "The Protestant Ethic and the 'Spirit' of Capitalism" proposed an economic theory based on collective ethnic or cultural behavior rather than on the individual rationality of classical economics.[27] While popular understandings of "The Protestant Ethic" take it for a theory of savings and investment, it is, in fact, a theory of devotion to profession, a theory of labor. Weber's text thus provides an answer to the questions about the control of free labor that the Verein für Sozialpolitik had been asking since the 1870s. Weber identified as the central feature of capitalism the unquestioning, even irrational, commitment to profession (*Berufspflicht*), whether as a worker or investor.[28] This irrationally rational economy began, as Weber famously argued, from a typically Protestant drive to "penetrate all spheres of private and public life to the greatest conceivable extent with endless burdensome and earnest regimentation of all of life."[29] This ascetic, worldly rationalism was accentuated by Luther's emphasis on the divine calling to profession (*Beruf*), and given fur-

ther power by a popular misinterpretation of Calvinist doctrines of pre-
destination, whereby success in career was thought to indicate salvation
in the afterlife.

In "The Protestant Ethic," Weber formulated a theory of economic motivation that rejected the individual calculating rationality fundamental
to the laissez-faire, classical political economy that the Verein für Sozialpolitik opposed. In perhaps the only piece of strictly economic theorizing
in the book, Weber cautioned against correlating individual wages with
labor productivity. Raising wages, Weber pointed out, had the paradoxical effect of decreasing the productivity of workers who are motivated
solely by economic gain, for workers will quickly realize they can work
less to achieve the standard of living to which they are accustomed. Low
wages are effective means to achieve increased productivity among such
workers for a brief period, for they will have to work harder to maintain
their standard of living. However, such a strategy begins to reduce worker
output as wages become "physiologically insufficient" and poor nutrition
undermines productivity and even leads to a de-evolutionary "selection
of the least fit." The low productivity of poorly paid and poorly fed Poles,
Weber offered, illustrated this outcome.[30]

Economic motivations could not, by themselves, increase the productivity of workers: only a "feeling of responsibility" could lead workers to
stop asking how to get a job done with the "maximum of comfort and a
minimum of achievement" and to begin to pursue work "as if it were an
absolute end in itself [*Sebstzweck*]—that is, a profession [*Beruf*]." Such a
feeling, according to Weber, was "not something occurring in nature"
but rather a result of Protestantism.[31] Protestantism did not merely teach
workers the commonplace that "doing good work, even with poor wages
. . . was something that pleased God," but, most importantly, it gave
workers "the psychological motivation that this work was a calling, and
was thus the superior, perhaps the only, means of achieving salvation."
At the same time, this Protestant ethic "legalized the exploitation of this
specific willingness to work, in that it also interpreted the acquisition of
wealth by the entrepreneur as 'calling.' "[32]

Such explicitly theological motivations became unconscious compul-
sions as the external technical apparatus of industry replaced internal religious motivations as the driving force behind capitalist behavior. Humans
found themselves enclosed, famously, in a "shell hard as steel" (*stahl-
hartes Gehäuse*—Talcott Parson's "iron cage"), possibly not to be released until "the last ton of fossil fuel has been consumed" and the material apparatus of capitalism collapses.[33] As long as fossil fuel remained
available and the apparatus of capitalism continued to function, however,
Weber and his colleagues in the Verein für Sozialpolitik could lay to rest
their concerns about the ill effects of free labor within Germany, and

worry instead about preventing corruption by Polish and other inferior workers. The concept of civilization, though seemingly flexible, functioned for Weber to separate groups as surely as the concept of race did. Differences of civilization might even, Weber speculated, ultimately rest on biological racial differences. Weber's schema suggested that only the Protestant could fully complete the colonial project of "educating to labor" (*Erziehung zur Arbeit*). Protestants, Weber implied, possessed the internal compunction required by free labor ideology, so that external coercion was only necessary outside the German imperialist core.

Max Weber first explicitly incorporated an interest in African American workers into his sociology of labor in a project on the "psychophysics of industrial labor." At the 1907 meeting of the Verein für Sozialpolitik, Weber's younger brother, Alfred, who had become Max's colleague at Heidelberg, initiated a study of the "intellectual and psychological qualities" necessary for industrial labor.[34] Max Weber had proposed expanding his brother's study to consider the "qualities resulting from the ethnic, social, and cultural provenance, the tradition, and the living conditions of workers." Rather than individual psychological studies, therefore, Weber recommended studying the economic efficiency of "ethnic, cultural, professional, and social groups" for various industrial employments, much as one might consider "the profitability of a variety of coal, ore, or other 'raw material.' "[35] Such a study, Max Weber promised, would not only offer new scientific insights, but would also help guide economic, cultural, and educational policy.[36] While it would be difficult, he acknowledged, to distinguish "differences 'inherited' in a biological sense" and "differences in tradition," Weber nonetheless insisted on the existence, "in principle," of "inheritable differences . . . in . . . nervous and psychic constitution" that influence "the varying tempo, steadiness, and certainty of reaction" which, in turn, influence the " 'disciplinability' [*Disziplinierbarkeit*] necessary for heavy industry."[37] Weber dubbed this study, borrowing a term from experimental psychologists, a "psychophysics."[38] He also hoped to incorporate recent advances in physical anthropology, physiology, and psychopathology into the study.

In his "Psychophysics," Weber returned to his earlier interest in race from the emphasis on religion that characterized his work on the "Protestant Ethic." Focusing on race allowed Weber to consider African Americans, the majority of whom were Protestant, after all, as a type of worker fundamentally different from white Protestants. While the study was only to consider various groups of white German workers, the possibility of such varying qualities of labor across groups obtained plausibility, Weber repeatedly stressed, from the example of "American Negroes." The example of the "well known experience of Negroes in the North American textile industry," Weber remarked, could allow no doubt of "the possibility—indeed the likelihood—that 'racial differences' play a role in competence for industrial work."[39] In fact, at this time, one of the myriad ways that white elites divided the southern working class was by reserving relatively high-paying jobs in textile mills for white workers, who were thus rewarded for participating in the exclusion of blacks. Weber maintained that the existence of hereditary mental illnesses among "North American Negroes" spoke for the biological foundation of differences among the labor capacities of various groups, although the general improvement of American blacks after emancipation, he allowed, provided evidence to the contrary. In any case, Weber hoped eventually to "determine different ethnic potentials for hysteria," supplementing, as he explained, Freud's theory that particular events in the life of an individual caused hysteria. Weber doubted that this "ethnic potential for hysteria" was a biological inheritance, reckoning that it might result instead from "culture (or rather lack of culture)."[40] Weber thus recommended, in this study of white workers, that researchers consider variations in social structure, culture, and tradition to account for the different working abilities of different groups.

Verein für Sozialpolitik members produced a number of case studies in this project, but not a general "psychophysics" of labor, in part because many workers and trade unions, perhaps suspecting the authoritarian and exploitative potential of such a study, refused to cooperate with data collection. None of the case studies reflected Weber's interest in the cultural-racial division of labor.[41] Nonetheless, in his methodological writings for the *Psychophysik* project, Weber continued to develop his racial sociology, both as a theoretical understanding of the world and as a practical guide to help managers select workers from groups deemed suitable for particular jobs.

Scholars often cite Max Weber's debate with the now infamous Social Darwinist Alfred Ploetz to suggest that the Heidelberg national economist opposed racism.[42] In fact, the debate indicates the importance race played in Weber's thought, and the sociological, rather than solely biological, nature of his racism. At the first German Sociological Congress in 1910, Ploetz presented, at the request of the organizers, his own view of the relation of race (*Rasse*) and society (*Gesellschaft*). While recognizing that races depend upon society to survive, Ploetz also endorsed the common Social Darwinistic fears that social welfare and Christian charity would undermine natural selection by allowing inferior individuals to flourish. Race, Ploetz asserted, ultimately trumped society in both normative and explanatory importance. Werner Sombart led the ensuing discussion, which challenged Ploetz's lecture in ways that had the speaker repeatedly interjecting shouts of "*Nein!*" Still, Sombart concluded, practically nobody at the congress, and certainly not his "friend Max Weber, whom he personally knows quite well," rejected "biology." "Quite true!" exclaimed Weber from the audience.[43] Weber never disputed the explanatory role of biological race, explicitly leaving the question open in many of his writings, and speculating that race played an important, if not all-determining, role in many social phenomena. Weber disagreed with Ploetz that welfare and charity worked against natural selection, but he did not dispute the role of natural selection in human society.

Weber and Ploetz, who had also spent time in the southern United States, agreed that blacks were inferior to whites, but disagreed about the causes of this inferiority. The two men shared the view, for example, that black people in America usually smelled worse than white people but debated the origin of this smell: for Ploetz the smell was biological, for Weber, it resulted from a habitual neglect of bathing. Weber explained that the supposed inferiority of African Americans stemmed from the limitations that whites placed on black access to education and social advancement, and cited W.E.B. Du Bois as "the most important sociological scholar anywhere in the southern states."[44] Yet Du Bois, as we have seen, did not exemplify African Americans for Max Weber or his wife, Marianne, but rather the "half-Negroes, quarter-Negroes, and one hundredth part Negroes whom no non-American can distinguish from whites."[45] Weber rejected the biologism of Ploetz and of the American "one drop rule," but in doing so worked out a social and economic racism that remains influential to this day.

In his 1920 *Sociology of Religion*, published posthumously, Weber brought together the various strands of his racial and cultural thought into a theory of economics and civilization that generalized many of the concerns of the Verein für Sozialpolitik and New South discussions about race and free labor. In the *Sociology of Religion* Weber proposed that economic differences among global regions resulted from differences among five civilizations, defined by major world religions: Confucianism, Hinduism, Buddhism, Christianity, and Islam. Weber also discussed Judaism, largely, he explained, because many of his contemporaries thought that Jews played a major role in the development of capitalism.[46] Weber revised earlier studies of Confucianism and Taoism, Hinduism, Buddhism, and ancient Judaism, as well as his 1904–1905 articles on Protestantism, to highlight why no region other than the West had created, in his view, the rational, capitalist economics of Protestant civilizations. In the preface to the *Sociology of Religion*, he expanded his notion of Protestant civilization to argue that the Occident alone possessed areas of civilization, such as science, art, and economics, that developed in directions of "*universal* meaning and validity."[47]

Religion had served Weber as a proxy variable for race in his 1895 Freiburg address, when he assumed that Protestants were German and Catholics were Polish to draw conclusions about, as he put it, "physical and mental race differences," from census data on religion.[48] In his *Sociology of Religion*, however, religion represented an essential characteristic of groups, not identical to race, but nearly as permanent and determining as race. Religion represented the ideas of the "bearers of civilization [*Kulturträger*]" and thus, Weber thought, could be used to characterize the six civilizations. Weber left open the possibility that these civilizational differences resulted from biological race, noting, indeed, that he was "personally and subjectively predisposed to attribute great importance to the meaning of biological heredity" but that knowledge about "racial-neurology and -psychology" did not yet suffice for such a study.[49] The worldly asceticism characteristic of Protestantism had given that civilization a commitment to work more fundamental than any brought about by economic motivation or other types of rational individual self-interest. Other civilizations lacked this Protestant drive to labor. Weber raised the project of authorities in colonial Africa and in the American New South of "educating the Negro to work"—*Erziehung des Negers zur Arbeit*— to a general cultural sociology of economics that continues to be at least as important as biological racism in enforcing and justifying global inequalities.[50]

Sociology for the Old South and the New

American sociology was not only a German import, and, indeed, southerners had long made use of sociology to discuss race and labor both before and after emancipation. In his 1854 *Sociology for the South; Or, The Failure of Free Society*, George Fitzhugh, an apologist for slavery, described society as a stable, hierarchical, and mutually beneficial organization of all humans, slave and free alike. Like members of the Verein für Sozialpolitik, Fitzhugh employed sociology to criticize laissez-faire economics for both its abstraction and for the chaotic individual freedom it promoted. Fitzhugh characterized Adam Smith, the founder of laissez-faire economics, as "absent, secluded and unobservant." Smith, Fitzhugh continued, "saw only that prosperous and progressive portion of society whom liberty or free competition benefited, and mistook its effects on them for its effects on the world." In fact, the dissolution of the social bonds of feudalism in Europe, brought about by the French Revolution, had only increased the misery of the poor and led to the subsequent revolutionary tumults of 1830 and 1848. Workers in the northern states suffered similar deprivation and threatened similar disorders. Slaves in the American South, meanwhile, Fitzhugh explained, were well cared for by their masters and thus content. Fitzhugh held slavery to be superior to free labor in all societies, for whites as well as for blacks, although he did write that blacks had special need of paternalistic masters. Slavery, according to Fitzhugh, "is a form, and the very best form, of socialism" and, indeed, in Europe, "socialism is the new fashionable name of slavery."[51] No member of the Verein für Sozialpolitik ever advocated slavery, as Fitzhugh did, but most did offer a hierarchical and paternalistic account of society that endorsed state socialism to prevent the disorder of laissez-faire economics and social democracy. Fitzhugh, like many German sociologists, offered advice for ordering and maintaining a hierarchical status quo against the freedom of labor.

Thinkers in the New South similarly employed sociology to address problems of race and free labor. At least since 1896, Booker T. Washington had regarded sociology as an important part of his efforts at Tuskegee Institute to improve the lives of African Americans. He had initially sought, as we have seen, to hire W.E.B. Du Bois to provide a sociological complement to George Washington Carver's efforts at agricultural transformation. When he failed to recruit W.E.B. Du Bois to Tuskegee, he engaged Robert E. Park, today regarded as one of the most important sociologists in the discipline's history in the United States. In 1908 Booker T. Washington hired a second sociologist, Monroe Nathan Work, on the strength of recommendations from Robert E. Park and Thomas Jesse Jones.[52] Work, the first African American to publish an article in the *American Journal of Sociology*, had studied at the University of Chicago from 1898 to 1903.[53] At the 1912 International Conference on the Negro, Work delivered a lecture on the Tuskegee expedition to Togo. In 1912 he began publishing an annual *Negro Year Book* that recorded the economic and political progress that African Americans had made since emancipation.[54] Work hoped that making such information easily available would challenge the prevailing racism in American social science and would also help African Americans overcome self-doubt with knowledge of the achievements of their race.[55] Work believed that sociology in public school education could make society "more harmonious, more just and proper" by imparting "information, relative to community matters" that "would act as a counterant to race, class, and other forms of social friction."[56] Washington, Work, Jones, Du Bois, and Park conceived of sociology as a discipline that both studied and changed society and thus agreed on its importance to shaping the New South, even if they disagreed on what this New South should look like.

The Southern Sociological Congress, which first met in May, 1912, a month after the International Conference on the Negro at Tuskegee, provided a forum for southern whites to apply sociology to the "Negro question" and the New South.[57] At the second annual conference, Samuel C. Mitchell, president of the University of South Carolina, praised Baron Karl vom Stein, architect of the Prussian reform of the century before, who, "on that October day in 1807 . . . did away with serfdom in Prussia, quickened the schools, abolished feudal abuses, unified the people, equalized the taxes, planned popular assemblies, inspired patriotism in all, and set free the energy in the individual will."[58] Speakers at the conferences routinely applauded the industrial education promoted by Hampton and Tuskegee Institutes for working at solving the "race question" with, as a professor from Louisiana State University, put it, "educational and economic improvement rather than by political methods."[59] Booker T. Washington addressed the Southern Sociological Congress in 1914, encouraging the group to "let the world understand that in proportion as the negro is educated he does not wish to intermingle with the white people in a purely social way." He drew the attention of the conferees to the international importance of their discussions to colonial rule, reminding them that, "There are millions of black people throughout the world. Everywhere, especially in Europe, people are looking to us here in the South, black and white, to show to the world how it is possible for two races, different in color, to live together on the same soil, under the same laws, and each race work out its salvation in justice to each other."[60] Robert E. Park would help meet this demand for a new global sociology of race and labor by synthesizing sociologies of the German East, the American South, and colonial Africa.

ROBERT E. PARK, FROM GERMANY TO AFRICA TO TUSKEGEE AND BACK AGAIN

Robert E. Park brought together the German and the southern traditions of sociological thought, thereby influencing American sociology and American racial thought to perhaps a greater extent than any other sociologist. Park, an American whose studies in Germany with members of the Verein für Sozialpolitik led him to an interest in black labor in Africa and in the United States, became acquainted with Booker T. Washington in the Congo Reform Association.[61] Park had grown up in Red Wing, Minnesota, about fifty miles southwest of Minneapolis. After graduating from the University of Michigan in 1887, he spent a decade as a journalist in Minneapolis and Detroit, specializing in the kind of portraits of social ills, so important to American Progressivism, that Theodore Roosevelt later dubbed muckraking. In 1898 Park enrolled as a philosophy student at Harvard University, where Du Bois had received a Ph.D. in history three years earlier. Like Du Bois, Park set out for Germany after completing a master's degree at Harvard. Park, unlike Du Bois, had been given the financial means to complete his studies in Germany, taking courses at the Universities of Berlin and Strassburg before completing a dissertation at

Heidelberg in 1903 on "The Crowd and the Public" under the philosopher Wilhelm Windelband.[62] Park, however, would later remember not
Windelband, but rather the leading Verein für Sozialpolitik member
Georg Friedrich Knapp, with whom he took courses in Strassburg, as one
of his two most important teachers (the other was Booker T. Washington):
"Knapp was positively the most fascinating and instructive lecturer I ever
had the opportunity of hearing," Park recalled "His lectures on the development of agriculture and particularly his accounts of the German peasant and peasant community were positively the most illuminating descriptions of any society that have ever come my way." When he went to
Tuskegee, Park discovered that Knapp's lectures had given him "the best
possible introduction to an understanding of the plantation Negro."[63]
After completing his degree in Germany, Park returned to the Harvard
philosophy department, where he taught for two years while revising his
dissertation for publication.

Park first applied his German sociological training to colonial Africa
and the New South in E. D. Morel's Congo Reform Association, where
he came to agree with Morel and Washington that industrial education
represented a humane alternative to the brutal colonialism practiced in
the Congo. As publicist and later secretary of the American branch of the
Congo Reform Association, Park authored pamphlets and articles
exposing the abuses occurring in King Leopold's Congo.[64] In the Association, Park began working with Booker T. Washington, penning articles
on the Congo for the principal of Tuskegee.[65] Park explained to Washington that articles published under his name, in which "a representative of
your race has come out openly in defense of the other members of your
race in Africa, will strike the imagination of the American people." "Furthermore," Park continued, "the more I look into the matter, the more I
believe that the only possible regeneration of the black race in Africa is
through an industrial education, such as you stand for, fostered by the
government of the various colonies."[66] Park had come to the conclusion
that "conditions in the Congo were not the result of mere administrative
abuses" but were, rather, "one of the more or less inevitable incidents of
the civilizing process," which could be ameliorated by industrial education.[67] Park visited Tuskegee Institute, where he realized, he later recalled,
that "the problem of the America Negro was merely an aspect or a phase
of the native problem in Africa." Park found that his studies of the German peasantry with Knapp had prepared him for his work with "the
Negro peasant." As Park wrote: "to put Mr. Kipling's phrase in reverse
. . . the things you learn from the whites will help you a lot with the brown
and the black."[68] Knapp's work on the German peasantry was itself, in
turn, informed by his own study of African Americans in slavery and in
freedom. In 1905 Washington hired Park to publicize the efforts of

Tuskegee Institute in the United States and abroad. To this end, Park corresponded with John W. Robinson, the most important member of the Tuskegee expedition in Togo.[69]

In 1910 Park arranged a two-month research trip to Europe "to show Dr. Washington the condition of the European peasant as I had come to know it through my studies with Knapp in Strassburg."[70] Park took Washington, in a sense, through the looking glass, to show him the labor conditions that had shaped not only his own understanding of African Americans, but also that of his teacher Knapp and numerous other German social scientists and policy makers interested in the New South. From the end of August to the middle of October, Washington and Park traveled from London to Andrew Carnegie's Skibo castle in the Highlands of Scotland, through Germany, Austria-Hungary, Naples, Sicily, and Denmark. This European tour resulted in Washington's 1911 *Man Farthest Down*, a book supposed to demonstrate that peasants in Europe generally had lower standards of living than their African American counterparts. In order to study "the man farthest down," Washington "registered a firm resolution" not to "enter a single palace, museum, gallery, or cathedral" in Europe and to restrict his observations to the lives of European peasants. He slipped only once, when what he took to be a salt mine near Krakow—of special interest because of his own childhood in the salt-mining town of Malden, West Virginia—turned out to be an underground cathedral carved out by salt miners.[71] Washington also observed Jewish life in Krakow and elsewhere in Europe with special interest, both because of the discrimination contemporary Jews faced and also because the liberation of the ancient Israelites from Egyptian bondage had long served African Americans as an image of their own liberation.[72] Indeed, Washington himself was sometimes referred to in both the United States and West Africa as a "Moses of his race."[73]

Washington, like many observers before him, understood ethnic Poles, living as a minority population in Prussia, Russia, and Austria, as analogous to African Americans. Extending what he regarded as the lessons of the New South to Europe, he found the Poles suffering under political oppression in Russia and Prussia to be far more prosperous than those in Austria who have "a free hand in the governance of the province." Where Poles had no political power, "progress has begun at the bottom," whereas in Austria, where there was, according to Washington, little national oppression, "the nobles are content with [the] opportunity to play at politics . . . and have not learned the necessity of developing the resources that exist in the masses of the people." Washington noted the resemblance of this situation to the United States. Blacks in Mississippi, he claimed, were more completely excluded from political participation than they were in any other state in the union, but enjoyed some of the most remarkable self-improvement of the "masses of the people" in the nation. Like their black Mississippi counterparts, Poles in Prussia, had learned "to take advantage of their disadvantages and make their difficulties their opportunities."[74]

The Man Farthest Down also served as a piece of New South boosterism, demonstrating that, despite the obstacles and privations they faced in the South, African Americans fared better than the peasants and poor of Europe. Although Robert Park, who had arranged the trip, wrote most of the book, Washington controlled its message. He not only reminded Park to write "in natural, easy, conversational style," but also insisted that Park emphasize "the contrast ... between the condition of the Negro in a city like New Orleans, New York or Washington, and the people who live in the crowded districts of the cities in Europe." "As I see it," Washington reminded Park, "the condition of the Negro in the cities of this country is many per cent better than it is in the crowded cities of Europe that we saw."[75] Park shared Washington's horror at rural poverty in Europe, particularly in southern Italy, but his private notes also indicate a fascination with ethnic conflict and social democracy during the trip.[76] Park apparently thought Washington a poor observer of Italian conditions, in contrast to the Tuskegee principal's keen understanding of the American South.[77] Park doubted, privately, Washington's assertion that the rural poor in Europe suffered worse conditions than rural blacks in the United States. While the European peasant was protected by custom, "the Negro's position," "as defined in law nowhere corresponds to his actual status as defined in custom."[78] Neither law nor custom offered a protected place for blacks in the New South, which, Park recognized, placed African Americans in a uniquely vulnerable position. Although Park may have intended the 1910 trip to bring Booker T. Washington closer to the social scientific perspective he had learned in Germany, it seems instead to have furthered Park's own transnational sociology of race and labor.

From the Global South to the Chicago School of Sociology

Park left Tuskegee shortly after the 1912 International Congress on the Negro, in order to develop his New South sociology of race and labor at the University of Chicago.[79] At the 1912 conference, Park, who lectured on the value of Tuskegee education for colonial Africa, met William I. Thomas, a University of Chicago sociologist who lectured on Polish peasants and workers living in Germany and the United States. Thomas's research on Polish peasants led him to conclude that "the peasant was and is mentally as backward as the Negro is or as he was in slavery." Thomas hoped pedagogues would "adjust educational policy not to mental traits in the biological sense but to the grades of culture existing among the different races."[80] Shortly after returning to Chicago from Tuskegee, Thomas wrote to Park that "the negro question beats the peasant question" and, resolving that "something is going to result from a comparison of the negro and the peasant," proposed a collaborative study with Park on "the negro and the peasant" in Africa, the United States, and the Caribbean.[81] Thomas, who had long been interested in race and racism, recruited Park to teach at the University of Chicago and encouraged him to resume more theoretical and social scientific work, which he had neglected during his years with the Congo Reform Association and at Tuskegee.[82]

Park continued to correspond with Washington and to support Tuskegee Institute, even after he left for the University of Chicago in 1912.[83] The African American writer Ralph Ellison, who had studied at Tuskegee, singled out Park in particular as "the man responsible for inflating Tuskegee into a national symbol, and who is sometimes spoken of as the 'power behind Washington's throne.'" To direct the "economic and political destiny" of African Americans, Ellison suggested, the North supported Tuskegee Institute and it "organized social science as an instrumentality to sanction its methods." "When we look at the connection between Tuskegee and our most influential school of sociology, the University of Chicago," wrote Ellison in 1944, "we are inclined to see more than an unconscious connection between economic interests and philanthropy, Negroes and social science."[84] This connection ran in both directions, and Park relied on the social thought of Tuskegee Institute and the New South as much as he promoted it.

Park and Thomas founded a highly influential school of sociology at the University of Chicago, based on their common interests in race and labor on both sides of the Atlantic.[85] At Chicago, Park relied on the agrarian sociology that he had learned in Germany from Georg Friedrich Knapp, using sociological questions about peasants to study African Americans, focusing on questions of land ownership and emancipation. "The Negro is the only example we have in America," Park told his students at Chicago, "of a peasant people," with the possible exception of French Canadians.[86] In his courses, Park compared African American slavery with serfdom in Prussia and Russia, finding that, beyond the obvious similarities, European serfs enjoyed more autonomy and economic independence than did their African American counterparts.[87]

Both Park and Thomas initially applauded rural communities as models of stability, and they disparaged the urbanization of groups, like Poles and blacks, that they regarded as inferior. Shortly after arriving at the

University of Chicago, Park wrote privately to Washington, contrasting African Americans in the South, whom he described as "a strong, vigorous, kindly and industrious people; simple minded, wholesome and good as God made them" and "very little infected with either disease or vice," with urban blacks, whom he found "very likely to be indifferent and frivolous, and disposed to live by their wits." Park predicted that, if the majority of blacks would remain in the rural South, "where they can grow up slowly and naturally, and be kept out of the cities where they will be forced along at a pace that will make them superficial and trifling, the race problem will eventually solve itself."[88]

Park had originally interested himself in African Americans as a model that might suggest means of ameliorating colonial atrocities in the Congo; at the University of Chicago, he made the Negro into a central and foundational figure of sociology. Park explained to his students that "the negro in America, representing as he does nearly every type of man from the primitive barbarian to the latest and most finished product of civilization, offers an opportunity to study primitive man in all the stages of progress from the lowest to the highest."[89] The Negro functioned in Park's sociology, however, not as a simple case study of human development, but rather as a deeply productive mystery. Here Park adhered to a long tradition of answering the "Negro question" with contradictions and obfuscations that grounded disciplinary and repressive regimes at least as effectively as clear, simplistic stereotypes might have. An essay prompt from one of Park's courses ran: "The Statement is frequently made of women by men that 'woman is a mystery,' and that the warp of women are beyond the ken of the male creature. The same statement is made by white men of Negroes. Women rarely if ever complain about their ability to understand men; Negroes do not complain of their inability to understand the white man. How do you interpret these facts?"[90] Blacks and women, Park remarked elsewhere, had intuitive rather than scientific knowledge of white men. "Clairvoyant," Park jotted in his notes, "animals, children, women and Negroes clairvoyant." These groups all had to be "clairvoyant," for the white man had to be "arbitrary . . . to maintain his authority." "The Negro discerned his habits."[91] White men, by contrast, were forced by their positions of authority to develop social science, rather than relying on intuition or "clairvoyance," to understand women and African Americans. The opacity and contradictions of the answers to the "Negro question" in the discussions of white elites had long served as part of a regime of oversupervised and underpaid labor. Park now made this opaque language serve the production of sociological knowledge.

At the 1918 meeting of the American Sociological Association at Richmond, Virginia, Park made his most widely quoted pronouncement: "The Negro is, so to speak, the lady among the races."[92] In this lecture, Park developed the concept of an innate, biological "racial temperament" that, along with social circumstances, modified the "content" or "inflection" of the "cultural forms" that a race took from "an alien civilization." Thus, for African Americans, "the temperament is African, but the tradition is American." Of the Negro, Park concluded, "He is primarily an artist, loving life for its own sake." (Five years earlier Du Bois had written similarly that "The Negro is primarily an artist" but criticized those who made this observation in order "to speak disdainfully of his sensuous nature.")[93] According to Park, "the education of the Negro in America and with the work of foreign missions" illustrated that any "cultural forms" a race takes from "an alien civilization" will always be modified by the group's innate, biologically grounded "racial temperament." Park concluded, surely thinking of Tuskegee's global program of "Negro" education, that pedagogies should be tailored for specific "racial temperaments."[94] As Armstrong had done almost three decades earlier at Mohonk, Park proposed a vague and even contradictory assessment of the nature of blacks, one that would continue to trap them in a position of subordination and exploitation while seeming to offer collective uplift.

Like Park, William I. Thomas, in the first volumes of his masterpiece, *The Polish Peasant in Europe and America*, coauthored with Polish sociologist Florian Znaniecki, found social stability in rural communities and disintegration in cities.[95] Polish villages, Thomas and Znaniecki held, no longer organized the lives of families and individuals, because both the seasonal migration of Sachsengänger and permanent migration overseas broke down the "primitive," extended family, which formally had encompassed and organized the lives of its members.[96] Echoing complaints they read in the Polish press, Thomas and Znaniecki argued that the emigration of marriageable men to the United States, combined with the mobility and independent income of young men and women employed seasonally in Prussia, led to a hedonistic sexuality based on personal inclination, often outside of marriage and in any case outside of the social patterns of the village. This economic and familial dislocation in turn engendered revolutionary desires for change, including, Thomas noted, resistance to the Prussian Settlement Commission.[97] Thomas and Znaniecki brought the politics of internal colonization and Sachsengängerei, which already indirectly influenced all German-trained sociologists in the United States, directly into what is perhaps the foundational work of American sociology.

In Chicago, Thomas and Znaniecki argued, Poles suffered demoralization even more severely than they had in Polish villages. Isolated in tenements, the nuclear family exercised insufficient control over the "sexual tendencies" of its members, leading to a "looseness of mores . . . among

Polish immigrants" that "astonishes the American social worker." This "looseness of mores" manifested itself most importantly in marital infidelity and divorce, which in turn caused further disorganization of all family members. A Polish immigrant would even be more likely to commit murder in America, the authors maintained, because he "feels himself here in a human wilderness, with nobody and nothing but his physical strength to rely upon." In school and at play on the city streets, Polish children went unsupervised, leading to "vagabondage and delinquency" among the boys, and "sexual immorality"—primarily extramarital sex— among girls.[98]

Thomas and Znaniecki offered their own work as a model for a series of sociological monographs on individual ethnic groups that would provide advice on how workers from various groups might best be made content with the economic status quo. "The modern division and organization of labor," Thomas and Znaniecki explained, "brings an enormous and continually growing quantitative prevalence of occupations which are almost completely devoid of stimulation." Rather than decrying this "economic organization," as a conservative "moralist" might, or trying to transform it, as communists did, sociology should, they affirmed, study the attitudes specific to various ethnic groups with a view toward reconciling them to the often tedious nature of capitalist labor. "The economic interests are only one class of human attitudes among others," they wrote, "and every attitude can be modified by an adequate social technique."[99] The socially integrative function appealed to, and may even have been inspired by, the social reformers at Hull House in Chicago. Thomas's wife, Harriet Park Thomas, was a close associate of the founder of Hull House, Jane Addams, and Helen Culver, a major supporter of the social settlement, financed Thomas's study with the enormous sum of $50,000 in 1908—equivalent to about a million dollars in 2007.[100]

For decades, many American sociologists regarded *The Polish Peasant in Europe and America* as the single most important work in their discipline, and to this day it is still regarded as path-breaking.[101] Thomas and Znaniecki's work shifted sociology, in the words of a 1985 review, from "a speculative to a research base."[102] So-called Chicago-school sociologists, as they came to be known, in the words of their "bible" of sociology, *Introduction to the Science of Sociology*, "directed their attention less to society than to societies, i.e. social groups." "This change," the text continued, "marks the transformation of sociology from a philosophy of history to a science of society."[103] The assumption shared by Thomas and Park that specific racial or ethnic groups differed fundamentally from one another, and that these differences had definite political and economic consequences, drove sociology to study individual groups, making it necessarily comparative and empirical. Society in general did not exist for Chicago-school sociology; society was, rather, a crazy quilt of distinct groups, each with a definite place in relation to the others.

THE GREAT MIGRATION AND THE TRANSFORMATION OF SOCIOLOGY

The history of the city of Chicago, of Polish and African American urban migration, and of the political forces unleashed in the First World War soon transformed the sociology that Park and Thomas taught. Under these external influences, Chicago-school sociology lost its pastoral reverence for rural stability and, in many cases, ceased offering itself as a guide to social control. University of Chicago sociology would become a distinctly urban discipline and one, as carried out by Thomas himself and by many of Park's students, that supported democratic political and economic transformations.

Thomas and Znaniecki's research on Poles was intimately bound up with the history of Polish migration in Europe and America, much like the early work of Max Weber and other members of the Verein für Sozialpolitik.[104] Chicago, to an even greater extent than anywhere in Germany, was a major destination for Polish migration. One of the volumes of Thomas and Znaniecki's work even consists of a lengthy autobiography of a former Polish Sachsengänger who moved to Chicago.[105] Thomas himself traveled in the Prussian province of Posen and, with his passable Polish, produced an article for the *American Journal of Sociology* on Polish resistance to the Prussian Settlement Commission, arguing that the implacable Polish national movement emerged as a response to Prussia's attempts to Germanize the region.[106]

While Thomas, along with Robert Park and many members of the Verein für Sozialpolitik, considered African Americans in the South as model docile rural laborers, African Americans did not play this role for long. Millions of African Americans rejected Booker T. Washington's advice to "cast down your buckets where you are" and fled the poverty, racism, and economic backwardness of the rural South to cities in the North. Between 1910 and 1920, tens of thousands of African Americans moved to Chicago, increasing the city's black population from 44,000 to 110,000.[107] Significant numbers of African Americans had always lived in cities, but with this dramatic urbanization, blacks themselves transformed the "Negro question" from a question of the rural South to a question of the urban North, much as Poles themselves transformed the peasant question, as Thomas had studied it, into an urban question.

International events also undermined the science of social control that Park and Thomas had initially offered. The United States had become increasingly reactionary in 1917, as it prepared to enter the First World War. Even W.E.B. Du Bois got caught up, to his later regret and embarrassment, in the nationalist hysteria, arguing that African Americans should "close ranks" and support the war effort of the United States.[108] The Espionage Act of 1917, passed a month after the Selective Service Act established the draft in America, made antiwar activity, including obstructing recruiting or the draft, a federal crime punishable by up to twenty years in prison. The Bolshevik Revolution of 1917 prompted a first American Red Scare and continued the government persecution of radicals in the United States in the years after the war. The Sedition Act of 1918 expanded the Espionage Act, declaring it a crime to "utter, print, write, or publish any disloyal, profane, scurrilous, or abusive language" about the U.S. government, flag, or military.

William I. Thomas himself suffered political persecution, most likely in large part because his wife, Harriet Park Thomas, served on the executive committee of the Woman's Peace Party, founded by Jane Addams in 1915 to oppose America's entry into the First World War.[109] After America declared war on Germany, in April 1917, the Woman's Peace Party came under criminal suspicion of violating the Espionage Act. Thomas himself was also widely criticized in the press and by his colleagues for his stance in favor of sexual liberty and equality between men and women.[110] In April 1918 the Bureau of Investigation (the agency later renamed the Federal Bureau of Investigation) arrested Thomas for registering in a Chicago hotel under a false name with a young woman with whom he was, apparently, in love. Agents of the Chicago Bureau had on at least one previous occasion used details gathered in the course of an investigation to charge a suspected political criminal with sex offenses when they could produce no other evidence against him.[111] Because of his reputation as a sexual libertine, this sort of tactic may have seemed especially appropriate to employ against Thomas. The court acquitted Thomas, who was defended by Clarence Darrow, of all charges, but the University of Chicago dismissed him because of the scandal.[112] Thomas remained in Chicago for some time, teaching sociology at private seminars arranged off campus by his former colleague, Louis Wirth.[113] He continued his distinguished career at the New School for Social Research in New York City and, later, at the University of California at Berkeley, until his death in 1947.

The volumes of the *Polish Peasant* published during and after Thomas's persecution reflect a growing sympathy for radical social and political change. When Thomas and Znaniecki wrote the preface to the first volume of the *Polish Peasant*, they claimed their sociology served the status quo. By the time the book appeared in print, the forces defending the status quo threatened Thomas himself. Thomas's sexual politics already put him at odds, to a certain extent, with conventional authorities, and his prosecution now pushed him further. Indeed, it was precisely around issues of sexuality and the family that Thomas first took his steps toward a more radical sociology. Thomas, in the volumes of the Polish Peasant written after his political persecution, no longer described the social disintegration experienced by Polish families in the United States in purely negative terms. Despite a litany of social ills that could have come from the pen of any conservative of the century before or since, Thomas and Znaniecki did not call for a return to rural households, extended families and pastoral values or, for that matter, for a nativist exclusion of immigrants. According to Thomas, modern urban life dissolved the organization of static, primitive communities like those of the Polish village, but it also presented possibilities for new, superior social organization and individual personality.

In the 1919 volume, Thomas and Znaniecki described two pathological types of modernity. The first, the "bohemian," rejected old organizations without embracing a new organization. The bohemian, "in its highest form," was an "artist, thinker, religious reformer, social revolutionist." Thomas and Znaniecki viewed with much more concern a second pathological type of modernity, the "limited, stable, self-satisfied philistine," the individual who stubbornly clings to a set social organization, regardless of its suitability to the modern, mobile world or its ability to facilitate satisfaction of basic human desires.[114] If the bohemian was a dangerously creative individual, the philistine was a dangerously narrow individual. The growth of philistinism constrained all members of society, and Thomas and Znaniecki cited as an example of philistinism "the sudden decay of intellectual life in American colleges and universities during the present war." The ever more specialized division of labor and social roles in capitalist society, the authors noted in the later volumes, had a marked tendency to produce philistines: "an individual whose character is formed by a modern professional group is the narrowest type of Philistine the world has ever seen," the two wrote.[115] Whereas the first volumes of the Polish Peasant had offered themselves as a means of preserving an economic status quo, with the ever growing tedium of its division of labor, the last volumes presented this status quo as a human pathology.

Thomas and Znaniecki preferred the "creative individual" to both the philistine and the bohemian. The "character" of the creative individual, the two sociologists explained, "is settled and organized but involves the possibility and even the necessity of evolution." Yet, the "creative individual" was nearly identical to the "highest form" of bohemianism, the difference being that the products of the "true creative type" would have greater "internal harmony and social importance" than those of the bohemian.[116] Thomas and Znaniecki might well have regarded, for example, the revolutionary speakers at Chicago's "bughouse square" as bohemians, surely more than a bit disorganized, but they also likely preferred them infinitely to philistines like the federal agents who locked these bohemians up. Thomas was, after all, a bohemian hounded by philistines eager to lock him up, too, and the later volumes of the *Polish Peasant* are, on one level, a plea for bohemianism written in the philistine years of America's first Red Scare.

The last two volumes of *The Polish Peasant*, published in the 1920s, after Znaniecki had returned to Poland and Thomas had been expelled from the university, suggest that the Polish peasant in America might not be a disorganized and demoralized threat to American society at all, but rather a source of modern forms of social organization to save America from its own growing philistinism.[117] The cooperative, an organization "based on free individual association for common aims," provided, the authors suggested, a flexible organization for a modern society that allowed for "mutual adjustment of [individual] aims." Thomas and Znaniecki praised "all immigrant groups, among them perhaps preeminently the Poles" because they "bring to this country precisely the attitudes upon which cooperative enterprises can be built." (This was exactly the sort of thing that the American right expected to prevent by limiting immigration with the 1921 Emergency Quota Act and the 1924 National Origins Act.) American society as a whole ought, they thought, to replace its old, hierarchical organizations with cooperatives: "A countrywide net of thousands, hundreds of thousands of small cooperative associations, with the active participation of various nationalities, coming together on a basis of real equality and united by serious common aims would do incomparably more for economic self-dependence, for the prevention of demoralization, for the development of active solidarity, for a genuine Americanization of the immigrant than anything that has ever been done to achieve these aims. It would, besides, contribute in a measure to the solution of many of the most difficult problems which American society itself is trying to solve at this moment.[118] If Thomas had become as sympathetic to anarchism or communist councils as he sounds in this passage, he would have kept these sympathies hidden in 1920, when expressing such political views could result in lengthy prison sentences.

Thomas and Znaniecki's descriptions of immigration and assimilation as a process of change for both the immigrant group and the United States, against nativist visions of a one-directional "Americanization," shaped the study of immigration in the sociology department at the University of Chicago, one of its most important topics of research.[119] The cooperative would not merely alleviate the temporary ills facing the Polish community in Chicago; it might cure the philistinism the United States in the age of

"100 percent Americanism," the Red Scare, and the waves of lynching and antiblack riots that swept the United States after the First World War. The Poles did not need to be saved by America; America needed saving by the Poles. Both Park and Thomas contributed to a series of "Studies of Methods of Americanization" commissioned by the Carnegie Corporation to endorse an Americanization that would "perpetuate no unchangeable political, domestic, and economic regime," but rather "a growing and broadening national life, inclusive of the best wherever found."[120] These new political attitudes were brought about by the mass migrations and revolutions of the groups that sociologists at the University of Chicago studied, not simply by changed intellectual attitudes on the part of Park, Thomas, and others.

Like Thomas, Park was forced by the urban migration of the group he studied, African Americans, to turn his attention to the city. He continued, however, to regard urban spaces as exceptional, even pathological, calling the city in 1915 "a laboratory or clinic in which human nature and social processes may be most conveniently and profitably studied" because it "shows the good and evil in human nature in excess"[121] In 1917, with his turn to urban issues, Park became the first president of the Chicago chapter of the Urban League. The Urban League encouraged black economic activity as an alternative to political challenges to the status quo. It thus represented an urban application of the approach Tuskegee Institute took to the problems of blacks in the rural South. Under Park's presidency, the League conducted research to help African American organizations accommodate black migrants from the rural South to urban life.[122]

Park, in contrast to many of his colleagues and students, rejected social reform that strayed from the Tuskegee Institute line. Park's "bias against do-gooders and also social workers" was legendary among his students, and he was known for his misogynist remarks about the women of Hull House.[123] This represented, in part, an effort to professionalize sociology by moving the discipline, as historian Mary O. Furner has described it, from "advocacy" to "objectivity."[124] By distancing sociology from social reform, Park also, in effect, took more than his share of credit for a kind of social study that had obvious antecedents in the research carried out by Jane Addams and other women at Hull House, as sociologist Mary Jo Deegan has shown, as well as in the work carried out at Tuskegee Institute.[125] A student who studied with Park in the 1930s remembered that Park "attacked the Quakers for their self-righteous meddling in the abolition movement and had a few things to say about all reformers in general, that the greatest damage done to the city of Chicago was not the product of corrupt politicians or criminals, but women reformers." This student remembered Park's particular anger at an "elderly woman" in the class who was "an aggressive reformer." Park also treated "a black student who had quite a lot of opinions which he aired with dignity . . . quite roughly and with such impatience that some of us wondered what he had against blacks."[126] Park's former student, Edgar T. Thompson, speculated in 1967 that "Park was a conservative and not a 'liberal' as that word is being used today."[127]

With his turn to urban sociology, Park began studying the processes of racial and cultural interaction, seeking, however, to preserve in the city the separation of individual groups that he saw in the rural South.[128] Park's students Winifred Raushenbush and Everett C. Hughes both confirm that Park did not, in the words of Raushenbush, believe in "total integration, a melting pot of races and the formation of a unified nation on American soil."[129] Park even gave qualified support to school segregation. "The Negro," Park explained in 1917, "under present conditions, requires an education which will enable him to resist and overcome the special obstacles to his racial progress and racial welfare which he meets in the white man's environment. This he does not always get in the white schools or white environment."[130] For Park, accommodation, in which social groups lived separately but in harmony, represented the highest social good, and would prove as desirable in "research in social conflicts, adjustments in labor problems, industrial relations, community organization, and political parties, as well as in the study of the social psychology of subordination and superordination, social status, social types, and leadership" as it had already in "studies of immigration, colonization, and race relations."[131] The multiracial structures of empire provided Park with a both normative and empirical model of society.

Rather than integration and assimilation, Park advocated maintaining separate but interdependent communities within a larger society, echoing Booker T. Washington's ideal of "separate as the fingers, yet one as the hand in all things essential to mutual progress." Park thus directed his students to write empirical dissertations on distinct social groups, including hoboes, plantations, slums, the wealthy "Gold Coast" neighborhood of Chicago, rural African Americans, and urban African Americans. The turn from "society . . . to societies, i.e. social groups" that Park encouraged was a political strategy as much as a social-scientific methodology, both describing and prescribing an imperial matrix of fixed and stable differences.[132] For the majority of University of Chicago sociologists, their city, and indeed the modern world, consisted of a mosaic of interacting, but relatively discrete groups, each of which could be subjected to monographic treatment.

Especially in the close confines of a city, hybridity and assimilation threatened Park's model of discrete ethnic and racial groups.[133] Before he relocated to Chicago, Park, living in the segregated South, claimed that hybridity, racial mixing, produced an undesirable "mulatto soul." "Negroes as soon as they get a little education," Park warned, acquire a "restlessness and an unhappiness" as they "attempt to conceal or explain away things in themselves that others criticize or that mark them as different from others." Booker T. Washington, according to Park, had successfully worked through the problems of his own "mulatto soul," while Du Bois had not yet done so.[134] One of Park's first students, Edward Byron Reuter, wrote a dissertation on "the Mulatto in the United States" that persuaded his mentor to take a more positive view of mixed-race individuals. Following a common American view, one to which Max Weber had also subscribed, Reuter argued that leaders and high achievers classified as black were actually "mulattos," by which he meant any African American with any white ancestry.[135] Where Park saw an unhappy mulatto, Reuter saw a black elite—an elite whose status came, however, from its whiteness. (Reuter's book was roundly criticized as both unscholarly and racist by the historian Carter G. Woodson and the sociologist Kelly Miller, both at Howard University.)[136] Reuter went on to a professorship at the University of Iowa before replacing Park at Fisk University after his mentor's death in 1944.

The situation in West Africa continued to inform the sociology that Park had brought to Chicago even after the conclusion of the Tuskegee expedition to German Togo. Hybridity remained as pressing a topic in West Africa as it was in the United States, for in both regions white elites sought to preserve a monopoly of political and economic power not only over black workers but also over black elites. Park's student Everett V. Stonequist recalled that he had arrived at his own interest in ethnic and racial hybridity after hearing a 1925 lecture by Frederick Lugard, the famous British colonial administrator and author on "Europeanized Africans."[137] He found these Africans physically defective—less fertile and with bad teeth—and politically dangerous. "American Negroes" demonstrated, to Lugard, the limitations of detribalized blacks, and he pointed to Booker T. Washington as an example of the weaknesses inherent in even the most successful "Europeanised or Americanised negro." Lugard judged Du Bois's *Souls of Black Folk* as an example of the "unhappiness and discontent" of this group. Lugard, famously, advocated what he called "indirect rule," ruling through individuals whom British administrators identified as traditional authorities, in large part to prevent the "detribalized," educated elites on the coast from gaining power.[138] Stonequist similarly asserted that American mulattoes were more likely to rebel than those he regarded as racially pure.[139]

When Park or his students did admit a grudging admiration for the hybridity of the city, they reimagined the "mulatto soul" as a white "marginal man." Park followed Stonequist in depicting this marginal man not as a "mulatto," but rather as a "Jew in the Diaspora," culturally hybrid but racially white. "The marginal man," Park admitted, "is always relatively the more civilized human being." Like the "mulatto" in Reuter's account, the marginal man was a cultural and political innovator.[140] Park saw in the "vast melting-pots of races and cultures, the metropolitan cities," the decline of "the sacred order of tribal custom" and the rise of "the rational organization which we call civilization."[141] Between Reuter, Park, and Stonequist, the mulatto became a more generalized "marginal man," elite, creative, and dangerous, much like the Bohemian described by Thomas and Znaniecki. Park, Reuter, and Stonequist, however, could not bring themselves to endorse hybridity, for it contradicted the basic methodological premise of their sociology, the study of discrete social groups, and perhaps also because hybridity simultaneously emerged from, supported, and threatened the political and economic status quo, much like Sachsengänger in Germany or black elites in West Africa.

Just as the Jew in the diaspora became the model for the "marginal man," the Jewish ghetto, as described by Park's student and later colleague at the University of Chicago, Louis Wirth, became the paradigm for the separate communities that made up society. The characteristics that Wirth identified in the Jewish neighborhood, he argued, held true for any group, not just Jews, living "in relations of mere externality" to the majority. This, of course, is the meaning of the term *ghetto* today. For Wirth, the ghetto provided "a laboratory specimen for the sociologist that embodies all the concepts and the processes of his professional vocabulary." Park, in his preface to Wirth's book, agreed, commenting, "Our great cities turn out, upon examination, to be a mosaic of segregated peoples."[142] The model of the culturally distinct and settled ghetto Jew supported the efforts of Park and some of his students to preserve in the city the separated and minority status of rural African Americans and the East Elbian peasants, which had made these groups models for transatlantic racial thought in the decades before the First World War and the Great Migration.

The dynamic nature of global capitalism itself continued, nonetheless, to threaten Park's model of discrete, settled social groups, and many of Park's own students pressed this challenge. Indeed, the first work in a series of urban studies by Chicago-trained sociologists treated the hobo, a figure of mobility no less politically threatening in the United States than the Polish Sachsengänger were in Poland.[143] Written by Nels Anderson, who had himself been a hobo before finding his way into college and finally graduate school at the University of Chicago, this work portrayed the hobo as a migrant laborer necessary to the United States economy, neither the "tramp," who wanders but does not work, nor the "bum," who neither wanders nor works. Chicago was the pushing-off point for these American Sachsengänger, who signed up for seasonal labor in harvesting, lumber, and other industries, most commonly in the western states. Whereas agents and overseers recruited and accompanied Sachsengänger, hoboes traveled from job to job by hopping trains illegally, taking advantage of industrial mobility while avoiding much of the regulation of the capitalist economy. In his introduction to Anderson's 1923 book, Park misrepresented the work as a study of the neighborhood in Chicago where hoboes live and of the problem of homelessness in the modern city. In fact, as Anderson makes clear, permanent homeless residents of Chicago did not represent typical hoboes; the migrant workers Anderson studied mocked these settled men as the "home guard."[144]

Like the Sachsengänger, the American hobo enjoyed an extraordinary mobility and freedom that was made possible by capitalism, was necessary to capitalism, and also, at the same time, threatened capitalism. Capitalism required the poverty and exploitation of hoboes, Sachsengänger, as well as many other workers, but these workers did not require poverty and exploitation. Hoboes, to a greater extent than Sachsengänger, organized themselves politically. The mobility of the hoboes not only facilitated their exploitation by capital, but also empowered their resistance to this exploitation. Chicago was the headquarters of the favored political organization of hoboes, the Industrial Workers of the World (the IWW or the Wobblies). The mobility of these workers meant that a local Wobbly fight could attract hundreds, as party comrades dropped their work at a moment's notice and hopped trains to great IWW actions in San Diego, Spokane, and elsewhere. The hobo was the ultimate bohemian, as William I. Thomas used that word, and, indeed, both the neighborhood in Chicago where hoboes lived when not traveling, as well as the larger world of the hoboes, was known as "Hobohemia." The hoboes were also sexually bohemian, and Anderson makes clear that sex between men was the norm, for it kept the hobo free from the social constraints of marriage and the family. Even more than sex with women, hoboes rejected the settled domesticity that heterosexuality implied, a domesticity incompatible with their economic and political mobility.[145] The figure of the hobo proved correct much of the dire assessments of migrant labor of the previous fifty years. Capitalism bred proletarianization, proletarianization bred mobility, and mobility bred communism. As Max Weber had lamented in 1894, "the much bemoaned 'mobilization' of rural workers is also the beginning of the mobilization for the class war."[146]

Park and Weber introduced a sociological understanding of race and labor, synthesizing the specific experiences of the German East, the American South, and, especially for Robert E. Park, colonial Africa, into a sociological model of empire. This sociology they offered as a means of both understanding and managing a global division of labor based on discrete minorities, devising methods of education and economic management for various racial, civilizational, or ethnic groups. The same mass mobilizations that the fixed differences of these sociologies alternately decried and obscured, however, also allowed other of Park's students, including Nels Anderson and, as we shall see, E. Franklin Frazier and Charles S. Johnson, to develop a radical social science that rejected both the sociology that Park and Weber had brought from the New South and the political, economic, and pedagogical projects of Tuskegee Institute. The revolutionary social science of Marx, Kautsky, and others, which haunted the colonial sociology of the global South since its inception in the years after the American Civil War, finally broke into the sociological mainstream in the years after the October Revolution.

Conclusion

PRUSSIAN PATHS OF CAPITALIST DEVELOPMENT: THE TUSKEGEE EXPEDITION TO TOGO BETWEEN TRANSNATIONAL AND COMPARATIVE HISTORY

IN THE PERIOD between the American Civil War and the First World War, people in many regions of the world, including the American South, the German East, and West Africa, cast off the political and economic unfreedom of slavery and serfdom. In response, elites, both new and old, invented ways to divert this newly won freedom into channels of state power and capital accumulation. The global South was an arbitrary creation of transnational actors committed to disseminating a racial division of labor modeled at least in part on the American New South. By imposing models of "development" devised for American freedpeople, understood as having nowhere to go but "up from slavery," colonial states blocked indigenous paths to prosperity and destroyed institutions of local political autonomy. Misunderstanding much of the world as the New South helped create what many now, more accurately than they perhaps know, call the global South. The Tuskegee cotton expedition to German Togo played a central role in the movement from New South to global South. The American South, however, served as a model not only for those who would globalize the New South of segregation, disfranchisement and sharecropping, but also, as we shall see, for those who would globalize African American efforts at self-emancipation, both during and after slavery.

Social scientists on both sides of the Atlantic played an important role in helping states and businesses transform elements of the New South into a global South. The movement from New South to global South also inspired some of the most important social scientists of the nineteenth and twentieth centuries, including Karl Marx, Gustav Schmoller, W.E.B. Du Bois, Max Weber, Karl Kautsky, Robert E. Park and, as we shall see shortly, Vladimir Ilyich Lenin. The work of these social scientists continues to inform the historiography of the American South and the global South. The entanglements of social science with the global South make problematic comparative histories of race and free labor because these so often rely on concepts that both emerged from, and helped to create, the capitalist world system they seek to describe. The social sciences of the global South are eminently practical, too close to their objects of study for analytic detachment. As historically immanent theoretical practices, helping to engineer the world that they also explain, however, these social sciences constitute objects of historical study in their own right. The proximity of knowledge and power in the global South also means that historians necessarily participate, if only to a limited extent, in the international politics of imperialism and neoimperialism.

Historians of the American South have for decades debated the extent to which the region followed a Prussian rather than an American path of capitalist agricultural development.[1] In societies following the "Prussian path," according to these historians, "feudal" landlords maintain much of their political and economic power even after the transition from feudalism to capitalism, or, in the American case, from slavery to free labor. In the "American path," by contrast, feudal landlords lose their power and property and are supplanted by a new class of capitalist farmers. No historian has argued that the American South followed such an American path.

In fact, the path of the New South was more Prussian, and the Prussian path more Southern, and both more African, than most historians have realized. Each of these regions were shaped by social scientists and political and economic authorities who looked to the examples set by the other two in devising means of checking the freedom of labor in capitalist agriculture in the wake of global emancipations. Historical understandings of the Prussian path have been profoundly influenced by the work of Verein für Sozialpolitik member Georg Friedrich Knapp, who employed the American South as an analytical and a practical model of postemancipation labor control in Prussia. Robert E. Park completed this circuit when he sent his student Edgar Tristam Thompson, who was writing a thesis on the Virginia plantation, to spend a summer in Germany east of the Elbe River, the territory of the large landed estates.[2] Though the dissertation studied the plantation in Virginia most closely, Thompson used the examples of Junker estates and the colonial plantations of his day to characterize the plantation generally as an industrial organization that used political control, often brought about by conquest and racial subordination, to organize labor for the production of an agricultural commodity.[3] Thompson's work, even more directly than Knapp's, continues to shape contemporary understandings of the plantation in the American South and around the world.[4] The Prussian path was southern long before historians debated whether it could be abstracted as a model for the American New South.

The question of whether the southern United States pursued a Prussian path, or, for that matter, whether Prussia and West Africa pursued a southern path, depends upon separating categories of knowledge from the transnational histories in which they emerged. The Prussian path, like the American path or the West African path, resulted from transnational networks of capital, social science, racial ideologies, and empire. Political and economic authorities themselves, with the help of many allies, abstracted categories of identity, sexuality, household, agriculture, and even capitalism to transform and standardize the lives and labor of the inhabitants of the regions they sought to dominate. Comparative analysis had a decidedly pragmatic agenda for those who employed it in creating a global South modeled on the American New South. The abstract categories employed by earlier comparative histories of capitalist agriculture arose from, but also threatened to obscure, a transnational history of sexuality, race, labor, and empire.

The concept of a Prussian path itself emerged from the transnational history of capitalist agriculture in eastern Germany, the American South, and West Africa. The distinction between a Prussian and an American Path was first drawn in 1908 by Vladimir Ilyich Lenin, one of the most important social democratic opponents of the new forms of rural labor control emerging in the wake of the emancipation of serfs in Russia in 1861. Lenin encouraged Russian Marxists to foster rural development in their own country along an American path by supporting a more complete bourgeois revolution on the land, thus ending all vestiges of feudal landlord power.[5] At that time, Lenin described American agriculture in rosy terms, similar to those employed by Karl Marx in his letter to Abraham Lincoln a half-century earlier, when the head of the First International had contrasted the small, independent farming in the North and the Midwest with the slave plantations of the South. Lenin may also have taken this characterization of American agriculture, ironically, from Verein für Sozialpolitik member Max Sering. Sering praised midwestern farming as a model for German internal colonization and pointed to the apparent success of the American family farm to counter the criticisms of small farming made in the agrarian program of the Social Democratic Party of Germany.[6]

More careful scrutiny of black tenant farming in the American South soon led Lenin to reject his earlier characterization of American agriculture. In his 1915 study, "Capitalism and Agriculture in the United States of America," Lenin focused on black sharecropping in the American South to suggest that the American path of capitalist agriculture, which he had advocated less than a decade earlier, also contained authoritarian, even "feudal" elements. After the American Civil War, Lenin noted, the American bourgeoisie restored "the most shameless and despicable oppression of the Negroes" within "'free,' republican-democratic capitalism." Lenin pointed to the sharecropping system in the United States, as well as to the inferior education provided for African Americans, as the principal means by which this special oppression continued, which he compared to the treatment of former serfs in Russia.[7] The condition of black sharecroppers in the American South, Lenin suggested, disproved the claims of Russian populists and bourgeois reformers that the growth of small family farming would ameliorate or even supplant capitalism on the land. Lenin classified sharecroppers and other semifree agricultural smallholders as workers rather than independent farmers, and thus, he argued, even in the countryside capitalism was growing and the proletariat increasing in number.[8]

In "Capitalism and Agriculture in the United States of America" Lenin abandoned the idealized concept of an American path of independent small farmers that he had borrowed, via Marx, from the American Free-Soilers and, via Max Sering, from the German Verein für Sozialpolitik. He recalled, instead, Kautsky's critical analysis of small farming in his 1899 *Agrarian Question*. Lenin, like Kautsky, observed that capitalist small farmers never lived entirely free of precapitalist constraints. Black sharecroppers of the American South, Lenin maintained, illustrated most clearly the gap between ideological representations of the independent family farm and the reality of labor in capitalist agriculture around the world. Lenin found, in 1915, that even the most advanced capitalist agriculture, whether or not precapitalist elites remained in power, included unfree or semifree labor, which Lenin characterized as feudal remnants. All capitalist agriculture occurred, in this sense, along what he had earlier called a Prussian path.[9] Lenin avoided overemphasizing Prussian peculiarities, not in order to applaud Junkers, but rather to reject a false dichotomy that tended to glorify "western" capitalism.[10] With this implicit rejection of his own earlier distinction between an American path and a Prussian path, Lenin was perhaps the first major Marxist theorist to recognize the modernity of the American South, that the South was no atavistic remnant of a feudal past but rather indicated with special clarity a general tendency of capitalist agriculture. New South boosters, theorists in the Verein für Sozialpolitik, and European colonial authorities had already realized this, with decidedly different practical aspirations, decades earlier.

The American South became important for the anticolonial Communist International that emerged after the Bolshevik Revolution, as it had been for the colonial global South and the liberal internationalism that gained new strength from the League of Nations. While the Soviet Union was brutally oppressive in many ways, it also helped inaugurate a revolutionary global South, one for which the "Negro question" was a question about strategies of emancipation rather than methods of exploitation and oppression. Though it is perhaps counterintuitive to describe emancipatory aspects of the Soviet Union, the new communist parties founded across the globe after the October Revolution challenged American racism and European colonialism more fundamentally and consistently than liberalism ever did.

While Lenin placed African Americans at the center of his analysis of capitalist agriculture, the Communist International addressed the status of African Americans as part of the closely related colonial question.[11] The Communist (Third) International, or Comintern, dominated by the Russian Communist Party, emerged in 1919 in the place of the by then defunct Socialist (Second) International, which had been dominated by the Social Democratic Party of Germany. At the second, 1920, congress of the Comintern, the American communist John Reed, author of *Ten Days that Shook the World*, called on his comrades to include African Americans among the colonized peoples whose "national-revolutionary" movements communists supported. Describing the particularly extreme oppression and exploitation that African Americans faced even after emancipation, Reed pointed to new black political activism in the first decades of the twentieth century. Previously, the only black political organizations were, Reed explained, "a semi-philanthropic educational association led by Booker T. Washington and supported by the white capitalists" that organized "schools in which the Negroes were brought up to be good servants of industry" and presented "with the good advice to resign themselves to the fate of an oppressed people." With the Great Migration, Reed continued, African Americans began to fight against racism and to organize as workers. For Reed, the African American socialist A. Philip Randolph, editor of the *Messenger* and soon to be founder of the Brotherhood of Sleeping Car Porters, exemplified this new political activism. Reed called on the Comintern to work more closely with African Americans struggling for "social and political equality."[12]

The fourth congress of the Comintern, in 1922, attended by Jamaican-born African American poet Claude McKay and the African American communist Otto Huiswood, gave party members "the special responsibility of closely applying the 'Theses on the Colonial Question' to the situation of the blacks" in the United States and in Africa. The "Theses on the Black Question" adopted by the congress argued that African Americans had been prepared by their history of "revolts, uprisings, and an underground struggle for freedom" to "play a major role in the liberation struggle of the entire African race" on both sides of the Atlantic. Booker T. Washington and many white elites argued that slavery had prepared African Americans to take a leading role in training colonial subjects to work in the global imperialist economy; the members of the Comintern turned this argument on its head, claiming that centuries of resistance to slavery and racial oppression might give African Americans a leading role in anticolonial revolutions. The Comintern set itself the task of linking the struggle of blacks against "capitalist and imperialist oppression" with the fight of "the oppressed non-white peoples of the colonies . . . against racial oppression, inequality and exploitation, and . . . for . . . political, economic and social emancipation and equality."[13]

The Comintern also began a fight against "white chauvinism" within national communist parties, and African American communists could rely on Moscow to support them in struggles against racists in the Communist Party of the United States (CPUSA). In 1925 the Comintern invited ten African American students to study at the Communist University of the Toilers of the East in Moscow, a university that trained party activists from among colonized peoples. In 1928, at its sixth congress, the Comintern decided to advocate the right of national self-determination for African Americans in the form of a black republic in the American South.[14] Delegates at the Sixth Congress, perhaps more importantly, subjected white American communists to withering criticism for their racism, their failure to organize African Americans, and their failure to fight against racism in the broader American labor movement. Strengthened and encouraged by the Comintern, the CPUSA fought against the oppression of African Americans, including defending the Scottsboro Nine in Alabama, organizing a communist sharecroppers' union, and fighting against "white chauvinism" in the communist and noncommunist labor movement more generally.[15]

The communist answer to the "Negro question" created a powerful response to the New South ideology that informed much academic social science on both sides of the Atlantic. Both the Second and the Third Internationals rejected the paternalist social science of the Verein für Sozialpolitik in favor of a revolutionary social science that treated workers as subjects of liberation rather than objects of study and control. Indeed, the communists of the Third International, like the socialists of the Second, continued to berate the German state socialism of Gustav Schmoller and others. Lenin had long criticized Schmoller and his colleagues for employing a holistic concept of society that committed them to preserving, or at most modifying, existing class hierarchies.[16] In 1927 Nikolai Bukharin, president of the Comintern, criticized the German historical school, and singled out Gustav Schmoller, for idealizing "the 'patriarchal' relations between landholders and farm workers" and for advocating state authority to support employers against workers, unions and the Social Democrats.[17] In 1928 Trotsky even criticized a "new propagandist school of Katheder-Sozialisten"—the name normally reserved for members of the Verein für Sozialpolitik—that emerged in the Soviet Union to support Stalin against the left of the party.[18] In his 1937 *Revolution Betrayed*, Trotsky maintained that much of the international support for Stalin came from "the spirit of the old-German *Katheder-Sozializmus*," which he found in the "conservatively pedantic socialism" of "the indefatigable Fabian couple, Beatrice and Sidney Webb."[19] Marxist socialists recognized in the state socialism of the Verein für Sozialpolitik an important adversary to, and, for Trotsky, a dangerous tendency within, Soviet communism.

When the Third International turned to the situation of African Americans, it provided a powerful antidote to Tuskegee strategies of racial accommodation. Communist discussions of African Americans often began by rejecting the political ideology associated with Tuskegee Institute, as John Reed had done when he first raised the topic at the 1920 Comintern congress. In *The Negroes in America*, a book Claude McKay wrote for the Comintern while in Moscow for the 1922 Congress, the author suggested that an unwillingness to take on the American ruling class hampered the struggle against racism carried out by Tuskegee Institute and even by the NAACP. McKay saw in the communist approach to the situation of African Americans a more thorough criticism and aggressive challenge to the forces and individuals oppressing blacks.[20] Leading African American communist Harry Haywood, in his autobiography *Black Bolshevik*, described his political education as a rejection of his father's devotion to Booker T. Washington and a challenge to the more elite, liberal politics of the NAACP.[21] The communist defense of the Scottsboro Nine, especially when contrasted with the tepid response of the NAACP to the case, made Marxism ever more relevant to the freedom struggles of even noncommunist African Americans and also made African American politics ever more relevant to European communists.[22]

In addition to its political activism, the CPUSA disseminated an uncompromising antiracism and revolutionary political strategy to scholars and activists outside its ranks. Revolutionary Marxism, as scholar Barbara Foley has demonstrated, provided a powerful political and theoretical vocabulary for many African American intellectuals, even those not affiliated with the Communist Party, to criticize and to combat racism, oppression, and exploitation.[23] Marxism itself, as Cedric Robinson has shown, did not simply bestow revolutionary consciousness upon blacks, but rather incorporated revolutionary traditions from Africa and the diaspora.[24] Many African Americans joined the party, but many more still drew on the insights of Marxist theory to create an emancipatory knowledge that contrasted with the conservative sociology that had emerged from Tuskegee Institute, the Verein für Sozialpolitik, and Chicago-school sociology.

The Red Summer of 1919—when a combination of racism, anticommunism, and bellicose patriotism following the end of the First World War led to a national wave of rural lynchings and urban white riots, including in Chicago—forced students of Robert E. Park to confront the volatile intersection of race and class more directly than their mentor had had to during his formative years at Tuskegee.[25] The Chicago Riot began on a lakeside beach, when white bathers attacked blacks determined to enjoy what had been customarily a whites-only beach, drowning a black teenager. As rumors of this incident circulated through the city, white gangs, known as "athletic clubs," saw a long awaited chance to carry out attacks on black Chicagoans. Armed with bricks and sticks, as well as firearms, white throngs surged through Chicago, beating and often killing any black person they could lay their hands on. White mobs murdered 23 blacks and injured 342 in a rampage carried out as an assault on an entire race. Fifteen whites were killed and 178 were injured, mostly by African Americans individuals defending themselves in their own neighborhoods.

The increasingly international politics of segregation played an important role in the Chicago Riot. As large numbers of African Americans had moved to Chicago during the Great Migration, housing shortages forced them to live outside Chicago's Southside "Black belt." Real estate agents had long maintained that the presence of blacks would reduce the value of local housing. In the two years preceding the riot, white vigilantes had already beaten and murdered individual blacks and had firebombed twenty-seven black-owned houses. White racists in Chicago may have felt emboldened by international outrage over the occupation of the German Rhineland by French troops of African descent after the First World War. E. D. Morel, the Congo reformer and enthusiast for Tuskegee Institute and German colonialism, joined this chorus of indignation, perversely similar to that aroused by colonial atrocities in the Congo. In a pamphlet describing alleged "Horrors on the Rhine," Morel described the misdeeds of black French soldiers carried out, according to the former head of the Congo Reform Association, to satisfy their "sexual requirements . . . upon the bodies of white women."[26] An anonymous group, in all likelihood an association of real estate agents, distributed a pamphlet by a less well known author, describing imagined racial atrocities in the Rhineland, titled "An Appeal of White Women to American Humanity." Evidently these brokers hoped the pamphlet would steel the resolve of its white readers to keep black residents out of their neighborhoods.[27]

Soon after the riots, a governor's committee appointed the African American sociologist Charles S. Johnson, a student of Robert E. Park's, to write a report on the causes of the Chicago riot. Under Johnson's direction, a group of researchers interviewed 274 black Chicago families, collecting family histories that included information on their relocation from the South and their housing conditions, since whites had been moved to mob action by blacks seeking housing outside the Southside. In spite of the misguided assumption that the cause of the riot could be discerned by studying its black victims rather than its white perpetrators, the official conclusions of the commission, published as *The Negro in Chicago*, made clear that the responsibility for the riots and the earlier racial tensions lay with Chicago's whites. The commission drew attention to the racism long endemic in the police force, in the school system, in labor unions, in the workplace, and in real estate markets. (The racist real estate market became an issue for the commission itself when it had trouble finding a building that would rent an office to a mixed-race group.)[28]

Charles S. Johnson has long been regarded as a relatively conservative sociologist, especially because he worked closely with the National Urban League and other organizations associated with the kind of white philanthropists who supported Tuskegee Institute. As editor of *Opportunity*, the journal of the New York Urban League, Johnson proved instrumental in promoting the work of Harlem Renaissance writers and artists. In 1928 Johnson became chair of the department of social science at Fisk University and, in 1946, president of the university until his death in 1956.[29] Yet, while Johnson himself, like many of his critics, highlighted the relatively conservative elements of his own thought, his work also contained decidedly radical elements that challenged the mostly accommodationist writings of his intellectual forebears Robert E. Park and Booker T. Washington.

In 1934 Johnson authored a study of Macon County, Alabama, the county in which Tuskegee is located, that unequivocally rejected the self-promotions of Tuskegee Institute and suggested a rebuke to the Chicago-school sociology that had emerged from the institute.[30] Publicists for Tuskegee Institute often emphasized its beneficial influence on Macon County. In 1913 Park had reported to the American Academy of Political and Social Science that, thanks to Tuskegee Institute, "a large proportion of colored farmers in Macon County live at present in neat four- and five-room cottages."[31] Two decades later, Johnson and four research assistants reported conditions in Macon County that undermined Park's assertions and, by implication, the strategies of Tuskegee Institute. Macon County, they learned, suffered from every sort of misery and had received little, if any, beneficial attention from Washington's institute. Johnson and his research assistants interviewed more than six hundred families from the county and, using lengthy quotations from these interviews, reconstructed a world wracked by poverty, malnutrition, and disease, and offering little opportunity for education. The only evidence of Tuskegee influence that Johnson and his assistants found in the county was the fading whitewash applied a quarter century earlier to cabins in a village called "Sambo," in preparation for a visit by Booker T. Washington. African Americans in Macon County, Johnson found, lived in conditions similar to, as he put it—invoking the famous work of William I. Thomas and Florian Znaniecki, as well as the transatlantic sociology of race and free labor from which it emerged—"the condition of the Polish peasant." To make matters worse, most residents grew cotton for a living, and they had to compete, according to Johnson, with "over fifty cotton-growing countries."[32] Johnson did not, it seems, recognize the important role that Tuskegee Institute had played in helping break the American cotton monopoly that had once, he maintained, buoyed the income of tenant farmers.

Johnson did not present the problems of Macon County as problems of education, or of the "accommodation" of different groups, or of the "civilizing process," as Robert Park might have. Johnson related the problems, instead, to the political economy of southern agriculture, and noted that New Deal policies did little to help black tenant farmers. Rather, the black tenant farmer, and indeed all farmers in the South, could be helped only by "a complete reorganization of agriculture," Johnson explained, "particularly in the Cotton Belt, in respect to both production and distribution" and particularly by "comprehensive planning, which affects not merely the South but the nation."[33] (This might have been Tuskegee's program, had Washington succeeded in bringing Du Bois and Carver together at Tuskegee and not succumbed to the colonial temptation offered by the German government.) There is little evidence that Johnson sympathized with the Communist Party, but he did employ a language of race and class that the Comintern helped bring to American political and social thought in order to criticize Tuskegee ideology and the conservative sociology of the University of Chicago.

Johnson was unaware that, as he and his students carried out their study, the infamous Tuskegee syphilis experiments were already under way. Johnson did know that the U.S. Public Health Service, working with the Rosenwald Fund, had administered mass syphilis tests in a number of Black-belt counties to study possibilities for mass treatment. The syphilis study had selected Macon County because of the cooperation of Tuskegee Institute, two local hospitals, and the local government. With 35 percent of residents infected with the disease, Macon County had the highest rate of syphilis of all the counties examined. Johnson also found that local residents were unaware that the disease was transmitted by sexual intercourse, attributing it, rather, to "bad blood."[34] The Public Health Service purposely withheld diagnosis from 399 male Macon County residents whom it had found to be infected with syphilis, in order to observe the cardiovascular and neurological damage they would suffer. A third of these men died of the disease before public exposure forced the Public Health Service to end the experiment in 1972. Tuskegee Institute cooperated with the study, lending what credibility it enjoyed among the residents of Macon County to assist the United States government in carrying out one of the greatest atrocities of medical experimentation.[35]

In his preface to Johnson's book, Robert E. Park maintained what he could of Tuskegee ideology in the face of Johnson's findings. Park described the population of Macon County as an example of one of America's remaining isolated societies—the Pennsylvania Dutch of Lancaster

County provided another—suffering from what to them seemed a catastrophe: the "sudden advent of a more highly civilized people intent upon their improvement and uplift by incorporating them into a more highly organized industrial society." The geography of empire remained paradigmatic for Park, who saw in Macon County the Belgian Congo all over again, not a scene of colonial atrocities but rather "one of the more or less inevitable incidents of the civilizing process," which industrial education could ameliorate. The African Americans of Macon County, alas, suffered from disorganization of their community, inhibited by "a tradition, embodied in the present plantation system," from progressing to a new organization in the South. Thus, "the Negro rural school, instead of creating a settled class of Negro peasant proprietors," Park lamented, "seems . . . to have conspired with other tendencies to hasten the movement from the rural South to the Northern cities." Like the German social scientists who had trained him, Park found that smallhold farming inhibited individual freedom and economic prosperity and also prevented the spread of social democracy: "If," Park concluded, "the agents of the 'Third International' find that such Negroes are as yet not ripe for communism, it is undoubtedly because they have not had as yet the opportunity to realize the evils of a free and competitive society."[36]

Johnson's study of Macon County, nonetheless allowed E. Franklin Frazier, another student of Robert Park's, to criticize openly the supposed "'realistic' approach" of Booker T. Washington by pointing out that "Tuskegee with its vast resources and idealism of service has been unable to change materially the life of the Negro farmers right at her door in Macon County."[37] Frazier, however, was a vocal critic of Johnson, and he sympathized with communism more openly than Johnson did. Indeed, Frazier even cited Lenin's "Capitalism and Agriculture in the United States of America" against Johnson's writings on cotton tenancy and accused Johnson, in my view incorrectly, of endorsing ideals "preached by Tuskegee and sanctioned by white friends of the Negro."[38] Neither Frazier nor Johnson were communists, but both used aspects of communist analysis to create an emancipatory sociology that broke with the conservative tradition of Tuskegee Institute as formulated by Robert E. Park. Years before he became a communist, W.E.B. Du Bois likewise employed Marxist categories in his 1935 *Black Reconstruction in America* to create perhaps the most important work of African American scholarship at the time, and the first study of the New South unburdened by the racist ideologies of white academics.[39]

The global effects of the Tuskegee expedition to Togo suggest how the historically minuscule can transform the historically enormous, how individuals and local events, through explicit and implicit comparisons, through imitations and even misunderstandings, produce transnational structures, which in turn set horizons of possibility for individuals and local events. Actors often shaped local situations according to their own sense that they were part of an interlinked macrohistorical world political economic system. When John W. Robinson of the Tuskegee expedition, for example, claimed to introduce sharecropping to Togo he, on the one hand, fundamentally misrepresented both American sharecropping and the forms of cotton farming forced on colonial subjects in German Togo. On the other hand, Robinson employed this misrepresentation to transform the political economy of Togo and thereby contributed to the processes by which the American New South refashioned itself as a model for the colonial global South.

Decolonization transformed aspects of the relation of the global South to the global North, a transformation registered, for example, by the differences between the Tuskegee expedition to Togo in 1901 and the emigration of W.E.B. Du Bois to independent Ghana, the former English Gold Coast, six decades later.[40] Du Bois traveled to Ghana on the invitation of its government, not as an auxiliary to a colonial ruler, and soon became a citizen of the newly independent state. In Ghana he collaborated with Africans on an *Encyclopedia Africana* to create an emancipatory social science, not to manipulate Africans for cotton growing or other colonial schemes. Du Bois died in August 1963, the night before Dr. Martin Luther King Jr. led the March on Washington. As a result of such efforts by African Americans, the first New South has been, in many respects, defeated. But the legacy of the New South in the global South, though dealt a heavy blow by decolonization, continues in new and myriad forms of neocolonialism. Indeed, cotton cultivation for the world market has been one of the most effective economic foundations of both colonialism and neocolonialism in West Africa.

The Tuskegee expedition to Togo sits at the junction of three great regional transformations, linking the racial political economies of the southern United States, eastern Germany, and colonial Africa. The expedition brought together three of the most powerful forces in the Atlantic world— German social science, African cash cropping, and the racial political economy of the New South—allowing each to transform the others. Each can be imagined as an arc, intersecting and supporting the other two, at a point marked by the Tuskegee expedition to Togo. One arc moves from German social science, through the expedition, to the University of Chicago and to a global sociology of race and labor; the second moves from the diverse and independent political economies of precolonial Africa to the economic dependency of primary product agriculture; the third from the New South to the global South. Each of these arcs would be invisible if viewed within the confines of just one of the regions the expedition brought together and incomprehensible if considered without the third. German social science became a global sociology of race and free labor, whose greatest representatives were Max Weber and Robert E. Park, through both the active participation of, and also the schemes of political economic control applied to, Africans and African Americans. Colonial authorities channeled the diverse potentials inherent in African cash cropping into economic dependency because German and American methods of constraining once bonded agricultural laborers converged on the recently emancipated political economy of Togo. The New South became a global South because Booker T. Washington and German elites adapted the racial politics of the southern United States to West Africa in a manner that appealed to powerful imperialist interests across the global North. Transnational history provides new ways of looking at old problems but also reveals new strata of actors, events, and processes that have been invisible to an academic historiography that has, until recently, remained beholden to the national states within which it emerged.

The global economy that emerged in the period between the American Civil War and the First World War resulted from the proliferation of forms of both mobility and immobility. Commodities, including palm oil, sugar, and cotton, moved with ever greater speed and in ever greater quantities over ever greater distances. International markets offered purchasers the contents of warehouses or even yet-to-be harvested crops halfway around the world. Political, economic, and intellectual elites moved almost as easily as these commodities, transporting European officials and businessmen to Africa, German and American social scientists back and forth across the Atlantic, and African American educators to Africa and Europe. Workers also moved across national frontiers and across oceans, whether as Polish migrants to Germany and the United States, Africans across the often artificial borders of European colonization, or African Americans in the Great Migration.

Yet this new mobility, constituting what is today often called globalization, depended, and still depends, on the proliferation of forms of immobility. These new forms of immobility allowed capital, commodities, workers, and ideas to move across a landscape of fixed differences and to remain stable across vast geographical distances. The type of social science that emerged in the Verein für Sozialpolitik, at Tuskegee and Hampton Institutes, and at the University of Chicago reflected, developed, and helped enforce categories of immobility, especially the cluster of kinship, gender, and race. Commodities markets could integrate the produce of various regions of the earth because experts, such as cotton classers, standardized the produce itself around fixed vocabularies. People changed geographical location more easily than ever before, and elites spared no effort to ensure that political and economic hierarchies survived these geographical dislocations. The dynamism of capitalism simultaneously contradicted, supported, and depended upon, static identities and stable commodities.

Political and economic elites existed only by virtue of their ability to appropriate the wealth and power resulting from the mobility and activity of African American farmers, Polish migrants, extended African households, and many other groups. But the productive activities from which these elites lived also threatened to overthrow the hierarchies that allowed them to appropriate wealth and power in the first place. It is for this reason that the powerful and the wealthy around the globe sneered almost unanimously at ambitious African Americans learning classical languages, at "black dandies" of West Africa, or at Westfaloki, the Polish seasonal migrants sporting fashionable clothes purchased in Germany. With these supposedly inappropriate extravagances workers retained some of the wealth they created and achieved a social mobility that elites feared. Economic and political rulers fostered patriarchal domesticity, with its train of racial, sexual, and economic constraints, as a way to prevent the free labor necessary for capital accumulation from becoming truly free labor, voluntary labor free from economic exploitation and political oppression. Those political and economic elites who tout the virtues of a free global economy have, in fact, much to lose from authentic economic freedom. The dense networks of empire that have shaped the global South are not systems, but rather parasitic growths on the spontaneous economic and political activities of multitudes; they are neither the causes nor the results of economic freedom but are rather reactions and obstacles to economic freedom.

NOTES

Introduction

1. The classic account of the Tuskegee expedition to Togo is Louis Harlan, "Booker T. Washington and the White Man's Burden," *American Historical Review* 71 (1966): 441–67. The Togolese historian Pierre Ali Napo discusses this first Tuskegee involvement in African development projects. Professor Napo's monograph marked the centenary of the expedition, for which Tuskegee University signed a Convention of Cooperation with the University of Lomé and unveiled a plaque dedicated to the members of the expedition at the University's Ecole Supérieure d'Agronomie. Pierre Ali Napo, *Togo, Land of Tuskegee Institute's International Technical Assistance Experimentation: 1900–1909* (Accra: Onyase Press, 2002). Translation of *Le Togo, Terre d'Experimentation de l'Assistance Technique Internationale de Tuskegee University en Alabama, USA 1900–1909* (Lomé: Editions Haho, 2001). Kendahl L. Radcliffe, "The Tuskegee-Togo Cotton Scheme, 1900–1909" (Ph.D. diss., University of California, Los Angeles, 1998) similarly treats the expedition as African American assistance to Africa. Milfred C. Fierce places the expedition in a longer history of relations between African Americans and West Africans in *The Pan-African Idea in the United States, 1900–1919: African-American Interests in Africa and Interaction with West Africa* (New York: Garland Publishing, Inc., 1993), 171–97. I share the view of Sven Beckert that the expedition was part of a larger global economic reorientation occasioned by the end of bonded labor. See Sven Beckert, "From Tuskegee to Togo: The Problem of Freedom in the Empire of Cotton," *Journal of American History* 92 (2005): 498–526. See also Andrew Zimmerman, "A German Alabama in Africa: The Tuskegee Expedition to German Togo and the Transnational Origins of West African Cotton Growers," *American Historical Review* 110 (2005): 1362–98. Donna J. E. Maier mentions the Tuskegee expedition in "Persistence of Precolonial Patterns of Production: Cotton in German Togoland, 1800–1914," in Allen F. Isaacman and Richard Roberts, eds., *Cotton, Colonialism, and Social History in Sub-Saharan Africa* (Portsmouth, NH: Heinemann, 1995), 82. Arthur J. Knoll discusses the Tuskegee cotton school in Togo in his *Togo under Imperial Germany 1884–1914: A Case Study in Colonial Rule* (Stanford: Hoover Institution Press, 1970), 144–47. Edward Graham Norris considers this cotton school in the context of a shift in the goals of colonial education from cultural continuity to managing social change, in *Die Umerziehung des Afrikaners: Togo 1895–1938* (Munich: Trickster, 1993), 141–49. The expedition is mentioned in a similar context in C. Adick, *Bildung und Kolonialismus in Togo* (Weinheim: Beltz, 1981), 192–93.

2. Alexander Walters, Henry B. Brown, H. Sylvester Williams, and W.E.B. Du Bois, "To the Nations of the World" (1900), in W.E.B. Du Bois, *An ABC of Color: Selections Chosen by the Author from Over a Half Century of His Writings* (New

York: International Publishers, 1969), 20; Richard Wright, *The Color Curtain: A Report on the Bandung Conference* (1956; Banner Books: University Press of Mississippi, 1994). On Tuskegee in Africa after the Togo expedition, see Kenneth James King, *Pan-Africanism and Education: A Study of Race Philanthropy and Education in the Southern States of America and East Africa* (Oxford: Clarendon Press, 1971) and Donald Spivey, *The Politics of Miseducation: The Booker T. Washington Institute of Liberia, 1929–1945* (Lexington: University Press of Kentucky, 1986). See also Edward H. Berman, "Tuskegee in Africa," *Journal of Negro Education* 41 (1972): 99–112. For the influence of Tuskegee in South Africa, see James Campbell, "Models and Metaphors: Industrial Education in the United States and South Africa," in Ran Greenstein, ed., *Comparative Perspectives on South Africa* (New York: St. Martin's, 1998), 90–134; R. Hunt Davis, Jr., "John L. Dube: A South African Exponent of Booker T. Washington," *Journal of African Studies* 2 (1975–76): 497–529; and Paul B. Rich, "The Appeals of Tuskegee: James Henderson, Lovedale, and the Fortunes of South African Liberalism, 1906–1930," *International Journal of African Historical Studies* 20 (1987): 271–92.

3. Historians have widely criticized American exceptionalism. See, for example, the essays collected in Thomas Bender, ed., *Rethinking American History in a Global Age* (Berkeley: University of California Press, 2002).

4. For a path-breaking interpretation of German imperialism and racism focusing on a transnational history of labor, see Sebastian Conrad, *Globalisierung und Nation im Deutschen Kaiserreich* (Munich: Beck, 2006). Christian Geulen offers an especially compelling account of the comparable development of racism in Germany and the United States in *Wahlverwandte: Rassendiskurs und Nationalismus im späten 19. Jahrhundert* (Hamburg: Hamburger Edition, 2004). John David Smith, focusing on the German anthropologist Felix von Luschan, shows that antiracism also emerged from transatlantic racial thought. See John David Smith, "Anthropologist Felix von Luschan and Trans-Atlantic Racial Reform," *Münchner Beiträge zur Völkerkunde* 7 (2002): 289–304; and Smith, "W.E.B. Du Bois, Felix von Luschan, and Racial Reform at the Fin de Siecle," *Amerikastudien/ American Studies* (2002): 23–38. The classic critique of the German *Sonderweg* is David Blackbourn and Geoff Eley, *The Peculiarities of German History: Bourgeois Society and Politics in Nineteenth-Century Germany* (New York: Oxford University Press, 1984). There have been many recent calls for placing German history in a transnational perspective, none more persuasive and forceful than Sebastian Conrad, "Doppelte Marginalisierung: Plädoyer für eine transnationale Perspektive auf die deutsche Geschichte," *Geschichte und Gesellschaft* 28 (2002): 145–69.

5. It was less than fifty years ago, it should be remembered, that the renowned British historian Hugh Trevor-Roper appeared on BBC television to warn students off of African history, which he described as the "unrewarding gyrations of barbarous tribes in picturesque but irrelevant corners of the globe." Hugh Trevor-Roper, *The Rise of Christian Europe* (London: Thames and Hudson, 1964), 9.

6. The best account of this global transformation of the cotton industry is Sven Beckert, "Emancipation and Empire: Reconstructing the Worldwide Web of Cotton Production in the Age of the American Civil War," *American Historical Review* 109 (2005): 1405–38.

7. The United States consumed a little over a fifth of its own production on the eve of the Civil War, and a full third by the last decade of the nineteenth century. Ernst von Halle, *Baumwollproduktion und Pflanzungswirtschaft in den nordamerikanischen Südstaaten* (Leipzig: Duncker & Humblot, 1897), 175, 182. See also Matthew Brown Hammond, *The Cotton Industry: An Essay in American Economic History* (New York: American Economics Association, 1897), 343.

8. John A. Todd, *The World's Cotton Crops* (London: A&C Black, 1915), 395, 416–17.

9. "Baron von Herman's Arrival," *Washington Post*, 14 August 1895. On the Herman family, see Ernst Heinrich Kueschke, *Neues allgemeines Deutsches Adels-Lexicon* (Leipzig: Friedrich Voigt, 1863), q.v. "Hermann, Herman auf Wein."

10. Baron Beno von Herman auf Wain, Washington, DC, to German Imperial Chancellor (*Reichskanzler*, hereafter chancellor) Hohenlohe-Schillingsfürst, 25 October 1895, Bundesarchiv, Berlin (hereafter BArch) R901/14543.

11. Baron von Herman, Washington, DC, to Chancellor Hohenlohe-Schillingsfürst, 24 June 1897, BArch R901/349.

12. Baron von Herman, "Memorandum über den Baumwollbau in den Vereinigten-Staaten und Deutsch Afrika," BArch R1001/8178, Bl. 200–4. Baron von Herman, "Bericht des Land- und Forstwirtschaftlichen Sachverständigen an der Kaiserlichen Botschaft," Washington, DC, 28 September 1899, BArch R901/350. He made a similar point in a report to Chancellor Hohenlohe-Schillingsfürst, 28 April 1900, BArch R901/14552. A copy of this report was also sent to the German government in Togo, Togo National Archives (microfilm copy), BArch R150 (hereafter TNA) FA 1–332, Bl. 105–9.

13. Baron von Herman, Württemberg, Germany, to Chancellor Bülow, 2 October 1901; Baron von Herman, Washington, DC, to Chancellor Bülow, 18 December 1901, BArch R1001/8179, Bl. 56–57, 91–97; "German Attache's Farewell Call," *Washington Post*, 20 December 1901.

14. On the KWK, see Richard V. Pierard, "A Case Study in German Economic Imperialism: The Colonial Economic Committee, 1896–1914," *Scandinavian Economic Review* 26 (1968): 155–67.

15. KWK, "Baumwoll-Expedition nach Togo" [1900], TNA FA 1–332, Bl. 88–102.

16. See the marginalia in KWK to the Colonial Section of the German Foreign Office, 11 October 1900, BArch R1001/8221, Bl. 11–13.

17. Baron von Herman to Booker T. Washington, 3 September 1900, in Harlan, ed., *The Booker T. Washington Papers*, 14 vols. (Urbana: University of Illinois Press, 1972–89), 5:633–36. These selections from the Booker T. Washington Papers in the Manuscript Division of the Library of Congress, Washington, DC, are now available online at http://www.historycooperative.org.

18. Baron von Herman to Booker T. Washington, 3 September 1900; Booker T. Washington to Baron von Herman, 20 September 1900 in Harlan, ed., *Booker T. Washington Papers* 5:633–36, 639–42.

19. Biographical information from a funeral program for James Nathan Calloway, which Constance Calloway Margerum made available to me, as well as from Harlan, ed., *Booker T. Washington Papers* 3:105n3. On the Marshall Farm, see Washington, *The Story of My Life and Work* (1900), in Harlan, ed., *Booker T. Washington Papers* 1:174.

20. W.E.B. Du Bois, *The Autobiography of W.E.B. Du Bois: A Soliloquy on Viewing My Life from the Last Decade of Its First Century* (1968; Oxford: Oxford University Press, 2007), 71.

21. Thomas J. Calloway to Booker T. Washington, 25 March 1909, Booker T. Washington Papers, Manuscript Division, Library of Congress, Washington, DC (hereafter Washington Papers, Library of Congress), Reel 34. For a selection of the photographs brought together by Du Bois for the exposition, see the Library of Congress with essays by David Levering Lewis and Deborah Willis, *Small Nation of People: W.E.B. Du Bois and African American Portraits of Progress* (New York: Harper Collins, 2003).

22. Harlan, ed., *Booker T. Washington Papers* 4:410n2. See also funeral program for James Nathan Calloway, Constance Calloway Margerum, Private Collection.

23. Harlan, ed., *Booker T. Washington Papers* 5:642n1.

24. On the marriage of Hiram Simpson's widow and Horace Greeley Griffin, see Radcliffe, "The Tuskegee-Togo Cotton Scheme," 91–94. Radcliffe bases her account on privately held papers of James N. Calloway. For the accident, see James N. Calloway to Booker T. Washington, 8 May 1902, in Harlan, ed., *Booker T. Washington Papers* 6: 455–56; Calloway, "Inspektion der Baumwollfarmen und Baumwollmärkte," in *Bericht II. Deutsch-koloniale Baumwoll-Unternehmungen 1902/03*, supplement to *Tropenpflanzer* 4 (1903): 112–22; James Nathan Calloway (Tuskegee Alabama) to Booker T. Washington, 17 March 1902, in Harlan, ed., *Booker T. Washington Papers* 6: 417–18, 418fn.

25. See Harlan, ed., *Booker T. Washington Papers* 2:105–6n3; Radcliffe, "The Tuskegee-Togo Cotton Scheme," 121–22.

26. Funeral program for James Nathan Calloway.

27. Emmett Jay Scott to George Washington Carver, 14 June 1902; George Washington Carver to Emmett Jay Scott, 14 June 1902, the George Washington Carver Papers, Tuskegee University, Alabama, Microfilm Edition, Manuscript Division, Library of Congress, Washington, DC (hereafter, Carver Papers), Reel 2.

28. When Calloway later told stories about his trip to Africa to his children, he related that Robinson and the two Tuskegee cotton growers who drowned in Togo had been devoured by a "water monster." Bud Calloway, "Tracking the Water Monster, or, J. N. Calloway and the Tuskegee Cotton Growing Expedition to Togo, West Africa, 1900," n.d., unpublished typescript. Before he died in 2004, Bud Calloway gave a copy of this manuscript to Dr. Michael Bieze of the Marist School, and I am grateful to Dr. Bieze for making this text available to me.

29. The essays in Isaacman and Roberts, eds., *Cotton, Colonialism, and Social History in Sub-Saharan Africa* are an excellent introduction to the marvelous work on imperialist cotton projects in Africa. See also Allen Isaacman, *Cotton Is the Mother of Poverty: Peasants, Work, and Rural Struggle in Colonial Mozambique, 1938–1961* (Portsmouth, NH: Heinemann, 1996); Thomas J. Bassett, *The Peasant Cotton Revolution in West Africa: Côte d'Ivoire, 1880–1995* (Cambridge: Cambridge University Press, 2001); Osumaka Likaka, *Rural Society and Cotton in Colonial Zaire* (Madison: University of Wisconsin Press, 1997); Elias C. Mandala, *Work and Control in a Peasant Economy: A History of the Lower Tchi Valley in Malawi, 1859–1960* (Madison: University of Wisconsin Press, 1990); and Rich-

ard L. Roberts, *Two Worlds of Cotton: Colonialism and the Regional Economy in the French Soudan, 1800–1946* (Palo Alto: Stanford University Press, 1996). For especially good accounts of the myriad ways colonial agriculture disrupts African economic life, see Paul Richards, "Ecological Change and the Politics of African Land Use," *African Studies Review* 26 (1983): 1–72, and John Tosh, "The Cash Crop Revolution in Tropical Africa: An Agricultural Reappraisal," *African Affairs* 79 (1980): 79–94. Benin, Burkina Faso, Chad, and Mali complained officially about the unfair terms of the international cotton market at the 2003 World Trade Organization Conference in Cancún. The official report of the conference is available at http://www.wto.org. On recent conditions for Togolese cotton growers, see Alfred Schwartz, *Le Paysan et la Culture du Coton au Togo: Approche Sociologique* (Paris: Institut Français de Recherche Scientifique pour le Développement en Coopération, 1985). Analysis by Oxfam confirms that reducing U.S. subsidies to cotton growers would significantly alleviate poverty in West Africa. See Julian M. Alston, Daniel A. Sumner, and Henrich Brunke, "Impacts of Reductions in US Cotton Subsidies on West Africa Cotton Producers," Oxfam Research Paper published June, 2007, online at: http://www.oxfamamerica.org.

30. See Tunde Adeleke, *UnAfrican Americans: Nineteenth-Century Black Nationalists and the Civilizing Mission* (Lexington: University Press of Kentucky, 1998).

31. Du Bois, *Autobiography*, 90.

32. See Robert J. Norrell, "Understanding the Wizard: Another Look at Booker T. Washington," in W. Fitzhugh Brundage, ed., *Booker T. Washington and Black Progress: Up from Slavery 100 Years Later* (Gainesville: University Press of Florida, 2003), 58–80, and Norrell, *Up from History: The Life of Booker T. Washington* (Cambridge: Harvard University Press, 2009).

33. Every student of Booker T. Washington is gratefully dependent on the excellent work of Louis R. Harlan. See his two-volume biography of Washington, *Booker T. Washington: The Making of a Black Leader, 1856–1901* (London: Oxford University Press, 1972) and *Booker T. Washington: The Wizard of Tuskegee, 1901–1915* (London: Oxford University Press, 1983). See also his fourteen-volume edition of selections from the Booker T. Washington Papers, *Booker T. Washington Papers.* Comparably important to this book is August Meier, *Negro Thought in America, 1880–1915: Racial Ideologies in the Age of Booker T. Washington* (1963; Ann Arbor: University of Michigan Press, 1988). C. Vann Woodward, whom Norrell also criticizes, offers a similarly complex, although necessarily more brief, interpretation of Washington in *Origins of the New South, 1877–1913*, rev. ed. (1951; Baton Rouge: Louisiana State University Press, 1972), passim, and *The Strange Career of Jim Crow*, 3rd ed. (1955; New York: Oxford University Press, 1974), passim. On Washington, see also Brundage, ed., *Booker T. Washington and Black Progress*; Kevern Verney, *The Art of the Possible: Booker T. Washington and Black Leadership in the United States, 1881–1925* (New York: Routledge, 2001); and Michael Rudolph West, *The Education of Booker T. Washington: American Democracy and the Idea of Race Relations* (New York: Columbia University Press, 2006).

34. St. Clair Drake, review of *Negro Thought in America, 1880–1915,* by August Meier (Ann Arbor, 1963), *American Sociological Review* 30 (1965): 329–30.

35. For the paradoxical humanitarian roots of European colonization in Africa, see especially Kevin Grant, *A Civilised Savagery: Britain and the New Slaveries in Africa, 1884–1926* (New York: Routledge, 2005).

36. See, for example, the text by the leading British abolitionist, Thomas Fowell Buxton, *The African Slave Trade, and Its Remedy* (London: John Murray, 1840).

37. On the American Colonization Society, see Eric Burin, *Slavery and the Peculiar Solution: A History of the American Colonization Society* (Gainesville: University Press of Florida, 2005). On colonization and racism, see George M. Fredrickson, *The Black Image in the White Mind: The Debate on Afro-American Character and Destiny, 1817–1914* (New York: Harper and Row, 1971), 1–42. On abolitionist opposition to the American Colonization Society, see Paul Goodman, *Of One Blood: Abolitionism and the Origins of Racial Equality* (Berkeley: University of California Press, 1998).

38. See, most recently, Eric Foner, "Lincoln and Colonization," in Foner, ed., *Our Lincoln: New Perspectives on Lincoln and His World* (New York: Norton, 2008), 135–66; and James Oakes, *The Radical and the Republican: Frederick Douglass, Abraham Lincoln, and the Triumph of Antislavery Politics* (New York: Norton, 2007).

39. For a study of German imperialism in English, see Woodruff D. Smith, *The German Colonial Empire* (Chapel Hill: University of North Carolina Press, 1978). In German, see Sebastian Conrad, *Deutsche Kolonialgeschichte* (Munich: C. H. Beck, 2008); Horst Gründer, *Geschichte der deutschen Kolonien*, 4th ed. (Stuttgart: UTB, 2000); and the now classic Hans-Ulrich Wehler, *Bismarck und der Imperialismus* (1969; Munich: Deutscher Taschenbuch Verlag, 1976).

40. My interpretation of German colonialism thus differs sharply from interpretations that give causal primacy to culture and ideas. For a brilliant interpretation of German colonialism that does pursue such an idealist agenda, explicitly to reject political-economic interpretations such as those pursued here, see George Steinmetz, *The Devil's Handwriting: Precoloniality and the German Colonial State in Qingdao, Samoa, and Southwest Africa* (Chicago: University of Chicago Press, 2007). It should be obvious that the present interpretation does not seek to sideline the role of ideas or culture in imperialism, but rather suggests a multicausal model more adequate to the historical complexities of empire than the cultural monism that has marked many recent studies.

41. Frank Lawrence Owsley, *King Cotton Diplomacy: Foreign Relations of the Confederate States of America*, 2nd ed. (Chicago: University of Chicago Press, 1959).

42. See the excellent account of this expedition by James T. Campbell, "Redeeming the Race: Martin Delany and the Niger Valley Exploring Party, 1859–60," *New Formations* 45 (Winter 2001–2002): 125–49.

43. Indeed, the British Church Missionary Society already exported some cotton from the region. See Judith A. Byfield, *The Bluest Hands: A Social and Eco-*

nomic History of Women Dyers in Abeokuta (Nigeria), 1890–1940 (Portsmouth, NH: Heinemann: 2002).

44. Martin R. Delany, *The Condition, Elevation, Emigration, and Destiny of the Colored People of the United States* and *Official Report of the Niger Valley Exploring Party*, Toyin Falola, Introduction (Amherst, NY: Humanity Books, 2004), 355. See also the account by the second leader of the Niger Valley expedition, Robert Campbell, *A Pilgrimage to My Motherland: An Account of a Journey among the Egbas and Yorubas of Central Africa, in 1859–1860* (New York: Thomas Hamilton, 1861).

45. Delany, *Condition, Elevation, Emigration, and Destiny of the Colored People of the United States*, 336–37.

46. See Roberts, *Two Worlds of Cotton*.

47. See Tarasankar Banerjee, "American Cotton Experiments in India and the American Civil War," *Journal of Indian History* 37 (1969): 425–32 and K. L. Tuteja, "American Planters and the Cotton Improvement Programme in Bombay Presidency in Nineteenth Century," *Indian Journal of American Studies* 28 (1998): 103–8. See also Arthur W. Silver, *Manchester Men and Indian Cotton, 1847–1872* (Manchester: Manchester University Press, 1966).

48. For good contemporary account of Egyptian cotton by a German cotton expert, see Moritz Schanz, *Cotton in Egypt and the Anglo-Egyptian Sudan* (Manchester: Taylor, Garnett, Evans, 1913). See also W. Lawrence Balls, *The Cotton Plant in Egypt: Studies in Physiology and Genetics* (London: MacMillan, 1912).

49. On this period as a precursor to contemporary globalization, see Paul Q. Hirst and Grahame Thompson, *Globalization in Question: The International Economy and the Possibilities of Governance*, 2nd ed. (Cambridge, UK: Polity, 1999).

50. The plantation, as a number of authors have shown, was in fact one of the earliest examples of industrial production, but a racial organization of labor, rather than the discipline of the factory and the machine, provided the primary instrument of labor control. See C.L.R. James, *The Black Jacobins: Toussaint L'Ouverture and the San Domingo Revolution*, 2nd ed. (1938; New York: Vintage Books, 1989), 85–86; and Sidney Mintz, *Sweetness and Power: The Place of Sugar in Modern History* (New York: Penguin, 1985).

51. Robert Miles, *Capitalism and Unfree Labour: Anomaly or Necessity?* (London: Tavistock, 1987).

52. See Benedict Anderson, *Imagined Communities: Reflections on the Origin and Spread of Nationalism*, 2nd ed. (New York: Verso, 1991).

53. Daniel R. Headrick, *The Tools of Empire: Technology and European Imperialism in the Nineteenth Century* (New York: Oxford University Press, 1981), 102–3.

54. On the development of international white solidarity in the late nineteenth and early twentieth centuries, see Marilyn Lake and Henry Reynolds, *Drawing the Global Colour Line: White Men's Countries and the International Challenge of Racial Equality* (Cambridge: Cambridge University Press, 2008).

55. Lewis Henry Morgan, *Ancient Society* (New York: H. Holt, 1877); Claude Lévi-Strauss, *Elementary Structures of Kinship*, James Harle Bell and John Richard von Sturmer, trans., Rodney Needham, ed. (1949; London: Eyre and Spottis-

woode, 1969); Gayle Rubin, "The Traffic in Women: Notes on the 'Political Economy' of Sex," in Rayna Rapp Reiter, ed., *Toward an Anthropology of Women* (New York: Monthly Review Press, 1975), 157–210; and Monique Wittig, *The Straight Mind and Other Essays* (Boston: Beacon Press, 1992).

56. Daniel Patrick Moynihan, U.S. Department of Labor, Office of Policy Planning and Research, *The Negro Family: A Case for National Action* (Washington, DC: Office of Policy Planning and Research, 1965), 29.

57. The links between households and the political economy of imperialism suggest that Claude Meillassoux was correct to see an articulation between household and capitalist economy, but also that he should have emphasized the dynamic interaction of the two spheres. See especially his *Maidens, Meal and Money* (1975; Cambridge: Cambridge University Press, 1981). The relations of household transformations, the gendered division of labor, and the political economy of imperialism in Africa were given classic treatment in Ester Boserup, *Woman's Role in Economic Development* (New York: St. Martin's, 1970). Jane I. Guyer, "Household and Community in African Studies," *African Studies Review* 24 (1981): 87–137, makes the excellent point that the household in Africa consists, in fact, of a set of historically specific rights and obligations of individuals defined as both within and without the household. Guyer has encouraged historians to understand the family in its political economic context while simultaneously following anthropologists in problematizing kinship. M. Anne Pitcher focuses on the gendered division of labor in household cotton production in "Conflict and Cooperation: Gendered Roles and Responsibilities within Cotton Households in Northern Mozambique," *African Studies Review* 39 (1996): 81–112. Jean Marie Allman and Victoria Tashjian demonstrate that even the basic theorization involved in periodization shifts when historical narratives privilege women. See *"I Will Not Eat Stone": A Women's History of Colonial Asante* (Portsmouth, NH: Heinemann, 2000). Nancy Rose Hunt considers the question of imperialism and reproduction in *A Colonial Lexicon of Birth Ritual, Medicalization, and Mobility in the Congo* (Durham: Duke University Press, 1999). The essays collected in Lisa A. Lindsay and Stephan F. Miescher, eds., *Men and Masculinities in Modern Africa* (Portsmouth, NH: Heinemann, 2003) focus on African men to show how they responded to shifting demands of household, political economy, imperialism, and identity. Colonial authorities and missionaries themselves were keenly aware of the connection between domesticity and political economy, and sought to shape both accordingly, reasoning that monogamous patriarchy in the former led to profitability in the latter, and vice versa. See the essays collected in Karen Tranberg Hansen, ed., *African Encounters with Domesticity* (New Brunswick: Rutgers University Press, 1992); Diana Jeater, *Marriage, Perversion, and Power: The Construction of Moral Discourse in Southern Rhodesia, 1894–1930* (Oxford: Clarendon Press, 1993); Henrietta L. Moore and Megan Vaughan, *Cutting Down Trees: Gender, Nutrition and Agricultural Change in the Northern Province of Zambia 1890–1990* (Portsmouth, NH: Heinemann, 1994); and John L. Comaroff and Jean Comaroff, *Of Revelation and Revolution*, vol. 1: *Christianity, Colonialism, and Consciousness in South Africa* (Chicago: University of Chicago Press, 1991); and especially vol. 2: *The Dialectics of Modernity on a South African Frontier* (Chicago: University of Chicago Press, 1997).

58. My findings thus differ from those of James C. Scott and others who treat peasant households as sources of resistance to larger political and economic systems. See especially James C. Scott, *Weapons of the Weak: Everyday Forms of Peasant Resistance* (New Haven: Yale University Press, 1985). My own findings agree more with the views of many authors in the *Journal of Peasant Studies*, including, as an excellent example, Christine Pelzer White, "Everyday Resistance, Socialist Revolution and Rural Development: The Vietnamese Case," *Journal of Peasant Studies* 13 (1986): 49–63. One of the journal's editors, Henry Bernstein, even bid "farewell to the peasantry," leaving the journal to locate the "economic form agricultural petty commodity production" (formerly known as peasant production) in "the shifting places of agriculture in the international divisions of labour of imperialism." Henry Bernstein, "Farewells to the Peasantry," *Transformation* 52 (2003): 1–19, here 14 and Bernstein and Terence J. Byres, "From Peasant Studies to Agrarian Change," *Journal of Agrarian Change* 1 (2001): 1–56. Bernstein has long maintained that there was no peasant mode of production and that peasants in Africa were, in fact, "wage labor equivalents." See Henry Bernstein, "African Peasantries: A Theoretical Framework," *Journal of Peasant Studies* 6 (1979): 421–43. Under the editorship of Tom Brass, the *Journal of Peasant Studies* has turned even more fiercely against peasant essentialism. See collected articles by Tom Brass in *Towards a Comparative Political Economy of Unfree Labour: Case Studies and Debates* (London, 1999) and *Peasants, Populism and Postmodernism: The Return of the Agrarian Myth* (London, 2000).

59. On the postemancipation plantation system, see especially Philip D. Curtin, *The Rise and Fall of the Plantation Complex: Essays in Atlantic History* (Cambridge: Cambridge University Press, 1990). Anne Phillips has persuasively argued that the British in West Africa fostered peasants as dependent petty commodity producers to prevent the emergence of either a politically organized proletariat or an economically autonomous landowning class. See *The Enigma of Colonialism: British Policy in West Africa* (London: James Currey, 1989). Other excellent attempts to grasp the complex and historically specific relations between peasant and worker, precapitalist and capitalist, and precolonial and colonial include: Victor L. Allen, "The Meaning of the Working Class in Africa," *Journal of Modern African Studies* 10 (1972): 169–89; Victoria Bernal, *Cultivating Workers: Peasants and Capitalism in a Sudanese Village* (New York: Columbia University Press, 1991); Colin Bundy, *The Rise and Fall of the South African Peasantry* (Berkeley: University of California Press, 1979); Frederick Cooper, "Back to Work: Categories, Boundaries and Connections in the Study of Labour," in Peter Alexander and Rick Halpern, eds. *Racializing Class, Classifying Race: Labour and Difference in Britain, the USA and Africa* (New York: St. Martin's Press, 2000), 213–35; Bill Freund, *The African Worker* (Cambridge: Cambridge University Press, 1988); and Ken Post, "Peasantization in West Africa," in Peter Gutkind and Peter Waterman, eds., *African Social Studies: A Radical Reader* (London: Heinemann, 1977), 241–50. There has also been some movement in the development community to reject both positivist modernization theory and the "farmer first" populism meant to challenge it, recognizing that "rural people's knowledge" and "western science" both "represent contrasting multiple epistemologies produced within particular agroecological, sociocultural and political economic settings." See Ian Scoones

and John Thompson, "Knowledge, Power, and Development—Towards a Theoretical Understanding," in Ian Scoones and John Thompson, eds., *Beyond Farmer First: Rural People's Knowledge, Agricultural Research and Extension Practice* (London: Intermediate Technology Publications, 1994), 16–32.

60. See Daniel T. Rodgers, *Atlantic Crossings: Social Politics in a Progressive Era* (Cambridge: Harvard University Press, 1998); Axel R. Schäfer, "W.E.B. Du Bois, German Social Thought, and the Racial Divide in American Progressivism, 1892–1909," *Journal of American History* 88 (2001): 925–49; and Axel R. Schäfer, *American Progressives and German Social Reform, 1875–1920: Social Ethics, Moral Control, and the Regulatory State in a Transatlantic Context* (Stuttgart: Franz Steiner, 2000). Still important is Jürgen Herbst, *The German Historical School in American Scholarship: A Study in the Transfer of Culture* (Ithaca: Cornell University Press, 1965).

61. Karl Marx and Friedrich Engels, *Manifesto of the Communist Party* (1848), trans. Samuel Moore (Chicago: Charles H. Kerr, 1906), 17. Nearly all the works by Karl Marx, Friedrich Engels, August Bebel, Karl Kautsky, Rosa Luxemburg, Clara Zetkin, and other Marxists that I cite in this book are available online in English at http://www.marxists.org and in the original German at http://www.mlwerke.de. These Web sites have been extraordinarily helpful in tracking down often obscure references in the voluminous works of these writers. In this book I use the more authoritative printed versions of these works rather than these Web sites (which, in cases where I compared, nonetheless turned out to be entirely accurate).

62. As Marx writes, with capitalism "grows the revolt of the working-class, a class always increasing in numbers, and disciplined, united, organized by the very mechanism of the process of capitalist production itself. The monopoly of capital becomes a fetter upon the mode of production, which has sprung up and flourished along with, and under it. The centralization of the means of production and the socialization of labour reach a point at which they become incompatible with their capitalist integument. This integument is burst asunder. The knell of capitalist private property sounds. The expropriators are expropriated." Karl Marx, *Capital*, vol. 1, Ben Fowkes, trans. (1867; New York: Penguin Books, 1992), 929.

CHAPTER 1
COTTON, THE "NEGRO QUESTION,"
AND INDUSTRIAL EDUCATION IN THE NEW SOUTH

1. William Tecumseh Sherman, *Memoirs of Gen. W. T. Sherman*, 2 vols., 4th ed. (New York: Charles L. Webster, 1892), 2:246.

2. For an excellent interpretation of the New South in the context of imperialism, see Natalie J. Ring, "The Problem South: Region, Race, and 'Southern Readjustment,' 1880–1930" (Ph.D. diss., University of California, San Diego, 2003). David Sehat uses a colonial framework to study the role of Tuskegee in the South in "The Civilizing Mission of Booker T. Washington," *Journal of Southern History* 73 (2007): 323–62. The classic work on the New South is C. Vann Woodward, *Origins of the New South*. For the debate around Woodward's work, see

John David Smith, ed., *When Did Southern Segregation Begin?* (New York: Bedford/St. Martin's, 2002). See also Edward L. Ayers, *The Promise of the New South: Life after Reconstruction* (New York: Oxford University Press, 1992); Foner, *Nothing but Freedom: Emancipation and Its Legacy* (Baton Rouge: Louisiana State University Press, 1983); and Julie Saville, *The Work of Reconstruction: From Slave to Wage Laborer in South Carolina, 1860–1870* (Cambridge: Cambridge University Press, 1994). On New South ideology and the "Negro question," see Fredrickson, *The Black Image in the White Mind*; Paul M. Gaston, *The New South Creed: A Study in Southern Mythmaking* (New York: Knopf, 1970); James M. McPherson, *The Abolitionist Legacy: From Reconstruction to the NAACP* (Princeton: Princeton University Press, 1975); John David Smith, *An Old Creed for the New South: Proslavery Ideology and Historiography, 1865–1918* (1985; Athens: University of Georgia Press, 1991); Ronald T. Takaki, "Civilization in the New South," ch. 9, in *Iron Cages: Race and Culture in Nineteenth-Century America*, rev. ed. (1979; New York: Oxford University Press, 2000), 194–214; and Joel Williamson, *The Crucible of Race: Black-White Relations in the American South since Emancipation* (New York: Oxford University Press, 1984).

3. On the political economy of the New South, see, especially, Gavin Wright, *Old South, New South: Revolutions in the Southern Economy Since the Civil War* (New York: Basic Books, 1986).

4. Todd, *The World's Cotton Crops*, 109. See also John A. Todd, "The Cost of Labour as Affecting the Cotton Crop (Especially in the United States)," *Transactions of the Third International Congress of Tropical Agriculture*, 3 vols. (London: John Bale, Sons and Danielsson, 1917), 2:493–502.

5. For an excellent history of African American political struggles, see Steven Hahn, *A Nation under Our Feet: Black Political Struggles in the Rural South from Slavery to the Great Migration* (Cambridge: Harvard University Press, 2003). See also Herbert Aptheker, *American Negro Slave Revolts* (1944; New York: International Publishers, 1983).

6. For one example of this common view, see Alfred Holt Stone, "The Negro and Agricultural Development," *Annals of the American Academy of Political and Social Science* 35 (1910): 8–15.

7. Many proponents of a New South hoped that the region would diversify its agriculture and expand its manufacturing, and some even dreamed of helping African Americans achieve political equality with whites. One famous proponent of this view of the New South was the Pennsylvania Radical Republican, William D. "Pig Iron" Kelley. See his "Cotton Growing and Agriculture Contrasted," in *The Old South and the New: A Series of Letters* (New York: G. P. Putnam's Sons: 1888), 112–62. Dominant versions of the New South, however, called for sustaining the region's two principal antebellum economic features, namely: coerced African American workers and industrial-grade cotton.

8. Donald Spivey, *Schooling for the New Slavery: Black Industrial Education, 1868–1915* (Westport, CT: Greenwood Press, 1978). Emphasizing education as an exclusive panacea for all the problems of freedpeople, as historian Ronald E. Butchart has argued, also appealed to many white elites because it did not challenge the dominant position of planters as land redistribution or even legal protection for black workers might have. See Butchart, *Northern Schools, Southern*

Blacks, and Reconstruction: Freedmen's Education, 1862–1875 (Westport, CT: Greenwood Press, 1980).

9. The four species of cotton cultivated by humans are: *G. herbaceum*, *G. arboreum*, *G. hirsutum*, and *G. barbadense*. For an excellent account of the history, biology, and cultivation of cotton, see C. Wayne Smith and J. Tom Cothren, eds., *Cotton: Origin, History, Technology, and Production* (New York: Wiley, 1999).

10. On the history of cotton in the European Middle Ages, see Maureen Fennell Mazzaoui, "The Cotton Industry of Northern Italy in the Late Middle Ages: 1150–1450," *Journal of Economic History* 32 (1972): 262–86 and Mazzaoui, *The Italian Cotton Industry in the Later Middle Ages, 1100–1600* (Cambridge: Cambridge University Press, 1981).

11. Joseph E. Inikori, "Slavery and the Revolution in Cotton Textile Production in England," *Social Science History* 13 (1989): 343–79. See also his *Africans and the Industrial Revolution in England: A Study in International Trade and Economic Development* (Cambridge: Cambridge University Press, 2002). On comparative labor costs, see Stephen Broadberry and Bishnupriya Gupta, "Cotton Textiles and the Great Divergence: Lancashire, India and the Shifting Comparative Advantage, 1600–1850," unpublished working paper, 11 May 2004. http:// www2.warwick.ac.uk/fac/soc/economics/staff/faculty/broadberry/wp/ cotdiv5.pdf, accessed 7/16/2004.

12. On gender and the household in the industrial revolution, with an excellent account of household textile production and its decline, see Anna Clarke, *The Struggle for the Breeches: Gender and the Making of the British Working Class* (Berkeley: University of California Press, 1995).

13. For a good nineteenth-century account of these developments in the textile industry, see Thomas Ellison, *The Cotton Trade of Great Britain* (1886; reprint, New York: A. M. Kelley, 1968), 14–32. For a more recent account emphasizing the social as well as the technological aspects of this industrial revolution, see Maxine Berg, *The Age of Manufactures: Industry, Innovation, and Work in Britain, 1700–1820* (New York: Oxford University Press, 1986), 198–263.

14. See Alwin Oppel, *Die deutsche Textilindustrie: Entwicklung, Gegenwärtiger Zustand, Beziehung zum Ausland und zur deutschen Kolonialwirtschaft* (Leipzig: Duncker and Humblot, 1912) and W. Lochmüller, *Zur Entwicklung der Baumwollindustrie in Deutschland* (Jena: Gustav Fischer, 1906). On the spinning industry in Saxony, see Rudolf Forberger, *Die Industrielle Revolution in Sachsen 1800–1861* (Berlin: Akademie-Verlag, 1982) and Heinrich Gebauer, *Die Volkswirtschaft im Königreiche Sachsen*, 3 vols. (Dresden: Wilhelm Baensch, 1893).

15. For differences between the British and German cotton textile industries, see John C. Brown, "Market Organization, Protection, and Vertical Integration: German Cotton Textiles before 1914," *Journal of Economic History* 52 (1992): 339–51, and Brown, "Imperfect Competition and Anglo-German Trade Rivalry: Markets for Cotton Textiles Before 1914," *Journal of Economic History* 55 (1995): 494–527. For a contemporary report on the German cotton textile industry, see R.M.R. Dehn, *The German Cotton Industry: A Report to the Electors of the Gartside Scholarships* (Manchester: Manchester University Press, 1913).

16. Andrew Ure, *The Philosophy of Manufactures: or, an Exposition of the Scientific, Moral, and Commercial Economy of the Factory System of Great Brit-*

ain (1835; New York: August M. Kelley, 1967), x, 367. On this text, and on labor discipline and machinery more generally, see Andrew Zimmerman, "The Ideology of the Machine and the Spirit of the Factory: Remarx on Babbage and Ure," *Cultural Critique* 37 (1997): 5–29. The most celebrated account of this political struggle in the industrial revolution remains E. P. Thompson, *The Making of the English Working Class* (New York: Vintage Books, 1963). Clarke, *The Struggle for the Breeches*, provides an excellent account of the interlinked struggles around gender and class in the same period.

17. The classic history of southern agriculture, which emphasizes the connection between slave labor and cotton production, is Lewis Cecil Gray, *History of Agriculture in the Southern United States to 1860*, 2 vols. (Washington: The Carnegie Institution of Washington, 1933).

18. On the history of ginning, including Eli Whitney's device, see Angela Lakwete, *Inventing the Cotton Gin: Machine and Myth in Antebellum America* (Baltimore: Johns Hopkins University Press, 2003). For the history of the gin in the United States after the Civil War, see Charles S. Aiken, "The Evolution of Cotton Ginning in the Southeastern United States," *Geographical Review* 63 (1973): 196–224. See also Aiken, *The Cotton Plantation South Since the Civil War* (Baltimore: Johns Hopkins University Press, 1998).

19. On this global cotton boom and its effects, see Beckert, "Emancipation and Empire." The transition from American to global cotton production spanned a greater time period, I believe, than Beckert suggests in that article, but he nonetheless provides an excellent and wide-ranging analysis of the concerns and processes that began this global transformation. See also Susan Archer Mann, "The Rise of Wage Labour in the Cotton South: A Global Analysis," *Journal of Peasant Studies* 14 (1987): 226–42.

20. On the Indian cotton boom during the Civil War, see Frenise A. Logan, "India—Britain's Substitute for American Cotton, 1861–65," *Journal of Southern History* 24 (1958): 472–80, and Frenise A. Logan, "India's Loss of the British Cotton Market After 1865," *Journal of Southern History* 31 (1965): 40–50.

21. J. W. McConnel, "Commerce and Science in Cotton Growing," *Transactions of the Third International Congress of Tropical Agriculture*, 2:361.

22. See S.R.B. Leadbetter, *The Politics of Textiles: The Indian Cotton-Mill Industry and the Legacy of Swadeshi, 1900–1985* (New Delhi: Sage, 1993). For contemporary observations on the difficulties the Swadeshi movement had with Indian cotton, see the report by W. A. Graham Clark, Special Agent of the Department of Commerce and Labor, *Cotton Fabrics in British India and the Philippines* (Washington: Government Printing Office, 1907), 48.

23. See Jason W. Clay, *World Agriculture and the Environment: A Commodity-by-Commodity Guide to Impacts and Practices* (Washington, DC: Island Press, 2004), 283–304.

24. William Cronon, in *Nature's Metropolis: Chicago and the Great West* (New York: W. W. Norton, 1992), gives a wonderful account of the role of commodity markets in transforming grain, lumber, and meat into commodities in Chicago. Cronon's account makes especially good use of the still very informative Henry Crosby Emery, "Speculation on the Stock and Produce Exchanges of the United States" (Ph.D. diss., Columbia University, 1896).

25. The city of Bremen employed cotton inspectors following New York standards since 1872, and the city founded its own cotton market in 1889. For a commemoration of the Bremen cotton market, see Hermann Schwarmann, *Eine Baumwollära: 125 Jahren Bremer Baumwollbörse* (Bremen: Hauschild, 1997).

26. On the New York cotton futures market, see Kenneth J. Lipartito, "The New York Cotton Exchange and the Development of the Cotton Futures Market," *Business History Review* 57 (1983): 50–72.

27. H. H. Willis, Gaston Gage, Vernette B. Moore, *Cotton Classing Manual* (Washington, DC: The Textile Foundation, 1938), 45. This text elaborates the regulations published in the USDA manual, *The Classification of Cotton* (Washington, DC: U.S. Department of Agriculture, 1938). For other information on cotton grading, see D. E. Earle and W. S. Dean, "The Classification and Grading of Cotton," U.S. Department of Agriculture Farmers' Bulletin, 591 (10 July 1914). James A. B. Scherer, *Cotton as a World Power: A Study in the Economic Interpretation of History* (1916; New York: Negro Universities Press, 1969), esp. 375n5.

28. The manual assured its readers that, "through experience, classers and mill-men become familiar with the characteristics of cotton that will and will not give good spinning results for their particular purposes." Willis, Gage, Moore, *Cotton Classing Manual*, 51–52. As this passage indicates, mills employed classers of their own, who mixed cotton from various bales to adjust more precisely the quality of cotton fed into machines.

29. T. S. Miller, *The American Cotton System Historically Treated* (Austin: Austin Printing Co. 1909), 45.

30. On seed control and the dangers of hybridization of cotton, see J. F. Duggar, *Descriptions and Classification of Varieties of American Upland Cotton*, Alabama Agricultural Experiment Station of the Alabama Polytechnic Institute, Auburn, Bulletin No. 140 (July 1907) (Opelika, AL: Post Publishing Co., 1907) and W. Lawrence Balls, *Studies of Quality in Cotton* (London: Macmillan, 1928). On cotton planting and picking, see James Thomas Broadbent, *Cotton Manual for Manufacturers and Students* (Boston: Lord and Nagle, 1905).

31. On the mechanization of cotton picking, see Donald Holley, *The Second Great Emancipation: The Mechanical Cotton Picker, Black Migration, and How They Shaped the Modern South* (Fayetteville: University of Arkansas Press, 2000).

32. Foner, *Reconstruction: America's Unfinished Revolution, 1863–1877* (New York: Harper, 1988), 3. Foner concurs here with W.E.B. Du Bois, *Black Reconstruction in America: An Essay toward a History of the Part which Black Folk Played in the Attempt to Reconstruct Democracy in America, 1860–1880* (New York: S. A. Russell, 1935). On the self-emancipation of slaves during the Civil War, see especially Hahn, *A Nation under Our Feet*, 62–115. On slavery as the cause of the Civil War, see, most recently, Chandra Manning, *What This Cruel War Was Over: Soldiers, Slavery, and the Civil War* (New York: Alfred A. Knopf, 2007).

33. There is much excellent work on free-labor ideology, race, and emancipation in the United States and around the world. See especially Frederick Cooper, *From Slaves to Squatters: Plantation Labor and Agriculture in Zanzibar and Kenya, 1890–1925* (1980; Portsmouth, NH: Heinemann, 1997); Frederick Cooper, Thomas C. Holt, and Rebecca J. Scott, *Beyond Slavery: Explorations of Race,*

Labor, and Citizenship (Chapel Hill: University of North Carolina Press, 2000); Seymour Drescher, The Mighty Experiment: Free Labor versus Slavery in British Emancipation (Oxford: Oxford University Press, 2002); Eric Foner, Free Soil, Free Labor, Free Men: The Ideology of the Republican Party before the Civil War (New York: Oxford University Press, 1970); Eric Foner, Nothing but Freedom: Emancipation and Its Legacy (Baton Rouge: Louisiana State University Press, 1983); Jonathan A. Glickstein, Concepts of Free Labor in Antebellum America (New Haven: Yale University Press, 1991); and Thomas C. Holt, The Problem of Freedom: Race, Labor, and Politics in Jamaica and Britain, 1832–1938 (Baltimore: Johns Hopkins University Press, 1992).

34. On the web of legal constraints in Europe and around the world that bound workers conventionally defined as free, see Douglas Hay and Paul Craven, "The Criminalization of 'Free' Labour: Master and Servant in Comparative Perspective," Slavery and Abolition 15 (1994): 71–101; Hay and Craven, "Master and Servant in England and the Empire: A Comparative Study," Labour 31 (1993): 175–84; Robert J. Steinfeld, The Invention of Free Labor: The Employment Relation in English and American Law and Culture, 1350–1870 (Chapel Hill: University of North Carolina Press, 1991); and Steinfeld, Coercion, Contract, and Free Labor in the Nineteenth Century (Cambridge: Cambridge University Press, 2001). See also the essays collected in Hay and Craven, eds., Masters, Servants, and Magistrates in Britain and the Empire, 1562–1955 (Chapel Hill: University of North Carolina Press, 2004).

35. See Foner, Reconstruction, 70–71, and Claude F. Oubre, Forty Acres and a Mule: The Freedmen's Bureau and Black Land Ownership (Baton Rouge: Louisiana State University Press, 1978).

36. See Robert Francis Engs, Freedom's First Generation: Black Hampton, Virginia, 1861–1890 (Philadelphia: University of Pennsylvania Press, 1979).

37. For a good account of the ambivalent relation of the Freedmen's Bureau to emancipation, see William S. McFeely, Yankee Stepfather: General O. O. Howard and the Freedmen (New Haven: Yale University Press, 1968). James M. McPherson, however, cautions against exaggerating the extent to which blacks were abandoned by their erstwhile white allies after Reconstruction in The Abolitionist Legacy.

38. Engs, Freedom's First Generation, 102–35.

39. On northern planters, see Lawrence N. Powell, New Masters: Northern Planters during the Civil War and Reconstruction (New Haven: Yale University Press, 1980).

40. See especially Jacqueline Jones, Labor of Love, Labor of Sorrow: Black Women, Work, and the Family from Slavery to the Present (New York: Basic Books, 1985); and Deborah G. White, Ar'n't I a Woman?: Female Slaves in the Plantation South, rev. ed. (1985; New York: Norton, 1999). The classic critique of earlier views that slavery created pathological families is Herbert G. Gutman, The Black Family in Slavery and Freedom, 1750–1925 (New York: Pantheon Books, 1976). Gutman takes immediate aim at Moynihan, The Negro Family. The African American sociologist E. Franklin Frazier, Gutman notes, made a similar argument in The Negro Family in the United States (Chicago: University of Chicago Press, 1939). Frazier, however, argued that the institution of slavery had

created pathological families to counter common racist assumptions about the inherent moral inferiority of African Americans.

41. See especially Jones, *Labor of Love, Labor of Sorrow.*

42. For contemporary observations of southern sharecropping, see Thomas J. Edwards, "The Tenant System and Some Changes since Emancipation," *Annals of the American Academy of Political and Social Science* 49 (1913): 38–46, and Charles S. Johnson, Edwin R. Embree, W. W. Alexander, *The Collapse of Cotton Tenancy: Summary of Field Studies and Statistical Surveys 1933–35* (Chapel Hill: University of North Carolina Press, 1935). Especially helpful for the present discussion of sharecropping have been William Cohen, *At Freedom's Edge: Black Mobility and the Southern White Quest for Racial Control, 1861–1915* (Baton Rouge: Louisiana State University Press, 1991); Pete Daniel, *In the Shadow of Slavery: Peonage in the South, 1901–1969* (1972; Urbana: University of Illinois Press, 1990); Pete Daniel, "The Metamorphosis of Slavery, 1865–1900," *Journal of American History* 66 (1979): 88–99; Barbara Jeanne Fields, "The Advent of Capitalist Agriculture: The New South in a Bourgeois World," Thavolia Glymph and John Kushma, eds., *Essays on the Postbellum Southern Economy* (College Station: Texas A&M University Press, 1985), 73–94; Daniel A. Novak, *The Wheel of Servitude: Black Forced Labor after Slavery* (Lexington: University Press of Kentucky, 1978); Roger L. Ransom and Richard Sutch, *One Kind of Freedom: The Economic Consequences of Emancipation*, 2nd ed. (1977; Cambridge: Cambridge University Press, 2001); Edward Royce, *The Origins of Southern Sharecropping* (Philadelphia: Temple University Press, 1993); Jonathan Wiener, *Social Origins of the New South: Alabama, 1860–1885* (Baton Rouge: Louisiana State University Press, 1978); and Wright, *Old South, New South.*

43. See Alex Lichtenstein, *Twice the Work of Free Labor: The Political Economy of Convict Labor in the New South* (London: Verso, 1996).

44. George Bigwood, *Cotton* (London: Constable, 1918), 30–31. See the similar argument by John A. Todd, "The Cost of Labour as Affecting the Cotton Crop (especially in the United States)," *Transactions of the Third International Congress of Tropical Agriculture* 2:493–502.

45. Wright, *Old South, New South*, 107.

46. Harvie Jordan, speech in *Official Report of the Fourth International Cotton Congress of Delegated Representatives of Master Cotton Spinners' and Manufacturers' Associations held in the Musikvereinsgebäude, Vienna, May 27–29, 1907* (n.p., n.d.), 31.

47. Johnson et al., *The Collapse of Cotton Tenancy*, 11.

48. John A. Todd, "The Cost of Labour as Affecting the Cotton Crop (especially in the United States)," *Transactions of the Third International Congress of Tropical Agriculture* 2: 493–502.

49. Henry W. Grady, "The New South" (1886), in Joel Chandler Harris, ed., *Henry W. Grady* (1890; New York: Haskell House, 1972), 87–88, 90–91. On Grady, see Harold E. Davis, *Henry Grady's New South: Atlanta: A Brave and Beautiful City* (Tuscaloosa: University of Alabama Press, 1990), and Raymond B. Nixon, *Henry W. Grady, Spokesman of the New South* (New York: Russell and Russell, 1969).

50. Lewis H. Blair, *A Southern Prophecy: The Prosperity of the South Dependent upon the Elevation of the Negro*, C. Vann Woodward, ed. (1889; Boston: Little, Brown, and Co., 1964), 26, 25.

51. See, for example, Booker T. Washington, "Atlanta Exposition Address" of 1895 in *Up from Slavery* (1901; Mineola: Dover, 1995), 106–9 and Booker T. Washington, "The Negro's Part in Southern Development," *Annals of the American Academy of Political and Social Science* 35 (1910): 124–33.

52. The classic work on the novelty of postwar racism is C. Vann Woodward, *The Strange Career of Jim Crow.* See also Woodward's *Origins of the New South.*

53. W.E.B. Du Bois, "Strivings of the Negro People," *Atlantic Monthly* (August 1897): 194–98, here 194. This essay was reprinted as "Of Our Spiritual Strivings" in *The Souls of Black Folk* (1903; Mineola: Dover, 1994), 1.

54. See Gerald David Jaynes, *Branches without Roots: Genesis of the Black Working Class, 1862–1882* (New York: Oxford University Press, 1986), as well as the literature cited in notes 33 and 34, above.

55. Steven Hahn makes clear the extent to which lynching was enmeshed in the broad struggle for black freedom in the South. See Hahn, *A Nation under Our Feet*, 425–31. On lynching, see W. Fitzhugh Brundage, *Lynching in the New South: Georgia and Virginia, 1880–1930* (Urbana: University of Illinois Press, 1993); Philip Dray, *At the Hands of Persons Unknown: The Lynching of Black America* (New York: Random House, 2002); and Leon Litwack, *Trouble in Mind: Black Southerners in the Age of Jim Crow* (New York: Knopf, 1998), 280–325.

56. On African American education in the South, see James D. Anderson, *The Education of Blacks in the South, 1860–1935* (Chapel Hill: University of North Carolina Press, 1988); Butchart, *Northern School, Southern Blacks*; Robert Francis Engs, *Educating the Disfranchised and Disinherited: Samuel Chapman Armstrong and Hampton Institute, 1839–1893* (Knoxville: University of Tennessee Press, 1999); Adam Fairclough, *A Class of Their Own: Black Teachers in the Segregated South* (Cambridge: Belknap Press of Harvard University Press, 2007); Louis R. Harlan, *Separate and Unequal: Public School Campaigns and Racism in the Southern Seaboard States 1901–1915* (Chapel Hill: University of North Carolina Press, 1958); Brian Kelly, "Sentinels for New South Industry: Booker T. Washington, Industrial Accommodation and Black Workers in the Jim Crow South," *Labor History* 44 (2003): 337–57; Robert C. Morris, *Reading, 'Riting, and Reconstruction: The Education of Freedmen in the South, 1861–1870* (Chicago: University of Chicago Press, 1976); Spivey, *Schooling for the New Slavery*; and Heather Andrea Williams, *Self-Taught: African American Education in Slavery and Freedom* (Chapel Hill: University of North Carolina Press, 2005).

57. Fairclough, *A Class of Their Own*, 64.

58. On the AMA see, especially, Joe Martin Richardson, *Christian Reconstruction: The American Missionary Association and Southern Blacks, 1861–1890* (Athens: University of Georgia Press, 1986).

59. Richardson, *Christian Reconstruction*, 124–25.

60. On the relation of Fisk and Tuskegee, see Harlan, *Booker T. Washington: The Making of a Black Leader*, 145–46, 179–80.

61. On Hampton and Tuskegee, see especially Anderson, *The Education of Blacks in the South*; Engs, *Educating the Disfranchised*; and Spivey, *Schooling for the New Slavery*.

62. John Dewey, *The School and Society* (1900), in *The School and Society and The Child and the Curriculum* (Chicago: University of Chicago Press, 1990). See also Lawrence A. Cremin, *The Transformation of the School: Progressivism in American Education, 1876–1957* (New York: Vintage, 1961), esp. ch. 2, "Education and Industry," 23–57. For contemporary praise of industrial education for all children, regardless of race, see Carroll D. Wright, "The Work of the National Society for the Promotion of Industrial Education," *Annals of the American Academy of Political and Social Science* 33, 1 (January 1909). Special Issue on Industrial Education: 13–22.

63. Paul Goodman, "The Manual Labor Movement and the Origins of Abolitionism," *Journal of the Early Republic* 13 (1993): 355–88 and Goodman, *Of One Blood*.

64. W.E.B. Du Bois, "Negro Education," review of *Negro Education*, by Jones (Washington, DC, 1917), *Crisis* 15 (1918): 177, in David Levering Lewis, ed., *W.E.B. Du Bois: A Reader* (New York: Henry Holt, 1995), 263.

65. On industrial education in Hawaii see Carl Kalani Beyer, "Manual and Industrial Education for Hawaiians during the Nineteenth Century," *Hawaiian Journal of History* 38 (2004): 1–34.

66. Great Britain, *Minutes of the Committee of Council on Education* (1847), quoted in King, *Pan-Africanism and Education*, 45.

67. Richard Armstrong to Reuben Chapman, 8 September 1848, Armstrong Family Papers, Williams College. Quoted Spivey, *Schooling for the New Slavery*, 18.

68. Samuel Chapman Armstrong, "Lessons from the Hawaiian Islands," *Journal of Christian Philosophy* (January 1884), 213–14. Quoted in part in Engs, *Educating the Disfranchised*, 74.

69. Armstrong, "Lessons from the Hawaiian Islands," 216.

70. Anderson, *The Education of Blacks in the South*, 75.

71. See Leslie H. Fishel, Jr., "The 'Negro Question' at Mohonk: Microcosm, Mirage, and Message," *New York History* 74 (1993): 277–314.

72. Booker T. Washington to George Washington Cable, 7 April 1890, in Harlan, ed., *Booker T. Washington Papers* 3:45.

73. Samuel Chapman Armstrong, "Industrial Training," in Barrows, ed., *First Mohonk Conference*, 13. Speakers at the Second Mohonk conference made points similar to the first. See Isabel C. Barrows, ed., *Second Mohonk Conference on the Negro Question, Held at Lake Mohonk, Ulster County, New York, June 3, 4, 5, 1891* (1891; reprint, New York: Negro Universities Press, 1969).

74. Harlan gives his birthdate as 1856. Washington gives "1858 or 1859" in *Up from Slavery*, 1. While many of Washington's publications were ghost-written, *Up from Slavery*, Harlan argues, was written largely by Washington himself. See Harlan, "Up from Slavery as History and Biography," in Brundage, ed., *Booker T. Washington and Black Progress*, 19–37.

75. Washington, *Up from Slavery*, 13.

76. Ibid., 25–26; 8; Booker T. Washington, *The Future of the American Negro* (1899; reprint, New York: Negro Universities Press, 1969), 72.

77. Washington, *Up from Slavery*, 36.

78. Harlan, *Booker T. Washington: The Making of a Black Leader, 1856–1901*, 82.

79. Washington, *Up from Slavery*, 43.

80. Andrew Carnegie, *The Empire of Business* (New York, 1902), 79–81. Quoted in Raymond E. Callahan, *Education and the Cult of Efficiency: A Study of the Social Forces that Have Shaped the Administration of the Public Schools* (Chicago: University of Chicago Press, 1962), 9.

81. *Verhandlungen üeber Fragen des höheren Unterrichts, Berlin 4. bis. 7. Dezember 1890* (Berlin, 1891), 770. Quoted in James C. Albisetti, *Secondary School Reform in Imperial Germany* (Princeton: Princeton University Press, 1983).

82. James D. Anderson has demolished the myth that antiracist northern philanthropists were forced to compromise with southern racism in their support of second-class schooling for blacks. As he shows in *Education of Blacks in the South*, northern philanthropists genuinely supported the Hampton-Tuskegee model. On the spread of the Tuskegee-Hampton model through northern philanthropy, see also Harlan, *Separate and Unequal*; Don Quinn Kelley, "Ideology and Education: Uplifting the Masses in Nineteenth-Century Alabama," *Phylon* 40 (1979): 147–58; J. M. Stephen Peeps, "Northern Philanthropy and the Emergence of Black Higher Education—Do-Gooders, Compromisers, or Co-Conspirators?" *Journal of Negro Education* 50 (1981): 251–69; Spivey, *Schooling for the New Slavery*; and William H. Watkins, *The White Architects of Black Education: Ideology and Power in America, 1865–1954*, Robin D. G. Kelley, foreword (New York: Teachers College Press, 2001). For a sympathetic interpretation of these white philanthropists, see Eric Anderson and Alfred A. Moss, Jr., *Dangerous Donations: Northern Philanthropy and Southern Black Education, 1902–1930*, Louis R. Harlan, foreword (Columbia: University of Missouri Press, 1999).

83. Edgar Gardner Murphy, head of the Southern Education Board, while professing educational equality for blacks and whites, remarked that, "Certain forms of industrial training may be emphasized the more clearly with the masses of our negroes; certain forms of scholastic training may be emphasized the more clearly with our white children." Edgar Gardner Murphy, *Problems of the Present South: A Discussion of Certain of the Educational, Industrial and Political Issues in the Southern States* (New York: Grosset and Dunlap, 1904), 89.

84. William H. Baldwin, "The Present Problem of Negro Education," *Journal of Social Science* 37 (1899): 52–68, here 58, quoted in Spivey, *The Politics of Miseducation*, 4.

85. B. C. Caldwell, "The Work of the Jeanes and Slater Funds," in James E. McCulloch, *The South Mobilizing for Social Service: Addresses Delivered at the Southern Sociological Congress, Atlanta, Georgia, April 25–29, 1913* (Nashville: Southern Sociological Congress, 1913), 427–31; Lance G. E. Jones, *The Jeanes Teacher in the United States, 1908–1933* (Chapel Hill: University of North Carolina Press, 1937); Stephen J. Wright, "The Development of the Hampton-Tuskegee Pattern of Higher Education," *Phylon* 10 (1949): 334–42; and Alice

Brown Smith, *Forgotten Foundations: The Role of Jeanes Teachers in Black Education* (New York: Vantage Press, 1997).

86. Donal F. Lindsey, *Indians at Hampton Institute, 1877–1923* (Urbana: University of Illinois Press, 1995).

87. Washington, *Up from Slavery*, 47.

88. Booker T. Washington, "The American Negro and His Economic Value," *International Monthly* 2 (1900): 672–86, here 673.

89. *Catalogue of the Tuskegee Normal and Industrial Institute* (1893–1894), 46, 65–66.

90. These statistics are taken from relevant issues of *Southern Letter*, the official newsletter of Tuskegee Institute, and the *Catalogue of the Tuskegee Normal and Industrial Institute*.

91. Booker T. Washington, "Chapters from My Experience," 6 parts, *The World's Work*, October 1910, 13505–22; November 1910, 13627–40; December 1910, 13783–94; January 1911, 13847–54; February 1911, 14032–39; April 1911, 14230–38, here November 1910, 13635.

92. See the complaints about the exclusion of blacks from the 1893 fair in Ida B. Wells, Frederick Douglass, Irvine Garland Penn, and Ferdinand L. Barnett, *The Reason Why the Colored American Is Not in the World's Columbian Exposition: The Afro-American Contribution to Columbian Literature* (1893), Robert W. Rydell, ed. (Urbana: University of Illinois Press, 1999).

93. Walter G. Cooper, *The Cotton States and International Exposition and South, Illustrated. Including the Official History of the Exposition* (Atlanta: The Illustrator Co., 1896), 57.

94. See, for example, the speech immediately following Washington's at the exposition by Judge Emory Speer, in Cooper, *Cotton States and International Exposition*, 101–8.

95. I. Garland Penn, "The Awakening of a Race," *Atlanta Constitution*, 22 September 1895, quoted in Cooper, *Cotton States and International Exposition*, 60.

96. See Cooper, *Cotton States and International Exposition*, 24, 8, 89, 91.

97. Alice Bacon, *The Negro and the Atlanta Exposition* (Baltimore: Trustees of the Slater Fund, 1896), 18–19. Bacon relates the reluctance of black artists to submit work to the exposition.

98. W.E.B. Du Bois, "Of Mr. Booker T. Washington and Others," in *The Souls of Black Folk*, 26, 32.

99. Washington's speech is printed in Cooper, 98–99, and in Washington, *Up from Slavery*, 106–9.

100. W.E.B. Du Bois, Wilberforce, to Booker T. Washington, 24 September 1895, in Harlan, ed., *Booker T. Washington Papers* 4:26.

101. Booker T. Washington to Edna Dow Littlehale Cheney, 15 October 1895, in Harlan, ed., *Booker T. Washington Papers* 4:56–57. Tuskegee Institute did not support black disfranchisement. Indeed, the Tuskegee Woman's Club, an organization of Tuskegee faculty, supported female suffrage, and some male Tuskegee personnel voted. See Adele Logan Alexander, "Adella Hunt Logan and the Tuskegee Woman's Club: Building a Foundation for Suffrage," in Mary Martha

Thomas, ed., *Stepping Out of the Shadows: Alabama Women, 1819–1990* (Tuscaloosa: University of Alabama Press, 1995), 96–113.

102. As Kevin Gaines has argued, black elites in this period called for racial solidarity and uplift precisely as a way to preserve and reproduce their own class status. The demand for solidarity was, for all its emancipatory potential, also a demand of obedience from working-class blacks. See Kevin K. Gaines, *Uplifting the Race: Black Leadership, Politics, and Culture in the Twentieth Century* (Chapel Hill: University of North Carolina Press, 1996). Booker T. Washington did reject explicitly racist portrayals of African Americans, including by the African American writer William Hannibal Thomas. See John David Smith, *Black Judas: William Hannibal Thomas and the American Negro* (Athens: University of Georgia Press, 2000; Chicago: Ivan R. Dee, 2002).

103. Booker T. Washington, *Atlanta Exposition Address*, Brown Seal Records, Broome Special Phonographic Records, n.d., 78 rpm, in the A.F.R. Lawrence Collection, Library of Congress, Washington, DC. This is a commercial pressing of a private recording made in the Columbia Studios in 1908, probably for use in Tuskegee fund-raising. See Tim Brooks, *Lost Sounds: Blacks and the Birth of the Recording Industry, 1890–1919* (Urbana: University of Illinois Press, 2004), 503–4. The recording can be heard on the compact disc that accompanies that book.

104. Washington, *Up from Slavery*, 60–62.

105. Carter G. Woodson, *The Mis-Education of the Negro* (Washington, DC: The Associated Publishers, 1933), xii.

106. The *Southern Workman* articles used to teach political economy at Hampton were collected in T. T. Bryce, *Economic Crumbs, Or Plain Talks for the People about Labor,—Capital,—Money, Tariff,—Etc.* (Hampton, VA: Hampton Steam Press, 1879), 3.

107. Daniel Putnam, *A Manual of Pedagogics*, Richard G. Boone, introduction (New York: Silver, Burdett and Co., 1895), 15, 31–32, 36–37.

108. Ruric Nevel Roark, *Method in Education: A Textbook for Teachers* (New York: American Book Co. 1899), 7, 37, 343.

109. Laughlin taught at Harvard until 1888 and the University of Chicago until 1916. "James L. Laughlin, Economist, is Dead," *New York Times*, 29 November 1933.

110. J. Laurence Laughlin, *The Elements of Political Economy: With Some Applications to the Questions of the Day*, rev. ed. (1887; New York: American Book Co., 1896–1920), 235, 371.

111. The ethics text was the unexceptional Francis Wayland, *The Elements of Moral Science* (Boston: Gould and Lincoln, 1860). Information on the Tuskegee curriculum comes from Catalogue of the Tuskegee Normal and Industrial Institute (1893–1914) and *Southern Letter* (1889–1904).

112. See chapter 4, below.

113. [Robert E. Park?], "What Negro Students Read," [1905?], Washington Papers, Library of Congress, Reel 64.

114. *Southern Letter* 9, no. 2 (February 1892).

115. "What Negro Students Read."

116. State commissioners restored the forbidden topics when they learned of these private efforts by faculty and students. Richard R. Wright Jr., *Eighty-Seven*

Years behind the Black Curtain: An Autobiography (Philadelphia: Rare Book Co., 1965), 41–45.

117. Monroe N. Work, "How Tuskegee Has Improved a Black Belt County," Monroe N. Work Papers, Box 3.

118. John Quincy Johnson, *Report of the Fifth Tuskegee Negro Conference 1896* (Baltimore: Trustees of the Slater Fund, 1896), 5. 13–14, 16–18, 25. For a description of the similar second conference, see "An Account of the Tuskegee Negro Conference," *Southern Workman* 22 (March 1893): 50–51, in Harlan, ed., *Booker T. Washington Papers* 3:294–99.

119. Du Bois, *Autobiography*, 286.

120. George Washington Carver, "Need of Scientific Agriculture in the South," Tuskegee Institute, Farmer's Leaflet 7 (Tuskegee, April 1902), Carver Papers, Reel 24. Reprinted from the *Review of Reviews*, 25 (1902): 320–22. Carver makes a similar point in "A Few Hints to Southern Farmers," *The Southern Workman* 28 (1899): 351–53, Carver Papers, Reel 24.

121. See Linda O. McMurry, *George Washington Carver, Scientist and Symbol* (New York: Oxford University Press, 1981), 75. Unless otherwise specified, information on Carver comes from McMurry's biography.

122. See the excellent article by Mark Hersey, "Hints and Suggestions to Farmers: George Washington Carver and Rural Conservation in the South," *Environmental History* 11 (2006): 239–68.

123. On Tuskegee extension work, see Hersey, "Hints and Suggestions to Farmers," as well as Allen W. Jones, "The Role of Tuskegee Institute in the Education of Black Farmers," *Journal of Negro History* 60 (1975): 252–67; and Robert E. Park, "Agricultural Extension Among the Negroes," *The World To-Day* 15 (1908): 820–26.

124. Hersey, "Hints and Suggestions to Farmers."

125. On Du Bois, see David Levering Lewis, *W.E.B. Du Bois: Biography of a Race, 1868–1919* (New York: Henry Holt, 1993) and *W.E.B. Du Bois: The Fight for Equality and the American Century, 1919–1963* (New York: Henry Holt, 2000). Unless otherwise specified all biographical information on Du Bois comes from these volumes.

126. W.E.B. Du Bois, *The Suppression of the African Slave-Trade to the United States of America, 1638–1870* (New York: Longmans, Green and Co., 1896).

127. W.E.B. Du Bois, *The Philadelphia Negro: A Social Study* (Philadelphia: University of Pennsylvania Press, 1899).

128. See Alfred A. Moss, *The American Negro Academy: Voice of the Talented Tenth* (Baton Rouge: Louisiana State University Press, 1981). For Crummell and his influence on Du Bois, see especially Wilson Jeremiah Moses, *The Golden Age of Black Nationalism, 1850–1925* (Hamden, CT: Archon Books, 1978).

129. Alexander Crummell, *Civilization the Primal Need of the Race* and *The Attitude of the American Mind toward the Negro Intellect* (Washington, DC: American Negro Academy, 1898), 3–4, 6, 14.

130. W.E.B. Du Bois, *The Conservation of Races* (Washington, DC: American Negro Academy, 1897), 7, 9, 10, 15.

131. W.E.B. Du Bois, *The Philadelphia Negro*, 390–96.

132. W.E.B. Du Bois, ed., *The Negro in Business* (Atlanta: Atlanta University Press, 1899). Reprinted in *The Atlanta University Publications* (New York: Arno Press, 1968).

133. "A Program for a Sociological Society," (1897) First Sociological Club, Atlanta University, Papers of W.E.B. Du Bois, University of Massachusetts, Amherst, microfilm edition, Manuscript Division, Library of Congress, Washington, DC (hereafter Du Bois Papers), Reel 80.

134. For an appreciation of Atlanta University, see W.E.B. Du Bois, "The Cultural Missions of Atlanta University," *Phylon* 3 (1942): 105–15.

135. See *Mortality among Negroes in Cities: Proceedings of the Conference for Investigation of City Problems, Held at Atlanta University, May 26–27 1896* (Atlanta: Atlanta University Press, 1896). Reprinted in *Atlanta University Publications* (New York: Arno Press, 1968).

136. On these efforts to bring Du Bois to Tuskegee, see Lewis, "Social Science, Ambition, and Tuskegee," ch. 9 in *W.E.B. Du Bois: Biography of a Race*, 211–37.

137. W.E.B. Du Bois, Wilberforce, to Booker T. Washington, 1 April 1896, in Harlan, ed., *Booker T. Washington Papers* 4:152–43.

138. W.E.B. Du Bois, "The Study of the Negro Problems," *Annals of the American Academy of Political and Social Science* 11 (January 1898): 1–23. On Du Bois's experience at Wilberforce, see Lewis, *W.E.B. Du Bois: Biography of a Race*, 153–54, 175–78.

139. Booker T. Washington to W.E.B. Du Bois, 26 October 1899, in Harlan, ed., *Booker T. Washington Papers* 5:245.

140. W.E.B. Du Bois to Booker T. Washington, 17 February 1900, in Harlan, ed., *Booker T. Washington Papers* 5:443–44.

141. Du Bois, review of *Up from Slavery*, by Booker T. Washington, *The Dial* 31 (16 July 1901): 53–55, in Harlan, ed., *Booker T. Washington Papers* 6:175–78.

142. Du Bois, *Autobiography*, 150–57.

143. Du Bois, "Of Mr. Booker T. Washington and Others," 31.

144. On this trip, see Harlan, *Booker T. Washington: The Making of a Black Leader*, 238–43.

145. Booker T. Washington, "Some European Observations and Experiences." Reprinted from the *New York Age*, the *Washington Colored American*, the *New Orleans Southwestern Christian Advocate*, the *Indianapolis Freeman*, and the *Tuskegee Student* (Tuskegee, AL: Tuskegee Institute Steam Press, 1900), 4, 9–13. In Pamphlets in American History, Biography, B 2337.

146. See Imanuel Geiss, *The Pan-African Movement: A History of Pan-Africanism in America, Europe and Africa*, trans. Ann Keep (1968; New York: Africana Publishing, 1974). See also the useful discussion in George Shepperson, "Pan-Africanism and 'Pan-Africanism': Some Historical Notes," *Phylon* 23 (1962): 346–58. Steven Hahn contextualizes African American interest in settling in Africa in the larger struggle against racism in the South. See Hahn, *A Nation under Our Feet*, 317–63.

147. On Garvey, see especially Judith Stein, *The World of Marcus Garvey: Race and Class in Modern Society* (Baton Rouge: Louisiana State University Press, 1986).

148. H. M. Turner, "Essay: The American Negro and the Fatherland," in J.W.E. Bowen, ed., *Africa and the American Negro: Addresses and Proceedings of the Congress on Africa Held under the Auspices of the Stewart Missionary Foundation for Africa of the Gammon Theological Seminary in Connection with the Cotton States and International Exposition December 13–15, 1895* (1896; reprint, Miami: Mnemosyne, 1969), 195–98.

149. Alexander Crummell, "Civilization as a Collateral and Indispensable Instrumentality in Planting the Christian Church in Africa," in Bowen, ed., *Africa and the American Negro*, 119.

150. See Booker T. Washington, N.B. Wood, and Fannie Barrier Williams, *A New Negro for a New Century: An Accurate and Up-to-Date Record of the Upward Struggles of the Negro Race* (Chicago: American Publishing House, 1900).

151. Washington, "The American Negro and His Economic Value," 672.

152. Thomas J. Calloway to Booker T. Washington, 25 March 1909, Washington Papers, Library of Congress, Reel 34.

153. Interview with Nathan Calloway, great-grandson of James Nathan Calloway, January 2007, Washington, DC. For a selection of the photographs brought together by Du Bois for the exposition, see Library of Congress, *Small Nation of People*.

154. Thomas J. Calloway, U.S. Commission to the Paris Exposition of 1900, "The American Negro Exhibit" (Washington, DC, 21 December 1899), Carver Papers, Reel 2.

155. W.E.B. Du Bois, "The American Negro at Paris," *American Monthly Review of Reviews* (New York) 22 (November 1900): 575–77, in Herbert Aptheker, ed., *Writings in Periodicals Edited by Others*, 4 vols. (Milwood, NY: Kraus-Thomas Organization, 1982), 1:86.

156. Thomas J. Calloway to Booker T. Washington, 23 August 1900, Washington Papers, Library of Congress, Reel 34.

157. Thomas J. Calloway to Booker T. Washington, 25 February 1901, and Thomas J. Calloway to Booker T. Washington, 28 September 1900, Washington Papers, Library of Congress, Reel 34.

158. Calloway chaired a committee of the London conference that sought, in the end unsuccessfully, to hold Pan-African conferences biennially. Thomas J. Calloway to Booker T. Washington, 25 July 1900, Washington Papers, Library of Congress, Reel 34.

159. Alexander Walters, Henry B. Brown, H. Sylvester Williams, W.E.B. Du Bois, "To the Nations of the World," 20.

CHAPTER 2

SOZIALPOLITIK AND THE NEW SOUTH IN GERMANY

1. For an excellent account showing how German nationalist activists used novels to depict Poles as racially different from Germans, see Kristen Kopp, "Constructing Racial Difference in Colonial Poland," in Eric Ames, Marcia Klotz, and Lora Wildenthal, eds. *Germany's Colonial Pasts* (Lincoln: University of Nebraska Press, 2005), 76–96.

2. Karl Marx, Preface to the first edition of *Capital*, vol. 1, Ben Fowkes, trans. (1867; New York: Penguin Books, 1992), 91.

3. [Karl Marx], "Address of the International Working Men's Association to Abraham Lincoln, President of the United States of America, 28 January 1865, in Karl Marx and Friedrich Engels, *The Civil War in the United States*, 3rd ed. (New York: International Publishers, 1961), 279.

4. On free labor, Free Soilers, and abolition, see Foner, *Free Soil, Free Labor, Free Men*.

5. Marx in London to Engels in Manchester, 23 April 1866, in Marx and Engels, *Collected Works*, vol. 42 (New York: International Publishers, 1987), 268–69.

6. See Marx and Engels, *Manifesto of the Communist Party*, 16.

7. Gustav Schmoller, "Nationalökonomische und socialpolitische Rückblicke auf Nordamerika," *Preußische Jahrbücher* 17 (1866): 38–75; 153–92; 519–47; 587–611, here 52–62 and 611

8. Marion W. Gray, "Prussia in Transition: Society and Politics under the Stein Reform Ministry of 1808," *Transactions of the American Philosophical Society*, New Series 76 (1986): 1–175, 25–26, 17–18.

9. William W. Hagen, *Ordinary Prussians: Brandenburg Junkers and Villagers, 1500–1840* (Cambridge: Cambridge University Press, 2002), has emphasized the power of serfs in Prussia. His work can be usefully compared with the findings of Eugene D. Genovese, *Roll, Jordan, Roll: The World the Slaves Made* (New York: Pantheon Books, 1974).

10. For the text of this so-called "Oktoberedikt," see Werner Conze, ed., *Quellen zur Geschichte der deutschen Bauernbefreiung* (Göttingen: Musterschmidt, 1957), 102–5. The classic work on agrarian reform in Prussia is Georg Friedrich Knapp, *Die Bauernbefreiung und der Ursprung der Landarbeiter in den älteren Theilen Preußens*, 2 vols. (1887; Munich: Duncker and Humblot, 1927). For more recent works, see Gray, "Prussia in Transition"; Reinhart Koselleck, *Preußen zwischen Reform und Revolution: Allgemeines Landrecht, Verwaltung und soziale Bewegung von 1791 bis 1848*, 2nd ed. (1967; Stuttgart: Klett-Cotta, 1975); Hanna Schissler, *Preußische Agrargesellschaft im Wandel: Wirtschaftliche, gesellschaftliche und politische Transformationsprozesse von 1763 bis 1847* (Göttingen: Vandenhoeck und Ruprecht, 1978); Frank B. Tipton, *Regional Variations in the Economic Development of Germany during the Nineteenth Century* (Middletown: Wesleyan University Press, 1976); and Hans-Ulrich Wehler, *Deutsche Gesellschaftsgeschichte*, vol. 3, *Von der "Deutsche Doppelrevolution" bis zum Beginn des Ersten Weltkrieges* (Munich: C.H. Beck, 1987).

11. See Gray, "Prussia in Transition," 32–35. For an important survey of German economic thought from the eighteenth to the twentieth centuries, see Keith Tribe, *Strategies of Economic Order: German Economic Discourse, 1750–1950* (Cambridge: Cambridge University Press, 1995).

12. Quoted in Koselleck, *Preußen zwischen Reform und Revolution*, 487.

13. Jonathan Osmond, "Land, Peasant and Lord in German Agriculture Since 1800," in Robert W. Scribner and Sheilagh C. Ogilvie, eds., *Germany: A New Social and Economic History*, vol. 3 (London: Arnold, 1996), 82.

14. On the case of the American South, see Powell, *New Masters*.

15. See Koselleck, *Preußen zwischen Reform und Revolution*, 641–59.

16. Wehler, *Deutsche Gesellschaftsgeschichte* 3:185–86.

17. See Klaus J. Bade, "German Emigration to the United States and Continental Immigration to Germany in the Late Nineteenth and Early Twentieth Centuries," *Central European History* 13 (1980): 348–77.

18. Frank B. Tipton Jr., "Farm Labor and Power Politics: Germany, 1850–1914," *Journal of Economic History* 34 (1974): 951–79, here 959.

19. Wehler, *Deutsche Gesellschaftsgeschichte* 3:56–59.

20. For the 1845 law and further discussion, see Robert J. Steinfeld, *Coercion, Contract, and Free Labor*, 244–45.

21. For the full text of the Employment Law of 1869, see Robert von Landmann, *Kommentar zur Gewerbeordnung für das Deutsche Reich*, 2 vols. (Munich: C. H. Beck, 1907). This law was passed by the North German League and applied to all the German states after German unification in 1871. On the use of household membership to subject workers to legal sanction, see Title VII, § 127d and § 134.

22. 1872 was the date of the meeting that founded the organization, which came into official existence in 1873. Especially helpful for my account of the *Verein für Sozialpolitik* has been Erik Grimmer-Solem, *The Rise of Historical Economics and Social Reform in Germany, 1864–1894* (Oxford: Clarendon Press, 2003). See also Abraham Ascher, "Professors as Propagandists: The Politics of the Kathedersozialisten," *Journal of Central European Affairs* 23 (1963): 282–302; Rüdiger vom Bruch, "Bürgerliche Sozialreform im deutschen Kaiserreich," in vom Bruch, ed., *Weder Kommunismus noch Kapitalismus: Bürgerliche Sozialreform in Deutschland vom Vormärz bis zur Ära Adenauer* (Munich: C. H. Beck, 1985), 61–179; Dieter Lindenlaub, *Richtungskämpfe in Verein für Sozialpolitik: Wissenschaft und Sozialpolitik im Kaiserreich vornehmlich vom Beginn des "Neuen Kurses" bis zum Ausbruch des Ersten Weltkrieges (1890–1914)* (Wiesbaden: Franz Steiner, 1967); Kevin Repp, *Reformers, Critics, and the Paths of German Modernity: Anti-Politics and the Search for Alternatives, 1890–1914* (Cambridge: Harvard University Press, 2000); Dietrich Rueschemeyer, "The Verein für Sozialpolitik and the Fabian Society: A Study in the Sociology of Policy-Relevant Knowledge," in Dietrich Rueschemeyer and Theda Skocpol, eds., *States, Social Knowledge, and the Origins of Modern Social Policies* (Princeton: Princeton University Press, 1996), 117–62; and James J. Sheehan, *The Career of Lujo Brentano: A Study of Liberalism and Social Reform in Imperial Germany* (Chicago: University of Chicago Press, 1966). Dieter Krüger discusses the critique of Marxism by German social scientists in *Nationalökonomen im Wilhelminischen Deutschland* (Göttingen: Vandenhoeck and Ruprecht, 1983), 49–73. Rüdiger vom Bruch offers rich discussions of academic politics, including of members of the Verein für Sozialpolitik, in Wilhelmine Germany. See his *Gelehrtenpolitik, Sozialwissenschaften und Akademische Diskurse in Deutschland im 19. und 20. Jahrhundert* (Stuttgart: Franz Steiner, 2006) and *Wissenschaft, Politik und Öffentliche Meinung: Gelehrtenpolitik im Wilhelminischen Deutschland (1890–1914)* (Husum: Matthiesen, 1980).

23. See the illuminating discussion in George Steinmetz, *Regulating the Social: The Welfare State and Local Politics in Imperial Germany* (Princeton: Princeton

University Press, 1993). On the earlier Prussian tradition, see Hermann Beck, *The Origins of the Authoritarian Welfare State in Prussia: Conservatives, Bureaucracy, and the Social Question, 1815–70* (Ann Arbor: University of Michigan Press, 1995).

24. Georg Friedrich Knapp, "Landarbeiter und innere Kolonisation" (1893), in Georg Friedrich Knapp, *Einführung in einige Hauptgebiete der Nationalökonomie: Siebenundzwanzig Beiträge zur Sozialwissenschaft* (Munich: Duncker and Humblot, 1925), 137.

25. Gustav Schmoller, "Eröffnungsrede," *Verhandlungen der Eisenacher Versammlung zur Besprechung der socialen Frage am 6. und 7. October 1872* (Leipzig: Duncker and Humblot, 1873), 1, 3–5.

26. See Lujo Brentano, "Abstracte und realistische Volkswirthe," *Zeitschrift des königlich-preußischen statistischen Bureaus* 11 (1871): 383–85. Online at: http://www.semverteilung.vwl.uni-muenchen.de. Apparently the first to characterize German supporters of free trade as the "Manchester School" was Gustav Friedrich von Schönberg, in *Arbeitsämter: Eine Aufgabe des deutschen Reichs* (Berlin: J. Buttentag, 1871).

27. Friedrich List, *Das nationale System der politischen Ökonomie* (1844; Berlin: Reimar Hobbing, 1930), 39–51.

28. On these German free traders, see Volker Hentschel, *Die deutschen Freihändler und der volkswirtschaftliche Kongress 1858 bis 1885* (Stuttgart: Klett, 1975); W. O. Henderson, "Prince Smith and Free Trade in Germany," *Economic History Review*, New Series 2 (1950): 295–302; Gustav Cohn, "Free Trade and Protection," *The Economic Journal* 14 (1904): 188–95; and Wilhelm Roscher, "Uebersicht der neuesten Entwicklungen," ch. 35 in *Geschichte der National-Oekonomik in Deutschland* (Munich: R. Oldenbourg, 1874), 1004–48.

29. For the first criticism of the group as "socialists of the lectern," see the 1871 *National-Zeitung* article republished as Heinrich Bernhard Oppenheim, *Der Katheder-sozialismus* (Berlin: R. Oppenheim, 1872).

30. On the Verein and its differences with the Social Democratic Party, see Guenther Roth, *The Social Democrats in Imperial Germany: A Study in Working-Class Isolation and National Integration* (Totowa, NJ: Bedminster Press, 1963), 136–43.

31. Brentano, "Abstracte und realistische Volkswirthe." See also the vigorous defense against the accusation of social democratic sympathies in Hans Delbrück, Gustav Schmoller and Adolph Wagner, *Ueber Die Stumm'sche Herrenhaus-Rede Gegen Die Kathedersozialisten* (Berlin: Georg Stilke, 1897).

32. On the image of the *pétroleuse*, see David A. Shafer, *The Paris Commune: French Politics, Culture, and Society at the Crossroads of the Revolutionary Tradition and Revolutionary Socialism* (New York: Palgrave Macmillan, 2005), 179.

33. Friedrich Engels, "Supplement and Addendum" (1895) to Karl Marx, *Capital*, vol. 3, David Fernbach, trans. (1894; New York: Penguin Books, 1981), 1031.

34. On Sombart's engagement with Marxism and the Social Democratic Party, as well as on Sombart generally, see Friedrich Lenger's outstanding biography, *Werner Sombart, 1863–1941: Eine Biographie* (Munich: C. H. Beck, 1994).

35. See Otto Hintze, "Gustav Schmoller," in *Soziologie und Geschichte* (Göttingen: Vandenhoeck and Ruprecht, 1964), 532, cited in David F. Lindenfeld, *The Practical Imagination: The German Sciences of State in the Nineteenth Century* (Chicago: University of Chicago Press, 1997), 226.

36. Rosa Luxemburg, "Hohle Nüsse" (1899), in *Gesammelte Werke*, 5 vols. (Berlin: Dietz, 1970), 1/1:487–92.

37. Rosa Luxemburg, "Im Rate der Gelehrten" (1903), in *Gesammelte Werke* 1/1:382–90.

38. Friedrich Engels, Introduction to the English edition (1892), *Socialism, Utopian and Scientific*, trans. Edward Aveling (Chicago: Charles H. Kerr, 1907), xxxv, xxxviii.

39. Antonio Labriola, "In memoria del Manifesto dei Comunisti," in *Scritti Filosofici e Politici*, ed. Franco Sbarberi, 2 vols. (Torino: Einaudi, 1973), 2: 24n1.

40. See conclusion, below.

41. On the "negative integration" of revolutionary workers through the Social Democratic Party, see Roth, *The Social Democrats in Imperial Germany*. On the turn to more conservative strategies in the SPD, see Carl E. Schorske, *German Social Democracy, 1905–1917: The Development of the Great Schism* (Cambridge: Harvard University Press, 1955).

42. Adolf Held, "Die Bestrafung des Arbeitscontractbruchs," *Verhandlungen der zweiten Generalversammlung des Vereins für Socialpolitik am 11. und 12. October 1874, Schriften des Vereins für Socialpolitik*, vol. 9 (Leipzig: Duncker and Humbolt, 1875), 13, 7. See also Lujo Brentano, "Gutachten," in Verein für Socialpolitik, *Die Reform des Lehrlingswesens: Sechszehn Gutachten und Berichte* (Leipzig: Duncker and Humblot, 1875), 49–71.

43. Ascher, "Professors as Propagandists."

44. On German anti-Semitism, see Massimo Ferrari Zumbini, *Die Wurzeln des Bösen: Gründerjahre des Antisemitismus: Von der Bismarckzeit zu Hitler* (Frankfurt am Main: Klostermann, 2003). On the German right, see Geoff Eley, *Reshaping the German Right: Radical Nationalism and Political Change after Bismarck* (1980; Ann Arbor: University of Michigan Press, 1990) and James N. Retallack, *The German Right, 1860–1920: Political Limits of the Authoritarian Imagination* (Toronto: University of Toronto Press, 2006). For a good overview see David Blackbourn, *The Long Nineteenth Century: A History of Germany, 1780–1918* (New York: Oxford University Press, 1998), 400–59.

45. On Knapp, see Hartmut Harnisch, "Georg Friedrich Knapp: Agrargeschichtsforschung und Sozialpolitisches Engagement im Deutschen Kaiserreich," *Jahrbuch fur Wirtschaftsgeschichte* 1 (1993): 95–132, and Kerstin Schmidt, "Georg Friedrich Knapp: Ein Pionier der Agrarhistoriker," *Zeitschrift für Geschichtswissenschaft* 37 (1989): 228–42.

46. Knapp, *Die Bauernbefreiung*.

47. Gustav Schmoller, "Der Kampf des preußischen Königthums um die Erhaltung des Bauernstandes," review of *Die Bauernbefreiung*, by Knapp, *Jahrbuch für Gesetzgebung, Verwaltung und Volkswirthschaft im Deutschen Reich* 12 (1888): 245–55, quoted in Harnisch, "Georg Friedrich Knapp," 127. According to Harnisch, Knapp wrote to Schmoller that he agreed with this characterization of his work. Schmoller wrote privately to Knapp of his admiration for *Die Bauernbefrei-*

ung in a letter of 18 March 1887, Geheime Staatsarchiv Preußischer Kulturbesitz, Berlin, Germany (hereafter GStA) VI. HA Nachlaß Schmoller (hereafter NL Schmoller), Nr. 131b, Bl. 48–51.

48. Georg Friedrich Knapp, "Die Landarbeiter bei der Stein-Hardenbergischen Gesetzgebung," in *Die Landarbeiter in Knechtschaft und Freiheit: Vier Vorträge* (Leipzig: Duncker and Humboldt, 1891), 86.

49. See Max Sering, *Landwirthschaftliche Konkurrenz Nordamerikas in Gegenwart und Zukunft: Landwirthschaft, Kolonisation und Verkehrswesen in den Vereinigten Staaten und in Britisch Nord-Amerika* (Leipzig: Duncker and Humblot, 1887); Max Sering, "Politik der Grundbesitzverteilung in den grossen Reichen," *Verhandlungen des Landes-Oekonomie-Kollegiums am 9. Februar 1912* (Berlin: Gebrüder Unger, 1912), in GStA PK, I. HA Rep. 87B, Nr. 9329, Bl. 13–41.

50. See especially Max Sering, "Die Agrarfrage und der Sozialismus," review of *Die Agrarfrage*, by Karl Kautsky (Stuttgart, 1899), *Jahrbuch für Gesetzgebung, Verwaltung, und Volkswirtschaft* 23 (1899): 1493–1556.

51. Schmoller, "Nationalökonomische und socialpolitische Rückblicke auf Nordamerika."

52. Knapp, bibliography of works on colonialism; notes on *Entwicklungsgeschichte der Kolonialpolitik des Deutschen Reiches*, by Charpentier (Berlin, 1886), 25 April 1886; notes on *Deutsche Interessen in der Südsee* (Berlin, 1885), 2 May 1888; notes on text on East Africa by [Friedrich] Fabri; notes on *Ein Jahr in Ostafrika* by E. Krenzler (Ulm, 1888), 10 May 1888, GStA VI. HA Nachlaß Knapp (hereafter NL Knapp), K. III, Bl. 664; 667–71; 673–80; 683–85, 643–49. Knapp, library slips, 12 May 1888–15 November 1888, NL Knapp, K. II, Bl. 192a–i, 194.

53. Georg Friedrich Knapp, "Der Ursprung der Sklaverei in den Kolonieen," in *Die Landarbeiter in Knechtschaft und Freiheit*, 15.

54. Knapp, "Der Ursprung der Sklaverei in den Kolonieen," 14–16. Knapp gave a similar lecture the following year. See Knapp, lecture notes, 5 June 1899, NL Knapp, K. III, Bl 567–70.

55. Knapp, notes on the history of the United States and on slavery, 30 July 1900, NL Knapp, K. II, Bl. 41–43.

56. Verein für Socialpolitik, *Bäuerliche Zustände in Deutschland*, vol. 1, *Schriften des Vereins für Socialpolitik*, vol. 22 (Leipzig: Duncker and Humblot, 1883), v.

57. "Massregeln der Gesetzgebung und Verwaltung zur Erhaltung des bäuerlichen Grundbesitzes," in *Verhandlungen der am 6. und 7. October 1884 abgehaltenen Generalversammlung des Vereins für Socialpolitik, Schriften des Vereins für Socialpolitik*, vol. 28 (Leipzig: Duncker and Humblot, 1884), 34.

58. Klaus Saul, "Der Kampf um das Landproletariat: Sozialistische Landagitation, Großgrundbesitz und preußische Staatsverwaltung 1890 bis 1903," *Archiv für Sozialgeschichte* 15 (1975): 163–208.

59. *Verhandlungen der Generalversammlung des Vereins für Socialpolitik am 24. und 25. September 1886.*

60. Gustav Schmoller, "Die preußische Kolonisation des 17. und 18. Jahrhundert," in Verein für Socialpolitik, *Zur Inneren Kolonisation in Deutschland: Erfahrungen und Vorschläge* (Leipzig: Duncker and Humblot, 1886), 1–2.

61. Sombart-Ermsleben, "Steesow, ein projektirtes Bauerndorf in der Priegnitz, Provinz Brandenburg," Verein für Socialpolitik, *Zur Inneren Kolonisation in Deutschland*, 183–229.

62. On the Kulturkampf, liberalism, and nationalism, see especially Michael B. Gross, *The War against Catholicism: Liberalism and the Anti-Catholic Imagination in Nineteenth-Century Germany* (Ann Arbor: University of Michigan Press, 2004) and Helmut Walser Smith, *German Nationalism and Religious Conflict: Culture, Ideology, Politics, 1870–1914* (Princeton: Princeton University Press, 1995).

63. Otto von Bismarck, *Gedanken und Erinnerungen*, 2 vols. (Stuttgart: Cotta, 1898), 2:127.

64. See Helmut Neubach, *Die Ausweisungen von Polen und Juden aus Preussen 1885/86: Ein Beitrag zu Bismarcks Polenpolitik und zur Geschichte des deutsch-polnischen Verhältnisses* (Wiesbaden: Otto Harrassowitz, 1967). On this and other Prussian anti-Polish measures, see Richard Blanke, *Prussian Poland in the German Empire (1871–1900)* (Boulder: East European Monographs, 1981), and William W. Hagen, *Germans, Poles, and Jews: The Nationality Conflict in the Prussian East, 1772–1914* (Chicago: University of Chicago Press, 1980).

65. Lars Olsson, "Labor Migration as a Prelude to World War I," *International Migration Review* 30 (1996): 875–900.

66. Of the 1.25 million who left Russian Poland for good in the period between 1871 and 1914, the vast majority, 800,000, relocated to the United States; 200,000 moved across the Atlantic to Brazil or Canada; another 200,000 traveled east into the Russian Empire; a mere 50,000 settled permanently in Germany. Of the 1.2 million Poles who left Galicia, the portion of Poland ruled by Austria, in the same period, one half went to western Germany, especially to industrial and mining jobs in Westphalia, with the remainder moving to the United States, Canada, or Brazil. Jerzy Zubrzycki, "Emigration from Poland in the Nineteenth and Twentieth Centuries," *Population Studies* 6 (1953): 248–72, 257–59.

67. Osmond, "Land, Peasant and Lord in German Agriculture Since 1800," 82.

68. On the history of the sugarbeet, see Eugene van Cleef, "The Sugar Beet in Germany, with Special Attention to Its Relation to Climate," *Bulletin of the American Geographical Society* 47 (1915): 241–58; 334–41; George H. Coons, "The Sugar Beet: Product of Science," *The Scientific Monthly* 68 (1949): 149–64; Noël Deerr, *The History of Sugar*, 2 vols. (London: Chapman and Hall, 1949–50); Edmund Oskar von Lippmann, *Geschichte des Zuckers seit den ältesten Zeiten bis zum Beginn der Rübenzucker-Fabrikation*, 2nd ed. (Berlin: J. Springer, 1929); E. Muriel Poggi, "The German Sugar Beet Industry," *Economic Geography* 6 (1930): 81–93.

69. August Meitzen, *Der Boden und die Landwirtschaftlichen Verhältnisse des preussischen Staates*, vol. 8 (Berlin: P. Parey, 1908), 85–137.

70. On this point, see Poggi, "The German Sugar Beet Industry," 85–86.

71. Richard Buerstenbinder, *Die Zuckerrübe: ein Handbuch für den praktischen Landwirt*, 3rd ed., Martin Ullmann, ed. (Hamburg: Lucas Gräfe and Sillem, 1896), 5. The European, and later the American, sugarbeet industry have always depended on tariffs and other state support to undermine competition from tropical sugarcane. Thanks to protective tariffs, beet sugar accounted for slightly more than half of the world's sugar consumption from 1883 until 1902, after which tariff reductions reduced the proportion of the world's sugar supply derived from beets to about a third. Jason Clay, "Sugarcane," ch. 7, in *World Agriculture and the Environment* (Washington, DC: Island Press, 2004), 155–72.

72. Johann Josef Fühling, *Der praktische Rübenbauer* (Bonn: Henry and Cohen, 1860), 80.

73. Poggi, "The German Sugar Beet Industry," 88.

74. Buerstenbinder, *Die Zuckerrübe*, 23–24.

75. On sugar beets, see, in addition to literature already cited, Ferdinand Knauer, *Der Rübenbau für Landwirte und Zuckerfabrikanten*, 6th ed. (Berlin: Paul Parey, 1886); K. Stammer, *Lehrbuch der Zuckerfabrikation*, 2 vols., 2nd ed. (1874; Braunschweig: Friedrich Vieweg und Sohn, 1887); and Theodor Roemer and A. Schaumburg, *Handbuch des Zuckerrübenbaues* (Berlin: Paul Parey, 1927). I also learned much from an October 2004 interview with Professor Ursula Mahlendorf, who worked in sugarbeet fields in her childhood.

76. Karl Kaerger, *Die Sachsengängerei: Auf Grund persönlicher Ermittlungen und statistischer Erhebungen* (Berlin: Paul Parey, 1890), 1–2. Kaerger's study is based on his own observations of Sachsengänger in western Prussia and in areas of eastern Prussia from which they originated. This book is, even today, regarded as the authoritative study of the Sachsengänger. Unless otherwise indicated, information below derives from Kaerger. See also Klaus Bade, "'Kulturkampf' auf dem Arbeitsmarkt: Bismarcks 'Polenpolitik' 1885–1890," in Otto Pflanze, ed., *Innenpolitische Probleme des Bismarck-Reiches* (Munich: R. Oldenbourg, 1983), 121–42; Bade, "'Preussengänger' und 'Abwehrpolitik': Ausländerbeschäftigung, Ausländerpolitik und Ausländerkontrolle auf dem Arbeitsmarkt in Preussen vor dem Ersten Weltkrieg," *Archiv für Sozialgeschichte* 24 (1984): 91–162; Ulrich Herbert, *A History of Foreign Labor in Germany, 1880–1980: Seasonal Workers/ Forced Laborers, Guest Workers*, William Templer, trans. (1986; Ann Arbor: University of Michigan Press, 1990); and Johannes Nichtweiss, *Die ausländische Saisonarbeiter in der Landwirtschaft der östlichen und mittleren Gebiete des Deutschen Reiches: Ein Beitrag zur Geschichte der preußisch-deutschen Politik von 1890–1914* (Berlin: Rütten and Loening, 1959).

77. See, for example, P. Müllendorff, "The Development of German West Africa (Kamerun)," *Journal of the African Society* 2 (1902–1903): 70–92, here 73, and Karstedt, "Betrachtungen zur Sozialpolitik in Ostafrika," *Koloniale Rundschau* 6 (1914): 133–41.

78. Martin Lezius, *Heimatsgebiete der Sachsengänger in Brandenburg, Posen und Schlesien* (Neudamm: Neumann, 1913), 68, 87–95.

79. See Bade, "'Preussengänger' und 'Abwehrpolitik,' " 122–28.

80. Elizabeth Bright Jones has shown that in Saxony young women were preferred as agricultural employees for most tasks. See "Gender and Agricultural Change in Saxony, 1900–1930" (Ph.D. diss., University of Minnesota, 2000).

81. Booker T. Washington and Robert E. Park, *Man Farthest Down: A Record of Observation and Study in Europe* (1911; Garden City: Doubleday, Page and Co., 1912), 55.

82. Kaerger, *Die Sachsengängerei*, 50–53; Lezius, *Heimatsgebiete der Sachsengänger*, 98–103.

83. Kaerger, *Die Sachsengängerei*, 62.

84. Regierungs-Präsident Christoph von Tiedemann, Bromberg, "Denkschrift betreffend einige Massregeln zur Germanisierung der Provinz Posen," 6 January 1886, GStA PK, I. HA Rep. 90 A, Nr. 3742, Bl. 6–36. See also Baron von Wilamowitz-Möllendorf, President of the Province of Posen, "Denkschrift betreffend die Grundsätze für das Verhalten der Staatsregierung gegenüber den Staatsangehörigen polnischer Muttersprache in der Provinz Posen," 23 November 1895, GStA PK, I. HA Rep. 90 A, Nr. 3743, Bl. 114–25; Sitzung des kgl. Staatsministeriums, 9 October 1900, GStA PK, I. HA Rep. 87ZB, Nr. 176, Bl. 84–94.

85. Meeting of the Prussian Ministry of State, 13 June 1900, GStA PK, I. HA Rep. 87ZB, Nr. 176, Bl. 57–63.

86. Lezius, *Heimatsgebiete der Sachsengänger*, 81.

87. Meeting of all Prussian Government Ministries, 13 February 1906, GStA PK, I. HA Rep. 87ZB, Nr. 178, Bl. 244–49. Poles who permanently settled in the West, some feared, also spread anti-German Polish nationalism, and also used their savings to fund anti-German efforts in Prussia. On worries that Polish "itinerant preachers" spread political discontent among Westphalian miners, see President of the Province of Westphalia, Münster, to Minister of Interior Baron von der Recke, 31 October 1896 (copy), GStA PK, I. HA Rep. 90 A, Nr. 3744, Bl. 38–52.

88. President of the Province Bromberg, Christoph von Tiedemann, "Denkschrift betreffend einige Massregeln zur Germanisierung der Provinz Posen," 6 January 1886, GStA PK, I. HA Rep. 90 A, Nr. 3742, Bl. 6–36. A similar point is made by Wittenburg, President of the Settlement Commission, to Wilamowitz, President of the Province of Posen, 12 May 1896 (copy), GStA PK, I. HA Rep. 90 A, Nr. 3743, Bl. 137–42.

89. Max Weber made this point explicitly in "Der Nationalstaat und die Volkswirtschaftspolitik" (1895), in Johannes Winckelmann, ed., *Gesammelte Politische Schriften*, 3rd ed. (Tübingen: J.C.B. Mohr, 1971), 1–25.

90. The publication of the Verein's volume on *Internal Colonization in Germany* had been reported in the German press and noted by the architects of the Prussian Settlement Commission as they began their work. See the *National Zeitung* clippings in the files related to the Settlement Commission, "Innere Kolonisation," 2 March 1886 and 24 October 1886, GStA PK, I. HA Rep. 87ZB, Nr. 183, Bl. 4, 6.

91. The law is quoted in Knapp, "Landarbeiter und innere Kolonisation," 138. On the confidential discussion within Bismarck's government prior to this law, see "Vertrauliche Besprechung des königlichen Staatsministeriums," 10 January 1886, Bismarck to Undersecretary Honmeyer, Ministry of State, 11 January 1886, "Vertrauliche Besprechung des königlichen Staatsministeriums," 24 January 1886, GStA PK, I. HA Rep. 90 A, Nr. 3742, Bl. 1–2, 70–72; Puttkamer, Minister of Interior, 21 January 1886, GStA PK, I. HA Rep. 87B, Nr. 173, Bl. 1–5;

"Denkschrift betreffend die Aufgaben der geistlichen, Unterrichts und Medizinalverwaltung in den polnischen Landestheilen," 22 January 1886, GStA PK, I. HA Rep. 87ZB, Nr. 169, Bl. 7–19. For a good overview of the activities of the Settlement Commission, see Blanke, *Prussian Poland in the German Empire*, 53–91; Hagen, *Germans, Poles, and Jews*, 134–35, and Robert Lewis Koehl, "Colonialism inside Germany: 1886–1918," *Journal of Modern History* 25 (1953): 255–72.

92. For a detailed account of these laws, naturally from a critical position, see the contemporary account by the leading Catholic Center Party deputy, Matthias Erzberger, *Der Kampf gegen den Katholizismus in der Ostmark: Material zur Beurteilung der Polenfrage durch die deutschen Katholiken* (Berlin: Germania, 1908).

93. King Friedrich Wilhelm of Prussia, 6 August 1841, GStA PK, I. HA Rep. 90 A, vol. II, Nr. 3742, Bl. 44.

94. Baron von Wilamowitz-Möllendorf, President of the Province of Posen, "Denkschrift betreffend die Grundsätze für das Verhalten der Staatsregierung gegenüber den Staatsangehörigen polnischer Muttersprache in der Provinz Posen," 23 November 1895, GStA PK, I. HA Rep. 90 A, Nr. 3743, Bl. 114–25.

95. The massive holdings of the archives of the Settlement Commission, GStA PK, I. HA Rep. 212, document the activities of estate managers through exhaustive regulations and circulars. See especially *Geschäfts-Anweisungen für die Ansiedlungsvermittler der königlichen Ansiedlungskommission* (Posen: L. Neumeyer, 1910), GStA PK, I. HA Rep. 212, Nr. 5224. Unless otherwise specified, all information on the activities of estate managers comes from this source.

96. See, however, the complaints about the poor hospitality shown to potential settlers by administrators. Settlement Commission to all Estate Administrators, 8 January 1904 and 18 May 1904, GStA PK, I. HA Rep. 212, Nr. 5127.

97. Martin Belgard, *Parzellierung und innere kolonisation in den 6 Östllichen provinzen Preussens, 1875–1906* (Leipzig: Duncker and Humblot, 1907), 84.

98. Settlement Commission to all Estate Administrators, 22 September 1903, GStA PK, I. HA Rep. 212, Nr. 5127.

99. Settlement Commission to all Estate Administrators, 24 February 1905, GStA PK, I. HA Rep. 212, Nr. 5127.

100. Settlement Commission to all Estate Administrators, 11 February 1900, GStA PK, I. HA Rep. 212, Nr. 5126.

101. Minister of Agriculture to all Ministers of State, 17 July 1909, GStA PK, I. HA Rep. 87ZB, Nr. 180, Bl. 2.

102. Printed tenancy agreement, sent on 20 March 1906, GStA PK, I. HA Rep. 212, Nr. 5142, Bl. a, 55–56.

103. "Geschäftsanweisung für die Oberverwalter der Ansiedlungskommission," 9 September 1907, GStA PK, I. HA Rep. 212, Nr. 5130.

104. Printed formula for family contract, n.d. [position in folder suggests 1907–1908], GStA PK, I. HA Rep. 212,, Nr. 5142, Bl. a, 86.

105. Settlement Commission to all Estate Administrators, 23 June 1906, GStA PK, I. HA Rep. 212, Nr. 5127.

106. Belgard, *Parzellierung und innere kolonisation*, 73, also attested to the supposed inferiority of these Russian Germans to local Poles.

107. Minister of Agriculture to Chancellor Bülow, July 1908, GStA PK, I. HA Rep. 87B, Nr. 9372, Bl. 79–84.

108. Settlement Commission to all Estate Administrators, 10 December 1908, GStA PK, I. HA Rep. 212, Nr. 5142, Bl. a, 100–1.

109. Belgard, *Parzellierung und innere kolonisation*, 69–71.

110. "Ueber innere Kolonisation mit Rücksicht auf die Erhaltung und Vermehrung des mittleren und kleineren ländlichen Grundbesitzes," *Verhandlungen der Generalversammlung des Vereins für Socialpolitik am 24. und 25. September 1886*, 77, 91, 102–36.

111. See, for example, Max Sering to the Minister of Agriculture, 6 March 1891, GStA PK, I. HA Rep. 87B, Nr. 9369, Bl. 1–2.

112. For an article in English advocating extending smallhold farming in Germany, but critical of the mechanisms of supervision built into previous efforts at parcelization and internal colonization, see Lujo Brentano, "Agrarian Reform in Prussia," 2 parts, *Economic Journal* 7 (1897): 1–20, 165–84.

113. Kaerger, *Die Sachsengängerei*, 24.

114. Karl Kaerger, *Die Arbeiterpacht: Ein Mittel zur Lösung der ländlichen Arbeiterfrage* (Berlin: Gergonne, 1893), 39, 201, 207. The sample contracts are on 235–83. See also Kaerger, "Die ländlichen Arbeiterverhältnisse in Nordwestdeutschland," *Die Verhältnisse der Landarbeiter*, vol. 1, *Schriften des Vereins für Socialpolitik*, vol. 53 (Leipzig: Duncker and Humblot, 1892), 1–239. On *Heuerling*, including interest in this form in eastern Germany, see Robert G. Moeller, *German Peasants and Agrarian Politics, 1914–1924: The Rhineland and Westphalia* (Chapel Hill: University of North Carolina Press, 1986).

115. Knapp, "Landarbeiter und innere Kolonisation," 137, 135.

116. Max Weber, *Die Verhältnisse der Landarbeiter im ostelbischen Deutschland*, vol. 3, *Schriften des Vereins für Socialpolitik*, vol. 55 (Leipzig: Duncker and Humblot, 1892), 804.

117. Georg Friedrich Knapp, "Landarbeiter und innere Kolonisation," 138–42.

118. See William I. Thomas, "The Prussian-Polish Situation: An Experiment in Assimilation," *American Journal of Sociology* 19 (1914): 624–39. Thomas does not give footnotes in this article, but was almost surely informed by the Polish sociologist Florian Znaniecki, who was conducting research on Polish nationalism for Thomas at that time. E. Strumpfe, *Polenfrage und Ansiedelungskommission* (Berlin: Dietrich Reimer, 1902) also discusses Polish parcelization banks.

119. See Wietusch, Police Headquarters, Posen, report of 21 November 1912, GStA PK, I. HA Rep. 87ZB, vol. 9, Nr. 181, Bl. 266–69, and President of the Province of Posen to the Minister of Agriculture, 31 December 1912, GStA PK, I. HA Rep. 87ZB, Nr. 181, Bl. 272–73.

120. *Lech* (Gniezno), 4 May 1906, quoted in Thomas, "The Prussian-Polish Situation," 636–37.

121. See Thomas, "The Prussian-Polish Situation," 639.

122. *Gazeta Świąteczna* (1892), excerpted and translated in William I. Thomas and Florian Znaniecki, *The Polish Peasant in Europe and America: Monograph*

of an Immigrant Group, vol. 4, *Disorganization and Reorganization in Poland* (Boston: Gordon Badger, 1920), 50–51.

123. Lezius, *Heimatsgebiete der Sachsengänger*, 68.

124. *Gazeta Świąteczna* (1903), excerpted and translated in Thomas and Znaniecki, *The Polish Peasant* 4:52–54.

125. *Gazeta Świąteczna* (1892).

126. *Gazeta Świąteczna* (1907), excerpted and translated in Thomas and Znaniecki, *The Polish Peasant* 4:33–34.

127. For a short story showing the ruin of a young female Sachsengänger, see Wilhelm von Polenz (1861–1903), "Sachsengänger," in *Sachsengänger: Erzählungen* (Berlin: Rütten and Loening, 1991), 152–65.

128. *Gazeta Świąteczna* (1903).

129. August Bebel, *Die Frau und der Sozialismus*, 10th ed. (1879; Stuttgart: Dietz, 1891).

130. This point is made forcefully in Anne Lopes and Gary Roth, *Men's Feminism: August Bebel and the German Socialist Movement* (Amherst, NY: Humanity Books, 2000).

131. Jean H. Quataert, *Reluctant Feminists in German Social Democracy, 1885–1917* (Princeton: Princeton University Press, 1979). Quataert offers an excellent and balanced account of socialist feminism in Germany. See also Richard J. Evans, "An Opposing Woman," ch. 1, in *Comrades and Sisters: Feminism, Socialism, and Pacifism in Europe, 1870–1945* (Brighton, Sussex: Wheatsheaf Books, 1987), 15–36.

132. Clara Zetkin, *Die Arbeiterinnen- und Frauenfrage der Gegenwart* (Berlin: Berliner Volks-Tribüne, 1889).

133. See Vernon L. Lidtke, "Invitation from the Right," ch. 6, in *The Outlawed Party: Social Democracy in Germany, 1878–1890* (Princeton: Princeton University Press, 1966), 155–75. For the longer history of social democracy and communism in Germany, see Eric D. Weitz, *Creating German Communism, 1890–1990: From Popular Protests to Socialist State* (Princeton: Princeton University Press, 1997).

134. *Sozialdemokrat*, 5 January 1882, cited in Horst Bartel, "Zur Politik und zum Kampf der deutschen Sozialdemokratie gegen die Bismarcksche Sozialreformpolitik und gegen den Rechtsopportunismus in den Jahren 1881/1884," *Zeitschrift für Geschichtswissenschaft* 5 (1957): 1100–1101.

135. *Sozialdemokrat*, 20 December 1883, cited in Bartel, "Zur Politik und zum Kampf der deutschen Sozialdemokratie," 1103–4.

136. See Karl Kautsky, *Die Agrarfrage: Eine Uebersicht über die Tendenzen der modernen Landwirtschaft und die Agrarpolitik der Sozialdemokratie*, 2nd ed. (1899; Stuttgart: J.H.W. Dietz, 1902), 325–28.

137. On rural agitation, see Saul, "Der Kampf um das Landproletariat" and Athar Hussain and Keith Tribe, "*Landagitation*," ch. 3 in *German Social Democracy and the Peasantry 1890–1907*, vol. 1 of *Marxism and the Agrarian Question* (Highlands, NJ: Humanities Press, 1981), 72–101.

138. Friedrich Engels, "Die Bauernfrage in Frankreich und Deutschland" (1894–95), in Karl Marx and Friedrich Engels, *Werke*, vol. 22 (Berlin: Dietz, 1972), 503.

139. V. I. Lenin, review of Karl Kautsky, *Die Agrarfrage* (Stuttgart, 1899), in *Collected Works*, 45 vols. (Moscow: Progress Publishers, 1960–70), 4:94–99.

140. Kautsky, *Agrarfrage*, 162–63, 165, 110, 185, 104–6, 316–17, 320.

141. Ibid., 192, 371.

142. Ibid., 364, 448–51.

143. Max Sering, who composed the response of the *Verein für Sozialpolitik* to Kautsky's text, evidently missed Kautsky's critique of the patriarchal household, focusing instead on the economics of small and medium sized farms. See Sering, "Die Agrarfrage und der Sozialismus."

144. For an excellent account of the role of Max Weber's family in shaping his ideas and career, see Guenther Roth, *Max Webers Deutsch-englische Familiengeschichte 1800–1950: Mit Briefen und Dokumenten* (Tübingen: Mohr Siebeck, 2001). On Max Weber's father and the Settlement Commission, see 441–43.

145. "Vertrauliche Besprechung des königlichen Staatsministeriums," 10 January 1886.

146. Marianne Weber, *Max Weber: A Biography*, Harry Zohn, trans. (1926; New York: John Wiley and Sons, 1975), 146–47. For an illuminating interpretation of Max Weber's work on agricultural labor, see Keith Tribe, "Prussian Agriculture-German Politics: Max Weber 1892–97," *Economy and Society* 12 (1983): 181–226.

147. C. Vann Woodward, *Origins of the New South* and *The Strange Career of Jim Crow*.

148. For an excellent study of anti-immigrant movements in the United States, see John Higham, *Strangers in the Land: Patterns of American Nativism, 1860–1925*, 2nd ed. (New Brunswick, NJ: Rutgers University Press, 1988).

149. Since the Second World War, scholars have almost universally ignored Weber's racism. Joachim Radkau's otherwise superb biography of Max Weber discusses Weber's anti-Polish racism but dismisses it as a feature of the Wilhelmine context rather than one of Weber's fundamental intellectual and political commitments. See Joachim Radkau, *Max Weber: Die Leidenschaft des Denkens* (Munich: Hanser, 2005), 131–43. Marianne Weber, in her biography, *Max Weber*, is quite explicit and unapologetic about her late husband's racism. She has been excoriated, unjustly in my view, especially by those who prefer the liberal, "value-free" social scientist of popular imagination to the racist-nationalist Weber that his widow presents. Indeed, Marianne Weber's biography of her husband led one of Max Weber's former colleagues to remark in 1926 that he "now had a better understanding for the Indian institution of widow burning." This remark is cited in Roth, *Max Webers Deutsch-englische Familiengeschichte*, 601–2. For exceptional accounts that acknowledge the importance of Weber's racism, or at least the centrality of anti-Polish politics to his thought, see Gary A. Abraham, "Max Weber: Modernist Anti-Pluralism and the Polish Question," *New German Critique* 53 (1991): 33–66; Bruch, *Gelehrtenpolitik*, 222–29; Hajime Konno, *Max Weber und die Polnische Frage (1892–1920): Eine Betrachtung zum Liberalen Nationalismus im Wilhelminischen Deutschland* (Baden-Baden: Nomos, 2004); and Wolfgang J. Mommsen, *Max Weber and German Politics, 1890–1920*, Michael S. Steinberg, trans. (1959; Chicago: University of Chicago Press, 1984).

150. Max Weber, "Zur Gründung einer National-Sozialen Partei" (1896), in Winckelmann, ed., *Gesammelte Politische Schriften*, 28–29.

151. Max Weber to the Pan-German League, 22 April 1899, cited in Marianne Weber, *Max Weber*, 224–25.

152. Quoted in Marianne Weber, *Max Weber*, 631–32.

153. Max Weber, "Entwicklungstendenz in der Lage der ostelbischen Landarbeiter" (1894), in *Gesammelte Aufsätze zur Sozial- und Wirtschaftsgeschichte* (Tübingen: J.C.B. Mohr, 1924), 492–93. Translated: Max Weber, "Developmental Tendencies in the Situation of East Elbian Rural Labourers," *Economy and Society* 8 (1979): 177–205.

154. Max Weber, "Die ländliche Arbeitsverfassung" (1893), in *Gesammelte Aufsätze zur Sozial- und Wirtschaftsgeschichte*, 457, 448.

155. Max Weber, *Die Verhältnisse der Landarbeiter im ostelbischen Deutschland*, 793, 795, 803–4.

156. Max Weber, "Die ländliche Arbeitsverfassung" (1893), 456–57.

157. Sering claims to disagree with Weber in this assertion, although the two men make nearly identical arguments. Max Sering, *Die Innere Kolonisation in östlichen Deutschland, Schriften des Vereins für Socialpolitik*, vol. 56 (Leipzig: Dunckerd and Humblot, 1893), 13, 14–16, 280.

158. Knapp, "Landarbeiter und innere Kolonisation," 125.

159. Max Weber, "Der Nationalstaat und die Volkswirtschaftspolitik," 2, 8, 10, 14, 12. For English translations, see "The Nation State and Economic Policy" (1895), in Weber, *Political Writings*, Peter Lassman and Ronald Speirs, eds. (Cambridge: Cambridge University Press, 1994), 1–28, and "The National State and Economic Policy," in *Reading Weber* (London: Routledge, 1989), 188–209.

160. Especially helpful for my account has been Barrington S. Edwards, "W.E.B. Du Bois, Empirical Social Research, and the Challenge to Race, 1868–1910" (Ph.D. diss., Harvard, 2001), 111–46 and Axel R. Schäfer, "W.E.B. Du Bois, German Social Thought, and the Racial Divide in American Progressivism, 1892–1909." See also Kenneth Barkin, "'Berlin Days,' 1892–1894: W.E.B. Du Bois and German Political Economy," *Boundary 2* 27, no. 3 (2000): 79–101; Barkin, "Germany on His Mind—'Das Neue Vaterland.'" *Journal of African American History* 91 (2006): 444–49; "W.E.B. Du Bois and the Kaiserreich," *Central European History* 31 (1998): 155–96; and "W.E.B. Du Bois's Love Affair with Imperial Germany," *German Studies* 28 (2005): 284–302; Thomas D. Boston, "W.E.B. Du Bois and the Historical School of Economics," *The American Economic Review* 81 (1991): 303–6; Francis L. Broderick, "The Academic Training of W.E.B. Du Bois," *Journal of Negro Education* 27 (1958): 10–16; Francis L. Broderick, "German Influence on the Scholarship of W.E.B. Du Bois," *The Phylon Quarterly* 19 (1958): 367–71; Barrington S. Edwards, "W.E.B. Du Bois between Worlds: Berlin, Empirical Social Research, and the Race Question," *Du Bois Review* 3 (2006): 395–424; and Sieglinde Lemke, "Berlin and Boundaries: sollen versus geschehen," *Boundary 2* 27, no. 3 (2000): 45–78.

161. W.E.B. Du Bois to President D. C. Gilman, Slater Fund, 28 October 1892, in Herbert Aptheker, ed., *The Correspondence of W.E.B. Du Bois*, 3 vols. (Amherst: University of Massachusetts Press, 1973), 1:20–21.

162. W.E.B. Du Bois to John F. Slater Fund, 10 March 1893, in Aptheker, ed., *The Correspondence of W.E.B. Du Bois*, 1:23–24.

163. W.E.B. Du Bois to John F. Slater Fund, 10 March 1893.

164. *Verhandlungen der am 20. und 21. März 1893 in Berlin abgehaltenen General Versammlung des Vereins für Socialpolitik über die ländliche Arbeiterfrage und über die Bodenbesitzverteilung und die Sicherung des Kleingrundbesitzes*, vol. 58, *Schriften des Vereins für Socialpolitik* (Leipzig: Duncker and Humblot, 1893), 1.

165. Du Bois, *Autobiography*, 102. W.E.B. Du Bois, *Dusk of Dawn: An Essay Toward an Autobiography of a Race Concept* (1940; New Brunswick, NJ: Transaction Publishers, 1983), 47.

166. Max Weber, "Die ländliche Arbeitsverfassung," 457.

167. Nichtweiss, *Die Ausländischen Saisonarbeiter*, 38–40; Herbert, *A History of Foreign Labor in Germany, 1880–1980*, 18.

168. Juhani Koponen, *Development for Exploitation: German Colonial Policies in Mainland Tanzania, 1884–1914* (Helsinki: Tiedekirja, 1994), 336–37.

169. Karl Kaerger, *Tangaland und die Kolonisation Deutsch-Ostafrikas: Thatsachen und Vorschläge* (Berlin: Herman Walther, 1892), 73. See also Karl Kaerger, *Die künstliche Bewässerung in den wärmeren Erdstrichen und ihre Anwendbarkeit in Deutsch-Ostafrika* (Berlin, Gergonne and cie., 1893). Two years after this meeting, in 1895, the German embassy in Buenos Aires, Argentina, hired Kaerger as agricultural attaché, making him the counterpart of Baron von Herman in Washington, who recruited Booker T. Washington for the Togo expedition. His reports from South America are collected in Karl Kaerger, *Landwirtschaft und Kolonisation im Spanischen Amerika*, 2 vols. (Leipzig: Duncker and Humboldt, 1901).

170. *Verhandlungen der am 20. und 21. März 1893 in Berlin abgehaltenen General Versammlung des Vereins für Socialpolitik*, 98–99.

171. *Verhandlungen der am 20. und 21. März 1893 in Berlin abgehaltenen General Versammlung des Vereins für Socialpolitik*, 99–100.

172. On Anton Sombart and the *Verein für Sozialpolitik*, see Lenger, *Werner Sombart*, 27–30 and passim; and Arthur Mitzman, *Sociology and Estrangement: Three Sociologists of Imperial Germany* (New Brunswick, NJ: Transaction, 1987), 140–42.

173. *Verhandlungen der am 20. und 21. März 1893 in Berlin abgehaltenen General Versammlung des Vereins für Socialpolitik*, 127.

174. W.E.B. Du Bois to John F. Slater Fund, 6 December 1893, in Aptheker, ed., *The Correspondence of W.E.B. Du Bois* 1:26.

175. Adolph Wagner, 28 March 1894, translated by W.E.B. Du Bois, in Aptheker, ed., *The Correspondence of W.E.B. Du Bois* 1:27–28.

176. Adolph Wagner, *Grundlegung der politischen Oekonomie*, 3rd ed., 2 vols. (Leipzig: C. F. Winter, 1894), 2:66.

177. Du Bois, *Autobiography*, 110. Du Bois notes that this classmate, Stanislaus Estreicher, was executed by the Germans during the Second World War.

178. Du Bois, *Suppression of the African Slave-Trade*, vi, 194, 70, 197.

179. Du Bois, *Autobiography*, 101–2.

180. This manuscript was first published as "The Socialism of German Social-ists," *Central European History* 31 (1998): 189–96.

181. "The Present Condition of German Politics," c. 1893, Du Bois Papers, Reel 87. This essay was published in *Central European History* 31 (1998): 171–87.

182. Du Bois, *Autobiography*, 102.

183. W.E.B. Du Bois, *The Conservation of Races*, 7, 9–10. Arnold Rampersad also suggests that Du Bois modeled his concept of folk, for *Souls of Black Folk*, on the German conception of *Volk*. See Rampersad, *The Art and Imagination of W.E.B. Du Bois* (Cambridge: Harvard University Press, 1976), 74.

184. Alexander Walters, Henry B. Brown, H. Sylvester Williams, W.E.B. Du Bois, "To the Nations of the World" (1900), in W.E.B. Du Bois, *An ABC of Color*.

185. Gustav Schmoller *Grundriß der allgemeinen Volkswirtschaftslehre*, 2 vols. (Leipzig: Duncker and Humblot, 1900), 1:38–39, 140–45.

186. Schmoller *Grundriß der allgemeinen Volkswirtschaftslehre* 1:158, 149–50.

CHAPTER 3
ALABAMA IN AFRICA: TUSKEGEE AND THE
COLONIAL DECIVILIZING MISSION IN TOGO

1. See Mahmood Mamdani, *Citizen and Subject: Contemporary Africa and the Legacy of Late Colonialism* (Princeton: Princeton University Press, 1996). For an important consideration of the construction of ethnicity that includes a case study of the Ewe, see Paul Nugent, "Putting the History Back into Ethnicity: Enslave-ment, Religion, and Cultural Brokerage in the Construction of Mandinka/Jola and Ewe/Agotime Identities in West Africa, c. 1650–1930," *Comparative Studies in Society and History* 50 (2008): 920–48.

2. On the role of the Asante Empire in defining the Togo-Ghana border, see Paul Nugent's superb *Smugglers, Secessionists and Loyal Citizens on the Ghana-Togo Frontier: The Lie of the Borderlands since 1914* (Oxford: James Currey, 2002), and Marion Johnson, "Ashante East of the Volta," *Transactions of the Historical Society of Ghana* 8 (1965): 33–39. The best general histories of Togo are the volumes written by the Department of History at the University of Lomé, Togo, under the direction of Nicoué Lodjou Gayibor, ed., *Histoire des Togolais des Origines à 1884* (Lomé: Université du Benin, 1997), and *Le Togo Sous Domi-nation Coloniale (1884–1960)* (Lomé: Université du Benin, 1997). See also the essays collected in François de Medeiros, ed., *Peuples du Golfe du Bénin: Aja-Ewe* (Paris: Éditions Karthala, 1984). The most complete account of German co-lonialism in Togo is the dissertation by Pierre Ali Napo, "Le Togo à l'epoche allemande (1884–1914)," 5 vols. (Ph.D. diss., Sorbonne, 1995). For one-volume histories of Togo, see Ralph Erbar, *Ein Platz an der Sonne? Die Verwaltungs- und Wirtschaftsgeschichte der deutschen Kolonie Togo, 1884–1914* (Stuttgart: Franz Steiner, 1991), Knoll, *Togo under Imperial Germany 1884–1914*, and Peter Se-bald, *Togo 1884–1914: Eine Geschichte der deutschen "Musterkolonie" auf der Grundlage amtlicher Quellen* (Berlin: Akademie-Verlag, 1988). Dennis Laumann

has conducted fascinating research on both German and Ewe historical memory of German colonialism. See his "A Historiography of German Togoland, or the Rise and Fall of a 'Model Colony,' " *History in Africa* 30 (2003): 195–211, and "Remembering and Forgetting the German Occupation of the Central Volta Region of Ghana" (Ph.D. diss., University of California, Los Angeles, 1999).

3. See Robin Law, *The Slave Coast of West Africa, 1550–1750* (Oxford: Oxford University Press, 1991). For figures on the slave trade, see especially Patrick Manning, "The Slave Trade in the Bight of Benin, 1640–1890," in Henry A. Gemery and Jan S. Hogendorn, eds., *The Uncommon Market: Essays in the Economic History of the Atlantic Slave Trade* (New York: Academic Press, 1979), 107–41. See also Philip D. Curtain, *The Atlantic Slave Trade: A Census* (Madison: University of Wisconsin Press, 1969); Herbert S. Klein, *The Atlantic Slave Trade* (Cambridge; Cambridge University Press, 1999); Patrick Manning, *Slavery and African Life: Occidental, Oriental, and African Slave Trades* (Cambridge: Cambridge University Press, 1990); and Paul E. Lovejoy, *Transformations in Slavery: A History of Slavery in Africa*, 2nd ed. (Cambridge: Cambridge University Press, 2000).

4. Information on the destinations of enslaved Africans from the Bight of Benin comes from David Eltis, Stephen D. Behrendt, David Richardson, and Herbert S. Klein, *The Trans-Atlantic Slave Trade: A Database on CD-ROM* (Cambridge: Cambridge University Press, 1999).

5. On the Haitian uprising, including the role of Vodou, see Laurent Dubois, *Avengers of the New World: The Story of the Haitian Revolution* (Cambridge: Harvard University Press, 2004).

6. Robin Law and Kristin Mann, "West Africa in the Atlantic Community: The Case of the Slave Coast," *William and Mary Quarterly*, 3rd Ser. 56, No. 2, African and American Atlantic Worlds (1999): 307–34. Afro-Brazilian families formed an elite in Togo, and included the Lawsons and the Olympios of Anecho and later Lome. See Alcione M. Amos, "Afro-Brazilians in Togo: The Case of the Olympio Family, 1882–1945," *Cahiers d'études africaines* 162 (2001). Online at: http://etudesafricaines.revues.org/document88.html.

7. Manning, *Slavery and African Life*, 66–69.

8. Michel Verdon rightly cautions against generalizing about the Ewe, which, in fact, he shows, differ significantly across three major geographical areas. See Michel Verdon, *The Abutia Ewe of West Africa: A Chiefdom that Never Was* (Berlin: Mouton, 1983). The best contemporary accounts of Ewe political economy from the German colonial period are Jakob Spieth, *Die Ewe-Stämme: Material zur Kunde des Ewe-Volkes in Deutsch-Togo* (Berlin: Dietrich Reimer, 1906), and Diedrich Westermann, *Die Glidyi-Ewe in Togo: Züge aus ihrem Gesellschaftsleben* (Berlin: Walter de Gruyter, 1935). Spieth was a missionary whose observations were made primarily in Ho, Matse, and Taviewe. Westerman, an instructor at the Seminar for Oriental Languages in Berlin, based his work on accounts he recorded in Berlin in the 1920s and 1930s from Bonifatius Foli from Glidyi, Togo. Unless otherwise noted, information on the Togolese economy comes from these two sources. On the Togolese economy, see also Peter Buhler, "The Volta Region of Ghana: Economic Change in Togoland, 1850–1914" (Ph.D. diss., University of California, San Diego, 1975) and M.B.K. Darkoh, "Togoland

under the Germans," 2 Parts, *Nigerian Geographical Journal* 10 (1967): 107–22 and 11 (1968): 153–68.

9. For a contemporary observation of these divided households, see Th. Schlegel, Kpatove station, "Warum ehren die Afrikaner ihre Frauen nicht und essen nicht mit ihnen zusammen?" n.d., Norddeutsche Missionsgesellschaft, Staatsarchiv Bremen, 7,1025 (hereafter NDM), 31/4.

10. Spieth, *Die Ewe-Stämme*, 209.

11. Heinrich Klose, *Togo unter deutscher Flagge* (Berlin: Dietrich Reimer, 1899), 250–55.

12. Westermann, *Die Glidyi-Ewe*, 77.

13. Spieth, *Die Ewe-Stämme*, 233.

14. Anna Knüsli, *Afrikanisches Frauenleben wie ich es in Togo gesehen habe* (Bremen: Norddeutschen Missions-Gesellschaft, 1907), 13. On Knüsli, see the obituary in *Monats-Blatt der Norddeutschen Missions-Gesellschaft* (hereafter MNDM) 69 (1908): 19–20.

15. Heinrich Seidel, "Pfandwesen und Schuldhaft in Togo: Nach den Erhebungen im Missionsbezirke Amedschovhe dargestellt," *Globus* 79 (1901): 309–13. Seidel based his account on information that an African mission teacher gathered at Amedschovhe. Carl Spiess also confirms the practice in "Einiges aus den Sitten und Gebräuchen der Evhe-Neger in Togo," *Deutsche Geographische Blätter* 29 (1906): 33–36. Beverly Grier discusses a similar situation among the Akan in "Pawns, Porters, and Petty Traders: Women in the Transition to Cash Crop Agriculture in Colonial Ghana," *Signs* 17 (1992): 304–28.

16. Donna J. E. Maier, "Slave Labor and Wage Labor in German Togo, 1885–1914," Arthur J. Knoll and Lewis H. Gann, eds., *Germans in the Tropics: Essays in German Colonial History* (New York: Greenwood, 1987), 76.

17. See the outstanding history of the West African palm oil trade, Martin Lynn, *Commerce and Economic Change in West Africa: The Palm Oil Trade in the Nineteenth Century* (Cambridge: Cambridge University Press, 1997).

18. J. M. Sarbah, "The Oil-Palm and Its Uses," *Journal of the Royal African Society* 8 (1909): 232–50. Sarbah was an important African merchant from Gold Coast.

19. Law and Mann, "West Africa in the Atlantic Community."

20. Lynn, *Commerce and Economic Change in West Africa*.

21. "Germany and the Palm Kernel Trade," *Journal of the Royal African Society* 14 (1915): 193–98.

22. A. H. Milbourne, "Palm Kernels from West Africa: Movement to Establish the Industry in Great Britain," *Journal of the Royal African Society* 15 (1916): 133–44.

23. Anthony G. Hopkins, *An Economic History of West Africa* (New York: Columbia University Press, 1973), 130.

24. Leonhard Harding, "Hamburg's West Africa Trade in the Nineteenth Century," in Gerhard Liesegang, H. Pasch, and Adam Jones, eds., *Figuring African Trade* (Berlin: Dietrich Reimer, 1986), 363–91.

25. An important early account of the Togo factories is Paul Heichen, "Togo," *Afrika Hand-Lexikon*, 3 vols. (Leipzig: Gressner and Schramm, 1885), 3:1270–

75. See also W. A. Crabtree, "Togoland," *Journal of the Royal African Society* 14 (1915): 168–84, here 171.

26. Westermann, *Die Glidyi-Ewe*, 97–99.

27. Klose, *Togo*, 332–33.

28. Westermann, *Die Glidyi-Ewe*, 81–82.

29. Edwidge Edorh portrays the lives of these wealthy female merchants in his novel *La Fille de Nana-Benz* (Lomé: Éditions Akpagnon, 1996).

30. Hugo Zöller, *Das Togoland und die Sklavenküste* (Berlin: W. Spemann, 1885), 207–8. Zöller confirms much of the account given in Heichen, "Togo."

31. See Ferdinand Goldberg, in Anecho, Togo, to the German Foreign Office, 1 August 1890 (copy), TNA FA 1–332, Bl. 21–34, and "Der Baumwollbau in Togo, seine bisheringe Entwicklung und sein jetziger Stand," *Deutsches Kolonialblatt* 22 (1911): 229–33, 282–87, here 229.

32. Paul Richards, "Ecological Change and the Politics of African Land Use," *African Studies Review* 26 (1983): 1–72, here 27.

33. Interplanting was widely reported by German observers. The details reported here come from Ferdinand Goldberg to the German Foreign Office, 1 August 1890.

34. For descriptions of Togolese interplanting, see "Bericht über die Ackerbauschule Nuatjä für das Berichtsjahr 1908/09," BArch R1001/6543; Pape to the Government of Togo, 19 August 1909, TNA FA 1–388, 72–73; and "Organisation des landwirtschaftlichen Versuchswesens in Togo," Berlin, 19 December 1910, BArch R1001/8224, Bl. 69–83.

35. On Togolese picking and spinning, see anon., report about cotton growing, n.d. (circa. 1904), TNA FA 1–89, Bl. 8–57; Heinrich Klose, "Industrie und Gewerbe in Togo" *Globus* 85 (1904): 69–73, 89–93; Spieth, *Die Ewe-Stämme*, 405–6; and Meg Gehrts, *A Camera Actress in the Wilds of Togoland* (London: Seeley, Service and Co., 1915), 86–95. Gehrts's account refers to the ethnographic films made by Hans Shomburgk while he was shooting thrillers in Togo in which Gehrts played the "white goddess."

36. See Spieth, *Die Ewe-Stämme*, 404–6.

37. The complete process of cotton growing, spinning, and weaving, with the exception of dying, was filmed by Hans Schmoburgk in Togo in 1913–14 for the short "Baumwoll-Industrie im Deutschen Sudan," now available as part of the film *In the German Sudan*, VHS (1912–14; Göttingen: IWF, 1977).

38. Hans Schomburgk filmed Togolese using this loom for "Baumwoll-Industrie im Deutschen Sudan."

39. Klose, "Industrie und Gewerbe in Togo," 72.

40. Eugen von Zimmerer, Imperial Commissioner of Togo, "Die Baumwollenkultur im Schutzgebiete," 9 November [1889], TNA FA 1–332, Bl. 3–6.

41. See G. Daueble, Praefect of the North German Mission in Togo, to Graef, acting governor of Togo, 11 March 1903, copy, BArch R1001/4079, Bl. 184–86, and Heichen, "Togo," 1274.

42. For a European missionary endorsing the cultural value of educating students to white-collar work, see Gottlob Härtter, "Leben und Wirken zweier Evhe-Lehrer," MNDM, 3rd series, 13 (1901): 83–86. For a similar view expressed by

an African mission teacher, see G. Chr. Mensa, "Unsere Stations-Schulen, ihr Lehr-gang und Erfolg," Akpafu, 7 October 1909, NDM 31/3.

43. Hans Gruner, Misahöhe, to the Government of Togo, 11 March 1907, TNA FA 1–363, 238–40.

44. "Schul- und Gehilfenordnung. 1913," NDM 39/2.

45. "Die katholische Missionen," Nr. 11 (August 1913), typewritten copy, Ghana Archive of the Basel Mission, Microfilm Edition (East Ardsley, UK: EP Microform Ltd., 1978), D-1, vol. 104.

46. "Lehrplan der Mädchenschule," n.d., NDM 39/1.

47. On the Hausa, see Mahdi Adamu, *The Hausa Factor in West African His-tory* (Zaria, Nigeria: Ahmadu Bello University Press, 1978). On the Hausa in Togo, see Klose, *Togo*, esp. 35–36, 216, 328–29.

48. Klose, *Togo*, 328–29.

49. In 1888, Jesco von Puttkamer, future head of the government of Togo, noted that the merchant clerks in the coastal cities chose to educate their children at the Wesleyan mission because they were "convinced of the value in business of a thorough knowledge of English." Puttkamer, Anecho, Togo, to Bismarck, 10 February 1888 (copy), BArch R1001/4076, Bl. 12–16. Based in Lagos, the Wesleyans had run a boys school in Anecho (then known as Little Popo) off and on since 1850. In 1890 they opened a girls' school in the city and also ran smaller schools in Gliji and Porto Seguro. Karl Ulbrich, District Superintendent of Anecho, to Gleim, acting head of the German Government of Togo, 28 May 1897 (copy), BArch R1001/4079, Bl. 44–46; "Die katholische und wesleyanisch-methodistische Mission in Deutsch-Togo," MNDM, 3rd series, 13 (1901): 41–42.

50. The best account of the Catholic Church in Togo is by a member of the Society of the Divine Word, Karl Müller, *Geschichte der katholischen Kirche in Togo* (Kaldenkirchen: Steyler Verlagsbuchhandlung, 1958). The greater numbers of Catholic students is also attested to by other sources. At this time the Catholics in Togo had five stations, eleven parishes, twenty regular schools, and a trade school. See "Die katholische und wesleyanisch-methodistische Mission in Deutsch-Togo." By 1911 the Catholic lead over the North German Mission had shrunk slightly, but remained at more than 7,000 Catholic students to the North Germans' 5,500. On English as the language of instruction for Catholics in Togo, see Hermann auf der Heide, *Die Missionsgesellschaft von Steyl: Ein Bild der ersten 25 Jahre ihres Bestehens* (Kaldenkirchen: Missionsdruckerei in Steyl, 1900), 404. By the end of the German colonial period, Catholics apparently also employed Ewe instructors, despite the unpopularity of instruction in this language, in part to make it more difficult for their students to leave Togo to seek work in Gold Coast or German Cameroon. See Müller, *Geschichte der katholischen Kirche in Togo*, 213–14.

51. See the figures sent by Karl Ulbrich, district superintendent of Anecho, to Gleim, acting head of the German government of Togo, 28 May 1897; Däuble, Keta, to Gleim, 15 June 1897, copy; Joh. Müller, Akropong, "Bericht über den Stand der Basler Missionsschulen im deutschen Togo-Gebiet, nach dem Stand vom 1. Januar 1897 bzw. Antworten auf Fragen, die vom Hohen Kais. Auswärtigen Amte gestellt wurden," 21 June 1897 (copy); Praefect J.H. Bücking to the Govern-

ment of Togo, 20 April 1903, copy, BArch R1001/4079, Bl. 44–46, 47–49, 38–43, 180–81.

52. On Togolese sending their children to Gold Coast for English education, see G. Rieker to the Government of Togo, 16 March 1903, copy, BArch R1001/4079, Bl. 188–89. On Gold Coast education, see F. Wright (the late inspector of schools, Gold Coast Colony), "The System of Education in the Gold Coast Colony," in Great Britain, Board of Education, *Educational Systems of the Chief Crown Colonies and Possessions of the British Empire, Including Reports on the Training of Native Races*, 3 vols., volumes 12–14 of *Special Reports on Educational Subjects* (London: Her Majesty's Stationery Office, 1905), 2:1–30.

53. See Philip Foster, *Education and Social Change in Ghana* (Chicago: University of Chicago Press, 1965). After the end of British rule in Ghana, C. K. Graham of University of Science and Technology, Kumasi, Ghana, criticized the inattention given to industrial and agricultural education during the colonial period in his *The History of Education in Ghana From the Earliest Times to the Declaration of Independence* (London: Frank Cass, 1971). British educational consultant Eric Ashby similarly lamented the emphasis given to "English, clerky education, developed by the missionaries," in *Universities: British, Indian, Africa: A Study in the Ecology of Higher Education*, with Mary Anderson (Cambridge: Harvard University Press, 1966), 153. Carol Summers shows how industrial education could also serve resistance against a missionary educational program that was by no means politically neutral. She draws special attention to the different politics of missionary education for women and for men, who risked being labeled "mission boys." See Summers, *Colonial Lessons: Africans' Education in Southern Rhodesia, 1918–1940* (Portsmouth, NH: Heinemann, 2002). T. O. Beidelman makes a related point about the fraught politics of the mission in *Colonial Evangelism: A Socio-Historical Study of an East African Mission at the Grassroots* (Bloomington: Indiana University Press, 1982). Gertrude Mianda shows a contrasting gendered politics of education in the Belgian Congo, where men sought to keep French a male preserve and successfully excluded women from Francophone literary culture. See "Colonialism, Education, and Gender Relations in the Belgian Congo: The Évolué Case," in Jean Allman, Susan Geiger and Nakanyike Musisi, eds., *Women in African Colonial Histories* (Bloomington: Indiana University Press, 2002), 144–63.

54. Stephanie Newell demonstrates that literary education did not merely function as vocational education for clerks, but also allowed for the emergence of reading groups that discussed English classics, which they then sought to apply to everyday moral problems. See Stephanie Newell, *Literary Culture in Colonial Ghana: "How to Play the Game of Life"* (Bloomington: Indiana University Press, 2002), esp. 1–63. On the intellectual culture of Gold Coast, see Robert W. July, *Origins of Modern African Thought: Its Development in West Africa during the Nineteenth and Twentieth Centuries* (New York: Frederick A. Praeger, 1967).

55. On the ambivalent position of cosmopolitan Africans in relation to the colonial state, see Roger Gocking, *Facing Two Ways: Ghana's Coastal Communities Under Colonial Rule* (Lanham, MD: University Press of America, 1999), and the essays collected in Benjamin N. Lawrance, Emily Lynn Osborn, and Rich-

ard L. Roberts, eds., *Intermediaries, Interpreters, and Clerks: African Employees in the Making of Colonial Africa* (Madison: University of Wisconsin Press, 2006).

56. "Our English- and German-speaking assistants," one German missionary noted, "have followed European newspapers for a long time, and native merchants on the coast read expensive English newspapers." "Nutifafa na mì: Das erste Eweblatt," MNDM, 3rd series, 15 (1903): 79–80.

57. "Grievances of Gold Coast Natives," *Gold Coast Chronicle*, 15 March 1901, 3. For a useful bibliography of the Gold Coast press, see K.A.B. Jones-Quartey, "The Gold Coast Press: 1822–c1930, and the Anglo-African Press: 1825–c1930—The Chronologies," *Institute of African Studies Research Review* 4, no. 2 (1968): 30–46. On these papers and the Pan-African political milieu from which they emerged see Geiss, *The Pan-African Movement*, 199–228; July, *Origins of Modern African Thought*, 327–457; and Stein, *The World of Marcus Garvey*, 7–23.

58. A Native of Anecho, "German Atrocities in Togoland," *African Times and Orient Review*, O.S., 2 (Nov–Dec. 1913), 201–3.

59. "Martin Aku aus Lome in Togo," in Diedrich Westermann, *Afrikaner erzählen ihr Leben* (Essen: Essner Verlagsanstalt, 1938), 351–52.

60. Klose, *Togo*, 257, 171. Zine Magubane has suggested that in South Africa blacks and white racists alike appropriated the image of the black dandy from American minstrel shows. Perhaps this was also the case for West Africa, or perhaps the black dandy and white hatred for black dandies were independent parallel inventions arising from similar racist divisions of labor across the Black Atlantic. See Zine Magubane, "What is (African) America to Me? Africans, African Americans, and the Rearticulation of Blackness," ch. 7, in *Bringing the Empire Home: Race, Class, and Gender in Britain and Colonial South Africa* (Chicago: University of Chicago Press, 2004), 153–84.

61. See, for example, Felix von Luschan, *Beiträge zur Völkerkunde der Deutschen Schutzgebiete* (Berlin: Dietrich Reimer, 1897), 21; Heinrich Hartert, "Betrachtungen über Negercharakter," *Deutsche Kolonialzeitung* 24 (1907): 376–77; Governor Theodor Seitz of Cameroon, "Wirtschaftliche und soziale Verhältnisse der Eingeborenen Kameruns," *Koloniale Rundschau* 1 (1909): 321–36; and Hans Gruner (Jena), Denkschrift on Togo, 14 April 1938, BArch R1001/4308, Bl. 186–93.

62. Such an attitude toward African appropriation of European culture was also common and long-lived among British observers. See, for example, Thomas Masterman Winterbottom, *An Account of the Native Africans in the Neighbourhood of Sierra Leone*, 2nd ed., 2 vols. (1803; New York: Barnes and Noble, 1969), and Frederick Lugard, *The Dual Mandate in British Tropical Africa* (Edinburgh: Blackwood, 1922), 79–84.

63. Dritter, *Jahresbericht über die Entwickelung der Schutzgebiete in Afrika und der Südsee im Jahre 1907/08. Teil D: Togo* (Berlin: Ernst Siegfried Mittler und Sohn, 1909), 26–27, BArch R1001/6543.

64. "A Word to the Wise," *Gold Coast Chronicle*, 6 December 1901, 2.

65. Schmoller *Grundriß der allgemeinen Volkswirtschaftslehre*, 149–50.

66. For an excellent account of the hybrid society that emerged from the encounter between the North German Mission and the Ewe, see Birgit Meyer,

Translating the Devil: Religion and Modernity Among the Ewe in Ghana (Trenton, NJ: African World Press, 1999) and Meyer, "Christianity and the Ewe Nation: German Pietist Missionaries, Ewe Converts and the Politics of Culture," *Journal of Religion in Africa* 32 (2002): 167–99. On the North German Mission, see also Hans W. Debrunner, *A Church between Colonial Powers: A Study of the Church in Togo* (London: Lutterworth Press, 1965).

67. Däuble, Keta, to Landeshauptmann Dr. Glaim, Lome, 15 June 1897, copy, BArch R1001/4079, Bl. 47–49; Martin Schlunk, *Das Schulwesen in den deutschen Schutzgebieten* (Hamburg: L. Friederichsen, 1914), 28–30.

68. Puttkamer applauded the North German Mission for offering relatively little instruction in English. Puttkamer, Anecho, to Bismarck, 10 February 1888 (copy), BArch R1001/4076, Bl. 12–16. He would have preferred that the mission offer no English instruction at all, but eliminating the language entirely would have driven many students to one of the competitor schools. See Zahn, Bremen, to Spieth 17 May 1894 (copy), BArch R1001/4078, Bl. 111–16.

69. Jakob Spieth and G. Daueble, Lome, 20 April 1894, to Chancellor Caprivi, BArch R1001/4078, Bl. 126–47. For government opposition to teaching English to Africans see also Imperial Commissioner of Togo to Bismarck, 26 July 1887 (copy), BArch R1001/4076, Bl. 5–7 and Colonial Section of the German Foreign Office, memo, 10 December 1889, BArch R1001/4076, Bl. 66. For the Bremen mission's response, see Zahn, Bremen, to the Colonial Section of the German Foreign Office, 24 September 1891, BArch R1001/4077, B. 25–29.

70. Governor Zech to the Colonial Section of the German Foreign Office, 11 March 1904, BArch R1001/4080, Bl. 8–17.

71. Missionaries agreed, however, to offer twelve hours of German a week and made vague promises of ending English instruction in the future. "Niederschrift über die Verhandlungen betreffend den deutschen Unterricht in den Missionsschulen," Lome, Togo, 15 March 1904, BArch R1001/4080, Bl. 23–33. English instruction continued in the Togo missions even after a 1905 law forbad the teaching of any language but German and the "language of the country" [*Landessprache*]. *Jahresbericht über die Entwickelung der Schutzgebiete in Afrika und der Südsee im Jahre 1906/07. Teil D: Togo* (Berlin: Ernst Siegfried Mittler und Sohn, 1908), 15, BArch R1001/6543.

72. R. Fiess, "Der erste Schulunterricht bei unseren Neger," *Deutsche Kolonialzeitung* 23 (1906): 296–97.

73. "Nutifafa na mì: Das erste Eweblatt," MNDM, 3rd series, 15 (1903): 79–80. On the Catholic newspaper, *Mia Hôlô*, see Benjamin N. Lawrance, *Locality, Mobility, and "Nation": Periurban Colonialism in Togo's Eweland, 1900–1960* (Rochester, NY: University of Rochster Press, 2007), 160–61.

74. As one North German missionary explained in 1891: "The bond of unity is the Ewe language, but only to the extent that the unity of language can be preserved in a *Volk* that is so splintered and that, because of this division, has no literature that would preserve the unity of language." "Das deutsche Schutzgebiet Togo," MNDM, 3rd series, 3 (1891): 39, 48.

75. Gottlob Härtter, "Welcher Dialekt der Evhesprachen verdient zur Schrift- und Verkehrssprache im Evheland (Togo) erhoben zu werden," *Beiträge zur Kolonialpolitik und Kolonialwirtschaft* 3 (1901/02): 342–47.

76. Benjamin N. Lawrance, "Most Obedient Servants: The Politics of Language in German Colonial Togo," *Cahiers d'Études Africaines* 159 (2000). Available online at: http://etudesafricaines.revues.org/document27.html.

77. On the creation of Ewe religion, see especially Meyer, *Translating the Devil*. For contemporary sources, see Jakob Spieth, *Die Religion der Eweer in Süd-Togo* (Göttingen: Vandenhoeck and Ruprecht, 1911), and Heinrich Seidel, "System der Fetischverbote in Togo: Ein Beitrag zur Volkskunde der Evhe," *Globus* 73 (1898): 340–44. See also Herold, "Bericht betreffend die religiöse Anschauungen und Gebräuche der deutschen Ewe-Neger," *Mitteilungen von Forschungsreisenden und Gelehrten aus den deutschen Schutzgebieten* 5 (1892): 141–60. On the concept of the fetish in West African religion and in European thought, see William Pietz, "The Problem of the Fetish, I," *Res* 9 (1985): 5–17; "The Problem of the Fetish, II," *Res* 13 (1987): 23–45; "The Problem of the Fetish, IIIa: Bosman's Guinea and the Enlightenment Theory of Fetishism," Res 16 (1988): 105–23. See also William Pietz, "Fetishism and Materialism: The Limits of Theory in Marx," in Emily Apter and William Pietz, eds., *Fetishism as Cultural Discourse* (Ithaca: Cornell University Press, 1993), 119–51. For a contemporary assessment of this transformation, see A. B. Ellis, *The Ewe-Speaking Peoples of the Slave Coast of West Africa: Their Religion, Manners, Customs, Laws, Languages, Etc.* (1890; Chicago: Benin Press, 1956), 33.

78. Sandra E. Greene, "Notsie Narratives: History, Memory and Meaning in West Africa," *South Atlantic Quarterly* 101 (2002) 1015–41; Greene, *Sacred Sites and the Colonial Encounter* (Bloomington: Indiana University Press, 2002); and Greene, *Gender, Ethnicity, and Social Change on the Upper Slave Coast: A History of the Anlo Ewe* (Portsmouth, NH: Heinemann, 1996).

79. Benjamin N. Lawrance, "Most Obedient Servants: The Politics of Language in German Colonial Togo," and Lawrance, *Locality, Mobility and "Nation."* See also D.E.J. Amenumey, *The Ewe Unification Movement: A Political History* (Accra: Ghana Universities Press, 1989); and Debrunner, *A Church Between Colonial Powers*, 122–42.

80. On the Yewe cult see Greene, *Gender, Ethnicity, and Social Change on the Upper Slave Coast*, 98–99. For contemporary German observations, see Carl Spiess, "Die Landschaft Tove bei Lome in Togo" and "Religionsbegriffe der Evheer in Westafrika," *Mitteilungen des Seminars für Orientalische Sprachen* 6 (1903): 109–27.

81. Louis Althusser's discussion of ideological "interpellation" through such institutions as the school has been helpful for the present discussion, although Althusser perhaps attributes too much efficacy to this process. See Althusser, "Ideology and Ideological State Apparatuses," in *Lenin and Philosophy*, Ben Brewster, trans. (New York: Monthly Review Press, 1971), 127–86. For further discussion of Althusser and identity in the colonial context, see Andrew Zimmerman, "A German Alabama in Africa: The Tuskegee Expedition to German Togo and the Transnational Origins of West African Cotton Growers," and Zimmerman, "What Do You Really Want in German East Africa, *Herr Professor?*"

82. On Tove, see anon., "Erstes Regen in Tove," MNDM, 3rd series, 6 (1894): 98–100; Albert Binder, letter from Tove, 24 June 1893; H. Schröder, Lome, Togo, to A. W. Schreiber, Inspector of Missions, North German Mission, 24 July 1905,

NDM 20/3; Carl Spiess, "Die Landschaft Tove bei Lome in Togo," *Deutsche Geographische Blätter* 25 (1902): 75–79.

83. Curt von François, *Ohne Schuß durch dick und dünn: Erste Erforschung des Togohinterlandes*, Götz von François, ed. (Esch-Waldems: Eigenverlag Dr. Götz von François, 1972), 19.

84. See Mary Gaunt, *Alone in West Africa* (London: T. Werner Laurie, 1912), 255. Klose, *Togo*, 162. See also Anthony G. Hopkins, *An Economic History of West Africa* (New York, Columbia University Press, 1973), ch. 2.

85. Moritz Schanz, *West-Afrika* (Berlin, 1903), 298–99.

86. Hans Gruner, *Vormarsch zum Niger: Die Memoiren des Leiters der Togo-Hinterlandexpedition 1894/95*, Peter Sebald, ed. (Berlin: Edition Ost, 1997).

87. Except where noted, the account of the battle comes from Klose, *Togo*, 160–67.

88. Hans Gruner claimed that he killed thirty people in his report on the battle, 1 April 1895, Nachlaß 250 (Hans Gruner) in Staatsbibliothek, Berlin, Germany (herafter NL Gruner), K. 7, Mappe 34, Bl. 5–7. In a 1981 interview, one of his African soldiers, Fritz Togbe, recalled the battle as particularly fierce with many deaths. See Dadja Halla-Kawa Simtaro, "Le Togo 'Musterkolonie': Souvenir de l'Allemagne dans la Société Togolaise," 2 vols. (Ph.D. diss., Université de Provence, Aix-Marseille I, 1982), 2:601. Simtaro conducted numerous fascinating oral history interviews, transcripts of which he generously provides in the second volume of this dissertation.

89. German colonial officers contributed thousands of body parts—heads, hands, feet, skin, and more—to the collections of the Berlin Anthropological Society. See Zimmerman, *Anthropology and Antihumanism in Imperial Germany* (Chicago: University of Chicago Press, 2001), ch. 7.

90. "Kwittah Terrible Revelations," *Gold Coast Chronicle*, 26 July 1895, 3, sent by F. M. Zahn, Bremen, to the Colonial Section of the German Foreign Office, 8 November 1895, BArch R1001/4307, Bl. 65–66. The article recounts German actions at Tove and the impression that they made in Togo.

91. Marion Johnson found in 1974 that "People still tell in Togo of the smashing of local pottery to create a market for the German imported hardware—and show the broken potsherds to prove it." Marion Johnson, "Cotton Imperialism in West Africa," *African Affairs* 73 (1974): 178–87, here 184.

92. Carl Spiess, "Die Landschaft Tove bei Lome in Togo," *Deutsche Geographische Blätter* 25 (1902): 75–79, here 75, and Klose, *Togo*, 163.

93. James N. Calloway, "Tuskegee Cotton-Planters in Africa," *Outlook* 70 (March 29, 1902): 772–76, here 774.

94. Calloway, "Tuskegee Cotton-Planters in Africa," 775.

95. Gaunt, *Alone in West Africa*, 254–55.

96. In 1897, thanks to this penetration of the hinterland, the German government promoted the highest official of Togo from a *Landeshauptmann* to a governor and, the following year, moved the capital of the colony from the old commercial center, Anecho (then known as Little Popo), to the newer city of Lome. See Schanz, *West-Afrika*, 297–98.

97. Historian Donna E. Maier has found that many groups from whom Togolese elites had formerly captured slaves provided forced labor for Germans on

behalf of their former masters. See Maier, "Slave Labor and Wage Labor in German Togo."

98. See, for example, Otto Warburg, "Zum neuen Jahre," *Der Tropenpflanzer* 6 (1902): 1–10, here 7.

99. Governor Julius von Zech, "Program für eine planmässige Entwicklung des Schutzgebietes innerhalb der nächsten 10 Jahre" sent to the German Colonial Office on 26 May 1907, BArch R1001/4235, Bl. 15–75. The German Colonial Office (*Reichskolonialamt*) replaced the Colonial Section of the Foreign Office (*Kolonalabteilung des Auswärtigen Amtes*) as the highest German colonial office in 1907.

100. Gruner, Misahöhe, to the Government of Togo, 2 April 1909, TNA FA 1–388, 5. For an English observation of the German taxation system, see "An Admirably Managed German Colony: Mr. Birtwistle on Togoland," *African Mail*, 16 April 1909, 273–74.

101. An Anti-Prussian, "The Germans in Togoland: Visit of the German Secretary of State for the Colonies to Togoland," *African Times and Orient Review*, O.S., 2 (Nov.–Dec. 1913), 251.

102. "Every idler or bad worker received a well deserved corporal punishment," recalled Fare Napo, a Togolese veteran of the German military, in a 1980 interview. See Simtaro, "Le Togo 'Musterkolonie' " 2:701–2.

103. KWK, "Baumwoll-Expedition nach Togo" [1900], TNA FA 1–332, Bl. 88–102. The German Foreign Office sent this document to the German government in Togo. Colonial Section of the Foreign Office to the Government of Togo, June 1900, TNA FA 1–332, Bl. 78.

104. For the use of the term "Negro" in German East Africa, see Andrew Zimmerman, " 'What do you really want in German East Africa, *Herr Professor*?' Counterinsurgency and the Science Effect in Colonial Tanzania," *Comparative Studies in Society and History* 48 (2006): 419–61.

105. For a discussion of this colonial literature, see Anton Markmiller, *"Die Erziehung des Negers zur Arbeit": Wie die koloniale Pädagogik afrikanische Gesellschaften in die Abhängigkeit führte* (Berlin: Dietrich Reimer, 1995). See also Fatima El-Tayeb, *Schwarze Deutsche: Der Diskurs um "Rasse" und nationale Identität 1890–1933* (Frankfurt: Campus, 2001).

106. James N. Calloway to KWK, 1 January 1902, in KWK, "Baumwoll-Expedition nach Togo. Bericht 1901," BArch R901/351.

107. Klose, *Togo*, 160.

108. Calloway, Lome, Togo, to KWK, 12 March 1901 (copy), BArch R1001/8221, Bl. 51.

109. John W. Robinson to Booker T. Washington, 26 May 1901, in Harlan, ed., *Booker T. Washington Papers* 6:126–29.

110. Calloway, "Tuskegee Cotton-Planters in Africa," 773.

111. John Robinson, Notsé, to Governor Zech, 17 January 1904, TNA FA 1–332, Bl. 295–301.

112. KWK, "Baumwoll-Expedition nach Togo," (copy), TNA FA 1–332, Bl. 88–102. Sent by Colonial Section of the Foreign Office to the Government of Togo, June 1900, TNA FA 1–332, Bl. 78.

113. The German colonial state even rejected the land claims of a German plantation company in order to preserve Volkskultur. For details on the founding of this company, see "Erster Geschäftsbericht der deutschen Togogesellschaft für die Zeit vom 29. Dezember 1902 bis 30. April 1903," BArch R1001/3642, Bl. 153. On the acquisition of land by the company in the nineteenth century, see Deutsche Togogesellschaft to the Colonial Section of the German Foreign Office, 28 April 1904, BArch R1001/3643, Bl. 15–19. On the opposition of small traders and missionaries to the plantation company, see Stefan Weißflog, "J. K. Vietor und sein Konzept des leistungsfähigen Afrikaners," Werner Ustorf, ed., *Mission im Kontext: Beiträge zur Sozialgeschichte der Norddeutschen Missionsgesellschaft im 19. Jahrhundert* (Bermen: Übersee Museum, 1986), 293–304.

114. Association of West African Merchants, Hamburg, to the Colonial Section of the German Foreign Office, 11 February 1903, BArch R1001/3642, Bl. 93–97. Governor Zech similarly stressed the educative value of smallholding, explaining that small farms also demonstrated improved farming techniques in a way comprehensible to the "Negro," who could not, he maintained, comprehend large-scale plantation agriculture. See Governor Zech to the editors of the *Deutschen Tageszeitung* in Berlin, 26 June 1909, BArch R1001/4308, Bl. 96–104.

115. Baron von Herman, "Plantagen und Eingeborenen-Kulturen in den Kolonien," *Verhandlungen des Deutschen Kolonialkongresses 1902 zu Berlin am 10. und 11. Oktober 1902* (Berlin, Dietrich Reimer, 1902), 507–17. Herman, comments on Emil Stark (Chemnitz), "Die Bedeutung der Baumwolle in der Weltwirtschaft," *Verhandlungen des Deutschen Kolonialkongresses 1902*, 712–27.

116. J. K. Vietor (Bremen), "Die Arbeiterfrage in den deutschen Kolonien," *Verhandlungen des Deutschen Kolonialkongresses 1902*, 526.

117. Schmoller, comments on Herman, "Plantagen und Eingeborenen-Kulturen in den Kolonien," *Verhandlungen des Deutschen Kolonialkongresses 1902*, 515–16.

118. J. K. Vietor, comment on Otto Warburg, "Die Landwirtschaft in den deutschen Kolonien," *Verhandlungen des Deutschen Kolonialkongresses 1905 zu Berlin am 5. 6. und 7. Oktober 1905* (Berlin: Dietrich Reimer, 1906), 603.

119. Otto Warburg, "Einführung der Pflugkultur in den deutschen Kolonien," *Verhandlungen des Kolonial-Wirtschaftlichen Komitees* (1906): 4–9, here 7.

120. Dr. Gerhard, "Charakterzüge des amerikanischen Negers," 2 parts, *Deutsche Kolonialzeitung* 21 (1904): 257–59, 456–57. See also Alexander Lion, *Die Kulturfähigkeit des Negers und die Erziehungsaufgaben der Kulturnationen* (Berlin: Wilhelm Süsserott, 1908). Others argued that this supposed tendency to imitate demonstrated the inherent inferiority of blacks. See Karl Oetker, *Die Neger-Seele und die Deutschen in Afrika: Ein Kampf gegen Missionen, Sittlichkeits-Fanatismus und Bürokratie vom Standpunkt moderner Psychologie* (Munich: J. F. Lehmann, 1907). One missionary cited the example of Booker T. Washington as argument against Oetker's well-known book. See P. O. Henning, "Zum Kampf um die Negerseele: Eine Antwort auf Dr. med. Oetkers 'Die Negerseele und die Deutschen in Afrika,' " *Flugschriften der Hanseastisch-Oldenburgischen Missions-Konferenz* (Bremen: J. Morgenbesser, 1907), 13.

121. Booker T. Washington, "The Economic Development of the Negro Race in Slavery," in Booker T. Washington and W.E.B. Du Bois, *The Negro in the South:*

His Economic Progress in Relation to His Moral and Religious Development (Philadelphia: George W. Jacobs & Co., 1907), 7–41.

122. James N. Calloway to Booker T. Washington, 3 February 1901, in Harlan, ed., *Booker T. Washington Papers* 6:26–27. See also James Calloway, "From the African Party," *Southern Letter*, 17, no. 4 (April 1901): 2–3.

123. J. K. Vietor, a German merchant active in Togo, transmitted African complaints about the lash and the chain gang to Governor Zech (who promised only to consider the possibility of using lighter chains). See J. K. Vietor, Bremen, to the North German Mission, Togo, 10 July 1905, NDM 98/1. On the use of the lash and other brutal means of rule in German Togo, see D.E.K. Amenumey, "German Administration in Southern Togo," *Journal of African History* 10 (1969): 623–39; Têtêvi Godwin Tété-Adjalogo, *De la colonisation allemande au Deutsche-Togo Bund* (Paris: Éditions L'Harmattan, 1998); and Trutz von Trotha, " 'One for Kaiser': Beobachtungen zur politischen Soziologie der Prügelstrafe am Beispiel des 'Schutzgebietes Togo,' " in Peter Heine and Ulrich van der Heyden, eds., *Studien zur Geschichte des deutschen Kolonialismus in Africa: Festschrift zum 60. Geburtstag von Peter Sebald* (Pfaffenweiler: Centaurus, 1995), 521–51.

124. An Anti-Prussian, "The Germans in Togoland: Visit of the German Secretary of State for the Colonies to Togoland," *African Times and Orient Review*, O.S., 2 (Nov.–Dec. 1913), 249–51.

125. "Verordnung betreffend die Auswanderung Eingeborenen des Togogebietes," 15 November 1899, R1001/3192, Bl. 121–22. See also Governor Doering to Deutsch Südamerikanische Telegraphen-Gesellschaft, 3 January 1911, R1001/3193, Bl. 44. Pastor Erhardt K. Paku of Palime, a Togolese who had grown up under German rule, remembered in 1981 that the parents of those who stayed in the Gold Coast longer than six months were punished. See Simtaro, "Le Togo 'Musterkolonie' " 2:554. On the limited success of German attempts to control emigration, see Governor Doering to the German Colonial Office, 12 May 1911, R1001/3193, Bl. 48–49. In the early years of German rule, the state did not seek to prevent this labor migration but rather to profit from it by charging recruiters a fee for each employee they took out. "Verweisung betreffend die Anwerbung von Eingeborenen des Togogebietes zu Diensten Ausserhalb des Schutzgebietes," 24 December 1891, R1001/3192, Bl. 61.

126. Governor Waldemar Horn (acting) to Colonial Section of the German Foreign Office, 24 October 1902, R1001/3193, Bl. 24–25; Gruner, Misahöhe District Office (*Bezirksamt*), to the North German Mission, Lome, Togo, 24 April 1914, NDM , 98/1.

127. Governor Doering to the German Colonial Office, 12 May 1911, R1001/3193, Bl. 48–49.

128. "Entwurf einer Dienstanweisung für Bezirksleiter," n.d. (printed) and "Pflichten und Rechte der Häuptlinge," n.d., NL Gruner, K. 7, Mappe 36, Bl. 171–82, 150. Curt von François agreed with Gruner on this point. See Curt von François, "Die Förderung der Eingeborenenkulturen durch Einführung der kommunalen Selbstverwaltung," *Deutsche Kolonialzeitung* 19 (1902): 203.

129. See Spieth, *Die Ewe-Stämme*, 404–6.

130. Calloway, "Tuskegee Cotton-Planters in Africa," 772.

131. Simtaro, "Le Togo 'Musterkolonie,' " 2:711.

132. Ibid, 715.

133. Robert Kwami, Amedschovhe, "Welche Nachtheile sind mit der Kultur-entwicklung unseres Landes verbunden?" 11 November 1909, NDM 31/3.

134. Robert Klu, Waya, "Warum können die Schwarzen ihre Kinder nicht erziehen?," 18 September 1909, NDM 31/3.

135. A Native of Anecho, "German Atrocities in Togoland," 203.

136. Governor Doering to the German Colonial Office, 12 May 1911, R1001/3193, Bl. 48–49.

137. Robert Kwami, Amedschovhe, "Welche Nachtheile sind mit der Kultur-entwicklung unseres Landes verbunden?," 11 November 1909, NDM 31/3.

138. Quashie, "Togo-Germans and Immoralism and Its Effect on the Gold Coast," Gold Coast Leader, 6 July 1912, BArch R1001/4308, Bl. 117.

139. Minutes of a meeting at the Misahöhe station between Gruner and local African leaders, the missionary Schosser, two teachers from the mission at Agu, and five teachers from the Catholic mission, 15 April 1904, BArch R1001/8222, Bl. 140–41.

140. Eduard Hahn, Die Entstehung der Pflugkultur (unsres Ackerbaus) (Heidelberg: Carl Winter's Universitätsbuchhandlung, 1909), 9–40. Hahn himself remained skeptical that Africans could adopt plow culture, because their agriculture was dominated by women. Eduard Hahn, Von der Hacke zum Pflug (Leipzig: Quelle and Meyer, 1914), 43–48.

141. Otto Warburg, "Einführung der Pflugkultur in den deutschen Kolonien," 4, 6.

142. Germany, Reichskolonialamt, Die Baumwollfrage: Denkschrift über Produktion und Verbrauch von Baumwolle Massnahmen gegen die Baumwollnot (Jena: Gustav Fischer: 1911), 131–32. The standard German reference work on tropical agriculture, one used by John Robinson during his work in Togo, warned that only white people could learn to use plows. Heinrich Semler, Die Tropische Agrikultur: Ein Handbuch für Pflanzer und Kaufleute, 2nd ed. revised by Richard Hindorf with Otto Warburg and M. Busemann, 4 vols. (1888–1892; Wismar: Hinstorff'sche Hofbuchhandlung Verlagsconto, 1897), 3: 260–63. The book is listed in an inventory of the Notsé school. See John Robinson, "Ackerbau-Schule-Nuatjä Inventarien-Verzeichnis," 3 April 1908, TNA FA 3/1000, Bl. 74–79. The KWK, however, encouraged the Tuskegee expedition to train Africans both to use plows and to care for draft animals. Karl Supf, "Deutsch-koloniale Baumwoll Unternehmungen, Bericht VII (Frühjahr 1906)," Der Tropenpflanzer 10 (1906): 355–69.

143. District Officer (Bezirksamtmann) Schlettwein, Lome, Togo, to the Government of Togo, 31 October 1911, BArch R1001/8673, Bl. 189–90.

144. KWK, "Baumwoll-Expedition nach Togo. Bericht 1901," BArch R901/351. See also Calloway, "Tuskegee Cotton-Planters in Africa" and "Farming in West Africa," New York Times, 30 March 1902.

145. Statistics collected in 1911, for example, show that nearly every draft animal that the expedition provided to African cotton growers had died. The majority of the cattle still alive at the time of the survey were recent replacements for the dead, and presumably soon met the same fate as their predecessors. "Stand der Siedlungen des Schutzgebietes Togo (Ende 1911)," BArch R1001/8673, Bl.

182–83. Also in TNA FA 1–366, Bl. 1–3. That the settlers could not use plows because the cattle mostly died is also confirmed in Sengmüller, Notsé, "Bericht über die Siedlungen ehemaliger Ackerbauschüler in das Jahr 1910/11," 1 July 1911, TNA FA 1–388, 269–74.

146. Albrecht Zimmermann, *Anleitung für die Baumwollkultur in den deutschen Kolonien*, 2nd ed. (1905; Berlin: KWK, 1910), 55.

147. In 1907 the expedition employed a dozen men to pull wagons to the coast and back. Karl Supf, Deutsch-Koloniale Baumwoll-Unternehmungen, Bericht IX (Herbst 1907), BArch R1001/8149, Bl. 39–70.

148. John W. Robinson, "Cotton Growing in Africa," *The Southern Letter* 21, no. 1 (January 1905).

149. C. Osswald, North German Mission, Lome, to A. W.: Schreiber, 26 July 1901 and 14 August 1901, NDM 20/1.

150. Governor Horn to the Colonial Section of the German Foreign Office, 24 November 1902, BArch R1001/8222, Bl. 14.

151. District Chief (*Bezirksleiter*) Geo A. Schmidt, Atakpame, Togo, to the Government of Togo, 10 November 1902 (copy), BArch R1001/8222, Bl. 15–22. Published in part in "Baumwoll-Expedition nach Togo," *Verhandlungen des Kolonial-Wirtschaftlichen Komitees* (1903) (22 January 1903): 12–16. Gruner, 5 August 1905, copy, TNA FA 1/303, Bl. 59–86.

152. Smend, Misahöhe station, to the Government of Togo, 20 March 1904, TNA FA 1–363, Bl. 17.

153. All information about Robinson's African family comes from personal communications of the author with Monica Eklou, great-granddaughter of Francisca Adjoa Robinson, in October 2005.

154. Gruner refers to his "*schwarze Frau*" in a telegram to a doctor asking for medical treatment for complications relating to the birth of a stillborn child. Hans Gruner, telegram to Külz, May 1905, copied in his diary, NL Gruner, K. 3, Mappe 19.

155. See the interviews with M. Emil Kossi Kuma Nutsua and Hans Komla Gruner in Simtaro, "Le Togo 'Musterkolonie' " 2:600–98.

156. Hans Komla Gruner described himself in a letter to his father as "one of your mulatto sons, whose appearance and place of birth you do not know." See Hans Komla Gruner to Hans Gruner, 12 September 1929, NL Gruner, K. 12, Nr. 71, Bl. 7. See also Hans Komla Gruner to Hans Gruner, 30 August 1937, NL Gruner, K. 12, Nr. 72, Bl. 31.

157. Eugenius Carl Winkler to Hans Gruner, 19 June 1929, NL Gruner, K. 12, Nr. 71, Bl. 12. On interracial marriage in the German empire, see especially Lora Wildenthal, *German Women for Empire, 1884–1945* (Durham: Duke University Press, 2001).

158. Warren Logan to Booker T. Washington, 13 June 1902, Booker T. Washington to Warren Logan, 14 July 1902, in Harlan, ed., *Booker T. Washington Papers* 6:480–81, 494.

159. Booker T. Washington, *Working with the Hands* (1904) (New York: Negro Universities Press, 1969), 226–30. Washington makes a similar point in "The Economic Development of the Negro Race in Slavery," 33–36.

160. James Calloway, "Inspektion der Baumwollfarmen und Baumwoll-märkte," in *Bericht II. Deutsch-koloniale Baumwoll-Unternehmungen* 1902/03, supplement to *Tropenpflanzer* 4 (1903): 112–22, here 113. Washington echoes this view in Booker T. Washington, "The African at Home," ch. 3 in *The Story of the Negro*, vol. 1 (1909; New York: Negro Universities Press, 1969), 36–56.

161. On the 1902 draught, see E. Anrima [?], teacher, Tove, to A. W. Schreiber, 2 March 1904, NDM 20/2 and Müller, *Geschichte der katholischen Kirche in Togo*, 213–14.

162. John Tosh, "The Cash Crop Revolution in Tropical Africa: An Agricul-tural Reappraisal," *African Affairs* 79 (1980): 79–94.

163. H. Schröder, Lome, Togo, to A. W. Schreiber, 24 July 1905, NDM 20/3.

164. E. Anrima [?] to A. W. Schreiber, 2 March 1904, NDM 20/2.

165. See Ferdinand Goldberg, Anecho, Togo, "Bericht über meine Thätigkeit in Togo-Gebiet vom 1. Juni bis 30. September 1891," 1 October 1891 (copy), TNA FA 1–332, Bl. 61–77; "Der Baumwollbau in Togo, seine bisherhige Ent-wicklung, und sein jetziger Stand," n.d., BArch R1001/8224. An abridged version of this text appeared as "Der Baumwollbau in Togo, seine bisheringe Entwicklung und sein jetziger Stand," *Deutsches Kolonialblatt* 22 (1911): 229–33, 282–87. See also "Baumwolle (Gossypium)," n.d. [in 1911/12 year], BArch R1001/7816, Bl. 38–45, and "Niederschrift über die Ergebnisse der Verhandlungen bei der Baumwollkonferenz 1904," Lomé, Togo, 29 April 1904 (copy), BArch R1001/8222, Bl. 142–48.

166. The Tuskegee plantation was also a producer of cotton in its own right, employing about a hundred workers. C. Osswald, North German Mission Society, Lome, to A. W. Schreiber, 26 July 1901 and 14 August 1901, NDM 20/1.

167. For early attempts at crossing Ho and American, see Smend, Misahöhe station, to KWK, 9 November 1903, TNA FA 1–332, Bl. 221–31. On the ubiquity of Ho cotton in Togo markets, see Zimmermann, *Anleitung für die Baumwoll-kultur in den deutschen Kolonien*, 20–23.

168. This new cotton varietal was called Sea-Island, even though it produced a staple equivalent to American Upland, because it had black rather than green seeds, which was an easy way to differentiate Sea-Island from Upland cotton in the United States. The color of Togo Sea-Island seeds is mentioned in Governor Zech to the German Colonial Office, 12 September 1909, BArch R1001/8223, 152–55. Togo Sea-Island, despite its name, came to be regarded as equivalent to American Upland. See, for example, the address by the German cotton expert, Moritz Schanz, *Cotton in the United States of North America: Report for the Fifth International Congress, Paris, 1st to 3rd June, 1908* (Manchester: Taylor, Garnett, Evens, and Co., [1908]).

169. Schwartz, *Le Paysan et la Culture du Coton au Togo*, 5.

170. See, for example, the following reports: Emil Stark (Chemnitz), "Die Be-deutung der Baumwolle in der Weltwirtschaft," *Verhandlungen des Deutschen Kolonialkongresses 1902*, 712–27; "Togo;" *Bulletin du Comité de l'Afrique Fran-çais* 12 (1902): 236; "Baumwollkultur in den deutschen Kolonien," *Deutsche Kolonialzeitung* 20 (1903): 433; Karl Supf, Deutsch-Koloniale Baumwoll-Unternehmungen, Bericht VI. (Herbst, 1905), BArch R1001/8147, Bl. 227–30.

171. Karl Supf, Deutsch-Koloniale Baumwoll-Unternehmungen, Bericht VI. (Herbst, 1905), BArch R1001/8147, Bl. 227–30. While this report suggested that Togo Sea-Island might be used as a substitute for Egyptian, subsequent measurements make clear that its staple length of 28–29mm placed it in the range of American Upland. For measurements of Togo Sea-Island, see Landeskulturanstalt Nuatjä, "Togo Sea-Island Baumwoll-Züchtung 1912/13," BArch R1001/8674, Bl.7–51.

172. Scheidt, German Consul, Galveston, memo, 1 July 1908, BArch R901/367, Bl. 51.

173. See "Der Baumwollbau in Togo, seine bisherhige Entwicklung, und sein jetziger Stand"; Doering to District Agronomists Maywald, Lumblatt, and Graness, 24 February 1911, BArch R1001/8224, Bl. 263–65 and Bl. 263–66; Pape, "Arbeitsplan für die neu anzulegenden Saatzuchtstellen in den Bezirken Misahöhe, Atakpame und Sokode," n.d., TNA FA 3/1013, Bl. 3–17. This tendency to hybridize is also discussed in "Baumwolle (Gossypium)," n.d. [in 1911/12 year], BArch R1001/7816, Bl. 38–45.

174. See Governor Zech to the German Colonial Office, 12 September 1909, BArch R1001/8223, Bl. 152–55; Governor Zech to the German Colonial Office, 12 May 1909, BArch R1001/8223, 141–42; and "Der Baumwollbau in Togo, seine bisheringe Entwicklung und sein jetziger Stand," *Deutsches Kolonialblatt* 22 (1911): 229–33, 282–87, here 282–87.

175. "Togo, La Production du Coton," *Agence Extérieure et Coloniale*, 29 October 1925, BArch R1001/8226, Bl. 189; "Aufzeichnung über die Besprechung mit den Herren Chefs der Togofirmen," 10 April 1908, TNA FA 1–88, Bl. 29–48; Germany, Reichskolonialamt, *Die Baumwollfrage.*

176. Supf, KWK, to Governor Zech, 7 January 1904, TNA FA 1–332, Bl. 334–38.

177. Acting Governor Doering to District Agronomists Maywald, Lumblatt, and Graness, 24 February 1911, BArch R1001/8224, Bl. 263–66. On teaching cotton picking, see District Agronomist Lumblatt, Atakpame, semiannual report, 11 October 1912, BArch R1001/8673, Bl. 215–17.

178. Deking, Sokode district agronomist, semiannual report, 17 December 1912, TNA FA 1–366, Bl. 122–31.

179. Maywald, Palime district agronomist, semiannual report, 11 October 1912, BArch R1001/8673, Bl. 219–20.

180. Sengmüller, report on the Kpedji area, 13 November 1913 (copy), BArch R1001/8226, Bl. 150–53.

181. See Verband Deutscher Baumwollverbraucher (Dresden) to Secretary Lindequist, the German Colonial Office, 22 October 1910, and Verband Deutscher Baumwollgarn-Verbraucher, Dresden, to Secretary Lindequist, 22 October 1910, BArch R1001/8224, Bd. 53–56, and Dr. Krueger and Dr. Simoneit, "Die Ursachen der Verschlecterung der Togo-Baumwolle und Vorschläge ihrer Verbesserung," Palime, 2 February 1911, BArch R1001/8225, Bl. 16–21.

182. Unsigned Report about cotton growing, n.d. (circa. 1904), TNA FA 1–89, Bl. 8–57.

183. G. H. Pape, *Anleitung für die Baumwollkultur Togo* (Berlin: KWK, 1911), 31–32, TNA FA1/384, Bl. 293ff. Still, most cotton pickers in Togo favored

the basket over the sack, and picking yields—and labor discipline—remained low. See "Leitfaden für den Landwirtschaftlichen Unterricht in Togo," n.d. [by position in folder, probably 1911 or 1912], TNA FA 1–366, Bl. 70–110.

184. Kolonialkomite, Berlin, telegram to the Government of Togo, 12 November 1901, TNA FA 1–332, Bl. 119; Karl Supf, KWK, to the Colonial Section of the Foreign Office, 15 November 1901 (copy), TNA FA 1–332, Bl. 130.

185. The state redoubled its cotton policing efforts after a temporary decline in the suitability of Togo cotton for industrial processing in 1910. Doering, on behalf of the German Government of Togo, to the German Colonial Office, 10 March 1911, BArch R1001/8224, Bl. 259–62. Walter Busse, "Aufzeichnung der Sitzung der Baumwollbau-Kommission des KWK," 21 November 1910, BArch R1001/8151, Bl. 51–56.

186. Doering, Atakpame station, to the Government of Togo, 11 June 1904, TNA FA1/297, Bl. 334–35.

187. Since 1903 the German government had forbidden Togolese from selling their cotton to merchants from the Gold Coast. See the Missionaries Smend and Martin, Kpandu, memo, 21 September 1903 (copy), TNA FA 1–332, Bl. 194–95. English merchants apparently did, nonetheless, attempt to purchase Togolese cotton. See "Baumwollkultur in den deutschen Kolonien," *Deutsche Kolonialzeitung* 20 (1903): 433. A 1911 law forbade the sale of cotton outside officially sanctioned markets and punished violators with a fine of up to six-hundred marks or six weeks of imprisonment—which in Togo meant forced labor. See "Bekanntmachung des Gouverneurs zur Durchführung der Verordnung betreffend den Handel mit Baumwolle vom 11. Januar 1911," *Amtsblatt für das Schutzgebiet Togo*, 3 February 1911, BArch R1001/8224, Bl. 237, and "Verordnung des Gouverneurs von Togo, betr. den handel mit Baumwolle, vom 11. Januar 1911," *Deutsches Kolonialblatt* 22 (1911): 268. See also Government of Togo to Atakpame District Office, 19 January 1911, TNA FA 3/1009, Bl. 157. A January, 1914, law gave the German government a monopoly over the distribution of cotton seed and prohibited the purchase of cotton in Togo without an official government license. Licensed purchasers were required to separate cotton into two classes. Europeans in violation of this law were to be fined up to fifteen hundred marks, while Togolese violators were to be given an unspecified punishment, which, in German Togo meant flogging, forced labor, or both. See "Verordnung des Gouverneurs betreffend den Handel mit und die Aufbereitung von Baumwolle, Lome, 9 January 1914," in *Amtsblatt für das Schutzgebiet Togo* 9 (1914): 19–20, BArch R1001/8226, Bl. 162–63. On at least one occasion cotton was confiscated from an unlicensed purchasing agent. See Wellbrecht, telegram to the Atakpame district office, [1914], TNA FA 3/1009, Bl. 157.

188. Marx, *Capital*, vol. 1, 279–80.

189. Supf, KWK to Governor Zech, 9 December 1903, TNA FA 1–332, Bl. 280; and KWK, Deutsch-Koloniale Baumwoll-Unternehmungen, Bericht III. 1903/04, BArch R1001/8147, Bl. 143–44.

190. Governor Horn to the district officer of Anecho, 15 February 1904, TNA FA 1–363, Bl. 5–7.

191. Walter Busse to KWK, 25 July 1904, TNA FA 1/303, Bl. 433–38.

192. Alex Johnston, "A Negro Exodus," *Journal of the Royal African Society* (London) 3 (1903–04): 398–409, here 402.

193. "Die African Methodist Episcopal Zion Church in Keta," MNDM, 3rd series, 14 (1902): 101–3. On Freeman, see also J. H., review of *Thomas B. Freeman*, by John Milum (London, n.d), *Evangelisches Missions-Magazin* (Basel) 38 (1894): 174–75; and Edwin W. Smith, *Aggrey of Africa: A Study in Black and White* (1929; reprint New York: Books for Libraries, 1971), 30, 43.

194. E. Anrima [?] to A. W. Schreiber, 2 March 1904, NDM 20/2.

195. "African Methodist Episcopal Zion Church," MNDM, 3rd series, 15 [*sic*—should be 16] (1904): 53.

196. "Afro-Americans and the Gold Coast," *African Times and Orient Review*, N.S., 1 (21 April 1914), 99–100.

197. Governor Zech to KWK, 7 February 1902 (copy), BArch R1001/8222, Bl. 107.

198. Governor Horn to the district officer of Anecho, 15 February 1904.

199. Schanz, *West-Afrika*, 299.

200. A North German missionary had visited Notsé as early as 1888, but found the king "so shamelessly beggarly" that he left the area after preaching only once. E. Bürgi, "Reisen an der Togoküste und im Ewegebiet," *Dr. A. Petermanns Mitteilungen aus Justus Perthes' Geographischer Anstalt* 34 (1888): 233–37. See Bürgi's similar comments on this trip in his letter to Franz Michael Zahn, inspector of missions, Bremen, 26 November 1891, NDM 41/4.

201. By 1909, German force allowed all but one of the major European commercial firms in Lome to open branches in Atakpame. See the report by a German Catholic missionary, P. Glanemann, "Atakpame," *Gott will es!* 21 (1909): 73–76.

202. "Bekanntmachung," 11 January 1900, TNA FA 3/1248, Bl. 2–3.

203. Atakpame station to the Government of Togo, 19 March 1901, TNA FA 3/1086, Bl. 14–15.

204. Geo A. Schmidt, "Notschä Unbotmaessigkeit" in *Schmidt gegen Roeren: Unter den kaudinischen Joch. Ein Kampf um Recht und Ehre* (Berlin: Swetschke und Sohn, 1907), 45–47, NL Gruner, K. 7, Mappe 35. As a result of these economic developments, made possible by the initial conquest, Atakpame gained the status of a district in 1908. "Bezirksamt-Atakpame," *Deutsche Kolonialzeitung* 25 (1908): 337.

205. Interview with Fare Napo in Simtaro, "Le Togo 'Musterkolonie' " 2:699–705.

206. On Chra, see Asmis, "Die Besserungssiedlung an der Chra (Schutzgebiet Togo). Ein Beitrag zur Lehre vom Strafvollzug in den Kolonien," *Koloniale Rundschau* 9 (1911): 528–40.

207. Hans Gruner, Misahöhe district office, "Pflichten und Rechte der Häuptlinge," n.d., NL Gruner, K. 7, Mappe 36, Bl. 150.

208. Interviews with Bewi Motom'Souwé Talbéwi Kondoi Lorenz and Amegan Sam Tiw, in Simtaro, "Le Togo 'Musterkolonie' " 2:754–75. Martin Schlunk noted the sorrow and homesickness of Chra residents in 1910. See Schlunk *Meine Reise durchs Eweland* (Bremen: Norddeutsche Missions-Gesellschaft, 1910), 54.

209. Asmis, "Die Besserungssiedlung an der Chra."

210. Sengmüller to Atakpame district office, 28 August 1911, TNA FA 3/1000, Bl. 204–5.

211. Doering later claimed that he had chosen to locate the penal colony at Chra because of its proximity to the "auspicious" (*zukunftsreichen*) region of Notsé. See Asmis, "Die Besserungssiedlung an der Chra," 533.

212. Governor Zech, circular to all district stations and offices, 4 March 1904, TNA FA 1–363, Bl. 9–10.

213. Doering, Atakpame station, [to the Government of Togo], 26 September 1905, TNA FA 1–363, Bl. 50–57.

214. Governor Zech to the German Colonial Office, 25 January 1908, BArch R1001/8673, Bl. 24–25. Further inquiry revealed that the two students, both from Misahöhe, were orphans, one of them, Gotthold Gogon, in poor health, the other one, Friedmund Adom, blinded in a childhood accident. These two Togolese had, it seems, no other possibility for livelihood than the cotton school, which apparently agreed to take them. Diehl, North German Mission Society, Agu, Togo, to Misahöhe district office, 5 April 1907; the Government of Togo to the KWK, Lome, Togo, 16 April 1907; [Governor Zech] to the district chief of Misahöhe, 15 March 1907, TNA FA 1–363, Bl. 255–58, 251–52, 227–29.

215. Anecho district office to the Government of Togo, 29 October 1909, TNA FA 1–388, 103.

216. Sansane-Mangu station to Governor Zech, February 28, 1906, BArch R150, TNA FA 1–363, Bl. 85–91.

217. Kete-Kratschi station to the Government of Togo, 8 November 1909, TNA FA 1–388, 112–13.

218. On Notsé and Ewe historical memory, see the outstanding work by Sandra E. Greene, "Notsie Narratives: History, Memory and Meaning in West Africa" and *Gender, Ethnicity, and Social Change on the Upper Slave Coast*.

219. The North German Missionary Society reported this Ewe origin story as early as 1877, before formal German rule, and before, apparently, any Germans had actually visited Notsé. Christian Hornberger, "Etwas aus der Geschichte der Anloer," *Quartalblatt der Norddeutschen Missionsgesellschaft* 82 (1877): 437–39. Translated and cited by Greene, "Notsie Narratives," 1023–24. Curiously, in the first months of 1914, Hans Gruner, one of the officials closest to the cotton expedition, took extensive oral histories about the exodus from Notsé. Gruner, "Wissenschaftliche Notizen (Geschichte)," 12 January 1914–17 February 1914; 15/2/1914–26/3/1914; 18/4/1914–17/7/1914; NL Gruner, K. 8, Nr. 42. For accounts by Ewe missionaries, see Arnold Binka, "Die Geschichte der Logbaer," n.d.; Valentin Agbesingale, "Geschichte von der Stammung der Gbedzigbe," Lehrer Robert Dotse, trans., n.d., NDM 31/4. For an account by a German missionary, see Carl Spiess, "Ein Beitrag zur Geschichte des Evhe-Volkes in Togo: Seine Auswanderung aus Notse," *Mitteilungen des Seminars für Orientalische Sprachen* 5 (1902): 278–83. For a British account, see Colonial Office, Great Britain, *Report on the British Mandated Sphere of Togoland for 1920–1921* (London: His Majesty's Stationery Office, 1922).

220. Agokoli III was interviewed by Ansa K. Asamoa, *The Ewe of South-Eastern Ghana and Togo on the Eve of Colonialism: A Contribution to the Marxist*

Debate on pre-Capitalist Socio-Economic Formations (Tema: Ghana Publishing Corporation, 1986).

221. See Greene, "Notsie Narratives."

222. Gottlob Härtter, "Einige Bausteine zur Geschichte der Ewe-Stämme (Togo)," *Beiträge zur Kolonialpolitik und Kolonialwirtschaft* 3 (1901/02): 432–48, 464–80, 492–514.

223. Governor Zech, 22 August 1904, to KWK, TNA FA 1–363, Bl. 22–37. Printed in "Deutsch-koloniale Baumwoll-Unternehmungen. Sonderbericht über die Baumwollschule in Nuatschä," BArch R1001/8673, Bl. 3–5.

224. John Robinson, Notsé, to Governor Zech, 17 January 1904, TNA FA 1–332, Bl. 295–301. At a final exam held publicly before the Governor of Togo and the head of Atakpame station, Notsé graduates demonstrated the skills they had acquired in harnessing draft animals, assembling and using plows, picking cotton, and using a steam-powered cotton gin and a cotton press. The students also answered questions, put to them in Ewe, about agriculture, and demonstrated their ability to give the German names for agricultural implements. "Aufzeichnugn über die am 19ten Dezember 1906 abgehaltene Prüfung der Ackerbau Schule in Nuatjä," TNA FA 1–363, 174–79; 211–13. The notes on the test in 1910 reveal that the program had not changed significantly. See "Prüfung der Ackerbauschule in Nuatjä," 2 January 1910, TNA FA 1–388, 133–38.

225. Robinson, memo, n.d., TNA FA 3/1008, Bl. 128–36.

226. Governor Zech, "Programm für die Einstellung, Ausbildung und spätere Verwendung von Landwirtschaftsschülern," 29 December 1906, TNA FA 1–363, 158–60; Governor Zech, "Lehrplan für die Baumwollschule in Nuatjä," (n.d.), TNA FA 1–363, 161–62.

227. John W. Robinson, "Tuskegee Graduates in Africa," *Southern Letter* 23, no. 4 (April 1907). The budget figures Robinson gives in that article are confirmed in Governor Zech to KWK, 23 August 1907 (copy), BArch R1001/8673, Bl. 9.

228. Personal correspondence with Monica Eklou, October 2005.

229. Governor Zech, 22 August 1904, to KWK, TNA FA, Bl. 22–37.

230. Dr. Sengmüller to the Government of Togo, 4 February 1912 (copy), BArch R1001/8673, Bl. 160–64.

231. "Ora et labora!" MNDM, 3rd series, 2 (1890): 71–76, here 71.

232. "Afrikanische Arbeiter," MNDM 13 (1888): 120–22, here 122. Diedrich Bavendamm makes a similar point in "Das Volk gewann ein Herz zu arbeiten," MNDM, 3rd series, 6 (1894): 18–19.

233. "Wirthschaftliche Aussichten für Deutsch-Togo," MNDM, 3rd series, 13 (1901): 19–21, here 21.

234. Booker T. Washington, "The Colored Ministry, Its Defects and Needs," *Christian Union* 42 (14 August 1890), 199–200; in Harlan, ed., *Booker T. Washington Papers* 3:73.

235. James Nathan Calloway to Booker T. Washington, 2 June 1901, in Harlan, ed., *Booker T. Washington Papers* 6:142–43.

236. J. K. Vietor, comment on O. Warburg, "Die Landwirtschaft in den deutschen Kolonien," *Verhandlungen des Deutschen Kolonialkongresses 1905*, 603.

237. "Kulturfortschritte in Deutsch-Togo," MNDM, 3rd series, 18 (1906): 5–6 and "Was verdankt die Togo-Mission der deutschen Kolonial-Regierung," MNDM, 69 (1908): 20–22.

238. A. W. Schreiber to the *Stations-Conferenzen*, 9 July 1907, NDM 39/4. The Bremen office also translated an article by Washington discussing the necessity of Christianity to the improvement of Africa, although what was done with this translation is unknown. See Booker T. Washington, "Freunde von Afrika," translation of a letter in the *New York Independent*, 15 March 1906, typescript, NDM 98/1.

239. "Die Neger in Nordamerika," MNDM, 69 (1908): 108–10, here 110. See also "Die Negerfrage in Nordamerika," MNDM, 71 (1910): 18–19.

240. E. Bürgi, Amedschovhe, "Bemerkungen zu einem Berichte Dr. Schossers über die praktische Ausbildung unserer Schüler," March 1906, NDM 39/4. The marginalia in this document indicate that the head of the mission in Bremen did not share Bürgi's reservations about industrial education.

241. A. W. Schreiber to the German Colonial Office, 21 August 1909, NDM 88/2.

242. E. Funke, H. Schröder, conference minutes, Amedschovhe, 3 March 1908, NDM 39/4.

243. Spiess and Poppinga, conference minutes, Ho, Bemerkungen zu Schossers Vorschlaege, March 1908, NDM 39/4.

244. Conference minutes, Ho, 27 August 1907, NDM 39/4. See also E. Bürgi, Amedschovhe, "Bemerkungen zu Herr Inspektors Asführungen über systematisch-pratische Ausbildung unserer Schüler," 29 August 1907, NDM 39/4; E. Funke, "Zur Reform unserers Schulsystems," Amedschovhe, 29 August 1907, NDM 39/4; Missionary from Akpafu, memorandum prepared for a conference held in Lome, 3–5 September 1907, NDM 39/4.

245. Forthmeier, Keta, "Die Arbeitsfrage in unsern Schulen," 1 October 1907, NDM 39/4. For the response from the head of the mission in Bremen, see A. W. Schreiber, to the managing board of the North German Mission, 16. November 1907, NDM 39/4.

246. Hans Gruner, Misahöhe, to the Government of Togo, 11 March 1907, TNA FA 1–363, 238–40.

247. On this summer program, see Pape, Notsé, 19 August 1909, NDM 8/6, and "Ferienkursus der Missionslehrer auf der Ackerbauschule in Nuatjä," MNDM, 71 (1910): 8.

248. See Reinhold Dzansi, Agu, "Thema: Der Landwirtschaftliche Kurs in Nuatjä," n.d., and Aaron A. Anku, Peki Dzake, "What Profit Brought the Agricultural Course at Aburi to You?" 15 October 1909, NDM 31/3.

249. Theophilus R. Asieni, "Wie verwerte ich meine Kenntnisse, die ich auf Ackerbauschule in Notschie erworben habe?" n.d., NDM 31/3.

250. "Die Erziehung der Schüler in Akpasu zur Arbeit," MNDM 68 (1907): 31.

251. Pfisterer and Dettmann, conference minutes, Atakpame, 24 February 1908, NDM 39/4. The missionaries may refer here to the title of Booker T. Washington's 1902 *Character Building*, which appeared in German two years later. Booker T. Washington, *Charakterbildung: Sonntags-Ansprachen an die Zöglinge*

der Normal- und Gewerbeschule von Tuskegee, Estelle Du Bois-Reymond, trans. (Berlin: Dietrich Reimer [Ernst Vohsen], 1910).

252. Even before the expedition arrived in Togo, one German official warned that getting Togolese to practice cotton culture as the Germans desired would require "gentle and even possibly strong pressure from the government." Geo A. Schmitt, Atakpame station, to the Government of Togo, 7 August 1900, TNA FA 1–332, Bl. 111–18.

253. See John W. Robinson, Notsé, to Governor Zech, 12 December 1904, TNA FA 1/303, Bl. 255–58, and the copy of this letter sent by the future governor Zech to Atakpame district office, 29 December 1904, TNA FA 3/1008, Bl. 114–18.

254. Atakpame station [to the Government of Togo], 25 September 1905, TNA FA 1–304, Bl. 60–63.

255. Governor Zech, "Programm für die Einstellung, Ausbildung und spätere Verwendung von Landwirtschaftsschülern," 29 December 1906, TNA FA 1–363, 158–60. See also the discussion recorded in "Aufzeichnung über die anlässlich des Bezirksleiter Versammlung in Lome am 5. Februar 1907 stattgehaltete Besprechung über Baumwollkultur und [illegible]," TNA FA 1–304, Bl. 372–90 and typescript Bl. 391–98.

256. District chief, Sokode-Basari station, to the Government of Togo, 23 October 1910, TNA FA 1–388, 277–91.

257. District officer, Atakpame to the Government of Togo, 24 October 1910, TNA FA 1–388, 321–29.

258. Kete-Kratschi station, [to the Government of Togo], 28 September 1909, TNA FA 1–388, 95–101.

259. District Chief Kittel of Kete-Kratschi, report on settlers to the Government of Togo, 10 October 1911 (copy), BArch R1001/8673, Bl. 184.

260. Governor Brückner to the German Colonial Office, 4 May 1912, BArch R1001/8673, Bl. 177–78.

261. For Pape's own account of his life, see G. H. Pape, College Station Texas, 6 May 1904, TNA FA 1/303, Bl. 250–51. See also D. F. Houston, Agricultural and Mechanical College of Texas, to Julius Runge, German Consul, Galveston, Texas, 25 May 1904 (copy), TNA FA 1/303, Bl. 253.

262. Pape, Notsé school, to the Government of Togo, 14 November 1908, TNA FA 1–402, 191–92.

263. District Officer Haering of Atakpame, 12 November 1911, BArch R1001/8673, Bl. 187–88.

264. Germany, Reichskolonialamt, *Der Baumwollbau in den deutschen Schutzgebieten: Seine Entwicklung seit dem Jahre 1910* (Jena: Gustav Fischer, 1914). Cotton remained the principal focus of the "Agricultural Institute" (*Landeskulturanstalt*), as the government renamed it. Sengmüller to the Government of Togo, 15 August 1911 (copy), BArch R1001/8673, Bl. 171–73. See also Dr. Sengmüller to the Government of Togo, 4 February 1912 (copy), BArch R1001/8673, Bl. 160–64. See "Bekanntmachung des Governors betreffend die Umgestaltung der Ackerbauschule Nuatjä," 4 May 1912, BArch R1001/8673, Bl. 180–81.

265. John Booth, Notsé, to the Government of Togo, 3 July 1911 (copy), TNA FA 1–388, 263–68.

266. Sengmüller, "Bericht über eine Reise in die Kpedji-Landschaft," 15 November 1913, TNA FA 1–366, Bl. 116–21.

267. The head of the school complained about the large numbers of escaped students in 1912. See Sengmüller to Atakpame district office, 7 June 1912, TNA FA 3/1000, Bl. 177, 275 (copy), and Sengmüller to Atakpame district office, 14 June 1911, TNA FA 3/1000, Bl. 180. The statistics collected at the end of 1911 indicate only ninety-eight individual settlers, although there should have been roughly two hundred graduates by then. Two are listed in the table as having "escaped" during the year, and this may have been the fate of a larger number. "Stand der Siedlungen des Schutzgebietes Togo (Ende 1911)," BArch R1001/8673, Bl. 182–83. The large number of escapees is also noted in Sengmüller, Notsé, "Bericht über die Siedlungen ehemaliger Ackerbauschüler in das Jahr 1910/11," 1 July 1911, TNA FA 1–388, 269–74.

268. Doehring, Atakpame station, 26 November 1906, TNA FA 1–363, 191–94.

269. District Officer Schlettwein, Lome district, to the Government of Togo, 31 October 1911, BArch R1001/8673, Bl. 189–90.

270. Sengmüller to the Government of Togo, 8 November 1911 (copy), BArch R1001/8673, Bl. 186.

271. Doering, on behalf of the Government of Togo, to the Atakpame district officer, 3 April 1911, TNA FA 3/1009, Bl. 215–16.

272. For the use of tax workers for cotton farming in Togo, including in graduates' settlements and the Notsé school itself, see Karl Supf, KWK, to the Colonial Section of the Foreign Office, 15 November 1901, copy sent to the Government of Togo, TNA FA 1–332, Bl. 130; Kete-Kratschi station to the Government of Togo, 28 September 1909, TNA FA 1–388, 95–101; Sengmüller, Notsé, "Bericht über die Siedlungen ehemaliger Ackerbauschüler in das Jahr 1910/11," 1 July 1911, TNA FA 1–388, 269–74; District Chief Kittel, Kete-Kratschi, "Bericht ueber der Ansiedler," to the Government of Togo, 10 October 1911 (copy), BArch R1001/8673, Bl. 184. The following volumes list each of the tax workers assigned to Notsé: TNA FA 3/1241, FA3/1315, FA 3/1321, FA 3/1322.

273. District officer, Atakpame to the Government of Togo, 24 October 1910, TNA FA 1–388, 321–29.

274. District Chief Kittel, Kete-Kratschi, "Baumwollkultur der Eingeborenen," n.d. [circa 1910], TNA FA 1–388, 312–14. In the North there was no railroad to transport cotton inexpensively to the coast. Mangu-Jendi District to the Government of Togo, 28 November 1907, TNA FA 1–402, 4–5.

275. Döhring, Atakpame station, to the Government of Togo 28 December 1907, TNA FA 1–402, 7–12. Similar conditions prevailed in Kete-Kratschi district. Kete-Kratschi station to the Government of Togo, 18 May 1909, TNA FA 1–388, 18–21.

276. These figures are based on Governor Zech to the German Colonial Office, 23 November 1909, BArch R1001/8223, 155–60; Wyndham R. Dunstan, *Report on the Present Position of Cotton Cultivation: Presented to the International Congress of Tropical Agriculture, Brussels, May 1910* (Paris: International Association of Tropical Agriculture and Colonial Development, 1910), 46–47 and N. M. Penzer, *Cotton in British West Africa, Including Togoland and the Cameroons*

(London: The Federation of British Industries, 1920). In "German Alabama in Africa" I gave figures for the kilogram output that I now regard as an underestimate. They were based on Dunstan, who, though agreeing with the two other sources on the annual percentage increase of cotton output, gives figures which are a fifth of the other two. Perhaps he simply miscalculated the conversion between kilograms and pounds.

277. Raymond E. Dumett, "Obstacles to Government-Assisted Agricultural Development in West Africa: Cotton-Growing Experimentation in Ghana in the Early Twentieth Century," *Agricultural History Review* 23 (1975): 156–72.

278. Cotton rose steadily as a percentage of the total value of commodities recorded by German customs officials exported from Togo, but never exceeded 10 percent of the total. Palm kernels and oil made up the bulk of the value of exports from Togo, although their place was sometimes challenged by rubber. Indeed, cotton lagged in value even behind the corn with which it was often interplanted, although it was more important than peanuts. See the figures given by the customs office of Togo, 26 August 1912, BArch R1001/7816, Bl. 89–90.

279. Commissariat de la République Française au Togo, *Guide de la Colonisation au Togo* (Paris: Émile Larose, 1924), 31; Victor Chazelas, *Territoires Africains sous Mandat de la France: Cameroun et Togo* (Paris: Société d'Éditions Géographiques, Maritimes et Coloniales, 1931), 216–18.

280. Supf of KWK to Governor Zech, 6 November 1908, BArch R1001/8223, Bl. 115. See also "Der derzeitige Stand der Baumwollfrage in unseren Kolonien," *Deutsche Kolonialzeitung* 25 (1908): 821–23. The intention to model this school on Notsé is also confirmed by Morris Schanz in *Official Report of the Seventh International Cotton Congress of Delegated Representatives of Master Cotton Spinners' and Manufacturers' Associations, Brussels, 6–8 June, 1910* (n.p., n.d.), 181. Governor Zech rejected the proposal that Robinson act as a wandering plow teacher, noting that even three years' education at Notsé had been insufficient to introduce the plow to Togolese. See Governor Zech to KWK, 13 December 1908, BArch R1001/8223, Bl. 116–17. He did, however, support the other work proposed for Robinson, which was, on his insistence, to be subordinate to the Sasane-Mangu station. See Governor Zech to the German Colonial Office, 19 December 1908, BArch R1001/8223, Bl. 114.

281. Freude, memo, Notsé, 29 September 1909 (copy), German original and English translation, Booker T. Washington Papers, Reel 68.; Booker T. Washington to Mrs. John W. Robinson, Macon, Mississippi, 30 September 1909, Booker T. Washington Papers, Reel 68. Robinson's missing body, as well as the existence of his Togolese family, made it difficult, and perhaps impossible, for his American wife Danella to collect his life insurance policy. See KWK to Booker T. Washington, 9 September 1910, and Booker T. Washington to KWK, 24 September 1910, Booker T. Washington Papers, Reel 68.

282. For a critique of this assumption, see especially Adeleke, *UnAfrican Americans*. For an excellent history of African American involvement with Africa, see James T. Campbell, *Middle Passages: African American Journeys to Africa, 1787–2005* (New York: Penguin, 2006). See also James T. Campbell, *Songs of Zion: The African Methodist Episcopal Church in the United States and South Africa* (New York: Oxford University Press, 1995); Lamin Sanneh, *Abolitionists*

Abroad: American Blacks and the Making of Modern West Africa (Cambridge: Harvard University Press, 1999); Elliot P. Skinner, *African Americans and U.S. Foreign Policy Toward Africa 1850–1924: In Defense of Black Nationality* (Washington, DC: Howard University Press, 1992); and Walter Williams, *Black Americans and the Evangelization of Africa, 1877–1900* (Madison: University of Wisconsin Press, 1982). For an excellent and critical account of American technical assistance in the global South, see David McBride *Missions for Science: U. S. Technology and Medicine in America's African World* (New Brunswick: Rutgers University Press, 2002).

283. Calling the Tuskegee expedition part of a "decivilizing mission" should not be taken to imply an endorsement of modernization theory or the possibility of an authentic "civilizing mission." I follow James Ferguson, who writes: "The modernization narrative was always a myth, an illusion, often even a lie. We should all learn to do without it. But if the academic rejection of modernization and development is not simply to reproduce at another level the global disconnects of capital, migration, and information flows, we must replace it with other ways of conceiving the relations of historical connectedness and ethical and political responsibility that link Africa and the rest of the world. If the people who have, in good faith, lived out the agonizing, failed plotline of development and modernization are not to be simply disconnected and abjected from the new world order, it will be necessary to find new ways of thinking about both progress and responsibility in the aftermath of modernism." James Ferguson, *Expectations of Modernity: Myths and Meanings of Urban Life on the Zambian Copperbelt* (Berkeley: University of California Press, 1999), 253–54.

* CHAPTER 4
FROM A GERMAN ALABAMA IN AFRICA TO A SEGREGATIONIST INTERNATIONAL:
THE LEAGUE OF NATIONS AND THE GLOBAL SOUTH

1. For an excellent survey of the *Musterkolonie* image, see Dennis Laumann, "A Historiography of German Togoland, or the Rise and Fall of a 'Model Colony,' " *History in Africa* 30 (2003): 195–211.

2. In the years between 1904 and 1908, the height of colonial cotton efforts, the United States continued to produce about 60 percent of the world's cotton supply, India about 20 percent, and Egypt about 7 percent, while sub-Saharan Africa in total, including German Togo, produced well below 1 percent. See Germany, Reichskolonialamt, *Die Baumwollfrage*, 151–53.

3. "Highways & Byways," *Chautauquan*, January 1901, 351, cited in "Colored Missionaries in Africa," *Friends' Intelligencer*, 19 October 1901, 674, and in "Negro Colonists in Africa," *Christian Advocate*, 14 February 1901, 256. The expedition was also praised, if not this excessively, by the American Geographical Society. See "Cotton Growing in German Togo" in "Geographical Record," *Bulletin of the American Geographical Society* 34 (1902): 249–57, and "Geographical Record," *Bulletin of the American Geographical Society* 38 (1906): 556–69. Similar American admiration appears in "Cotton Growing in Africa," *Zion's Herald*

17 June 1903, 739; "Engineering Notes," *Scientific American* 84, no. 1 (5 January 1901); and "Affairs in Africa," *Current Literature* 35 (August 1903), 144.

4. See Governor Adolf von Götzen of German East Africa to the Colonial Section of the German Foreign Office, 8 August 1901 and 15 October 1901, BArch R1001/8179, Bl. 16–17, Bl. 56–57; Weydig (in Rhodes, Illinois) to KWK, 4 July 1902 (copy), BArch R1001/8179, Bl. 191–95; *Arbeitsplan und Organization der Baumwoll-Kulturversuche 1910, 1911, 1912* (Berlin: KWK, n.d.), BArch R1001/8150, Bl. 123; Moritz Schanz, "Baumwollbau in deutschen Kolonien," *Zeitschrift für Kolonialpolitik, Kolonialrecht und Kolonialwirtschaft* 12 (1910): 1–28; Germany, Reichskolonialamt, *Die Baumwollfrage*, 114–15; Draft of "Die Entwickelung der Gouvernementsbaumwollstationen Mpanganya, Myombo und Mabama, der Landwirtschaftlichen Versuchstation Kibongoto und der Fruchtkulturstation Morogoro im Jahre 1912," sent by Governor Heinrich Schnee of German East Africa to the Imperial Colonial Office, 10 January 1913, Tanzanian National Archives, Dar es Salaam, Tanzania, German Records, G8/33, Bl. 178–90. On the cotton programs in German East Africa, see also Thaddeus Sunseri, *Vilimani: Labor Migration and Rural Change in Early Colonial Tanzania* (Portsmouth, NH: Heinemann, 2002), 119–30; and Thaddeus Sunseri, "Peasants and the Struggle for Labor in Cotton Regimes of the Rufiji Basin, Tanzania (1890–1918)," in Isaacman and Roberts, eds., *Cotton, Colonialism, and Social History in Sub-Saharan Africa,* 180–99.

5. As the British *African Mail* wrote, "it may be remembered that the Colonial Agricultural Committee took over in 1900 the introduction of cotton growing in the German colonies on a plan systematically prepared beforehand. They not only gave an impetus to the European cotton growing Associations, but also set an example by their method of work. This service of the Committee is recognised abroad." "Germany and Empire-Grown Cotton," *African Mail*, 15 May 1908, 312. See also Todd, *The World's Cotton Crops*, 183–84. With the preeminent cotton textile industry in the world in the middle of the previous century, Britain had sought longest to break the American monopoly on industrial-grade cotton. A Cotton Supply Association, founded in 1857—even before the cotton famine brought about by the American Civil War—recognized that Indian cotton could not meet British industrial needs and turned hopeful attention to West African cotton. See Isaac Watts, *The Cotton Supply Association: Its Origins and Progress* (Manchester: Tubbs and Brook, 1871).

6. On British explanations of German success, see "African Topics Reviewed," *Journal of the African Society* 3 (1903–1904): 198–99. On the British request for Tuskegee personnel, see Booker T. Washington, "The Successful Training of the Negro," *World's Work* 6 (1903): 3731–51, here 3747. See also "Bericht über englische Baumwollkultur-versuche," in *Bericht II. Deutsch-koloniale Baumwoll-Unternehmungen 1902/03*, supplement to *Tropenpflanzer* 4 (1903): 144–46.

7. "British Officer Here to Study Cotton," *New York Times*, 31 July 1904; E. L. Blackshear and J. Wesslay Hoffman, *Industrial Training of African Natives: Copies of Letters to Sir Alfred L. Jones* (Prairie View, Texas, n.p., 1909). The officer, John Wesslay Hoffman, had taught agriculture and biology at Tuskegee from 1894 to 1895. See Harlan, ed., *Booker T. Washington Papers* 3:414n.1;

John P. Power, "Tuskegee Institute Graduates in the Egyptian Soudan," *Southern Letter*, 23, no. 6 (June 1907).

8. See "Cotton Raising in Africa," *London Times—New York Times Special Cablegram*, 26 November 1902; "Vom Baumwollbau in Westafrika," *Deutsche Kolonialzeitung* 16 (1903); W. H. Himbury, "Empire Cotton," *Journal of the Royal African Society* 17 (1918): 262–75; and N. M. Penzer, *Cotton in British West Africa*, 10.

9. See the following articles from the *Bulletin du Comité de l'Afrique Français*, the African journal of the Parti Colonial: "La culture du coton" 10 (1900): 406; "Togo" 11 (1901): 26–27; "Togo" 11 (1901): 134; "Togo" 11 (1901): 245; "Togo" 11 (1901): 389; "Togo" 12 (1902): 155–56; "Togo" 12 (1902): 236; Emile Baillaud, "L'Exploitation du Coton en Afrique Occidental" 13 (1903): 37–44; "Les entreprises cotonnières dans les colonies allemandes" 13 (1903): 323–24; "Togo" 13 (1903): 102–3; "Togo" 13 (1903): 289; "Possessions Allemandes: Le culture du coton" 15 (1905): 284–85.

10. On the ACC see Richard Roberts, "French Colonialism, Imported Technology, and the Handicraft Textile Industry in the Western Sudan, 1898–1918," *Journal of Economic History* 47 (1987): 461–72.

11. Henry Bloud, *Le Problème Cotonnier et l'Afrique Occidentale Française: Une Solution Nationale* (Paris: Emile Larose, 1925), 79–89, 212–41.

12. E. D. Morel, *Red Rubber: The Story of the Rubber Slave Trade Flourishing on the Congo in the Year of Grace 1906*, Harry H. Johnston, Introduction (1906; New York: Negro Universities Press, 1969).

13. For a recent example, see Adam Hochschild, *King Leopold's Ghost: A Story of Greed, Terror, and Heroism in Colonial Africa* (Boston: Houghton Mifflin, 1998).

14. E. D. Morel, *King Leopold's Rule in Africa* (New York: Funk and Wagnalls, 1905), 3, 7.

15. See the splendid discussion of Morel, human rights, and imperialism in Kevin Grant, *A Civilised Savagery: Britain and the New Slaveries in Africa, 1884–1926* (New York: Routledge, 2005).

16. On this group, see Kenneth Dike Nworah, "The Liverpool 'Sect' and British West African Policy 1895–1915," African Affairs 70 (1971): 349–64; Kenneth Dike Nworah, "The West African Operations of the British Cotton Growing Association, 1904–1914," *African Historical Studies* 4 (1971): 315–30; and Anne Phillips, *The Enigma of Colonialism*.

17. C. T. Hagberg Wright, "German Methods of Development in Africa," *Journal of the African Society* 1 (1901): 23–38.

18. A. Chevalier, "The Cultivation of the Cotton Plant and the Agricultural Future of Senegambia and of the Soudan," *Journal of the African Society* 1 (1901–1902): 431–43.

19. P. Müllendorff, "The Development of German West Africa (Kamerun)," 78.

20. Morel thus viewed Germany as a natural ally of Great Britain in Africa and in the crusade against atrocities in the Congo. See Morel's editorials, "The Attitude of Germany," *Official Organ of the Congo Reform Association* N.S. 4 (October 1909): 311–16; and "Germany and the Congo," *Official Organ of the Congo Reform Association* N.S. 5 (January 1910): 431–33.

21. "Herr Dernburg on German Rule and Prospects in Africa," *African Mail*, 5 February 1909, 171–72.

22. Morel applauded German colonialism as an alternative to both the "Belgian school" and "the Peters School," the abusive practices associated with Carl Peters in German East Africa before the turn of the century. See "Reichstag Notes: Herr Dernburg's Success," *West African Mail*, 14 December 1906, 906–7; [E. D. Morel], "Editorial: Wise Words," *The African Mail*, 28 February 1908, 201; [E. D. Morel], "Herr Dernburg on German Rule and Prospects in Africa," *African Mail*, 5 February 1909, 171–72.

23. "Morel on the Congo v. Morel on the Gold Coast," *Gold Coast Nation*, 18 April 1912. See also "Mr. Morel's West African Campaign," *Gold Coast Nation*, 28 November 1912.

24. E. D. Morel, *Affairs of West Africa* (London, W. Heinemann, 1902), 196–200. This work is discussed in Anne Phillips, *The Enigma of Colonialism*, 177–82. See also Morel, "The European and the Native in the Economy of West Africa," *African Mail*, 23 April 1909, 283–84;

25. This has led William Roger Louis to term Morel a "pro-German radical." See William Roger Louis, "Great Britain and German Expansion in Africa, 1884–1919," in Prosser Gifford and William Roger Louis, with Alison Smith, eds., *Britain and Germany in Africa: Imperial Rivalry and Colonial Rule* (New Haven: Yale University Press, 1967), 35. Louis cites a letter of 7 October 1912 from Morel to John Holt. See also Catherine Ann Cline, introduction to *Truth and the War*, by E. D. Morel (1916; New York: Garland Publishing, 1972).

26. William Roger Louis, *Great Britain and Germany's Lost Colonies, 1914–1919* (Oxford: Clarendon, 1967), 35.

27. John H. Harris, *Dawn in Darkest Africa* (1912; reprint, London: Frank Cass, 1968), 87–90, 294–303.

28. Lord Cromer, Preface to *Dawn in Darkest Africa*, viii–xi.

29. On the early attempts to employ African Americans for the Congo Free State, see German Embassy in Belgium to Chancellor Bülow, 16 November 1903, BArch R901/353. On the attempt to hire students from Tuskegee Institute, see Booker T. Washington, "The Successful Training of the Negro," 3247. On the American growers in the Congo, see Jean de Hemptinne, "Cotton Growing in the Belgian Congo," *Official Report of the First International Cotton Congress of Delegated Representatives of Master Cotton Spinners' and Manufacturers' Associations held at the Tonhalle, Zürich, May 23–27, 1904* (n.p., n.d.), 90–96. The Belgian Congo continued to employ American cotton experts even after the First World War. See *Official Report of the Tenth International Cotton Congress of Delegated Representatives of Master Cotton Spinners' and Manufacturers' Associations, Zurich, 9–11 June 1920* (Manchester: Taylor, Garnett, Evans, & Co., n.d.), 333–36.

30. Harlan, ed., *Booker T. Washington Papers* 1:271.

31. Thomas Jesse Jones, Hampton Institute, to Robert Park, 10 July 1905, Robert Ezra Park Collection, Special Collections Research Center, University of Chicago Library (hereafter Park Collection), Box 15, Folder 2. It is virtually certain that Park advised Jones to decline the offer.

32. "Congo to Have a Tuskegee Institute," London, 31 December 1912, News Clipping File, Tuskegee Institute Archive, Reel 1, frame 386.

33. Park recruited Mark Twain at the suggestion of E. D. Morel. See E. D. Morel to Robert Park, 17 October [1904], Park Collection, Box 14, Folder 9.

34. Morel, *Affairs of West Africa*, 198–200.

35. Roscoe Conkling Bruce to Booker T. Washington, 3 April 1903, Washington Papers, Library of Congress, Reel 32.

36. Roscoe Conkling Bruce to Tuskegee academic faculty, 10 January 1905, Washington Papers, Library of Congress, Reel 32.

37. John W. Hubert to Roscoe Conkling Bruce, 12 January 1905; Leslie P. Hill, Division of Education, to Roscoe Conkling Bruce, 14 January 1905, Washington Papers, Library of Congress, Reel 32. Harlan discusses Bruce's intervention in the Tuskegee curriculum in *Booker T. Washington* 2:145–48.

38. Harlan, ed., *Booker T. Washington Papers* 4:391n1.

39. See McMurry, *George Washington Carver*, 82–83. In 1915 Carver wrote that "More Cotton Per Acre at Less Cost, and Better Prices" followed only "literacy and food self-reliance" in importance for Alabama. Carver, *A New and Prolific Variety of Cotton* (Tuskegee: Tuskegee Institute Steam Press, 1915), Carver Papers, Reel 24. For Carver's cotton recommendations, see Carver, *How to Make Cotton Growing Pay* (Tuskegee: Tuskegee Institute Steam Press, 1908) and *Cotton Growing for Rural Schools* 20 (Tuskegee: Tuskegee Institute Steam Press, 1911) Carver Papers, Reel 24.

40. John W. Robinson, Lome, Togo, to George Washington Carver, 24 June 1905, Carver Papers, Reel 3.

41. The Anganka Dhampala, School of Arts and Agriculture, Benares, India [to George Washington Carver], 4 August 1904, Carver Papers, Reel 2.

42. George B. Cowles, Adams Mission Station, Durban, Natal, South Africa, to George Washington Carver, 12 November 1904, Carver Papers, Reel 2; A. Kol., Russian Government, Assistant Agricultural Commissioner, St. Louis, Mo., to George Washington Carver, 11 February 1910, Carver Papers, Reel 4.

43. George Washington Carver to Emmett Jay Scott, 24 September 1910, Carver Papers, Reel 4. This letter is cited in McMurry, *George Washington Carver*, 88; Booker T. Washington, Vienna, Austria, to George Washington Carver, 11 September 1910 (photocopy), Carver Papers, Reel 4.

44. Booker T. Washington to newspapers of Toronto, Ottawa, and Montreal, December 1 1905, Washington Papers, Library of Congress, Reel 64. See also Park to Washington, 25 September 1905, Washington Papers, cited in King, *Pan-Africanism and Education*, 15, and Booker T. Washington to Robert E. Park, 28 September 1905, in Harlan, ed., *Booker T. Washington Papers* 8:378.

45. Robert E. Park, "Tuskegee's Notable Celebration," *Congregationalist and Christian World*, 21 April 1906, 578. The lecture was published as John W. Robinson, "A Tuskegee Graduate in West Africa," *Colored American Magazine* 10:5 (May, 1906): 355–59.

46. Moritz Schanz, "Nordamerikanische Neger für Westafrika," *Deutsche Kolonialzeitung*, 25 (1908): 364–65. On Tuskegee's international students, see Washington, "The Successful Training of the Negro," 3747, and the *Catalogue of the*

Tuskegee Normal and Industrial Institute, 1903–4, 1904–5, 1905–6, 1911–12, 1913–14.

47. Booker T. Washington, "Relation of Industrial Education to National Progress," *Annals of the American Academy of Political and Social Science* 33 (1909): 1–12, here 8–9.

48. Moritz Schanz, "Eine ungehaltene Rede von Booker Washington in Berlin," *Der Tropenpflanzer* 14 (1910): 641–45, 643–44.

49. Washington and Park, *Man Farthest Down*, 146–47.

50. Edgar Gardner Murphy, "Ascendancy," ch. 11, in *The Basis of Ascendancy: A Discussion of Certain Principles of Public Policy Involved in the Development of the Southern States* (New York: Longmans, Green, and Co., 1909), 222–23.

51. *Foreign Affairs* has been the official journal of the Council on Foreign Relations since 1922.

52. George H. Blakeslee, "Introduction," *Journal of Race Development* 1 (1910–11): 1–4, here 2.

53. George Washington Carver to Emmett Jay Scott, 1 October 1910, Carver Papers, Reel 4. See also "Problems of the Far East to be Discussed at Historical Conference at Clark University," *New York Times*, 19 November 1911.

54. "Go Separately to Liberia," *New York Times*, 22 April 1909. On the trip to Liberia, see Peter J. Duignan and Lewis Henry Gann, *The United States and Africa: A History* (Cambridge: Cambridge University Press and Hoover Institution, 1985), 195–96.

55. Booker T. Washington to President William Howard Taft, 19 April 1912 in Harlan, ed., *Booker T. Washington Papers* 11:522–23. On the conference, see Maurice S. Evans, "International Conference on the Negro," *Journal of the African Society* 11 (1911–12): 413–29, and Geiss, *The Pan-African Movement*, 218–21.

56. Booker T. Washington, "The Opening Address of the International Conference on the Negro," 17 April 1912, in Harlan, ed., *Booker T. Washington Papers* 11:520–22. See also Booker T. Washington, "An Announcement of a Conference at Tuskegee," ca. March 1911, in Harlan, ed., *Booker T. Washington Papers* 11:520–22; the notice in "Editorial Notes," *Journal of the African Society* 10 (1911): 352–64, here 364; and the earlier article proposing international cooperation around the issue of industrial education for Africa, Booker T. Washington, "Industrial Education in Africa," *Independent* 40 (15 March 1906).

57. The text of the lecture was not preserved. Because the program of the conference is not available, it is not possible to determine with certainty if this lecture was simply planned but never delivered. However, given the importance of the expedition to Togo in the international reputation of Tuskegee Institute, it would be surprising if these efforts were not addressed at the conference. See Emmett Jay Scott to Robert E. Park, 29 February 1912, and reply by Park (n.d.), Washington Papers, Library of Congress, Reel 66.

58. Leo J., letter to the editor, *African Times and Orient Review* 2 (1913): 175.

59. Quashie, "Togo-Germans and Immoralism and Its Effect on the Gold Coast," *Gold Coast Leader*, 6 July 1912, in BArch R1001/4308, Bl. 117.

60. Casely Hayford, "Our National Crisis," review of *West African Celebrities* by Attoh Ahuma, *Gold Coast Leader*, 23 June 1906, cited in Geiss, *The Pan-African Movement*, 203.

61. Booker T. Washington has long enjoyed a reputation in Africa as an advocate of black self-help. See W. Manning Marable, "Booker T. Washington and African Nationalism," *Phylon* 35 (1974): 398–406; Donald Spivey, "The African Crusade for Black Industrial Schooling," *Journal of Negro History* 63 (1978): 1–17; and Michael O. West, "The Tuskegee Model of Development in Africa: Another Dimension of the Africa/African-American Connection," *Diplomatic History* 16 (1992): 371–87.

62. E. W. Blyden, "West Africa before Europe," *Journal of the African Society* 2 (1903): 359–74; Geiss, *The Pan-African Movement*, 218–21.

63. J. E. Casely Hayford, quoted in "The Negro Conference at Tuskegee Institute," *African Times and Orient Review*, Old Series, 1 (July 1912): 10–12. As early as 1905, Casely Hayford had dismissed both Booker T. Washington and W.E.B. Du Bois as "exclusive and provincial" because they addressed the condition of blacks only in the United States. J. E. Casely Hayford, preface to Edward Wilmot Blyden, *West Africa before Europe and Other Addresses, Delivered in England in 1901* (C. M. Phillips, 1905), i. This passage is more widely known from Casely Hayford's novel, *Ethiopia Unbound: Studies in Race Emancipation* (1911; London: Routledge, 1969), 163.

64. *Gold Coast Nation*, 6 February 1913, cited in Geiss, *The Pan-African Movement*, 476n.119.

65. "The Coming Together of West Africa," *Gold Coast Nation*, 23 May 1912. For Washington as Moses, see, for example, F. A. Pinanko, "An Address Delivered at the International Conference on the Negro, held at Tuskegee, Ala.," *Gold Coast Nation*, 6 February 1913. J. E. Casely Hayford warned that there could be no Gold Coast Tuskegee without a Gold Coast university to train the teachers for such an institute. See Casely-Hayford in *Sierra Leone Weekly*, quoted in "An African on His Race," in E. D. Morel's newspaper *African Mail*, 19 June 1908, 367.

66. On Dusé Mohamed Ali, see Geiss, *The Pan-African Movement*, 221–28.

67. "The Negro Conference at Tuskegee Institute," *African Times and Orient Review*, Old Series, 1 (July 1912): 10–12.

68. Dusé Mohamed Ali to Booker T. Washington, 1 May 1912, Washington Papers, Library of Congress, Reel 66; Emmett Jay Scott to Robert E. Park, 13 May 1912, Washington Papers, Library of Congress, Reel 66; "The Negro Conference at Tuskegee Institute," African Times and Orient Review, Old Series, 1 (July 1912): 10–12; and Booker T. Washington, "Tuskegee Institute" *African Times and Orient Review*, 1 (1912), 48–54, Monroe N. Work Papers, Box 9.

69. On Marcus Garvey, Dusé Mohamed Ali, and black nationalism, see Stein, *The World of Marcus Garvey*.

70. Park also invited Franz Boas, who did not attend, Park explained, because he was out of the country at the time. Park to Washington, 13 June 1912, Washington Papers, Library of Congress, Reel 66.

71. "Morel on the Congo v. Morel on the Gold Coast," *Gold Coast Nation*, 18 April 1912.

72. Morel did not attend the conference or deliver this lecture, but it was printed as one of the four major contributions from the 1912 conference. See E. D. Morel, "The Future of Tropical Africa," *Southern Workman* 41 (1912): 353–62.

73. Maurice S. Evans, "Education among the Bantu of Southeast Africa," *Southern Workman* 41 (1912): 363–68, here 367–68.

74. Maurice S. Evans, "International Conference on the Negro," *Journal of the African Society* 11 (1911–12): 413–29, 429.

75. Maurice S. Evans, "Natal," in Evans, Dr. Hardy, and Dr. Karstedt, *Natal, Rhodesien, Britisch-Ostafrika*, part 3 of *Die Ansiedlung von Europäern in den Tropen, Schriften des Vereins für Socialpolitik*, vol. 147 (Munich: Duncker and Humblot, 1913), 1–46.

76. Maurice S. Evans, *Black and White in the Southern States: A Study of the Race Problem in the United States from a South African Point of View* (1915), introduction by George M. Fredrickson (Columbia: University of South Carolina Press, 2001), 273–81. In his annotated bibliography, arranged by importance rather than alphabetical order, Evans cited Booker T. Washington as his first authority. See also Maurice S. Evans, "Black and White in South Africa," *International Review of Missions* 4 (1915): 177–99. Robert E. Park, reviewing Evans's text for the *American Journal of Sociology*, rejected the segregationist's work as relying on "political dogma" rather than "matters of fact" and denied his claim that Booker T. Washington would support maintaining blacks in the United States as "a nation within a nation." See Park, review of *Black and White in the Southern States, a Study of the Race Problem in the United States from a South African Point of View*, by Maurice S. Evans (London, 1915), *American Journal of Sociology* 21 (1916): 696–97.

77. Robert E. Park, "Education by Cultural Groups," *Southern Workman* 41 (1912): 369–77, here 369–70, 377.

78. William I. Thomas, "Education and Racial Traits," *Southern Workman* 41 (1912): 378–86, here 378, 383–85. Thomas presented similar views, as well as practical recommendations for study, in his article "Race Psychology: Standpoint and Questionnaire, with Particular Reference to the Immigrant and the Negro," *American Journal of Sociology* 17 (May 1912): 725–75.

79. Morel's organization reported favorably on Vohsen's Congo reform efforts and on the German *Kongo-Liga*. See the following articles in *Official Organ of the Congo Reform Association*: "The Attitude of Germany," N.S. 4 (October 1909): 311–16; "Germany and the Congo," N.S. 5 (January 1910): 431–33; and "Memorial to the German Chancellor from the German Congo Reform League," N.S. 10 (August 1912): 840–46. Similarly, Vohsen published translations of Morel in *Koloniale Rundschau*. See E. D. Morel, "Die Grundbedingung europäischer Herrschaft im tropischen Afrika," *Koloniale Rundschau* 1 (1909): 76–88, and, after the First World War, when Morel defended German colonialism against its new detractors: "E. D. Morel gegen den Deutschenhaß," *Koloniale Rundschau* (1918): 136–40; E. D. Morel, "Ein Ausweg," *Koloniale Rundschau* (1918): 284–96; and E. D. Morel, "Afrika und der europäische Friede," *Koloniale Rundschau* (1919): 129–45.

80. On Vohsen, see Otto Jöhlinger et al., "Ernst Vohsen, Ein Lebensbild," *Koloniale Rundschau* (1919): 67–128.

81. Booker T. Washington, *Vom Sklaven Empor: Eine Selbstbiographie*, Estelle Du Bois-Reymond, trans. (Berlin: Dietrich Reimer [Ernst Vohsen], 1902), vi. By 1914 *Up from Slavery* had been translated into French, German, Spanish, Italian, Dutch, Hindi and Norwegian. Emmett Jay Scott to Mr. J. S. Johnson, Paramount Pictures Corporation, 22 October 1914, Washington Papers, Library of Congress, Reel 14.

82. Booker T. Washington, *Charakterbildung: Sonntags-Ansprachen an die Zöglinge der Normal- und Gewerbeschule von Tuskegee*, Estelle Du Bois-Reymond, trans. (Berlin: Dietrich Reimer [Ernst Vohsen], 1910), and Booker T. Washington, *Handarbeit: Fortsetzung des Buches "Sklaven Empor" und Schilderung der Erfahrungen des Verfassers bei dem gewerblichen Unterricht in Tuskegee*, Estelle Du Bois-Reymond, trans. (Berlin: Dietrich Reimer [Ernst Vohsen], 1913). An excerpt of *Character Building* also appeared as "Der Wert der Einfachheit" in *Koloniale Rundschau* 2 (1910): 493–97.

83. Alexander Tille, "Die Wettbewerb weisser, gelber und schwarzer Arbeit in der industriellen Produktion," *Verhandlungen des Deutschen Kolonialkongresses 1902*, 792–93.

84. See especially Tille, "Die Wettbewerb weisser, gelber und schwarzer Arbeit"; Moritz Schanz, "Die Baumwollfrage in den Kolonien," *Verhandlungen des Deutschen Kolonialkongresses 1905*, 698–710; and D. Richter, "Das Problem der Negerseele und die sich daraus für die Emporentwickelung des Negers ergebenden Folgerungen," *Verhandlungen des Deutschen Kolonialkongresses 1910 zu Berlin am 6., 7. und 8. Oktober 1910* (Berlin: Dietrich Reimer, 1910), 609–28. For other German discussions of African Americans relevant to colonial labor policy, see Hermann Gerhard, "Die volkswirtschaftliche Entwicklung des Südens der Vereinigten Staaten von Amerika von 1860 bis 1900, mit besonderer Berücksichtigung der Negerfrage" (Ph.D. diss., University of Heidelberg, 1903); Alexander Kuhn, *Zum Eingeborenenproblem in Deutsch-Südwestafrika: Ein Ruf an Deutschlands Frauen* (Berlin: Dietrich Reimer, 1905). I could not obtain a copy of this book, which was reviewed in *Deutsche Kolonialzeitung* 22 (1905): 198; Georg von Skal, "Die Rassenfrage in den Vereinigten Staaten," *Die Zukunft* Nr. 52–53 (1905), reprinted in *Politisch-Anthropologische Revue* 5 (1906/1907): 53–54; Hermann Gerhard, "Die Negerfrage in den Vereinigten Staaten," *Politisch-Anthropologische Revue* 5 (1906/1907): 268–81; "Die soziale Hebung der Negerrasse," *Politisch-Anthropologische Revue* 4 (1905/06): 528; Eugen Fischer, *Die Rehobother Bastards und das Bastardisierungsproblem beim Menschen* (Jena, 1913), 297. For a good discussion of this literature, see El-Tayeb, *Schwarze Deutsche*.

85. P. Müllendorff, "The Development of German West Africa," 73, 78.

86. Karstedt, "Betrachtungen zur Sozialpolitik in Ostafrika," *Koloniale Rundschau* 6 (1914): 133–41.

87. Useful information on Rohrbach's life before the First World War may be gleaned from Walter Mogk, *Paul Rohrbach und das "Größere Deutschland: Ethischer Imperialismus in Wilhelminischen Zeitalter: Ein Beitrag zur Geschichte des Kulturprotestantismus* (Munich: Wilhelm Goldmann, 1972). Mogk, however, barely alludes to Rohrbach's racism or to his later support for National Socialism.

88. Paul Rohrbach, *Deutsche Kolonialwirtschaft*, vol. 1, *Südwest-Afrika* (Berlin: Buchverlag der "Hilfe," 1907), viii.

89. Paul Rohrbach, *Deutsche Kolonialwirtschaft: Kulturpolitische Grundsätze für die Rassen- und Missionsfragen* (Berlin: Buchverlag der "Hilfe," 1909), 44.

90. Rohrbach, *Deutsche Kolonialwirtschaft; Kulturpolitische Grundsätze für die Rassen- und Missionsfragen*, 7, 13, 40–43. See also the similar praise for the Notsé school in Rohrbach, *Das Deutsche Kolonialwesen* (Leipzig: G. A. Gloeckner, 1911), 95–96, 103.

91. Paul Rohrbach, *Deutschlands koloniale Forderung* (Hamburg: Hanseatische Verlagsanstalt, 1935), 48. The Togo cotton project, though not the school itself, is discussed in A. Marcus, "Die Baumwolle in Africa," in Paul Rohrbach, ed., *Afrika: Beiträge zu einer praktischen Kolonialkunde* (Berlin: Werner and Co., 1943), 168–72.

92. See Klaus Epstein, "Erzberger and the German Colonial Scandals, 1905–1910," *The English Historical Review* 74 (1959): 637–63, and Müller, *Geschichte der katholischen Kirche in Togo*, 161, 175. As John Lowry has shown, Africans themselves, in Togo as well as Tanzania, Namibia, and Cameroon, played a role in the Reichstag dissolution of 1906–1907. See John S. Lowry, "African Resistance and Center Party Recalcitrance in the Reichstag Colonial Debates of 1905/06," *Central European History* 39 (2006): 244–69.

93. "To Raise Cotton in Africa," *New York Times*, 29 March 1902.

94. See "What Is Doing in Society," *New York Times*, 7 March 1902. On the Carnegie Hall meeting, see "Hampton and Tuskegee," *New York Times*, 3 March 1902.

95. On Henry's visit, see "Prince's Delight," *Boston Globe*, 10 March 1902; "Vanderbilts Have Prince at Dinner," *Atlanta Constitution*, 10 March 1902; "He Likes Our Songs," *Los Angeles Times*, 10 March 1902; "Farming in West Africa," *New York Times*, 30 March 1902; James Nathan Calloway, "Cotton Raising in Togoland," *Southern Workman* 31 (1902): 332–38, here 333; Robert D. Evans, "Prince Henry's American Impressions," *McClure's Magazine* 29, no. 1 (May 1902): 27–37.

96. "Hits at Business Men," *New York Times*, 2 June 1907. "German Ire is Stirred," *Chicago Daily Tribute*, 2 June 1907. For a biography of Dernburg, see Werner Schiefel, *Bernhard Dernburg 1865–1937: Kolonialpolitiker und Bankier im wilhelminischen Deutschland* (Zürich: Atlantis, 1974).

97. On the reception of Dernburg's appointment in the United States and in Germany, see "Banker in the Kaiser's Cabinet; Herr Dernburg, a Jew, the New Colonial Office Director," *New York Times*, 4 September 1906; "Triumph of Americanism," *Washington Post*, 5 September 1906; "Kaiser's Choice a Surprise," *Chicago Daily Tribune*, 5 September 1906. In his Rosh Hashanah address, a New York rabbi lauded Dernburg's appointment as evidence of decreasing anti-Semitism in Western Europe. See "New Year of Jews Begins This Evening," *Washington Post*, 19 September 1906.

98. Both quoted in "An American Triumph at the German Court," *New York Times*, 5 September 1906, 5. For a report on German receptions, see also "Dernburg Appointment Meets Approval Here," *New York Times*, 7 September 1906.

99. See Rudolph von Elphberg, "German Colonies Reek with Graft," *Chicago Daily Tribune*, 25 November 1906. That Dernburg's appointment suggested a turn for the better is also suggested in "Colonial Difficulties," *Daily Mirror*, quoted in *West African Mail*, 30 November 1906, 857.

100. "Germany's Great Man," *New York Times*, 11 February 1907.

101. Stenographic report of the Reichstag debate of 3 December 1906, NL Gruner, K. 7, Mappe 35. See also the point-by-point response to Center-Party deputy Hermann Roeren's criticisms of the Togo administration by Geo A. Schmidt, district officer of Atakpame, in *Schmidt gegen Roeren*.

102. "Dernburg Kissed by Kaiser," *New York Times*, 26 December 1906. The *Times* took this account from an unnamed Leipzig newspaper.

103. See "Letter of Marquise de Fontenoy," *Chicago Daily Tribune*, 10 January 1907; "Elections in Germany," *Los Angeles Times*, 20 January 1907; "Kaiser Uses Threats," *Washington Post*, 20 January 1907.

104. Centralbureau der Nationalliberalen Partei, *Kolonialpolitik seit der Reichstagsauflösung von 1906* (Berlin: Buchhandlung der Nationalliberalen Partei, 1909), 3, 24.

105. Winfried Becker, "Kulturkampf als Vorwand: Die Kolonialwahlen von 1907 und das Problem der Parlamentarisierung des Reiches," *Historisches Jahrbuch* 106 (1986): 59–84.

106. The recent work of Erik Grimmer-Solem has been important for this account of the Verein für Sozialpolitik, the Colonial-Political Action Committee, and the elections of 1907. See his "The Professors' Africa: Economists, the Elections of 1907, and the Legitimation of German Imperialism," *German History* 25 (2007): 313–47 and "Imperialist Socialism of the Chair: Gustav Schmoller and German Weltpolitik, 1897–1905," in Geoff Eley and James Retallack, eds., *Wilhelminism and Its Legacies: German Modernities, Imperialism, and the Meanings of Reform, 1890–1930* (New York: Berghahn Books, 2003), 106–22.

107. E. Struve, "Geschäftsbericht des Kolonialpolitischen Aktionskomitees," n.d., NL Schmoller, Nr. 13, Bd. II, Bl. 277–93. On the membership of he CPAC, see "Mitgliederverzeichnis des Kolonialpolitischen Aktionskomitees," January 1907, NL Schmoller, Nr. 13, Bd. II, Bl. 101–13.

108. Kolonialpolitisches Aktionskomitee, *Kolonialpolitischer Führer* (Berlin: Wedekind, 1907), 6–7, 20–21, NL Schmoller, Nr. 13, Bd. II, Bl. 43–74.

109. Gustav Schmoller, Bernhard Dernburg, Walter Delbrück, et al. *Reichstagsauflösung und Kolonialpolitik. Offener stenographische Bericht über die Versammlung in der Berliner Hochschule für Musik am 8. Januar 1907* (Berlin: Wedekind, 1907), 5.

110. "Germans Cite Our Colonies," *New York Times*, 9 January 1907; "Kaiser Fears Our Rivalry," *New York Times*, 22 January 1907; Edward T. Heyn, "German Colonial Issue," *Chicago Daily Tribune*, 27 January 1907.

111. *Reichstagsauflösung und Kolonialpolitik*, 6–8. This passage is also discussed in El-Tayeb, 49.

112. The CPAC distributed the text of Dernburg's speech to every public-school (*Volksschule*) teacher and to non-socialist workers' organizations. Kolonialpolitisches Aktionskomitee, Printed circular letters from Schmoller, 17 January 1907, and 18 January 1907, NL Schmoller, Nr. 13, Bd. II, Bl. 76–77. Somebody—

the CPAC suspected a Center Party member—managed to slip anticolonial leaflets into a set of these pamphlets sent out by the right-wing Navy League. Minutes of the meeting of the executive council of the CPAC, 2 February 1907, NL Schmoller, Nr. 13, Bd. II, Bl. 10–11.

113. *Reichstagsauflösung und Kolonialpolitik*, 24–32.

114. Dernburg to the Hamburg Senate, 12 July 1907 (copy), Staatsarchiv Hamburg, Germany, 364–66, A I 1, "Einrichtung eines Kolonialinstitutes in Hamburg," 61–65.

115. Grimmer-Solem, "The Professors' Africa."

116. Karl Rathgen, lecture to the Institut Solvay, March 1909, *Koloniale Rundschau* 1 (1909): 303; Karl Rathgen, *Les Nègres et la Civilisation européenne. Conférence fait à l'Institut Solvay, le 14 Mars 1909. Extrait de la Revue de l'Université de Hambourg Mai–Juin 1909* (Liége: La Meuse, 1909).

117. Park to Washington, 31 December 1913, Washington Papers, Library of Congress, Reel 66; William Anthony Aery to Robert E. Park, 10 March 1914, Park Collection, Box 8, Folder 2.

118. On Colonial Office support for the study, see the minutes of a meeting of 3 January 1911 between the representatives of the *Verein für Sozialpolitik* and the Colonial Office; Verein für Sozialpolitik, "Einladung zur nächsten Ausschußsitzung am 4. Januar 1911"; German Colonial Office to German Foreign Office, 20 January 1912; Solf to Sering, 30 January 1912, BArch R1001/6281, Bl. 31–33, 3–4, 7, 8–10. The completed results are *Die Ansiedlung von Europäern in den Tropen, Schriften des Vereins für Socialpolitik*, vol. 147, 5 parts (Munich: Duncker and Humblot, 1912–15): Part 1: Lindequist, *Deutsch-Ostafrika als Siedlungsgebiet für Europäer unter Berücksichtigung Britisch-Ostafrikas und Nyassalands* (1912); Part 2: Karl Sapper, D. van Blom. and J. A. Nederburgh, *Mittelamerika, Kleine Antillen, Niederlädisch-West- und Ostindien* (1912); Part 3: Maurice S. Evans, Dr. Hardy, and Dr. Karstedt, *Natal, Rhodesien, Britisch-Ostafrika* (1913); Part 4: Johannes Spanuth, *Britisch-Kaffraria und seine deutschen Seidlungen* (1914); Part 5: Ernst Wagemann, *Die deutschen Kolonisten im brasilianischen Staate Espirito Santo* (1915).

119. G. K. Anton, "Die Bedeutung von Zwang und Freiheit, Plantagen- und Volkskulturen für die koloniale Arbeiterfrage," *Koloniale Rundschau* 6 (1914): 196–221. This article was sent by the author to Colonial Secretary Solf on 22 April 1914 and became the basis for an oral conversation about colonial labor. See Solf to Anton, 25 April 1914, and 2 June 1914. This correspondence is in BArch R1001/6286, Bl. 182, 184–85.

120. Moritz Schanz, "Lebenslauf," 5 March 1918, Sammlung Darmstaedter C 1891. Schanz is referred to as the owner of a spinning mill in "Die Neger in Nordamerika," MNDM, 69 (1908): 108–10 and as an industrialist in "Die Negerfrage in Nordamerika," MNDM, 71 (1910): 18–19.

121. Moritz Schanz, "Negererziehung in Nordamerika und Booker T. Washington," 2 parts, *Der Tropenpflanzer* 12 (1908): 214–26; 270–80.

122. Schanz repeats Washington's warning about Du Bois and gives a version of Du Bois's report in "Nordamerikanische Neger für Westafrika," *Deutsche Kolonialzeitung* 25 (1908): 364–65. Most of this version is confirmed by a letter of Du Bois to Schanz of 24 October 1907, Du Bois Papers, Reel 1. The portions not

contained in that letter may have been based on discussions between Schanz and Du Bois in Atlanta.

123. Moritz Schanz, "Die Negerfrage in Nordamerika," *Der Tropenpflanzer* 13 (1909): 573–85, here 576–77. See also Schanz, *Der Neger in den Vereinigten Staaten von Nordamerika* (Essen: G. D. Baedeker, 1911).

124. William P. Pickett, *The Negro Problem: Abraham Lincoln's Solution* (1909; New York: Negro Universities Press, 1969), 334, 337–39, 397–98. Pickett's book was also cited in [Diedrich Westermann?], "Fortschritte der nordamerikanischen Neger," *Koloniale Rundschau* 2 (1910): 3–14.

125. Schanz discussed Pickett's *Negro Problem* and the 1910 riots in at least two lectures: Moritz Schanz "Der koloniale Baumwolle," *Verhandlungen des Deutschen Kolonialkongresses 1910*, 829–30; and *Official Report of the Eighth International Cotton Congress of Delegated Representatives of Master Cotton Spinners' and Manufacturers' Associations, Barcelona, 8–10 May 1911* (n.p., n.d.), 154. This was not the first time a German observer surmised that America was on the verge of a civil war between blacks and whites. See "Die Neger-Unruhen in Amerika," and "Das Rassenproblem in Amerika," *Politisch-Anthropologische Revue* 5 (1906/1907): 532–33.

126. Booker T. Washington to Colonial Committee, 30 September 1909, Booker T. Washington Papers, Reel 68; "German Officials Here to Study Cotton," *New York Times*, 4 October 1909; "Financial Notes," *New York Times*, 6 October 1909.

127. Bernhard Dernburg, "Bericht über die Studienreise des Staatssekretärs des Reichs-Kolonialamts Wirklichen Geheimen Rats Dernburg in die Baumwollgebiete von Nordamerika 1909," in Germany, Reichskolonialamt, *Die Baumwollfrage*, 227–28. This portion of Dernburg's report was reproduced in "Baumwollproduktion und Negerfrage in den Vereinigten Staaten," *Zeitschrift für Socialwissenschaft* n.s.:2 (1911), 349–50.

128. *Official Report of the Seventh International Cotton Congress of Delegated Representatives of Master Cotton Spinners' and Manufacturers' Associations, Brussels, 6–8 June, 1910* (n.p., n.d.), 186.

129. *Official Report of the Fifth International Cotton Congress of Delegated Representatives of Master Cotton Spinners' and Manufacturers' Associations held in the Salle des Ingeniéurs Civils de France, Paris, June 1st, 2nd, & 3rd, 1908* (n.p., n.d.), 235–36.

130. Dernburg, "Bericht über die Studienreise," 229–54.

131. "A German Bourbon: Herr Dernburg Shows Aristocratic Narrowness," *Brooklyn Times*, 6 January 1910, BArch R1001/8253, Bl. 19.

132. Adeleke, *UnAfrican Americans*.

133. On those Social Democrats who did embrace imperialism, see Roger Fletcher, *Revisionism and Empire: Socialist Imperialism in Germany, 1897–1914* (London: George Allen and Unwin, 1984). On discussions of colonialism and socialism in the SPD and the 1906–1907 elections, see Frank Oliver Sobich, *"Schwarze Bestien, Rote Gefahr": Rassismus und Antisozialismus im Deutschen Kaiserreich* (Frankfurt: Campus, 2006). The Social Democratic Party was more tolerant of individual expressions of racism and imperialism than, for example, the Communist Party would be. The SPD did not expel even the racist Ludwig

Wohltman, although his views diverged sharply from the party mainstream. On Wohltmann, see El-Tayeb, *Schwarze* Deutsche, 69–76. El-Tayeb, in my view, exaggerates the importance of Wohltmann and of racism and imperialism in the Social Democratic Party in the period before the First World War.

134. Henri van Kol, originally an engineer who had worked in Java, had also led discussions of colonialism at the 1900 and 1904 Socialist Congresses. In 1900 he had rejected colonialism and called on the International to help organize socialist parties in the colonies. *Internationaler Sozialisten-Kongress zu Paris, 23. bis 27. September 1900* (Berlin: Vorwärts, 1900). In 1904, already, he indicated his rightward shift, suggesting that socialists in the metropole try to foster a more benevolent colonialism. *Internationaler Sozialisten-Kongress zu Amsterdam, 14. bis 20. August 1904* (Berlin: Vorwärts, 1904), 23–24.

135. Marchlewski spoke under his pseudonym Karski. For a selection of his writings on Poles in Prussia, see Julian Baltazar Marchlewski (J. Karski), *Zur Polenpolitik der Preussischen Regierung: Auswahl von Artikeln aus den Jahren 1897 bis 1923* (Berlin: Dietz, 1957).

136. *Internationaler Sozialisten-Kongress zu Stuttgart, 18. bis 24. August 1907* (Berlin: Vorwärts, 1907), 25–39.

137. Karl Kautsky, *Sozialismus und Kolonialpolitik: Eine Auseinandersetzung* (Berlin: Vorwärts, 1907), 18–20.

138. Louis, *Great Britain and Germany's Lost Colonies*, 16, 89n31.

139. German modernity has long served the ideological needs of liberalism, as an externalizing projection of the negative features of the capitalism and modernity that are, in fact, central to liberalism. This ideological use of German history is highlighted critically by David Blackbourn and Geoff Eley, *Peculiarities of German History*, and Margaret Anderson and Kenneth Barkin, "The Myth of the Puttkamer Purge and the Reality of the *Kulturkampf*," *Journal of Modern History* 54 (1982): 647–86.

140. Frederick D. Lugard, *The Dual Mandate in British Tropical Africa* (London: W. Blackwood and Sons, 1922).

141. George Louis Beer, *African Questions at the Paris Peace Conference with Papers on Egypt, Mesopotamia, and the Colonial Settlement* (1923; reprint, New York: Negro Universities Press, 1969), 179, 279–80.

142. Germany, Reichskolonialministerium, *Deutsche und französische Eingeborenenbehandlung: Eine Erwiderung auf die im "Journal Officiel de la République Française" vom 8. November 1918 und 5. Januar 1919 veröffentlichten Berichte* (Berlin: Dietrich Reimer, 1919).

143. Frederick D. Lugard, *The Rise of Our East African Empire*, 2 vols. (1893; London: Frank Cass, 1968), 1:402–3. The commissioner of British East Africa, Charles Eliot, expressed similar sentiments in his *The East Africa Protectorate* (1905; reprint, New York: Barnes and Noble, 1966), 229, 256–58.

144. See Lake and Reynolds, *Drawing the Global Colour Line*, 284–309, and Naoko Shimazu, *Japan, Race, and Equality: The Racial Equality Proposal of 1919* (London: Routledge, 1998).

145. For a comparison of segregation in South Africa and the American South, see John W. Cell, *The Highest Stage of White Supremacy: The Origins of Segrega-*

tion in South Africa and the American South (Cambridge: Cambridge University Press, 1982).

146. Antonio Gramsci, "Americanism and Fordism," in *Selections from the Prison Notebooks* (New York: International Publishers, 1971), 279–316. George Ritzer, *The McDonaldization of Society: An Investigation into the Changing Character of Contemporary Social Life* (Newbury Park: Pine Forge Press, 1993).

147. Franklin Henry Giddings, *The Elements of Sociology: A Text-Book for Colleges and Schools* (London: MacMillan, 1898), vi, 107–18.

148. For an especially good account of Jones and his relation to Giddings and Hampton social studies, see Donald Johnson, "W.E.B. Du Bois, Thomas Jesse Jones, and the Struggle for Social Education, 1900–1930," *Journal of Negro History* 85 (2000): 71–95.

149. "Race War Coming, Dr. Giddings Says. Sociologist Declares Enfranchisement of Negro was a Great Mistake," *New York Times*, 26 September 1912, Park Collection, Box 1, Folder 5.

150. Thomas Jesse Jones, "Negro Population in the United States," *Annals of the American Academy of Political and Social Science* 49 (1913): 1–9.

151. Thomas Jesse Jones, *Social Studies in the Hampton Curricula* (Hampton: Hampton Institute Press, 1908), 3, 5, 7–15, 17, 40. These lessons in subordination became part of all public school curricula when, as historian of education Michael Lybarger has shown, the U.S. Bureau of Education took up the social studies developed by Thomas Jesse Jones as a component of secondary education throughout the United States even into the 1970s. Michael Lybarger, "Origins of Modern Social Studies 1900–1916," *History of Education Quarterly* 23 (1983): 455–68.

152. On the Phelps Stokes Fund, see, especially, Eric S. Yellin, "The (White) Search for (Black) Order: The Phelps-Stokes Fund's First Twenty Years, 1911–1931," *The Historian* 65 (2002): 319–52.

153. See Thomas Jesse Jones, *Negro Education: A Study of the Private and Higher Schools for Colored People in the United States*, 2 vols., Department of the Interior, Bureau of Education, Bulletin, 1916 (Washington, DC: Government Printing Office, 1917) 2:1, 23. Booker T. Washington, in a private letter to Anson Phelps Stokes Jr., praised the survey as a means for the "killing out of the poorer schools . . . through a process of placing emphasis upon the efficient ones." Booker T. Washington to Anson Phelps Stokes, Jr., 15 May 1911, Washington Papers, Library of Congress, Reel 79.

154. W.E.B. Du Bois, "Negro Education," review of *Negro Education*, by Jones (Washington, DC, 1917), *Crisis* 15 (1918), in Lewis, ed., *W.E.B. Du Bois: A Reader*, 261–69.

155. Carter G. Woodson, "Thomas Jesse Jones," *Journal of Negro History* 35 (1950): 107–9. When Jones was alive, Woodson was more blunt: "He will be lauded by his white friends and execrated and abhorred by Negroes who suffer from his career in Negro Life." Carter G. Woodson, review of *Progress in Negro Status and Race Relations, 1911–1946: The Thirty-five Year Report of the Phelps Stokes Fund*, by Anson Phelps Stokes et al. (New York, 1948), *Journal of Negro History* 34 (1949): 367–69.

156. For an excellent account of Jones and his activities in Africa, see King, *Pan-Africanism and Education*.

157. Thomas Jesse Jones, *Educational Adaptations: Report of Ten Years' Work of the Phelps-Stokes Fund, 1910–1920* (New York: Phelps-Stokes Fund, [1920]), 23.

158. Thomas Jesse Jones, *Education in Africa: A Study of the West, South, and Equatorial Africa by the African Education Commission, under the Auspices of the Phelps-Stokes Fund and Foreign Mission Societies of North America and Europe* (New York: Phelps-Stokes Fund, 1922), xxiii, 16. See also Thomas Jesse Jones, *Education in East Africa: A Study of East, Central and South Africa by the Second African Education Commission under the Auspices of the Phelps-Stokes Fund, in Cooperation with the International Education Board* (New York: Phelps-Stokes Fund, 1925). For Jones's understanding of pedagogy, see Thomas Jesse Jones, *Four Essentials of Education*, preface by Franklin H. Giddings (New York: Scribner's Sons, 1926). Giddings's preface provides a succinct account of principles that Jones elaborates at length. See viii.

159. Jones, *Education in East Africa*, xiii.

160. James T. Campbell has argued that the importance of Tuskegee and Hampton Institutes in South Africa lay in their roles as pedagogical models rather than in their direct influence. See Campbell, "Models and Metaphors: Industrial Education in the United States and South Africa." Maurice Evans, who had attended the 1912 conference at Tuskegee, and Charles T. Loram were especially important in bringing the language of the New South to South Africa. See Cell, *The Highest Stage of White Supremacy*, and R. Hunt Davis Jr., "Charles T. Loram and an American Model for African Education in South Africa," *African Studies Review* 19 (1976): 87–99. See also Charles T. Loram, *The Education of the South African Native* (1917; reprint, New York: Negro Universities Press, 1969). Shula Marks has shown how John L. Dube, a Zulu educator sometimes called the Booker T. Washington of South Africa, in fact differed significantly from his American counterpart, especially in his political activism, in "The Ambiguities of Dependence: John L. Dube of Natal," *Journal of Southern African Studies* 1 (1975): 162–80. She thus opposes R. Hunt Davis, Jr., "John L. Dube: A South African Exponent of Booker T. Washington," *Journal of African Studies* 2 (1975–76): 497–529. More recently Heather Hughes has shown that not only white elites, but also elite African politicians, played a central role for Dube, in "Doubly Elite: Exploring the Life of John Langalibalele Dube," *Journal of Southern African Studies* 27 (2001): 445–58.

161. On the Booker Washington Institute, see Spivey, *The Politics of Miseducation*.

CHAPTER 5
FROM INDUSTRIAL EDUCATION FOR THE NEW SOUTH TO A
SOCIOLOGY OF THE GLOBAL SOUTH

1. See especially Rodgers, *Atlantic Crossings*.

2. Etienne Balibar, "Is There a 'Neo-Racism'?" in Balibar and Immanuel Wallerstein, *Race, Nation, Class: Ambiguous Identities*, Chris Turner, trans. (1988; London: Verso, 1999), 22.

3. Imperial racism, as Michael Hardt and Antonio Negri have argued, operates through differentiation and inclusion, rather than through the binaries, hierarchies, and exclusions of imperialist or colonialist racism. See especially the section on "Imperial Racism" in Michael Hardt and Antonio Negri, *Empire* (Cambridge: Harvard University Press, 2000), 190–95.

4. Imperialism could function as what David Harvey calls a "spatial fix" for capital (or, for that matter, for culture, the state, or anything else) because it operated in, as Harvey also maintains, previously differentiated spaces. See David Harvey, *The Limits to Capital*, 2nd ed. (1982; London: Verso, 1999), esp. ch. 13, "Crises in the Space Economy of Capitalism: The Dialectics of Imperialism," 413–45.

5. Radkau, *Max Weber*, 254. Radkau treats Weber's mental health extensively, 253–315. After a year at the University of Freiburg, in 1896, Max Weber had moved to the University of Heidelberg.

6. On the Webers' trip to America, see Marianne Weber, *Max Weber: A Biography*, Harry Zohn, trans. (1926; New York: John Wiley and Sons, 1975), 279–304. Especially important for the present discussion is Lawrence Scaff, "Max Weber's *Amerikabild* and the African American Experience," in David McBride et al., *Crosscurrents: African Americans, Africa, and Germany in the Modern World* (Columbia: Camden House, 1998), 82–94. See also Wolfgang Mommsen, "Die Vereinigten Staaten von Amerika," in *Max Weber: Gesellschaft, Politik und Geschichte* (Frankfurt: Suhrkamp, 1974), 72–96; Radkau, *Max Weber*, 371–80; Guenther Roth, "Transatlantic Connections: A Cosmopolitan Context for Max and Marianne Weber's New York Visit 1904," *Max Weber Studies* 5 (2005): 81–112; and Lawrence Scaff, "The 'Cool Objectivity of Sociation': Max Weber and Marianne Weber in America," *History of the Human Sciences* 11 (1998): 61–82.

7. International Congress of Arts and Science, *Program and List of Speakers* (St. Louis: 1904).

8. See Paul A. Kramer, "Tensions of Exposition: Mixed Messages at the St. Louis World's Fair," ch. 4, in *The Blood of Government: Race, Empire, the United States, and the Philippines* (Chapel Hill: The University of North Carolina Press, 2006), 229–84, and Robert W. Rydell, *All the World's a Fair: Visions of Empire at American International Expositions, 1876–1916* (Chicago: University of Chicago Press, 1984).

9. William I. Thomas, "The Province of Social Psychology," Howard J. Rogers, ed., *Congress of Arts and Science: Universal Exposition, St. Louis, 1904*, 8 vols. (Boston: Houghton, Mifflin, and Co., 1905–07), 5:863.

10. Bernard Moses, "The Control of Dependencies Inhabited by the Less Developed Races," and Paul Reinsch, "The Problems of Colonial Administration," in Rogers, ed. *Congress of Arts and Science* 7:387–98, 399–416. The quotation is from Reinsch, 399.

11. Albert G. Keller's short presentation, "The Value of the Study of Colonies from a Sociological Standpoint," is noted but not reprinted in Rogers, ed. *Congress of Arts and Science* 7: 416. For Keller's work on German colonialism, see his "The Beginnings of German Colonization" *Yale Review* (May 1901) and "The Colonial Policy of the Germans," *Yale Review* (February 1902): 390–415. See

also Keller's *Colonization: A Study in the Founding of New Societies* (Boston: Ginn and Co., 1908).

12. Marianne Weber, *Max Weber*, 290. Wolfgang Mommsen surmises that many of these points were removed from the published version. See Mommsen, "Die Vereinigten Staaten von Amerika," 72–96.

13. Max Weber, "The Relations of the Rural Community to Other Branches of Social Science," Charles W. Seidenadel, trans, in Rogers, ed. *Congress of Arts and Science* 7:725–26, 733, 730, 745–46. This awkward English translation is the only available record of Weber's original German lecture.

14. Marianne Weber, *Max Weber*, 295.

15. Marianne Weber, Asheville, North Carolina, to her mother, 12 October 1904, and Max Weber, Asheville, NC, to his mother, 13 October 1904, GStA, VI HA, Nachlaß Weber, Nr. 6, Bl. 52–58. Marianne Weber quotes from the latter in *Max Weber*, 296.

16. The quotations are from Marianne Weber, *Max Weber*, 295, part of which quotes Max Weber, Asheville, NC, to his mother, 13 October 1904; Marianne Weber to her mother, 12 October 1904; and Marianne Weber, *Max Weber*, 295.

17. On the Fallensteins, as well as on the American and English connections of Max Weber's family, see Guenther Roth, *Max Webers Deutsch-englische Familiengeschichte*. In 1976 Professors Larry Keeter and Steve Hall of nearby Appalachian State University interviewed two members of the Fallenstein family, Lola and Maggie, who had been present during the Webers' visit. Keeter and Hall produced a video on the visit, which is available at Michael Wise, "Max Weber Visits America: A Review of the Video," *Sociation Today* 4:2 (Fall 2006), http://www.ncsociology.org/sociationtoday/v42/wise.htm. In 1995 sociology students at Appalachian State University placed a historical marker in front of the house where the Webers had stayed, financed by funds collected from sociology departments across the United States.

18. The German original is "Nigger-Englisch." Marianne Weber, *Max Weber: Ein Lebensbild* (Heidelberg: Lambert Schneider, 1926), 312. The English translator of the biography, Harry Zohn, places a *sic* after Marianne Weber's "Nigger-English. " Zohn explained: "The author presumably meant that Weber's English was primitive and perhaps even 'exotic' and droll." See Marianne Weber, *Max Weber*, 299n28. As I argue elsewhere, Zohn's *sic* is a result of liberal fantasies about Max Weber. In the age of the minstrel show, "Nigger-English" was likely far more entertaining than an awkward German accent. See Zimmerman, "Decolonizing Weber," *Postcolonial Studies* 9 (2006): 53–79.

19. Harry H. Johnston, *The Story of My Life* (London: Chatto and Windus, 1923), 422–23. Johnston praised the near absence of American accents among all Tuskegee and Hampton students in *The Negro in the New World* (1910; reprint, New York: Johnson Reprint, 1969), 396.

20. Max Weber, New York City, to W.E.B. Du Bois, n.d. [November, 1904], Du Bois Papers, Reel 3.

21. Max Weber to W.E.B. Du Bois, 20 March 1905, in Herbert Aptheker, ed., *The Correspondence of W.E.B. Du Bois*, 3 vols. (Amherst: University of Massachusetts Press, 1973), 1:106–7.

22. Max Weber, New York City, to W.E.B. Du Bois, n.d. [November, 1904], Du Bois Papers, Reel 3.

23. Max Weber, New York City, to W.E.B. Du Bois, 17 November 1904, Du Bois Papers, Reel 3.

24. W.E.B. Du Bois, "Die Negerfrage in den Vereinigten Staaten," *Archiv für Sozialwissenschaft und Sozialpolitik* 22 (1906): 31–79, here 43, 75, 79.

25. *Souls of Black Folk* was not translated into German until 2003. W.E.B. Du Bois, *Die Seelen der Schwarzen* (Freiburg: Orange-Press, 2003).

26. Max Weber to W.E.B. Du Bois, 30 March 1905, in Aptheker, ed., *The Correspondence of W.E.B. Du Bois*, I: 106–7. Aptheker incorrectly dates the letter as 20 March 1905. Facsimile in W.E.B. Du Bois, *Die Seelen der Schwarzen* (Freiburg: Orange-Press, 2003). Original in Du Bois Papers, Reel 3. See also Du Bois's response, n.d., Du Bois Papers, Reel 3. The works Weber proposed for his review included Du Bois's *Souls of Black Folks*, Booker T. Washington's *Character Building*, and Thomas Nelson Page, *The Negro: The Southerner's Problem* (New York: Charles Scribner's Sons, 1904). Of Page's book, Weber wrote: "very superficial methinks." Du Bois suggested Weber add to his list: William A. Sinclair, *The Aftermath of Slavery* (Boston: Small, Maynard, and Co., 1905); Edward Austin Johnson, *Light Ahead for the Negro* (New York: Grafton, 1904); and Winfield Hazlitt Collins, *Domestic Slave Trade of the United States* (New York: Broadway, 1904).

27. "Die protestantische Ethik und der 'Geist' des Kapitalismus," 2 parts, *Archiv für Sozialwissenschaft und Sozialpolitik* 20 (1904): 1–54; 21 (1905) 1–110.

28. Max Weber, "Die protestantische Ethik," *Archiv*, part 1, 17.

29. Ibid., part 1, 3.

30. Ibid., 20–25.

31. Ibid., 23.

32. Ibid., part 2, 106.

33. Ibid., 108.

34. Heinrich Herkner, Gustav Schmoller, Alfred Weber, "Vorwort," in Marie Berneys, *Untersuchungen über Auslese und Anpassung (Berufswahl und Berufsschicksal) der Arbeiter in den verschiedenen Zweigen der Grossindustrie Dargestellt an den Verhältnissen der "Gladbacher Spinnerei und Weberei," A.G. zu München-Gladbach im Rheinland, Schriften des Vereins für Socialpolitik*, vol. 133 (Leipzig: Duncker and Humblot, 1910), vii–xv. This project would lead to Alfred Weber's most famous work, *Über den Standort der Industrien* (Tübingen: J.C.B. Mohr, 1909).

35. Max Weber, "Zur Psychophysik der industriellen Arbeit" (1908–1909), in *Gesammelte Aufsätze zur Soziologie und Sozialpolitik* (Tübingen: J.C.B. Mohr, 1924), 68, 123, 125–26.

36. Max Weber, "Methodologische Einleitung für die Erhebungen des Vereins für Sozialpolitik über Auslese und Anpassung (Berufswahlen und Berufsschicksal) der Arbeiterschaft der geschlossenen Großindustrie" (1908), in *Gesammelte Aufsätze zur Soziologie und Sozialpolitik*, 1–2.

37. Max Weber, "Methodologische Einleitung," 27–28.

38. Weber borrowed the term from his colleague at Heidelberg, Emil Kraeplin, the man who had initially diagnosed his depression. Max Weber, "Zur Psychophysik der industriellen Arbeit," 61–64.

39. Max Weber, "Methodologische Einleitung," 27–28.

40. Max Weber, "Zur Psychophysik der industriellen Arbeit," 247–52.

41. For the results, see *Untersuchungen über Auslese und Anpassung (Berufs-wahl und Berufsschicksal) der Arbeiter in den verschiedenen Zweigen der Gross-industrie, Schriften des Vereins für Socialpolitik*, vols. 133–35 (Leipzig: Duncker and Humblot, 1910–12). See also Anthony Oberschall, "Max Weber and the Problem of Industrial Work," ch. 6, in *Empirical Social Research in Germany 1848–1914* (Paris: Mouton and Co., 1965), 111–36.

42. For a less laudatory, more accurate account of Weber's views on race, see Ernst Moritz Manasse, "Max Weber on Race," *Social Research* 14 (1947): 191–221.

43. Alfred Ploetz, "Die Begriffe Rasse und Gesellschaft und einige damit zu-sammenhängende Probleme," 21 October 1910, in *Verhandlungen des Ersten Deutschen Soziologentages vom 19–22. Oktober 1910 in Frankfurt a.M.* (Tü-bingen: J.C.B. Mohr, 1911), 111–36.

44. See the Discussion of Ploetz, "Die Begriffe Rasse und Gesellschaft," in *Ver-handlungen des Ersten Deutschen Soziologentages*, 137–65. Max Weber's contri-butions to this discussion are reprinted in Max Weber, "Diskussionsrede dort-selbst zu dem Vortrag von A. Ploetz über 'Die Begriffe Rasse und Gesellschaft,' " in *Gesammelte Aufsätze zur Soziologie und Sozialpolitik*, 456–62. For English translations of Max Weber's remarks, see Benjamin Nelson, "Max Weber on Race and Society," *Social Research* 38 (1971): 30–41, and Nelson, "Max Weber, Dr. Alfred Ploetz and W.E.B. Du Bois," *Sociological Analysis* 34 (1973): 308–12.

45. Max Weber, Asheville, NC, to his mother, 13 October 1904, quoted in Marianne Weber, *Max Weber*, 296.

46. Max Weber, "Die Wirtschaftsethik der Weltreligionen," *Gesammelte Auf-sätze zur Religionssoziologie*, 3 vols., 2nd ed. (1920; Tübingen: J.C.B. Mohr, 1922) 1:237–38.

47. Max Weber, "Vorbemerkung," *Religionssoziologie* 1:1.

48. Max Weber, "Der Nationalstaat und die Volkswirtschaftspolitik" (1895), 2–3. In "Protestant Ethic," however, Weber specifically rejected the case of Ger-mans and Poles in eastern Prussia as an example of religiously determined eco-nomic differences, which he attributed, instead, to the "degree of cultural develop-ment." Weber, "Die protestantische Ethik," *Archiv*, part 1, p. 2. Weber repeated this point in the 1920 edition, "Die protestantische Ethik und der Geist des Kapi-talismus," *Religionssoziologie* 1:19.

49. Max Weber, "Vorbemerkung," *Religionssoziologie* 1:12, 14–15.

50. The American political scientist Samuel Huntington has, perhaps more than any other contemporary political thinker, embraced—even if in a crude form—Weber's cultural-economic thinking. In a 1993 article for *Foreign Affairs*, since expanded into a book, Huntington outlined a future world politics based on what he calls a "Clash of Civilizations." Samuel P. Huntington, "The Clash of Civilizations? " *Foreign Affairs* 72, Nr. 3 (Summer 1993): 22–49. A collection of essays co-edited by Huntington under the title *Culture Matters* follows Weber in attributing poverty in the United States, Latin America, Africa, and elsewhere to noneconomic "cultural factors" that authors discern behind these economic inequalities. Lawrence E. Harrison and Samuel P. Huntington, eds., *Culture Mat-*

ters: How Values Shape Human Progress (New York: Basic Books, 2000). This scholarship is perhaps less well known in academic circles than those more intellectually rigorous treatments, from Talcott Parsons to Jürgen Habermas, that take aspects of Weber's thought to develop a non- or even anti-Marxist functionalist sociology. Talcott Parsons, *The Structure of Social Action: A Study in Social Theory with Special Reference to a Group of Recent European Writers* (New York: McGraw-Hill, 1937). Jürgen Habermas, *The Theory of Communicative Action,* 2 vols., Thomas McCarthy, trans. (Boston: Beacon Press, 1984).

51. George Fitzhugh, *Sociology for the South; Or, The Failure of Free Society* (Richmond: A. Morris, 1854), 7, 10, 34–44, 164–68, 82–95, 27, 42.

52. On Monroe N. Work, see Linda O. McMurry, *Recorder of the Black Experience: A Biography of Monroe Nathan Work* (Baton Rouge: Louisiana State University Press, 1985). See also Monroe N. Work, "An Autobiographical Sketch," typescript, circa June 1942, Monroe N. Work Papers, Box 1 and Jessie P. Guzman, "Monroe Nathan Work and His Contributions: Background and Preparation for Life's Career," *Journal of Negro History* 34 (1949): 428–61.

53. Monroe N. Work, "Crime Among the Negroes of Chicago. A Social Study," *American Journal of Sociology* 6 (1900): 204–23.

54. This research culminated in Monroe N. Work's *Bibliography of the Negro in Africa and America* (New York: H. W. Wilson, 1928), a reference work still in wide use today.

55. Monroe N. Work, "Why a Negro Year Book? Why a Bibliography of the Negro in Africa and America? " Harmon Award acceptance speech, 12 February 1929, Monroe N. Work Papers, Box 1.

56. Monroe N. Work, "Sociology in the Common Schools," n.d., Monroe N. Work Papers, Box 3.

57. James E. McCulloch, ed., *The Call of the New South: Addresses Delivered at the Southern Sociological Congress, Nashville, Tennessee, May 7 to 10, 1912* (1912; reprint, Westport, CT: Negro Universities Press, 1970).

58. Samuel C. Mitchell, "The Challenge of the South for a Better Nation," in James E. McCulloch, ed., *The South Mobilizing for Social Service: Addresses Delivered at the Southern Sociological Congress, Atlanta, Georgia, April 25–29, 1913* (Nashville: Southern Sociological Congress, 1913), 44.

59. William O. Scroggs, "Desirable Civic Reforms in the Treatment of the Negro," in *The South Mobilizing for Social Service*, 419.

60. Booker T. Washington, "The Southern Sociological Congress as a Factor for Social Welfare," in James E. McCulloch, ed., *Battling for Social Betterment. Southern Sociological Congress, Memphis, Tennessee, May 6–10, 1914* (Nashville: Southern Sociological Conference, 1914), 156, 158–59.

61. See especially Fred H. Matthews, "Robert Park, Congo Reform and Tuskegee: The Molding of a Race Relations Expert, 1905–1913," *Canadian Journal of History* 8 (1973): 37–65, and Winifred Raushenbush, *Robert E. Park: Biography of a Sociologist* (Durham: Duke University Press, 1979), 37–42.

62. Park's dissertation is available in English in Robert E. Park, *The Crowd and the Public*, Henry Elsner Jr., ed. (Chicago: University of Chicago Press, 1972).

63. Robert E. Park, "Life History," February 1929, The Ernest W. Burgess Papers, Special Collections Research Center, University of Chicago Library (here-

after, Burgess Papers), Box 17, Folder 1. Also in Paul J. Baker, "The Life Histories of W. I. Thomas and Robert E. Park," *American Journal of Sociology* 79 (1973): 243–60. See also Robert E. Park, "Methods of Teaching: Impressions and a Verdict," *Social Forces* 20 (1941): 36–46.

64. E. D. Morel and Robert E. Park, *The Treatment of Women and Children in the Congo State 1895–1904: An Appeal to Women of the United States of America* (Boston: Congo Reform Association, 1904); Robert E. Park, "Recent Atrocities in the Congo State," *The World To-Day* 8 (1904): 1328–31; "A King in Business: Leopold II of Belgium, Autocrat of the Congo and International Broker," *Everybody's Magazine* 15 (1906): 624–33; "The Terrible Story of the Congo," *Everybody's Magazine* 15 (1906): 763–72; "The Blood-Money of the Congo," *Everybody's Magazine* 16 (1907): 60–70. These and other texts are also in Stanford M. Lyman, *Militarism, Imperialism, and Racial Accommodation: An Analysis and Interpretation of the Early Writings of Robert E. Park* (Fayetteville: University of Arkansas Press, 1992). Park's wife, Clara Cahill Park, also wrote a pamphlet appealing to American women to address the Congo abuses, *Native Women in Africa: Their Hard Lot in the March of Progress* (Boston: Congo Reform Association, 1904).

65. Robert E. Park to Booker T. Washington, 18 July 1904, Washington Papers, Library of Congress, Reel 64; Booker T. Washington to Robert E. Park, 19 July 1904, Washington Papers, Library of Congress, Reel 64. [Robert E. Park], "Suggestion for an address to the President of the United States by Representative negroes, in regard to conditions in the Congo," n.d., Washington Papers, Library of Congress, Reel 396; [Robert E. Park], "Memorial to the Congress of the United States of America," January 1905, Washington Papers, Library of Congress, Reel 64.

66. Robert E. Park to Booker T. Washington, 10 September 1904, Washington Papers, Library of Congress, Reel 396. The article Park included was published as Booker T. Washington, "Cruelty in the Congo Country," *Outlook* (1904): 375–77, in Harlan, ed., *Booker T. Washington Papers* 8:85–90.

67. Robert E. Park, "Methods of Teaching"; see also Robert E. Park, "An Autobiographical Note," in Everett C. Hughes et al., eds., *The Collected Works of Robert Ezra Park*, 3 vols. (New York: Arno Press, 1974), 1:v–ix. Washington confirms Park's account in Washington and Park, *The Man Farthest Down*, 14.

68. Park, "Methods of Teaching," 41. Washington expressed a similar view about the similarities between the situation of Africans and that of African Americans in a letter to Grace Lathrop Dunham Luling, 28 January 1905, in Harlan, ed., *Booker T. Washington Papers* 8:184–85.

69. See John W. Robinson to Robert Park, 6 March 1907, and Robinson to Park, 8 July 1908, Park Collection, Box 14, Folder 5; and John W. Robinson to Robert Park, 20 November 1908, Park Collection, Box 14, Folder 5. Park also encouraged Washington to give prominent place to the work of Tuskegee Institute in Africa in *Story of the Negro*. See Park to Washington, 2 June 1908, Washington Papers, Library of Congress, Reel 65.

70. Robert E. Park, "Life History," February 1929, Burgess Papers, Box 17, Folder 1. Washington discussed his collaboration with Park on this trip in Washington and Park, *Man Farthest Down*, 14–17. Park determined their European

itinerary in consultation with Edward A. Steiner, a professor of "Applied Christianity" at Grinnell College, originally from Austria, who provided them with English-speaking contacts and advice for studying rural populations in Eastern Europe. Edward A. Steiner, Grinnell College, Grinnell, Iowa, to Booker T. Washington, n.d. (copy) Park Collection, Box 14, Folder 6.

71. Washington and Park, *Man Farthest Down*, 10–11.

72. In his private notebooks, Park also found Polish Jews especially fascinating, physically distinct from the surrounding population in ways that made clear to him that "Jews were intellectually a superior race." Robert E. Park, European notebook, 1910, Park Collection, Box 16, Folder 4.

73. See, for example, James Creelman, "South's New Epoch," *New York World*, 18 September 1895, reprinted in Harlan, ed., *Booker T. Washington Papers* 4:3–15 and F. A. Pinanko, "An Address delivered at the International Conference on the Negro, held at Tuskegee, Ala.," *Gold Coast Nation*, 6 February 1913.

74. Washington and Park, *Man Farthest Down*, 291–95.

75. Washington to Park, 24 October 1910, Washington Papers, Library of Congress, Reel 65; Washington to Park, 2 December 1910, Park Collection, Box 15, Folder 10.

76. Park, European notebook, 1910, Park Collection, Box 16, Folder 3.

77. This according to the recollection of Park's student, Edgar T. Thompson, Duke University, to Winifred Raushenbush, 9 October 1967, Park Collection, Box 19, Folder 3.

78. Robert E. Park, "Life History," February 1929, Burgess Papers, Box 17, Folder 1.

79. Park to Scott, 5 July 1913, Washington Papers, Library of Congress, Reel 66.

80. William I. Thomas, "Education and Racial Traits," *Southern Workman* 41 (1912): 378–86, here 378, 383–85. Thomas presented similar views, as well as practical recommendations for study, in his article "Race Psychology: Standpoint and Questionnaire, With Particular Reference to the Immigrant and the Negro," *American Journal of Sociology* 17 (May 1912): 725–75.

81. William I. Thomas to Robert E. Park, 23 April 1912, Park Collection, Box 14, Folder 7. Also quoted in Raushenbush, *Robert E. Park*, 68.

82. Thomas to Park, 24 April 1912, Park Collection, Box 14, Folder 7. Also quoted in Raushenbush, *Robert E. Park*, 68; Thomas to Park, 16 May 1912, Park Collection, Box 14, Folder 7. Quoted in part in Raushenbush, *Robert E. Park*, 70.

83. Robert Park to Booker T. Washington, 25 February 1905, in Harlan, ed., *Booker T. Washington Papers* 8:203. According to Park biographer Fred H. Matthews, Park devoted about half of his work to Tuskegee even after he left for Chicago. See Matthews, *Quest for an American Sociology: Robert E. Park and the Chicago School* (Montreal: McGill-Queen's University Press, 1977), 84. On Robert Park's collaboration with Booker T. Washington, see also St. Clair Drake, "The Tuskegee Connection: Booker T. Washington and Robert E. Park" *Society* 20 (1983): 4: 82–92; Stanford M. Lyman, *Militarism, Imperialism, and Racial Accommodation*; Fred H. Matthews, "Robert Park, Congo Reform and Tuskegee"; Raushenbush, *Robert E. Park*.

84. Ralph Ellison, "An American Dilemma: A Review," unpublished manuscript written for the *Antioch Review* in 1944, in Ellison, *Shadow and Act* (New York: Random House, 1964), 306–7. University of Chicago sociologist Morris Janowitz, while defending the Chicago school as a whole, confirmed Ellison's view when he speculated that one of the sociology instructors at Tuskegee had used Park and Burgess's textbook "to justify his Uncle Tom attitude." Janowitz, review of *Shadow and Act*, by Ralph Ellison (New York, 1964), in *American Journal of Sociology* 70 (1965): 732–34. According to Ellison biographer Arnold Rampersad, Ellison had argued with his Tuskegee sociology instructor specifically about Park's characterization of "the Negro" as "the lady among the races." Rampersad, *Ralph Ellison: A Biography* (New York: Alfred A. Knopf, 2007), 77–78.

85. On sociology at the University of Chicago, see especially Stow Persons, *Ethnic Studies at Chicago, 1905–45* (Urbana: University of Illinois Press, 1987). Equally important for my own thinking is the account of sexuality, race, class, and Chicago-school sociology by Roderick A. Ferguson, *Aberrations in Black: Toward a Queer of Color Critique* (Minneapolis: University of Minnesota Press, 2004). See also Barbara Ballis Lal, *The Romance of Culture in an Urban Civilization: Robert E. Park on Race and Ethnic Relations in Cities* (London: Routledge, 1990); Rolf Lindner, *The Reportage of Urban Culture: Robert Park and the Chicago School*, Adrian Morris, trans. (1990; Cambridge: Cambridge University Press, 1996); and R. Fred Wacker, "The Sociology of Race and Ethnicity in the Second Chicago School," in Gary Alan Fine, ed., *A Second Chicago School? The Development of a Postwar American Sociology* (Chicago: University of Chicago Press, 1995), 136–63. For a persuasive interpretation of Chicago-school sociology as emerging from Hull House, see Mary Jo Deegan, *Jane Addams and the Men of the Chicago School, 1892–1918* (New Brunswick: Transaction Books, 1988) and *Race, Hull-House, and the University of Chicago: A New Conscience against Ancient Evils* (Westport, CT: Praeger, 2002). Andrew Abbott focuses especially on later generations of Chicago sociologists in *Department and Discipline: Chicago Sociology at One Hundred* (Chicago: University of Chicago Press, 1999). On American social science more broadly, see Dorothy Ross, *Origins of American Social Science* (Cambridge: Cambridge University Press, 1991) and Mary O. Furner, *Advocacy and Objectivity: A Crisis in the Professionalization of American Social Science, 1865–1905* (Lexington: University Press of Kentucky, 1975).

86. Park, notes on the Negro, n.d., Park Collection, Box 1, Folder 7. See also Park, "The Course," n.d, Park Collection Papers, Box 1, Folder 4; Park, course notes, n.d., Park Collection, Box 1, Folder 4; Park, notebook written in Tuskegee, n.d., Park Collection, Box 11, Folder 1.

87. Park, manuscript on the "Negro in America" [n.d.], Park Collection, Box 1, Folder 4. The text is written on Tuskegee Institute stationery, suggesting that it was from his early years at the University of Chicago. See also Park, "Racial Assimilation in Secondary Groups: With Particular Reference to the Negro," *American Journal of Sociology* 19 (1914): 606–23.

88. Park, notes, n.d., Park Collection, Box 1, Folder 7.

89. Park, "Problem I," n.d., Park Collection, Box 1, Folder 8.

90. "Interaction," n.d., Park Collection, Box 1, Folder 8.

91. On this "lady among the races" statement, Morris Janowitz remembered, "Park regretted it again and again." See Morris Janowitz, review of *Shadow and Act*, by Ralph Ellison (New York, 1964), *American Journal of Sociology* 70 (1965): 732–34.

92. W.E.B. Du Bois, "The Negro in Literature and Art," *Annals of the American Academy of Political and Social Science* 49 (1913): 233–37, here 233.

93. Robert E. Park, "The Conflict and Fusion of Cultures with Special Reference to the Negro," *Journal of Negro History* 4 (1919): 111–33, here 130, 112.

94. Park to Washington, 29 May 1913, Washington Papers, Library of Congress, Reel 66.

95. Florian Znaniecki had come to Chicago from Poland in 1915, when Warsaw, then part of Russia, fell to the Germans. Znaniecki, head of the Bureau for the Protection of Emigrants in Warsaw, had been conducting research for Thomas in Poland since 1913, and he continued working for Thomas in the United States. Znaniecki returned to Poland in 1919, and worked as a professor in Poznan until the Germans invaded for the second time, in 1939, after which he permanently relocated to the United States until his death in 1958. See "Florian Znaniecki, Sociologist, Dead," *New York Times*, 25 March 1958. Thomas later presented Znaniecki as a research assistant rather than a true coauthor, and their common project was indeed carried out at Thomas's initiative and under his direction. Sociologist Howard Becker, however, later quipped that Thomas had been able to "reap nearly all the credit" for the work because he was "the man whose name had alphabetical priority and was easiest to pronounce with confidence." Howard Becker, review of *Cultural Sciences: Their Origin and Development*, by Florian Znaniecki (Urbana, 1952), in *Social Forces* 31 (1953): 289–92, here 289. Znaniecki later became an important sociologist in his own right. Many sociologists of science will be familiar with his *The Social Role of the Man of Knowledge* (New York: Columbia University Press, 1940), which is still a classic in the field.

96. Thomas and Znaniecki, *The Polish Peasant in Europe and America* 2:288, 296–97, 433–34.

97. Ibid., vol. 4.

98. Ibid., 5:222, 256, 292, 294–317, 318–39.

99. Ibid., 1:77–81.

100. William I. Thomas to Dorthy Swaine Thomas, January (?) 1935, copy, Individual Archives Collections, William I. Thomas Papers, Special Collections Research Center, University of Chicago Library, Box 1, Folder 1. Relative value calculations based on the Consumer Price Index and GDP deflator currency converters at the Economic History Services Web site: http://eh.net, accessed 29 January 2009. Harriet Park Thomas would work with Jane Addams in the Women's Peace Party after 1916 and admired Addams's research. See her positive review: Harriet Park Thomas, review of *The Spirit of Youth and the City Streets*, by Jane Addams (New York, 1909), in *American Journal of Sociology* 15 (1910): 550–53.

101. Less than a decade after its publication, the book was widely referred to as a classic, and, in 1939, the Social Science Research Council selected it, based on a survey of leading sociologists, as the first in a planned series of critical ap-

praisals of great recent works of sociology. Herbert Blumer, "Introduction to the Transaction Edition," *Critiques of Research in the Social Sciences: An Appraisal of Thomas and Znaniecki's the Polish Peasant* (1939; reprint, New Brunswick, NJ: Transaction Publishers, 1979), v. For reviews hailing the work as a nearly instant classic, see Ellsworth Faris, review of *The Polish Peasant in Europe and America*, by William I. Thomas and Florian Znaniecki, 2nd ed. (1927), in *American Journal of Sociology* 33 (1928): 816–19, and Theodore Abel, review of *The Polish Peasant in Europe and America*, by William I. Thomas and Florian Znaniecki, 2nd ed. (1927), in *American Journal of Psychology* 41 (1929): 665–66. The book's instant "classic" status was commented on in Konstantin Symmons-Symonolewicz, review of *The Polish Peasant in Europe and America*, by William I. Thomas and Florian Znaniecki, reprint of 2nd ed. (New York, 1958), in *American Slavic and East European Review* 19 (1960): 128–30.

102. Lester R. Kurtz, review of *The Polish Peasant in Europe and America*, by William I. Thomas and Florian Znaniecki, edited and abridged by Eli Zaretsky (Urbana, 1984), *American Journal of Sociology* 91 (1985): 476–79.

103. Robert E. Park and Ernest W. Burgess, *Introduction to the Science of Sociology* (Chicago: University of Chicago Press, 1921), 43–44. Morris Janowitz relates that University of Chicago Sociology students referred to this text as the "green bible." See his introduction to the 3rd, 1969, edition of the text.

104. In the early years of the study, Thomas had focused extensively on the Polish question in Germany. Thomas was assisted by both Florian Znaniecki and Samuel N. Harper, a Russian specialist and son of the founding president of the University of Chicago. See Samuel N. Harper, *The Russia I Believe In: The Memoirs of Samuel N. Harper, 1902–1941*, Paul V. Harper, ed. (Chicago: University of Chicago Press, 1945), 77–80. Thomas's correspondence with Harper is preserved in the Samuel N. Harper Papers, Special Collections Research Center, University of Chicago Library, Box 1, Folders 15, 16, 18, 20 and Box 2, Folder 2; Box 7, Folder 6; Box 8, Folder 5.

105. Thomas and Znaniecki, *The Polish Peasant in Europe and America*, vol. 3.

106. William I. Thomas, "The Prussian-Polish Situation: An Experiment in Assimilation," *American Journal of Sociology* 19 (1914): 624–39.

107. Chicago Commission on Race Relations, *The Negro in Chicago: A Study of Race Relations and a Race Riot* (Chicago: University of Chicago Press, 1922), 2.

108. For a discussion of Du Bois's motives in this political turn, see Mark Ellis, " 'Closing Ranks' and 'Seeking Honors': W.E.B. Du Bois in World War I," *Journal of American History* 79 (1992): 96–124.

109. "Code for Peace Party," *Washington Post*, 9 June 1916, 9.

110. In 1907 Thomas had aroused nationwide scandal by suggesting, in the *American Journal of Sociology*, that women and "savages" were both wrongfully blamed for an inferiority that resulted, in fact, from their unjust exclusion from education and civilization. He denounced especially the inferior status accorded women, which was based entirely on unfounded misogynistic prejudice, pure and simple, even when masquerading as "chivalry and chaperonage." These customs of patriarchal sexuality were, in Thomas's view, "the persistence of the old race

habit of contempt for women, and of their intellectual sequestration." William I. Thomas, "The Mind of Woman and the Lower Races," *American Journal of Sociology* 12 (1907): 435–69, here 463. For the response to Thomas, see Hildegard Hawthorne, "Sex and Society," *New York Times Book Review*, 16 February 1907, and anon., "Women and the Intellectual Life," *New York Times*, 10 February 1907. Thomas's writing on sex and sexuality are collected, in slightly modified form, in William I. Thomas, *Sex and Society: Studies in the Social Psychology of Sex* (Chicago: University of Chicago Press, 1907). See also William I. Thomas to Albion Small, 5 July 1915 and 17 June 1915, and "Women Bitterly Opposed to New Ideas of Dr. Thomas," *Chicago Examiner*, 10 June 1915, University Presidents' Papers, 1889–1925, Special Collections Research Center, University of Chicago Library, Box 64, Folder 4.

111. See "Lynar's 'Plot' Amazes," *Washington Post*, 28 April 1917. According to Chicago-trained sociologist Kimball Young, Thomas also suspected the Bureau's interest was in his wife's pacifist politics rather than in his own sexual activities. Fred B. Lindstrom, Ronald A. Hardert, and Kimball Young, "Kimball Young on Founders of the Chicago School," *Sociological Perspectives* 31 (1988): 269–97, here 293–94.

112. "Prof. Thomas Freed by Court," *Washington Post*, 20 April 1918.

113. Everett C. Hughes, memorandum, 12 February 1977, Everett Cherrington Hughes Papers, Special Collections Research Center, University of Chicago Library, Box 1, Folder 13.

114. Thomas and Znaniecki identified as four fundamental human wishes: the "desire for new experience"; "the desire for stability"; the "desire for response" from family and the immediate social group; and "desire for recognition" from society at large. Thomas and Znaniecki, *The Polish Peasant in Europe and America*, 3:26–27, 33, 56. These four wishes became a central concept of Chicago-school sociology.

115. Ibid., 3:61–64.

116. Ibid., 3:27–28, 48.

117. Znaniecki continued to work on the final volumes even after he had returned to Poland. See Florian Znaniecki to William I. Thomas, 26 January 1920, Florian Znaniecki Papers, Special Collections Research Center, University of Chicago Library, Box 8, Folder 13.

118. Thomas and Znaniecki, *The Polish Peasant in Europe and America*, 4: 305; 5:345, 344.

119. The connection of anti-immigrant and antidemocratic politics is central to John Higham's classic *Strangers in the Land: Patterns of American Nativism, 1860–1925*, 2nd ed. (New Brunswick: Rutgers University Press, 1988).

120. Publisher's note, Robert E. Park, *The Immigrant Press and Its Control* (New York: Harper and Brothers, 1922), v. See also William I. Thomas, Robert Park, and Herbert Miller, *Old World Traits Transplanted* (1921; Montclair, New Jersey: Patterson Smith, 1971).

121. Robert E. Park, "The City: Suggestions for the Investigation of Human Behavior in the City Environment," *American Journal of Sociology* 20 (1915): 577–612.

122. Touré F. Reed argues that the sociology of Park and Thomas played a more important role in the Urban League than did the closely related social thought associated with Tuskegee Institute. See Reed, *Not Alms but Opportunity: The Urban League and the Politics of Racial Uplift, 1910–1950* (Chapel Hill: University of North Carolina Press, 2008). See also Arvarh E. Strickland, *History of the Chicago Urban League* (Urbana: University of Illinois Press, 1966), and Nancy J. Weiss, *The National Urban League, 1910–1940* (New York: Oxford University Press, 1974).

123. Winifred Raushenbush to Edgar T. Thompson, 26 August 1967, Park Collection, Box 19, Folder 3. See also Mary Wirth to Winifred Raushenbush, 13 August 1966, Park Collection, Box 19, Folder 3.

124. Furner, *Advocacy and Objectivity*.

125. See Deegan, *Jane Addams and the Men of the Chicago School* and *Race, Hull-House, and the University of Chicago*.

126. Theodor K. Noss to Winifred Raushenbush, 5 November 1969, Park Collection, Box 19, Folder 2. Also cited in Raushenbush, *Robert E. Park*, 97.

127. Edgar T. Thompson, Duke University, to Winifred Raushenbush, 11 August 1967, Park Collection, Box 19, Folder 3.

128. One of Park's most famous contributions to sociology is a so-called race relations cycle that he worked out with William I. Thomas. The earliest version of this cycle described three stages through which two groups passed when brought into contact with each other: isolation, before contact between two groups; crisis, in the immediate aftermath of contact; and accommodation, as the two groups learned to live alongside each other. Thomas to Park, 16 May 1912, Park Collection, Box 14, Folder 7. Quoted in part in Raushenbush, *Robert E. Park*, 70. Isolation was, for Park and Thomas, a naive and primitive period ruled by group custom. Crisis (a stage Park would later divide into conflict and competition) was a potentially revolutionary period, in which groups had "exaggerated self-consciousness." Accommodation, for Park, was the ultimate goal, in which the two groups lived in practical harmony. [Robert E. Park], "Accommodation," n.d., Burgess Papers, Box 17, Folder 1. Park took the term *accommodation* from Franklin H. Giddings, Thomas Jesse Jones's teacher, who used it to describe the Americanization of European immigrants. Franklin Henry Giddings, *The Elements of Sociology: A Text-book for Colleges and Schools* (Macmillan, 1898), 52–53. According to Park, the political thought of W.E.B. Du Bois and the French Revolution were both examples of crisis, while the pedagogical and political strategies advocated by Booker T. Washington were examples of accommodation. See Robert Park to William I. Thomas, 6 October 1912, Park Collection, Box 14, Folder 7, quoted in part in Raushenbush, *Robert E. Park*, 70. Park would later add assimilation as a stage beyond accommodation, a stage that he did not, however, regard as particularly desirable. See the account of the race relations cycle in Park and Burgess, *Introduction to the Science of Sociology*, chs. 8–11.

129. [Winifred Raushenbush] to Werner J. Cahnman, 3 September 1966, Park Collection, Box 18, Folder 7. Everett C. Hughes, Memorandum, dictated 12 February 1977, Everett Cherrington Hughes Papers, University of Chicago, Box 1, Folder 13.

130. Robert E. Park, review of *The Psychology of the Negro: An Experimental Study*, by George Oscar Ferguson, Jr. (New York, 1916), *American Journal of Sociology* 22 (1917): 680–85, here 685.

131. [Robert E. Park], "Accommodation," n.d., Burgess Papers, Box 17, Folder 1.

132. Park and Burgess, *Introduction to the Science of Sociology*, 43–44.

133. Homi Bhabha has drawn attention to this subversive aspect of hybridity in numerous essays. See, for example, Homi K. Bhabha, "Sly Civility," in *The Location of Culture* (London: Routledge, 1994), 93–101.

134. Park to Thomas, 6 October 1912, Park Collection, Box 14, Folder 7. Quoted in part in Raushenbush, *Robert E. Park*, 70.

135. Edward Byron Reuter, *The Mulatto in the United States* (1918; New York: Haskell House, 1969).

136. Carter G. Woodson, review of *The Mulatto in the United States*, by Edward Byron Reuter (New York, 1918), in *Mississippi Valley Historical Review* 7 (1920): 175–76. Kelly Miller, review of *The Mulatto in the United States*, by Edward Byron Reuter (New York, 1918), in *American Journal of Sociology* 25 (1919): 218–24.

137. Everett V. Stonequist, Preface to *The Marginal Man: A Study in Personality and Culture Conflict* (1937; New York: Russell and Russell, 1961). Stonequist developed this book from his 1930 dissertation.

138. Frederick Lugard, *The Dual Mandate in British Tropical Africa* (Edinburgh: Blackwood, 1922), 79–84.

139. Stonequist, *The Marginal Man*, 29, 59–65.

140. Park, Preface to Stonequist, *The Marginal Man*, xvii–xviii.

141. Robert E. Park, "Human Migration and the Marginal Man," *American Journal of Sociology* 33 (1928): 881–93, here 890.

142. Louis Wirth, *The Ghetto* (Chicago: University of Chicago Press, 1928), 282–83, 287, ix.

143. For recent assessments of the hobo in American history, see Todd DePastino, *Citizen Hobo: How a Century of Homelessness Shaped America* (Chicago: University Of Chicago Press, 2005), and Frank Tobias Higbie, *Indispensable Outcasts: Hobo Workers and Community in the American Midwest, 1880–1930* (Urbana: University of Illinois Press, 2003).

144. Nels Anderson's book for Park's series is *The Hobo* (Chicago: University of Chicago Press, 1923). This became his M.A. thesis in 1925. He received his Ph.D. from New York University in 1930. Anderson wrote a more lighthearted account of the hobo under the pseudonym Dean Stiff—*The Milk and Honey Route: A Handbook for Hobos* (New York: The Vanguard Press, 1930). Excerpts from these and other works by Anderson on hoboes are collected in Raffaele Rauty, ed., *On Hobos and Homelessness* (Chicago: University of Chicago Press, 1998).

145. For the importance role of homosexuality in the sociology of the University of Chicago, see Chad Heap, "The City as a Sexual Laboratory: The Queer Heritage of the Chicago School," *Qualitative Sociology* 26 (2003): 457–87.

146. Weber, "Entwicklungstendenz in der Lage der ostelbischen Landarbeiter," 492–93.

CONCLUSION
PRUSSIAN PATHS OF CAPITALIST DEVELOPMENT: THE TUSKEGEE EXPEDITION
TO TOGO BETWEEN TRANSNATIONAL AND COMPARATIVE HISTORY

1. See especially Jonathan M. Wiener, *Social Origins of the New South: Alabama, 1860–1885* (Baton Rouge: Louisiana State University Press, 1978); Wiener, "Class Structure and Economic Development in the American South, 1865–1955," *American Historical Review* 84 (1979): 970–92; and Shearer Davis Bowman, *Masters and Lords: Mid-Nineteenth-Century U.S. Planters and Prussian Junkers* (New York: Oxford University Press, 1993). See also the excellent articles by Steven Hahn, "Class and State in Postemancipation Societies: Southern Planters in Comparative Perspective," *American Historical Review* 95 (1990): 75–98, and Anthony Winson, "The 'Prussian Road' of Agrarian Development: A Reconsideration," *Economy and Society* 11 (1982): 381–408. Winson points to Roger Bartra as the first historian to use the "Prussian path" concept in his 1974 *Agrarian Structure and Political Power in Mexico*, Stephen K. Ault, trans. (Baltimore: Johns Hopkins University Press, 1993). For an important comparison of the Russian and American cases in the period of serfdom and slavery, see Peter Kolchin, *Unfree Labor: American Slavery and Russian Serfdom* (Cambridge: Harvard University Press, 1987). The concept of a "Prussian Path" is sometimes incorrectly attributed to Barrington Moore, *The Social Origins of Dictatorship and Democracy: Lord and Peasant in the Making of the Modern World* (Boston: Beacon Press, 1966).

2. Edgar T. Thompson, Duke University, to Winifred Raushenbush, 13 November 1966, Park Collection, Box 19, Folder 3.

3. Edgar T. Thompson, "The Plantation" (Ph.D. diss., University of Chicago, 1932).

4. For discussion of the influence of Thompson on studies of the plantation, see Jay R. Mandle, *Not Slave, Not Free: The African American Economic Experience Since the Civil War* (Durham: Duke University Press, 1992), 59–60. Many of Thompson's most influential articles are collected in *Plantation Societies, Race Relations, and the South* (Durham: Duke University Press, 1975).

5. Vladimir Ilyich Lenin, *The Agrarian Programme of Social-Democracy in the First Russian Revolution, 1905–1907* (1908), in *Collected Works*, 13: 238–42. Lenin made a similar point in the 1907 preface to the second edition of his 1899 *The Development of Capitalism in Russia*, *Collected Works*, 3:31–34.

6. See especially Max Sering, "Die Agrarfrage und der Sozialismus." See also Sering, *Landwirthschaftliche Konkurrenz Nordamerikas in Gegenwart und Zukunft*; and Sering, "Politik der Grundbesitzverteilung in den grossen Reichen." Lenin cites Sering in *The Development of Capitalism in Russia*, 267–75, and discusses Sering in his *Notebooks on the Agrarian Question, 1900–1916*, *Collected Works* 40:239, 248, 266, 268, 398.

7. Vladimir Ilyich Lenin, "Capitalism and Agriculture in the United States of America," in *Collected Works*, 22:25–26. Lenin made a similar point in "Russians and Negroes" (1913), *Collected Works*, 18:543–44.

8. Lenin, "Capitalism and Agriculture in the United States of America," 27–43.

9. In his 1920, Lenin noted that "survivals of medieval, semi-feudal exploitation" of small farmers exist "in all capitalist countries, even the most advanced." He cited German cottagers, or *Instleute*, French *métayers*, and "the sharecroppers in the United States (not only Negroes, who, in the Southern States, are mostly exploited in this way, but sometimes whites too)." Lenin, "Preliminary Draft Theses on the Agrarian Question for the Second Congress of the Communist International" (1920), *Collected Works*, 31:152–64.

10. In this sense, Lenin's strategy resembels that of Blackbourn and Eley, *The Peculiarities of German History*.

11. Unless otherwise specified, all information on African Americans, the Communist Party, and the Soviet Union comes from the excellent and comprehensive Mark I. Solomon, *The Cry Was Unity: Communists and African Americans, 1917–36* (Jackson: University Press of Mississippi, 1998). See also Philip S. Foner and James S. Allen, eds., *American Communism and Black Americans: A Documentary History, 1919–1929* (Philadelphia: Temple University Press, 1987). Other important analyses include Kate A. Baldwin, *Beyond the Color Line and the Iron Curtain: Reading Encounters between Black and Red, 1922–1963* (Durham: Duke University Press, 2002); and Glenda Elizabeth Gilmore, *Defying Dixie: The Radical Roots of Civil Rights, 1919–1950* (New York: Norton, 2008).

12. Communist International, *Second Congress of the Communist International: Minutes of the Proceedings* (London: New Park Publications, 1977). That fall, at a Comintern Congress of "the Peoples of the East," held in Baku, Azerbaijan, Reed again spoke on the oppression of African Americans, this time as a warning to those "peoples of the East" who might mistakenly anticipate "that 'free America' will govern better, will liberate the peoples of the colonies, will feed and defend them." *Congress of the Peoples of the East. Baku, September 1920. Stenographic Report* (London: New Park Publications, 1977).

13. "The Black Question," Fourth Congress of the Communist International, 30 November 1922, in Communist International, *Theses, Resolutions, and Manifestos of the First Four Congresses of the Third International* (London: Ink Links, 1980), 328–31.

14. Of the African Americans present at the Sixth Congress, only one, Harry Haywood, endorsed national self-determination for African Americans. See Harry Haywood, *Black Bolshevik: Autobiography of an Afro-American Communist* (Chicago: Liberator Press, 1978).

15. See the superb treatment of the Scottsboro case by James A. Miller, Susan D. Pennybacker, and Eve Rosenhaft, "Mother Ada Wright and the International Campaign to Free the Scottsboro Boys, 1931–1934," *American Historical Review* 106 (2001): 387–430. On the sharecroppers' union, see Robin D.G. Kelley, *Hammer and Hoe: Alabama Communists during the Great Depression* (Chapel Hill: University of North Carolina Press, 1990).

16. Vladimir Ilyich Lenin, "Gems of Narodnik Project-Mongering" (1898), in *Collected Works*, 2:459–90; Lenin, review of *A Short Course of Economic Science*, by A. Bogdanov (Moscow, 1897) (1898), in *Collected Works*, 4:46–54. Lenin, *What Is to Be Done? Burning Questions of Our Movement* (1902; New York: International Publishers, 1969), 13–14.

17. Nikolai Bukharin, *The Economic Theory of the Leisure Class* (1927; New York: Monthly Review Press, 1972), 17–22, 175n4. Bukharin's text is primarily a critique of the Austrian school of economics and discusses the German historical school only briefly.

18. Leon Trotsky, *The Third International After Lenin* (1929; New York, Pathfinder Press, 1970), 298.

19. Leon Trotsky, *The Revolution Betrayed* (1937; New York: Pathfinder Press, 1972), 10.

20. The English original of McKay's report does not survive, but a Russian translation has been retranslated into English. See Claude McKay, *The Negroes in America* (Port Washington, NY: Kennikat Press, 1979). McKay discusses his sympathy for, but also indicates his distance from, the Communist Party in his *A Long Way from Home* (1937; New York: Arno Press, 1969), 153–84.

21. Haywood, *Black Bolshevik*, 27, 349, 421–23. The African American communist Hosea Hudson describes Communist-Party work with the more elite NAACP in the 1930s. See Hudson, *The Narrative of Hosea Hudson: His Life as a Negro Communist in the South*, Nell Irvin Painter, ed. (Cambridge: Harvard University Press, 1979), 269–81.

22. See Miller, Pennybacker, and Rosenhaft, "Mother Ada Wright and the International Campaign to Free the Scottsboro Boys."

23. Barbara Foley, *Spectres of 1919: Class and Nation in the Making of the New Negro* (Urbana: University of Illinois Press, 2003).

24. Cedric J. Robinson, *Black Marxism: The Making of the Black Radical Tradition* (1983; Chapel Hill: University of North Carolina Press, 2000).

25. On the Chicago Riot, see William M. Tuttle Jr., *Race Riot: Chicago in the Red Summer of 1919* (1970; Urbana: University of Illinois Press, 1996). Chicago Commission on Race Relations, *The Negro in Chicago*, also gives a good account of the riots. Also noteworthy is the account by the great poet of Chicago, Carl Sandburg, *The Chicago Race Riots, July, 1919* (1919; New York: Harcourt, Brace and World, 1969).

26. E. D. Morel, *The Horror on the Rhine*, foreword by Arthur Ponsonby (London: Union of Democratic Control, 1920), 10.

27. Chicago Commission on Race Relations, *The Negro in Chicago*, 639.

28. Ibid., 639–51, xvii–xviii. The book did not appear under Johnson's name, but it bears all the marks of the Chicago school of sociology and points to Johnson as the main author.

29. On Johnson, see especially Patrick J. Gilpin and Marybeth Gasman, *Charles S. Johnson: Leadership beyond the Veil in the Age of Jim Crow* (Albany: State University of New York Press, 2003), and Richard Robbins, *Sidelines Activist: Charles S. Johnson and the Struggle for Civil Rights* (Jackson: University Press of Mississippi, 1996). Johnson, as Barbara Foley has shown, connected race and class oppression in a decidedly radical manner. When Alain Locke published the seminal collection of essays of the Harlem Renaissance, the 1925 *New Negro*, he edited a number of contributions to mute their leftist political arguments. Johnson's essay on "Black Workers and the City," previously published in *Survey Graphic*, became, in Locke's collection, "The New Frontage on American Life." Foley, *Spectres of 1919*, 227–28. In 1931 Johnson praised the communist-led Na-

tional Miners Union for working across racial boundaries, including appointing an African American vice president. See Solomon, *The Cry Was Unity*, 103–5. In 1936 Johnson brought Park, then emeritus from the University of Chicago, to Fisk University. After Park died in 1944, Johnson renamed the social sciences building after him. The building has since been renamed Park-Johnson Hall.

30. Charles S. Johnson, *Shadow of the Plantation*, new introduction by Joseph S. Hines (1934; New Brunswick: Transaction Publishers, 1996).

31. Robert E. Park, "Negro Home Life and Standards of Living," *Annals of the American Academy of Political and Social Science* 49 (1913): 147–63, here 153.

32. Johnson, *Shadow of the Plantation*, 13, 144, 148, 208, 212.

33. Ibid., 212.

34. See, for example, ibid., 188, 201–2.

35. James Jones, *Bad Blood: The Tuskegee Syphilis Experiment* (New York: Free Press, 1981).

36. Park, preface to Johnson, *Shadow of the Plantation*, xx, xxiii, xxviii–xxix.

37. E. Franklin Frazier, "A Critical Summary of Articles Contributed to Symposium on Negro Education," *Journal of Negro Education*, 5 (1936): 531–33, here 533. Frazier, like Johnson, has sometimes been misunderstood as a conservative, particularly because his *The Negro Family in the United States* (Chicago: University of Chicago Press, 1939) was a source for the infamous "Moynihan Report" (Moynihan, *The Negro Family*). Such an interpretation distorts both the context and the arguments of *Negro Family* and, more generally, the life and work of E. Franklin Frazier. On Frazier, see especially Anthony M. Platt, *E. Franklin Frazier Reconsidered* (New Brunswick: Rutgers University Press, 1991).

38. E. Franklin Frazier, "Seventy Years Too Late," review of *Collapse of Cotton Tenancy*, by Charles S. Johnson et al. (Chapel Hill, 1935), *Journal of Negro Education* 5 (1936): 273–75.

39. Du Bois, *Black Reconstruction in America*.

40. On Du Bois's move to Ghana and his turn to Soviet Communism, see David Levering Lewis, *W.E.B. Du Bois: The Fight for Equality and the American Century, 1919–1963*, 554–71.

BIBLIOGRAPHY

ARCHIVES AND UNPUBLISHED MANUSCRIPTS

Bundesarchiv, Berlin, Germany
  R901, Auswärtiges Amt
  R1001, Reichskolonialamt
  R150, Togo National Archives (microfilm copy)
Geheimes Staatsarchiv, Preußischer Kulturbesitz, Berlin, Germany
  Georg Friedrich Knapp Papers
  Gustav Schmoller Papers
  Max Weber Papers
  Rep. 87ZB, Ministerium für Landwirtschaft, Domänen und Forsten, Die Mass-
    nahmen zur Bekämpfung der Ausbreitung des Polenthums und die Beförde-
    rung deutscher Ansiedlugnen in den Provinzen Westpreussen und Polen
  Rep. 90 A, Staatsministerium, Jüngere Registratur, Verwaltung der ehemals pol-
    nischen Gebietsteile. Politische Zustände und Polenpolitik
  Rep. 212, Ansiedlungskommission für Westpreussen und Posen
Library of Congress, Manuscript Division, Washington, DC
  Booker T. Washington Papers
  George Washington Carver Papers, Tuskegee University, Microfilm Edition
  Papers of W.E.B. Du Bois, University of Massachusetts, Amherst, Microfilm
    Edition
  The Ghana Archive of the Basel Mission
Narodna in univerzitetna knjižnica, Ljubljana, Slovenia. Photography Collection
  of Anton Codelli
Slovenski etnografski muzej, Ljubljana, Slovenia. Photography Collection of
  Anton Codelli
Staatsarchiv, Bremen
  Papers of the Norddeutsche Missionsgesellschaft
  Photography Collection of the Norddeutsche Missionsgesellschaft
Staatsarchiv, Hamburg
  "Einrichtung eines Kolonialinstitutes in Hamburg"
  "Universität"
Staatsbibliothek, Berlin
  Hans Gruner Papers
  Sammlung Darmstaedter
Tanzania National Archives, Dar es Salam, Tanzania. German Records
Tuskegee University, Tuskegee, Alabama
  Monroe N. Work Papers
  News Clipping File
University of Chicago Library, Special Collections Research Center
  Ernest W. Burgess Papers

Samuel N. Harper Papers
Everett Cherrington Hughes Papers
Robert Ezra Park Collection
William I. Thomas Papers
University Presidents' Papers, 1889–1925
Florian Znaniecki Papers

SERIALS

African Mail
African Times and Orient Review
American Journal of Sociology
Archiv für Sozialwissenschaft und Sozialpolitik
Atlanta Constitution
Boston Globe
Bulletin du Comité de l'Afrique Français
Catalogue of the Tuskegee Normal and Industrial Institute
Chicago Daily Tribune
Deutsche Kolonialzeitung
Deutsches Kolonialblatt
Globus
Gold Coast Chronicle
Gold Coast Leader
Gold Coast Nation
Journal of the African Society
Journal of the Royal African Society
Koloniale Rundschau
Los Angeles Times
Monats-Blatt der Norddeutschen Missions-Gesellschaft
New York Times
Official Organ of the Congo Reform Association
Politisch-Anthropologische Revue
Schriften des Vereins für Socialpolitik
Southern Letter
Southern Workman
Tropenpflanzer
Wall Street Journal
Washington Post
West African Mail
The World's Work

PRIMARY SOURCES

Abel, Theodore. Review of *The Polish Peasant in Europe and America* by William I. Thomas and Florian Znaniecki. *American Journal of Psychology* 41 (1929): 665–66.

Anderson, Nels. *The Hobo.* Chicago: University of Chicago Press, 1923.

—— (under the pseudonym Dean Stiff). *The Milk and Honey Route: A Handbook for Hobos.* New York: The Vanguard Press, 1930.

Anon. "Colored Missionaries in Africa." *Friends' Intelligencer,* 19 October 1901, 674.

Anon. "Cotton Growing in German Togo" in "Geographical Record." *Bulletin of the American Geographical Society* 34 (1902): 249–57.

Anon. "Geographical Record." *Bulletin of the American Geographical Society* 38 (1906): 556–69.

Anon. "Negro Colonists in Africa." *Christian Advocate,* 14 February 1901, 256.

Anon. *Internationaler Sozialisten-Kongress zu Paris, 23. bis 27. September 1900.* Berlin: Vorwärts, 1900.

Anon. *Internationaler Sozialisten-Kongress zu Stuttgart, 18. bis 24. August 1907.* Berlin: Vorwärts, 1907.

Anon. *Official Report of the First International Cotton Congress of Delegated Representatives of Master Cotton Spinners' and Manufacturers' Associations held at the Tonhalle, Zürich, May 23–27, 1904.* n.p., n.d.

Anon. *Official Report of the Fourth International Cotton Congress of Delegated Representatives of Master Cotton Spinners' and Manufacturers' Associations held in the Musikvereinsgebäude, Vienna, May 27–29, 1907.* n.p., n.d.

Anon. *Official Report of the Fifth International Cotton Congress of Delegated Representatives of Master Cotton Spinners' and Manufacturers' Associations held in the Salle des Ingeniéurs Civils de France, Paris, June 1st, 2nd, and 3rd, 1908.* n.p., n.d.

Anon. *Official Report of the Sixth International Cotton Congress of Delegated Representatives of Master Cotton Spinners' and Manufacturers' Associations, Milan, 17–19 May, 1909.* n.p., n.d.

Anon. *Official Report of the Seventh International Cotton Congress of Delegated Representatives of Master Cotton Spinners' and Manufacturers' Associations, Brussels, 6–8 June, 1910.* n.p., n.d.

Anon. *Official Report of the Eighth International Cotton Congress of Delegated Representatives of Master Cotton Spinners' and Manufacturers' Associations, Barcelona, 8–10 May 1911.* n.p., n.d.

Anon. *Official Report of the Tenth International Cotton Congress of Delegated Representatives of Master Cotton Spinners' and Manufacturers' Associations, Zurich, 9–11 June 1920.* Manchester: Taylor, Garnett, Evans, and Co., n.d.

Anon. *Transactions of the Third International Congress of Tropical Agriculture.* 3 vols. London: John Bale, Sons and Danielsson, 1917.

Anon. *Verhandlungen des Deutschen Kolonialkongresses 1902 zu Berlin am 10. und 11. Oktober 1902.* Berlin: Dietrich Reimer, 1902.

Anon. *Verhandlungen des Deutschen Kolonialkongresses 1905 zu Berlin am 5. 6. und 7. Oktober 1905.* Berlin: Dietrich Reimer, 1906.

Anon. *Verhandlungen des Deutschen Kolonialkongresses 1910 zu Berlin am 6. 7. und 8. Oktober 1910.* Berlin: Dietrich Reimer, 1910.

Anon. *Verhandlungen des Ersten Deutschen Soziologentages vom 19.–22. Oktober 1910 in Frankfurt A.M.* Tübingen: J.C.B. Mohr, 1911.

Anon. "Highways & Byways." *The Chautauquan,* January 1901, 351.

Anon. "Cotton Growing in Africa." *Zion's Herald*, 17 June 1903, 739.

Anon. "Affairs in Africa." *Current Literature* 35 (August 1903): 144.

Armstrong, Samuel Chapman. "Lessons from the Hawaiian Islands." *Journal of Christian Philosophy* (January 1884): 200–29.

Atlanta University Publications. New York: Arno Press, 1968.

Bacon, Alice. *The Negro and the Atlanta Exposition*. Baltimore: Trustees of the Slater Fund, 1896.

Baker, Paul J. "The Life Histories of W. I. Thomas and Robert E. Park." *American Journal of Sociology* 79 (1973): 243–60.

Balls, W. Lawrence. *The Cotton Plant in Egypt: Studies in Physiology and Genetics*. London: MacMillan, 1912.

———. *Studies of Quality in Cotton*. London: Macmillan, 1928.

Barrows, Isabel C., ed. *First Mohonk Conference on the Negro Question, Held at Lake Mohonk, Ulster County, New York, June 4, 5, 6, 1890*. 1890. Reprint, New York: Negro Universities Press, 1969.

———, ed. *Second Mohonk Conference on the Negro Question, Held at Lake Mohonk, Ulster County, New York, June 3, 4, 5, 1891*. 1891. Reprint, New York: Negro Universities Press, 1969.

Bebel, August. *Die Frau und der Sozialismus*. 1879. 10th ed. Stuttgart: Dietz, 1891.

Becker, Howard. Review of *Cultural Sciences: Their Origin and Development* by Florian Znaniecki (Urbana, 1952). *Social Forces* 31 (1953): 289–92.

Beer, George Louis. *African Questions at the Paris Peace Conference with Papers on Egypt, Mesopotamia, and the Colonial Settlement*. 1923. Reprint, New York: Negro Universities Press, 1969.

Belgard, Martin. *Parzellierung und innere kolonisation in den 6 Östllichen provinzen Preussens, 1875–1906*. Leipzig: Duncker and Humblot, 1907.

Bigwood, George. *Cotton*. London: Constable, 1918.

Bismarck, Otto von. *Gedanken und Erinnerungen*. 2 vols. Stuttgart: Cotta, 1898.

Blackshear, E. L., and J. Wesslay Hoffman. *Industrial Training of African Natives: Copies of Letters to Sir Alfred L. Jones*. Prairie View, Texas: n.p., 1909.

Blair, Lewis H. *A Southern Prophecy: The Prosperity of the South Dependent upon the Elevation of the Negro*. 1889. Edited by C. Vann Woodward. Boston: Little, Brown, and Co., 1964.

Blakeslee, George H. "Introduction." *Journal of Race Development* 1 (1910–11): 1–4.

Bloud, Henry. *Le Problème Cotonnier et l'Afrique Occidentale Française: Une Solution Nationale*. Paris: Emile Larose, 1925.

Blumer, Herbert. *Critiques of Research in the Social Sciences: An Appraisal of Thomas and Znaniecki's the Polish Peasant*. 1939. Reprint, New Brunswick, NJ: Transaction Publishers, 1979.

Blyden, Edward Wilmot. *West Africa Before Europe and Other Addresses, Delivered in England in 1901*. London: C. M. Phillips, 1905.

Bowen, J.W.E., ed. *Africa and the American Negro: Addresses and Proceedings of the Congress on Africa Held under the Auspices of the Stewart Missionary Foundation for Africa of the Gammon Theological Seminary in Connection with the Cotton States and International Exposition December 13–15, 1895.* 1896. Reprint, Miami: Mnemosyne, 1969.

Brentano, Lujo. "Abstracte und realistische Volkswirthe." *Zeitschrift des königlich-preußischen statistischen Bureaus* 11 (1871): 383–85.

———. "Agrarian Reform in Prussia." 2 parts. *The Economic Journal* 7 (1897): 1–20, 165–84.

Broadbent, James Thomas. *Cotton Manual for Manufacturers and Students.* Boston: Lord and Nagle, 1905.

Bryce, T. T. *Economic Crumbs, Or Plain Talks for the People about Labor,— Capital,—Money, Tariff,—Etc.* Hampton, VA: Hampton Steam Press, 1879.

Buerstenbinder, Richard. *Die Zuckerrübe: ein Handbuch für den praktischen Landwirt.* 3rd ed. Edited by Martin Ullmann. Hamburg: Lucas Gräfe and Sillem, 1896.

Bukharin, Nikolai. *The Economic Theory of the Leisure Class.* 1927. New York: Monthly Review Press, 1972.

Bürgi, E. "Reisen an der Togoküste und im Ewegebiet." *Dr. A. Petermanns Mitteilungen aus Justus Perthes' Geographischer Anstalt* 34 (1888): 233–37.

Buxton, Thomas Fowell. *The African Slave Trade, and Its Remedy.* London: John Murray, 1840.

Calloway, James N. "Tuskegee Cotton-Planters in Africa." *Outlook* 70 (March 29, 1902): 772–76.

Campbell, Robert. *A Pilgrimage to My Motherland: An Account of a Journey among the Egbas and Yorubas of Central Africa, in 1859–1860.* New York: Thomas Hamilton, 1861.

Chazelas, Victor. *Territoires Africains sous Mandat de la France: Cameroun et Togo.* Paris: Société d'Éditions Géographiques, Maritimes et Coloniales, 1931.

Chicago Commission on Race Relations. *The Negro in Chicago: A Study of Race Relations and a Race Riot.* Chicago: University of Chicago Press, 1922.

Clark, W. A. Graham. *Cotton Fabrics in British India and the Philippines.* Washington: Government Printing Office, 1907.

Cleef, Eugene van. "The Sugar Beet in Germany, with Special Attention to Its Relation to Climate." *Bulletin of the American Geographical Society* 47 (1915).

Cohn, Gustav. "Free Trade and Protection." *Economic Journal* 14 (1904): 188–95.

Communist International. *Second Congress of the Communist International: Minutes of the Proceedings.* London: New Park Publications, 1977.

———. *Theses, Resolutions, and Manifestos of the First Four Congresses of the Third International.* London: Ink Links, 1980.

Congress of the Peoples of the East. Baku, September 1920. Stenographic Report. London: New Park Publications, 1977.

Coons, George H. "The Sugar Beet: Product of Science." *Scientific Monthly* 68 (1949): 149–64.

Cooper, Walter G. *The Cotton States and International Exposition and South, Illustrated. Including the Official History of the Exposition.* Atlanta: The Illustrator Co., 1896.

Crummell, Alexander. *Civilization the Primal Need of the Race* and *The Attitude of the American Mind Toward the Negro Intellect*. Washington, DC: American Negro Academy, 1898.

Deerr, Noël. *The History of Sugar.* 2 vols. London: Chapman and Hall, 1949–50.

Dehn, R.M.R. *The German Cotton Industry: A Report to the Electors of the Gartside Scholarships*. Manchester: Manchester University Press, 1913.

Delbrück, Hans, Gustav Schmoller, and Adolph Wagner. *Ueber Die Stumm'sche Herrenhaus-Rede Gegen die Kathedersozialisten*. Berlin: Georg Stilke, 1897.

Delany, Martin R. *The Condition, Elevation, Emigration, and Destiny of the Colored People of the United States* and *Official Report of the Niger Valley Exploring Party*. Introduction by Toyin Falola. Amherst, NY: Humanity Books, 2004.

Dernburg, Bernhard. "Baumwollproduktion und Negerfrage in den Vereinigten Staaten." *Zeitschrift für Socialwissenschaft* n.s.2 (1911): 349–50.

Dewey, John. *The School and Society and The Child and the Curriculum*. Chicago: University of Chicago Press, 1990.

Drake, St. Clair. Review of *Negro Thought in America, 1880–1915*, by August Meier. *American Sociological Review* 30 (1965): 329–30.

Du Bois, W.E.B. *An ABC of Color: Selections Chosen by the Author from Over a Half Century of His Writings*. New York: International Publishers, 1969.

———. *The Autobiography of W.E.B. Du Bois: A Soliloquy on Viewing My Life from the Last Decade of Its First Century*. 1968. Oxford: Oxford University Press, 2007.

———. *Black Reconstruction in America: An Essay Toward a History of the Part which Black Folk Played in the Attempt to Reconstruct Democracy in America, 1860–1880*. New York: S.A. Russell, 1935.

———. *The Conservation of Races*. Washington, DC: American Negro Academy, 1897.

———. *The Correspondence of W.E.B. Du Bois* 3 vols. Edited by Herbert Aptheker. Amherst: University of Massachusetts Press, 1973.

———. "The Cultural Missions of Atlanta University." *Phylon* 3 (1942): 105–15.

———. *Dusk of Dawn: An Essay Toward an Autobiography of a Race Concept*. 1940. New Brunswick: Transaction Publishers, 1983.

———. "Die Negerfrage in den Vereinigten Staaten." *Archiv für Sozialwissenschaft und Sozialpolitik* 22 (1906): 31–79.

———. "The Negro in Literature and Art." *Annals of the American Academy of Political and Social Science* 49 (1913): 233–37.

———. *The Philadelphia Negro: A Social Study*. Philadelphia: University of Pennsylvania Press, 1899.

———. "The Present Condition of German Politics." *Central European History* 31 (1998): 171–87.

———. *Die Seelen der Schwarzen*. Freiburg: Orange-Press, 2003.

———. *The Souls of Black Folk*. 1903. Mineola: Dover, 1994.

———. "Strivings of the Negro People." *Atlantic Monthly* (August 1897): 194–98.

————. "The Study of the Negro Problems." *Annals of the American Academy of Political and Social Science* 11 (January 1898): 1–23.

————. *The Suppression of the African Slave-Trade to the United States of America, 1638–1870.* New York: Longmans, Green and Co., 1896.

————. *W.E.B. Du Bois: A Reader.* Edited by David Levering Lewis. New York: Henry Holt, 1995.

————. *Writings in Periodicals Edited by Others.* Edited by Herbert Aptheker. 4 vols. Milwood, NY: Kraus-Thomas Organization, 1982.

Duggar, J. F. *Descriptions and Classification of Varieties of American Upland Cotton.* Alabama Agricultural Experiment Station of the Alabama Polytechnic Institute, Auburn. Bulletin No. 140 (July 1907). Opelika, AL: Post Publishing Co., 1907.

Dunstan, Wyndham R. *Report on the Present Position of Cotton Cultivation: Presented to the International Congress of Tropical Agriculture, Brussels, May 1910.* Paris: International Association of Tropical Agriculture and Colonial Development, 1910.

Earle, D. E., and W. S. Dean. "The Classification and Grading of Cotton." *United States Department of Agriculture Farmers' Bulletin,* 591 (July 10, 1914).

Edorh, Edwige. *La Fille de Nana-Benz.* Lomé: Éditions Akpagnon, 1996.

Edwards, Thomas J. "The Tenant System and Some Changes since Emancipation." *Annals of the American Academy of Political and Social Science* 49 (1913): 38–46.

Eliot, Charles. *The East Africa Protectorate.* 1905. Reprint, New York: Barnes and Noble, 1966.

Ellis, A. B. *The Ewe-Speaking Peoples of the Slave Coast of West Africa: Their Religion, Manners, Customs, Laws, Languages, Etc.* 1890. Chicago: Benin Press, 1956.

Ellison, Ralph. "An American Dilemma: A Review." In *Shadow and Act,* 303–17. New York: Random House, 1964.

Ellison, Thomas. *The Cotton Trade of Great Britain.* 1886. Reprint, New York: A. M. Kelley, 1968.

Emery, Henry Crosby. "Speculation on the Stock and Produce Exchanges of the United States." Ph.D. diss., Columbia University, 1896.

Engels, Friedrich. "Die Bauernfrage in Frankreich und Deutschland" (1894–95). In Karl Marx and Friedrich Engels, *Werke.* Vol. 22. Berlin: Dietz, 1972.

————. *Socialism, Utopian and Scientific.* Translated by Edward Aveling. Chicago: Charles H. Kerr, 1907.

Erzberger, Matthias. *Der Kampf gegen den Katholizismus in der Ostmark: Material zur Beurteilung der Polenfrage durch die deutschen Katholiken.* Berlin: Germania, 1908.

Evans, Maurice S. "Black and White in South Africa." *International Review of Missions* 4 (1915): 177–99.

————. *Black and White in the Southern States: A Study of the Race Problem in the United States from a South African Point of View.* 1915. Introduction by George M. Fredrickson. Columbia: University of South Carolina Press, 2001.

Evans, Maurice S., Dr. Hardy, and Dr. Karstedt. *Natal, Rhodesien, Britisch-Osta-frika*, part 3 of *Die Ansiedlung von Europäern in den Tropen, Schriften des Vereins für Socialpolitik*. Vol. 147. Munich: Duncker and Humblot, 1913.

Evans, Robert D. "Prince Henry's American Impressions." *McClure's Magazine* 29, no. 1 (May 1902): 27–37.

Extension Department, Tuskegee Normal and Industrial Institute. *The Negro Rural School and Its Relation to the Community*. Tuskegee, 1914.

Fitzhugh, George. *Sociology for the South; Or, The Failure of Free Society*. Richmond: A. Morris, 1854.

François, Curt von. *Ohne Schuß durch dick und dünn: Erste Erforschung des Togohinterlandes*. Edited by Götz von François. Esch-Waldems: Eigenverlag Dr. Götz von François, 1972.

Frazier, E. Franklin. "A Critical Summary of Articles Contributed to Symposium on Negro Education." *Journal of Negro Education* 5 (1936): 531–33.

———. *The Negro Family in the United States*. Chicago: University of Chicago Press, 1939.

———. "Seventy Years too Late." Review of *Collapse of Cotton Tenancy* by Charles S. Johnson et al. (Chapel Hill, 1935). *Journal of Negro Education* 5 (1936): 273–75.

Fühling, Johann Josef. *Der praktische Rübenbauer*. Bonn: Henry and Cohen, 1860.

Gaunt, Mary. *Alone in West Africa*. London: T. Werner Laurie [1912].

Gehrts, Meg. *A Camera Actress in the Wilds of Togoland*. London: Seeley, Service and Co., 1915.

Gerhard, Hermann. "Die volkswirtschaftliche Entwicklung des Südens der Vereinigten Staaten von Amerika von 1860 bis 1900, mit besonderer Berücksichtigung der Negerfrage." Ph.D. diss., University of Heidelberg, 1903.

Germany. Reichskolonialamt. *Der Baumwollbau in den deutschen Schutzgebieten: Seine Entwicklung seit dem Jahre 1910*. Jena: Gustav Fischer, 1914.

———. *Die Baumwollfrage: Denkschrift über Produktion und Verbrauch von Baumwolle Massnahmen gegen die Baumwollnot*. Jena: Gustav Fischer: 1911.

Germany. Reichskolonialministerium. *Deutsche und französische Eingeborenenbehandlung: Eine Erwiderung auf die im "Journal Officiel de la République Française" vom 8. November 1918 und 5. Januar 1919 veröffentlichten Berichte*. Berlin: Dietrich Reimer, 1919.

Giddings, Franklin Henry. *The Elements of Sociology: A Text-book for Colleges and Schools*. Macmillan, 1898.

Glanemann, P. "Atakpame." *Gott will es!* 21 (1909): 73–76.

Great Britain, Colonial Office. *Report on the British Mandated Sphere of Togoland for 1920–1921*. London: His Majesty's Stationery Office, 1922.

Gruner, Hans. *Vormarsch zum Niger: Die Memoiren des Leiters der Togo-Hinterlandexpedition 1894/95*. Edited by Peter Sebald. Berlin: Edition Ost, 1997.

H. J. Review of *Thomas B. Freeman*, by John Milum (London, n.d). *Evangelisches Missions-Magazin* 38 (1894): 174–75.

Habermas, Jürgen. *The Theory of Communicative Action*. 2 vols. Translated by Thomas McCarthy. Boston: Beacon Press, 1984.

Hahn, Eduard. *Die Entstehung der Pflugkultur (unsres Ackerbaus)*. Heidelberg: Carl Winter's Universitätsbuchhandlung, 1909.

———. *Von der Hacke zum Pflug*. Leipzig: Quelle and Meyer, 1914.

Halle, Ernst von. *Baumwollproduktion und Pflanzungswirtschaft in den nordamerikanischen Südstaaten*. Leipzig: Duncker and Humblot, 1897.

Hammond, Matthew Brown. *The Cotton Industry: An Essay in American Economic History*. New York: American Economics Association, 1897.

Harper, Samuel N. *The Russia I Believe In: The Memoirs of Samuel N. Harper, 1902–1941*. Edited by Paul V. Harper. Chicago: University of Chicago Press, 1945.

Harris, Joel Chandler, ed. *Henry W. Grady*. 1890. New York: Haskell House, 1972.

Harris, John H. *Dawn in Darkest Africa*. 1912. Reprint, London: Frank Cass, 1968.

Harrison, Lawrence E., and Samuel P. Huntington, eds. *Culture Matters: How Values Shape Human Progress*. New York: Basic Books, 2000.

Härtter, Gottlob. "Einige Bausteine zur Geschichte der Ewe-Stämme (Togo)." *Beiträge zur Kolonialpolitik und Kolonialwirtschaft* 3 (1901/02): 432–48, 464–80, 492–514.

———. "Welcher Dialekt der Evhesprachen verdient zur Schrift- und Verkehrssprache im Evheland (Togo) erhoben zu werden." *Beiträge zur Kolonialpolitik und Kolonialwirtschaft* 3 (1901/02): 342–47.

Hayford, J. E. Casely. *Ethiopia Unbound: Studies in Race Emancipation*. 1911. London: Routledge, 1969.

Haywood, Harry. *Black Bolshevik: Autobiography of an Afro-American Communist*. Chicago: Liberator Press, 1978.

Heichen, Paul. "Togo." *Afrika Hand-Lexikon*. vol. 3, 1270–75. Leipzig: Gressner and Schramm, 1885.

Heide, Hermann auf der. *Die Missionsgesellschaft von Steyl: Ein Bild der ersten 25 Jahre ihres Bestehens*. Kaldenkirchen: Missionsdruckerei in Steyl, 1900.

Henning, P. O. "Zum Kampf um die Negerseele: Eine Antwort auf Dr. med. Oetkers 'Die Negerseele und die Deutschen in Afrika.' " *Flugschriften der Hanseastisch-Oldenburgischen Missions-Konferenz*. Bremen: J. Morgenbesser, 1907.

Hentschel, Volker. *Die deutschen Freihändler und der volkswirtschaftliche Kongress 1858 bis 1885*. Stuttgart: Klett, 1975.

Herold. "Bericht betreffend die religiöse Anschauungen und Gebräuche der deutschen Ewe-Neger." *Mitteilungen von Forschungsreisenden und Gelehrten aus den deutschen Schutzgebieten* 5 (1892): 141–60.

Hudson, Hosea. *The Narrative of Hosea Hudson: His Life as a Negro Communist in the South*. Edited by Nell Irvin Painter. Cambridge: Harvard University Press, 1979.

Huntington, Samuel P. "The Clash of Civilizations?" *Foreign Affairs* 72, Nr. 3 (Summer 1993): 22–49.

International Congress of Arts and Science. *Program and List of Speakers*. St. Louis, 1904.

Johnson, Charles S. *Shadow of the Plantation*, New Introduction by Joseph S. Hines. 1934. New Brunswick: Transaction Publishers, 1996.

Johnson, Charles S., Edwin R. Embree, W. W. Alexander. *The Collapse of Cotton Tenancy: Summary of Field Studies and Statistical Surveys 1933–35.* Chapel Hill: University of North Carolina Press, 1935.

Johnson, John Quincy. *Report of the Fifth Tuskegee Negro Conference 1896.* Baltimore: Trustees of the Slater Fund, 1896.

Johnston, Harry H. *The Negro in the New World.* 1910. Reprint, New York: Johnson Reprint, 1969.

———. *The Story of My Life.* London: Chatto and Windus, 1923.

Jones, Thomas Jesse. *Education in Africa: A Study of the West, South, and Equatorial Africa by the African Education Commission, under the Auspices of the Phelps-Stokes Fund and Foreign Mission Societies of North America and Europe.* New York: Phelps-Stokes Fund, 1922.

———. *Education in East Africa: A Study of East, Central and South Africa by the Second African Education Commission under the Auspices of the Phelps-Stokes Fund, in Cooperation with the International Education Board.* New York: Phelps-Stokes Fund, 1925.

———. *Educational Adaptations: Report of Ten Years' Work of the Phelps-Stokes Fund, 1910–1920.* New York: Phelps-Stokes Fund [1920].

———. *Four Essentials of Education.* Preface by Franklin H. Giddings. New York: Scribner's Sons, 1926.

———. *Negro Education: A Study of the Private and Higher Schools for Colored People in the United States.* 2 vols. Department of the Interior, Bureau of Education, Bulletin, 1916. Washington, DC: Government Printing Office, 1917.

———. "Negro Population in the United States." *Annals of the American Academy of Political and Social Science* 49 (1913): 1–9.

———. *Social Studies in the Hampton Curriculum.* Hampton: Hampton Institute Press, 1908.

Jones-Quartey, K.A.B. "The Gold Coast Press: 1822–c1930, and the Anglo-African Press: 1825–c1930—The Chronologies." *Institute of African Studies Research Review* 4, no. 2 (1968): 30–46.

Kaerger, Karl. *Die Arbeiterpacht: Ein Mittel zur Lösung der ländlichen Arbeiterfrage.* Berlin: Gergonne, 1893.

———. *Die künstliche Bewässerung in den wärmeren Erdstrichen und ihre Anwendbarkeit in Deutsch-Ostafrika.* Berlin: Gergonne and cie., 1893.

———. "Die ländlichen Arbeiterverhältnisse in Nordwestdeutschland." Vol. 1. of *Die Verhältnisse der Landarbeiter.* Vol. 53 of *Schriften des Vereins für Socialpolitik.* Leipzig: Duncker and Humblot, 1892.

———. *Landwirtschaft und Kolonisation im Spanischen Amerika.* 2 vols. Leipzig: Duncker and Humboldt, 1901.

———. *Die Sachsengängerei: Auf Grund persönlicher Ermittlungen und statistischer Erhebungen.* Berlin: Paul Parey, 1890.

———. *Tangaland und die Kolonisation Deutsch-Ostafrikas: Thatsachen und Vorschläge.* Berlin: Herman Walther, 1892.

Kautsky, Karl. *Die Agrarfrage: Eine Uebersicht über die Tendenzen der modernen Landwirtschaft und die Agrarpolitik der Sozialdemokratie.* 1899. 2nd ed. Stuttgart: J.H.W. Dietz, 1902.

———. *Sozialismus und Kolonialpolitik: Eine Auseinandersetzung.* Berlin: Vorwärts, 1907.

Keller, Albert G. "The Beginnings of German Colonization" *Yale Review* (May 1901): 30–52.

———. "The Colonial Policy of the Germans." *Yale Review* (February 1902): 390–415.

———. *Colonization: A Study in the Founding of New Societies.* Boston: Ginn and Co., 1908.

Kelley, William D. *The Old South and the New: A Series of Letters.* New York: G. P. Putnam's Sons, 1888.

Klose, Heinrich. *Togo unter deutscher Flagge.* Berlin: Dietrich Reimer, 1899.

Knapp, Georg Friedrich. *Die Bauernbefreiung und der Ursprung der Landarbeiter in den älteren Theilen Preußens.* 2 vols. 1887. Munich: Duncker and Humblot, 1927.

———. *Die Landarbeiter in Knechtschaft und Freiheit: Vier Vorträge.* Leipzig: Duncker and Humboldt, 1891.

———. *Einführung in einige Hauptgebiete der Nationalökonomie: Siebenundzwanzig Beiträge zur Sozialwissenschaft.* Munich: Duncker and Humblot, 1925.

Knauer, Ferdinand. *Der Rübenbau für Landwirte und Zuckerfabrikanten.* 6th ed. Berlin: Paul Parey, 1886.

Knüsli, Anna. *Afrikanisches Frauenleben wie ich es in Togo gesehen habe.* Bremen: Norddeutschen Missions-Gesellschaft, 1907.

Kueschke, Ernst Heinrich. *Neues allgemeines Deutsches Adels-Lexicon.* Leipzig: Friedrich Voigt, 1863.

Kuhn, Alexander. *Zum Eingeborenenproblem in Deutsch-Südwestafrika: Ein Ruf an Deutschlands Frauen.* Berlin: Dietrich Reimer, 1905.

Labriola, Antonio. "In memoria del Manifesto dei Comunisti." In *Scritti Filosofici e Politici.* vol. 2, 469–530. Edited by Franco Sbarberi. Torino: Einaudi, 1973.

Lance G. E. *The Jeanes Teacher in the United States, 1908–1933.* Chapel Hill: University of North Carolina Press, 1937.

Landmann, Robert von. *Kommentar zur Gewerbeordnung für das Deutsche Reich.* 2 vols. Munich: C. H. Beck, 1907.

Laughlin, J. Laurence. *The Elements of Political Economy: With Some Applications to the Questions of the Day.* 1887. Rev. ed. New York: American Book Co., 1896–1920.

Lenin, Vladimir Ilyich. *Collected Works.* 45 vols. Moscow: Progress Publishers, 1960–1970.

———. *What Is to Be Done? Burning Questions of Our Movement.* 1902. New York: International Publishers, 1969.

Lezius, Martin. *Heimatsgebiete der Sachsengänger in Brandenburg, Posen und Schlesien.* Neudamm: Neumann, 1913.

Lion, Alexander. *Die Kulturfähigkeit des Negers und die Erziehungsaufgaben der Kulturnationen.* Berlin: Wilhelm Süsserott, 1908.

Lippmann, Edmund Oskar von. *Geschichte des Zuckers seit den ältesten Zeiten bis zum Beginn der Rübenzucker-Fabrikation.* 2nd ed. Berlin: J. Springer, 1929.

List, Friedrich. *Das nationale System der politischen Ökonomie.* 1844. Berlin: Reimar Hobbing, 1930.

Lochmüller, W. *Zur Entwicklung der Baumwollindustrie in Deutschland.* Jena: Gustav Fischer, 1906.

Loram, Charles T. *The Education of the South African Native.* 1917. Reprint, New York: Negro Universities Press, 1969.

Lugard, Frederick D. *The Dual Mandate in British Tropical Africa.* Edinburgh: Blackwood, 1922.

———. *The Rise of Our East African Empire.* 2 vols. 1893. London: Frank Cass, 1968.

Luschan, Felix von. *Beiträge zur Völkerkunde der Deutschen Schutzgebiete.* Berlin: Dietrich Reimer, 1897.

Luxemburg, Rosa. *Gesammelte Werke.* 5 vols. Berlin: Dietz, 1970.

Marchlewski, Julian Baltazar (J. Karski). *Zur Polenpolitik der Preussischen Regierung: Auswahl von Artikeln aus den Jahren 1897 bis 1923.* Berlin: Dietz, 1957.

Marx, Karl. *Capital.* Vol. 1. Translated by Ben Fowkes. 1867. New York: Penguin Books, 1992.

———. *Capital.* Vol. 3. Translated by David Fernbach. 1894. New York: Penguin Books, 1981.

———. *The Civil War in the United States.* 3rd ed. New York: International Publishers, 1961.

———. *Collected Works.* Vol. 42. New York: International Publishers, 1987.

Marx, Karl, and Friedrich Engels. *Manifesto of the Communist Party.* 1848. Translated by Samuel Moore. Chicago: Charles H. Kerr, 1906.

McCulloch, James E., ed. *The Call of the New South: Addresses Delivered at the Southern Sociological Congress, Nashville, Tennessee, May 7 to 10, 1912.* 1912. Reprint, Westport, CT: Negro Universities Press, 1970.

———, ed. *The South Mobilizing for Social Service: Addresses Delivered at the Southern Sociological Congress, Atlanta, Georgia, April 25–29, 1913.* Nashville: Southern Sociological Congress, 1913.

———, ed. *Battling for Social Betterment.* Southern Sociological Congress, Memphis, Tennessee, May 6–10, 1914. Nashville: Southern Sociological Conference, 1914.

McKay, Claude. *A Long Way from Home.* 1937. New York: Arno Press, 1969.

———. *The Negroes in America.* Port Washington, NY: Kennikat Press, 1979.

Meitzen, August. *Der Boden und die Landwirthschaftlichen Verhältnisse des preußischen Staates.* Vol. 8. Berlin: P. Parey, 1908.

Miller, T. S. *The American Cotton System Historically Treated.* Austin: Austin Printing Co., 1909.

Mitzman, Arthur. *Sociology and Estrangement: Three Sociologists of Imperial Germany.* New Brunswick, NJ: Transaction, 1987.

Moeller, Robert G. *German Peasants and Agrarian Politics, 1914–1924: The Rhineland and Westphalia.* Chapel Hill: University of North Carolina Press, 1986.

Moore, Henry F. *Affairs of West Africa.* London: W. Heinemann, 1902.

———. *The Horror on the Rhine.* Foreword by Arthur Ponsonby. London: Union of Democratic Control, 1920.

———. *King Leopold's Rule in Africa.* New York: Funk and Wagnalls, 1905.

———. "Paper on Agricultural and Technical Education in the Colonies." *Journal of the Royal Colonial Institute* 22 (1891): 119–54.

———. *Red Rubber: The Story of the Rubber Slave Trade Flourishing on the Congo in the Year of Grace 1906*. Introduction by Harry H. Johnston. 1906. New York: Negro Universities Press, 1969.

Moore, Henry F., and Robert E. Park. *The Treatment of Women and Children in the Congo State 1895–1904: An Appeal to Women of the United States of America. Selections from a Pamphlet by E. D. Morel, of the Congo Reform Association of Great Britain, with comment by Robert E. Park, Ph.D., of the American Congo Reform Association*. Boston, 1904.

Morgan, Lewis Henry. *Ancient Society*. New York: H. Holt, 1877.

Moynihan, Daniel Patrick, U.S. Department of Labor, Office of Policy Planning and Research. *The Negro Family: A Case for National Action*. Washington, DC: Office of Policy Planning and Research, 1965.

Müller, Karl. *Geschichte der katholischen Kirche in Togo*. Kaldenkirchen: Steyler Verlangsbuchhandlung, 1958.

Murphy, Edgar Gardner. *The Basis of Ascendancy: A Discussion of Certain Principles of Public Policy Involved in the Development of the Southern States*. New York: Longmans, Green, and Co., 1909.

———. *Problems of the Present South: A Discussion of Certain of the Educational, Industrial and Political Issues in the Southern States*. New York: Grosset and Dunlap, 1904.

Nationalliberale Partei, Centralbureau. *Kolonialpolitik seit der Reichstagsauflösung von 1906*. Berlin: Buchhandlung der Nationalliberalen Partei, 1909.

Neubach, Helmut. *Die Ausweisungen von Polen und Juden aus Preussen 1885/ 86: Ein Beitrag zu Bismarcks Polenpolitik und zur Geschichte des deutschpolnischen Verhältnisses*. Wiesbaden: Otto Harrassowitz, 1967.

Oetker, Karl. *Die Neger-Seele und die Deutschen in Afrika: Ein Kampf gegen Missionen, Sittlichkeits-Fanatismus und Bürokratie vom Standpunkt moderner Psychologie*. Munich: J. F. Lehmann, 1907.

Oppel, Alwin. *Die deutsche Textilindustrie: Entwicklung, Gegenwärtiger Zustand, Beziehung zum Ausland und zur deutschen Kolonialwirtschaft*. Leipzig: Duncker and Humblot, 1912.

Oppenheim, Heinrich Bernhard. *Der Katheder-sozialismus*. Berlin: R. Oppenheim, 1872.

Pape, G. H. *Anleitung für die Baumwollkultur Togo*. Berlin: KWK, 1911.

Park, Clara Cahill. *Native Women in Africa: Their Hard Lot in the March of Progress*. Boston: Congo Reform Association, 1904.

Park, Robert E. "Agricultural Extension Among the Negroes." *The World To-Day* 15 (1908): 820–26.

———. "The Blood-Money of the Congo." *Everybody's Magazine* 16 (1907): 60–70.

———. *The Collected Works of Robert Ezra Park*. 3 vols. Edited by Everett C. Hughes et al. New York: Arno Press, 1974.

———. "The Conflict and Fusion of Cultures with Special Reference to the Negro." *Journal of Negro History* 4 (1919): 111–33.

Park, Robert E. *The Crowd and the Public.* Edited by Henry Elsner Jr. Chicago: University of Chicago Press, 1972.

———. *The Immigrant Press and Its Control.* New York: Harper and Brothers, 1922.

———. "A King in Business: Leopold II of Belgium, Autocrat of the Congo and International Broker." *Everybody's Magazine* 15 (1906): 624–33.

———. "Methods of Teaching: Impressions and a Verdict." *Social Forces* 20 (1941): 36–46.

———. "Negro Home Life and Standards of Living." *Annals of the American Academy of Political and Social Science* 49 (1913): 147–63.

———. *Race and Culture.* Glencoe, IL: The Free Press, 1950.

———. "Racial Assimilation in Secondary Groups: With Particular Reference to the Negro." *American Journal of Sociology* 19 (1914): 606–23.

———. "Recent Atrocities in the Congo State." *The World To-Day* 8 (1904): 1328–31.

———. "The Terrible Story of the Congo." *Everybody's Magazine* 15 (1906): 763–72.

———. "Tuskegee International Conference on the Negro." *Journal of Race Development* 3 (1912–13): 117–20.

Park, Robert E., and Ernest W. Burgess. *Introduction to the Science of Sociology.* Chicago: University of Chicago Press, 1921.

Park, Robert E., Ernest W. Burgess, and Roderick D. McKenzie. *The City.* Chicago: University of Chicago Press, 1928.

Parsons, Talcott. *The Structure of Social Action: A Study in Social Theory with Special Reference to a Group of Recent European Writers.* New York: McGraw-Hill, 1937.

Penzer, N. M. *Cotton in British West Africa, Including Togoland and the Cameroons.* London: The Federation of British Industries, 1920.

Pickett, William P. *The Negro Problem: Abraham Lincoln's Solution.* 1909. New York: Negro Universities Press, 1969.

Poggi, E. Muriel. "The German Sugar Beet Industry." *Economic Geography* 6 (1930): 81–93.

Polenz, Wilhelm von. "Sachsengänger." In *Sachsengänger: Erzählungen,* 152–65. Berlin: Rütten and Loening, 1991.

Putnam, Daniel. *A Manual of Pedagogics.* Introduction by Richard G. Boone. New York: Silver, Burdett and Co., 1895.

Rathgen, Karl. *Les Nègres et la Civilisation européenne. Conférence fait à l'Institut Solvay, le 14 Mars 1909. Extrait de la Revue de l'Université de Hambourg Mai–Juin 1909.* Liége: La Meuse, 1909.

République Française au Togo, Commissariat. *Guide de la Colonisation au Togo.* Paris: Émile Larose, 1924.

Reuter, Edward Byron. *The Mulatto in the United States.* 1918. New York: Haskell House, 1969.

Roark, Ruric Nevel. *Method in Education: A Textbook for Teachers.* New York: American Book Co. 1899.

Robinson, John W. "Cotton Growing in Africa." In *Tuskegee and Its People: Their Ideals and Achievements*, 184–99. Edited by Booker T. Washington. 1905. Freeport, NY: Books for Libraries Press, 1971.

———. "A Tuskegee Graduate In West Africa." *Colored American Magazine* 10:5 (May 1906): 355–59.

Roemer, Theodor, and A. Schaumburg. *Handbuch des Zuckerrübenbaues*. Berlin: Paul Parey, 1927.

Rogers, Howard J., ed. *Congress of Arts and Science: Universal Exposition, St. Louis, 1904*. 8 vols. Boston: Houghton, Mifflin, and Co., 1906.

Rohrbach, Paul. *Das Deutsche Kolonialwesen*. Leipzig: G. A. Gloeckner, 1911.

———. *Deutsche Kolonialwirtschaft*. Vol. 1, *Südwest-Afrika*. Berlin: Buchverlag der "Hilfe." 1907.

———. *Deutsche Kolonialwirtschaft: Kulturpolitische Grundsätze für die Rassen- und Missionsfragen*. Berlin: Buchverlag der "Hilfe." 1909.

———. *Deutschlands koloniale Forderung*. Hamburg: Hanseatische Verlagsanstalt, 1935.

———, ed. *Afrika: Beiträge zu einer praktischen Kolonialkunde*. Berlin: Werner and Co., 1943.

Roscher, Wilhelm. *Geschichte der National-Oekonomik in Deutschland*. Munich: R. Oldenbourg, 1874.

Sandburg, Carl. *The Chicago Race Riots July, 1919*. 1919. New York: Harcourt, Brace and World, 1969.

Schanz, Moritz. "Baumwollbau in deutschen Kolonien." *Zeitschrift für Kolonialpolitik, Kolonialrecht und Kolonialwirtschaft* 12 (1910): 1–28.

———. *Cotton in Egypt and the Anglo-Egyptian Sudan*. Manchester: Taylor, Garnett, Evans, 1913.

———. *Cotton in the United States of North America. Report for the Fifth International Congress, Paris, 1st to 3rd June, 1908*. Manchester: Taylor, Garnett, Evens, and Co. [1908].

———. *Der Neger in den Vereinigten Staaten von Nordamerika*. Essen: G. D. Baedeker, 1911.

———. *West-Afrika*. Berlin: Wilhelm Süsserott, 1903.

Scherer, James A. B. *Cotton as a World Power: A Study in the Economic Interpretation of History*. 1916. New York: Negro Universities Press, 1969.

Schlunk, Martin. *Das Schulwesen in den deutschen Schutzgebieten*. Hamburg: L. Friederichsen, 1914.

———. *Meine Reise durchs Eweland*. Vol. 1 of *Die Norddeutsche Mission in Togo*. Bremen: Norddeutsche Missions-Gesellschaft, 1910.

Schmidt, Geo A. *Schmidt gegen Roeren: Unter den kaudinischen Joch. Ein Kampf um Recht und Ehre*. Berlin: Swetschke und Sohn, 1907.

Schmoller, Gustav. *Grundriß der allgemeinen Volkswirtschaftslehre*. 2 vols. Leipzig: Duncker and Humblot, 1900–1904.

———. "Nationalökonomische und socialpolitische Rückblicke auf Nordamerika." *Preußische Jahrbücher* 17 (1866): 38–75, 153–92, 519–47, 587–611.

Schmoller, Gustav, Bernhard Dernburg, Walter Delbrück, et al. *Reichstagsauflösung und Kolonialpolitik. Offener stenographische Bericht über die Versam-*

mlung in der Berliner Hochschule für Musik am 8. Januar 1907. Berlin: Wedekind, 1907.

Schomburgk, Hans. "In the German Sudan." 1912–14. VHS. Göttingen: IWF, 1977.

Schönberg, Gustav Friedrich von. *Arbeitsämter. Eine Aufgabe des deutschen Reichs.* Berlin: J. Buttentag, 1871.

Seidel, Heinrich. "System der Fetischverbote in Togo: Ein Beitrag zur Volkskunde der Evhe." *Globus* 73 (1898): 340–44.

Semler, Heinrich. *Die Tropische Agrikultur: Ein Handbuch für Pflanzer und Kaufleute.* 2nd ed. Revised by Richard Hindorf with Otto Warburg and M. Busemann. 4 vols. 1888–92. Wismar: Hinstorff'sche Hofbuchhandlung Verlagsconto, 1897.

Sering, Max. "Die Agrarfrage und der Sozialismus." Review of *Die Agrarfrage,* by Karl Kautsky (Stuttgart, 1899). *Jahrbuch für Gesetzgebung, Verwaltung, und Volkswirtschaft* 23 (1899): 1493–1556.

————. *Die Innere Kolonisation in östlichen Deutschland.* Vol. 56 of *Schriften des Vereins für Socialpolitik.* Leipzig: Duncker and Humblot, 1893.

————. *Landwirthschaftliche Konkurrenz Nordamerikas in Gegenwart und Zukunft: Landwirthschaft, Kolonisation und Verkehrswesen in den Vereinigten Staaten und in Britisch Nord-Amerika.* Leipzig: Duncker and Humblot, 1887.

Sherman, William Tecumseh. *Memoirs of Gen. W. T. Sherman.* 2 vols. 4th ed. New York: Charles L. Webster, 1892.

Spiess, Carl. "Die Landschaft Tove bei Lome in Togo." *Deutsche Geographische Blätter* 25 (1902): 75–79.

————. "Ein Beitrag zur Geschichte des Evhe-Volkes in Togo: Seine Auswanderung aus Notse." *Mitteilungen des Seminars für Orientalische Sprachen* 5 (1902): 278–83.

————. "Einiges aus den Sitten und Gebräuchen der Evhe-Neger in Togo." *Deutsche Geographische Blätter* 29 (1906): 33–36.

————. "Religionsbegriffe der Evheer in Westafrika." *Mitteilungen des Seminars für Orientalische Sprachen* 6 (1903): 109–27.

Spieth, Jakob. *Die Ewe-Stämme: Material zur Kunde des Ewe-Volkes in Deutsch-Togo.* Berlin: Dietrich Reimer, 1906.

————. *Die Religion der Eweer in Süd-Togo.* Göttingen: Vandenhoeck and Ruprecht, 1911.

Stammer, K. *Lehrbuch der Zuckerfabrikation.* 2 vols. 1874. 2nd ed. Braunschweig: Friedrich Vieweg und Sohn, 1887.

Stone, Alfred Holt. "The Negro and Agricultural Development." *Annals of the American Academy of Political and Social Science* 35 (1910): 8–15.

Stonequist, Everett V. *The Marginal Man: A Study in Personality and Culture Conflict.* 1937. New York: Russell and Russell, 1961.

Strumpfe, E. *Polenfrage und Ansiedelungskommission.* Berlin: Dietrich Reimer, 1902.

Symmons-Symonolewicz, Konstantin. Review of *The Polish Peasant in Europe and America* by William I. Thomas and Florian Znaniecki. *American Slavic and East European Review* 19 (1960): 128–30.

Thomas, Harriet Park. *Review of The Spirit of Youth and the City Streets* by Jane Addams. *American Journal of Sociology* 15 (1910): 550–53.

Thomas, William I. "The Prussian-Polish Situation: An Experiment in Assimilation." *American Journal of Sociology* 19 (1914): 624–39.

———. *Sex and Society: Studies in the Social Psychology of Sex*. University of Chicago, 1907.

Thomas, William I., Robert Park, and Herbert Miller. *Old World Traits Transplanted*. 1921. Montclair, New Jersey: Patterson Smith, 1971.

Thomas, William I., and Florian Znaniecki. *The Polish Peasant in Europe and America: Monograph of an Immigrant Group*. 5 vols. Boston: Gordon Badger, 1918–20.

Thompson, Edgar T. "The Plantation." Ph.D. diss., University of Chicago, 1932.

———. *Plantation Societies, Race Relations, and the South*. Durham: Duke University Press, 1975.

Todd, John A. *The World's Cotton Crops*. London: A&C Black, 1915.

Trevor-Roper, Hugh. *The Rise of Christian Europe*. London: Thames and Hudson, 1964.

Trotsky, Leon. *The Revolution Betrayed*. 1937. New York: Pathfinder Press, 1972.

———. *The Third International after Lenin*. 1929. New York: Pathfinder Press, 1970.

United States. Department of Agriculture. *The Classification of Cotton*. Washington, DC: U.S. Department of Agriculture, 1938.

Ure, Andrew. *The Philosophy of Manufactures: or, an Exposition of the Scientific, Moral, and Commercial Economy of the Factory System of Great Britain*. 1835. New York: August M. Kelley, 1967.

Verein für Sozialpolitik. *Die Ansiedlung von Europäern in den Tropen*. 5 parts. Vol. 147 of *Schriften des Vereins für Socialpolitik*. Munich: Duncker and Humblot, 1912–15.

———. *Bäuerliche Zustände in Deutschland*. vol. 1. Vol. 22 of *Schriften des Vereins für Socialpolitik*. Leipzig: Duncker and Humblot, 1883.

———. *Die Reform des Lehrlingswesens: Sechszehn Gutachten und Berichte*. Leipzig: Duncker and Humblot, 1875.

———. *Untersuchungen über Auslese und Anpassung (Berufswahl und Berufsschicksal) der Arbeiter in den verschiedenen Zweigen der Grossindustrie*. Vols. 133–35 of *Schriften des Vereins für Socialpolitik*. Leipzig: Duncker and Humblot, 1910–1912.

Verhandlungen der am 6. und 7. October 1884 abgehaltenen Generalversammlung des Vereins für Socialpolitik. Vol. 28 of *Schriften des Vereins für Socialpolitik*. Leipzig: Duncker and Humblot, 1884.

Verhandlungen der am 20. und 21. März 1893 in Berlin abgehaltenen General Versammlung des Vereins für Socialpolitik über die ländliche Arbeiterfrage und über die Bodenbesitzverteilung und die Sicherung des Kleingrundbesitzes. Vol. 58 of *Schriften des Vereins für Socialpolitik*. Leipzig: Duncker and Humblot, 1893.

———. *Verhandlungen der Eisenacher Versammlung zur Besprechung der socialen Frage am 6. und 7. October 1872*. Leipzig: Duncker and Humblot, 1873.

Verein für Sozialpolitik. *Verhandlungen der Generalversammlung des Vereins für Socialpolitik am 24. und 25. September 1886.* Vol. 33 of *Schriften des Vereins für Socialpolitik.* Leipzig: Duncker and Humblot, 1887.

———. *Verhandlungen der zweiten Generalversammlung des Vereins für Socialpolitik am 11. und 12. October 1874.* Vol. 9 of *Schriften des Vereins für Socialpolitik.* Leipzig: Duncker and Humbolt, 1875.

———. *Zur Inneren Kolonisation in Deutschland: Erfahrungen und Vorschläge.* Leipzig: Duncker and Humblot, 1886.

Wagner, Adolph. *Grundlegung der politischen Oekonomie.* 2 vols. 3rd ed. Leipzig: C. F. Winter, 1894.

Warburg, Otto. "Einführung der Pflugkultur in den deutschen Kolonien." *Verhandlungen des Kolonial-Wirtschaftlichen Komitees* (1906): 4–9.

Washington, Booker T. "The American Negro and His Economic Value." *International Monthly* 2 (1900): 672–86.

———. *Atlanta Exposition Address.* Brown Seal Records, Broome Special Phonographic Records, n.d. 78 rpm. A.F.R. Lawrence Collection, Library of Congress, Washington, DC.

———. *The Booker T. Washington Papers.* 14 vols. Edited by Louis R. Harlan. Urbana: University of Illinois Press, 1972–89.

———. *Charakterbildung: Sonntags-Ansprachen an die Zöglinge der Normal- und Gewerbeschule von Tuskegee.* Translated by Estelle Du Bois-Reymond. Berlin: Dietrich Reimer (Ernst Vohsen), 1910.

———. *The Future of the American Negro.* 1899. Reprint, New York: Negro Universities Press, 1969.

———. *Handarbeit: Fortsetzung des Buches "Sklaven Empor" und Schilderung der Erfahrungen des Verfassers bei dem gewerblichen Unterricht in Tuskegee.* Translated by Estelle Du Bois-Reymond. Berlin: Dietrich Reimer (Ernst Vohsen), 1913.

———. "Industrial Education in Africa." *Independent* 40 (15 March 1906): 616–19.

———. "The Negro's Part in Southern Development." *Annals of the American Academy of Political and Social Science* 35 (1910): 124–33.

———. "Relation of Industrial Education to National Progress." *Annals of the American Academy of Political and Social Science* 33, 1 (January 1909): 1–12.

———. "Some European Observations and Experiences." Tuskegee, AL: Tuskegee Institute Steam Press, 1900. In Pamphlets in American History. Biography. B 2337.

———. *The Story of the Negro.* 2 vols. 1909. New York: Negro Universities Press, 1969.

———. "The Successful Training of the Negro." *World's Work* 6 (1903): 3731–51.

———. *Up from Slavery.* 1901. Mineola: Dover, 1995.

———. *Vom Sklaven Empor: Eine Selbstbiographie.* Translated by Estelle Du Bois-Reymond. Berlin: Dietrich Reimer (Ernst Vohsen), 1902.

———. *Working with the Hands.* 1904. New York: Negro Universities Press, 1969.

Washington, Booker T., and Robert E. Park. *Man Farthest Down.* 1911. Garden City: Doubleday, Page and Co., 1912.

Washington, Booker T., and W.E.B. Du Bois. *The Negro in the South: His Economic Progress in Relation to His Moral and Religious Development*. Philadelphia: George W. Jacobs and Co., 1907.

Washington, Booker T., and N. B. Wood, and Fannie Barrier Williams. *A New Negro for a New Century: An Accurate and Up-To-Date Record of the Upward Struggles of the Negro Race*. Chicago: American Publishing House, 1900.

Watts, Isaac. *The Cotton Supply Association: Its Origins and Progress*. Manchester: Tubbs and Brook, 1871.

Wayland, Francis. *The Elements of Moral Science*. Boston: Gould and Lincoln, 1860.

Weber, Alfred. *Über den Standort der Industrien*. Tübingen: J.C.B. Mohr, 1909.

Weber, Marianne. *Max Weber: A Biography*. Translated by Harry Zohn. New York: John Wiley and Sons, 1975.

————. *Max Weber: Ein Lebensbild*. Heidelberg: Lambert Schneider, 1926.

Weber, Max. "Developmental Tendencies in the Situation of East Elbian Rural Labourers." *Economy and Society* 8 (1979): 177–205.

————. *Gesammelte Aufsätze zur Religionssoziologie*. 3 Vols. 1920. 2nd ed. Tübingen: J.C.B. Mohr, 1922.

————. *Gesammelte Aufsätze zur Sozial- und Wirtschaftsgeschichte*. Tübingen: J.C.B. Mohr, 1924.

————. *Gesammelte Aufsätze zur Soziologie und Sozialpolitik*. Tübingen: J.C.B. Mohr, 1924.

————. *Gesammelte Politische Schriften*. Edited by Johannes Winckelmann. 3rd ed. Tübingen: J.C.B. Mohr, 1971.

————. *Political Writings*. Edited by Peter Lassman and Ronald Speirs. Cambridge: Cambridge University Press, 1994.

————. "Die protestantische Ethik und der 'Geist' des Kapitalismus." 2 parts. *Archiv für Sozialwissenschaft und Sozialpolitik* 20 (1904): 1–54; 21 (1905): 1–110.

————. *Die Verhältnisse der Landarbeiter im ostelbischen Deutschland*. Vol. 55 of *Schriften des Vereins für Socialpolitik*. Leipzig: Duncker and Humblot, 1892.

Wells, Ida B., Frederick Douglass, Irvine Garland Penn, and Ferdinand L. Barnett. *The Reason Why the Colored American is Not in the World's Columbian Exposition: The Afro-American Contribution to Columbian Literature*. 1893. Edited by Robert W. Rydell. Urbana: University of Illinois Press, 1999.

Westermann, Diedrich. *Afrikaner erzählen ihr Leben*. Essen: Essner Verlagsanstalt, 1938.

————. *Die Glidyi-Ewe in Togo: Züge aus ihrem Gesellschaftsleben*. Berlin: Walter de Gruyter, 1935.

Willis, H. H., Gaston Gage, Vernette B. Moore. *Cotton Classing Manual*. Washington, DC: The Textile Foundation, 1938.

Winterbottom, Thomas Masterman. *An Account of the Native Africans in the Neighbourhood of Sierra Leone*. 2 vols. 1803. New York: Barnes and Noble 1969.

Wirth, Louis. *The Ghetto*. Chicago: University of Chicago Press, 1928.

Woodson, Carter G. Review of *Progress in Negro Status and Race Relations, 1911–1946 the Thirty-five Year Report of the Phelps Stokes Fund* by Anson

Phelps Stokes et al. (New York, 1948). *Journal of Negro History* 34 (1949): 367–69.

———. Review of *The Mulatto in the United States*, by Edward Byron Reuter (New York, 1918). *Mississippi Valley Historical Review* 7 (1920): 175–76.

———. "Thomas Jesse Jones." *Journal of Negro History* 35 (1950): 107–9.

Woofter, T. J. Jr. *Landlord and Tenant on the Cotton Plantation*. Washington, DC: Works Progress Administration, 1936.

Work, Monroe N. *Bibliography of the Negro in Africa and America*. New York: H. W. Wilson, 1928.

———. "Crime among the Negroes of Chicago. A Social Study." *American Journal of Sociology* 6 (1900): 204–23.

Wright, Caroll D. "The Work of the National Society for the Promotion of Industrial Education." *Annals of the American Academy of Political and Social Science* 33, 1 (January 1909): 13–22.

Wright, F. "The System of Education in the Gold Coast Colony." In Great Britain, Board of Education, *Educational Systems of the Chief Crown Colonies and Possessions of the British Empire, Including Reports on the Training of Native Races*. 3 vols. Vols. 12–14 of *Special Reports on Educational Subjects*. London: Her Majesty's Stationery Office, 1905.

Wright Jr., Richard R. *Eighty-seven Years behind the Black Curtain: An Autobiography*. Philadelphia: Rare Book Co., 1965.

Zetkin, Clara. *Die Arbeiterinnen- und Frauenfrage der Gegenwart*. Berlin: Berliner Volks-Tribüne, 1889.

Zimmermann, Albrecht. *Anleitung für die Baumwollkultur in den deutschen Kolonien*. 2nd ed. Berlin: Kolonial-Wirtschaftliches Komitee, 1910.

Znaniecki, Florian. *The Social Role of the Man of Knowledge*. New York: Columbia University Press, 1940.

Zöller, Hugo. *Das Togoland und die Sklavenküste*. Berlin: W. Spemann, 1885.

SECONDARY SOURCES

Abbott, Andrew. *Department and Discipline: Chicago Sociology at One Hundred*. Chicago: University of Chicago Press, 1999.

Abraham, Gary A. "Max Weber: Modernist Anti-Pluralism and the Polish Question." *New German Critique* 53 (1991): 33–66.

Adamu, Mahdi. *The Hausa Factor in West African History* (Zaria, Nigeria: Ahmadu Bello University Press, 1978.

Adeleke, Tunde. *UnAfrican Americans: Nineteenth-Century Black Nationalists and the Civilizing Mission*. Lexington: University Press of Kentucky, 1998.

Adick, C. *Bildung und Kolonialismus in Togo*. Weinheim: Beltz, 1981.

Agbodeka, F. "The Origins of the Republic Idea in Eweland: The North Western Region." In *Peuples du Golfe du Bénin: Aja-Ewe*. Edited by François de Medeiros. Paris: Éditions Karthala, 1984.

Aiken, Charles S. *The Cotton Plantation South since the Civil War*. Baltimore: Johns Hopkins University Press, 1998.

———. "The Evolution of Cotton Ginning in the Southeastern United States." *Geographical Review* 63 (1973): 196–224.

Albisetti, James C. *Secondary School Reform in Imperial Germany*. Princeton: Princeton University Press, 1983.

Alexander, Adele Logan. "Adella Hunt Logan and the Tuskegee Woman's Club: Building a Foundation for Suffrage." In *Stepping Out of the Shadows: Alabama Women, 1819–1990*, 96–113. Edited by Mary Martha Thomas. Tuscaloosa: University of Alabama Press, 1995.

Allen, Victor L. "The Meaning of the Working Class in Africa." *Journal of Modern African Studies* 10 (1972): 169–89.

Allman, Jean Marie and Victoria Tashjian. " 'I Will Not Eat Stone': A Women's History of Colonial Asante*. Portsmouth: Heinemann, 2000.

Allman, Jean Marie, Susan Geiger, and Nakanyike Musisi, eds. *Women in African Colonial Histories*. Bloomington: Indiana University Press, 2002.

Alston, Julian M., Daniel A. Sumner and Henrich Brunke. "Impacts of Reductions in U.S. Cotton Subsidies on West Africa Cotton Producers." Oxfam Research Paper. June, 2007. Online at: http://www.oxfamamerica.org.

Althusser, Louis. "Ideology and Ideological State Apparatuses." In *Lenin and Philosophy*, 127–86. Translated by Ben Brewster. New York: Monthly Review Press, 1971.

Amenumey, D.E.J. *The Ewe Unification Movement: A Political History*. Accra: Ghana Universities Press, 1989.

———. "German Administration in Southern Togo." *Journal of African History* 10 (1969): 623–39.

Amos, Alcione M. "Afro-Brazilians in Togo: The case of the Olympio family, 1882–1945." *Cahiers d'études africaines* 162 (2001). Online at: http://etudesafricaines.revues.org/document88.html.

Anderson, Benedict. *Imagined Communities: Reflections on the Origin and Spread of Nationalism*. 2nd ed. New York: Verso, 1991.

Anderson, Eric, and Alfred A. Moss Jr. *Dangerous Donations: Northern Philanthropy and Southern Black Education, 1902–1930*. Foreword by Louis R. Harlan. Columbia: University of Missouri Press, 1999.

Anderson, James D. *The Education of Blacks in the South, 1860–1935*. Chapel Hill: University of North Carolina Press, 1988.

Anderson, Margaret, and Kenneth Barkin. "The Myth of the Puttkamer Purge and the Reality of the *Kulturkampf*." *Journal of Modern History* 54 (1982): 647–86.

Aptheker, Herbert. *American Negro Slave Revolts*. 1944. New York: International Publishers, 1983.

Asamoa, Ansa K. *The Ewe of South-Eastern Ghana and Togo on the Eve of Colonialism: A Contribution to the Marxist Debate on pre-Capitalist Socio-Economic Formations*. Tema: Ghana Publishing Corporation, 1986.

Ascher, Abraham. "Professors as Propagandists: The Politics of the Kathedersozialisten." *Journal of Central European Affairs* 23 (1963): 282–302.

Ashby, Eric, in association with Mary Anderson. *Universities: British, Indian, Africa: A Study in the Ecology of Higher Education*. Cambridge: Harvard University Press, 1966.

Bade, Klaus J. "German Emigration to the United States and Continental Immigration to Germany in the Late Nineteenth and Early Twentieth Centuries." *Central European History* 13 (1980): 348–77.

———. " 'Kulturkampf' auf dem Arbeitsmarkt: Bismarcks 'Polenpolitik' 1885–1890." In *Innenpolitische Probleme des Bismarck-Reiches*, 121–42. Edited by Otto Pflanze. Munich: R. Oldenbourg, 1983.

———. " 'Preussengänger' und 'Abwehrpolitik': Ausländerbeschäftigung, Ausländerpolitik und Ausländerkontrolle auf dem Arbeitsmarkt in Preussen vor dem Ersten Weltkrieg." *Archiv für Sozialgeschichte* 24 (1984): 91–162.

Baldwin, Kate A. *Beyond the Color Line and the Iron Curtain: Reading Encounters between Black and Red, 1922–1963*. Durham: Duke University Press, 2002).

Balibar, Etienne. "Is There a 'Neo-Racism'?" In *Race, Nation, Class: Ambiguous Identities*, by Balibar and Immanuel Wallerstein. Translated by Chris Turner, 1988. London: Verso, 1999.

Banerjee, Tarasankar. "American Cotton Experiments in India and the American Civil War." *Journal of Indian History* 37 (1969): 425–32.

Barkin, Kenneth D. " 'Berlin Days,' 1892–1894: W.E.B. Du Bois and German Political Economy." *Boundary* 2 27 (2000): 79–101.

———. *The Controversy over German Industrialization, 1890–1902*. Chicago: University of Chicago Press, 1970.

———. "Introduction: Germany on His Mind—'Das Neue Vaterland'." *Journal of African American History* 91 (2006): 444–49.

———. "W.E.B. Du Bois's Love Affair with Imperial Germany." *German Studies* 28 (2005): 284–302.

———. "W.E.B. DuBois and the Kaiserreich." *Central European History* 31 (1998): 155–96.

Bartel, Horst. "Zur Politik und zum Kampf der deutschen Sozialdemokratie gegen die Bismarcksche Sozialreformpolitik und gegen den Rechtsopportunismus in den Jahren 1881/1884." *Zeitschrift für Geschichtswissenschaft* 5 (1957): 1100–1101.

Bartra, Roger. *Agrarian Structure and Political Power in Mexico*. Translated by Stephen K. Ault. Baltimore: Johns Hopkins University Press, 1993.

Bassett, Thomas J. *The Peasant Cotton Revolution in West Africa: Côte d'Ivoire 1880–1995*. Cambridge: Cambridge University Press, 2001.

Beck, Hermann. *The Origins of the Authoritarian Welfare State in Prussia: Conservatives, Bureaucracy, and the Social Question, 1815–70*. Ann Arbor: University of Michigan Press, 1995.

Becker, Winfried. "Kulturkampf als Vorwand: Die Kolonialwahlen von 1907 und das Problem der Parlamentarisierung des Reiches." *Historisches Jahrbuch* 106 (1986): 59–84.

Beckert, Sven. "Emancipation and Empire: Reconstructing the Worldwide Web of Cotton Production in the Age of the American Civil War." *American Historical Review* 109 (2005): 1405–38.

———. "From Tuskegee to Togo: The Problem of Freedom in the Empire of Cotton." *Journal of American History* 92 (2005): 498–526.

Beidelman, T.O. *Colonial Evangelism: A Socio-Historical Study of an East African Mission at the Grassroots*. Bloomington: Indiana University Press, 1982.

Bender, Thomas, ed. *Rethinking American History in a Global Age*. Berkeley: University of California Press, 2002.

Berg, Maxine. *The Age of Manufactures: Industry, Innovation, and Work in Britain, 1700–1820*. New York: Oxford University Press, 1986.

Berman, Edward H. "Tuskegee in Africa." *Journal of Negro Education* 41 (1972): 99–112.

Bernal, Victoria. *Cultivating Workers: Peasants and Capitalism in a Sudanese Village*. New York: Columbia University Press, 1991.

Bernstein, Henry. "African Peasantries: A Theoretical Framework." *Journal of Peasant Studies* 6 (1979): 421–43.

———. "Farewells to the Peasantry." *Transformation* 52 (2003) 1–19.

Bernstein, Henry, and Terence J. Byres. "From Peasant Studies to Agrarian Change." *Journal of Agrarian Change* 1 (2001): 1–56.

Beyer, Carl Kalani. "Manual and Industrial Education for Hawaiians during the Nineteenth Century." *Hawaiian Journal of History* 38 (2004): 1–34.

Bhabha, Homi K. *The Location of Culture*. London: Routledge, 1994.

Blackbourn, David. *The Long Nineteenth Century: A History of Germany, 1780–1918*. New York: Oxford University Press, 1998.

Blackbourn, David, and Geoff Eley. *The Peculiarities of German History: Bourgeois Society and Politics in Nineteenth-Century Germany*. New York: Oxford University Press, 1984.

Blanke, Richard. *Prussian Poland in the German Empire (1871–1900)*. Boulder: East European Monographs, 1981.

Bockman, Johanna K. "Neoliberalism and Socialism." Unpublished manuscript.

———."The Origins of Neoliberalism between Soviet Socialism and Western Capitalism: 'A Galaxy without Borders.'" *Theory and Society* 36 (2007): 343–71.

Bockman, Johanna K., and Michael Bernstein. "Scientific Community in a Divided World: Economists, Planning, and Research Priority during the Cold War." *Comparative Studies in Society and History* 50 (2008): 581–613.

Bockman, Johanna K., and Gil Eyal. "Eastern Europe as a Laboratory for Economic Knowledge: The Transnational Roots of Neo-Liberalism." *American Journal of Sociology* 108 (2002): 310–52.

Boserup, Ester. *Woman's Role in Economic Development*. New York: St. Martin's, 1970.

Boston, Thomas D. "W.E.B. Du Bois and the Historical School of Economics." *American Economic Review* 81 (1991): 303–6.

Bowman, Shearer Davis. *Masters and Lords: Mid-Nineteenth-Century U.S. Planters and Prussian Junkers*. New York: Oxford University Press, 1993.

Brass, Tom, ed. *Towards a Comparative Political Economy of Unfree Labour: Case Studies and Debates*. London: Frank Cass, 1999.

———. *Peasants, Populism and Postmodernism: The Return of the Agrarian Myth*. London: Frank Cass, 2000.

Broadberry, Stephen, and Bishnupriya Gupta. "Cotton Textiles and the Great Divergence: Lancashire, India and the Shifting Comparative Advantage, 1600–

1850." Unpublished Working Paper, 11 May 2004. http://www2.warwick
.ac.uk/fac/soc/economics/staff/faculty/broadberry/wp/cotdiv5.pdf, accessed 7/
16/2004.

Broderick, Francis L. "The Academic Training of W.E.B. Du Bois." *Journal of Negro Education* 27 (1958): 10–16.

———. "German Influence on the Scholarship of W.E.B. Du Bois." *Phylon Quarterly* 19 (1958): 367–71.

Brooks, Tim. *Lost Sounds: Blacks and the Birth of the Recording Industry, 1890–1919*. Urbana: University of Illinois Press, 2004.

Brown, John C. "Imperfect Competition and Anglo-German Trade Rivalry: Markets for Cotton Textiles Before 1914." *Journal of Economic History* 55 (1995): 494–527.

———. "Market Organization, Protection, and Vertical Integration: German Cotton Textiles Before 1914." *Journal of Economic History* 52 (1992): 339–51.

Bruch, Rüdiger vom. "Bürgerliche Sozialreform im deutschen Kaiserreich." In *Weder Kommunismus noch Kapitalismus: Bürgerliche Sozialreform in Deutschland vom Vormärz bis zur Ära Adenauer*, 61–179. Edited by Rüdiger vom Bruch. Munich: C. H. Beck, 1985.

———. *Gelehrtenpolitik, Sozialwissenschaften und Akademische Diskurse in Deutschland im 19. und 20. Jahrhundert*. Stuttgart: Franz Steiner, 2006.

———. *Wissenschaft, Politik und Öffentliche Meinung: Gelehrtenpolitik im Wilhelminischen Deutschland (1890–1914)*. Husum: Matthiesen, 1980.

Brundage, W. Fitzhugh, ed. *Booker T. Washington and Black Progress: Up from Slavery 100 Years Later*. Gainesville: University Press of Florida, 2003.

———. *Lynching in the New South: Georgia and Virginia, 1880–1930*. Urbana: University of Illinois Press, 1993.

Buhler, Peter. "The Volta Region of Ghana: Economic Change in Togoland, 1850–1914." Ph.D. diss., University of California, San Diego, 1975.

Bundy, Colin. *The Rise and Fall of the South African Peasantry*. Berkeley: University of California Press, 1979.

Burin, Eric. *Slavery and the Peculiar Solution: A History of the American Colonization Society*. Gainesville: University Press of Florida, 2005.

Butchart, Ronald E. *Northern Schools, Southern Blacks, and Reconstruction: Freedmen's Education, 1862–1875*. Westport, CT: Greenwood Press, 1980.

Byfield, Judith A. *The Bluest Hands: A Social and Economic History of Women Dyers in Abeokuta (Nigeria), 1890–1940*. Portsmouth, NH: Heinemann: 2002.

Callahan, Raymond E. *Education and the Cult of Efficiency: A Study of the Social Forces that Have Shaped the Administration of the Public Schools*. Chicago: University of Chicago Press, 1962.

Calloway, Bud. "Tracking the Water Monster, or, J. N. Calloway and the Tuskegee Cotton Growing Expedition to Togo, West Africa, 1900." Unpublished manuscript.

Campbell, James T. "Models and Metaphors: Industrial Education in the United States and South Africa." In *Comparative Perspectives on South Africa*, 90–134. Edited by Ran Greenstein. New York: St. Martin's, 1998.

———. *Middle Passages: African American Journeys to Africa, 1787–2005*. New York: Penguin, 2006.

———. "Redeeming the Race: Martin Delany and the Niger Valley Exploring Party, 1859–60." *New Formations* 45 (Winter 2001–2002): 125–49.

———. *Songs of Zion: The African Methodist Episcopal Church in the United States and South Africa.* New York: Oxford University Press, 1995.

Cell, John W. *The Highest Stage of White Supremacy: The Origins of Segregation in South Africa and the American South.* Cambridge: Cambridge University Press, 1982.

Clarke, Anna. *The Struggle for the Breeches: Gender and the Making of the British Working Class.* Berkeley: University of California Press, 1995.

Clay, Jason W. *World Agriculture and the Environment: A Commodity-by-Commodity Guide to Impacts and Practices.* Washington, DC: Island Press, 2004.

Cline, Catherine Ann. Introduction to *Truth and the War*, by E. D. Morel. 1916. New York: Garland Publishing, 1972.

Cohen, William. *At Freedom's Edge: Black Mobility and the Southern White Quest for Racial Control, 1861–1915.* Baton Rouge: Louisiana State University Press, 1991.

Comaroff, John L., and Jean Comaroff. *Of Revelation and Revolution.* 2 vols. Chicago: University of Chicago Press, 1991–97.

Conrad, Sebastian. *Deutsche Kolonialgeschichte.* Munich: C. H. Beck, 2008.

———. "Doppelte Marginalisierung: Plädoyer für eine transnationale Perspektive auf die deutsche Geschichte." *Geschichte und Gesellschaft* 28 (2002): 145–69.

———. *Globalisierung und Nation im Deutschen Kaiserreich.* Munich: Beck, 2006.

Conze, Werner, ed. *Quellen zur Geschichte der deutschen Bauernbefreiung.* Göttingen: Musterschmidt, 1957.

Cooper, Frederick, Thomas C. Holt, and Rebecca J. Scott. *Beyond Slavery: Explorations of Race, Labor, and Citizenship.* Chapel Hill: University of North Carolina Press, 2000.

———. "Back to Work: Categories, Boundaries and Connections in the Study of Labour." In *Racializing Class, Classifying Race: Labour and Difference in Britain, the USA and Africa*, 213–35. Edited by Peter Alexander and Rick Halpern. New York: St. Martin's Press, 2000.

———. *From Slaves to Squatters: Plantation Labor and Agriculture in Zanzibar and Kenya, 1890–1925.* 1980. Portsmouth, NH: Heinemann, 1997.

Cremin, Lawrence A. *The Transformation of the School: Progressivism in American Education, 1876–1957.* New York: Vintage, 1961.

Cronon, William. *Nature's Metropolis: Chicago and the Great West.* New York: W. W. Norton, 1992.

Curtain, Philip D. *The Atlantic Slave Trade: A Census.* Madison: University of Wisconsin Press, 1969.

———. *The Rise and Fall of the Plantation Complex: Essays in Atlantic History.* Cambridge: Cambridge University Press, 1990.

Daniel, Pete. "The Metamorphosis of Slavery, 1865–1900." *Journal of American History* 66 (1979): 88–99.

———. *In the Shadow of Slavery: Peonage in the South, 1901–1969.* 1972. Urbana: University of Illinois Press, 1990.

Darkoh, M.B.K. "Togoland under the Germans." 2 parts. *Nigerian Geographical Journal* 10 (1967): 107–22 and 11 (1968): 153–68.

Davis, Harold E. *Henry Grady's New South: Atlanta: A Brave and Beautiful City.* Tuscaloosa: University of Alabama Press, 1990.

Davis, R. Hunt, Jr. "Charles T. Loram and an American Model for African Education in South Africa." *African Studies Review* 19 (1976): 87–99.

———. "John L. Dube: A South African Exponent of Booker T. Washington." *Journal of African Studies* 2 (1975–76): 497–529.

Debrunner, Hans W. *A Church between Colonial Powers: A Study of the Church in Togo.* London: Lutterworth Press, 1965.

Deegan, Mary Jo. *Jane Addams and the Men of the Chicago School, 1892–1918.* New Brunswick: Transaction Books, 1988.

———. *Race, Hull-House, and the University of Chicago: A New Conscience against Ancient Evils.* Westport, CT: Praeger, 2002.

DePastino, Todd. *Citizen Hobo: How a Century of Homelessness Shaped America.* Chicago: University Of Chicago Press, 2005.

Diana Jeater. *Marriage, Perversion, and Power: The Construction of Moral Discourse in Southern Rhodesia, 1894–1930.* Oxford: Clarendon Press, 1993.

Drake, St. Clair. "The Tuskegee Connection: Booker T. Washington and Robert E. Park." *Society* 20 (1983) 4: 82–92.

Dray, Philip. *At the Hands of Persons Unknown: The Lynching of Black America.* New York: Random House, 2002.

Drescher, Seymour. *The Mighty Experiment: Free Labor versus Slavery in British Emancipation.* Oxford: Oxford University Press, 2002.

Dubois, Laurent. *Avengers of the New World: The Story of the Haitian Revolution.* Cambridge: Harvard University Press, 2004.

Duignan, Peter J., and Lewis Henry Gann. *The United States and Africa: A History.* Cambridge: Cambridge University Press and Hoover Institution, 1985.

Dumett, Raymond E. "Obstacles to Government-Assisted Agricultural Development in West Africa: Cotton-Growing Experimentation in Ghana in the Early Twentieth Century." *Agricultural History Review* 23 (1975): 156–72.

Edwards, Barrington S. "W.E.B. Du Bois between Worlds: Berlin, Empirical Social Research, and the Race Question." *Du Bois Review* 3 (2006): 395–424.

———. "W.E.B. Du Bois, Empirical Social Research, and the Challenge to Race, 1868–1910." Ph.D. diss., Harvard, 2001.

El-Tayeb, Fatima. *Schwarze Deutsche: Der Diskurs um "Rasse" und nationale Identität 1890–1933.* Frankfurt: Campus, 2001.

Eley, Geoff. *Reshaping the German Right: Radical Nationalism and Political Change after Bismarck.* 1980. Ann Arbor: University of Michigan Press, 1990.

Ellis, Mark. " 'Closing Ranks' and 'Seeking Honors': W.E.B. Du Bois in World War I." *Journal of American History* 79 (1992): 96–124.

Eltis, David, Stephen D. Behrendt, David Richardson, and Herbert S. Klein. *The Trans-Atlantic Slave Trade: A Database on CD-ROM.* Cambridge: Cambridge University Press, 1999.

Engs, Robert Francis. *Educating the Disfranchised and Disinherited: Samuel Chapman Armstrong and Hampton Institute, 1839–1893.* Knoxville: University of Tennessee Press, 1999.

————. *Freedom's First Generation: Black Hampton, Virginia, 1861–1890.* Philadelphia: University of Pennsylvania Press, 1979.

Epstein, Klaus. "Erzberger and the German Colonial Scandals, 1905–1910." *English Historical Review* 74 (1959): 637–63.

Erbar, Ralph. *Ein Platz an der Sonne? Die Verwaltungs- und Wirtschaftsgeschichte der deutschen Kolonie Togo, 1884–1914.* Stuttgart: Franz Steiner, 1991.

Evans, Richard J. *Comrades and Sisters: Feminism, Socialism, and Pacifism in Europe, 1870–1945.* Brighton, Sussex: Wheatsheaf Books, 1987.

Fairclough, Adam. *A Class of Their Own: Black Teachers in the Segregated South.* Cambridge, MA: Belknap Press of Harvard University, 2007.

Ferguson, James. *Expectations of Modernity: Myths and Meanings of Urban Life on the Zambian Copperbelt.* Berkeley: University of California Press, 1999.

Ferguson, Roderick A. *Aberrations in Black: Toward a Queer of Color Critique.* Minneapolis: University of Minnesota Press, 2004.

Fields, Barbara Jeanne. "The Advent of Capitalist Agriculture: The New South in a Bourgeois World." In *Essays on the Postbellum Southern Economy*, 73–94. Edited by Thavolia Glymph and John Kushma. College Station: Texas A&M University Press, 1985.

Fierce, Milfred C. *The Pan-African Idea in the United States, 1900–1919: African-American Interests in Africa and Interaction with West Africa.* New York: Garland Publishing, Inc., 1993.

Fishel, Leslie H., Jr. "The 'Negro Question' at Mohonk: Microcosm, Mirage, and Message." *New York History* 74 (1993): 277–314.

Fletcher, Roger. *Revisionism and Empire: Socialist Imperialism in Germany, 1897–1914.* London: George Allen and Unwin, 1984.

Foley, Barbara. *Spectres of 1919: Class and Nation in the Making of the New Negro.* Urbana: University of Illinois Press, 2003.

Foner. Eric. *Free Soil, Free Labor, Free Men: The Ideology of the Republican Party before the Civil War.* New York: Oxford University Press, 1970.

————. "Lincoln and Colonization." In *Our Lincoln: New Perspectives on Lincoln and his World*, 135–66. Edited by Foner. New York: Norton, 2008.

————. *Nothing but Freedom: Emancipation and Its Legacy.* Baton Rouge and London: Louisiana State University Press, 1983.

————. *Reconstruction: America's Unfinished Revolution, 1863–1877.* New York: Harper, 1988.

Foner, Philip S. and James S. Allen, eds. *American Communism and Black Americans: A Documentary History, 1919–1929.* Philadelphia: Temple University Press, 1987.

Forberger, Rudolf. *Die Industrielle Revolution in Sachsen 1800–1861.* Berlin: Akademie-Verlag, 1982.

Foster, Philip. *Education and Social Change in Ghana.* Chicago: University of Chicago Press, 1965.

Fredrickson, George M. *The Black Image in the White Mind: The Debate on Afro-American Character and Destiny, 1817–1914.* New York: Harper and Row, 1971.

Freund, Bill. *The African Worker.* Cambridge: Cambridge University Press, 1988.

Furner, Mary O. *Advocacy and Objectivity: A Crisis in the Professionalization of American Social Science, 1865–1905*. Lexington: University Press of Kentucky, 1975.

Gaines, Kevin K. *Uplifting the Race: Black Leadership, Politics, and Culture in the Twentieth Century*. Chapel Hill: University of North Carolina Press, 1996.

Gaston, Paul M. *The New South Creed: A Study in Southern Mythmaking*. New York: Knopf, 1970.

Gayibor, Nicoué Lodjou. *Histoire des Togolais des Origines à 1884*. Lomé: Université du Benin, 1997.

———. *Le Togo Sous Domination Coloniale (1884–1960)*. Lomé: Université du Benin, 1997.

Gebauer, Heinrich. *Die Volkswirtschaft im Königreiche Sachsen*. 3 vols. Dresden: Wilhelm Baensch, 1893.

Geiss, Imanuel. *The Pan-African Movement: A History of Pan-Africanism in America, Europe and Africa*. Translated by Ann Keep. 1968. New York: Africana Publishing, 1974.

Genovese, Eugene D. *Roll, Jordan, Roll. The World the Slaves Made*. New York: Pantheon Books, 1974.

Geulen Christian. *Wahlverwandte: Rassendiskurs und Nationalismus im späten 19. Jahrhundert*. Hamburg: Hamburger Edition, 2004.

Gilmore, Glenda Elizabeth. *Defying Dixie: The Radical Roots of Civil Rights, 1919–1950*. New York: Norton, 2008.

Gilpin, Patrick J., and Marybeth Gasman. *Charles S. Johnson: Leadership beyond the Veil in the Age of Jim Crow*. Albany: State University of New York Press, 2003.

Glickstein, Jonathan A. *Concepts of Free Labor in Antebellum America*. New Haven: Yale University Press, 1991.

Gocking, Roger. *Facing Two Ways: Ghana's Coastal Communities under Colonial Rule*. Lanham, MD: University Press of America, 1999.

Goodman, Paul. "The Manual Labor Movement and the Origins of Abolitionism." *Journal of the Early Republic* 13 (1993): 355–88.

———. *Of One Blood: Abolitionism and the Origins of Racial Equality*. Berkeley: University of California Press, 1998.

Graham, C. K. *The History of Education in Ghana from the Earliest Times to the Declaration of Independence*. London: Frank Cass, 1971.

Gramsci, Antonio. "Americanism and Fordism." In *Selections from the Prison Notebooks*, 279–316. New York: International Publishers, 1971.

Grant, Kevin. *A Civilised Savagery: Britain and the New Slaveries in Africa, 1884–1926*. New York: Routledge, 2005.

Gray, Lewis Cecil. *History of Agriculture in the Southern United States to 1860*. 2 vols. Washington: Carnegie Institution of Washington, 1933.

Gray, Marion W. "Prussia in Transition: Society and Politics under the Stein Reform Ministry of 1808." *Transactions of the American Philosophical Society*, New Series 76 (1986): 1–175.

Greene, Sandra E. *Gender, Ethnicity, and Social Change on the Upper Slave Coast: A History of the Anlo Ewe*. Portsmouth: Heinemann, 1996.

———. "Notsie Narratives: History, Memory and Meaning in West Africa." *South Atlantic Quarterly* 101 (2002) 1015–41.

———. *Sacred Sites and the Colonial Encounter*. Bloomington: Indiana University Press, 2002.

Grier, Beverly. "Pawns, Porters, and Petty Traders: Women in the Transition to Cash Crop Agriculture in Colonial Ghana." *Signs* 17 (1992): 304–28.

Grimmer-Solem, Erik. "Imperialist Socialism of the Chair: Gustav Schmoller and German Weltpolitik, 1897–1905." In *Wilhelminism and Its Legacies: German Modernities, Imperialism, and the Meanings of Reform, 1890–1930*, 106–22. Edited by Geoff Eley and James Retallack. New York: Berghahn Books, 2003.

———. "The Professors' Africa: Economists, the Elections of 1907, and the Legitimation of German Imperialism." *German History* 25 (2007): 313–47.

———. *The Rise of Historical Economics and Social Reform in Germany, 1864–1894*. Oxford: Clarendon Press, 2003.

Gross, Michael B. *The War against Catholicism: Liberalism and the Anti-Catholic Imagination in Nineteenth-Century Germany*. Ann Arbor: University of Michigan Press, 2004.

Gründer, Horst. *Geschichte der deutschen Kolonien*. 4th ed. Stuttgart: UTB, 2000.

Gutman, Herbert G. *The Black Family in Slavery and Freedom, 1750–1925*. New York: Pantheon Books, 1976.

Guyer, Jane I. "Household and Community in African Studies." *African Studies Review* 24 (1981): 87–137.

Guzman, Jessie P. "Monroe Nathan Work and His Contributions: Background and Preparation for Life's Career." *Journal of Negro History* 34 (1949): 428–61.

Hagen, William W. *Germans, Poles, and Jews: The Nationality Conflict in the Prussian East, 1772–1914*. Chicago: University of Chicago Press, 1980.

———. *Ordinary Prussians: Brandenburg Junkers and Villagers, 1500–1840*. Cambridge: Cambridge University Press, 2002.

Hahn, Steven. "Class and State in Postemancipation Societies: Southern Planters in Comparative Perspective." *American Historical Review* 95 (1990): 75–98.

———. *A Nation under Our Feet: Black Political Struggles in the Rural South from Slavery to the Great Migration*. Cambridge: Harvard University Press, 2003.

Hansen, Karen Tranberg, ed. *African Encounters with Domesticity*. New Brunswick: Rutgers University Press, 1992.

Harding, Leonhard. "Hamburg's West Africa Trade in the Nineteenth Century." In *Figuring African Trade: Proceedings of the Symposium on the Quantification and Structure of the Import and Export and Long Distance Trade in Africa 1800–1912*, 363–91. Edited by Gerhard Liesegang, H. Pasch and Adam Jones. Berlin: Dietrich Reimer, 1986.

Hardt, Michael, and Antonio Negri. *Empire*. Cambridge: Harvard University Press, 2000.

Harlan, Louis R. "Booker T. Washington and the White Man's Burden." *American Historical Review* 71 (1966): 441–67.

Harlan, Louis R. *Booker T. Washington: The Making of a Black Leader, 1856–1901*. London: Oxford University Press, 1972.

———. *Booker T. Washington: The Wizard of Tuskegee, 1901–1915*. London: Oxford University Press, 1983.

———. *Separate and Unequal: Public School Campaigns and Racism in the Southern Seaboard States 1901–1915*. Chapel Hill: University of North Carolina Press, 1958.

Harnisch, Hartmut. "Georg Friedrich Knapp: Agrargeschichtsforschung und Sozialpolitisches Engagement im Deutschen Kaiserreich." *Jahrbuch fur Wirtschaftsgeschichte* (1993): 95–132.

Harvey, David. *The Limits to Capital*. 2nd ed. 1982. London: Verso, 1999.

Hay, Douglas S., and Paul Craven. "The Criminalization Of 'Free' Labour: Master and Servant in Comparative Perspective." *Slavery and Abolition* 15 (1994): 71–101.

———. "Master and Servant in England and the Empire: A Comparative Study." *Labour* 31 (1993): 175–84.

———, eds. *Masters, Servants, and Magistrates in Britain and the Empire, 1562–1955*. Chapel Hill: University of North Carolina Press, 2004.

Headrick, Daniel R. *The Tools of Empire: Technology and European Imperialism in the Nineteenth Century*. New York: Oxford University Press, 1981.

Heap, Chad. "The City as a Sexual Laboratory: The Queer Heritage of the Chicago School." *Qualitative Sociology* 26 (2003): 457–87.

Henderson, W. O. "Prince Smith and Free Trade in Germany." *Economic History Review*, New Series 2 (1950): 295–302.

Herbert, Ulrich. *A History of Foreign Labor in Germany, 1880–1980: Seasonal Workers/Forced Laborers, Guest Workers*. Translated by William Templer. 1986. Ann Arbor: University of Michigan Press, 1990.

Herbst, Jürgen. *The German Historical School in American Scholarship: A Study in the Transfer of Culture*. Ithaca: Cornell University Press, 1965.

Hersey, Mark. "Hints and Suggestions to Farmers: George Washington Carver and Rural Conservation in the South." *Environmental History* 11 (2006): 239–68.

Higbie, Frank Tobias. *Indispensable Outcasts: Hobo Workers and Community in the American Midwest, 1880–1930*. Urbana: University of Illinois Press, 2003.

Higham, John. *Strangers in the Land: Patterns of American Nativism, 1860–1925*. 2nd ed. New Brunswick: Rutgers University Press, 1988.

Hirst, Paul Q., and Grahame Thompson. *Globalization in Question: The International Economy and the Possibilities of Governance*. 2nd ed. Cambridge, UK: Polity, 1999.

Hochschild, Adam. *King Leopold's Ghost: A Story of Greed, Terror, and Heroism in Colonial Africa*. Boston: Houghton Mifflin, 1998.

Holley, Donald. *The Second Great Emancipation: The Mechanical Cotton Picker, Black Migration, and How They Shaped the Modern South*. Fayetteville: University of Arkansas Press, 2000.

Holt, Thomas C. *The Problem of Freedom: Race, Labor, and Politics in Jamaica and Britain, 1832–1938*. Baltimore: Johns Hopkins University Press, 1992.

Hopkins, Anthony G. *An Economic History of West Africa*. New York, Columbia University Press, 1973.

Hughes, Heather. "Doubly Elite: Exploring the Life of John Langalibalele Dube." *Journal of Southern African Studies* 27 (2001): 445–58.

Hunt, Nancy Rose. *A Colonial Lexicon of Birth Ritual, Medicalization, and Mobility in the Congo*. Durham: Duke University Press, 1999.

Hussain, Athar, and Keith Tribe. *German Social Democracy and the Peasantry 1890–1907*. Vol. 1 of *Marxism and the Agrarian Question*. Highlands, NJ: Humanities Press, 1981.

Inikori, Joseph E. *Africans and the Industrial Revolution in England: A Study in International Trade and Economic Development*. Cambridge: Cambridge University Press, 2002.

———. "Slavery and the Revolution in Cotton Textile Production in England." *Social Science History* 13 (1989): 343–79.

Isaacman, Allen F. *Cotton Is the Mother of Poverty: Peasants, Work, and Rural Struggle in Colonial Mozambique, 1938–1961*. Portsmouth: Heinemann, 1996.

Isaacman, Allen F., and Richard Roberts, eds. *Cotton, Colonialism, and Social History in Sub-Saharan Africa*. Portsmouth, NH: Heinemann, 1995.

James, C.L.R. *The Black Jacobins: Toussaint L'Ouverture and the San Domingo Revolution*. 1938. 2nd ed. New York: Vingate Books, 1989.

Jaynes, Gerald David. *Branches without Roots: Genesis of the Black Working Class, 1862–1882*. New York: Oxford University Press, 1986.

Johnson, Donald. "W.E.B. Du Bois, Thomas Jesse Jones, and the Struggle for Social Education, 1900–1930." *Journal of Negro History* 85 (2000): 71–95.

Johnson, Marion. "Ashante East of the Volta." *Transactions of the Historical Society of Ghana* 8 (1965): 33–39.

———. "Cotton Imperialism in West Africa." *African Affairs* 73 (1974): 178–87.

Jones, Allen W. "The Role of Tuskegee Institute in the Education of Black Farmers." *Journal of Negro History* 60 (1975): 252–67.

Jones, Elizabeth Bright. "Gender and Agricultural Change in Saxony, 1900–1930." Ph.D. diss., University of Minnesota, 2000.

Jones, Jacqueline. *Labor of Love, Labor of Sorrow: Black Women, Work, and the Family from Slavery to the Present*. New York: Basic Books, 1985.

Jones, James. *Bad Blood: The Tuskegee Syphilis Experiment*. New York: Free Press, 1981.

July, Robert W. *Origins of Modern African Thought: Its Development in West Africa during the Nineteenth and Twentieth Centuries*. New York: Frederick A. Praeger, 1967.

Kelley, Don Quinn. "Ideology and Education: Uplifting the Masses in Nineteenth-Century Alabama." *Phylon* 40 (1979): 147–58.

Kelley, Robin D. G. *Hammer and Hoe: Alabama Communists During the Great Depression*. Chapel Hill: University of North Carolina Press, 1990.

Kelly, Brian. "Sentinels for New South Industry: Booker T. Washington, Industrial Accommodation and Black Workers in the Jim Crow South." *Labor History* 44 (2003): 337–57.

King, Kenneth James. *Pan-Africanism and Education: A Study of Race Philanthropy and Education in the Southern States of America and East Africa*. Oxford: Clarendon Press, 1971.

Klein, Herbert S. *The Atlantic Slave Trade*. Cambridge: Cambridge University Press, 1999.

Knoll, Arthur J. *Togo under Imperial Germany 1884–1914: A Case Study in Colonial Rule*. Stanford: Hoover Institution Press, 1970.

Koehl, Robert Lewis. "Colonialism inside Germany: 1886–1918." *Journal of Modern History* 25 (1953): 255–72.

Kolchin, Peter. *Unfree Labor: American Slavery and Russian Serfdom*. Cambridge: Harvard University Press, 1987.

Konno, Hajime. *Max Weber und die Polnische Frage (1892–1920): Eine Betrachtung zum Liberalen Nationalismus im Wilhelminischen Deutschland*. Baden-Baden: Nomos, 2004.

Kopp, Kristen. "Constructing Racial Difference in Colonial Poland." In *Germany's Colonial Pasts*, 76–96. Edited by Eric Ames, Marcia Klotz, and Lora Wildenthal. Lincoln: University of Nebraska Press, 2005.

Koselleck, Reinhart. *Preußen zwischen Reform und Revolution: Allgemeines Landrecht, Verwaltung und soziale Bewegung von 1791 bis 1848*. 1967. 2nd ed. Stuttgart: Klett-Cotta, 1975.

Kramer, Paul A. *The Blood of Government: Race, Empire, the United States, and the Philippines*. Chapel Hill: The University of North Carolina Press, 2006.

Krüger Dieter. *Nationalökonomen im Wilhelminischen Deutschland*. Göttingen: Vandenhoeck and Ruprecht, 1983.

Lake, Marilyn, and Henry Reynolds. *Drawing the Global Colour Line: White Men's Countries and the International Challenge of Racial Equality*. Cambridge: Cambridge University Press, 2008.

Lakwete, Angela. *Inventing the Cotton Gin: Machine and Myth in Antebellum America*. Baltimore: Johns Hopkins University Press, 2003.

Lal, Barbara Ballis. *The Romance of Culture in an Urban Civilization: Robert E. Park on Race and Ethnic Relations in Cities*. London: Routledge, 1990.

Laumann, Dennis. "A Historiography of German Togoland, or the Rise and Fall of a 'Model Colony.' " *History in Africa* 30 (2003): 195–211.

———. "Remembering and Forgetting the German Occupation of the Central Volta Region of Ghana." Ph.D. diss., University of California, Los Angeles, 1999.

Law, Robin. *The Slave Coast of West Africa, 1550–1750*. Oxford: Oxford University Press, 1991.

Law, Robin, and Kristin Mann. "West Africa in the Atlantic Community: The Case of the Slave Coast." *William and Mary Quarterly*, 3rd Ser. 56, No. 2, African and American Atlantic Worlds (1999): 307–34.

Lawrance, Benjamin N. *Locality, Mobility, and "Nation": Periurban Colonialism in Togo's Eweland, 1900–1960*. Rochester: University of Rochster Press, 2007.

———. "Most Obedient Servants: The Politics of Language in German Colonial Togo." *Cahiers d'Études Africaines* 159 (2000). Online at: http://etudesafricaines.revues.org/document27.html.

Lawrance, Richard, Emily Lynn Osborn, and Richard L. Roberts, eds. *Intermediaries, Interpreters, and Clerks: African Employees in the Making of Colonial Africa.* Madison: University of Wisconsin Press, 2006.

Leadbetter, S.R.B. *The Politics of Textiles: The Indian Cotton-Mill Industry and the Legacy of Swadeshi, 1900–1985.* New Delhi: Sage, 1993.

Lemke, Sieglinde. "Berlin and Boundaries: sollen versus geschehen." *Boundary 2* 27, no. 3 (2000): 45–78.

Lenger, Friedrich. *Werner Sombart, 1863–1941: Eine Biographie.* Munich: C. H. Beck, 1994.

Lewis, David Levering. *W.E.B Du Bois: Biography of a Race, 1868–1919.* New York: Henry Holt, 1993.

———. *W.E.B. Du Bois: The Fight for Equality and the American Century, 1919–1963.* New York: Henry Holt, 2000.

Lévi-Strauss, Claude. *Elementary Structures of Kinship.* 1949. Translated by James Harle Bell and John Richard von Sturmer. Edited by Rodney Needham. London: Eyre and Spottiswoode, 1969.

Library of Congress with essays by David Levering Lewis and Deborah Willis. *Small Nation of People: W.E.B. Du Bois and African American Portraits of Progress.* New York: Harper Collins, 2003.

Lichtenstein, Alex. *Twice the Work of Free Labor: The Political Economy of Convict Labor in the New South.* London: Verso, 1996.

Lidtke, Vernon L. *The Outlawed Party: Social Democracy in Germany, 1878–1890.* Princeton: Princeton University Press, 1966.

Likaka, Osumaka. *Rural Society and Cotton in Colonial Zaire.* Madison: University of Wisconsin Press, 1997.

Lindenfeld, David F. *The Practical Imagination: The German Sciences of State in the Nineteenth Century.* Chicago: University of Chicago Press, 1997.

Lindenlaub, Dieter. *Richtungskämpfe in Verein für Sozialpolitik: Wissenschaft und Sozialpolitik im Kaiserreich vornehmlich vom Beginn des "Neuen Kurses" bis zum Ausbruch des Ersten Weltkrieges (1890–1914).* Wiesbaden: Franz Steiner, 1967.

Lindner, Rolf. *The Reportage of Urban Culture: Robert Park and the Chicago School.* Translated by Adrian Morris. 1990. Cambridge: Cambridge University Press, 1996.

Lindsay, Lisa A., and Stephan F. Miescher, eds. *Men and Masculinities in Modern Africa.* Portsmouth, NH: Heinemann, 2003.

Lindsey, Donal F. *Indians at Hampton Institute, 1877–1923.* Urbana: University of Illinois Press, 1995.

Lindstrom, Fred B., Ronald A. Hardert, Kimball Young. "Kimball Young on Founders of the Chicago School." *Sociological Perspectives* 31 (1988): 269–97.

Lipartito, Kenneth J. "The New York Cotton Exchange and the Development of the Cotton Futures Market." *Business History Review* 57 (1983): 50–72.

Litwack, Leon. *Trouble in Mind: Black Southerners in the Age of Jim Crow.* New York: Knopf, 1998.

Logan, Frenise A. "India—Britain's Substitute for American Cotton, 1861–65." *Journal of Southern History* 24 (1958): 472–80.

Logan, Frenise A. "India's Loss of the British Cotton Market After 1865." *Journal of Southern History* 31 (1965): 40–50.

Lopes, Anne, and Gary Roth. *Men's Feminism: August Bebel and the German Socialist Movement.* Amherst, NY: Humanity Books, 2000.

Louis, William Roger. "Great Britain and German Expansion in Africa, 1884–1919." In *Britain and Germany in Africa: Imperial Rivalry and Colonial Rule.* Edited by Prosser Gifford and William Roger Louis, with Alison Smith. New Haven: Yale University Press, 1967.

———. *Great Britain and Germany's Lost Colonies, 1914–1919.* Oxford: Clarendon, 1967.

Lovejoy, Paul E. *Transformations in Slavery: A History of Slavery in Africa.* 2nd ed. Cambridge: Cambridge University Press, 2000.

Lowry, John S. "African Resistance and Center Party Recalcitrance in the Reichstag Colonial Debates of 1905/06." *Central European History* 39 (2006): 244–69.

Lybarger, Michael. "Origins of Modern Social Studies 1900–1916." *History of Education Quarterly* 23 (1983): 455–68.

Lyman, Stanford M. *Militarism, Imperialism, and Racial Accommodation: An Analysis and Interpretation of the Early Writings of Robert E. Park.* Fayetteville: University of Arkansas Press, 1992.

Lynn, Martin. *Commerce and Economic Change in West Africa: The Palm Oil Trade in the Nineteenth Century.* Cambridge: Cambridge University Press, 1997.

Magubane, Zine. *Bringing the Empire Home: Race, Class, and Gender in Britain and Colonial South Africa.* Chicago: University of Chicago Press, 2004.

Maier, Donna J. E. "Persistence of Precolonial Patterns of Production: Cotton in German Togoland, 1800–1914." In *Cotton, Colonialism, and Social History in Sub-Saharan Africa*, 71–95. Edited by Allen Isaacman and Richard Roberts. Portsmouth, NH: Heinemann, 1995.

———. "Slave Labor and Wage Labor in German Togo, 1885–1914." In *Germans in the Tropics: Essays in German Colonial History*, 73–91. Edited by Arthur J. Knoll and Lewis H. Gann. New York: Greenwood, 1987.

Mamdani, Mahmood. *Citizen and Subject: Contemporary Africa and the Legacy of Late Colonialism.* Princeton: Princeton University Press, 1996.

Manasse, Ernst Moritz. "Max Weber on Race." *Social Research* 14 (1947): 191–221.

Mandala, Elias C. *Work and Control in a Peasant Economy: A History of the Lower Tchi Valley in Malawi, 1859–1960.* Madison: University of Wisconsin Press, 1990.

Mandle, Jay R. *Not Slave, Not Free: The African American Economic Experience since the Civil War.* Durham: Duke University Press, 1992, 59–60.

Mann, Susan Archer. "The Rise of Wage Labour in the Cotton South: A Global Analysis." *Journal of Peasant Studies* 14 (1987): 226–42.

Manning, Chandra. *What This Cruel War Was Over: Soldiers, Slavery, and the Civil War.* New York: Alfred A. Knopf, 2007.

Manning, Patrick. "The Slave Trade in the Bight of Benin, 1640–1890." In *The Uncommon Market: Essays in the Economic History of the Atlantic Slave*

Trade, 107–41. Edited by Henry A. Gemery and Jan S. Hogendorn. New York: Academic Press, 1979.

———. *Slavery and African Life: Occidental, Oriental, and African Slave Trades.* Cambridge: Cambridge University Press, 1990.

Marable, W. Manning. "Booker T. Washington and African Nationalism." *Phylon* 35 (1974): 398–406.

Markmiller, Anton. *"Die Erziehung des Negers zur Arbeit": Wie die koloniale Pädagogik afrikanische Gesellschaften in die Abhängigkeit führte.* Berlin: Dietrich Reimer, 1995.

Marks, Shula. "The Ambiguities of Dependence: John L. Dube of Natal." *Journal of Southern African Studies* 1 (1975): 162–80.

Matthews, Fred H. *Quest for an American Sociology: Robert E. Park and the Chicago School.* Montreal: McGill-Queen's University Press, 1977.

———. "Robert Park, Congo Reform and Tuskegee: The Molding of a Race Relations Expert, 1905–1913." *Canadian Journal of History: Annales Canadiennes d'Histoire* 8 (1973): 37–65.

Mazzaoui, Maureen Fennell. "The Cotton Industry of Northern Italy in the Late Middle Ages: 1150–450." *Journal of Economic History* 32 (1972): 262–86.

———. *The Italian Cotton Industry in the Later Middle Ages, 1100–1600.* Cambridge: Cambridge University Press, 1981.

McBride, David. *Missions for Science: U. S. Technology and Medicine in America's African World.* New Brunswick: Rutgers University Press, 2002.

McFeely, William S. *Yankee Stepfather: General O. O. Howard and the Freedmen.* New Haven: Yale University Press, 1968.

McMurry, Linda O. *George Washington Carver, Scientist and Symbol.* New York: Oxford University Press, 1981.

———. *Recorder of the Black Experience: A Biography of Monroe Nathan Work.* Baton Rouge: Louisiana State University Press, 1985.

McPherson, James M. *The Abolitionist Legacy: From Reconstruction to the NAACP.* Princeton: Princeton University Press, 1975.

Medeiros François de, ed. *Peuples du Golfe du Bénin: Aja-Ewe.* Paris: Éditions Karthala, 1984.

Meier, August. *Negro Thought in America, 1880–1915: Racial Ideologies in the Age of Booker T. Washington* 1963. Ann Arbor: University of Michigan Press, 1988.

Meillassoux, Claude. *Maidens, Meal and Money.* 1975. Cambridge: Cambridge University Press, 1981.

Meyer, Birgit. "Christianity and the Ewe Nation: German Pietist Missionaries, Ewe Converts and the Politics of Culture." *Journal of Religion in Africa* 32 (2002): 167–99.

———. *Translating the Devil: Religion and Modernity Among the Ewe in Ghana.* Trenton, NJ: African World Press, 1999.

Miles, Robert. *Capitalism and Unfree Labour: Anomaly or Necessity?* London: Tavistock, 1987.

Miller, James A., Susan D. Pennybacker, and Eve Rosenhaft. "Mother Ada Wright and the International Campaign to Free the Scottsboro Boys, 1931–1934." *American Historical Review* 106 (2001): 387–430.

Mintz, Sidney. *Sweetness and Power: The Place of Sugar in Modern History.* New York: Penguin, 1985.

Mogk, Walter. *Paul Rohrbach und das "Größere Deutschland: Ethischer Imperialismus in Wilhelminischen Zeitalter: Ein Beitrag zur Geschichte des Kulturprotestantismus.* Munich: Wilhelm Goldmann, 1972.

Mommsen, Wolfgang J. *Max Weber and German Politics, 1890–1920.* Translated by Michael S. Steinberg. 1959. Chicago: University of Chicago Press, 1984.

———."Die Vereinigten Staaten von Amerika." In *Max Weber: Gesellschaft, Politik und Geschichte*, 72–96. Frankfurt: Suhrkamp, 1974.

Moore, Barrington. *The Social Origins of Dictatorship and Democracy: Lord and Peasant in the Making of the Modern World.* Boston: Beacon Press, 1966.

Moore, Henrietta L. and Megan Vaughan. *Cutting Down Trees: Gender, Nutrition and Agricultural Change in the Northern Province of Zambia 1890–1990.* Portsmouth, NH: Heinemann, 1994.

Morris, Robert C. *Reading, 'Riting, and Reconstruction: The Education of Freedmen in the South, 1861–1870.* Chicago: University of Chicago Press, 1976.

Moses, Wilson Jeremiah. *The Golden Age of Black Nationalism, 1850–1925.* Hamden, CT: Archon Books, 1978.

Moss, Alfred A. *The American Negro Academy: Voice of the Talented Tenth.* Baton Rouge: Louisiana State University Press, 1981.

Napo, Pierre Ali. "Le Togo à l'epoche allemande (1884–1914)." 5 vols. Ph.D. diss., Paris, Sorbonne, 1995.

———. *Togo, Land of Tuskegee Institute's International Technical Assistance Experimentation: 1900–1909.* Accra: Onyase Press, 2002. Translation of *Le Togo, Terre d'Experimentation de l'Assistance Technique Internationale de Tuskegee University en Alabama, USA 1900–1909.* Lomé: Editions Haho, 2001.

Nelson, Benjamin. "Max Weber, Dr. Alfred Ploetz and W.E.B. Du Bois." *Sociological Analysis* 34 (1973): 308–12.

———. "Max Weber on Race and Society." *Social Research* 38 (1971): 30–41.

Newell, Stephanie. *Literary Culture in Colonial Ghana: "How to Play the Game of Life."* Bloomington: Indiana University Press, 2002.

Nichtweiss, Johannes. *Die ausländische Saisonarbeiter in der Landwirtschaft der östlichen und mittleren Gebiete des Deutschen Reiches: Ein Beitrag zur Geschichte der preußisch-deutschen Politik von 1890–1914.* Berlin: Rütten and Loening, 1959.

Nixon, Raymond B. *Henry W. Grady, Spokesman of the New South.* New York: Russell and Russell, 1969.

Norrell, Robert J. *Up from History: The Life of Booker T. Washington.* Cambridge: Harvard University Press, 2009.

Norris, Edward Graham. *Die Umerziehung des Afrikaners: Togo 1895–1938.* Munich: Trickster, 1993.

Novak, Daniel A. *The Wheel of Servitude: Black Forced Labor after Slavery.* Lexington, KY: University Press of Kentucky, 1978.

Nugent, Paul. "Putting the History Back into Ethnicity: Enslavement, Religion, and Cultural Brokerage in the Construction of Mandinka/Jola and Ewe/Agotime Identities in West Africa, c. 1650–1930." *Comparative Studies in Society and History* 50 (2008): 920–48.

———. *Smugglers, Secessionists and Loyal Citizens on the Ghana-Togo Frontier: The Lie of the Borderlands since 1914*. Oxford: James Currey, 2002.

Nworah, Kenneth Dike. "The Liverpool 'Sect' and British West African Policy 1895–1915." *African Affairs* 70 (1971): 349–64.

———. "The West African Operations of the British Cotton Growing Association, 1904–1914." *African Historical Studies* 4 (1971): 315–30.

Oakes, James. *The Radical and the Republican: Frederick Douglass, Abraham Lincoln, and the Triumph of Antislavery Politics*. New York: Norton, 2007.

Oberschall, Anthony. *Empirical Social Research in Germany 1848–1914*. Paris: Mouton and Co., 1965.

Olsson, Lars. "Labor Migration as a Prelude to World War I." *International Migration Review* 30 (1996): 875–900.

Osmond, Jonathan. "Land, Peasant and Lord in German Agriculture Since 1800." In *Germany: A New Social and Economic History*. vol. 3, 71–105. Edited by Robert W. Scribner and Sheilagh C. Ogilvie. London: Arnold, 1996.

Oubre, Claude F. *Forty Acres and a Mule: The Freedmen's Bureau and Black Land Ownership*. Baton Rouge: Louisiana State University Press, 1978.

Owsley, Frank Lawrence. *King Cotton Diplomacy: Foreign Relations of the Confederate States of America*. 2nd ed. Chicago: University of Chicago Press, 1959.

Peeps, J. M. Stephen. "Northern Philanthropy and the Emergence of Black Higher Education—Do-Gooders, Compromisers, or Co-Conspirators?" *Journal of Negro Education* 50 (1981): 251–69.

Persons, Stow. *Ethnic Studies at Chicago, 1905–45*. Urbana: University of Illinois Press, 1987.

Phillips, Anne. *The Enigma of Colonialism: British Policy in West Africa*. London: James Currey, 1989.

Pierard, Richard V. "A Case Study in German Economic Imperialism: The Colonial Economic Committee, 1896–1914." *Scandinavian Economic Review* 26 (1968): 155–67.

Pietz, William. "Fetishism and Materialism: The Limits of Theory in Marx." In *Fetishism as Cultural Discourse*, 119–51. Edited by Emily Apter and William Pietz. Ithaca: Cornell University Press, 1993.

———. "The Problem of the Fetish, I." *Res* 9 (1985): 5–17.

———. "The Problem of the Fetish, II." *Res* 13 (1987): 23–45.

———. "The Problem of the Fetish, IIIa: Bosman's Guinea and the Enlightenment Theory of Fetishism." *Res* 16 (1988): 105–23.

Pitcher, M. Anne. "Conflict and Cooperation: Gendered Roles and Responsibilities within Cotton Households in Northern Mozambique." *African Studies Review* 39 (1996): 81–112.

Platt, Anthony M. *E. Franklin Frazier Reconsidered*. New Brunswick: Rutgers University Press, 1991.

Post, Ken. "Peasantization in West Africa." In *African Social Studies: A Radical Reader*, 241–50. Edited by Peter Gutkind and Peter Waterman. London: Heinemann, 1977.

Powell, Lawrence N. *New Masters: Northern Planters during the Civil War and Reconstruction*. New Haven: Yale University Press, 1980.

Quataert, Jean H. *Reluctant Feminists in German Social Democracy, 1885–1917*. Princeton: Princeton University Press, 1979.

Radcliffe, Kendahl L. "The Tuskegee-Togo Cotton Scheme, 1900–1909." Ph.D. diss., University of California, Los Angeles, 1998.

Radkau, Joachim. *Max Weber: Die Leidenschaft des Denkens*. Munich: Carl Hanser, 2005.

Rampersad, Arnold. *The Art and Imagination of W.E.B. Du Bois*. Cambridge: Harvard University Press, 1976.

———. *Ralph Ellison: A Biography*. New York: Alfred A. Knopf, 2007.

Ransom, Roger L., and Richard Sutch. *One Kind of Freedom: The Economic Consequences of Emancipation*. 1977. 2nd ed., Cambridge: Cambridge University Press, 2001.

Raushenbush, Winifred. *Robert E. Park: Biography of a Sociologist*. Durham: Duke University Press, 1979.

Rauty, Raffaele, ed. *On Hobos and Homelessness*. Chicago: University of Chicago Press, 1998.

Reed, Touré F. *Not Alms but Opportunity: The Urban League and the Politics of Racial Uplift, 1910–1950*. Chapel Hill: University of North Carolina Press, 2008.

Repp, Kevin. *Reformers, Critics, and the Paths of German Modernity: Anti-Politics and the Search for Alternatives, 1890–1914*. Cambridge: Harvard University Press, 2000.

Retallack, James N. *The German Right, 1860–1920: Political Limits of the Authoritarian Imagination*. Toronto: University of Toronto Press, 2006.

Rich, Paul B. "The Appeals of Tuskegee: James Henderson, Lovedale, and the Fortunes of South African Liberalism, 1906–1930." *The International Journal of African Historical Studies* 20 (1987): 271–92.

Richards, Paul. "Ecological Change and the Politics of African Land Use." *African Studies Review* 26 (1983): 1–72.

Richardson, Joe Martin. *Christian Reconstruction: The American Missionary Association and Southern Blacks, 1861–1890*. Athens: University of Georgia Press, 1986.

Ring, Natalie J. "The Problem South: Region, Race, and 'Southern Readjustment,' 1880–1930." Ph.D. diss., University of California, San Diego, 2003.

Ritzer, George. *The McDonaldization of Society: An Investigation into the Changing Character of Contemporary Social Life*. Newbury Park: Pine Forge Press, 1993.

Robbins, Richard. *Sidelines Activist: Charles S. Johnson and the Struggle for Civil Rights*. Jackson: University Press of Mississippi, 1996.

Roberts, Richard L. "French Colonialism, Imported Technology, and the Handicraft Textile Industry in the Western Sudan, 1898–1918." *Journal of Economic History* 47 (1987): 461–72.

———. *Two Worlds of Cotton: Colonialism and the Regional Economy in the French Soudan, 1800–1946.* Palo Alto: Stanford University Press, 1996.

Robinson, Cedric J. *Black Marxism: The Making of the Black Radical Tradition.* 1983. Chapel Hill: University of North Carolina Press, 2000.

Rodgers, Daniel T. *Atlantic Crossings: Social Politics in a Progressive Era.* Cambridge: Harvard University Press, 1998.

Ross, Dorothy. *Origins of American Social Science.* Cambridge: Cambridge University Press, 1991.

Roth, Guenther. *Max Webers Deutsch-englische Familiengeschichte 1800–1950: Mit Briefen und Dokumenten.* Tübingen: Mohr Siebeck, 2001.

———. *The Social Democrats in Imperial Germany: A Study in Working-Class Isolation and National Integration.* Totowa, NJ: Bedminster Press, 1963.

———. "Transatlantic Connections: A Cosmopolitan Context for Max and Marianne Weber's New York Visit 1904." *Max Weber Studies* 5 (2005): 81–112.

Royce, Edward. *The Origins of Southern Sharecropping.* Philadelphia: Temple University Press, 1993.

Rubin, Gayle. "The Traffic in Women: Notes on the 'Political Economy' of Sex." In *Toward an Anthropology of Women*, 157–210. Edited by Rayna Rapp Reiter. New York: Monthly Review Press, 1975.

Rueschemeyer, Dietrich. "The Verein für Sozialpolitik and the Fabian Society: A Study in the Sociology of Policy-Relevant Knowledge." In *States, Social Knowledge, and the Origins of Modern Social Policies*, 117–62. Edited by Dietrich Rueschemeyer and Theda Skocpol. Princeton: Princeton University Press, 1996.

Rydell, Robert W. *All the World's a Fair: Visions of Empire at American International Expositions, 1876–1916.* Chicago: University of Chicago Press, 1984.

Sanneh, Lamin. *Abolitionists Abroad: American Blacks and the Making of Modern West Africa.* Cambridge: Harvard University Press, 1999.

Saul, Klaus. "Der Kampf um das Landproletariat: Sozialistische Landagitation, Großgrundbesitz und preußische Staatsverwaltung 1890 bis 1903." *Archiv für Sozialgeschichte* 15 (1975): 163–208.

Saville, Julie. *The Work of Reconstruction: From Slave to Wage Laborer in South Carolina, 1860–1870.* Cambridge: Cambridge University Press, 1994.

Scaff, Lawrence. "The 'Cool Objectivity of Sociation': Max Weber and Marianne Weber in America." *History of the Human Sciences* 11 (1998): 61–82.

———. "Max Weber's *Amerikabild* and the African American Experience." In *Crosscurrents: African Americans, Africa, and Germany in the Modern World*, 82–94. Edited by David McBride et al. Columbia: Camden House, 1998.

Schäfer, Axel Rolf. *American Progressives and German Social Reform, 1875–1920: Social Ethics, Moral Control, and the Regulatory State in a Transatlantic Context.* Stuttgart: Franz Steiner, 2000.

———. "W.E.B. Du Bois, German Social Thought, and the Racial Divide in American Progressivism, 1892–1909." *Journal of American History* 88 (2001): 925–49.

Schiefel, Werner. *Bernhard Dernburg 1865–1937: Kolonialpolitiker und Bankier im wilhelminischen Deutschland.* Zürich: Atlantis, 1974.

Schissler, Hanna. *Preußische Agrargesellschaft im Wandel: Wirtschaftliche, gesell-schaftliche und politische Transformationsprozesse von 1763 bis 1847*. Göttingen: Vandenhoeck und Ruprecht, 1978.

Schmidt, Kerstin. "Georg Friedrich Knapp: Ein Pionier der Agrarhistoriker." *Zeitschrift für Geschichtswissenschaft* 37 (1989): 228–42.

Schorske, Carl E. *German Social Democracy, 1905–1917: The Development of the Great Schism*. Cambridge: Harvard University Press, 1955.

Schwarmann, Hermann. *Eine Baumwollära: 125 Jahren Bremer Baumwollbörse*. Bremen: Hauschild, 1997.

Schwartz, Alfred. *Le Paysan et la Culture du Coton au Togo: Approche Sociologique*. Paris: Institut Français de Recherche Scientifique pour le Développement en Coopération, 1985.

Scoones, Ian, and John Thompson. "Knowledge, Power, and Development—Towards a Theoretical Understanding." In *Beyond Farmer First: Rural People's Knowledge, Agricultural Research and Extension Practice*, 16–32. Edited by Ian Scoones and John Thompson. London: Intermediate Technology Publications, 1994.

Scott, James C. *Weapons of the Weak: Everyday Forms of Peasant Resistance*. New Haven: Yale University Press, 1985.

Sebald, Peter. *Togo 1884–1914: Eine Geschichte der deutschen "Musterkolonie" auf der Grundlage amtlicher Quellen*. Berlin: Akademie-Verlag, 1988.

Sehat David. "The Civilizing Mission of Booker T. Washington." *Journal of Southern History* 73 (2007): 323–62.

Shafer, David A. *The Paris Commune: French Politics, Culture, and Society at the Crossroads of the Revolutionary Tradition and Revolutionary Socialism*. New York: Palgrave Macmillan, 2005.

Sheehan, James J. *The Career of Lujo Brentano: A Study of Liberalism and Social Reform in Imperial Germany*. Chicago: University of Chicago Press, 1966.

Shepperson, George. "Pan-Africanism and 'Pan-Africanism': Some Historical Notes." *Phylon* 23 (1962): 346–58.

Shimazu, Naoko. *Japan, Race, and Equality: The Racial Equality Proposal of 1919*. London: Routledge, 1998.

Silver, Arthur W. *Manchester Men and Indian Cotton, 1847–1872*. Manchester: Manchester University Press, 1966.

Simtaro, Dadja Halla-Kawa. "Le Togo 'Musterkolonie': Souvenir de l'Allemagne dans la Société Togolaise." 2 vols. Ph.D. diss., Université de Provence, Aix-Marseille I, 1982.

Skinner, Elliot P. *African Americans and U.S. Foreign Policy toward Africa 1850–1924: In Defense of Black Nationality*. Washington, DC: Howard University Press, 1992.

Smith, Alice Brown. *Forgotten Foundations: The Role of Jeanes Teachers in Black Education*. New York: Vantage Press, 1997.

Smith, C. Wayne, and J. Tom Cothren, eds. *Cotton: Origin, History, Technology, and Production*. New York: Wiley, 1999.

Smith, Edwin W. *Aggrey of Africa: A Study in Black and White*. 1929. Reprint, New York: Books for Libraries, 1971.

Smith, Helmut Walser. *German Nationalism and Religious Conflict: Culture, Ideology, Politics, 1870–1914*. Princeton: Princeton University Press, 1995.

Smith, John David. "Anthropologist Felix von Luschan and Trans-Atlantic Racial Reform." *Münchner Beiträge zur Völkerkunde* 7 (2002): 289–304.

———. *Black Judas: William Hannibal Thomas and the American Negro*. Athens: University of Georgia Press, 2000.

———. *An Old Creed for the New South: Proslavery Ideology and Historiography, 1865–1918*. 1985. Athens: University of Georgia Press, 1991.

———. "W.E.B. Du Bois, Felix von Luschan, and Racial Reform at the Fin de Siecle." *Amerikastudien/American Studies* (2002): 23–38.

———, ed. *When Did Southern Segregation Begin?* New York: Bedford/St. Martin's, 2002.

Smith, Woodruff D. *The German Colonial Empire*. Chapel Hill: University of North Carolina Press, 1978.

Sobich, Frank Oliver. *"Schwarze Bestien, Rote Gefahr": Rassismus und Antisozialismus im Deutschen Kaiserreich*. Frankfurt: Campus, 2006.

Solomon, Mark I. *The Cry Was Unity: Communists and African Americans, 1917–36*. Jackson: University Press of Mississippi, 1998.

Spivey, Donald. "The African Crusade for Black Industrial Schooling." *Journal of Negro History* 63 (1978): 1–17.

———. *The Politics of Miseducation: The Booker T. Washington Institute of Liberia, 1929–1945*. Lexington: University Press of Kentucky, 1986.

———. *Schooling for the New Slavery: Black Industrial Education, 1868–1915*. Westport, CT: Greenwood Press,1978.

Stein, Judith. *The World of Marcus Garvey: Race and Class in Modern Society*. Baton Rouge: Louisiana State University Press, 1986.

Steinfeld, Robert J. *Coercion, Contract, and Free Labor in the Nineteenth Century*. Cambridge: Cambridge University Press, 2001.

———. *The Invention of Free Labor: The Employment Relation in English and American Law and Culture, 1350–1870*. Chapel Hill: The University of North Carolina Press, 1991.

Steinmetz, George. *The Devil's Handwriting: Precoloniality and the German Colonial State in Qingdao, Samoa, and Southwest Africa*. Chicago: University of Chicago Press, 2007.

———. *Regulating the Social: The Welfare State and Local Politics in Imperial Germany*. Princeton: Princeton University Press, 1993.

Strickland, Arvarh E. *History of the Chicago Urban League*. Urbana: University of Illinois Press, 1966.

Summers, Carol. *Colonial Lessons: Africans' Education in Southern Rhodesia, 1918–1940*. Portsmouth, NH: Heinemann, 2002.

Sunseri, Thaddeus. *Vilimani: Labor Migration and Rural Change in Early Colonial Tanzania*. Portsmouth, NH: Heinemann, 2002.

Swatos, William H., Jr. "Sects and Success: Missverstehen in Mt. Airy." *Sociological Analysis* 43 (1982): 375–79.

Takaki, Ronald T. *Iron Cages: Race and Culture in Nineteenth-Century America*. 1979. Rev. ed. New York: Oxford University Press, 2000.

Tété-Adjalogo, Têtêvi Godwin. *De la colonisation allemande au Deutsche-Togo Bund*. Paris: Éditions L'Harmattan, 1998.

Thompson, E. P. *The Making of the English Working Class*. New York: Vintage Books, 1963.

Tipton, Frank B., Jr. "Farm Labor and Power Politics: Germany, 1850–1914." *Journal of Economic History* 34 (1974): 951–79.

———. *Regional Variations in the Economic Development of Germany during the Nineteenth Century*. Middletown: Wesleyan University Press, 1976.

Tosh, John. "The Cash Crop Revolution in Tropical Africa: An Agricultural Reappraisal." *African Affairs* 79 (1980): 79–94.

Tribe, Keith. "Prussian Agriculture-German Politics: Max Weber 1892–7," *Economy and Society* 12 (1983): 181–226.

———. *Strategies of Economic Order: German Economic Discourse, 1750–1950*. Cambridge: Cambridge University Press, 1995.

Trotha, Trutz von. " 'One for Kaiser': Beobachtungen zur politischen Soziologie der Prügelstrafe am Beispiel des 'Schutzgebietes Togo.' " In *Studien zur Geschichte des deutschen Kolonialismus in Africa: Festschrift zum 60. Geburtstag von Peter Sebald*, 521–51. Edited by Peter Heine and Ulrich van der Heyden. Pfaffenweiler: Centaurus, 1995.

Tuteja, K. L. "American Planters and the Cotton Improvement Programme in Bombay Presidency in Nineteenth Century." *Indian Journal of American Studies* 28 (1998): 103–8.

Tuttle, William M., Jr. *Race Riot: Chicago in the Red Summer of 1919* (1970). Urbana: University of Illinois Press, 1996.

Verdon, Michel. *The Abutia Ewe of West Africa: A Chiefdom that Never Was*. Berlin: Mouton, 1983.

Verney, Kevern. *The Art of the Possible: Booker T. Washington and Black Leadership in the United States, 1881–1925*. New York: Routledge, 2001.

Wacker, R. Fred. "The Sociology of Race and Ethnicity in the Second Chicago School." In *A Second Chicago School? The Development of a Postwar American Sociology*, 136–36. Edited by Gary Alan Fine. Chicago: University of Chicago Press, 1995.

Watkins, William H. *The White Architects of Black Education: Ideology and Power in America, 1865–1954*. Forward by Robin D. G. Kelley. New York: Teachers College Press, 2001.

Wehler, Hans-Ulrich. *Bismarck und der Imperialismus*. 1969. Munich: Deutscher Taschenbuch Verlag, 1976.

———. *Deutsche Gesellschaftsgeschichte*. Vol. 3, *Von der "Deutsche Doppelrevolution" bis zum Beginn des Ersten Weltkrieges*. Munich: C. H. Beck, 1987.

Weiss, Nancy J. *The National Urban League, 1910–1940*. New York: Oxford University Press, 1974.

Weißflog, Stefan. "J. K. Vietor und sein Konzept des leistungsfähigen Afrikaners." In *Mission im Kontext: Beiträge zur Sozialgeschichte der Norddeutschen Missionsgesellschaft im 19. Jahrhundert*, 293–304. Edited by Werner Ustorf. Bermen: Übersee Museum, 1986.

Weitz, Eric D. *Creating German Communism, 1890–1990: From Popular Protests to Socialist State*. Princeton: Princeton University Press, 1997.

West, Michael O. "The Tuskegee Model of Development in Africa: Another Dimension of the Africa/African-American Connection." *Diplomatic History* 16 (1992): 371–87.

West, Michael Rudolph. *The Education of Booker T. Washington: American Democracy and the Idea of Race Relations.* New York: Columbia University Press, 2006.

White, Christine Pelzer. "Everyday Resistance, Socialist Revolution and Rural Development: The Vietnamese Case." *Journal of Peasant Studies* 13 (1986): 49–63.

White, Deborah G. *Ar'n't I a Woman?: Female Slaves in the Plantation South.* 1985. Rev. ed. New York: Norton, 1999.

Wiener, Jonathan M. "Class Structure and Economic Development in the American South, 1865–1955." *American Historical Review* 84 (1979): 970–92.

———. *Social Origins of the New South: Alabama, 1860–1885.* Baton Rouge: Louisiana State University Press, 1978.

Wildenthal, Lora. *German Women for Empire, 1884–1945.* Durham: Duke University Press, 2001.

Williams, Heather Andrea. *Self-Taught: African American Education in Slavery and Freedom.* Chapel Hill: University of North Carolina Press, 2005.

Williams, Walter. *Black Americans and the Evangelization of Africa, 1877–1900.* Madison: University of Wisconsin Press, 1982.

Williamson, Joel. *The Crucible of Race: Black-White Relations in the American South since Emancipation.* New York: Oxford University Press, 1984.

Winson, Anthony. "The 'Prussian Road' of Agrarian Development: A Reconsideration." *Economy and Society* 11 (1982): 381–408.

Wise, Michael. "Max Weber Visits America: A Review of the Video." *Sociation Today* 4:2 (Fall 2006). Online at: http://www.ncsociology.org/sociationtoday /v42/wise.htm.

Wittig, Monique. *The Straight Mind and Other Essays.* Boston: Beacon Press, 1992.

Woodson, Carter G. *Mis-Education of the Negro.* Washington, DC: The Associated Publishers, 1933.

Woodward, C. Vann. *Origins of the New South, 1877–1913.* 1951. Rev. ed. Baton Rouge: Louisiana State University Press, 1972.

———. *The Strange Career of Jim Crow.* 1955. 3rd ed. New York: Oxford University Press, 1974.

Wright, Gavin. *Old South, New South: Revolutions in the Southern Economy Since the Civil War.* New York: Basic Books, 1986.

Wright, Richard. *The Color Curtain: A Report on the Bandung Conference.* 1956. Banner Books: University Press of Mississippi, 1994.

Wright, Stephen J. "The Development of the Hampton-Tuskegee Pattern of Higher Education." *Phylon* 10 (1949): 334–42.

Yellin, Eric S. "The (White) Search for (Black) Order: The Phelps-Stokes Fund's First Twenty Years, 1911–1931." *Historian* 65 (2002): 319–52.

Zimmerman, Andrew. *Anthropology and Antihumanism in Imperial Germany.* Chicago: University of Chicago Press, 2001.

Zimmerman, Andrew. "Decolonizing Weber." *Decolonizing German Theory.* Edited by George Steinmetz. Special Issue of *Postcolonial Studies* 9 (2006): 53–79.

———. "A German Alabama in Africa: The Tuskegee Expedition to German Togo and the Transnational Origins of West African Cotton Growers." *American Historical Review* 110 (2005): 1362–98.

———. "The Ideology of the Machine and the Spirit of the Factory: Remarx on Babbage and Ure." *Cultural Critique* 37 (1997): 5–29.

———. " 'What Do You Really Want in German East Africa, *Herr Professor?*' Counterinsurgency and the Science Effect in Colonial Tanzania." *Comparative Studies in Society and History* 48 (2006): 419–61.

Zubrzycki, Jerzy. "Emigration from Poland in the Nineteenth and Twentieth Centuries." *Population Studies* 6 (1953): 248–72.

Zumbini, Massimo Ferrari. *Die Wurzeln des Bösen: Gründerjahre des Antisemitismus: Von der Bismarckzeit zu Hitler.* Frankfurt am Main: Klostermann, 2003.

INDEX